Musicians
& Composers
of the 20th Century

Musicians & Composers
of the 20th Century

Volume 1
Will Ackerman—John Denver

Editor

Alfred W. Cramer
Pomona College

SALEM PRESS

Pasadena, California   Hackensack, New Jersey

Editorial Director: Christina J. Moose
Developmental Editor: Jeffry Jensen
Acquisitions Editor: Mark Rehn
Manuscript Editor: Constance Pollock
Research Assistant: Keli Trousdale

Photograph Editor: Cynthia Breslin Beres
Production Editor: Andrea E. Miller
Page Design: James Hutson
Layout: William Zimmerman

Cover photo: Leonard Bernstein (Erich Auerbach/Getty Images)

Library of Congress Cataloging-in-Publication Data

Musicians and composers of the 20th century / editor Alfred W. Cramer.
    p. cm.
  Includes bibliographical references and index.
  ISBN 978-1-58765-512-8 (set : alk. paper) — ISBN 978-1-58765-513-5 (vol. 1 : alk. paper) —
ISBN 978-1-58765-514-2 (vol. 2 : alk. paper) — ISBN 978-1-58765-515-9 (vol. 3 : alk. paper) —
ISBN 978-1-58765-516-6 (vol. 4 : alk. paper) — ISBN 978-1-58765-517-3 (vol. 5 : alk. paper) —
1. Music—20th century—Bio-bibliography—Dictionaries. I. Cramer, Alfred William.
  ML105.M883 2009
  780.92′2—dc22

  [B]

2009002980

First Printing

PRINTED IN THE UNITED STATES OF AMERICA

Contents

Publisher's Note

Musicians and Composers of the 20th Century offers in-depth biographical and critical essays on those men and women who made an enduring impact on music from 1901 to 2000. Covering more than 600 musical artists in detailed essays ranging from three to five pages in length, this A-Z reference will provide an entry point for students seeking the basics on musicians in all genres, worldwide.

Scope of Coverage

Musicians and Composers of the 20th Century features 608 essays on 614 individuals from around the world who have gained significance as composers, performers, instrumentalists, vocalists, and teachers. They have made contributions to a variety of musical genres, from classical to jazz, opera to musical theater, blues to soul, folk to rock, traditional regional forms to contemporary country. New Age, rap, reggae, and world music, relative newcomers on the scene, are covered as well.

The 101 women and 513 men covered in these five volumes are musically classified into one or more of the following categories or genres: accordion players (1), arrangers (16), avant-garde musicians (10), bandleaders (15), banjoists (7), bebop musicians (16), bluegrass musicians (7), blues musicians (40), boogie-woogie musicians (7), cabaret singers (3), calypso singers (1), cellists (8), Celtic singers (1), choral directors (4), Christian music performers (6), clarinetists (4), classical composers (111), other classical musicians (57), conductors (36), cornetists (3), country and country-western musicians (52), disco musicians (4), drummers and other percussionists (12), dulcimer players (1), electronic and electroacoustic musicians (13), experimental musicians (8), film composers (45), flutists (4), folk-rock musicians (8), folksingers (35), funk musicians (16), glam-rock musicians (5), gospel musicians (9), grunge-rock musicians (2), guitarists (245), hard-bop musicians (8), harmonica players (6), harpsichordists (3), hip-hop musicians (19), instrument makers (3), jazz composers (59), other jazz musicians (57), keyboardists (13), Latin jazz musicians (13), Latin popular musicians (5), librettists (6), lute players (3), lyricists (36), mandolinists (1), mariachi musicians (2), minimalist composers (4), multimedia artists (1), music educators (8), musical-theater composers (42), musical-theater singers (12), musicologists (7), New Age musicians (8), new wave musicians (3), opera composers (57), opera singers (17), organists (2), performance artists (2), pianists (86), pop-rock musicians (13), popular composers (14), popular singers (59), punk-rock musicians (7), ragtime musicians (7), rappers (25), record producers (8), reggae musicians (3), rhythm-and-blues musicians (44), rock musicians (93), rockabilly musicians (9), salsa musicians (6), sarod musicians (1), saxophonists (21), serial and atonal composers (10), singer-songwriters (230), sitar players (1), ska musicians (2), songwriters (28), soul singers (22), swing musicians (18), synthesizer musicians (5), television composers (3), trombonists (3), trumpeters (8), vibraphonists (2), viol players (3), violinists (19), and musicians identified with the relatively new genre of world music (19).

The persons covered in these volumes are equally diverse geographically, identified with one or more of the following countries or regions: Africa (5), Argentina (4), Australia (3), Austria (11), Bangladesh (1), Belgium (2), Brazil (5), Canada (9), China (2), Cuba (4), Czech Republic (4), Denmark (2), Egypt (1), England (49), Estonia (1), Finland (2), France (20), Germany (19), Greece (3), Hungary (7), Iceland (1), India (2), Ireland (2), Israel (3), Italy (12), Jamaica (4), Japan (3), Korea (1), Lithuania (1), Mexico (5), Middle East (4), Netherlands (2), Nigeria (1), Northern Ireland (2), Norway (1), Pakistan (1), Panama (1), Poland (5), Puerto Rico (2), Romania (2), Russia (15), Scotland (2), South Africa (3), Spain (4), Sweden (1), Switzerland (2), Ukraine (2), United Kingdom (53), United States (428), and/or the West Indies and Caribbean (9).

Essay Length and Format

Each essay ranges in length from three to five pages (1,500 to 2,500 words) and displays standard ready-reference top matter offering easy access to biographical information:

- **Name:** Every essay is headed by the name of the musician as best known in standard English-language sources.

- **Identification line:** Every essay's heading is followed by an identification line that lists the individual's nationality and his or her musical identity, from arranger to blues musician to classical or jazz composer to singer-songwriter.
- **Summary description:** A brief italicized paragraph encapsulates the individual's significance in the history of music.
- **Born and Died lines** list the most accurate dates of birth and death available, followed by the precise locations of birth and death; both contemporary and modern place-names (where different) are listed.
- **Also known as** lists additional names—including full names, birth names, alternative spellings, pseudonyms, nicknames, and other monikers.
- **Member of** lists principal groups, such as bands or choirs, with which the musician is associated.
- **Principal works** or **Principal recordings** (sometimes both) lists, by genre or type (such as "albums" or "orchestral works" or "operatic roles") the individual's major works or recordings, including first performance dates and (for foreign-language works) any common English translations. For collaborative works, primary "coauthors" such as lyricists and librettists are listed in parentheses. "Writings of interest" appear at the ends of these listings for those musicians who produced books about their lives and music. These extensive listings form one of the set's major features.
- **The Life** introduces the main text of the essay, providing biographical facts about the individual's life from birth through death.
- **The Music**, the heart of the essay, offers analytical commentary on the musician's work as a whole as well as core selected works, such as famous compositions, key performances, and notable recordings.
- **Musical Legacy** describes the musician's influence on styles, genres, and subsequent generations of musicians, as well as his or her impact on popular culture.
- **Byline:** All essays are signed by the scholars who wrote them (who are also listed, with their academic affiliations, in the front matter to Volume 1).
- **Further Reading:** This section sends readers to key books and other print resources for students wishing to conduct additional study. All entries

are annotated to guide readers to particular areas of interest.
- **See also** lists cross-references to related musicians covered in *Musicians and Composers of the 20th Century*—an especially useful feature for popular band members and musical-theater collaborators.

Special Features

Musicians and Composers of the 20th Century is illustrated with more than 400 photographs of the musicians scattered throughout the five volumes. In addition, several resources and finding aids for users of this encyclopedia appear at the end of Volume 5, including a General Bibliography, a Glossary, a Chronological List of Musicians by birth year, an annotated list of Electronic Resources, a Category Index classifying musicians into more than 90 genres, a Geographical Index of 50 countries and regions represented, a Personages and Groups Index listing both musicians discussed in the text and musical groups such as bands, and finally a Works Index listing all major works that receive significant text discussion.

Acknowledgments

Salem Press would like to extend its appreciation to all involved in the development of this work. Special thanks go to Alfred W. Cramer, Associate Professor of Music at Pomona College, Claremont, California, who developed and monitored the contents list for contributing writers to ensure the set's relevance to a broad range of high school and undergraduate curricula. Professor Cramer teaches courses in the history of twentieth century music and music theory. The recipient of the Society for Music Theory's 2004 Outstanding Publication Award, he received his B.A. in music from Yale University in 1987 and his Ph.D. in music theory from the University of Pennsylvania in 1997. He is also an accomplished violinist and has soloed with the National Repertory Orchestra and played in several regional orchestras.

The essays were written and are signed by more than 200 music scholars and other academicians, a list of whom will be found in the following pages, accompanied by their academic affiliations. Without their contributions, a project of this magnitude would not be possible.

Editor's Introduction

Musicians and Composers of the 20th Century examines the work of more than six hundred artists representing classical art, jazz, rock, folk, blues, soul, gospel, country, Latin, New Age, reggae, and world music as well as music for film and musical theater. If someone at the start of the twentieth century had envisioned a future encyclopedia of twentieth century musicians, it would not have had this scope. Although anyone could have anticipated that music would evolve, no one could have anticipated the surprising ways in which the basic concept of music changed during the century.

Consider the fundamental changes in the way music was experienced. In 1900 virtually all music was live music. When people wanted to hear music, they played or sang it themselves, or they went to a public event—a graduation, a parade, a religious service, or, of course, a concert. The technology of sound recording was barely two decades old, and the idea that recordings might play music was more recent than that. By the late 1920's, it had become common to experience music through recordings. The first radio broadcasts began in about 1919. Recorded sound was routinely synchronized to films by the late 1920's. Beginning in the 1950's, tape recording made possible new ways to edit and manipulate sound. By the 1990's, widely available computers had given millions of people the ability to make sophisticated recordings or to create music without singing or playing an instrument.

In 1900 most people thought of music as notated. At that time, classical music, written down by composers, had more prestige; popular songs, published as sheet music, made more money. Nevertheless, there was plenty of unnotated music, mostly considered folk music. To those concerned with high art, folk music was valuable primarily as the raw material on which a nation's refined culture could be built. It was largely through attention to their common folk culture that the separate kingdoms of Germany had come together as a nation during the nineteenth century; and, with Germany's example in mind, composers such as Bedřich Smetana and Antonín Dvořák in Bohemia and Jean Sibelius in Finland had developed national styles of art music rooted in folk idioms.

From 1892 to 1895, Dvořák lived in America, where he turned American attention toward Native American and African American music as the likely raw material for an American art music that would validate America as a nation.

Thus, a prognosticator from 1900 might have expected some folk musicians to appear in this encyclopedia, in a deferential position to the classical musicians, who would by far take up most of the pages. The variety of styles found here would have been inconceivable. Such a broad mix also might have raised eyebrows during the middle decades of the twentieth century, when, amazingly, many people referred to the music of high culture as "good" music, considering it a more accurate term than "classical." (Interestingly, jazz musicians called it "long-hair" music.) By that time, this encyclopedia would have been conceivable in more or less its present form. Many of the key changes had taken place by 1940, the year Woody Guthrie met Pete Seeger.

During the Great Depression, Seeger's father, Charles, and stepmother, Ruth Crawford Seeger, sought to join ranks with those who were suffering economically, largely by bringing to them a brand of avowedly dissonant modernist music. Perhaps not surprisingly, such music did not catch on, so the Seegers set about rethinking their assumptions about composing. They decided that anyone who changed a few notes here or a few words there to a folk song was engaging in the authentic process of composition. This meant that folk music was no longer considered static raw material bound by tradition, but rather it was a living body of music being created anew by ordinary people. Pete Seeger put this idea into practice with his singalong performances of folk music, while Guthrie, Leadbelly, and other singers were lauded as folk music composers. This transformation of folk music (and, by extension, of American music) from quaint, Romanticized ballads to earthy, often raucous statements signaled a fundamental shift in attitude: A song did not have to be performed by a refined singer in order to be realized at its fullest. The homespun sound of the folk performer was no embarrassment but in fact an integral part of the musical expression. When folksinger Bob Dylan got an amplifier and began to transform rock music, he helped rock music make a similar claim to the status of serious high art, despite its lack of conventional refined singing.

This history says more about the concept of folk music than it says about the music's sound, creation, or dissemination. The folk songs collected by John and Alan Lomax, the Seegers, and others were a mix of Appalachian music sung by folks of British origin, blues sung by African Americans, cowboy songs of the Western United States, and more, but much of this music was already available on commercial recordings and radio broadcasts by the late 1920's. It was marketed to niche audiences: white, non-urban audiences for the country music of artists such as the Carter Family, black audiences for the blues of Bessie Smith, and so on. Seen in this light, the folk music movement of the late 1930's to early 1950's was an attempt to counter the commercialization of traditional music by the recording and broadcast industries, as well as an attempt to fight against the racial and economic divisions that were perpetuated by the marketing of the music.

Even the folk music movement itself could not withstand such commercialization; by the late 1960's, "folk" was yet another label on a bin in the record store. Rather than identifying a certain type of creative process, as the Seegers would have had it, folk music was now identified by its style, which most often began with a solo singer and an acoustic guitar. Ethnicity was also still at the heart of commercial categorizations, and "folk music" was predominantly associated with white singers. Indeed, the commercial classification of music continues to invoke ethnicity. To some extent, this is no surprise; after all, if musical traditions are handed down within communities, it stands to reason that they be associated with the ethnicities of those communities, although the dynamics may be quite complex. For example, hip-hop culture developed during the 1970's as a way for urban African Americans and Latinos to interact in a positive way, yet rap, the music of hip-hop, is generally labeled African American—even while other groups (such as Asian Americans) adopt the style as an expression of their own identities.

It is unlikely that a 1900 prognosticator could have imagined anything like hip-hop, let alone envisioned the inclusion of rap artists in an encyclopedia such as this one. Even today, there is debate over whether the recited lyrics of rap can be considered music; and the rap artists' use of disc-jockey techniques and electronic manipulation of preexisting recordings is a long way from what constituted composition in 1900. One could fill many pages discussing the precursors of rap's musicalization of the spoken word in African American history. Nevertheless, rap music is also a reminder that technology has continually changed not only the way musicians work but also what they think music is.

A 1900 prognosticator would have thought much differently about genre (a French word that means "type" or "category"). In 1900 attempts to categorize music tended to focus on national style or on the different forms of classical music—templates for composition such as the brief symphonic overture, the storytelling symphonic poem, and the long, four-movement symphony; for small groups of solo instruments, the sonata, trio, and quartet; for solo instrument accompanied by orchestra, the concerto; for voice (usually with instrumental accompaniment), the song or aria; and the grandest spectacle of all, opera, a staged story set to music. The differences among such forms seem to matter less now, although many listeners respond quickly to the differences among the country, rock, blues, and musical-theater templates for songs. Today listeners encounter a wider range of music than ever before, with the result that they tend to categorize music by broad traditions rather than by the different forms within those traditions. Moreover, the Romantic notion of music as universal expression makes us reluctant to pigeonhole different kinds of music in separate compartments. Miles Davis quite rightly observed that music is "just music."

Davis was understandably concerned that categorizations of music were likely to get something wrong. Nevertheless, it is necessary to recognize differences in genre and style in order to understand music. Just as one needs to know the language of a speaker in order to respond to what the speaker is saying, one needs familiarity with a musical genre in order to respond fully to its expression. The sound of a slide guitar in a country song recorded in Nashville expresses something quite different from the same sound in Hawaiian music. In fact, a number of twentieth century classical composers relied on the genres they inherited from the nineteenth century to give their works meaning—especially the symphony. Aaron Copland developed a sound that is now iconic of America by working out a style of melody rooted in folk songs and dance tunes and fitting such melodies into symphonies, ballets, and other forms. In the "neoclassical" movement begun in the 1920's, composers such as Igor Stravinsky, Paul Hindemith, and Ottorino Respighi revived many of the forms of the eighteenth century and earlier as a way of drawing attention away from the Romantic expressivism that they regretted inheriting from the nineteenth century. In the Soviet Union, the symphony genre, which had connoted heroism ever since Ludwig van Beethoven's *Eroica* symphony of 1805, provided the kind of heroic expression that the dictator Joseph Stalin desired for the Soviet state. Dmitri Shostakovich composed such works; indeed, compared with other symphonies his works often seem overly heroic—so much so that listeners who know the genre well sometimes feel that he was secretly thumbing his nose at the Soviet regime.

Developments in music, of course, have much to do with the other events of history. By 1900 the United States had the world's largest economy. England, France, and the Netherlands held vast colonies around the globe, while Japan and the United States were beginning to annex territories. Many European countries were already republican or parliamentary democracies, but Germany, Austria, and Russia were still imperial monarchies while aristocrats and gentlemen dominated other countries as well. People behaved as though the foundations of society had been securely established, and all that was needed was perpetual improvement of the details. Nevertheless, the cracks were showing for anyone willing to look: poverty, mistrust between nations, and the inequality of women and minorities were at odds with most of these societies' stated progressive principles. Seemingly local revolutions kept undermining foundations: in politics, the spontaneous 1905 uprising in Russia; in science, Albert Einstein's 1905 theories of relativity and quantum mechanics; in painting, cubism and expressionism. Three of the century's greatest composers—Arnold Schoenberg, Stravinsky, and Béla Bartók—produced some of their most daring works before 1914, the year when the onset of World War I changed everything. All the countries involved in the war suffered horrific losses, and the war brought down the monarchies of Germany and Austria (which became democratic) as well as that of Russia (which became the totalitarian Soviet Union). During the 1920's, the economies of those three countries failed to recover, and the economic depression spread around the globe by the early 1930's.

Thus, during the 1920's and 1930's, society and its institutions seemed broken and ready for reinvention. If music before World War I tended toward the large striking statement or at least the small sentimental statement, music between the world wars was often fashioned with a view toward reinventing music's social function. This encyclopedia tells how musicians such as Hindemith and Francis Poulenc sought to take classical music off its pedestal and make it useful to people. Zoltan Kodály, Carl Orff, and others in central Europe got involved in teaching music to small children, as did Shin'ichi Suzuki, who was studying in Germany at the time. Darius Milhaud, Kurt Weill, the young Copland, and many others incorporated jazz elements into their work. It was not just that jazz's driving, syncopated rhythms captured something about modern life during the Jazz Age of the 1920's. Jazz also represented the promise of a new, less racialized social structure. (This aspect of jazz was celebrated in Europe more than in America, where most jazz performance was racially segregated well past World War II.) Furthermore, because it was new, not yet codified, and evolving swiftly, jazz represented possibility. George Gershwin aimed to elevate jazz by fitting it to the templates of "good" music—rhapsody, concerto, symphonic poem, and opera. Even the notion that jazz involved improvisation was not clear; by the late 1920's, the now-standard jazz form in which soloists improvise over the chord changes of a popular tune was just being tested by Louis Armstrong and others. The image of jazz at the time belonged to Bing Crosby as much as to Armstrong.

World War II (1939-1945) brought the Great Depression to an end, and with the rising prosperity of the 1950's came less attention to music's social function and more attention to the intrinsic properties of music itself. In the classical realm, the more populist styles lost prominence to the more structurally complex music of composers such as Pierre

Boulez, Karlheinz Stockhausen, and Milton Babbitt—composers who were little concerned with reaching a wide audience. Jazz was dominated by bebop and its successors; this music of Charlie Parker, Max Roach, Dizzy Gillespie, Thelonious Monk, Davis, and John Coltrane was not dance music but was rather created to stand on its own.

From the 1960's to the end of the century, musicians increasingly saw their work as commentary on the state of the world. The folk music movement had long seen itself as a vehicle for rally and protest, and this concept spread into rock music (notably in the work of John Lennon) and eventually into rap and other popular styles. Although no catastrophes on the scale of the world wars took place during the second half of the twentieth century, there was a tone of anxiety as people came to understand the possibility of nuclear annihilation or man-made environmental catastrophe. There were laments and anger over the various regional wars that did occur; George Crumb's *Black Angels: Thirteen Images from the Dark Land* is a particularly striking lament over the Vietnam War. There was soul-searching as Europeans tried to come to terms with the Nazi holocaust of the 1930's and 1940's and to build new relationships with their former colonies, and as Americans sought to end racial injustice. The 1970's brought the most powerful women's rights movement yet. (By the end of the century, significant numbers of women could be composers, finally.) There was a sense that the world was shrinking, as jet airplane travel became routine and as human beings even traveled to the moon. Thus Steve Reich sought to bring to classical music the cyclically repeated rhythmic and melodic patterns of African and Indonesian music; Julia Wolfe and others sought to bridge the stylistic gap between classical music and rock-inflected popular music; and Tan Dun and Osvaldo Golijov attempted syntheses of different styles from around the world.

Much music after 1950 sounded decidedly different from anything heard early in the century. This was especially true of experimental music by composers such as Harry Partch, John Cage, Pauline Oliveros, and Alvin Lucier. Nowhere was sonic unfamiliarity more significant than in rock music, whose amplified sound and raw energy seemed to some more liberating and to others more threatening than almost anything else going on in the world. A 1900 prognosticator could scarcely have imagined these sounds or their diversity.

Early twentieth century historians sought to retrace the deepest, longest channel of the wide river of music, and it was understood that that deep channel belonged to the great European composers. Halfway through the century, people began to think music was not a single river; they began to talk of the world's "musics," in the plural. It is now difficult to identify a single main channel of music history. How would one decide what the main channel is? Is it the music that sells the most recordings? Is it the most sophisticated, advanced music? The most expressive music? Expressive for whom?

In fact, this is an age of musical eclecticism. *Musicians and Composers of the 20th Century* contains articles about musicians from many musical traditions, each with its own rich living history, and many people are quite familiar with a good deal of music from outside their traditions. Thus, the musicians chosen for inclusion represent the eclectic mixture of styles likely to be encountered by American audiences. The few entries on world music, for example, cannot possibly do justice to all the musics of the world, but they can stand for the large amount of world music that is being heard in America.

Many musical reference volumes from 1900 to the present have focused on the lives of important musicians. *Musicians and Composers of the 20th Century* does so with a special emphasis on their music. Now that the twentieth century is over, such an emphasis on the music offers an invitation to find historical patterns and connections that may not yet be obvious. This introduction has tried to show some relationships among disparate musical traditions. Readers may find other patterns of coherence or choose to focus on one particular genre or group of musicians without reference to other connections (a project facilitated by the Category Index and the Geographical Index at the end of Volume 5). Both kinds of research will be essential as new histories of the twentieth century are written. With its manageable and informative guides to further reading, this encyclopedia is meant to get readers started on such research. At the same time, this encyclopedia will have succeeded if it inspires readers to listen to some unfamiliar music or to hear something new in music they already know.

Alfred W. Cramer

Contributors

Michael Adams
CUNY Graduate Center

Bland Addison
Worcester Polytechnic Institute

Joshua Addison
Apple Hill Center for Chamber Music

Stephen Arthur Allen
Rider University

David E. Anderson
Seymour, Indiana

Abby Anderton
University of Michigan, Ann Arbor

Andy Argyrakis
Tribune Media Services

Erica K. Argyropoulos
University of Kansas

Sylvia P. Baeza
Applied Ballet Theater

Christa A. Banister
Saint Paul, Minnesota

John W. Barker
University of Wisconsin—Madison

Samantha Ryan Barnsfather
University of Florida

Maryanne Barsotti
Warren, Minnesota

Amy M. Bauer
University of California, Irvine

Michael Baumgartner
University of British Columbia

Alvin K. Benson
Utah Valley University

Luke Berryman
Boston University

Margaret Boe Birns
New York University

Nicholas Birns
The New School

Dan Blim
University of Michigan

Joseph A. Bognar
Valparaiso University

Jonathan W. Boschetto
Princeton University

Delbert S. Bowers
University of Southern California

Joel J. Brattin
Worcester Polytechnic Institute

Howard Bromberg
University of Michigan Law School

Gwynne Kuhner Brown
University of Puget Sound

Karina Bruk
Rutgers University

Thomas W. Buchanan
Ancilla Domini College

Richard R. Bunbury
Boston University

Gary W. Burdette
University of Kansas

Laura Burns
Chicago, Illinois

Justin D. Burton
Rutgers University

Susan Butterworth
Salem State College

Brian G. Campbell
Saint John's University

Carey L. Campbell
Weber State University

Daniela Candillari
Indiana University

Louis R. Carlozo
Loyola University Chicago

William S. Carson
Coe College

Christopher W. Cary
University of Florida

Eric Charry
Wesleyan University

John L. Clark, Jr.
Connecticut College

Gretchen Rowe Clements
SUNY, Buffalo

Bud Coleman
University of Colorado at Boulder

Michael Conklin
The College of New Jersey

Alfred W. Cramer
Pomona College

Rebecca Cypess
Yale University

Mary Virginia Davis
University of California, Davis

Frank Day
Clemson University

Lisa de Alwis
University of Southern California

Terry L. Dean
University of Georgia

Paul Dellinger
Wytheville, Virginia

Andrew Raffo Dewar
Wesleyan University

Marcia B. Dinneen
Bridgewater State College

Joy M. Doan
University of Michigan

Slawomir P. Dobrzanski
Kansas State University

Brian Doherty
Arizona State University

Ryan Scott Ebright
Peabody Institute

Robert P. Ellis
Northborough Historical Society

Thomas L. Erskine
Salisbury University

Oran Etkin
Brooklyn Conservatory

William A. Everett
*University of Missouri—Kansas City,
    Conservatory of Music & Dance*

Jack Ewing
Boise, Idaho

Sandra J. Fallon
Brandeis University

Dennis E. Ferguson
Boston University

Susan M. Filler
Chicago, Illinois

Frances Conover Fitch
Longy School of Music

Luminita Florea
Eastern Illinois University

Anthony J. Fonseca
Nicholls State University

Kate Friedricks
Tujunga, California

Gary Galván
LaSalle University

Cory M. Gavito
Oklahoma City University

Samantha Giarratani
Saint Anselm College

Dilek Göktürk
University of Florida

Sheldon Goldfarb
University of British Columbia

Melissa Ursula Dawn Goldsmith
Nicholls State University

Lewis L. Gould
University of Texas at Austin

S. Andrew Granade
*University of Missouri—Kansas City,
    Conservatory of Music & Dance*

Eben Graves
Tufts University

Jasmine L. Hagans
Northeastern University

Christopher Hailey
Franz Schreker Foundation

Fusako Hamao
Santa Monica, California

Brian Timothy Harlan
University of Southern California

Marcus Desmond Harmon
University of California, Los Angeles

Rob Haskins
University of New Hampshire

Diane Andrews Henningfeld
Adrian College

Eduardo Herrera
*University of Illinois at
    Urbana-Champaign*

Teri A. Herron
Indiana University, Bloomington

Dane O. Heuchemer
Kenyon College

Michael Hix
Troy University

Matthew Ryan Hoch
Shorter College

Peter J. Hoesing
Florida State University

John R. Holmes
Franciscan University of Steubenville

Lisa Hooper
Indiana University, Bloomington

Gregory D. Horn
*Southwest Virginia Community
    College*

Julie H. Huang
Oklahoma City University

Kelly A. Huff
University of Kansas

Mark Humphrey
Santa Monica, California

Stephen Husarik
University of Arkansas—Fort Smith

Raymond Pierre Hylton
Virginia Union University

Mitsutoshi Inaba
University of Oregon

Margaret R. Jackson
Troy University

Ron Jacobs
Asheville, North Carolina

Jeffry Jensen
Glendale Community College

Sheila Golburgh Johnson
Santa Barbara, California

Jeffrey Daniel Jones
University of Kentucky

Joseph E. Jones
*University of Illinois at
Urbana-Champaign*

Alexander Kahn
University of California, Berkeley

Ajay Kalra
University of Texas at Austin

Ryan R. Kangas
University of Texas at Austin

Paul E. Killinger
Western Illinois University

Mary J. King
California Baptist University

Joseph Klein
University of North Texas

Phillip J. Klepacki
University of Florida

Grove Koger
Boise State University

Helena Kopchick
University of Oregon

Madeleine Kuhns
Chicago, Illinois

Hedy Law
University of Chicago

Michael Lee
University of Oklahoma

Sonia Lee
*University of Illinois at
Urbana-Champaign*

Cara Lemon
ChoiceStream

James Leve
Northern Arizona University

Roberta L. Lindsey
Indiana University

Alexander Raymond Ludwig
Brandeis University

Paige Clark Lush
University of Kentucky

R. C. Lutz
Madison Advisors

Clyde S. McConnell
University of Calgary

Thomas MacFarlane
New York University

David W. Madden
California State University, Sacramento

Claire D. Maiers
Tufts University

Siu-Yin Mak
University of Southern California

Victoria Malawey
Kenyon College

Martin J. Manning
United States Department of State

Andrew R. Martin
Inver Hills Community College

Sonya Mason
Manhattan School of Music

LeeAnn Maton
Chicago, Illinois

Joseph R. Matson
University of Iowa

Michael Mauskapf
University of Michigan, Ann Arbor

Matthew Mihalka
University of Minnesota—Twin Cities

Sam Miller
Wesleyan University

Susan W. Mills
Appalachian State University

Don Allan Mitchell
Delta State University

Rachel E. Mitchell
*University of Illinois at
Urbana-Champaign*

Andrea Moore
Camerata Pacifica

Alice Myers
Bard College at Simon's Rock

John Myers
Bard College at Simon's Rock

Philip D. Nauman
Boston University

Leslie Neilan
*Virginia Polytechnic Institute and State
University*

William Nelles
*University of Massachusetts—
Dartmouth*

Byron Nelson
West Virginia University

Matthew Nicholl
Berklee College of Music

Ann Glazer Niren
Indiana University Southeast

Eric Novod
Rutgers University

Daniel Nuñez
University of Colorado at Boulder

Arsenio Orteza
St. Thomas More High School

Robert J. Paradowski
Rochester Institute of Technology

Jessica Payette
Stanford University

Alyson Payne
Southwestern Michigan College

Jonathan G. Secora Pearl
Perceptral LLC

Edward Pearsall
University of Texas at Austin

Michael Pelusi
Philadelphia, Pennsylvania

Amanda M. Pence
University of Kansas

Ray Pence
University of Kansas

Mark E. Perry
University of Kansas

Mark A. Peters
Trinity Christian College

Barbara Bennett Peterson
California State University, San Bernardino, Palm Desert Campus

John R. Phillips
Purdue University Calumet

Anastasia Pike
Patrick Henry College

Constance Pollock
Glendale, California

Mark D. Porcaro
University of Dayton

Luke A. Powers
Tennessee State University

April L. Prince
University of Texas at Austin

Bryan Proksch
McNeese State University

Sarah Caissie Provost
Brandeis University

P. Brent Register
Clarion University

Rosemary M. Canfield Reisman
Charleston Southern University

Betty Richardson
Southern Illinois University, Edwardsville

Diane M. Ricks
Georgia Southern University

Edward A. Riedinger
Ohio State University

Jerry E. Rife
Rider University

Gregory Rivkin
Rutgers University

R. Todd Rober
Kutztown University of Pennsylvania

Richard Allen Roe
Rockville, Maryland

J. Griffith Rollefson
University of Wisconsin—Madison

Ryan Ross
University of Illinois at Urbana-Champaign

Jason Salter
University of Calgary

Mark C. Samples
University of Oregon

Richard Sax
Lake Erie College

Peter Schimpf
Metropolitan State College of Denver

Eric Olds Schneeman
University of Southern California

Lacy Schutz
Sterling and Francine Clark Art Institute

Elizabeth Scoggin
Boston University

Laurie R. Semmes
Appalachian State University

R. Baird Shuman
University of Illinois at Urbana-Champaign

Douglas D. Skinner
Texas State University—San Marcos

Frederick Key Smith
Lake City Community College

Joanna R. Smolko
University of Pittsburgh

Tim J. Smolko
University of Georgia

Jennifer L. Smull
University of Texas at Austin

Juliana Snapper
University of California, San Diego

Staci A. Spring
McMurry University

Stephanie N. Stallings
Florida State University

James Stanlaw
Illinois State University

Jill Stapleton-Bergeron
University of Tennessee

August W. Staub
University of Georgia

David Steffens
Oklahoma City University

Eric S. Strother
University of Kentucky

Jonathan A. Sturm
Iowa State University

Tim Sullivan
University of Michigan

Janine Tiffe
Florida State University

Contributors

Monica T. Tripp
Spelman College

Judy Tsui
Chicago, Illinois

Jamshed Turel
McGill University

Stephen Valdez
University of Georgia

Yiorgos Vassilandonakis
*University of California,
   Berkeley*

Francesco Dalla Vecchia
University of Iowa

Daniel R. Vogel
Edinboro University of Pennsylvania

Mary H. Wagner
University of Michigan—Flint

Zachary Wallmark
University of Oregon

Gabriel Weiner
University of Southern California

David J. Weisberg
William Paterson University

Twyla R. Wells
University of Northwestern Ohio

Tyrone Williams
Xavier University

Mary A. Wischusen
Wayne State University

Mandy Suzanne Wong
University of California, Los Angeles

Sandra S. Yang
*California State Polytechnic
   University*

Elizabeth Anne Yeager
University of Kansas

Robert Young
Los Angeles, California

Jeremy Yudkin
Boston University

Key to Pronunciation

Many of the names of personages covered in *Musicians and Composers of the 20th Century* may be unfamiliar to students and general readers. For these unfamiliar names, guides to pronunciation have been provided upon first mention of the names in the text. These guidelines do not purport to achieve the subtleties of the languages in question but will offer readers a rough equivalent of how English speakers may approximate the proper pronunciation.

Vowel Sounds

Symbol	Spelled (Pronounced)
a	answer (AN-suhr), laugh (laf), sample (SAM-puhl), that (that)
ah	father (FAH-thur), hospital (HAHS-pih-tuhl)
aw	awful (AW-fuhl), caught (kawt)
ay	blaze (blayz), fade (fayd), waiter (WAYT-ur), weigh (way)
eh	bed (behd), head (hehd), said (sehd)
ee	believe (bee-LEEV), cedar (SEE-dur), leader (LEED-ur), liter (LEE-tur)
ew	boot (bewt), lose (lewz)
i	buy (bi), height (hit), lie (li), surprise (sur-PRIZ)
ih	bitter (BIH-tur), pill (pihl)
o	cotton (KO-tuhn), hot (hot)
oh	below (bee-LOH), coat (koht), note (noht), wholesome (HOHL-suhm)
oo	good (good), look (look)
ow	couch (kowch), how (how)
oy	boy (boy), coin (koyn)
uh	about (uh-BOWT), butter (BUH-tuhr), enough (ee-NUHF), other (UH-thur)

Consonant Sounds

Symbol	Spelled (Pronounced)
ch	beach (beech), chimp (chihmp)
g	beg (behg), disguise (dihs-GIZ), get (geht)
j	digit (DIH-juht), edge (ehj), jet (jeht)
k	cat (kat), kitten (KIH-tuhn), hex (hehks)
s	cellar (SEHL-ur), save (sayv), scent (sehnt)
sh	champagne (sham-PAYN), issue (IH-shew), shop (shop)
ur	birth (burth), disturb (dihs-TURB), earth (urth), letter (LEH-tur)
y	useful (YEWS-fuhl), young (yuhng)
z	business (BIHZ-nehs), zest (zehst)
zh	vision (VIH-zhuhn)

Complete List of Contents

Volume 1

Volume 2

Contents xxxv

Volume 3

Volume 4

Volume 5

Musicians
& Composers
of the 20th Century

A

Will Ackerman

American New Age composer and guitarist

Ackerman is one of the seminal figures in contemporary instrumental, or New Age, music. As a guitarist and composer, he focused on expression and emotion in his music; as a businessman and founder of a record label, he was responsible for promoting and producing notable artists in the genre.

Born: November 1, 1949; West Germany (now in Germany)

Principal recordings

ALBUMS (solo): *In Search of the Turtle's Navel*, 1976; *It Takes a Year*, 1977; *Childhood and Memory*, 1979; *Passage*, 1981; *Past Light*, 1983; *Conferring with the Moon: Pieces for Guitar*, 1986; *Imaginary Roads*, 1990; *The Opening of Doors*, 1992; *Sound of the Wind Driven Rain*, 1998; *Hearing Voices*, 2001; *Returning*, 2004.

The Life

Of European heritage, William Ackerman (AK-ur-man) was adopted as an infant by an American family. His adoptive father was an English professor at Stanford University; his adoptive mother committed suicide when he was young, so he was sent to live at a boarding school in Massachusetts. There he was involved in competitive swimming, and he also took an interest in poetry and guitar. Equally important to his brief musical experiences at this time was his growing attraction to the New England countryside.

After attending Stanford University, he worked for several years as a carpenter and a general contractor before settling in Windham County, Vermont. Largely self-taught as a guitarist—his only formal training was one lesson with Robbie Basho—Ackerman began a career as a composer and performer while at Stanford, although he did not know how to read music. In 1975 Ackerman founded Windham Hill Records and, as one of the pioneers of a musical movement that became known as New Age, profoundly impacted the American musical landscape. While managing the record label for more than two decades, Ackerman recorded several of his own albums and produced albums by such notable musicians as Alex de Grassi, Michael Hedges, Liz Story, and George Winston. After Ackerman sold Windham Hill Records in 1992, he recorded and produced music from his Imaginary Road studio in Vermont.

The Music

Though his music is often categorized as New Age, Ackerman's style might best be described as a lyrically emotional and primarily acoustic fusion of folk, jazz, and classical. Ackerman acknowledged that he was influenced by the American guitarists Basho, John Fahey, and Leo Kottke, as well as the French composer Erik Satie. Particularly noteworthy is Ackerman's use of a different open guitar tuning for almost every one of his compositions, resulting in music that relies—for Ackerman and the listener—more on emotion than on intellect. In performance, this usually requires the aid of an off-stage guitar tuner, and it lends an air of spontaneity and freshness to his music, whether live or recorded.

Early Albums. Ackerman's first two albums, *In Search of the Turtle's Navel* and *It Takes a Year*, are generally considered landmarks in New Age music, and they provided the foundation to the establishment of the Windham Hill label. Both recordings feature Ackerman's solo guitar on songs in miniature that are highly original and personal, especially the former's "Processional" (written as incidental music for a production of William Shakespeare's *Romeo and Juliet*) and the latter's "The Bricklayer's Beautiful Daughter" (perhaps his most famous piece) and "The Impending Death of the Virgin Spirit" (inspired by the suicide of his mother). Stylistically, both albums reflect a fusion of folk, bluegrass, and the blues.

Past Light. Ackerman fully embraced composing for ensemble settings on his fifth album, *Past Light*. Expanding the vocabulary of his music, as well as its timbres and textures, Ackerman reached out to guest performers for *Past Light*. Particularly noteworthy on *Past Light*, the strongest of Ackerman's ensemble albums, are the tracks "Visiting," "Garden," "Ventana," and "Night Slip." Following albums featured a notable list of guest artists, including Charles Bisharat, Chuck Greenberg, Michael Hedges, Michael Manring, Paul McCandless, Tim Story, Russel Walder, George Winston, and the Kronos Quartet.

Sound of the Wind Driven Rain *and* Hearing Voices. Both nominated for Grammy Awards, these albums are marked by the addition of the human voice. On the heels of several ensemble-based albums, *Sound of the Wind Driven Rain* finds Ackerman's guitar taking the central melodic role, and the album is supported by the earthy vocals of African musician Samite and various guest instrumentalists. *Hearing Voices* also includes the vocal work of Samite and six other singers. Though *Hearing Voices* includes texts in such languages as Luganda, Gaelic, Arabic, Hebrew, Italian, Hindi, and Sanskrit, the meaning of the words is secondary to the manner in which their sounds blend with the guitar and other instruments.

Returning. In 2004 Ackerman revisited eleven pieces from previous albums, reinterpreting and rerecording them as intimate solo expressions. The result is an album in which each track is imbued with new meaning and emotion. Despite the fact that *Returning* contains no new music, it reaffirmed Ackerman's personal style and demonstrated his mature reinterpretations. The technology and instruments employed give a fresh sound to the pieces.

Musical Legacy

With numerous gold and platinum albums to his name, as well as two Grammy nominations and a Grammy Award for *Returning*, Ackerman established himself as a popular and successful guitarist. He performed at such notable venues as the Imperial Palace in Japan, the Kremlin, the Montreux Jazz Festival, Carnegie Hall, and the Hollywood Bowl. As an artist and the founder and principal producer of Windham Hill Records, Ackerman played a sig-

nificant role in the establishment and perpetuation of the style of instrumental music known as New Age. Perhaps most noteworthy, however, was Ackerman's focus on writing and performing music that emphasized emotion over intellect without sacrificing quality.

Frederick Key Smith

Further Reading

Bank, Rena F. "Shhh! Don't Call His Music 'New Age.'" *The New York Times*, Sepember 11, 1988, p. NJ19. Informative article discusses Ackerman's music, including his compositional style, in the context of New Age music.

Bronstein, Scott. "Making Money Out of 'Mellow.'" *The New York Times*, May 4, 1986, p. F4. Discusses the success of the Windham Hill label, focusing on Ackerman's influence on the company.

Cohen, Jonathan. "Six Questions with Will Ackerman." *Billboard*, November 19, 2005: 42. Provides a basic overview of Ackerman's creation of and involvement with the Windham Hill label.

Kleinfield, N. R. "Soft Music: What a Grind." *The New York Times*, November 8, 1992, p. 391. An informative and largely biographical article on Ackerman, before and after his involvement with Windham Hill.

Taylor, Chuck. "At Twenty-five, Windham Hill Keeps Its Spirit Alive." *Billboard*, July 21, 2001: 1. A retrospective look at the Windham Hill label, including material on Ackerman's life and music.

See also: Satie, Erik.

Roy Acuff

American country singer, songwriter, and fiddle player

Acuff grew up immersed in the rich musical climate of southeast Tennessee: lonesome mountain ballads, fiddle tunes, and church hymns. After World War II, when country artists were going for a smooth, pop-oriented style, Acuff never abandoned his Southern roots.

Born: September 15, 1903; Maynardville,
  Tennessee
Died: November 23, 1992; Nashville, Tennessee
Also known as: Roy Claxton Acuff (full name);
  King of Country Music
Member of: Roy Acuff and His Smokey
  Mountain Boys

Principal recordings

ALBUMS (solo): *Old Time Barn Music*, 1951; *Songs of
  the Smokey Mountains*, 1955; *Great Speckled Bird*,
  1958; *Once More It's Roy Acuff*, 1961; *That Glory
  Bound Train*, 1961; *Hymn Time*, 1962; *Country
  Music Hall of Fame*, 1963; *Hand-Clapping Gospel
  Songs*, 1963; *Roy Acuff Sings American Folk
  Songs*, 1963; *Star of the Grand Ol' Opry*, 1963; *The
  World Is His Stage*, 1963; *Great Train Songs*, 1965;
  Roy Acuff, 1965; *The Voice of Country Music*,
  1965; *Roy Acuff Sings Hank Williams*, 1966;
  Waiting for My Call to Glory, 1966; *I Saw the
  Light*, 1970; *Roy Acuff Time*, 1970; *Sunshine
  Special*, 1970; *Time*, 1970; *Back in the Country*,
  1974; *Smokey Mountain Memories*, 1975; *That's
  Country*, 1975; *Wabash Cannonball*, 1975; *So
  Many Times*, 1995; *Fireball Mail*, 2004; *Just a
  Closer Walk with Thee*, 2006.
ALBUMS (with Roy Acuff and His Smokey
  Mountain Boys): *Fly Birdie Fly*, 1990; *Hear the
  Mighty Rush of Engine*, 2001.

The Life

Roy Claxton Acuff (AK-uhf) was born in a small
town in the Smokey Mountains near Knoxville,
Tennessee. Acuff's main interests as a child were
sports, and he excelled at baseball. He was scheduled for a tryout with the Yankees, but severe sun-
stroke contracted on a fishing trip in Florida, and a
subsequent nervous breakdown, confined him to
bed for all of 1930. He picked up his father's fiddle
to pass the time, and when he recovered he was
good enough to join Doc Haur's traveling medicine
show. Acuff found he enjoyed pitching the cure-all
Mocoton Tonic and entertaining crowds. He honed
his showmanship skills and his singing on the road,
and in 1932 he formed his own band, the Crazy Ten-
nesseans. After they performed for local radio stations, they were asked to try out for the Grand Ole
Opry in 1938, and they were hired.

The 1940's were a productive period for Acuff.

During World War II, he was as popular as the big
band leaders among the soldiers. It is said that Japanese soldiers in Pacific would taunt U.S. Marines by
shouting, "To hell with Roy Acuff!" In 1942, with
songwriter Fred Rose, Acuff formed Acuff-Rose
Music Publishing, turning country-music songwriting into a professional business. By 1985 the
company held twenty thousand copyrights.

After touring in the 1950's and 1960's—including shows with Elvis Presley—Acuff observed record sales declining, so he decided to perform
mainly at the Grand Ole Opry. However, the folk
boom in the 1960's gave acoustic music new life and
a new audience: urbanites and college students. In
1971 Acuff sang on the Nitty Gritty Dirt Band's
crossover album "Will the Circle Be Unbroken"
with several other veteran country stars, exposing
him to a new generation of fans.

The Music

Acuff grew up immersed in the rich musical climate of southeast Tennessee: lonesome mountain
ballads, fiddle tunes, and church hymns. After the
war, when many country artists were going for a
smooth, pop-oriented style, Acuff never abandoned his Southern roots.

"Great Speckled Bird." A famous and widely
performed song in the country-music canon,
"Great Speckled Bird" clearly demonstrates early
country's close connections to gospel and Anglo-
American ballads. The title refers to a phrase from
the King James Version of the Bible (Jeremiah 12:9),
allegorically describing the persecution of the
Christian church. Acuff heard the song performed
by Charlie Swain and his group, the Black Shirts, in
1935, paying fifty cents for a copy, and he immediately incorporated the song into his repertoire. A
talent scout for the American Record Company
(which later became Columbia Records) looking for
the song signed Acuff and recorded his rendition in
1936.

"Wabash Cannonball." When Acuff and his
band first recorded this song in 1936, Sam "Dynamite" Hatcher handled the vocals. Published in
1904, and recorded by several country artists, including the Carter Family in 1929, this song is still a
bluegrass and country standard. Though the Wabash Railroad did have a Cannonball speedster
running in the 1880's between various Midwest lo-

cations, the song exaggerates its exploits, making it America's mythical train. Acuff recorded his version in 1947, with its memorable train-whistle introduction. This was one of Acuff's most requested numbers, played at every public performance. In 1965, after being asked how many times he had played the song, Acuff supposedly said, "About three times a day, 365 days a year, for thirty years."

"Precious Jewel." As a boy Acuff said that he had wondered how the earth could hold all sorts of treasures, but when a body is buried, it cannot contain the soul. While driving in the car late one night in 1940, with band members Pete "Bashful Brother Oswald" Kirby and "Sister" Rachel Veal, Acuff imagined an inspirational tune about the premature death of a young woman, a jewel on earth and in heaven. Within half an hour, he finished writing the song. Acuff and his band recorded "Precious Jewel" in April, and it became one of their most enduring pieces. In the 1980's, Acuff experienced the death of his wife and his band members Howdy Forrester and Jimmie Riddle. He rereleased this poignant song in 1987, this time as a duet with fellow veteran country superstar Charlie Louvin (a video came out in 1989). This version hit number eighty-seven on the country charts, the last time Acuff would appear on the charts.

"Wreck on the Highway." In 1938 the Dixon brothers recorded a maudlin song about a severe drunk-driving car accident in rural North Carolina. Their "I Didn't Hear Anybody Pray" met with only modest success. However, Acuff, thinking it was in the public domain, changed the melody slightly, deleted several stanzas, and altered the words in a few places. His more powerful version—"Wreck on the Highway"—went on to become a hit in 1942. In 1946 Acuff became concerned that Dorsey Dixon was indeed the composer, and he arranged for Dixon to receive credit. The song has many of the indispensable features of folk and early country music: the pain of needless and violent death always present in the background of daily life, the evils of drink, and the perils of neglecting Jesus.

Musical Legacy

In 1943 the governor of Tennessee, Prentice Cooper, declared that hillbilly music was disgracing the state. In protest Acuff entered the gubernatorial primaries in 1944. In 1948 he won the Republican nomination, although he was soundly defeated in the election. While Acuff's political career was modest, he left an impressive musical impact. In 1962 he was inducted into the Country Music Hall of Fame (the first living person ever elected). He received a Lifetime Achievement Grammy Award from the National Academy of Recording Arts and Sciences in 1987; in 1998 it gave him a Hall of Fame Award for "Wabash Cannonball." He was the first recipient of the Minnie Pearl Humanitarian Award in 1989. He received the American National Medal of the Arts from the National Endowment of the Arts in 1991. Acuff starred in eight films, and he has a star on the Hollywood Walk of Fame (at 1541 Vine Street). He performed before President Richard Nixon in 1974, and President George H. W. Bush gave him a Kennedy Center Honors Award in 1991.

James Stanlaw

Further Reading

Brown, Garrett, ed. *Legends of Classic Country*. Richmond, Va.: Time-Life Books, 2000. An illustrated history of country music until the 1970's that has a chapter on Acuff by a country-music scholar Charles Wolfe.

Dunkleberger, A. C. *King of Country Music: The Life Story of Roy Acuff*. Nashville, Tenn.: Williams, 1971. Acuff tells the story of his life, with details about his family and his life on the road.

Kingsbury, Paul, and Alanna Nash, eds. *Will the Circle Be Unbroken: Country Music in America*. New York: DK, 2006. Beautifully written and illustrated history of "America's sound track," with excellent material on Acuff.

Schlappi, Elizabeth. *Roy Acuff: The Smoky Mountain Boy*. Gretna, La.: Pelican, 1993. This well-researched biography is by a longtime collector of Acuff memorabilia. Includes a detailed discography until 1977 of some four hundred songs.

See also: Carter, Maybelle; Jones, George; Presley, Elvis; Scruggs, Earl; Watson, Doc; Williams, Hank.

John Adams

American classical composer and conductor

Adams's musical career embraces a wide range of musical genres, including the opera, the concerto, and works for chamber and symphony orchestras. His large-scale compositions are both innovative and deeply connected to the traditions of Western music.

Born: February 15, 1947; Worcester, Massachusetts
Also known as: John Coolidge Adams (full name)

Principal works

CHAMBER WORKS: Piano Quintet, 1970; *American Standard*, 1973 (for unspecified ensemble); *Grounding, 1975* (for three solo voices, instruments, and electronics); *China Gates*, 1977; *Phrygian Gates*, 1977; *Shaker Loops*, 1978.

ELECTRONIC WORK: *Onyx 4-Channel Tape*, 1976.

OPERA (MUSIC): *Nixon in China*, 1987 (libretto by Alice Goodman); *The Death of Klinghoffer*, 1991 (libretto by Alice Goodman); *I Was Looking at the Ceiling and Then I Saw the Sky*, 1995 (libretto by June Jordan); *Doctor Atomic*, 2005 (libretto by Peter Sellars).

ORATORIO (music): *El Niño*, 2000 (libretto by Peter Sellars).

ORCHESTRAL WORKS: *Common Tones in Simple Time*, 1979; *Shaker Loops*, 1983 (for string orchestra); *Harmonielehre*, 1985; *Eros Piano*, 1989 (for piano and orchestra); Violin Concerto, 1994; *On the Transmigration of Souls*, 2002; *The Dharma at Big Sur*, 2003 (for violin); *My Father Knew Charles Ives*, 2003.

VOCAL WORKS: *Harmonium*, 1981 (for chorus and orchestra); *Grand Pianola Music*, 1982; *The Wound-Dresser*, 1988 (for baritone and orchestra).

The Life

John Coolidge Adams was born in Worcester, Massachusetts, on February 15, 1947, and raised in Woodstock, Vermont, and East Concord, New Hampshire. Devoted amateur musicians, his par-ents encouraged their son's musical interests. His father taught Adams the clarinet, and the composer remembers singing alongside his mother in a community production of the musical *South Pacific*. Adams also remembers sitting on a piano bench next to Duke Ellington when the legendary jazz musician and composer came to perform at a dance hall run by Adams's grandfather.

During his teenage years Adams's musical experiences were centered on Boston, where he took clarinet lessons and attended concerts. His instrumental skills and familiarity with orchestral music allowed him to be called upon occasionally to play as a substitute clarinetist in the Boston Symphony Orchestra. Entering Harvard University, he studied with composer Leon Kirchner and others, absorbing—finally, with serious misgivings—the twelve-tone serialism that at the time dominated the teaching of composition in many university music departments.

Attracted by the experimental arts scene in the San Francisco Bay Area, Adams headed west in his Volkswagen Beetle after completing his undergraduate studies at Harvard. First supporting himself by operating a forklift in a warehouse, he began teaching within a year at the San Francisco Conservatory of Music, where he also led a new music ensemble and explored electronic sound. Among his influences at the time were the works of composer John Cage, who embraced the notion of chance events in the creation of art, and the compositions of such minimalists as Steve Reich and Terry Reilly.

With the appearance of mature compositions such as *Shaker Loops* and *Harmonium* in the early 1980's, Adams became a prominent musical personality in the San Francisco area. In 1983, after several years as an artistic adviser to the San Francisco Symphony, he became its first composer-in-residence. While remaining closely identified with the Bay Area, where he has settled with his wife and two children, Adams has also forged a strong relationship with Los Angeles and its Philharmonic Orchestra, which he has conducted on several occasions.

Living in California inspired Adams to learn to read and speak Spanish, and his growing affinity for Latin American culture led to the composition of an oratorio, *El Niño*, with texts in Spanish, Latin, and English. He has also established strong ties

John Adams. (Hulton Archive/Getty Images)

with Europe as both conductor and composer. In 2003 Adams was awarded the Pulitzer Prize for his composition *On the Transmigration of Souls*, a work commissioned by the New York Philharmonic in memory of the victims of the terrorist attacks of September 11, 2001. The premiere recording of the work received three Grammy awards in 2005.

The Music

Adams began composing by the age of ten, and by fourteen he had written a suite for string orchestra and heard it performed by a local community orchestra. Early influences included American popular music as well as the traditional repertoire of the European classics. Adams has always been an avid student of what he has called "vernacular" music, but exposure to the great symphonic works of such composers as Jean Sibelius and Anton Bruckner was especially formative. Adams remarks that his life was "utterly transformed" by the availability of long-playing recordings of classical music, which

had become commonplace and affordable in the mid-1950's.

While Adams attended Harvard University in the late 1960's, he absorbed the music of European and American modernism while also listening to pop, soul, and rock music. The contrast between the exuberance of popular music and the seemingly exhausted, uncommunicative language of contemporary classical music weighed upon him, and in 1972 he determined that he needed a change of scene. Instead of traveling to Europe—where he felt he would find music of the same unappealing, intellectual modernism—he went to California, which he made his home in 1972.

Shaker Loops. One of the experimental musical trends that Adams encountered in California was minimalism. Characterized by a devotion to pulse, repetition, and sustained diatonic harmony, minimalism was deeply attractive to Adams. Though he was younger than most of his minimalist colleagues, he soon became recognized as a significant contributor to the movement. His initial exploration of the minimalist idiom took the form of a work for strings called *Wavemaker*, which was soon withdrawn. In 1977 *Shaker Loops*, for string sextet, was completed and attracted immediate attention. A 1983 adaptation of the work for string orchestra is widely regarded as a classic of the minimalist idiom. Among the technical ideas underlying *Shaker Loops*, and contributing to its title, is the "tape loop" familiar from earlier works by Reich and others in which a piece of audiotape cycles repeatedly through a playback head.

Harmonielehre. Beginning in the 1980's, Adams completed large-scale works almost yearly. These vary widely in mood and artistic intention, but their progress is marked by Adams's increasing confidence in using large orchestral forces. *Harmonium* for orchestra and chorus sets poems by the Englishman John Donne and the American Emily Dickinson. *Harmonielehre*, another commission from the San Francisco Symphony, appeared just over three years later. The title, translated as "theory of harmony," is a reference to an influential book by Austrian composer Arnold Schoenberg. Adams said that this composition was "the culmination—so far—of my teaching myself about harmony." However, *Harmonielehre* seems to address harmony not just in Adams's musical practice but also in his personal experiences: The composer related that it was an intense dream that unlocked the composition of this work after months of creative blockage.

Nixon in China *and* The Death of Klinghoffer. First presented in 1987 and 1991 respectively, these operas established Adams as an artist willing to address unconventional subject matter and to challenge the public with novel musical gestures. The idea for *Nixon in China* originated not with the composer but with stage director Peter Sellars. The action of the opera takes place over a few days in February, 1972, when U.S. president Richard Nixon traveled to China to meet with Chinese leader Mao Zedong. The representation of an historic event in an opera while many of its participants were still living was rightly thought to be artistically daring, and Adams's aggressive score lives up to Sellars's conception and the libretto by poet Alice Goodman. Adams collaborated again with Sellars and Goodman for *The Death of Klinghoffer*, but this time difficulties beset the project because of its subject matter: the hijacking by terrorists of the cruise liner *Achille Lauro* in 1985, during which an American passenger, Leon Klinghoffer, was murdered and thrown overboard. Many who heard the opera, and others who only read about it, took exception to its representation of the terrorists, and some even asserted that the terrorists were more sympathetically portrayed than the victims. Regardless of this intractable political and social controversy, *The Death of Klinghoffer* is a resonant and theatrically effective work.

Violin Concerto. In writing a violin concerto, Adams was acutely aware of the standard set by the great Romantic and early twentieth century composers, and more than one aspect of Adams's composing practices might have precluded him from the task. For example, Adams did not think of himself as a natural melodist, and he was not accustomed to setting out in advance the detailed architecture of a piece. Moreover, he was not a string player—though he was fascinated by the violin and prepared for this composition by listening to many performances of non-Western bowed string instruments. It was Adams's initial conception to follow a fast first movement with concluding slower movements, but the work eventually exhibited the familiar fast-slow-fast three-movement form, with the middle section assuming an intensely lyrical, rhapsodic character contrasting strongly with the pyrotechnical, virtuosic writing in the outer movements. A measure of the work's artistic success is that it was played by more than a dozen violin soloists in the three years following its first performance.

Doctor Atomic. This work is centered on J. Robert Oppenheimer, director of the Manhattan Project, which developed the atomic bombs dropped on Hiroshima and Nagasaki, Japan, in August, 1945. The theme of the opera was suggested to Adams by the director of the San Francisco Opera, and the work was composed in less than eighteen months. Using diverse documentary and literary sources, Adams and director Sellars sought to evoke the personalities and emotions of the story's characters as they prepared for the weapons test at the Trinity site in July, 1945. Adams's first inspirations came from the music of science-fiction films of the post-World War II era and from the works of the French-born American composer Edgard Varèse, whose *Déserts* (1954) suggested to Adams a "post-nuclear holocaust landscape." Like several other Adams works, *Doctor Atomic* employs synthesizers, amplified voices, acoustic instruments, and taped sounds and music. Its premiere took place at the San Francisco Opera on October 1, 2005.

The Dharma at Big Sur *and* My Father Knew Charles Ives. These works, both from 2003, can be paired on the basis of how they reflect, respectively, Adams's productive encounter with California and the West and his New England origins. *The Dharma at Big Sur* is an indirect homage to Beat writer Jack Kerouac and, more directly, to California composer Lou Harrison. It is essentially a violin concerto written for a six-string electric violin tuned in Just Intonation, a system of tuning long favored by Harrison. The composition of the work was inspired by Adams's collaboration with the virtuoso violinist Tracy Silverman and embodies aspects of West Coast landscape and culture that are close to the composer's heart.

The title of *My Father Knew Charles Ives* refers to an innovative and somewhat eccentric composer who is a central figure in the history of American music. Noting that his father did not actually know Ives but might well have found him to be a delightful companion, Adams intends this composition to call to mind Ives's 1914 masterpiece, *Three Places in New England.*

Musical Legacy

Though performances of Adams's compositions are relatively frequent and widespread, recordings are the principal means through which listeners come to know his work. Adams's recordings of his own work are well supported not only by thorough, well-written liner notes but also by an expertly designed Web site run by Adams's technical organization. A meticulous attention to modern communications media is hardly unique to Adams, but the adequacy and transparency of this communication indicates an awareness not just of marketing but also of the need to bridge the distance between artists and the public. Adams's works are undoubtedly his most significant legacy, but the public form of his career has also notably contributed to the vitality of the contemporary music scene.

Clyde S. McConnell

Further Reading

Adams, John. "John Adams." http://www.earbox .com. Adams's official Web site offers biographical information, lists of works and recordings, links, and more.

May, Thomas, ed. *The John Adams Reader: Essential Writings on an American Composer.* Pompton Plains, N.J.: Amadeus Press, 2006. Engrossing book brings together reminiscences, reviews, and concert programs, though it lacks in-depth analysis.

Ross, Alex. "The Harmonist." *The New Yorker* 76, no. 41 (January 8, 2001): 40-46. Ross is a brilliant and sympathetic observer of Adams as musician and cultural figure.

Schiff, David. "Memory Spaces: John Adams's *On the Transmigration of Souls* Finds Redemption in September 11, and Should Bring Contemporary Classical Music to a New Audience." *The Atlantic Monthly* 291, no. 3 (April, 2003): 127-130. Describes Adams's "9/11" work and explains it in the context of the composer's earlier compositions.

Taruskin, Richard. "Music's Dangers and the Case for Control." *The New York Times*, December 9, 2001. A professor of music history at the University of California, Berkeley, articulates his belief that works such as *The Death of Klinghoffer* should be withheld from certain audiences, some of the time.

See also: Cage, John; Ellington, Duke; Nancarrow, Conlon; Reich, Steve; Salonen, Esa-Pekka; Schoenberg, Arnold.

Cannonball Adderley

American jazz saxophonist and composer

Adderley was a pioneer of the hard-bop, funky style of jazz prevalent in the 1960's and 1970's. At a time when popular interest in jazz was waning, he helped reestablish jazz music in the mainstream with a blues- and gospel-influenced sound.

Born: September 15, 1928; Tampa, Florida
Died: August 8, 1975; Gary, Indiana
Also known as: Julian Edwin Adderley (full name)

Principal recordings

ALBUMS: *The Adderleys: Cannonball and Nat*, 1955 (with Nat Adderley); *Cannonball Adderley and Strings*, 1955; *Presenting Cannonball*, 1955; *Julian Cannonball Adderley*, 1955; *In the Land of Hi-Fi*, 1956; *Cannonball En Route*, 1957; *Cannonball's Sharpshooters*, 1958; *Somethin' Else*, 1958 (with Miles Davis, Hank Jones, Sam Jones, and Art Blakey); *Alabama Concerto*, 1958; *Jump for Joy*, 1958; *Things Are Getting Better*, 1958 (with Milt Jackson); *Cannonball and Coltrane*, 1959 (with John Coltrane); *Cannonball Adderley Collection, Vol. 6: Cannonball Takes Charge*, 1959; *Cannonball Adderley Collection, Vol. 1: Them Dirty Blues*, 1960; *Cannonball Adderley Collection, Vol. 4: The Poll Winners*, 1960; *Cannonball Adderley Collection, Vol. 5: The Quintet at the Lighthouse*, 1960; *Know What I Mean?*, 1961; *African Waltz*, 1961; *The Quintet Plus*, 1961; *Nancy Wilson/ Cannonball Adderley*, 1961; *The Lush Side of Cannonball*, 1962; *Cannonball Adderley Collection, Vol. 2: Bossa Nova*, 1962; *Cannonball Adderley*

Collection, Vol. 7: Cannonball in Europe, 1962; *Cannonball Adderley Collection, Vol. 3: Jazz Workshop Revisited*, 1962; *Cannonball Adderley*, 1962; *Two for the Blues*, 1963; *Jazz Workshop Revisited*, 1963; *Fiddler on the Roof*, 1964; *Domination*, 1965; *Great Love Themes*, 1966; *Mercy, Mercy, Mercy! Live at "The Club,"* 1966; *74 Miles Away/Walk Tall*, 1967; *Why Am I Treated So Bad!*, 1967; *Accent on Africa*, 1968; *Country Preacher*, 1969; *The Happy People*, 1970; *Experience the E, Tensity, Dialogues*, 1970; *Inside Straight*, 1973; *Cannonball Adderley and Friends*, 1973; *Pyramid*, 1974; *Phenix*, 1975; *Lovers*, 1975; *Big Man*, 1975; *Bohemia After Dark*, 2003; *Cannonball Plays Zawinul*, 2004.

The Life

Julian Edwin "Cannonball" Adderley (AD-dur-lee) was born in Tampa, Florida, to musical parents. He began playing music as a child, and later he joined his high school's jazz group. After attending Florida A&M in Tallahassee, he directed the jazz band at Dillard High School in Fort Lauderdale from 1948 to 1956. During this time, while he studied at the U.S. Naval Academy School of Music, he played his saxophone in military bands and in other groups.

Adderley first arrived on the New York jazz scene in 1955, intending to accompany his brother, Nat, also a jazz instrumentalist, and start graduate school at New York University. By chance, he landed a gig with Oscar Pettiford and his band after sitting in with them at Club Bohemia, and this led to a recording contract. When Miles Davis first heard Adderley's saxophone, he was interested in collaborating. However, Adderley went back to Florida to teach, so it was not until October of 1957 that Adderley joined Davis's legendary group.

Adderley's career was launched by his participation in several influential recordings with Davis, including *Kind of Blue* (1959). Adderley went on to make several records under his own name, joining forces with his brother. They recorded and toured successfully until 1975. Later in his career, Adderley returned to teaching, which he loved, by incorporating lectures and workshops in his concerts on college campuses.

Adderley's nickname comes from childhood, when friends in Florida started calling him "Cannibal" because of his large appetite. This was then slurred into "Cannonball." Despite his aggressive-sounding nickname, Adderley was a jovial, intelligent, and kind gentleman. He died in 1975 after a massive stroke.

The Music

Adderley's musical style was rooted in gospel, blues, and jazz. He began listening to and collecting jazz records at a young age. At the same time, he was dancing to gospel music every Sunday night at the Tabernacle Baptist Church. When he first arrived in New York in the 1950's, Adderley was called the "new Bird" (after Charlie "Yardbird"

Cannonball Adderley. (Hulton Archive/Getty Images)

Parker, a popular jazz saxophonist who had recently died), but Adderley's warm sound and controlled style of improvisation guaranteed that he was a unique artist. His later releases under his own name were characterized by a funky, bluesy hard-bop style that appealed to both casual audiences and jazz purists.

Early Works. Although Adderley produced several records under his own name in the late 1950's, it was as a sideman for Davis that Adderley grew as an artist by contributing his sound to such successful albums as *Kind of Blue*. Playing alongside the remarkable tenor saxophonist John Coltrane greatly challenged Adderley and influenced the sound and style of his improvisations. Addeley's soul-infused, hard-swinging solos countered Coltrane's lengthy explorations, while the pair's impassioned playing provided a balance to the laid-back style of Davis.

Mercy, Mercy, Mercy! Live at "The Club." One might be easily fooled by the liner notes for this album, which place the setting of this live recording at "The Club." However, Adderley pretended to have recorded this album there as a favor to the Chicago club's owner, who was in need of business. The album was recorded in a Hollywood studio in 1966, with an audience invited to contribute the spirit of an appreciative crowd to the sound of the album. It became one of the top-selling jazz albums, and the title cut, written by Austrian-born pianist Joe Zawinul, was a Top 10 single. Other contributions to the album were Cannonball's "Sack o' Woe" and "Sticks," as well as Nat Adderley's "Fun" and "Games." The album reflected the spirit of the gospel and blues tradition, and it also explored the harmonic language of bebop.

Country Preacher. Recorded live at a Saturday-morning session of the Operation Breadbasket organization in 1969, this album melds Adderley's sociopolitical activism and his artistry. His group appeared at this event in conjunction with the Reverend Jesse Jackson, who was promoting justice and freedom for African Americans. The album contains stirring, uplifting, and poignant music, from the upbeat march "Walk Tall" to the bluesy "Country Preacher." The electric-piano stylings of Zawinul and Adderley's interactions with the audience enhance the soul-jazz, church-style feel of this album. The four-part "Afro-Spanish Omelette" explores avant-garde musical territory.

Musical Legacy

Witty and articulate, Adderley was a consummate bandleader, able to establish rapport with audiences while entertaining them as a creative soloist. Many of his works became leading sellers on the Riverside Records label, and his albums and singles often appeared on *Billboard* charts. At a time when jazz was moving toward more avant-garde styles, Adderley used the music of traditional African American culture in a modern context. He kept conventional concepts of melody and harmony in his music, and he expanded his blues foundation to include a variety of expressions from jazz, Latin, and pop traditions. His music reflected the pride of black Americans in the wake of the Civil Rights movement. Through his records, touring, and teaching in America and abroad, Adderley spread his legacy of social awareness.

Staci A. Spring

Further Reading

Baker, David N. *The Jazz Style of Cannonball Adderley: A Musical and Historical Perspective.* Miami, Fla.: Studio 224, 1980. Includes musical transcriptions for the study of Adderley's style. Bibliography, discography.

DeMichael, Don. "Cannonball Adderley: The Responsibilities of Success." *Down Beat* 63, no. 1 (January, 1996): 34. This reprint of a 1962 interview with the saxophonist gives highlights of his career and includes Adderley's views on his responsibility toward his audience.

Jones, Ryan Patrick. "'You Know What I Mean?' The Pedagogical Canon of 'Cannonball.'" *Current Musicology* 79/80 (Spring/Fall, 2005): 169. Explores the way Adderley applied his teaching methods to his everyday professional career.

Price, Tim, ed. *Julian "Cannonball" Adderley Collection.* Milwaukee, Wis.: Hal Leonard, 1995. Includes twenty-four solo transcriptions, performance notes, photographs, and an interview with Nat Adderley.

Sheridan, Chris. *Dis Here: A Bio-discography of Julian "Cannonball" Adderley.* Westport, Conn.: Greenwood Press, 2000. Annotated discography lists every Adderley recording session. Provides anecdotes and details of Adderley's daily life during his professional career.

Williams, Gene A. "Julian 'Cannonball' Adderley

(1928-1975)." *The Black Perspective in Music 4*, no. 3 (Autumn, 1976): 307. An article published shortly after his death comments on Adderley's life, music, and contributions to the African American community.

See also: Coltrane, John; Davis, Miles; Jones, Hank; Parker, Charlie.

Toshiko Akiyoshi

American jazz composer, pianist, and bandleader

A leading composer, Akiyoshi blends Japanese musical and cultural elements into her jazz compositions.

Born: December 12, 1929; Darien, China
Also known as: Toshiko Mariano
Member of: The Toshiko Akiyoshi Jazz Orchestra

Principal recordings

ALBUMS (solo): *Toshiko's Piano*, 1953; *Amazing Toshiko Akiyoshi*, 1954; *Toshiko, Her Trio, Her Quartet*, 1956; *The Many Sides of Toshiko*, 1957; *United Nations*, 1958; *Toshiko Mariano and Her Big Band: Recorded in Tokyo*, 1965; *Road Time*, 1976; *March of the Tadpoles*, 1977; *Salted Gingko Nuts*, 1978; *From Toshiko with Love*, 1981; *Remembering Bud/Cleopatra's Dream*, 1992; *Desert Lady/Fantasy*, 1993; *Monopoly Game*, 2001; *Shio Ginnan*, 2001.

ALBUMS (with the Lew Tabackin Big Band): *Kogun*, 1974; *Long Yellow Road*, 1975; *Insights*, 1976; *Tales of a Courtesan*, 1976; *Farewell to Mingus*, 1980; *European Memoirs*, 1982.

ALBUMS (with the Toshiko Akiyoshi Jazz Orchestra featuring Lew Tabackin): *Wishing Peace*, 1986; *Four Seasons of Morita Village*, 2001; *Hiroshima: Rising from the Abyss*, 2003.

WRITINGS OF INTEREST: *Life with Jazz*, 1996 (autobiography).

The Life

Toshiko Akiyoshi (toh-shee-koh a-kih-yoh-shee) was born in the Manchuria region of China to a family that, among others, profited from Japan's occupation of the region. Akiyoshi benefited from a substantial and strict educational system, and music was part of her curriculum, starting at age seven with training in classical piano.

With the collapse of the Japanese empire in 1945, her family lost everything, and it relocated to Japan. Akiyoshi remained interested in music, but she lacked an instrument. This motivated her to join a band that played popular tunes for American military personnel. Initially she kept this job a secret from her family, but it was decided later that Akiyoshi could play until she entered medical school. The family's difficult financial situation led to her advanced education being repeatedly postponed, however, and Akiyoshi began contemplating a career in music. Although she had focused on classical piano, Akiyoshi began exploring jazz after hearing several recordings, including Teddy Wilson's "Sweet Lorraine."

Akiyoshi soon moved to Tokyo, and by 1951 she was leading a combo, although listening to recordings remained her primary training tool (particularly those of Bud Powell). In 1953 Oscar Peterson heard Akiyoshi play, and he suggested to record producer Norman Granz that she be recorded. Granz recorded Akiyoshi later that year. In 1956 she entered Boston's Berklee School of Music, where she learned about jazz composition. She also found some professional success, with opportunities to play with many established artists (including Charles Mingus). Stereotyped as a woman and a foreigner, Akiyoshi was prevented from reaching the status she desired. In 1959, Akiyoshi married saxophonist Charlie Mariano. Forming a quartet, they enjoyed some success, finding an outlet for Akiyoshi's compositional endeavors.

Akiyoshi returned to Japan in 1964, where she recorded an album for the Jazz in Japan series, and she gave birth to a daughter, Michiru Mariano. Akiyoshi spent the second half of the decade working in Boston, New York, and Tokyo. She continued to find employment, but the number of people who saw beyond her gender and ethnicity remained a fairly small circle, jazz critic Leonard Feather being among the most notable. Her marriage soon ended, and much of her subsequent activity was focused on a 1967 New York big band debut.

In 1969 she married saxophonist Lew Tabackin,

and they moved to Los Angeles in 1972. There, they formed a quartet and a big band, which they initially organized as a rehearsal ensemble for Akiyoshi's continued compositional development. In 1974 the band's first album, *Kogun*, was released in Japan, where it was a commercial success. Other recordings followed, and by 1976 the band was winning *Down Beat* polls, and its albums were beginning to garner significant awards.

In 1982 Tabackin and Akiyoshi decided to move to New York, where they reorganized the ensemble as the Toshiko Akiyoshi Jazz Orchestra featuring Lew Tabackin. Although the group remained active until 2003, it did not achieve its previous level of commercial success. Nevertheless, Akiyoshi's works continued to earn critical acclaim. One of her longer compositions, *Hiroshima: Rising from the Abyss*, garnered considerable attention, and *Four Seasons of the Morita Village* won the *Swing Journal* Silver Award. Akiyoshi received fourteen Grammy Award nominations, and in 2007 she was named a National Endowment of the Arts Jazz Master.

The Music

Akiyoshi's gradual career development provided for a methodical and thorough musical growth. Her many years of piano practice resulted in an impressive level of technical ability and stylistic flexibility. Akiyoshi's compositional output includes works in swing, swing-shuffle, blues, waltz, Latin, ballad, and bebop styles, and her abilities are clearly revealed through her recordings, particularly those of Akiyoshi with the Lew Tabackin Big Band. Her scores point to many influences, including Mingus, Duke Ellington, Gil Evans, and Thelonious Monk.

Akiyoshi has composed works of modest and longer length. *Road Time*, *Insights*, and *Farewell to Mingus*, for example, include works ten minutes and longer. *Minimata*, a three-movement suite released on *Insights*, and "Henpecked Old Man," from the live album *Road Time*, have a recorded duration in excess of twenty-one minutes. Many of Akiyoshi's compositions, however, include extended sections available for improvised solos. "Henpecked Old Man," for example, features eight minutes of improvisation prior to the ensemble's entrance, and the work showcases several soloists. While Akiyoshi and Tabackin each displayed im-

provisational skills in these recordings (Tabackin was a particularly powerful soloist, on both tenor saxophone and flute), Akiyoshi devoted considerable space to featuring other members of the band, including Bobby Shew, Steven Huffsteter, Bill Byrne, and Bill Reichenbach. Although Akiyoshi's compositions lend much variety to the band's recorded legacy, it must also be noted that the quality of improvisation is very strong.

"Strive for Jive." Composed in a fast bebop style, this up-tempo song from *Tales of a Courtesan* evokes much of the Charlie Parker-Dizzy Gillespie tradition. In thirty-two-measure *aaba* form, the harmonic rhythm is fast, and the writing for the ensemble embraces bebop virtuosity. Although the voicings are rich in harmonic content, the composite shape of the harmonized melody recalls a standard bebop rendition of the tune. This work is among Akiyoshi's more virtuosic compositions of her early mature style.

Minimata. Akiyoshi's incorporation of Japanese music elements, played by Japanese musicians as well as imitated in stylized renditions by the band's players, gave the band's sound a unique identity. Appearing on *Insights* and organized in three movements, entitled "Peaceful Village," "Prosperity and Consequence," and "Epilogue," *Minimata* opens with a child (Akiyoshi's daughter) singing a traditional Japanese melody, which then transitions into a duet (for trumpet and flute), playing a variant of the opening tune in unison. The resulting imperfections in intonation between the two players bear a resemblance to the Japanese heterophonic performance style. In the final movement, traditional Japanese vocals and percussion (provided by No artists, from Japanese musical dramas) are superimposed upon Tabackin's final solo (with the rhythm section) and the ensemble's concluding tutti.

Japanese Sound. "Kisarazu Jink," a composition included in *Toshiko Mariano and Her Big Band: Recorded in Tokyo*, is built on a traditional Japanese tune, but Akiyoshi made no attempt to project the Japanese elements as authentic. Instead, Akiyoshi's nonmetrical piano introduction is followed by a hard-driving swing style, in 5/4 meter. *Tales of a Courtesan* is among the first of her recordings to reveal Akiyoshi's experiments in including Japanese elements within the big band environment, although the interest seems primarily focused on the philosophical side rather than in the musical vocabulary. In the live recording *Road Time*, and specifically in "Kogun," Japanese musical elements possess deeper compositional value. While Akiyoshi initially tended to keep the Japanese-oriented sections distinct from those in more traditional jazz styles, she did begin to blend them to a greater degree as the band's repertoire continued to expand.

While her charts present the players with considerable challenges, and the use of Japanese music elements can be viewed as her most notable contribution to jazz, in other areas Akiyoshi seems relatively conservative. Formally, outside of sections in which Japanese music elements are featured, she tends to write within standard jazz structures, sometimes sprinkled with phrase extensions and other formal alterations. Similarly, while she makes liberal use of extended harmonies, rich chromatically altered chords, tritone substitutions, and other reharmonization techniques, her works are quite tonal.

"Studio J." "Studio J" was inspired, according to Feather, by Akiyoshi's memories of improvisational training at the Berklee School of Music. Composed in the standard thirty-two-measure *aaba* form, this piece, which appears on *Insights*, features a mixture of traditional jazz harmony with more ambitious chromaticism and substantial use of extended harmonies. There is frequent use of contrary motion when the ensemble tutti is in voicings, and the rhythmic style is dense and complex. The extended solo section is followed by an energetic shout chorus, and Akiyoshi concludes the work by reprising the ensemble's opening idea.

Musical Legacy

Akiyoshi's greatest legacy lies in her original contribution to the field of jazz. As a woman, she is considered an exceptional musician and a pioneer. Her Japanese nationality presented another hurdle in achieving success in jazz, but she persevered. As a composer, she balanced convention with her own voice, releasing nothing that was not of excellent quality. Finally, her interest in blending Japanese elements into the big band compositional vehicle provided an early example for those artists active in the crossover movement.

Dane O. Heuchemer

Further Reading

Feather, Leonard. *The Passion for Jazz*. New York: Horizon, 1980. Feather was among Akiyoshi's most avid supporters, and this interview from 1976, with both Akiyoshi and Tabackin, concentrates on their careers up to the point where their big band was finally finding success. Feather also wrote the album notes for many of the Akiyoshi-Tabackin Big Band recordings, and his comments provide considerable background and insight into her works.

Koplewitz, Laura. "Toshiko Akiyoshi: Jazz Composer, Arranger, Pianist, and Conductor." In *The Musical Woman: An International Perspective, Volume II, 1984-85*, edited by Judith Lang Zaimont. New York: Greenwood Press, 1985. This is a fairly comprehensive treatment of Akiyoshi, including biographical information and a discussion of her approach to composition, her style, and more. The information is relevant to the Akiyoshi-Tabackin Big Band era.

Koyama, Kiyoshi. "Jazz in Japan." In *The Oxford Companion to Jazz*, edited by Bill Kirchner. Oxford, England: Oxford University Press, 2000. While Akiyoshi is just one of the musicians discussed, this article provides context for the atmosphere in which she began her career and found substantial popularity.

Lyons, Len. *The Great Jazz Pianists: Speaking of Their Lives and Music*. New York: Da Capo Press, 1983. An interview with Akiyoshi concentrates primarily on her style as a pianist, an issue that is understated in the study of her career.

See also: Ellington, Duke; Evans, Bill; Gillespie, Dizzy; Mingus, Charles; Monk, Thelonious; Parker, Charlie; Peterson, Oscar; Powell, Bud.

Herb Alpert

American trumpet player and record producer

In addition to pioneering an eclectic mix of mariachi, jazz, and rock and roll known as Ameriachi in the 1960's, Alpert cofounded A&M Records, which became a leading independent record label.

Born: March 31, 1935; Los Angeles, California
Also known as: Herbert Alpert (full name)
Member of: Herb Alpert and the Tijuana Brass

Principal recordings

ALBUMS (solo): *Just You and Me*, 1976; *Herb Alpert/ Hugh Masekala*, 1978; *Rise*, 1979; *Beyond*, 1980; *Magic Man*, 1981; *Fandango*, 1982; *Blow Your Own Horn*, 1983; *Wild Romance*, 1985; *Keep Your Eye on Me*, 1987; *Under a Spanish Moon*, 1988; *My Abstract Heart*, 1989; *North on South Street*, 1991; *Midnight Sun*, 1992; *Second Wind*, 1996; *Passion Dance*, 1997.

ALBUMS (with the Tijuana Brass): *The Lonely Bull*, 1962; *Herb Alpert's Tijuana Brass, Vol. 2*, 1963; *South of the Border*, 1964; *Going Places*, 1965; *Whipped Cream and Other Delights*, 1965; *S. R. O.*, 1966; *Tijuana Brass*, 1966; *What Now My Love*, 1966; *Herb Alpert's Ninth*, 1967; *Sounds Like*, 1967; *Beat of the Brass*, 1968; *Christmas Album*, 1968; *The Brass Are Comin'*, 1969; *Warm*, 1969; *Summertime*, 1971; *Solid Brass*, 1972; *You Smile, the Song Begins*, 1974; *Coney Island*, 1975; *Noche de amor*, 1983; *Bullish*, 1984; *Colors*, 1999.

SINGLES (solo): "This Guy's in Love with You," 1968; "I Need You," 1973 (with the Tijuana Brass); "Rotation/Angelina," 1979; "North on South St.," 1991; "Jump St.," 1991.

The Life

Born in Los Angeles in 1935, Herbert Alpert (AL-purt) grew up in a family of amateur musicians. His Russian father played mandolin, his mother played the violin, his sister played piano, and his brother played drums. Alpert began playing trumpet at age eight. Later, after two years of study at the University of Southern California, he left school to enlist as a trumpeter in the Sixth Army Band in San Francisco. His teachers over the years included Harold "Pappy" Mitchell, Ben Klatzkin, Lou Maggio, and Carmine Caruso.

In 1962 Alpert cofounded, with Jerry Moss, A&M Records (for Alpert and Moss). Each invested a paltry one hundred dollars in the venture, which was launched in Alpert's garage. The label's first record, *The Lonely Bull*, featured Alpert on trumpet with sounds from a live bullfight and a backing group of studio musicians dubbed the Tijuana Brass. Over the next three decades, A&M Records

discovered and signed a number of prominent musicians, including the Carpenters, Sting, Janet Jackson, and Garbage. By 1966 A&M Records was worth an estimated twenty million dollars, and in 1990 the label was sold to PolyGram for more than five hundred million dollars.

Active as a recording artist from 1958 to 1999, Alpert sold more than seventy-two million records worldwide. His accolades include seven Grammy Awards, sixteen Grammy nominations, fourteen platinum albums, five number-one albums, and a number-one single. With the sale of 13.7 million albums in 1966, he had an astonishing five albums at one time on the *Billboard* Top 20. His recording of "This Guy's in Love with You," by Burt Bacharach and Hal David, hit number one on the charts in 1968. In the 1970's he added other artistic expressions to his life, working in painting and sculpture. In 1988 he played "The Star Spangled Banner" at Super Bowl XXII in San Diego.

Alpert used his wealth to promote the performing arts, primarily through the Herb Alpert Foundation. In 1994 he funded the Alpert Award in the Arts through the California Institute of the Arts, an annual monetary prize that goes to five independent artists in the fields of dance, film-video, music, theater, and the visual arts. In 2007 he gave thirty million dollars to the University of California, Los Angeles, where the school of music was renamed in his honor.

The Music

Alpert's career divides roughly into three periods. From 1962 to the mid-1970's Alpert and the Tijuana Brass popularized Ameriachi, a fusion of jazz, mariachi, and rock and roll. Its brilliant sound of multiple mariachi trumpets over a Latin-rock accompaniment of acoustic guitar and drums drew a wide audience. In 1965 *Whipped Cream and Other Delights* captured the group at its height, and its racy cover, which featured an apparently naked woman covered in whipped cream, attracted popular attention. Alpert's solo career followed in the 1970's, a time during which Alpert recorded with trumpeter Hugh Masekela and produced the disco-funk-inspired sound epitomized by his album *Rise*. After a brief period of inactivity, Alpert made a comeback in 1996, issuing several albums featuring an eclectic mix of jazz, salsa, and hip-hop.

Going Places. The definitive Tijuana Brass album *Going Places* exhibits the musical formula that propelled Alpert to fame. The opening track, "Tijuana Taxi," composed by band member Ervan Coleman, commences with a honking horn over a shuffle drumbeat followed by the group's distinctive trumpeting over a marimba-guitar accompaniment. Composed in thirty-two-bar *aaba* form, this ditty moves forward on the sequencing of a short, catchy riff. Each *a* section features the seven-note riff in sequence. The bridge section includes an antiphonal call-and-response between the trumpets and the trombone, punctuated by the taxi horn. The following *a* sections explore different textures, employing solo marimba and dueting trumpets. "Spanish Flea" follows the same formula: a sequenced two-bar riff, a trumpet duet, a bridge featuring the trumpets with the answering trombone, a concluding section with solo balalaika and another trumpet duet, and continual punctuation points provided by the bass drum.

Rise. The release of *Rise* in 1979 solidified Alpert's solo career, propelling him back to the top of the charts after an extended absence. His newfound sound, with its heavy reliance on disco and funk, is evident in the opening moments of the album's first track, "1980," an Alpert composition. The classic Tijuana Brass instruments are now replaced by an electronically altered trumpet sound (with a heavy reverb and occasionally synthesized), an electric piano, and a synthesized bass. However, "1980" includes many of Alpert's tried-and-true formulas: a prominent trumpet duet toward the end of the track, a repeated sequenced riff, phrase punctuations played by the snare drum, and a bridge section juxtaposing the trumpet and the bass. Alpert's Tijuana Brass roots reappear in the background of the album's title track, which includes a marimba, mariachi-inspired turn figures on the trumpet, and nonmusical source material, including talking and a clap track.

The Late Albums. Alpert shows an interest in a variety of musical styles in *Second Wind*, *Passion Dance*, and *Colors*. Much of *Second Wind* draws on jazz fusion, especially late Miles Davis, while *Passion Dance* turns to salsa. The difference between Alpert's late recordings and his 1980's-era albums is apparent in "Route 101," a cover from *Fandango*. Latin sounds, together with elements of hip-hop,

return in *Colors*. The album is almost completely electronic, including an electronic accordion on "Libertango," though the cover of "Magic Man" uses Alpert's more familiar laid-back Latin sound. None of these late albums achieved the notoriety of his earlier recordings. All were released on another Alpert-Moss venture, the short-lived Almo Sounds label.

Musical Legacy

Alpert's musical legacy is threefold. First, he demonstrated the economic viability and popular potential of purely instrumental music, blazing a new trail that made possible the careers of instrumentalists such as Chuck Mangione, Kenny G, and Chris Botti. Second, his work as a record executive at A&M Records led to the discovery of a number of highly influential musicians. Finally, much of Alpert's legacy is still being written, as his foundation has shaped the paths of young musicians through endowments, scholarships, and grants.

Bryan Proksch

Further Reading

Erdmann, Tom. "A Passion for Creativity: An Interview with Herb Alpert." *International Trumpet Guild Journal* 29, no. 2 (2005): 21-30. A lengthy interview with Alpert on a wide range of topics.

Gridley, Mark, Robert Maxham, and Robert Hoff. "Three Approaches to Defining Jazz." *Musical Quarterly* 73 (1989): 513-531. This article challenges the popular notion that Alpert's music can be defined as jazz.

Lewis, George H. "Ghosts, Ragged but Beautiful: Influences of Mexican Music on American Country-Western and Rock and Roll." *Popular Music and Society* 15, no. 4 (1991): 85-103. Brief discussion of Alpert's musical influences in the 1960's.

Roberts, John Storm. *The Latin Tinge*. Oxford, England: Oxford University Press, 1979. Outline of Alpert's career, including his fall from popularity in the early 1970's.

Rollin, Betty. "Small Band, Big Sound: The Tijuana Brass." *Look*, June 14, 1966, 104-110. An account of Alpert's rocketlike rise to popularity.

See also: Bacharach, Burt; Carpenter, Karen; David, Hal; Getz, Stan; Iglesias, Julio; Jennings, Waylon; Masekela, Hugh; Notorious B.I.G.; Sting; Warwick, Dionne.

Trey Anastasio

American rock guitarist, songwriter, and jazz composer

A founding member of the jamband Phish, Anastasio remains an integral figure in the development of America's contemporary jamband scene, creating music that allows relentless improvisation, challenges commercial genre boundaries, and strives for a communal intimacy that blurs the lines between the stage and the audience.

Born: September 30, 1964; Fort Worth, Texas
Also known as: Ernest Joseph Anastasio III (full name)
Member of: Phish; Oysterhead

Principal recordings

ALBUMS (solo): *One Man's Trash*, 1998; *Trampled by Lambs and Pecked by the Doves*, 2000; *Trey Anastasio*, 2002; *Plasma*, 2003; *Seis de Mayo*, 2004; *Shine*, 2005; *Bar 17*, 2006; *The Horseshoe Curve*, 2007.

ALBUM (with Oysterhead): *The Grand Pecking Order*, 2001.

ALBUMS (with Phish): *Junta*, 1988; *A Picture of Nectar*, 1991; *Lawn Boy*, 1991; *Rift*, 1993; *Hoist*, 1994; *A Live One*, 1995; *Billy Breathes*, 1996; *Slip, Stitch, and Pass*, 1997; *The Story of the Ghost*, 1998; *Phish (The White Tape)*, 1998; *Farmhouse*, 2000; *The Siket Disc*, 2000; *Round Room*, 2002; *Undermind*, 2004.

The Life

In the summer of 1966, Ernest and Dina Anastasio (an-ah-STAH-zyoh) moved their family to Princeton, New Jersey. Ernest was an executive vice president of the Educational Testing Service, and Dina was an editor of *Sesame Street* magazine. They enrolled their son, Ernest Joseph Anastasio III, at the Princeton Day School in the fifth grade, Anastasio became close friends with his future songwriting partner, Tom Marshall, and Anastasio developed his musical abilities by joining the jazz band and serving as the drummer in the school's production of the musical *Carnival*. For high school, Anastasio transferred to the Taft School, and he started an eight-member band, Red Tide, which, by his senior year, evolved into the band Space Antelope.

From 1983 to 1986 Anastasio attended the University of Vermont. These years were pivotal for his musical growth, with the university's student lounge serving as the launching pad for the group Phish. In the fall of 1986, Anastasio transferred to Goddard College, from where, upon completion of his senior study, "The Man Who Stepped into Yesterday," he graduated in 1988.

Anastasio spent the better portion of the 1990's developing music and touring with Phish. On August 13, 1994, he married Susan Eliza Statesir. They became parents to daughters Eliza Jean and Isabella.

Phish's millennium New Year's celebration "Big Cypress" left Anastasio remorseful that the band might have reached its creative and musical pinnacle. Already independently exploring new musical outlets, he used the time afforded by the band's self-imposed hiatus at the end of 2000 to explore solo side projects.

By the summer of 2001 he was fully immersed in a self-billed tour with an eight-piece band. There was a Phish reunion on December 31, 2002, and Anastasio continued to play until Phish's final performance on August 15, 2004, while juggling other commitments to his side projects and those of husband and father.

Post-Phish, Anastasio was arrested on December 15, 2006, for driving under the influence and for drug possession. In attempts to heal and move on with his life, Anastasio handled the legal proceedings and his drug treatment privately. In late 2007 Anastasio reappeared on the jamband scene, playing with the Dave Matthews Band and Phil Lesh and Friends.

The Music

Passing time in suburban shopping malls while a teen, Anastasio listened to Top 40 radio stations, and through friends he grew fond of the Allman Brothers Band, Led Zeppelin, and the Grateful Dead. He also developed an interest in the classical orchestration and composition of Maurice Ravel. This cross-fertilization of musical identities led Anastasio to create music that valued discipline, composition, and improvisation.

"First Tube." While the origins of "First Tube" are often debated by fans, the same claim cannot be made about fan reception of the song. Many believe "First Tube" was the first song that Anastasio performed with the Phish side project, the Eight Foot Fluorescent Tubes, in Winooski, Vermont, in 1994. Others cite the absence of lyrical content from the official studio version of "First Tube" as distinguishing it from any similar melodic versions that followed. Released in 2000 as the final track on Phish's *Farmhouse*, "First Tube" was played at more than a third of the band's concerts that year, and without inciting complaints from fans. The extended guitar crescendo provides ample space for Anastasio to shine while routinely returning to the song's recurring rhythmic base groove. Also appearing on *Plasma*, a two-disc compilation of live music Anastasio performed with his band during Phish's hiatus, "First Tube" demonstrates both musical and popular longevity with the addition of horn and percussion sections.

Gamehendge. Gamehendge is the fictional land of Lizards, Colonel Forbin, and the evil tyrant Wilson. It serves as the backdrop to numerous Phish songs, including "The Man Who Stepped into Yesterday," "Colonel Forbin's Ascent," "The Lizards," "Wilson," "Tela," "AC/DC Bag," "Fly Famous Mockingbird," "The Sloth," "Possum," and "McGrupp and the Watchful Hosemasters." When performed by the band live in narrative order, the song cycle is commonly referred to as the Gamehendge Saga. "Gamehendge" debuted on March 12, 1988, before a live audience and has since been performed in various forms with additions such as "Axilla (I)," "Axilla (II)," "Divided Sky," "Harpua," and "Llama." "Gamehendge" is an important part of Phish lore, for the band and fans.

"You Enjoy Myself." Anastasio wrote "You Enjoy Myself" (or YEM) after he and Jon Fishman spent the summer of 1985 in Europe. After it debuted on February 3, 1986, YEM—which combines improvisation, complex time signatures, nonsensical lyrics, and trampolines—became a Phish staple and a fan favorite. It appears on several albums, including *Phish (The White Tape)*, *Junta*, and *A Live One*. Broken into four sections (intro, jam, bass and drums, and lyrical vocal jam), the song varies in length from ten to more than twenty minutes when performed live, depending on the extent of improvisation. Revealing his own desire for perfection, Anastasio stopped the band mid-note during a January 2, 2003, performance of the song and restarted it.

Musical Legacy

Anastasio's blend of disciplined improvisation, varied genre arrangements, and humor marks a unique space in American music culture. Afraid of becoming a nostalgia act, Anastasio chose to in 2004 leave Phish and begin a new chapter in his life. The experimentation and perfection Anastasio so relentlessly sought are embraced by jambands and their fans alike, solidifying a grassroots desire to look beyond the status quo and seek out innovative musicals styles and sounds.

Elizabeth Anne Yeager

Further Reading

Budnick, Dean. "Phish." In *Jambands: The Complete Guide to the Players, Music, and Scene*. San Francisco: Backbeat Books, 2003. Contains biographies of Anastasio and Phish, with an annotated bibliography.

_____. *The Phishing Manual*. New York: Hyperion, 1996. A detailed account of Phish's formative years, including song origins and statistics.

_____. "Trey Anastasio." In *Jambands: The Complete Guide to the Players, Music, and Scene*. San Francisco: Backbeat Books, 2003. Band biography and annotated discography.

Mockingbird Foundation. *The Phish Companion: A Guide to the Band and Their Music*. 2d ed. San Francisco: Backbeat Books, 2004. Song and venue statistics, band member bios, interviews, and show reviews through 2004.

See also: Garcia, Jerry; Ravel, Maurice.

Laurie Anderson

American performance artist, singer-songwriter, and violinist

Anderson is known primarily as a multimedia performance artist, and her large-scale works mix sounds, music, storytelling, and multimedia visuals, all of which use her multiple talents as a visual artist, singer, composer, filmmaker, and inventor.

Born: June 5, 1947; Glen Ellyn, Illinois
Also known as: Laura Phillips Anderson (full name)

Principal recordings

ALBUMS: *You're the Guy I Want to Share My Money With*, 1981; *Big Science*, 1982; *Mister Heartbreak*, 1984; *United States Live*, 1984; *Home of the Brave*, 1986; *Strange Angels*, 1989; *Bright Red*, 1994; *The Ugly One with the Jewels and Other Stories*, 1995; *Talk Normal: Laurie Anderson Anthology*, 2000; *Life on a String*, 2001; *Live at Town Hall NYC*, 2001; *Live in New York*, 2002.

SINGLES: "Big Science," 1981; "O Superman (For Massenet)," 1981; "Sharkey's Day," 1984; "Language Is a Virus," 1986; "Babydoll," 1989; "Strange Angels," 1989; "Beautiful Red Dress," 1990; "In Our Sleep," 1994.

WRITINGS OF INTEREST: *Stories from the Nerve Bible: A Retrospective, 1972-1992*, 1994.

The Life

Laura Phillips Anderson grew up in a suburb of Chicago, Illinois, the second of eight children born to Mary Louise and Arthur Anderson. A gifted musician and artist, she played violin in the Chicago Youth Orchestra and took painting classes at the Chicago Art Institute. By 1966, after a brief stint as a premedical student at Mills College, she enrolled in the art history program at Barnard College, New York, which was followed by a graduate degree in sculpture from Columbia University. Upon graduating, she wrote art reviews and taught art history.

Soon, however, Anderson began developing and performing art installations that involved the spoken word. One of her earliest works from 1974, which examined the idea of balance, was called *Duets on Ice* (1974-1975) and involved her standing in ice skates on blocks of ice while playing an electronically altered violin and telling stories. At this time, Anderson also met Bob Bielecki, who would become her longtime collaborator in the invention of new instruments.

In 1978, Anderson performed in an important festival of avant-garde performers in New York, where she met novelist William S. Burroughs, who would later become a collaborator. A year later, *Americans on the Move*, a performance piece about Anderson's extensive travels across America, premiered at Carnegie Recital Hall; it incorporated music, media, and the spoken word. This piece would eventually be reworked into *United States*, an epic portrait of America and its people that was premiered at the Brooklyn Academy of Music in 1983. Anderson's success during this time, however, was catapulted to unprecedented heights by 1981 with the crossover hit single "O Superman," which reached number two on the London pop charts and led to a multialbum deal with Warner Bros. Records.

After touring with *United States*, Anderson continued to generate large performance pieces throughout the 1980's, such as *Mister Heartbreak* (also the title of her second solo album), which developed into a self-directed video, *Home of the Brave*, released in 1986. Her most elaborate computer-generated stage and sound effects piece was her book *Stories from the Nerve Bible* (1994), which continued Anderson's concentration on themes of politics, war, and anonymity in a world of mass culture. By the end of the 1980's, however, Anderson was tired of the grueling touring schedules and the pressure of being a huge commercial success, and she began to turn her attention toward art installations and less overtly political topics.

In 1995, Anderson was one of the first artists to explore what was then the new technology of CD-ROMs: The release of *Puppet Motel* (1995), which consisted of thirty-three virtual rooms that allowed users to interface with various audio and visual elements related to her own works and interests. In 1998, Anderson developed art installation *Del Vivo*, as well as the performance piece *Songs and Stories from Moby Dick* (1999-2000), which was her first large work that did not directly comment on current political issues. In 2003 Anderson became an artist-in-residence for the National Aeronautics and Space Administration (NASA), a role that culminated in the performance piece *The End of the Moon*. In 2005 she was artist-in-residence at the New School in New York. In 2007, she toured with the work *Homeland*. In April, 2008, she married longtime partner Lou Reed.

The Music

Even though it is difficult to discuss Anderson's music separately from the other media in which she works, it is possible to trace important musical developments. A pioneer in electronically generated sound and invented instruments, Anderson did not specifically aspire to become a musician, and many of her album recordings concentrate on either the speaking voice as instrument or manipulated versions of her own voice to portray certain characters. However, after taking lessons with a voice coach in 1986, Anderson discovered her singing voice and shortly thereafter released *Strange Angels* (1989), which was considered a breakthrough not only because of the use of her natural voice but also because of her extensive collaborations with other artists. Aside from her solo albums and multimedia performances, Anderson has composed for film, theater, and orchestra.

Big Science. This album was Anderson's first solo recording, released by Warner Bros. Records in 1982, and it contains the unlikely eight-minute-long hit single "O Superman." This album comprises mostly spoken words over hypnotic electronically generated beats that suggest simplicity. When other instruments are brought in, however, the effects are dramatic, and in the "It Tango" the uneven brass initiates the mix-ups ahead, and an off-key saxophone solo in "From the Air" anticipates the threat of a plane crash. With her words, Anderson has an ability to make epiphanic revelations by saying very little. In "Walking and Falling," Anderson points out that "You're walking/ And you don't always realize it/ but you're always falling." *Big Science* was rereleased for its twenty-fifth anniversary with enhanced audio, the bonus track "Walk the Dog" (the original B side of the single "O Superman"), and the "O Superman" video clip.

"O Superman." Released both as a single and on the album *Big Science*, "O Superman" brought Anderson international attention. It is an ominous digital chant about the intrusion of technology into everyday life and the miscommunications of a family who converse with one another only through answering machines (which, at the time the song was released, were just becoming standard equipment in people's homes). The intentional irony is that this piece was made through the use of technological resources, including the manipulation of Anderson's voice.

United States. There is no video version of the original and seminal 1983 performance of *United States*; however, there is a box set of the original live performance (1984); the album *Big Science*, which contains a sampling of the musical pieces; and a book (1984) of images and sketches from the actual performance. The original eight-hour staged performance was premiered at the Brooklyn Academy of Music over two nights and featured a series on

Laurie Anderson. (AP/Wide World Photos)

intertwined visual and sound worlds that attempted to capture modern America at the beginning of the 1980's, with its new technological possibilities, emerging mass culture, and conservative political environment. Presented in four parts—"Transportation," "Politics," "Money," and "Love"—and performed by Anderson accompanied by five musicians, *United States* combined slide projections, video, graphics, animation, and musical numbers (sometimes spoken, sometimes sung), interspersed with spoken monologues.

Anderson often utilized her own technology-inspired inventions, such as her headlight glasses, which made her appear as though her eyes were light beams; the battery-operated light that she wore behind her teeth to make them glow; the tape-bow violin (one of her many manipulated violins); and the vocoder, which altered Anderson's voice. The result was a successful mix of high and low arts that encapsulated modern cultural issues such as national identity, miscommunication, suspicions that language often confuses rather than reveals, and the anonymity of living in a mass culture.

The Collected Videos. In 1990, Anderson released a collection of her film and video work from 1980 to 1990. It includes music videos from many well-known songs, including "O Superman," "Language Is a Virus," and "Sharkey's Day" (the later two are from *Home of the Brave*), as well as works initially seen only on television. The best of these are the acerbic public service announcements and *What You Mean We?*, which featured Anderson having a conversation with a clone of herself.

The public service announcements were produced in lieu of regular advertisements for Anderson's compact disc (CD) *Strange Angels*. In the kitchen of a busy coffee shop, Anderson makes humorous and ironic conversation with herself about military research, the national debt, women and money, and the national anthem.

What You Mean We? was broadcast on the television series *Alive from Off-Center*, which showcased performance videos by artists and was hosted by Anderson. Anderson often generated electronically manipulated versions of herself so that she could create personas to voice to the opinions that she felt uncomfortable expressing as herself. This video also includes the artist giving a tour of her home studio.

Song and Stories from Moby Dick. This performance piece was premiered at the Brooklyn Academy of Music in 1999 and represents a shift from previous works for three reasons: It does not raise overtly political issues; it is based on a preexisting text, the novel by Herman Melville of 1851; and it uses actors to act out the story on stage.

Songs and Stories from Moby Dick is a deeply philosophical piece; in the concert program's liner notes, Anderson describes being attracted to the "dark conclusions about the meaning of life, love, and obsession." Anderson occasionaly quotes long passages of Melville's text verbtim; overall, however, she uses little of the actual text, sometimes taking single phrases to initiate a new song or simply writing something new. Musically, the whole is completely computer-generated yet has a lush, graceful quality to it. Anderson used a new invention called the talking stick, a wireless instrument that can replicate any preprogrammed sound when touched and that is also used as an acting prop (such as a staff or a harpoon) as well as a light source. Two of the songs from this work were released on the 2001 CD *Life on a String*.

Musical Legacy

Laurie Anderson was single-handedly responsible for redefining performance art. A largely twentieth century genre, performance art had a history of being somewhat obscure and esoteric, often taking a hostile stance toward audiences, as in the Dada movement of the 1920's and the Fluxus movement of the 1960's. In Anderson's work, high and low multimedia arts are successfully merged, and communication and accessibility are at the core of her staged performances.

Anderson has also been key in developing new electronic sound worlds both from digital sources and in her manipulation of the violin, and she is a leader at voicing the cultural concerns of the modern world, whether in her staged performances, her art installations, or her video shorts. She has fundamentally changed the way music and narration are performed together on stage.

Anderson has been the recipient of many awards, including grants from the National Endowment for the Arts and a Guggenheim Fellowship.

Sonya Mason

Further Reading

Berghaus, Günter. "Laurie Anderson." In *Avant-Garde Performance: Live Events and Electronic Technologies*. New York: Palgrave Macmillan, 2005. An excellent resource geared toward college students. Includes an interview with Anderson, which discusses how Anderson integrates her thoughts into artworks. Encourages readers to compare the writings with various other artists from within the book.

Celent, Germano. *Laurie Anderson: Del Vivo*. Milan: Fondazione Prada, 1998. Compiled to coincide with the installation of the same name, which focuses on the live image of a prisoner being projected via cable to an exhibition space nearby. The project explored issues of incarnation, imprisonment, and voyeurism. Includes a detailed description of the project, background on the prison, and biographies of both Anderson and the prisoner, Santino Stefanini.

Duckworth, William. "Laurie Anderson." In *Talking Music: Conversations with John Cage, Philip Glass, Laurie Anderson, and Five Generations of American Experimental Composers*. New York: Schirmer, 1995. An interview with Anderson from the late 1980's that reveals much about her early influences and development. Places Anderson's work in the context of five generations of other experimental musicians.

Goldberg, RoseLee. *Laurie Anderson*. New York: Abrams, 2000. This comprehensive volume was written in close collaboration with the artist. It traces Anderson's chronological development through the use of extensive interviews, pictures, and photographs. Includes lists of records, films, videos, scores, songs, and CD-ROMs.

Howell, John. *Laurie Anderson*. New York: Thunder's Mouth Press, 1992. A thorough study of Anderson, including a biographical essay by the author, an interview with the artist, and an essay by curator Janet Kardon about the visual themes in Anderson's work. Also includes storyboards and sketches from *United States* and *Home of the Brave* and a time line of events and productions.

Huxley, Michael, and Noel Witts, eds. "Laurie Anderson: The Speed of Change." In *The Twentieth-Century Performance Reader*. New York: Routledge, 2002. Contains a short but important and interesting section on Anderson, placing her in the context of avant-garde performance history.

Summer, Melody, Kathleen Burch, and Michael Sumner, eds. "Laurie Anderson." In *The Guests Go to Supper*. Oakland, Calif.: Burning Books, 1986. Includes a transcription of an interview in which she discusses working with technology, along with a list of eight song lyrics with notes by the artist.

See also: Byrne, David; Reed, Lou; Reich, Steve.

Leroy Anderson

American classical composer

A master at light orchestral music, Anderson wrote sparkling arrangements and clever compositions for band and orchestra.

Born: June 29, 1908; Cambridge, Massachusetts
Died: May 18, 1975; Woodbury, Connecticut

Principal works

BAND WORKS: *Ticonderoga March*, 1945; *Governor Bradford March*, 1948; *A Trumpeter's Lullaby*, 1949; *Bugler's Holiday*, 1954; *March of the Two Left Feet*, 1970.

MUSICAL THEATER (music): *Goldilocks*, 1958 (libretto by Walter Kerr and Jean Kerr).

ORCHESTRAL WORKS: *Jazz Pizzicato*, 1938; *Jazz Legato*, 1939; *Promenade*, 1945 (for strings and trumpet); *The Syncopated Clock*, 1945 (with Mitchell Parish); *Fiddle-Faddle*, 1947; *The Irish Suite*, 1947 (additional movements, 1949); *Old MacDonald Had a Farm*, 1947; *Sleigh Ride*, 1948 (with Parish); *The Typewriter*, 1950; *The Waltzing Cat*, 1950 (with Parish); *Belle of the Ball*, 1951 (with Parish); *Blue Tango*, 1951 (with Parish); *The Penny-Whistle Song*, 1951; *Plink, Plank, Plunk!*, 1951; *Song of the Bells*, 1951; *Girl in Satin*, 1953; *Summer Skies*, 1953; *The Bluebells of Scotland*, 1954; *The First Day of Spring*, 1954; *Sandpaper Ballet*, 1954; *Arietta*, 1962; *Clarinet Candy*, 1962; *Home Stretch*, 1962.

PIANO WORKS: *Concerto in C Major*, 1953; *Forgotten Dreams*, 1954 (with Parish).

The Life

Leroy Anderson was born in 1908 to Swedish immigrant parents who came to the United States when they were children. His father, Bror Anton Anderson, was a postal clerk who played the mandolin. His mother, Anna Margareta Anderson, played the organ at the Swedish Church in Cambridge, and her son's first musical training was on the organ. With these musical influences at home, Anderson was ready for piano lessons, which he began at the New England Conservatory of Music in 1919. He attended the Cambridge High and Latin School, graduating in 1925. For his graduation ceremonies, he orchestrated the school song, and he conducted the school's orchestra in a rousing rendition of it. Anderson's father bought his son a trombone while he was in high school, in hopes Anderson would earn a front-row seat in the Harvard Band.

Fulfilling his father's wishes, Anderson did enter Harvard, playing both the trombone in the band and double bass in the orchestra, and singing with the Harvard Glee Club. He studied counterpoint with Edward Ballantine, who had been a student of pianist Artur Schnabel. Ballantine's music was noted for its humorous quality, which had a major influence on Anderson. When he was a senior, Anderson became the conductor of the Harvard Band, and for it he arranged some traditional Harvard songs, along with tunes from other Ivy League colleges. These were so fresh and original that they laid the foundation for his career. His arrangements attracted the attention of Arthur Fiedler, the director of the Boston Pops Orchestra.

Anderson continued his education at Harvard, studying composition with Walter Piston, who also taught composer and conductor Leonard Bernstein. At the time, the United States was entering the Great Depression, and although Anderson had obtained a master's degree in music, he doubted his ability to make a living in the field. With a great facility for languages, Anderson began his Ph.D. studies in German and the Scandinavian languages, hoping to make a living as a language teacher. Eventually he learned to speak Danish,

Leroy Anderson. (© Oscar White/CORBIS)

Norwegian, Icelandic, German, French, Italian, and Portuguese.

In World War II Anderson was drafted into the U.S. Army, and the military took advantage of his linguistic ability. He was stationed in Iceland to serve as a translator and an interpreter. His excellent abilities prompted the U.S. government to offer him the job of U.S. attaché to Sweden after the war. Anderson declined the position, although he was sent to Washington, D.C., to work in intelligence at the Pentagon. He was discharged from the Army when the war ended.

Determined to forge a career in music, Anderson began to write original works and to contribute more arrangements to the Boston Pops Orchestra. In addition, Fiedler asked him to conduct. During the 1950's Anderson gained international fame for his light concert music and for his songs. He recorded for Decca Records, and his *Blue Tango* went gold in 1952.

In the 1960's, Anderson augmented his arranging and compositional activities with guest-conducting for several orchestras near his home in Connecticut and in such venues as the Hollywood Bowl. In the 1970's, the Boston Pops invited Anderson to guest-conduct during a televised concert tribute to his career. Anderson told his wife that it was "the most important evening of my life."

Anderson married Eleanor Firke in 1942, and they had four children: Jane, Eric, Rolf, and Kurt. He composed and conducted until the end of his life, dying of cancer in 1975.

The Music

Anderson was a skilled arranger, and he brought a pronounced sense of play to his compositions, eliciting unexpected sounds from an orchestra. He scored for nontraditional instruments, such as a manual typewriter, which takes center stage for *The Typewriter*. The soloist taps the keys in rhythm, and the instrumentalists help to sound the margin bell and to imitate the clunk of the carriage as it returns at the end of a line. For *Sandpaper Ballet*, Anderson was inspired by vaudeville dancers who sprinkled sand on the stage to accent their steps. The orchestra's percussionists used sandpaper-covered blocks to scrape out their parts, the composer indicating fine, medium, and coarse grade to achieve the desired effect. *The Waltzing Cat* rivals any Viennese waltz, with violins imitating "meows," and Anderson finds the perfect coda: an instrumental bark that sends the musical feline scurrying.

Jazz Pizzicato. Anderson was still in college when Fiedler heard his arrangements for the Harvard Band. That led to an invitation to compose a work for the Boston Pops string section, with Anderson creating a sprightly one-minute, forty-five-second flurry of plucked strings that Fiedler immediately added to the Pops' repertoire. This launched a decades-long working relationship between Fiedler and Anderson, with the eminent conductor introducing Anderson to music publishers. In the wake of *Jazz Pizzicato* came *Jazz Legato*, which Anderson wrote as a companion piece.

Sleigh Ride. This perennial holiday classic may be Anderson's best-known composition. In 1948, the first time Fiedler and the Boston Pops played it, the enthusiastic audience demanded that they play it again. In three minutes, the work depicts a sleigh, drawn by horses, skimming over a snowy landscape and fading into the distance. Within the delightful melody, Anderson scored horse whinnies,

the clip-clop of horse hooves, and the smart crack of a whip, elements that are often obscured in the later version, which included lyrics by Mitchell Parish. The renditions of "Sleigh Ride"` by Gene Autry, Karen Carpenter, and other singers are still heard on the radio at Christmastime, and the Ventures performed it rock style. Anderson claimed he composed it during a heat wave.

The Syncopated Clock. One day, while he was serving in military intelligence at the Pentagon, Anderson was distracted by the ticking of a clock, and he conceived the idea of a timepiece that did not keep a regular beat. This time, he thought of the title first, and then he composed the rhythmically complex song for orchestra to go with it. For a few years, *The Syncopated Clock* was played by the Boston Pops and other orchestras. In 1950 Decca Records asked Anderson to record an album entirely of his music, and he included this work. An executive at CBS heard it and wanted to use it as a theme song for a program of old movies the network was about to debut called *The Late Show*. After the first program, CBS received dozens of phone calls—not about the movie but about the memorable theme. *The Syncopated Clock* became attached to the program, and it became widely recognized, enhancing Anderson's reputation. Later, the onomatopoeic "Plink, Plank, Plunk!" became the theme for a long-running television game show, *I've Got a Secret*.

Blue Tango. Written while he was still in the Army, *Blue Tango* showcased Anderson's facility for combining various musical elements in one piece. As the title indicates, there were South American rhythms and blues phrasings. He added some jazz aspects, with swelling dynamics and an irresistible beat. The danceable song became a favorite on radio and on jukeboxes, and it reportedly was the first instrumental record to sell a million copies. No one was more surprised at the success of *Blue Tango* than its unassuming composer, who watched in amazement as it climbed up the charts. Anderson claimed he wrote concert music, not pop music. He underestimated the infectious quality that permeates all his work.

Concerto in C Major. Written in 1953, Concerto in C Major for piano was Anderson's attempt at a full-scale orchestral work. He completed it just two weeks before it premiered in Chicago, played by the Grant Park Symphony Orchestra. For the composer, it was an ambitious work, including solo piano, one piccolo, two flutes, two oboes, two clarinets, two bassoons, four horns, three trumpets, three trombones, one tuba, timpani, suspended cymbals, maracas, claves, snare drum, strings, and cowbell. It had four-part fugues, tango rhythms, and, as evidenced by the cowbell, a hoedown theme. Although Concerto in C Major was performed two more times, Anderson was dissatisfied, withdrawing it with the intention of revising what he considered its weak spots. He never returned to it; after his death, his family released the work.

Goldilocks. In 1958 Anderson tried his hand at a Broadway show. The book was written by Walter and Jean Kerr, and the musical starred Don Ameche and Elaine Stritch. The story involved a comical feud between a stage actress and a movie director trying to find the financing to make an epic film about ancient Egypt. Anderson's score featured several songs and even a ballet. The show closed after 161 performances. Critics were generally positive about the music for *Goldilocks*, one calling it "charming," although most agreed the story was flawed.

Musical Legacy

Film composer John Williams, who conducted the Boston Pops Orchestra for several years, said that Anderson's music "remains forever as young and fresh as the very day on which it was composed." More than sixty years after he created them, his arrangements for the Harvard Band remain a part of its repertoire, and its new band quarters were named the Anderson Band Center in 1995. In 2003 Anderson's hometown of Cambridge dedicated the corner near his boyhood home as Leroy Anderson Square. Extensively recorded and performed, Anderson's music retains its timeless quality.

Constance Pollock

Further Reading

Anderson, Leroy. "How to Spoil Your Concert." *The Instrumentalist* 44, no. 1 (August, 1989): 69. An interesting perspective from Anderson the conductor about how concert presentations can be improved for the audience.

_____. *"The Syncopated Clock* Still Ticks." *Music Journal* 26, no. 9 (September, 1968): 30-31. Ander-

son describes how he conceived one of his most recognized pieces and how it migrated to television.

Biegel, Jeffrey. "Composer Leroy Anderson Went from Harvard to the Boston Pops." *Clavier* 34, no. 6 (July/August, 2004): 20-21, 24. A brief but thoughtful overview of Anderson's life, including an analysis of individual works.

Tommasini, Anthony. "Tuneful Gems from a Master of a Lost Art." *The New York Times*, March 10, 1996. In an album review of a collection of Anderson's music, the writer describes several of the composer's most famous works.

See also: Fiedler, Arthur.

Marian Anderson

American classical and opera singer

Known for her rich contralto voice, Anderson used her passion for music to transcend racial, gender, and national boundaries.

Born: February 27, 1897; Philadelphia, Pennsylvania
Died: April 8, 1993; Portland, Oregon

Principal works

OPERATIC ROLE: Ulrica in Giuseppe Verdi's *Un ballo in maschera*, 1955 (*The Masked Ball*).

Principal recordings

ALBUMS: *He's Got the Whole World in His Hands and Eighteen Other Spirituals*, 1962; *Snoopycat*, 1963.

SINGLES: "My Lord, What a Mornin'," 1924; "Nobody Knows the Trouble I Seen," 1924; "Heav'n Heav'n," 1928; "Ave Maria," 1935; "The Cuckoo," 1935; "My Soul's Been Anchored in the Lord," 1936; "Every Time I Feel the Spirit," 1937; "I Know the Lord Laid His Hands on Me," 1937; "Lord, I Can't Stay Away," 1937; "Were You There?," 1937; "I Don't Feel Noways Tired," 1938; "My Old Kentucky Home," 1941; "O What a Beautiful City," 1941; "Hear the Wind Whispering," 1945; "Nobody Knows the Trouble I Seen," 1947; "The First Nöel," 1951; "O Little Town of Bethlehem," 1952; "None But the Lonely

Heart," 1955; "Over the Mountains," 1955; "The Lord's Prayer," 1956; "Angels We Have Heard on High," 1961; "He's Got the Whole World in His Hands," 1961; "I Want Jesus to Walk with Me," 1961; "Joy to the World," 1961; "O Come All Ye Faithful," 1961; "He'll Bring It to Pass," 1964; "Oh, Heaven Is a Beautiful Place," 1964.

The Life

Marian Anderson was born in 1897 in Philadelphia to John and Anna Anderson. She began singing in the junior choir at church at the age of six. Two years later, although the family could not afford any music lessons, her father bought her a piano. Anderson began to teach herself music, eventually receiving formal training until the age of seventeen. She began to perform in public in 1914, singing solo roles in performances of George Frideric Handel's *Messiah* (1742) and Felix Mendelssohn's *Elijah* (1846). In 1915 she took lessons with the soprano Mary Saunders Patterson. Because Anderson could not afford the one-dollar lesson fee, Patterson taught her free of charge. After six months, at Patterson's suggestion, Anderson continued her singing lessons with the contralto Agnes Reifsnyder, with whom she studied through 1918. In the summer of 1919, Anderson studied with Oscar Sanger at the Chicago Conservatory of Music, and in the following year Giuseppe Boghetti, who analyzed her vocal tones, improved her breathing techniques and expanded her repertory. In 1921 Anderson graduated from South Philadelphia High School for Girls.

By the late 1920's, Anderson realized that a career for a contralto could be found in Europe, not in America. In October, 1927, she sailed to London, where she performed "Air de Lia" from Claude Debussy's *L'Enfant prodigue* (1884). In 1930 she went to study lieder with Michael Raucheison and Sverre Jordon in Berlin on a scholarship from the Julius Rosenwald Fund. In Germany she met Norwegian manager Rule Rassmussen. With his help, she undertook concert tours to Norway, Sweden, Finland, and Denmark. She obtained critical acclaim in Scandinavia in 1933, giving twenty concerts within two years, during which she learned from Kosti Vehanen songs by the Finnish composer Jean Sibe-

Marian Anderson. (Library of Congress)

lius. Two years later, at an afternoon concert in a hotel in Salzburg, Austria, she experienced a defining moment in her career. The conductor Arturo Toscanini heard her sing, famously exclaiming that "a voice like hers is heard only once in a hundred years." With the critical acclaim she obtained in Europe, the American impresario Sol Hurok launched her career in America in the 1935-1936 season. In 1938 Anderson gave seventy recitals in the United States alone, an unprecedented number for any concert singer.

Anderson toured in Europe in 1936 and 1949; in the 1950's and early 1960's she toured in Canada, the United States, Scandinavia, Europe, South America, Jamaica, the West Indies, Japan, Thailand, Burma, Vietnam, Korea, Philippines, Malaysia, India, Israel, Morocco, Tunisia, and Australia. She concluded her singing career in a yearlong farewell tour in 1964, with the final recital on Easter Sunday, April 19, 1965, at Carnegie Hall. She died on April 8, 1993, of heart failure. She was ninety-six.

The Music

Anderson was passionate about singing. While singing at church when she was young, she had the range to sing any parts in the choir. In addition to having an extended range, she could sing in diverse styles, ranging from German lieder by Ludwig van Beethoven, Johannes Brahms, Robert Schumann, Hugo Wolf, Richard Strauss, French arias by Francis Poulenc, Italian songs by Girolamo Frescobaldi, to English songs by Henry Purcell and Paul Hindemith. She was not primarily an opera singer, but her operatic repertory included "Ah! mon fils" from Giacomo Meyerbeer's *Le Prophète* (1849). She understood the emotional significance of spirituals, and therefore she was eager to learn and perform folk songs in her concert tours. Her dark, sweet contralto voice was particularly suitable for moving her audiences through folk songs. At her first concert in Helsinki, Finland, in 1931, for example, Anderson sang the household Finnish folk song "Läksin minä kesäyönä käymään" (one summer's night I went walking) in Finnish.

"America." By the late 1930's Anderson was one of the most prominent singers in the United States. Hurok, her manager, wanted to make history by arranging for her to sing in Constitutional Hall in Washington, D.C., on Easter Sunday of 1939. However, the management—the Daughters of the American Revolution—canceled Anderson's performance because of her race, a decision that infuriated many people, including First Lady Eleanor Roosevelt, who resigned from the Daughters of the American Revolution and arranged Anderson to give a free open-air concert at the Lincoln Memorial on the day she was supposed to perform at the Constitutional Hall. This event was widely advertised, and it drew an audience of seventy-five thousand, the largest crowd that had ever gathered in the capital. Accompanied by only her pianist, Vehanen, Anderson sang with the audience "The Star-Spangled Banner." Then she performed with great control "America," "O mio Fernando," and Franz Schubert's "Ave Maria" in German, a song that showcased her thick contralto timbre and her powerful dynamic range. After a brief intermission, she sang a group of spirituals, including "Gospel Train," "Trampin'," and "My Soul's Been Anchored in de Lord." For an encore, she chose the spiritual "Nobody Knows the Trouble I Seen." The powerful performance presented a strong testimony against racial inequality.

"Der Erlkönig." In the late 1920's, Anderson worked hard to master German lieder. She learned how to portray the complex psychological journey of one character from serenity to self-doubt in Franz Schubert's "Die junge Nonne," a lied that prepared her for interpreting lieder that involved multiple characters: the narrator, the queen, and the dwarf in "Der Zwerg" (1822), and the narrator, the dying boy, the anxious father, and the sinister spirit in "Der Erlkönig" (1821) In these complex lieder, Anderson made good use of her broad range, expressive power, and dramatic intensity to contrast markedly different personalities. Impressed by her performance of "Der Erlkönig" in Tokyo in 1953, a critic remarked that she created the illusion of four distinct dramatic characters through her voice. Her penetrating interpretation of "Der Erlkönig" remains one of her most notable artistic achievements.

Un ballo in maschera. Anderson was the first African American to break the racial barrier at the New York Metropolitan Opera. Approached by the general manager of the Metropolitan Opera, Rudolf Bing, at a party in September, 1954, she agreed to sing her operatic debut as Ulrica in Giuseppe Verdi's *Un ballo in maschera* (1859) on January 7, 1955. Although Ulrica is a minor role, it is critical to the opera's dramaturgy, vocally demanding, and hence suitable to Anderson's considerable talent. The music world was well aware of the historical significance of the performance. She received one thousand dollars per performance, which made her the highest-paid opera singer at the Metropolitan Opera at that time. Her debut became the selling point of the 1955-1956 season: Tickets were sold out within days; journalists from as far as the West Indies came to New York to witness the historical moment. Celebrities such as President Harry Truman's daughter Margaret Truman, the Duchess of Windsor, and First Lady Eleanor Roosevelt attended her debut. As soon as the curtain rose at the beginning of act 2, showing Ulrica's cave, the audience gave Anderson an enthusiastic five-minute ovation. At the end of the act, she came out for her curtain call, receiving another round of thunderous applause. After her stunning performance, she received two thousand telegrams of congratulations from across the world.

"Deep River." Anderson's deep voice was particularly suited to conveying the sorrow portrayed in spirituals, and "Deep River" showcased her skill. It was the performance of this song that impressed her first serious singing teacher, Giuseppe Boghetti, in 1920. Over the span of her career, she sang a repertory of more than one hundred spirituals arranged by Harry T. Burleigh, Nathaniel Dett, and Hall Johnson. Anderson followed the tradition established by her black predecessors, including Roland Hayes, and concluded her concerts with a series of spirituals, even when she had been warned specifically not to do so during tours in the Soviet Union in 1934. Nevertheless, the Russians responded with great enthusiasm by joining her in singing "Deep River" with their deep voices. During her tour to Israel in 1955, her performances of spirituals were an exotic appeal to students, many of whom heard black music for the first time in her concerts. This tradition continues in concerts by such African American vocalists as Jessye Norman, Kathleen Battle, and William Warfield. A recording of Anderson's performance of "Deep River" closed her memorial in the Union Baptist Church in June, 1993.

Musical Legacy

One of the first African American women to have a distinguished international singing career, Anderson used her voice to promote equality and justice across the world. In July, 1939, Anderson received the Spingarn Medal of the National Association of the advancement of Colored People from Eleanor Roosevelt. From the late 1930's to the 1950's, she received honorary doctorate degrees in music from Howard University (1938), Rutgers University (1957), New York University (1958), and the University of Pennsylvania (1958). In 1957 she received an honorary doctor of law degree from Saint Mary's College. Outside the United States, her artistic achievement was recognized by the Finnish government in 1949, and in 1952 she received from King Gustav of Sweden his government's Litteris et Artibus medal. Five years later, in 1957, she was invited by the U.S. Department of State to do a ten-week tour of India and the Far East as a goodwill ambassador, and she was given the Albert Einstein Commemorative Award. Her ambassadorial work was recognized repeatedly by the U.S. government. President Dwight Eisenhower appointed her a del-egate to the United Nations Human Rights Committee, and she delivered a speech at the United Nations in 1958. In 1963 President Lyndon Johnson awarded her the American Medal of Freedom. In 1977 Congress awarded her a gold medal in celebration of her birthday. In 1980 the U.S. Treasury Department coined a half-ounce gold commemorative medal with her image. Her successful singing career was marked by the Kennedy Center Honors she received in 1978, followed by the National Medal of Arts from President Ronald Reagan in 1986 and a Grammy Award for Lifetime Achievement in 1991. The Marian Anderson Award was established in 1998 to honor eminent artist-humanitarians in the United States.

Hedy Law

Further Reading

Anderson, Marian. *My Lord, What a Morning: An Autobiography*. Madison: University of Wisconsin Press, 1992. Anderson's autobiography was originally written in 1956, after her debut at the New York Metropolitan Opera. This is a passionate, emotional, and honest account of an extraordinary talent.

Emerson, Isabelle. *Five Centuries of Women Singers*. Westport, Conn.: Praeger, 2005. A study of twenty classical female singers from the sixteenth through the mid-twentieth century. The book provides a historical overview of the business of music, and it explains the achievements of notable singers within their historical context. This includes a reference to Anderson's remarkable career.

Freedman, Russell. *The Voice That Challenged a Nation: Marian Anderson and the Struggle for Equal Rights*. New York: Clarion Books, 2004. An accessible biography of Anderson written for young readers. Each of the eight chapters discusses one major event of her life.

Gill, Glenda Eloise. *No Surrender! No Retreat! African American Pioneer Performers of Twentieth Century American Theater*. New York: St. Martin's Press, 2000. A study documents how fifteen African American performing artists, including Anderson, overcame oppression in the course of their careers. Includes archival documents and interviews.

Keiler, Allan. *Marian Anderson: A Singer's Journey.*

New York: Scribner, 2000. A thorough biography, this offers detailed primary and secondary research that chronicles Anderson's life, and it includes interviews with Anderson. An indispensable resource for those interested in the social history of black Americans.

Roosevelt, Eleanor. *Courage in a Dangerous World: The Political Writings of Eleanor Roosevelt.* Edited by Allida M. Black. New York: Columbia University Press, 1999. Situates Anderson and the Daughters of the American Revolution within the history of women in twentieth century America. This book helps us understand the historical significance of Anderson's performance in 1939 from Roosevelt's perspective.

Ware, Susan. *Letter to the World: Seven Women Who Shaped the American Century.* New York: W. W. Norton, 1998. This book chronicles the lives of seven women of extraordinary achievements— Eleanor Roosevelt, Dorothy Thompson, Margaret Mead, Katherine Hepburn, Babe Dedrikson Zaharias, Martha Graham, and Anderson. It shows how each woman created a persona critical to her success and emphasizes how each balanced her public and her private lives.

See also: Hindemith, Paul; Norman, Jessye; Odetta; Poulenc, Francis; Toscanini, Arturo.

Dame Julie Andrews

English musical-theater and pop singer

Andrews is a gifted interpreter of musical roles and songs, with an remarkable ability to deliver story through melody in stage productions and on film.

Born: October 1, 1935; Walton-on-Thames, England

Also known as: Julia Elizabeth Wells (birth name); Julie Edwards (married name)

Principal works

MUSICAL THEATER (singer): *The Boy Friend*, 1954 (libretto, music, and lyrics by Sandy Wilson); *My Fair Lady*, 1956 (libretto and lyrics by Alan Jay Lerner; music by Frederick Loewe); *Camelot*, 1960 (libretto and lyrics by Lerner;

music by Loewe); *Victor/Victoria*, 1995 (libretto by Blake Edwards; music by Henry Mancini; lyrics by Leslie Bricusse).

Principal recordings

ALBUMS: *The Lass with the Delicate Air*, 1957; *Julie Andrews Sings*, 1958; *Broadway's Fair Julie*, 1961; *Don't Go in the Lion's Cage Tonight*, 1962; *Heartrending Ballads and Raucous Ditties*, 1962; *A Christmas Treasure*, 1968; *Darling Lili*, 1970; *Christmas with Julie Andrews*, 1982; *Love Me Tender*, 1982; *Love, Julie*, 1989; *Broadway: The Music of Richard Rodgers*, 1994; *Here I'll Stay: The Words of Alan Jay Lerner*, 1996; *Julie Andrews Selects Her Favorite Disney Songs*, 2005.

WRITINGS OF INTEREST: *Home: A Memoir of My Early Years*, 2008.

The Life

Julie Andrews was born Julia Elizabeth Wells, to Edward Wells, who taught woodworking and metalsmithing, and Barbara Mores, a pianist. She had a younger brother, John. When Andrews was five, her parents divorced.

During World War II, when Andrews's stepfather, Ted Andrews, led community singing in air-raid shelters, he noticed his stepdaughter's remarkable vocal ability and her four-octave range. After the war, Andrews began singing in her mother and stepfather's vaudeville act; she soon took her stepfather's name, Andrews, professionally. Andrews spent the next several years singing in various musical revues, including the Starlight Roof revue at the London Hippodrome. In November, 1948, she participated in a Royal Command Performance, hosted by Danny Kaye, at the London Palladium. Andrews also appeared in pantomimes (musical fairy tales), a type of children's entertainment popular in Britain.

While appearing in an unsuccessful play in the English provinces in 1954, Andrews was offered a role in an upcoming American production of *The Boy Friend* (1954), a cheerful spoof of 1920's musicals that was already a smash hit in London. At first Andrews was reluctant to take the part. She thought she was too young for the role, and the show would be her first appearance outside of England. Nevertheless, she signed a one-year contract, and *The Boy Friend* opened at Broadway's

Royale Theatre on September 30, 1954. New York critics were delighted with *The Boy Friend*, and they were especially charmed by Andrews as Polly, a wealthy young woman who fears she will be loved only for her money. Though *The Boy Friend* was an ensemble piece, with several actors having equally large parts, Andrews was given featured billing on the Royale Theatre's marquee a few weeks after the show opened. As soon as her contract expired, she returned to England. The visit was short, because she was besieged with job offers back in the United States. In one of these, Andrews played a supporting role in the television special *High Tor* (1956), a musical version of the Maxwell Anderson play that starred Bing Crosby as a romantic dreamer and Andrews as the ghost of a beautiful girl from the seventeenth century with whom he falls in love. By the time *High Tor* aired on CBS in early March, 1956, Andrews was back on Broadway in *My Fair Lady* (1956), the Alan Jay Lerner and Arthur Loewe musical play based on George Bernard Shaw's *Pygmalion* (1913).

In May, 1959, during a vacation from the London production of *My Fair Lady*, Andrews married Tony Walton, a theatrical set designer; they had one daughter, Emma, born in November, 1962. The couple worked together professionally, most notably on *Mary Poppins* (1964), but they divorced in 1968. The next year, Andrews married film director Blake Edwards. They adopted two daughters from Vietnam, Joanna and Amy.

At this time, Andrews worked in television, appearing in a number of specials, a variety series in the early 1970's that was critically acclaimed but not popular with the public, and a situation comedy in 1992 that lasted only a few weeks. The majority of her screen appearances since the late 1960's have been in films directed by Edwards, including such ribald comedies as 1979's *10* and 1981's *S.O.B.*

In 1974 Andrews published her first children's book, *The Last of the Really Great Whangdoodles*. It was followed in 1989 by *Mandy*, and she has published several more, including *The Great American Mousical*, an introduction to the theater for children. At the American Library Association's annual conference in June, 2007, Andrews announced that her publisher, HarperCollins, has established the Julie Andrews Collection, a book series, as an incentive to encourage children to read.

In 1997, near the end of her two-year run on Broadway with *Victor/Victoria*, Andrews was diagnosed with a noncancerous growth on her vocal cords. She wrapped up the musical in June, and she had surgery shortly afterward. Even though she had been told her vocal cords would not be compromised, Andrews lost her singing voice. Early in 2000, she filed a lawsuit against her doctor and his associates, but she accepted an undisclosed settlement, dropped the lawsuit, and moved on to other projects.

Andrews has worked on behalf of many charities, including Operation USA, the United Nations Children's Fund, and Save the Children. Andrews received many honors for her charity work as well as for her contributions to entertainment. In 2000 she was made a Dame Commander of the British Empire by Queen Elizabeth II, and in 2001 she received an Honor Award from the John F. Kennedy Center for Performing Arts in Washington, D.C. On January 28, 2007, Andrews won the Lifetime Achievement Award from the Screen Actors Guild.

The Music

My Fair Lady. The now classic production of *My Fair Lady* opened at Broadway's Mark Hellinger Theatre on March 15, 1956, to nearly unanimous praise. *My Fair Lady* retained much of Shaw's original dialogue, and the part of Eliza Doolittle demanded more acting ability than the average musical comedy role, and certainly more than Andrews had when she started rehearsals. Andrews had extensive experience as a singer, but almost none as an actress. Andrews later admitted in interviews that she had problems trying to learn the role and dealing with the prickly leading man, Rex Harrison, who wanted her to be replaced with someone more experienced. To help Andrews with her characterization, director Moss Hart gave her a grueling week of private coaching, going over every line of dialogue and nuance of the role. In gratitude, his leading lady later acknowledged that Hart made her Eliza Doolittle. The musical enjoyed an original run of 2,717 performances, and it garnered wonderful notices for Andrews. She returned to England to star in the London production of *My Fair Lady*, which opened April 30, 1958, at the Drury Lane Theatre, beginning a run of 2,281 performances. In total, Andrews spent three and half years performing in *My Fair Lady*.

Cinderella. In February, 1957, Andrews began rehearsals for the title role in the Richard Rodgers and Oscar Hammerstein II musical *Cinderella* (1957) while still doing eight shows a week in *My Fair Lady*. *Cinderella* was the celebrated team's only original production for television, and the producers surrounded Andrews with a stellar cast of actors, including Ilka Chase and Broadway legends Howard Lindsay and Dorothy Stickney. It was broadcast live on CBS on Sunday, March 31, 1957.

Camelot. Andrews returned to Broadway to play Guenevere in Lerner and Loewe's Arthurian musical *Camelot* (1960), which opened at the Majestic Theatre on December 3, 1960. Though *Camelot* did not repeat the triumph of *My Fair Lady*, it was a solid hit. Andrews immensely enjoyed the year and a half she spent with the lavish show, one of the costliest Broadway productions up to that time. Andrews befriended her Welsh-born leading man, Richard Burton, as King Arthur, whom she found affable and approachable. Andrews left *Camelot* when she discovered that she was pregnant.

While Andrews was appearing in the final months of *Camelot*, producer Jack L. Warner started to cast the film version of *My Fair Lady*. Although Andrews was tested for the role of Doolittle, Warner wanted for the part a big star who could guarantee big box-office receipts. He ensured this by hiring Audrey Hepburn, whose musical numbers were dubbed by Marni Nixon. Controversy over this decision continued until the Academy Awards ceremony, when Andrews's stage costar, Harrison, received his Best Actor Oscar for repeating his role in the film version and graciously thanked "two fair ladies." Similarly, Warner did not select Andrews for the role of Guenevere when he was producing the film version of *Camelot* in 1967. Instead, he signed British actress Vanessa Redgrave, another nonsinger.

Mary Poppins. Although Andrews was disappointed at not being hired to portray Doolittle on film, she accepted an offer from Walt Disney, who had admired Andrews's performance in *Camelot*, to star in his musical film version of *Mary Poppins* (1964), based on the P. L. Travers books. The score was written by Richard and Robert Sherman. This was Andrews's first motion picture, and the combination of live action and animation proved popular, making it one of Disney's most successful films. The great critical and commercial success of *Mary Poppins*, which costarred Dick Van Dyke, turned the loss of starring in the motion picture *My Fair Lady* into a stroke of good fortune for Andrews. She won the Best Actress Academy Award (one of the film's five wins) for her portrayal of the magical nanny who brings joy to a stuffy family in Edwardian London; it was a rare instance of a performer in a musical film being so honored. In addition, Andrews was the first Disney actress to be given an acting honor that was not honorary, an immense achievement.

The Sound of Music. After *Mary Poppins*, Andrews appeared in a World War II black comedy, *The Americanization of Emily*, in a nonsinging role, opposite frequent Andrews costar James Garner. Released in November, 1964, after *Mary Poppins* and before *The Sound of Music* (1965), *The Americanization of Emily* was generally well-received. The film version of Rodgers and Hammerstein's musical *The Sound of Music*, the tale of a rambunctious novice nun who becomes the nanny to an aristocratic Austrian family and then marries their father, reached theaters in March, 1965. Although critics were not enthusiastic, it became one of the most beloved films of all time. The 1959 musical was based on the story of the singing Von Trapp family, who left Austria before World War II and emigrated to the United States, ending up in Stowe, Vermont. The film version was shot on location in Salzburg, Austria, where the family estate was located. Some of the musical numbers were photographed in a series of locations that moved the story along, a novelty at the time.

The reviews praised the film's breathtaking Alpine scenery but criticized its sugary plot. Nevertheless, global audiences turned out in record-breaking numbers. It became the highest-grossing musical up to that time. There are even sing-along events, in which audience members dress up as characters in the film and sing along while the lyrics appear on the screen. Andrews got an Academy Award nomination for her role as Maria, and the film earned the Best Picture award. This is the film role for which Andrews is best known, although it did tend to lock her remarkable talent into a stereotype of the singing governess from which she had trouble escaping.

Thoroughly Modern Millie. Two nonmusical roles followed: *Torn Curtain* (1966), a suspense drama directed by Alfred Hitchcock and costarring Paul Newman, and *Hawaii* (1966), a big-budget epic about New England missionaries on the Pacific island, with Richard Harris and Max Von Sydow. Andrews came back to her musical roots with a 1920's spoof similar to *The Boy Friend*, called *Thoroughly Modern Millie* (1967), costarring Carol Channing, Mary Tyler Moore, James Fox, and the great British comedian Beatrice Lillie. It was one of the most popular films of the year, and its bouncy title tune, sung by Andrews over the opening credits, became a popular commercial success. The film featured Andrews in the title role as a 1920's flapper. Although the film received lackluster reviews, its score, by Elmer Bernstein, won an Academy Award. *Thoroughly Modern Millie* typified the film-musical genre, whose popularity peaked at the height of Andrews's vocal powers.

Star! The highly touted 1968 film *Star!*, based on the life of stage actor Gertrude Lawrence, teamed Andrews with her *The Sound of Music* director, Robert Wise, but the film was poorly received. She superbly re-created Lawrence's Broadway musical triumphs, with a far superior singing voice than Lawrence possessed, but Andrews was generally lambasted by critics as too ladylike for the role. Her costar, Daniel Massey, won a Best Supporting Actor nomination for his role as Noël Coward, and their scenes together invigorated a rather dramatically weak and inaccurate film.

After she married Edwards, Andrews appeared in several of his films, and she became a regular guest star on television, most notably in a series of specials with her friend, Carol Burnett, and in many specials, such as *The Julie Andrews Hour* (1972-1973), *Julie on Sesame Street* (1973), and *Julie Andrews: The Sound of Music* (1987).

Victor/Victoria. The most successful film effort of Andrews and Edwards, *Victor/Victoria*, broke with her ladylike image. In the 1982 musical farce, Andrews plays a down-on-her-luck opera singer who turns to female impersonation to earn a living, *Victor/Victoria* offered her a sophisticated and edgy role that allowed her to break away from her wholesome image. Her effectiveness in pretending to be a man who is pretending to be a woman earned Andrews a Best Actress Academy Award nomination, and it provided her with one of her best film roles in years, appearing opposite Garner again and Robert Preston in a brilliant turn as her gay mentor and friend. The role solidified Andrews's status as a serious and accomplished actor.

Back on Broadway. In the 1990's, with a less-pressing domestic situation, Andrews made a long-awaited return to the theater. She participated in the off-Broadway production *Putting It Together* (1993), a revue of Stephen Sondheim songs, as one of an ensemble cast of five singers, in a limited run of twelve weeks. Two years later, Andrews returned to the theater with the stage version of *Victor/Victoria*, a large-scale production that totally revolved around her character. Although expectations were high, *Victor/Victoria*, directed by her husband and with music and lyrics by Henry Mancini and Leslie Bricusse, opened on Broadway on October 25, 1995, to mixed reviews. Andrews was praised, and she received a Tony Award nomination, although she declined to accept the nomination when she discovered she was the only one the show nominated.

Later Projects. In 1998, for the stage musical *Dr. Dolittle* in London, she performed the voice of Polynesia the parrot, recording some seven hundred sentences and sounds, which were placed on a computer chip that sat in the mechanical bird's mouth. In 1999 she teamed with Garner to make *One Special Night*, a television film, for CBS. In 2001 Andrews and her *The Sound of Music* costar, Christopher Plummer, were reunited for a live television broadcast of the play *On Golden Pond* (1979).

Andrews returned to films in 2001 as the royal grandmother in *The Princess Diaries*, the story of a gawky teenager who learns that her long-absent father, who has died, was the prince of a small European country. In 2004 Andrews reprised her role as Queen Clarisse Renaldi in *The Princess Diaries 2: Royal Engagement*, and she also starred as the voice of Queen Lillian in *Shrek 2*.

Musical Legacy

Andrews was blessed with a beautiful soprano voice and crystal-clear diction that were especially suited to both film and stage musicals. Although her peak of popularity was in the 1960's, her career extended well beyond. She proved that she could mature beyond her typecasting as the singing governess, gaining strength as an actor at a time in her career when many women would be overlooked.

Andrews will always be remembered for her contributions to musical theater on the strength of her performances in the phenomenally popular Broadway musicals *My Fair Lady* and *Camelot* and the film musicals *The Sound of Music* and *Mary Poppins*. In addition, she has proved her creative versatility, with her roles in films aimed at the youth market and as a respected children's author.

Martin J. Manning

Further Reading

Arntz, James, and Thomas S. Wilson. *Julie Andrews*. Chicago: Contemporary Books, 1995. With a foreword by Burnett, the book covers the life and career of Andrews, concluding that she is a successful author, dedicated to her charities, and a fine actress not wholly appreciated for her non-singing dramatic abilities.

Lerner, Alan Jay. *The Street Where I Live*. New York: Da Capo Press, 1994. This book, originally published in 1978, offers behind-the-scenes details on the making of Andrews's two important stage productions, *My Fair Lady* and *Camelot*. Lerner's respect and love for his leading lady is apparent, and he expresses his dismay about the fact that she was not hired for the film version of *My Fair Lady*.

Spindle, Les. *Julie Andrews: A Bio-Bibliography*. New York: Greenwood, 1989. Comprehensive on Andrews's career up to 1989.

Wilk, Max. *The Making of "The Sound of Music."* New York: Routledge, 2007. Interesting story on the making of the successful film, with good material on Andrews.

Windeler, Robert. *Julie Andrews: A Life on Stage and Screen*. New York: Carol, 1997. Full coverage of Andrews's life up to 1997, although it falls short in later events, such as her vocal problems and her films for Disney.

See also: Bernstein, Elmer; Hammerstein, Oscar, II; Lerner, Alan Jay; Loewe, Frederick; Mancini, Henry; Rodgers, Richard; Sondheim, Stephen.

Martha Argerich

Argentine pianist

A prodigiously gifted pianist and a fiery and impetuous performer, Argerich is known for her powerful technique and her sensitive phrasing.

Born: June 5, 1941; Buenos Aires, Argentina

Principal recordings

ALBUMS: *Schumann: Kinderszenen, Kreisleriana,* 1987; *Mendelssohn: Concerto for Violin and Piano; Violin Concerto in D Minor,* 1989; *Beethoven: Piano Concertos Nos. 1 and 2,* 1995; *Rachmaninoff: Piano Concerto No. 3 in D Minor, Op. 30; Tchaikovsky: Piano Concerto No. 1 in B-flat Minor, Op. 23,* 1995; *Chopin: Piano Concerto No. 1; Liszt: Piano Concerto No. 1,* 1996; *Prokofiev: Piano Concerto No. 3; Ravel: Piano Concerto in G; Gaspard de la Nuit,* 1997.

The Life

Martha Argerich (AHR-gur-ihch) began playing the piano at age three, and she started lessons at age five with Vincenzo Scaramuzza. She remained his student until she was age ten. She gave her debut concert in 1949 at age eight, playing Ludwig van Beethoven's Piano Concerto in C Major, Op. 15 (1798). The following year she played Wolfgang Amadeus Mozart's Piano Concerto No. 20 in D Minor (1785), and Johann Sebastian Bach's French Suite No. 5 in G Major (1722). In 1955 Argerich's family moved to Europe, where she studied with Friedrich Gulda in Austria. When the eight-year-old Argerich played the last movement of Beethoven's Sonata in E-Flat, Op. 31, No. 3 for legendary pianist Walter Gieseking, he noticed that she was resistant to being pushed to play in public, and he encouraged those responsible for her training to be sensitive to these tendencies. His advice was not heeded, and the young Argerich often resorted to creative methods for avoiding practicing, such as putting water-soaked blotter paper into her shoes in the hope of inducing illness. At musical soirées, the girl so disliked playing for others that she hid under the table, while the young Daniel Barenboim, who loved performing, soaked up the praise of those present.

Although Argerich loved playing the piano, she wanted to be a doctor, not a pianist, and her contradictory relationship with the instrument for which she possesses such immense talent has manifested itself in various ways in her career. Argerich often distinguishes between her love for playing the piano and her dislike for many aspects of the profession of pianist.

In 1957 Argerich won within three weeks both the Geneva International Music Competition and the Ferruccio Busoni International Competition. Shortly thereafter, she suffered a major depression, certain that she would quit the piano and use her language skills to become a secretary. Teacher Stefan Askenase's wife Anny helped Argerich to regain her confidence, to overcome her illness, and to return to the piano after having been away from it for three years. She went on to win the International Frédéric Chopin Piano Competition in 1965.

Argerich's tempestuous personal life has been a matter of interest: She has been married three times, to composer Robert Chen, to conductor Charles Dutoit, and to pianist Stephen Kovacevich. She has three daughters, one from each marriage.

The Music

Performance. Argerich is famous for the speed and ease with which she learns music. She attributes this to never knowing as a child if a piece was difficult or not, and therefore she was not fearful of its complexities. Pianistic legends regarding this ability abound: that she learned a concerto just by studying it on a plane and then performed it upon arrival; that she initially learned Sergei Prokofiev's Concerto No. 3 (1921) by hearing a roommate practice it incessantly; that she can learn new music just a few hours before she performs it. Regardless of the veracity of these stories, their existence attests to her unique talent. Argerich admits that she never practices more than two hours a day.

Beginning in 1981, Argerich mostly eschewed solo literature, and she has played mostly concerti and chamber music. She cites a feeling of extreme loneliness on stage as the reason for avoiding solo performances. One notable exception was a Carnegie Hall concert in 2000 in which the first half consisted of her playing solo repertoire. This benefit concert for the John Wayne Cancer Institute was presented in gratitude by Argerich for the successful treatment of her melanoma, a disease from which she suffered for ten years.

Shrouded in the mystique created by her impassioned performances, commanding personality, and attractive appearance, Argerich also gained notoriety for canceling a considerable number of performances each season. One of the most highly acclaimed performers of her time, Argerich has never signed a contract, and thus she is never obligated to perform.

Recordings. Although her live solo performances are rare, Argerich's recordings are extensive, about fifty albums on various major labels, such as Deutsche Grammophone, Sony, Philips, Teldec, and EMI. She has recorded many compositions from the standard repertoire, and her discography includes works by Johann Sebastian Bach, Béla Bartók, Beethoven, Johannes Brahms, Chopin, Manuel de Falla, César Franck, Joseph Haydn, Franz Liszt, Witold Lutosławski, Niccolò Paganini, Prokofiev, Sergei Rachmaninoff, Maurice Ravel, Franz Schubert, Robert Schumann, and Peter Ilich Tchaikovsky. She regularly performs and records chamber music with a select group of musi-

Martha Argerich. (AP/Wide World Photos)

cians who are also her friends, among them pianists Nelson Freire, Kovacevich, Nicolas Economou, Alexis Golovin, and Alexandre Rabinovitch; flutist James Galway; violinists Ruggiero Ricci, Ivry Gitlis, and Gidon Kremer; and cellist Mischa Maisky.

Musical Legacy

One of the most sought-after performers in classical music, Argerich has permanent invitations to play with prestigious orchestras in North America, Europe, and Japan. She is known primarily for her passionate and expressive performances of many works from the standard repertoire of the nineteenth and twentieth centuries. Argerich is also involved in a number of music festivals: She became artistic director of the Beppu Festival in Japan in 1998. In 1999 she created the International Piano Competition and Festival Martha Argerich in Buenos Aires, and in 2002 she founded the Progetto Martha Argerich as part of the Lugano Festival in Switzerland. In 2002, in collaboration with EMI, Argerich promoted the talents of selected young pianists in a series of albums titled *Martha Argerich Presents.*

Argerich has won three Grammy Awards: in 1999 for her recording of Prokofiev's Piano Concerto No. 1 and Piano Concerto No. 3 and Bartók's Piano Concerto No. 3 with Charles Dutoit; in 2004 for piano duo works by Prokofiev and Ravel with Mikhail Pletnev; and in 2005 for Beethoven's Piano Concerto No. 2 and Piano Concerto No. 3 with Claudio Abbado. Among her other distinguished awards are Musician of the Year in 2001 from *Musical America* and Commandeur de l'Ordre des Arts et des Lettres in 2004 from the French government.

Lisa de Alwis

Further Reading

Dyer, Richard. "Argerich Captivates with Focus, Virtuosity." *The Boston Globe*, August 24, 2004. A review of Argerich's performance at a Tanglewood concert describes her agility at the piano and her ability to create a variety of colors with her playing.

Manildi, Donald. "Musician of the Year 2001: Martha Argerich." *Musical America* (2001). A comprehensive overview of Argerich's life and career. Manildi writes engagingly and takes great care with the details.

Ross, Alex. "Madame X." *The New Yorker* (November 12, 2001). Interview with the pianist contains biographical information and a discussion of her performance style, her effect on other musicians, and her charismatic personality.

See also: Barenboim, Daniel; Busoni, Ferruccio; Galway, Sir James; Perlman, Itzhak; Prokofiev, Sergei.

Harold Arlen

American musical-theater composer, pianist, and singer

Arlen developed the musical fusion created by George Gershwin—blending the high and the low, the black and the white sounds of American music. In more than four hundred songs, he perfected a style known as blue-eyed soul, and he was the most jazz-oriented of the Tin Pan Alley songwriters.

Born: February 15, 1905; Buffalo, New York
Died: April 23, 1986; New York, New York

Principal works

MUSICAL THEATER (music): *The 9:15 Review,* 1929 (lyrics by Ted Koehler); *Rhythmania,* 1931 (lyrics by Koehler); *You Said It,* 1931 (lyrics by Jack Yellen); *Americana,* 1932 (lyrics by Edgar "Yip" Harburg and Johnny Mercer); *The Cotton Club Parade,* 1932 (lyrics by Koehler); *Earl Carroll's Vanities of 1932,* 1932 (lyrics by Koehler); *The Great Magoo,* 1933 (lyrics by Harburg and Billy Rose); *Life Begins at 8:40,* 1934 (lyrics by Harburg and Ira Gershwin); *Bloomer Girl,* 1944 (lyrics by Sig Herzig and Harburg; libretto by Fred Saidy); *St. Louis Woman,* 1946 (lyrics by Countée Cullen and Mercer; libretto by Arna Bontemps); *House of Flowers,* 1954 (lyrics by Truman Capote); *Jamaica,* 1957 (lyrics by Harburg; libretto by Harburg and Saidy); *Saratoga,* 1959 (lyrics by Mercer).

PIANO WORKS: *Minor Gaff,* 1926 (blues fantasy; with Dick George); *Rhythmic Moments,* 1928; *Mood in Six Minutes,* 1935; *American Minuet,* 1939; *Bon-Bon,* 1960; *Ode,* 1960.

SONGS (music): "I Love a Parade," 1931 (lyrics by
Ted Koehler); "Lydia, the Tattooed Lady," 1939
(lyrics by Edgar "Yip" Harburg); "Over the
Rainbow," 1939 (lyrics by Harburg); "Blues in
the Night," 1941 (lyrics by Johnny Mercer);
"That Old Black Magic," 1942 (lyrics by
Mercer); "Dissertation on the State of Bliss,"
1954 (lyrics by Ira Gershwin); "The Man That
Got Away," 1954 (lyrics by Gershwin).

VOCAL WORK: *American Negro Suite: Four Spirituals,
a Dream, and Lullaby*, 1941 (six songs for voice
and piano; lyrics by Koehler).

The Life

The son of Samuel and Celia Arluck, Hyman
Arluck began to follow his father's footsteps as a
cantor by singing in synagogue at the age of seven.
Young Arluck was given piano lessons and loved to
sing, but he was much more interested in jazz than
classical music. At sixteen, Arluck dropped out of
school and played at cafés in Buffalo, New York,
with a group called the Snappy Trio. He arrived in
New York City at the age of twenty with the
Buffalodians, an eleven-piece dance band for which
Arluck was singer, pianist, and arranger. His first
published work was the solo piano piece *Minor
Gaff*, written with Dick George. It was during this
period that he changed his name from Arluck to
Arlen (AHR-luhn). Bandleader Arnold Johnson
heard Arlen at the Palace Theatre and hired him to
be a vocalist, pianist, and arranger for his orchestra,
which was currently playing for the *George White
Scandals of 1928*.

Arlen left the *George White Scandals of 1928* in order to pursue his dream: to be a singer. As a single
act in vaudeville, he was popular, but when he and
Ted Koehler signed with a publishing firm as a
songwriting team, Arlen realized he had to give up
his singing career. Nevertheless, he occasionally recorded his own songs (usually with the Leo Reisman Orchestra) in his unique singing style.

Arlen first met the beautiful model and showgirl
Anya Taranda in 1932, but the shy, soft-spoken
composer did not rush into their courtship. Cantor
Arluck was not pleased that his son was in love
with a Catholic girl, but the happy couple finally
wed in 1937 and moved to California. Friends with
the Berlins, the Gershwins, the Kerns, Dorothy
Fields, and Moss Hart, the attractive Arlens lived

the high life. A natty dresser, Arlen was often seen
with a walking cane and sporting a flower in his
buttonhole.

Around 1950 Anya began to have violent out-
bursts, serious enough to have her institutionalized
in 1953, and Arlen began to drink heavily. By 1961
Anya was well enough for the couple to move back
to Manhattan. Although she refused to see a doctor
concerning a nervous tic, Anya was able to resume
her social life. Her condition worsened, however, in
1969; she was diagnosed with a brain tumor and
died in 1970. After suffering for years from Parkin-
son's disease, the reclusive Arlen died of cancer in
1986 at the age of eighty-one.

The Music

Arlen's musical background gave him an unusually rich palette from which to paint as a composer.
Citing his cantor father as one of the most inspired
improvisers he knew, Arlen sang not only as a cantor but also with bands and in vaudeville. Along
with his intimate knowledge of and respect for
singers, Arlen was classically trained as a pianist
and yet had a deep love of jazz. Although he
thought in terms of melody, he also wrote orchestrations and did arrangements during the early
part of his career. Arlen's compositions were
shaped by American jazz and blues, the big band
sound, and popular song. Classic Arlen embraces
lush harmonic changes, unusual intervals, minor
tonalities, and sweeping melody lines.

Early Works. Cast as a singer in the Broadway
musical *Great Day*, Arlen volunteered to be the rehearsal pianist when the show's regular one did not
come to work. The show's musical director encouraged him to write down a song he had been improvising at the piano. Fortunately, he was introduced
to lyricist Ted Koehler, who created words for
Arlen's tune. So it was that Arlen's first song composition, "Get Happy," became his first song to appear in a Broadway show, *The 9:15 Revue*.

Arlen and Koehler replaced the team of Jimmy
McHugh and Dorothy Fields to write the Cotton
Club's shows, where they created the next eight re-
vues (1930-1934). For many years the Cotton Club
was wildly popular as white audiences went to
Harlem to drink bootleg liquor and see black per-
formers. Hits from this period include "I've Got the
World on a String" for Aida Ward, "Minnie the

Harold Arlen. (Library of Congress)

Moocher's Wedding Day" for Cab Calloway, "Stormy Weather" for Ethel Waters, and "As Long as I Live" for sixteen-year-old Lena Horne.

When E. Y. "Yip" Harburg broke up with Vernon Duke in 1934, he asked Arlen to join him in writing the musical revue *Life Begins at 8:40*, starring Ray Bolger and Bert Lahr (who would both later star in the 1939 film *The Wizard of Oz*). Since George Gershwin was writing *Porgy and Bess*, Ira Gershwin joined his college classmate Harburg as co-lyricist. The trio created "Let's Take a Walk Around the Block" and "What Can You Say in a Love Song?" Working with such thoroughbreds as Harburg and Gershwin clearly brought out his best, so Arlen ended his partnership with Koehler.

Film Work. While Arlen had been writing for film since 1931's *Manhattan Parade* ("I Love a Parade") and 1933's *Take a Chance* ("It's Only a Paper Moon"), in 1938 he decided to move to Hollywood. For the Marx brothers, Arlen and Harburg created the score for *At the Circus* (1939) and a song that would henceforth be associated with Groucho, "Lydia, the Tattooed Lady."

Jerome Kern was originally slated to write *The Wizard of Oz*, but when he had a minor stroke, Metro-Goldwyn-Mayer turned to Arlen and Harburg. In only fourteen weeks the team turned out a string of memorable songs, but "Over the Rainbow" was a hard sell. The original children's book by L. Frank Baum did not mention rainbows, the sweeping ballad was perceived to be out of character for a little Kansas farm girl, and Louis B. Mayer did not like the song. Even though it had been cut repeatedly in previews, assistant producer Arthur Freed insisted it remain. The song won the Academy Award for best song in 1939, has been named the number-one Song of the Century by the Recording Industry Association of America, and tops the American Film Institute's 100 Years, 100 Songs list.

Arlen and Johnny Mercer had written a song together in 1932 for the Shubert revue *Americana*, so they decided to team up again in 1941. While Arlen was comfortable with the standard *aaba* thirty-two-bar song format, he occasionally experimented. "Blues in the Night" (written for the film *Blues in the Night*) is unusual in that it is fifty-eight measures long, is *abcca* in form, and contains two measures that are whistled. (Dinah Shore's recording was her first to sell a million units.) Mercer heard Arlen play only a sensuous seventy-two bars of "That Old Black Magic" (in the film *Star Spangled Rhythm*) once before he began sketching out the lyrics.

Arlen's other successful film work includes *Cabin in the Sky* (1943) and *Here Come the Waves* (1944). For the former, Arlen and Harburg wrote three new songs to add to those written by Vernon Duke for the original stage version; "Happiness Is a Thing Called Joe" was another hit for Ethel Waters. For the latter, Mercer and Arlen wrote "Ac-Cent-Tchu-Ate the Positive" (inducted in the Grammy Hall of Fame in 1998). Another great Arlen-Mercer collaboration was "One for My Baby (and One More for the Road)," which appeared in *The Sky's the Limit* (1943). Harburg brought more of a concert-hall sound out of the composer, while Mercer encouraged the blues and jazz.

Reunited with Judy Garland after fifteen years, in 1954 Arlen teamed with Ira Gershwin for *A Star Is Born* because Harburg was blacklisted, a casualty of the communist witch hunts of the time. While "The Man That Got Away" is the best-known song from this film, other standouts include "It's a New

World," "Here's What I'm Here For," and "Lose That Long Face." The movie that was supposed to be Garland's big comeback almost ended her film career, and "The Man That Got Away" was nominated for but did not win the Academy Award.

More Broadway. In 1944 Arlen's Civil War-era musical *Bloomer Girl*, with lyrics by Harburg, book by Sig Herzig and Fred Saidy, and choreography by Agnes de Mille, hit Broadway. Following the success of *Oklahoma!* (1943), audiences flocked to this nostalgic show for 654 performances; "The Eagle and Me" and "Evelina" are highlights of the score. *St. Louis Woman* contained a terrific score by Arlen and Mercer, but Arna Bontemps and Countée Cullen's book was weak. Despite a superior cast— Pearl Bailey, Lena Horne, the Nicholas brothers— and a string of stunning songs—such as "Any Place I Hang My Hat Is Home," "Legalize My Name," "I Had Myself a True Love," "Come Rain or Come Shine," "It's a Woman's Prerogative," "I Wonder What Became of Me"—the musical had a run of only 113 performances on Broadway. Margaret Whiting's recording of "Come Rain or Come Shine" gave that song a life independent of the stage flop. Arlen and Mercer took their wonderful material and refashioned it into *Free and Easy*, a "blues opera," that proved to be equally unsuccessful in Europe.

With a book by Truman Capote and lyrics by Capote and Arlen, *House of Flowers* was notable for the excellent songs "I Never Has Seen Snow," "Don't Like Goodbyes," "Two Ladies in de Shade of de Banana Tree," and "A Sleepin' Bee." However, neither the direction of Peter Brook nor the presence of Pearl Bailey and Diahann Carroll could keep the show running past 165 performances. An Off-Broadway revival in 1968 was equally unsuccessful, but a 2003 concert version by Encores! proved the songs to be top-notch.

Arlen's last success on Broadway was *Jamaica* (with 557 performances), with Harburg as lyricist and starring Lena Horne. Although not as strong as *House of Flowers*, this score nevertheless contains "Push de Button," "Little Biscuit," "I Don't Think I'll End It All Today," and the show's finest, "Cocoanut Sweet." His last collaboration with Harburg produced the haunting ballad "Paris Is a Lonely Town" for the forgotten animated film *Gay Purr-ee* (1962).

Late in his career, Arlen finally had the opportunity to team up again with Mercer. *Saratoga* contains many fine songs—"Love Held Lightly" and "Goose Never Be a Peacock"—but it was to be his final Broadway production. After a couple more films, Arlen withdrew into retirement in the mid-1960's.

Piano Compositions. Like his idol Gershwin, Arlen was a Tin Pan Alley songwriter who also wrote "highbrow" piano compositions: *Mood in Six Minutes, American Minuet, American Negro Suite: Four Spirituals, a Dream, and a Lullaby* (lyrics by Koehler), *Ode,* and *Bon-Bon.*

Musical Legacy

When Lincoln Center inaugurated its American Songbook series in 1999, it chose to start with Harold Arlen. *New York Times* critic Stephen Holden applauded this choice, noting Arlen "is probably the most underappreciated composer as well the one most deeply connected to contemporary pop." Arlen created more shows with all-black casts— eight Cotton Club revues, *St. Louis Woman, Jamaica, House of Flowers, Free and Easy*—than any other major composer. Ethel Waters once remarked that Arlen was "the Negro-est white man I ever knew." When Arlen died in 1986, Irving Berlin remarked, "He wasn't as well known as some of us, but he was more talented than most of us, and he will be missed by all of us."

Bud Coleman

Further Reading

Friedwald, Will. *Stardust Melodies: The Biography of Twelve of America's Most Popular Songs.* New York: Pantheon Books, 2002. One chapter tells the story of Koehler and Arlen's "Stormy Weather."

Furia, Philip, and Michael Lasser. *America's Songs: The Stories Behind the Songs of Broadway, Hollywood, and Tin Pan Alley.* New York: Routledge, 2006. Contains the backstory and brief analysis of twenty-eight Arlen tunes.

Hischak, Thomas S. *The American Musical Film Song Encyclopedia.* Westport, Conn.: Greenwood Press, 1999. Sixty-one of Arlen's songs are briefly described, including who originally sang them, in which film they appeared, and who subsequently recorded them.

Jablonski, Edward. *Harold Arlen: Rhythm, Rainbows, and Blues*. Boston: Northeastern University Press, 1996. An expanded version of his 1961 biography *Harold Arlen: Happy with the Blues*.

Suskin, Steven. *Show Tunes, 1905-1985: The Songs, Shows, and Careers of Broadway's Major Composers*. New York: Dodd, Mead, 1986. According to Suskin, Gershwin used gimmicks in his writing, while the same elements were used organically in Arlen's work because of his superior imagination.

Wilder, Alec. *American Popular Song: The Great Innovators, 1900-1950*. Edited by James T. Maher. New York: Oxford University Press, 1972. Wilder believes Arlen surpassed Gershwin and that Arlen's talents as a singer and orchestrator gave him a range and richness as a composer that set him apart from his peers. Points out the irony that the composer's most popular song, "Over the Rainbow," is not representative of the distinctive Arlen style, although it does contain his signature octave jump.

See also: Bennett, Tony; Fitzgerald, Ella; Gershwin, George; Gershwin, Ira; Horne, Lena; Kern, Jerome; Lee, Peggy; Mercer, Johnny; Peterson, Oscar; Previn, Sir André; Streisand, Barbra; Tatum, Art; Webb, Jimmy.

Louis Armstrong

American jazz trumpeter and composer

A virtuoso trumpet player and innovative vocalist, Armstrong was an influential jazz musician who popularized the improvised solo and scat singing. With his showmanship and unquenchable determination to bring joy to the lives of others, Armstrong performed constantly throughout the United States and abroad, appeared in twenty-eight feature films, wrote dozens of articles and reminiscences, and became one of the world's most recognized and beloved Americans.

Born: August 4, 1901; New Orleans, Louisiana
Died: July 6, 1971; New York, New York
Also known as: Daniel Louis Armstrong (full name); Ambassador Satch; Satchmo

Principal recordings

ALBUMS: *New Orleans Jazz*, 1940; *Satchmo Serenades*, 1949; *New Orleans Days*, 1950; *New Orleans Nights*, 1950; *New Orleans to New York*, 1950; *Latter Day Louis*, 1954; *Louis Armstrong Plays W. C. Handy*, 1954; *Louis Armstrong Sings the Blues*, 1954; *Ambassador Satch*, 1955; *Satch Plays Fats: The Music of Fats Waller*, 1955; *Ella and Louis*, 1956 (with Ella Fitzgerald); *Ella and Louis Again*, 1957 (with Fitzgerald); *Louis and the Angels*, 1957; *Louis Armstrong Meets Oscar Peterson*, 1957; *Louis Under the Stars*, 1957; *Porgy and Bess*, 1957 (with Fitzgerald); *Satchmo in Style*, 1959; *Louis and the Dukes of Dixieland*, 1960; *Paris Blues*, 1960 (music by Duke Ellington); *The Great Reunion*, 1961 (with Ellington); *The Real Ambassadors*, 1961 (with Dave Brubeck, Dave Lambert, Jon Hendricks, and Annie Ross); *Together for the First Time*, 1961 (with Ellington); *Blueberry Hill*, 1962; *Hello, Dolly!*, 1963; *Louis*, 1964; *Satchmo*, 1964; *I Will Wait for You*, 1967; *What a Wonderful World*, 1970.

SINGLES: "Weary Blues," 1926; "Potato Head Blues," 1927; "Savoy Blues," 1927; "Willie the Weeper," 1927; "Weather Bird," 1928; "West End Blues," 1928.

The Life

Daniel Louis (LEW-ee) Armstrong was born in 1901 in New Orleans, the cradle of jazz. His father, William Armstrong, abandoned his mother, Mayann, so Louis was listed as illegitimate on his Catholic baptismal certificate. He was raised by Mayann and his grandmother Josephine in "Back o' Town," the African American section of Storyville, the prostitute district of New Orleans. Louis sang in church services from an early age.

At about the age of seven, Armstrong began working for the Karnoffsky family, Jewish immigrants who owned a junkyard and treated him kindly. They gave Armstrong a tin horn, which he would blow from the top of their junk wagon to attract business. At some point, Morris Karnoffsky bought Armstrong a used B-flat cornet. Armstrong dropped out of school in the fifth grade and began singing and playing his cornet on street corners.

On January 1, 1913, Armstrong fired a pistol in a New Year's street celebration, for which he was arrested and sent to the Colored Waifs' Home, a juvenile detention facility. While there, Armstrong assiduously practiced the bugle and cornet, advancing to bandleader. Upon his release on June 16, 1914, Armstrong began performing at New Orleans events, while working odd jobs. In 1918 Armstrong was invited to play cornet in Edward "Kid" Ory's popular band, the Brown Skinned Babies. He also married Daisy Parker, a prostitute, and took on the responsibility of raising his unwed cousin's child, Clarence Hatfield.

After starring in various New Orleans bands and Fate Marabel's Mississippi River steamboat band, Armstrong joined Joe "King" Oliver's band in Chicago in 1922, the same year Armstrong and Daisy divorced. Armstrong recorded his first songs with Oliver's band and married jazz pianist Lil Hardin in 1924. Over the next few years, Armstrong performed in Chicago and New York with such stars as Fletcher Henderson, Sidney Bechet, Ma Rainey, Alberta Hunter, Bessie Smith, and Fats Waller, in the process switching from the cornet to the trumpet. His recordings as Louis Armstrong's Hot Five and Hot Seven from 1925 to 1928 revolutionized jazz.

By then the most famous jazz musician in America, he formed his own big band in Chicago. In 1931 Armstrong made his film debut in Hollywood, where he was convicted of possession of marijuana. He also developed chronic lip ailments as a result of his hard-blowing style.

In 1934 Joe Glaser became his manager, starting a lifetime partnership. In 1938 Armstrong divorced Lil to marry his mistress Alpha Smith. In 1942 Armstrong divorced Alpha to marry chorus girl Lucille Wilson. In 1947 Glaser formed the "All Stars" band, with which Armstrong would perform the rest of his life. Showing no interest in the advent of bebop, Armstrong stayed with traditional and popular favorites in some three hundred concerts a year.

In 1960 the U.S. State Department made Armstrong a goodwill ambassador, prompting him to conduct musical tours of Africa and Asia. Although sometimes maligned for his easygoing spirit, Armstrong did speak out against segregation, most notably in 1957, when he criticized President Dwight Eisenhower for his inaction in the Little Rock, Arkansas, school integration controversy.

Declining health began to interfere with Armstrong's frenetic concert schedule, and in 1971 he died of heart failure. His funeral was broadcast throughout the world to international mourning.

The Music

Louis Armstrong completed the transformation of New Orleans ragtime and Dixieland music into twentieth century jazz. He became a unique musical personality, endowing each performance with trumpet mastery, heartfelt singing, and infectious enthusiasm.

Hot Five and Hot Seven Recordings. Although jazz legends such as Charles "Buddy" Bolden began the process, Armstrong completed the evolution of New Orleans rag music into modern jazz. This transformation can be heard in Armstrong's revolutionary Hot Five and Hot Seven recordings made in Chicago, birthplace of the new style. The classic New Orleans format consisted of ensemble playing in 2/2 time, during which the musicians played variations of the melody, collectively and one by one. Armstrong transformed this pattern in three ways. First, in the ensemble introduction, Armstrong's trumpet soared above the other musicians, with the melody a platform for his imaginative attacks in syncopated 4/4 time. In "Struttin' with Some Barbecue," Armstrong began with a bold twelve-bar melodic introduction that flew over the traditional New Orleans counterpoint of clarinet and trombone before surging ahead with ascending triplet notes. In the closing ensemble, his trumpet embellished the melody with his exuberant tone.

Second, and even more daringly, Armstrong liberated the solo from mere repetition of the arranged melody into an improvisational piece capable of telling a dramatic story. His innovative solos from these recordings opened with beautiful flights, developed with tension and anticipation, and were resolved in climaxes of soaring high notes and swooping harmonic changes. In "Potato Head Blues," Armstrong's stop-time solo chorus discarded the melody entirely as his trumpet cascaded though brilliant chord progressions (explorations of the underlying harmonies) before rejoining the ensemble in a poignant close. Likewise in the minor-key "Tight Like This," Armstrong built on a suggestive vocal dialogue with a dramatic three-chorus trumpet solo that began with ominous growls before ascending into an explosive climax

Louis Armstrong. (Library of Congress)

that the vocalists proclaimed to be "tight like that." Third, Armstrong in "Heebie Jeebies" added a new element to jazz: scat, which consisted of nonsense-syllable, rhythmic singing.

All of these new elements can be heard in the celebrated "West End Blues," which began with Armstrong's inspired nine-measure trumpet cadenza, filled with rapid and difficult glissandi. This introduction was followed by a duet between the clarinet and Armstrong's vocal, in which Armstrong's lilting scat syllables reached a new level of expressiveness. He concluded his second solo with tense and sustained high notes that swept the length of the song beneath it. The brilliance of "West End Blues" was equaled by the more contemplative interplay of the duet "Weatherbird," which Armstrong recorded with Earl "Fatha" Hines one year later.

Louis Armstrong and His Orchestra. Capitalizing on the rise of big band swing, Armstrong began fronting his own big band in 1929, eventually to be known as Louis Armstrong and His Orchestra. These polished recordings from 1929 to 1931 showed Armstrong at his finest. His fierce staccato blasts, alternating with a high C note sustained for ten measures, in "Mahogany Hall Stomp," his blistering arpeggios in "St. Louis Blues," his bravura vocal and trumpet solos in "Ain't Misbehavin'"

(which regularly stole the show in the revue *Hot Chocolate*), and his haunting opening cadenza in "Blue Again," all displayed the power and imagination of his Hot Five and Hot Seven sessions without their occasional mistakes and rawness. During the 1930's and 1940's, Armstrong continued to play jazz classics such as "St. James Infirmary" and "When the Saints Go Marching In" but also added novelty numbers such as "I'm a Ding Dong Daddy (from Dumas)" and "I'll Be Glad When You're Dead, You Rascal You." Most significantly, he gravitated to popular standards that he would make his own, such as his inspired recording of Hoagy Carmichael's "Stardust" in 1931. He also performed his trademark biographical numbers at nearly every concert, such as "Shine," "Black and Blue," and "When It's Sleepy Time Down South." Armstrong endowed his trumpet with the expressiveness and narrative capability of the human voice and his singing with glissandi, obligatos, and vibratos that attain the quality of a musical instrument.

The big band era ended with World War II, and following a successful Town Hall concert in New York City on May 17, 1947, Glaser formed Louis Armstrong and His All-Stars as a six-piece band. With a succession of all-stars over the succeeding decades, including Hines, Jack Teagarden, Barney Bigard, Sid Catlett, Trummy Young, Billy Kyle, Milt Hinton, Danny Barcelona, and vocalist Velma Middleton, Armstrong recorded such popular hits as "Blueberry Hill," "Mack the Knife," and "Hello, Dolly!" (which hit number one on the *Billboard* chart on May 9, 1964).

"What a Wonderful World." Perhaps Armstrong's most emblematic recording was "What a Wonderful World," written specifically for him and recorded shortly before his death. It is a sentimental number with strings, as Armstrong forgoes his trumpet to sing joyously of life. It sold fewer than a thousand records in the United States but was a major hit in England and other international markets. With its relentlessly upbeat lyrics, it might be considered saccharine, but it showcased Armstrong's sincerity, as his gravelly voice glided over each syllable and embraced it with moving vibrato. The exuberant cheerfulness of "What a Wonderful World" made it both a Christmas-season favorite and an ironic touch in such film sound tracks as *Good Morning, Vietnam* (1987).

Musical Legacy

Armstrong's impact on jazz has never been disputed. He revolutionized the solo, thereby transforming Dixieland collective playing into modern jazz featuring improvised composition. Elements of swing, bebop, and even free jazz were prefigured in his soaring trumpet harmonics. With a unique vocal style, he popularized scat singing and influenced generations of pop, jazz, and swing singers. Although some critics accuse Armstrong of commercially misusing his talents for the last three decades of his life, in fact he was expanding, not abandoning, his New Orleans roots. The incredible musical environment of early New Orleans—with its extravagant mix of spirituals, blues, funeral marches, quadrilles, field hollers, work songs, physical clowning, even Voodoo influences—contributed to Armstrong's unique musicality and showmanship. Armed with his trademark white handkerchief, mugging joyfully at the top of the stage, Armstrong brought his exuberant New Orleans spirit to each performance.

Armstrong is one of the few American musicians to become an international icon. In spite of his deprived Storyville upbringing and the oppression that African Americans suffered, Armstrong focused on the affirmative, joyful, wonderful experiences of life. In that way he was truly an ambassador of jazz and American culture.

Howard Bromberg

Further Reading

Armstrong, Louis. *Satchmo: My Life in New Orleans*. New York: Da Capo Press, 1986. Reprint of Armstrong's 1954 memoir of his gritty and colorful youth.

Bergreen, Laurence. *Louis Armstrong: An Extravagant Life*. New York: Broadway Books, 1997. In-depth portrait by a talented biographer of other American twentieth century figures such as Al Capone, James Agee, and Irving Berlin.

Boujut, Michael. *Louis Armstrong*. New York: Rizzoli International, 1998. Originally published in France, includes time line, photographs, interview with contemporary trumpeter Wynton Marsalis, discography, and filmography.

Brothers, Thomas. *Louis Armstrong's New Orleans*. New York: W. W. Norton, 2006. Biography of Armstrong's early years, emphasizing the lifelong influence that New Orleans's heady mix of African American musical culture would exert on Armstrong. Draws on extensive archives and interviews.

_____, ed. *Louis Armstrong in His Own Words: Selected Writings*. Oxford, England: Oxford University Press, 1999. Collection of Armstrong's prolific writings.

Collier, James Lincoln. *Louis Armstrong: An American Genius*. New York: Oxford University Press, 1983. Insightful analysis of early Armstrong recordings, but assesses Armstrong's later musical career as too commercial.

Giddins, Gary. *Satchmo: The Genius of Louis Armstrong*. New York: Da Capo Press, 2001. A noted jazz critic analyzes Armstrong's influence on twentieth century musical development.

Meckna, Michael. *Satchmo: The Louis Armstrong Encyclopedia*. Westport, Conn.: Greenwood Press, 2004. A comprehensive reference work with more than fifteen hundred entries and appendixes including discography, chronology, filmography, bibliography, and Web listings.

Panassié, Hugues. *Louis Armstrong*. New York: Charles Scribner's Sons, 1971. A leading French critic of jazz incisively analyzes Armstrong's recordings.

Ratliff, Ben. *Jazz: A Critic's Guide to the Hundred Most Important Recordings*. New York: Henry Holt, 2002. This volume in *The New York Times'* Essential Library Series includes chapters on Armstrong's "Complete Hot Five and Hot Seven Recordings" (1925-1929) and "Complete RCA Victor Recordings" (1930-1956), highlighting Armstrong's originality as soloist and vocalist.

See also: Basie, Count; Bechet, Sidney; Beiderbecke, Bix; Cole, Nat King; Cooke, Sam; Crosby, Bing; Domino, Fats; Fitzgerald, Ella; Gillespie, Dizzy; Goodman, Benny; Gordon, Dexter; Hampton, Lionel; Handy, W. C.;

Hawkins, Coleman; Henderson, Fletcher; Holiday, Billie; Hunter, Alberta; Jefferson, Blind Lemon; Johnson, Lonnie; Jordan, Louis; Lee, Peggy; Lewis, John; Masekela, Hugh; Mingus, Charles; Peterson, Oscar; Piaf, Édith; Rainey, Ma; Rodgers, Jimmie; Smith, Bessie; Waits, Tom; Waller, Fats; Whiteman, Paul; Williams, Mary Lou.

Eddy Arnold

American country guitarist, vocalist, and songwriter

Arnold had a significant impact on country-western music, scoring 147 singles on the country charts, twenty-eight of which reached number one. In addition, his recordings from the mid-1960's on made him a pop star who transcended genres.

Born: May 15, 1918; Madisonville, Tennessee
Died: May 8, 2008; Nashville, Tennessee
Also known as: Richard Edward Arnold (full name); Tennessee Plowboy

Principal recordings

ALBUMS: *Anytime*, 1955; *The Chapel on the Hill*, 1955; *Wanderin'*, 1955; *A Little on the Lonely Side*, 1956; *My Darling, My Darling*, 1957; *When They Were Young*, 1957; *Praise Him, Praise Him*, 1958; *Have Guitar, Will Travel*, 1959; *Thereby Hangs a Tale*, 1959; *More Eddy Arnold*, 1960; *You Gotta Have Love*, 1960; *Christmas with Eddy Arnold*, 1961; *Let's Make Memories Tonight*, 1961; *One More Time*, 1961; *Our Man Down South*, 1962; *Cattle Call*, 1963; *Faithfully Yours*, 1963; *Folk Song Book*, 1964; *Sometimes I'm Happy, Sometimes I'm Blue*, 1964; *The Easy Way*, 1965; *My World*, 1965; *I Want to Go with You*, 1966; *The Last Word in Lonesome*, 1966; *Somebody Like Me*, 1966; *Lonely Again*, 1967; *Turn the World Around*, 1967; *The Everlovin' World of Eddy Arnold*, 1968; *The Romantic World of Eddy Arnold*, 1968; *Walkin' in Love Land*, 1968; *Songs of the Young World*, 1969; *The Glory of Love*, 1969; *The Warmth of Eddy*, 1969; *Love and Guitars*, 1970; *Standing Alone*, 1970; *Loving Her Was Easier*, 1971; *Portrait of My Woman*, 1971; *Welcome to My World*, 1971; *Eddy Arnold Sings for Housewives and Other Lovers*, 1972; *Lonely People*, 1972; *The World of Eddy Arnold*, 1973; *I Wish That I Had Loved You Better*, 1974; *She's Got Everything I Need*, 1974; *The Wonderful World of Eddy Arnold*, 1975; *Eddy*, 1976; *I Need You All the Time*, 1977; *Many Tears Ago*, 1985; *Hand Holdin' Songs*, 1990; *You Don't Miss a Thing*, 1991; *After All These Years*, 2005.

SINGLES: "Cattle Call," 1945; "Each Minute Seems a Million Years," 1945; "I'll Hold You in My Heart (Till I Hold You in My Arms)," 1947.

The Life

Richard Edward Arnold was born in 1918 on his father's two-hundred-acre farm in Henderson, Tennessee. The family fell from prosperity, however, when in 1924 Arnold's father put up the farm as collateral to ease the debt of an older son by a previous marriage. The father's failing health in the late 1920's led to default, and in the depths of the Great Depression of the 1930's, Arnold lost both his father and his family homestead.

Later, Arnold made a name for himself by playing his guitar at local dances, and when a salesman from the *Jackson Sun* newspaper heard Arnold play, he arranged an audition with radio station WTJS, which was owned by the newspaper, in 1937. Arnold played first on WTJS, then on KWK in St. Louis in 1938, and finally he joined Pee Wee King's Golden West Cowboys in Nashville, becoming a popular radio singer known as the Tennessee Plowboy. He began recording country-western hits in 1945, and a decade later he attempted to get into the New York market with a more fully orchestrated sound. He finally succeeded in crossing over to the popular music charts in the mid-1960's. With sales of more than eighty-five million records over his lifetime, he became one of the best-selling recording artists in history. Arnold died on May 8, 2008, just a few days before his ninetieth birthday.

The Music

Despite his radio origins as the Tennessee Plowboy, Arnold endeavored from the start of his recording career to appeal to a wider audience. His first recording, "Each Minute Seems a Million Years," reached number five on the country charts, but two years later he made a significant impact on the popular music world. Of the top twenty country songs of 1947-1948, thirteen were Arnold's; six of those reached number one on the country charts, and of those six, four crossed over to the pop side. Arnold totally dominated the country charts at this time, his three number-one hits of 1947 staying at the top. "I'll Hold You in My Heart (Till I Hold You in My Arms" was on the country charts a staggering forty-six weeks, remaining number one nearly half that time (twenty-one weeks). In 1948 Arnold's singles were in the number-one position a total of forty weeks. This phenomenal success led country impresario Colonel Tom Parker (later the promotional genius behind Elvis Presley) to become Arnold's manager.

New York and Rock and Roll. Arnold's determination to succeed outside the world of country music brought mixed reactions from his fans. He had been one of the catalysts who made Nashville a major center of the recording industry, so when he went to New York in 1955 to record with the Hugo Winterhalter Orchestra, many fans called it selling out. However, the lush arrangements with full orchestra made songs such as "Cattle Call" and "That Do Make It Nice"—both number-one country hits—sell beyond the country market (though only "Cattle Call" charted on the pop side, reaching number forty-two). In addition, television widened Arnold's appeal; he appeared on a number of shows, and in 1954 he hosted *Eddy Arnold Time*, a music variety show. Just as he was catching on in the mass market, however, rock and roll revolutionized popular music, cutting into the sales of all other types of music, Arnold's included. As a result, Arnold's manager, Parker, began paying more attention to Presley.

New Management. In the early 1960's Arnold slowly began to regain his stature on the country charts—though never the top spot and never crossing over to the pop list, now known as the Top 40. In 1964 he changed management, signing with Jerry Purcell and working with producer Chet Atkins. Floyd Cramer, who

five years earlier had taken a country instrumental, "Last Date," to number two on the Top 40, supplied his "slip-note" piano style, and the Anita Kerr Singers sang background for what would become Arnold's biggest hit: "Make the World Go Away." It brought Arnold back to the top of the country charts, and it reached number six on the popular side. In fact, another song from the same session reached number one the same year: "What's He Doing in My World?" For the next four years, all of Arnold's country hits would also make the pop charts, though some barely made it into the Top 100. In 1966 Arnold was inducted into the Country Music Hall of Fame, which persuaded the singer to publish his autobiography—though some of his biggest hits were still to come. Arnold continued to score country hits into the 1970's and 1980's, before retiring in 1999, the year his remake of "Cattle Call" with seventeen-year-old LeAnn Rimes hit number eighteen in the country market. In mid-May of

Eddy Arnold. (AP/Wide World Photos)

2008, a week after Arnold's death, RCA released Arnold's "To Life," which two weeks later hit number forty-nine on the country charts.

Musical Legacy

Arnold's influence on American popular music can be measured by his popularity. Only George Jones had more country hits than Arnold, although Arnold's hits had more staying power. Another part of Arnold's legacy is the number and quality of artists in and out of country music who recorded his music. His signature tune, "Make the World Go Away," was recorded in 1971 by Presley, in 1975 by Donny and Marie Osmond (their version peaked at number forty-four), and in 2005 by Martina McBride. At the 2008 Country Music Awards show, Carrie Underwood and Brad Paisley sang a duet of the song as a tribute to Arnold. In 2003 Country Music Television chose the Forty Greatest Men of Country Music, ranking Arnold at number twenty-two. Although his crossover success was considered controversial, it was largely responsible for creating the string-sweetened Nashville sound that remans vital in country music.

John R. Holmes

Further Reading

Arnold, Eddy. *It's A Long Way from Chester County.* Old Tappan, N.J.: Hewitt House, 1969. A readable autobiography capturing Arnold's gentle personality. Includes photographs.

Kosser, Michael. *How Nashville Became Music City, USA: 50 Years of Music Row.* Milwaukee, Wis.: Hal Leonard, 2006. A history of the revolution in country-music recording that Arnold helped to foment.

St. John, Lauren. *Walkin' After Midnight: A Journey to the Heart of Nashville.* London: Picador, 2000. A British view of the Nashville sound that is Arnold's legacy.

Streissguth, Michael. *Eddie Arnold: Pioneer of the Nashville Sound.* New York: Schirmer Books, 1997. A detailed biography that includes a thorough sessionography and discography of Arnold's recordings.

See also: Atkins, Chet; Jones, George; Monroe, Bill; Presley, Elvis.

Vladimir Ashkenazy

Russian classical composer, pianist, and conductor

Born and educated in the Soviet Union, Ashkenazy forged an international career as a pianist and conductor, and he is renowned for his immense body of recorded repertoire in several genres.

Born: July 6, 1937; Gorki, Soviet Union (now Russia)

Principal recordings

ALBUMS (as conductor): *Mozart: Piano Concertos Nos. 20, 21, 23, 24, 25,* 1989; *Tchaikovsky: Nutcracker; Glazunov: The Seasons,* 1992; *Brahms: Symphony No. 1; Dvořák; Othello Overture,* 1993; *Essential Tchaikovsky,* 1993; *Borodin: Symphonies 1 and 2, In the Steppes,* 1994; *Rachmaninov: Piano Concerto No. 2; Paganini: Rhapsody,* 1994; *Shostakovich: Symphony No. 2, October, Etc.,* 1994; *Szymanowski: Symphonies, Etc.; Lutosławski,* 1997; *Sibelius: The Symphonies Nos. 1, 2, and 4, Etc.,* 1998.

ALBUMS (as pianist): *Prokofiev: Five Piano Concertos,* 1975; *Études,* 1984; *Prokofiev: Piano Concertos,* 1989; *Rachmaninov: Piano Concertos,* 1989; *Scriabin: Piano Sonatas,* 1989; *Chopin Favourites,* 1990; *Beethoven: Piano Concertos 4 and 5, "Emperor,"* 1991; *Favourite Rachmaninov,* 1992; *Ten Waltzes; Seven Nocturnes,* 1992; *Brahms: Piano Trios,* 1994; *Violin Sonatas Nos. 9 and 10,* 1994 (with Itzhak Perlman); *Piano Concertos Nos. 1-4,* 1995 (with André Previn and the London Symphony Orchestra); *Twenty-four Préludes; Piano Sonata No. 2,* 1995; *Eine Alpensinfonie; Don Juan; Salome's Dance,* 1996 (with the Cleveland Orchestra); *Capriccio Italien; The Tale of Tsar Sultan; Polovtsian Dances, Etc.,* 1996 (with the Royal Philharmonic Orchestra; Philharmonia Orchestra); *Chopin: Mazurkas,* 1996; *Symphony No. 7,* 1997 (with the St. Petersburg Philharmonic Orchestra); *Chopin for Lovers,* 1998; *The Art of Ashkenazy,* 1999; *Twenty-four Preludes and Fugues,* 1999; *Waltzes; Scherzos; Preludes,* 1999; *Four Ballades; Four Scherzi, Etc.,* 2000.

The Life

Vladimir Ashkenazy (VLA-dih-mihr ash-keh-NAH-zee) was born in Gorki, the first child of pianist David Ashkenazy and actress-singer Evstolia Plotnova. The family moved to Moscow in 1940, but it was forced to evacuate the following year because of the Nazi invasion. While his father supported the family by traveling and performing with the national Estrada entertaining troupe, Ashkenazy and his mother wandered throughout the Soviet Union as evacuees, settling in Tashkent for several months before returning to Moscow in 1943. His sister, Elena, was born in 1949.

In 1945 Ashkenazy entered the Central School of Music in Moscow, where he studied with Anaida Sumbatian until 1955. In his final year, he placed second in the fifth International Frédéric Chopin Competition in Warsaw. Shortly after, he entered the studio of Lev Oborin at the Moscow Conservatory, where he remained until his immigration to London. During his years at the conservatory, Ashkenazy took first prize at the 1956 Queen Elizabeth Competition in Brussels and joint first prize at the 1962 Tchaikovsky Competition in Moscow. He defected to London in 1963 during a concert tour, although, because of his celebrity status, he was able to retain his Soviet citizenship while living abroad.

In 1968, after approximately five years in London, Ashkenazy relocated to Reykjavík, Iceland, where he became a naturalized citizen in 1972. In Reykjavík, Ashkenazy became increasingly involved with the musical community, serving as artistic adviser to the Reykjavík Music Festival, while he continued to concertize throughout Europe. During this time, he launched his conducting career with a position as volunteer conductor of the Iceland Symphony Orchestra. Engagements as guest conductor followed, with orchestras such as the Royal Liverpool Philharmonic and the Swedish Radio Orchestra.

In 1978 Ashkenazy left Iceland to settle in Lucerne, Switzerland. From 1978 to 1982, he conducted the Philharmonia Orchestra of London regularly and almost exclusively, serving as principal guest conductor from 1981 to 1983.

Ashkenazy married Thorunn (Dody) Johannsdottir in 1961. They would have five children: Vladimir, Nadia, Dimitri, Sonia, and Sascha.

The Music

Performance. Ashkenazy's pianistic repertoire concentrates on music of the classical and Romantic eras, particularly the works of Ludwig van Beethoven, Wolfgang Amadeus Mozart, Frédéric Chopin, and Aleksandr Scriabin. He orchestrated his own version of Modest Mussorgsky's *Pictures at an Exhibition* (1874), conducting it to much acclaim with the Royal Liverpool Philharmonic at the Royal Festival Hall in 1982.

Conducting. As a conductor, Ashkenazy has noticeably favored repertoire of the nineteenth and early twentieth centuries. Beginning in the 1970's, his conducting career incorporated an extensive repertoire with a large number of prolific orchestras, including the Concertgebuow Orchestra (guest conductor, 1979), Royal Philharmonic Orchestra (principal conductor and music director, 1987-1994), Berlin Radio Symphony Orchestra/Deutches Symphonie-Orchester (chief conductor, 1988-1994; chief conductor and music director, 1994-1996), Czech Philharmonic Orchestra (chief conductor, 1998-2003), Cleveland Orchestra (principal guest conductor), and NHK Symphony Orchestra (music director). He was appointed conductor laureate of the Philharmonia Orchestra (2000), the Iceland Symphony Orchestra (2002), and the NHK Symphony Orchestra (2007).

Recordings. In 1962 Ashkenazy began to record exclusively for Decca Records, as both pianist and conductor. His piano recordings include the complete concerti of Beethoven, Chopin, Mozart, Béla Bartók, Johannes Brahms, Sergei Prokofiev, and Sergei Rachmaninoff. In addition, he has recorded complete collections of Johann Sebastian Bach's *The Well-Tempered Clavier* (1722), Beethoven's sonatas, the Chopin solo-piano works, and Dmitri Shostakovich's preludes and fugues. His chamber music recordings include complete sets of the Beethoven piano trios and the songs of Rachmaninoff and Peter Ilich Tchaikovsky. As a conductor, he has recorded the symphonies of Beethoven, Prokofiev, Rachmaninoff, and Jean Sibelius. His recordings have received numerous Grammy Awards: in 1979, 1982, and 1988 for Best Chamber Music Performance and in 1986 and 2000 for Best Instrumental Solo Performance.

Educational Endeavors. Ashkenazy's television projects, designed to appeal to children and adult audiences, include *Music After Mao* (1979), a program centered on his experiences visiting and teaching in Shanghai; the *Ashkenazy in Moscow* series, documenting his first return to Moscow in 1989; a *Superteachers* (1999) educational program, about children in inner-city London; and a documentary inspired by his Prokofiev and Shostakovich Under Stalin concert series. He has collaborated regularly with producer Christopher Nupen to produce more than twenty music-themed intimate portrait films, among them *We Want the Light* (2005), which depicts the linkage between German music and the Jewish prisoners incarcerated in Nazi concentration camps.

Musical Legacy

As a pianist, Ashkenazy has performed to critical acclaim throughout the world, especially in England, in Scandinavia, and in the Low Countries. His recording repertory spans more than one hundred recordings for piano alone, predominantly eighteenth and nineteenth century works, and it encompasses a number of complete, large-scale sets, such as the thirty-two sonatas of Beethoven and the complete symphonies Sibelius.

In the community, Ashkenazy has worked with broadcast media to promote traditional classical music to a mainstream audience, through documentaries and educational youth programs. He has developed orchestral concert projects such as Prokofiev and Shostakovich Under Stalin (performed in London, Cologne, New York, Vienna, Moscow in 2003) and Rachmaninoff Revisited (in New York in 2002). Since its inception in 1991, he served as president of the Rachmaninoff Society.

Siu-Yin Mak

Further Reading

Dumm, Robert. "The Teachers and Artists of Russia: Of Russian Music and Pianists." *Clavier* (July, 2000): 28. This article discusses Russian technique and training with Ashkenazy and other pianists.

Ho, Allan, Dmitry Feofanov, and Vladimir Ashkenazy. *Shostakovich Reconsidered*. London: Toccata Press, 1998. An analysis of Shostakovich and his music, co-authored by Ashkenazy.

Mach, Elyse. "Vladimir Ashkenazy." In *Great Contemporary Pianists Speak for Themselves*. New York: Dover, 1980. Ashkenazy offers a discussion about piano technique.

Noyle, Linda. *Pianists on Playing: Interviews with Twelve Concert Pianists*. Metuchen, N.J.: Scarecrow Press, 1987. Contains an interview with Ashkenazy about the personal and professional aspects of life as a concert artist.

Parrott, Jasper, and Vladimir Ashkenazy. *Beyond Frontiers*. New York: Atheneum, 1985. Biographical memoirs of Ashkenazy, with significant focus on the general mentality of life within the former Soviet Union.

Sadie, Stanley, and Vladimir Ashkenazy. *The Billboard Illustrated Encyclopedia of Classical Music*. New York: Watson-Guptill, 2000. An illustrated reference text jointly compiled by Sadie and Ashkenazy. Brief introductions of topics throughout the classical music genre.

See also: Perlman, Itzhak; Prokofiev, Sergei; Shostakovich, Dmitri.

Chet Atkins

American country guitarist, vocalist, and songwriter

Perhaps the best technical guitarist of his generation, Atkins was instrumental in making country music mainstream.

Born: June 20, 1924; Luttrell, Tennessee
Died: June 30, 2001; Nashville, Tennessee
Also known as: Chester Burton Atkins (full name)

Principal recordings

ALBUMS: *Chet Atkins' Gallopin' Guitar*, 1953; *Stringin' Along with Chet Atkins*, 1953; *A Session with Chet Atkins*, 1954; *Chet Atkins in Three Dimensions*, 1955; *Finger Style Guitar*, 1956; *Chet Atkins at Home*, 1957; *Hi Fi in Focus*, 1957; *Chet Atkins in Hollywood*, 1959; *Hum and Strum Along with Chet Atkins*, 1959; *Mister Guitar*, 1959; *The Other Chet Atkins*, 1960; *Teensville*, 1960; *Chet Atkins' Workshop*, 1961; *Christmas with Chet Atkins*, 1961; *The Most Popular Guitar*, 1961;

Caribbean Guitar, 1962; *Down Home*, 1962; *The Guitar Genius*, 1963; *Our Man in Nashville*, 1963; *Teen Scene*, 1963; *Travelin'*, 1963; *The Early Years of Chet Atkins and His Guitar*, 1964; *Guitar Country*, 1964; *My Favorite Guitar*, 1964; *Progressive Pickin'*, 1964; *Chet Atkins Picks on the Beatles*, 1965; *More of That Guitar Country*, 1965; *From Nashville with Love*, 1966; *Music from Nashville, My Hometown*, 1966; *The Pops Goes Country*, 1966; *Chet Atkins*, 1967; *Class Guitar*, 1967; *It's a Guitar World*, 1967; *Hometown Guitar*, 1968; *Solid Gold '68*, 1968; *Solo Flights*, 1968; *Chet Atkins and C. E. Snow*, 1969; *Chet Picks on the Pops*, 1969; *Lover's Guitar*, 1969; *Solid Gold '69*, 1969; *C. B. Atkins and C. E. Snoe by Special Request*, 1970; *Me and Jerry*, 1970; *Solid Gold '70*, 1970; *Yesourgroovin'*, 1970; *For the Good Times and Other Country Moods*, 1971; *This Is Chet Atkins*, 1971; *Chet Atkins Picks on the Hits*, 1972; *Alone*, 1973; *Strum Along Guitar Method*, 1973; *Atkins-Travis Traveling Show*, 1974; *Chet Atkins Picks on Jerry Reed*, 1974; *The Night Atlanta Burned*, 1975; *Chet Atkins Goes to the Movies*, 1976; *Guitar Monsters*, 1976; *Chester and Lester*, 1977 (with Les Paul); *Me and My Guitar*, 1977; *First Nashville Guitar Quartet*, 1979; *Reflections*, 1980; *Country After All These Years*, 1981; *East Tennessee Christmas*, 1983; *Great Hits of the Past*, 1983; *Work It out with Chet Atkins*, 1983; *Stay Tuned*, 1985; *Street Dreams*, 1986; *Sails*, 1987; *C. G. P.*, 1988; *Neck and Neck*, 1990; *Sneakin' Around*, 1991; *Read My Licks*, 1994; *Almost Alone*, 1996; *The Day Finger Pickers Took Over the World*, 1997; *Discover Japan*, 2002; *Solo Sessions*, 2003.

The Life

Chester Burton Atkins was born into a musical farm family in rural Union County, Tennessee. His first instruments were the ukulele and violin, and in 1932 he got a budget Silvertone guitar from his brother, for which he traded a year's worth of milking chores.

Atkins was about fifteen when he first heard guitarist Merle Travis on the radio. Travis's style of playing bass notes with the thumb and of rolling the first three fingers over the other strings, picking individual notes, produced a sound that impressed the fledgling musician, and it gave Atkins the direc-

tion he needed to perfect his style. By the time he left high school, he was quite musically accomplished, and in 1942 he got his first professional job on WNOX in Knoxville, playing fiddle. When the station manager heard Atkins playing guitar in the back of the tour bus, he immediately appointed Atkins WNOX staff guitarist. For the next three years, this position required Atkins to master a new song every day, which rapidly boosted his repertoire and his technique.

Later, Atkins moved to KWTO in Springfield, Missouri, where he picked up the nickname Chet (instead of Ches). His style, however, seemed too polished and sophisticated for that audience, and he was soon let go. In 1948 Atkins returned to Knoxville to play with Homer and Jethro and with the Carter Sisters (the group Maybelle Carter formed after the Carter Family broke up). They joined the Grand Ole Opry in Nashville in 1950. Once in Nashville, Atkins's talents as a sideman became in demand.

Atkins's own records were selling well by the mid-1950's. From 1957 to 1982, Atkins worked as producer and manager at RCA Records. His production skills became critical as rock and roll had eroded country music's audience. In 1982 Atkins left RCA to resume his performing career, creating what came to be known as the Nashville sound and collaborating with others to transform country music. Atkins died of cancer in Nashville, his longtime home, on June 30, 2001.

The Music

In an effort to gain broad appeal, Atkins changed the arrangements of much of the country canon, replacing the traditional instrumentation and harmonies of country music (such as fiddles, banjos, steel guitars, mandolins, and brother duets) with orchestra string sections or vocal choruses. This so-called Nashville sound diluted much of the difference between country and pop music until the 1990's.

Early Works. Atkins's first hit record was his instrumental version of the pop song "Mister Sandman," which reached number thirteen on the charts in 1955. This was followed closely by his guitar duet with Hank Snow, "Silver Bell." Seminal albums appeared, including *Finger Style Guitar*, *Mister Guitar*, *Chet Atkins' Workshop*, and *Guitar Country*.

Chet Atkins. (AP/Wide World Photos)

"Yakety Axe." By 1965 Atkins's career was well established. After an appearance at the Newport Jazz festival, Atkins took Nashville studio musician Boots Randolph's jazz saxophone standard, "Yakety Sax," and made it a signature piece. Calling it "Yakety Axe"—axe being guitarists' slang for their instrument—the song became a Top 5 hit in 1965.

Stay Tuned. Atkins left RCA in the 1980's because the label was reluctant to let him make a jazz album. With *Stay Tuned*, a jazz-rock fusion project, Atkins's wish was fulfilled. The record featured duets with the next generation of guitarists, such as George Benson, Earl Klugh, Mark Knopfler, Brent Mason, and Steve Lukather. Songs included "Sunrise" and "Quiet Eyes." When he premiered the album, newspaper headlines proclaimed that Atkins had transformed Nashville once again. Atkins and Knopfler received the Grammy Award for Best Country Instrumental Performance for the track "Cosmic Square Dance" in 1985.

Neck and Neck. In November, 1990, Atkins released an album of duets with Dire Straits' guitarist Mark Knopfler. This was his biggest success since 1966, and it introduced Atkins's new renditions on a number of classic country and pop standards, some new material, and a rather different version of

"Yakety Axe." The track "So Soft, Your Goodbye" won Atkins and Knopfler a country instrumental Grammy Award, while "Poor Boy Blues" won the Best Country Vocal Collaboration Award.

Solo Sessions. After his death in 2001, twenty-eight solo songs Atkins had recorded in his home studio from 1982 to 1992 were discovered. These were released as a two-album set in 2003. They included instrumental examples of almost every genre of music, from show tunes and spirituals to jazz standards and country-bluegrass songs. There was even a cover of the 1963 Japanese hit in America, "Sukiyaki." The range of material and the way Atkins approaches it show the depth of Atkins musical sensitivity.

Musical Legacy

A master musician, Atkins left a recorded output of some one hundred forty albums and a style of playing that is still emulated. He was one of the most recorded solo instrumentalists and session players in history, appearing on hundreds of recordings, starting with Hank Williams, Sr., and Elvis Presley in the 1950's and continuing through the 1990's.

As an RCA music executive, Atkins produced such varied artists as Eddy Arnold, Bobby Bare, Perry Como, Roy Orbison, Willie Nelson, and Dolly Parton. He was the youngest person ever inducted into the Country Music Hall of Fame in 1973. He was inducted into the Rock and Roll Hall of Fame in 2002 as a sideman. From 1967 to 1996, Atkins won fourteen Grammy Awards (most for Best Instrumental Performance and a Lifetime Achievement Award in 1993) and nine Country Music Association Awards. A street in Nashville is named after him: Chet Atkins Place. He also developed a line of signature guitars for Gibson, including the revolutionary acoustic-electric SST, which ran from 1987 to 2006.

James Stanlaw

Further Reading

Atkins, Chet, and Michael Cochran. *Chet Atkins: Me and My Guitars.* Milwaukee, Wis.: Hal Leonard, 2003. Part autobiography and part homage to the more than one hundred guitars he has used over the years, this is Atkins's collection of stories and anecdotes, illustrated with beautiful photographs of some of the instruments Atkins made famous.

Atkins, Chet, and Bill Neely. *Country Gentleman.* Chicago: Henry Regnery, 1974. Atkins's early autobiography, which is a valuable source of information on his life and his musical development.

Johnson, Chad. *The Best of Chet Atkins: A Step-by-Step Breakdown of the Styles and Techniques of the Father of Country Guitar.* Milwaukee, Wis.: Hal Leonard, 2004. Intended for guitarists, this book offers transcriptions and analyses of a dozen Atkins trademark songs, including "Mister Sandman," "Yakety Axe," "Country Gentleman," and "Galloping on the Guitar."

Kienzle, Rich. "Chet Atkins." In *The Encyclopedia of Country Music: The Ultimate Guide to the Music.* New York: Oxford University Press. 1998. Summary article on Atkins's life and work from a standard source.

McClellan, John, and Devan Bratic. *Chet Atkins in Three Dimensions: Fifty Years of Legendary Guitar, Volumes 1 and 2.* Pacific, Mo.: Mel Bay, 2004. A fascinating collection of about four dozen interviews with artists who worked with Atkins over the years, including nearly fifty transcriptions of his songs.

Wolf, Charles, and William Ivey. "The Nashville Sound." In *The Illustrated History of Country Music.* New York: Random House, 1995. Good discussion of Atkins's work as a music producer and executive and his creation of a crossover style that changed the face of country music.

See also: Arnold, Eddy; Carter, Maybelle; Cline, Patsy; Eddy, Duane; Everly, Don and Phil; Jennings, Waylon; Miller, Roger; Nelson, Willie; Orbison, Roy; Parton, Dolly; Paul, Les; Presley, Elvis; Pride, Charley; Travis, Merle; Watson, Doc; Williams, Hank.

Hoyt Axton

American country songwriter, guitarist, and vocalist

Singer-songwriter Axton blended elements of country, folk, pop, and rock in his music. His simple melodies and catchy hooks appealed to legions of fans.

Born: March 25, 1938; Duncan, Oklahoma
Died: October 26, 1999; Victor, Montana

Principal recordings

ALBUMS: *The Balladeer,* 1962; *Saturday's Child,* 1963; *Thunder and Lightnin',* 1963; *Explodes,* 1964; *Sings Betty Smith,* 1964; *Greenback Dollar,* 1965; *Long Old Road,* 1965; *Mr. Greenback Dollar Man,* 1965; *My Griffin Is Gone,* 1969; *Country Anthem,* 1971; *Joy to the World,* 1971; *Less than the Song,* 1973; *Life Machine,* 1974; *Southbound,* 1975; *Fearless,* 1976; *Road Songs,* 1977; *Snowblind Friend,* 1977; *Free Sailin',* 1978; *Rusty Old Halo,* 1979; *Where Did the Money Go?,* 1980; *Pistol Packin' Mama,* 1982; *Never Been to Spain,* 1986; *Spin of the Wheel,* 1990; *American Originals,* 1993; *Jeremiah Was a Bullfrog,* 1995; *Lonesome Road,* 1995.

The Life

Hoyt Axton was born in Duncan, Oklahoma, to John and Mae Boren Axton, public school teachers, and he was raised in Jacksonville, Florida. His songwriting was influenced by his mother, who, with lyricist Tommy Durden, composed Elvis Presley's first number-one single, "Heartbreak Hotel." Axton studied classical piano as a child, but he soon switched to guitar. A talented football player, he attended Oklahoma State University on a football scholarship, but he left school to join the Navy in 1958. While in the Navy, he remained athletically active as a boxer, becoming the heavyweight champion for his fleet.

After his discharge in 1961, Axton was drawn to the folk and coffeehouse scenes in San Francisco and Los Angeles. In 1962 the folk group the Kingston Trio recorded Axton's "Greenback Dollar," leading him to consider seriously a career in music. By the end of the 1960's, Axton was touring as the opening act for Three Dog Night. In the 1970's, based on the success of the songs he had written for other artists, his musical career began to soar. In 1979 he established his own record label, Jeremiah Records.

A talented artist, Axton published three books of drawings. A talented character actor, he appeared in numerous roles, in such television series as *Bonanza*, *McCloud*, *Murder, She Wrote*, and *WKRP in Cincinnati*. He was featured in the films *The Black Stallion* (1979), *Gremlins* (1984), and *We're No Angels* (1989).

A man of strong social conscience, Axton contributed to many causes, including the United Nations Children's Fund (UNICEF) and programs supporting drug and alcohol rehabilitation, the environment, prison-inmate welfare, and animal rights. He suffered a stroke in 1996, after which he was confined to a wheelchair and his health steadily declined. Axton died after a series of heart attacks in 1999 at the age of sixty-one.

The Music

Axton's voice was a rich baritone that he could infuse with a throaty, gravelly sound. His fairly narrow singing range and his slight Oklahoma twang fit the mood of his songs. Axton wrote mostly narrative songs, with clearly defined characters and situations. His chord progressions were simple, fusing elements of country, folk, rock, and pop, and his songs featured catchy hooks and memorable melodies. Though many of his songs are humorous, he also wrote serious songs about the dangers of substance abuse, including "The Pusher," "Snowblind Friend," "Boozers Are Losers," and "No No Song."

Songwriter. Although a talented singer, Axton is best known for his songs that were recorded by others. Axton's first big hit was "Greenback Dollar," cowritten with Ken Ramsey and recorded in 1962 by the folk group the Kingston Trio. His antiheroin song, "The Pusher," was recorded in 1968 by the hard-rock group Steppenwolf on its self-titled first album; the song was also featured prominently on the sound track to the film *Easy Rider* (1969). Steppenwolf then recorded Axton's anticocaine song, "Snowblind Friend," on the album *Steppenwolf 7* (1971). While opening for Three Dog Night in

1969, Axton offered the group the song "Joy to the World," which rose to the number-one spot on the *Billboard* pop chart. The group later recorded Axton's song "Never Been to Spain," which hit the Top 20. Ringo Starr recorded Axton's "No No Song" for his album *Goodnight Vienna*; and the single placed on the *Billboard* Top 20 chart.

Albums. Axton's development as a songwriter can be traced through his numerous recordings. His earliest were on small labels and demonstrated his folk style of writing. In 1962 he signed on with Horizon Records, which released *The Balladeer* (with his version of "Greenback Dollar"), *Thunder and Lightnin'*, and *Saturday's Child*. He signed to Vee-Jay Records in 1964 and released *Explodes* and *Greenback Dollar*. He moved to Surrey Records the next year to release *Mr. Greenback Dollar Man*. Axton later signed with Columbia Records for the album *My Griffin Is Gone* and recorded *Joy to the World* and *Country Anthem* for Capitol Records.

In 1973 Axton signed with A&M Records and released a series of successful recordings: *Less than the Song*, *Life Machine*, *Southbound*, *Fearless*, and *Road Songs*. *Life Machine* contained the songs "When the Morning Comes" and the humorous "Boney Fingers," both of which hit the Top 10 on the *Billboard* country-music chart. He signed to MCA Records and released *Snowblind Friend* and *Free Sailin'*. In 1979 Axton started his own label, Jeremiah Records, the name and logo taken from the opening line of his huge hit "Joy to the World." He released the album *Rusty Old Halo*, which was immensely popular, remaining on the country-album chart for a year. Also popular were the singles "Della and the Dealer" and "Rusty Old Halo," both Top 20 hits. He followed *Rusty Old Halo* with *Where Did the Money Go?* (including the hit singles "Where Did the Money Go?" and "Evangelina") and *Pistol Packin' Mama*. In between his numerous film and television appearances, Axton toured in the 1980's and early 1990's, until his death in 1999.

Musical Legacy

On stage, Axton defied categorization: He was not just a country singer or a folksinger or a rock performer. He managed to combine all these traditions in his popular performances. He is better known for the songs he wrote that were recorded by others, especially "Joy to the World," which is heard frequently in film sound tracks and on television commercials. As a songwriter, he created works that spanned a number of different styles: folk, folk-rock, rock, country, and pop. He worked with a variety of musicians, from Johnny Cash and Linda Ronstadt to Elvis Costello. His face is recognizable from his many appearances on television and in films.

Stephen Valdez

Further Reading

Clifford, Mike. *The Illustrated Encyclopedia of Rock.* New York: Harmony Books, 1976. Brief entry on Axton, with selective discography of Axton's recordings.

McCloud, Barry. *Definitive Country.* New York: Perigree Books, 1995. This encyclopedia of country music contains a short but informative entry on Axton, with brief discography.

See also: Cash, Johnny; Costello, Elvis.

Charles Aznavour

French pop and cabaret vocalist, songwriter, and film-score composer

A major figure in French popular music, Aznavour continued the tradition of the chanson, expanding the art form by incorporating musical elements of various ethnic traditions.

Born: May 22, 1924; Paris, France
Also known as: Shahnour Varenagh Aznavourian (birth name)

Principal works

FILM SCORES: *Délit de fiute*, 1959; *Gosse de Paris*, 1961; *Zarte Haut in Schwarzer Seide*, 1961; *Le Diable et les dix commandments*, 1962; *Les Quatre Vérités*, 1962; *Caroline chérie*, 1968.

MUSICAL THEATER (music and lyrics): *Lautrec*, 2000 (libretto by Shaun McKenna).

Principal recordings

ALBUMS: *La Mamma*, 1963; *'65*, 1965; *The World of Charles Aznavour*, 1965; *Of Flesh and Soul*, 1969;

A Tapestry of Dreams, 1974; *Charles Aznavour*, 1983; *Aznavour*, 1986; *Aznavour*, 1990; *En Español*, Vol. 1, 1991; *En Español*, Vol. 2, 1991; *En Español*, Vol. 3, 1991; *Memento si, momenti no*, 1991; *'92*, 1992; *Old Fashioned Way*, 1992; *Yesterday When I Was Young*, 1992; *Tu te laisses aller*, 1992; *Toi et moi*, 1994; *La Bohème*, 1995; *Hier encore*, 1995; *Idiote je t'aime*, 1995; *Il faut savior*, 1995; *Je m'voyais déjà*, 1995; *Aznavour*, 2000; *Charles Aznavour/Pierre Roche*, 2003; *Je voyage*, 2003; *Plus bleu que tes yeux*, 2003 (*Bluer than Your Eyes*); *Qui?*, 2004; *Insolitement votre*, 2005; *Premiéres chansons*, 2006; *Colore ma vie*, 2007.

SINGLES: "Sur ma vie," 1955; "Les Deux Guitars," 1962 ("Two Guitars"); "Je bois," 1965; "La Bohème," 1965; "Comme ils disent," 1972; "Hier encore," 1972; "Les Plaisirs démodés," 1972; "She," 1974; "Tous les visages de l'amour," 1974; "Pour toi Armenie," 1989.

WRITINGS OF INTEREST: *Aznavour by Aznavour*, 1972; *Yesterday When I Was Young*, 1979.

The Life

Shahnour Varenagh Aznavourian, later to be known as Charles Aznavour (az-nuh-vohr), was born into an artistic family: His father was a singer, and his mother was an actress. Through his parents, Charles and his sister, Aïda, were introduced to the theater. Aznavour's first appearance was at the Champs Élysées Studio at the age of nine in the play *Emil and the Detectives*, based on a 1929 book for children. After that, he worked as an extra in various films, and he appeared in plays at the performing school for boys that he attended. At one of the rehearsals for *Ça c'est Marseille*, Aznavour encountered Charles Trenet, a singer-songwriter, who became his role model.

During the German occupation of France in the early 1940's, Aznavour met pianist Pierre Roche, and they formed a duo, often performing at Club de la Chanson in Paris. Because Aznavour could not find enough suitable songs and Roche was not motivated enough to look for them, Aznavour started writing himself. First he would write the lyrics, and then he would compose the melody, to which Roche would add the harmonies. In 1941 Aznavour and Roche wrote the song "J'ai bu," which brought them to the attention of Édith Piaf. She recognized a great talent in Aznavour, and she took the singer and pianist on a tour throughout France as her opening act. Eventually, the duo followed Piaf to the United States, where they first performed at the Society Room in New York. However, Aznavour and Roche were laughed at because the audience thought they were trying to imitate French singers. When they went on to Montréal, they enjoyed success. Influenced by Piaf, Aznavour stopped working with Roche, and Aznavour returned to Paris to become Piaf's secretary and companion. During this period he made several successful stage appearances.

At the same time, Aznavour appeared in many films, among them *Adieu, Cherie* (1946), *Une Gosse Sensass* (1957), *Paris Music Hall* (1957), and *La Tête contre les murs* (1959). His most notable role was that of a piano player, Charlie Kohler/Edouard Saroyan, in François Truffaut's adaptation of David Goodis's novel *Tirez sur le pianiste* (1960). This film became a box-office hit in France and in the United States. For many films Aznavour also served as a composer and arranger: *Gosse de Paris*, *Les Quatre Vérités*, and *Caroline chérie*. In 1986 he cowrote and provided music for the film *Yiddish Connection* (1986), and he starred in the Canadian-French film *Ararat* (2002).

An advocate for his parents' homeland, Armenia, Aznavour founded a charity organization, Aznavour pour Armenie. Following the devastating 1988 earthquake in Armenia, Aznavour and his brother-in-law Georges Garvarentz wrote the song "Pour toi Armenie."

In the autumn of 2006, Aznavour started his global farewell tour, which continued into 2007 with concerts in Japan and Asia. During the second half of 2007, Aznavour returned to Paris for twenty concerts at Le Palais des Congrés.

The Music

Known for his interest in various musical styles, Aznavour has pursued a diverse career. He collaborated with opera singer Plácido Domingo and Norwegian soprano Sissel Kyrkjebø in a Christmas in Vienna concert in the 1994. Aznavour recorded a song from the eighteenth century Armenian poet Sayat Nova, and in 2006 he recorded with Cuban pianist Chucho Valdes in the album *Colore ma vie*. Aznavour appeared in the musical *Monsieur Carnaval* (1965), featuring his hit "La Bohème," and he wrote the music and lyrics for the musical *Lautrec* (2000).

Despite his untrained voice and noncommercial style, Aznavour maintained a successful career. His songs are usually written with a simple melody and basic harmonies. The early songs, written with Roche in swing style, responded to the musical trends of the time. Later, he wrote self-reflective ballads, many based on everyday experiences. "Hier encore," written in 1961, was inspired by the romance between Piaf and actor Eddie Constantine.

"Les Deux Guitars." Written on a Russian tune, the song consists of five verses with short refrains, in which one line is repeated. Aznavour uses this form often for his songs; other examples are "La Bohème" and "Comme ils disent." In addition to the text inspired by Gypsy music, the arrangement recalls the group Hot Five Club of France, which was popular in the 1930's.

Charles Aznavour. (AP/Wide World Photos)

"Les Plaisirs démodés." Written in 1972 by Garvarentz and Aznavour, this song is a mix of the modern rock sound and the French chanson of the 1930's. Both correspond with the text. In the rock section, Aznavour uses words such as trance, spectacle, curious propriety, and psychedelic. The second section has more intimate language, and it becomes tender and elegant, describing the mood of lovers dancing in a quiet setting. In this way it corresponds to the title, which translates to "Old Fashioned Way." This song, along with "She," brought Aznavour international acclaim.

"Fado." On *Colore ma vie*, Aznavour combines Cuban traditional music with French prose. Songs present short stories, and this particular track juxtaposes an element of fado music, the urban folk music of Portugal, with a lyrical nostalgia.

Musical Legacy

Aznavour wrote close to a thousand songs. Some were great successes for Piaf, including *Il Pleut* (1949), *C'est Un Gars* (1949) and *Il y avait* (1950). He wrote *Je hais les dimanches* in 1950 for Piaf. When she refused it, the song went to Juliette Greco, who made it a hit. In his work Aznavour followed the style of the chanson genre: sentimental lyrics that are more important than the melody. He often used instruments such as the accordion to evoke a sense of nostalgia. His influence is felt in the continuing art of French song, which incorporates elements such as rap, world music, and rock.

Daniela Candillari

Further Reading

Aznavour, Charles. *Memories of My Life*. London: Omnibus, 2005. Accounting of Aznavour's life in a series of sketches.

Crosland, Margaret. *Piaf*. New York: G. P. Putnam's Sons, 1985. Biography of Piaf includes information about her relationship with Aznavour.

See also: Domingo, Plácido; Piaf, Édith; Reed, Jimmy.

B

Milton Babbitt

American classical composer

A progenitor of integral serialism, Babbitt is a pioneer in the field of electroacoustic music. His work has had a profound influence on composers in Europe and America, and his compositions reflect his philosophy that music is an evolving, increasingly complex, and specialized art form.

Born: May 10, 1916; Philadelphia, Pennsylvania
Also known as: Milton Byron Babbitt (full name)

Principal works

CHAMBER WORKS: *Composition for Four Instruments*, 1948; Woodwind Quartet, 1953; *All Set*, 1957; *Sextets*, 1966 (for violin and piano); *Arie da capo*, 1974; *Dual*, 1980 (for cello and piano); *The Head of the Bed*, 1982 (for soprano, wind, and strings); *The Joy of More Sextets*, 1986 (for violin and piano); *The Crowded Air*, 1988; *Consortini*, 1989; *Soli e Duettini*, 1989 (for flute and guitar); *Soli e Duettini*, 1990 (for violin and viola); *None but the Lonely Flute*, 1991; *Swan Song No. 1*, 2003 (for wind and strings).

INSTRUMENTAL WORKS: *Three Compositions for Piano*, 1947; *Partitions*, 1957 (for piano); *Composition for Synthesizer*, 1961 (for synthesizer and four-track tape); *Reflections*, 1975 (for piano and synthesized tape); *My Ends Are My Beginnings*, 1978 (for clarinet); *Beaten Paths*, 1988 (for marimba); *Play It Again, Sam*, 1989 (for viola).

MUSICAL THEATER (music): *Fabulous Voyage*, 1946 (lyrics by Richard S. Childs; libretto by Richard Koch; based on Homer's *Odyssey*).

ORCHESTRAL WORKS: *Composition for Twelve Instruments*, 1948; *Relata I*, 1965; *Relata II*, 1968; *Ars combinatoria*, 1981; Concerto for Piano and Orchestra, 1985; Concerto for Orchestra, 2004.

VOCAL WORKS: *Philomel*, 1964 (for soprano and four-track tape); *Phonemena*, 1970 (for soprano and piano); *Phonemena*, 1975 (for soprano and tape); *A Solo Requiem*, 1977 (for soprano and two pianos).

WRITINGS OF INTEREST: *Milton Babbitt: Words About Music*, 1987 (edited by Stephen Dembski and Joseph N. Straus); *The Collected Essays of Milton Babbitt*, 2003 (edited by Stephen Peles).

The Life

Milton Byron Babbitt (BAB-biht) was born in Philadelphia, but he grew up in Jackson, Mississippi. The members of his immediate family were active in both music and mathematics, two fields whose influences are readily apparent in Babbitt's career and compositional output. He began his musical studies at an early age on the violin and later the clarinet and saxophone. While his compositions and writings are rooted primarily in the world of classical music, his knowledge of American popular music and his formidable skills in jazz are widely known. Early in his career he composed both jazz and popular music.

Babbitt began his college career as a mathematician at the University of Pennsylvania. However, he soon changed both the location and the focus of his studies, transferring to New York University and taking up music composition under the tutelage of Marion Bauer and Philip James. He took an early interest in the music of Igor Stravinsky, Edgard Varèse, and the composers of the Second Viennese School (Arnold Schoenberg, Anton von Webern, and Alban Berg). He earned the bachelor of arts in 1935, after which he began studying with Roger Sessions privately. He continued his studies with Sessions at Princeton University, earning a master of fine arts in 1942. While his dissertation for the Ph.D. was completed in 1946, the degree was not conferred until 1992. Apocryphal accounts assert that the dissertation was so complex that it lay unread on the desk of Oliver Strunk, the music faculty member involved in its consideration.

Babbitt's first academic post was at Princeton in 1943, not as a member of the music faculty but rather in the mathematics department. He later joined the music faculty in 1948 and the composition faculty at the Juilliard School in 1973. In addition to writing compositions during this time, some using electronic instruments, he composed theoretical works involving the development of the twelve-tone system.

Babbitt's interest in the electronic medium is of significant historical importance as he was instrumental in the establishment of the Columbia-Princeton Electronic Music Center, one of the most important institutions of its kind. It was originally founded as the Columbia University Studio in 1952 by Otto Luening and Vladimir Ussachevsky. The merger occurred in 1959 and was facilitated by the acquisition of the RCA Mark II synthesizer, an instrument that Babbitt had a hand in developing.

His numerous awards include a Guggenheim Fellowship (1960-1961), a Pulitzer Prize Special Citation in 1982 for "his life's work as a distinguished and seminal American composer," and a MacArthur Foundation Fellowship in 1986. He was also appointed Conant Professor of Music at Princeton (succeeding Sessions in this post). His students include many prominent composers, such as Paul Lanky, Peter Westergaard, and Stephen Sondheim.

The Music

Three Compositions for Piano. Completed in 1947, this stands as the earliest work in which the relationships of a twelve-tone row are applied systematically to other musical parameters. Many of Babbitt's European contemporaries (Olivier Messiaen, Pierre Boulez, and Karlheinz Stockhausen) did the same, but this piece is the first completed work. It stands as evidence supporting Babbitt's assertion that the first steps toward integral serialism, as it became known, were taken in America. Schoenberg's twelve-tone method ordered a row of twelve pitches and expressed their various transformations (transposition, inversion, retrograde, and combinations of these, such as retrograde inversion), which kept their intervallic content largely intact. Integral serialism (heretofore referred to simply as serialism) applied the properties of the row to musical parameters other than just pitch (such as rhythm, dynamics, articulation, and instrumentation).

In this piece, Babbitt serialized a set of rhythms throughout. The sequence 5-1-4-2 is inverted (in this case. by subtracting the number from 6) to get 1-5-2-4. The retrograde is simply the sequence backward, or 2-4-1-5, and the retrograde inversion is the inversion backward, or 4-2-5-1. These four combinations are used in the different "voices" of the work. For example, the first phrase in the lowest voice in the piano has a statement of five pitches, then one, then four, and then two, each grouping separated with tied notes or rests. Each variant is also imbued with a different character using other musical parameters such as articulation and dynamics.

In this work Babbitt also utilized combinatoriality, a technique created by Schoenberg, which gives the work a high degree of chromaticism. This technique is utilized in nearly every work of Babbitt since and is discussed in many of his theoretical publications.

Composition for Four Instruments *and* Composition for Twelve Instruments. These works display Babbitt's progression to a system where the materials are all inherently related. Both signifi-

Milton Babbitt. (© Oscar White/CORBIS)

cantly advanced and refined the method by which Babbitt would derive rhythms from the pitch material in the twelve-tone row. After *Three Compositions for Piano*, 1948's *Composition for Four Instruments* displays a technique that Babbitt referred to as partitioning, splitting the musical material of the row into different voices. Each voice so derived then exhibits a certain character as determined by other musical parameters. His *Composition for Twelve Instruments* explores the use of a duration scale. These explorations led to his development of the time-point system.

All Set. Babbitt was fond of puns, and the title of this piece represents several. Written for jazz ensemble, it is often what the bandleader asks of the band before beginning (many conductors of this piece cannot resist the temptation to do so in good humor). Jazz ensembles also often perform their numbers in sets, with breaks in between. The title also refers to the twelve-tone set used by Babbitt in its construction. *All Set* is one of the first of Babbitt's works to use his time-point system, in which rhythms are derived explicitly from the intervals of the twelve-tone set and relationships are directly proportional. Partitioning is used here as well, dividing the six solo instruments into voices (alto saxophone, tenor saxophone, trumpet, trombone, vibraphone, and piano). The piano, bass, and drums form the rhythm section, as is typical in a traditional jazz tune (although this is not). The main body of the work is then followed by a drum solo and a bass solo, then a coda with all of the instruments. *All Set* stands as one of the first examples of third-stream music. "Third stream" was coined by Gunther Schuller in 1957 (the same year *All Set* was completed) to describe a new category of music that embodied basic elements of jazz and Western art music.

Philomel. Many of the most important works of the early pioneers in the field of electroacoustic music have a vocal component, and *Philomel* is a pivotal one. Its inclusion of a soprano is only one of the aspects that gives it a human quality one might not expect from a work in which electronic synthesis and processes are integral. It is written for soprano, recorded soprano, and synthesized sound. The soprano's voice in the recorded part is processed using various electronic enhancements, creating an unusually otherworldly effect. The synthesized part utilizes many complex serial techniques for which Babbitt is known—the electronic medium provided him with the possibility for unparalleled complexity, as the limitations of the human performer are not in effect here.

John Hollander wrote the text for this work, which is based on the sixth book of Ovid's *Metamorphoses*, which describes the legend of Philomel, princess of Athens. Tereus, king of Thrace, is sent by his wife, Procne, to bring her sister Philomel back from Athens. During the return, Tereus forces Philomel into the woods, where he rapes her and cuts out her tongue, rendering her unable to tell the tale. Upon their return, she weaves a tapestry that depicts the events, and the sisters exact their revenge: Tereus is served the limbs of his son for dinner. He chases them into the woods, and the gods intercede, changing them all into birds—Tereus becomes a hoopoe, Procne becomes a swallow, and Philomel is transformed into a nightingale. The work was commissioned by Bethany Beardslee, whose premiere performance of the work in 1964 and whose virtuosic recording indelibly mark this piece.

Musical Legacy

Babbitt took Schoenberg's twelve-tone method and developed it into a full-fledged system in which all of the aspects of a musical composition are intrinsically connected. Through his explorations with synthesizers, he was able to fully realize his vision of integral serialism. The impact of his music and of the Columbia-Princeton Electronic Music Center is clear: Among the list of prominent composers who have studied there are Varèse, Luciano Berio, Charles Wuorinen, Wendy Carlos, and Mario Davidovsky. Nearly all of the composers who worked there were influenced not only by Babbitt's techniques with electronic music synthesizers but also by his compositional methods and philosophies in general.

In an unfortunate turn of events, he will always be remembered as the author of an article he entitled "The Composer as Specialist." Without Babbitt's consent or knowledge, the editors of the magazine *High Fidelity* renamed the article "Who Cares If You Listen?" It is likely that the new title helped sell many magazines, although it did not reflect Babbitt's true message. In the article he asserted that the field of the contemporary composer had become very specialized, analogous to what had occurred in other fields, such as philosophy and mathematics. He encouraged composers to withdraw from mainstream venues, as they placed unreasonable demands and limitations on their creative expression. Just as math professors and other scholars should not edit an academic journal so that, if read aloud, it would sell a sufficient number of seats at Lincoln Center, composers should not simplify or alter their compositional vision to do the same. Babbitt's musical output and philosophy influenced and emancipated many composers, resulting in a generation whose compositions exhibit remarkable complexity.

David J. Weisberg

Further Reading

Babbitt, Milton. *The Collected Essays of Milton Babbitt*. Edited by Stephen Peles, Stephen Dembski, Andrew Mead, and Joseph N. Strauss. Princeton, N.J.: Princeton University Press, 2003. Essays written by Babbitt himself, dating from 1949 to 1999. His writing is often extremely technical, although the topics in this collection range from highly complex descriptions of his compositional methods and analyses to heartfelt memorials.

Boretz, Benjamin. "Milton Babbitt." In *Dictionary of Contemporary Music*, edited by John Vinton. New York: E. P. Dutton, 1974. General article about Babbitt's life and work by a former student of the composer and cofounder of *Perspectives of New Music*.

Mead, Andrew Washburn. *An Introduction to the Music of Milton Babbitt*. Princeton, N.J.: Princeton University Press, 1994. Discusses Babbitt's influences, theories, and compositions. Excellent introduction to the twelve-tone method and Babbitt's development of it.

See also: Berg, Alban; Boulez, Pierre; Carlos, Wendy; Carter, Elliott; Dodge, Charles; Messiaen, Olivier; Rzewski, Frederic; Schoenberg, Arnold; Sondheim, Stephen; Stockhausen, Karlheinz; Stravinsky, Igor; Webern, Anton von.

Babyface

American rhythm-and-blues vocalist, guitarist, keyboardist, and songwriter

Babyface revolutionized the soul and rhythm-and-blues genres during the late 1980's and into the 1990's, crossing over into pop and rock spectrums with his own material and outside collaborations. In all arenas, he has found massive sales and widespread acclaim, making him a consistently sought-after talent in the studio, onstage, and behind the scenes.

Born: April 10, 1958; Indianapolis, Indiana
Also known as: Kenneth Brian Edmonds (birth name)
Member of: Manchild; the Deele

Principal recordings

ALBUMS (solo): *Lovers*, 1986; *Tender Lover*, 1989; *A Closer Look*, 1991; *For the Cool in You*, 1993; *The Day*, 1996; *Christmas with Babyface*, 1998; *Face2Face*, 2001; *A Love Story*, 2004; *Grown and Sexy*, 2005; *Playlist*, 2007.

ALBUMS (with Manchild): *Manchild 1*, 1972; *Power and Love*, 1977; *Feel the Phunn*, 1978.

ALBUMS (with the Deele): *Street Beat*, 1984; *Material Thangz*, 1985; *Eyes of a Stranger*, 1987.

The Life

Kenneth Brian Edmonds was born in the working-class environment of Indianapolis, Indiana, the fifth of six brothers. Soul, gospel, and rhythm and blues were regular listening staples in his household, and they fostered interests in songwriting and performance as Edmonds tipped into his teenage years. Though several local projects did not blossom outside the area, the hopeful Edmonds became a prolific songwriter while attending North Central High School.

His first major break came during a stint backing Bootsy Collins, the funk-soul star who gave Edmonds the moniker "Babyface," inspired by the teen's boyish looks. After finding footing as a session player, Babyface joined the funk outfit Manchild in 1977, though after a few unsuccessful albums, they parted company. From there, he joined the funk-flanked rhythm-and-blues group the Deele, along with fellow hopeful Antonio "L.A." Reid. The pair quickly formed a song-writing partnership that led to superstardom.

Babyface and Reid found fame as song-writers outside The Deele and quickly became highly sought after, while Babyface kept a solo career going, which surged into the 1990's. During his ascent to fame, Babyface met Tracey McQuarn; they were married on September 5, 1992, and had two sons, Brandon and Dylan Michael. The couple forged a business partner-ship as the Edmonds Entertainment Group, Inc., which specialized in producing movies.

During the late 1990's into the 2000's, the pair's personal and professional lives flour-ished, but in 2005 Tracey filed for divorce. Since then Babyface has been writing, recording, and touring.

The Music

Babyface's career took off in the mid-1980's, starting with the 1986 solo debut *Lovers*, which placed four rhythm-and-blues singles moder-ately on the charts. A double dose of chart suc-cess came with songwriting partner Antonio "L.A." Reid and their late-1980's radio staples "Girlfriend" (recorded by dance-diva Pebbles) and "Rock Steady" (cut by vocal group The Whispers). With the momentum behind these singles, Babyface scored credits for Bobby Brown's "Every Little Step," Sheena Easton's "The Lover in Me," plus Karyn White's "Superwoman" and "The Way You Love Me."

Tender Lover. Babyface's stock continued to rise with the rhythm-and-blues-chart-topping solo sin-gles "It's No Crime" and "Tender Lover," along with Top 5 tunes "Whip Appeal" and "My Kinda Girl," from the album *Tender Lover*. In 1989 Babyface and Reid started their own record label, LaFace, which soared at the turn of the decade thanks to breakout albums from Toni Braxton and TLC (both of which benefitted from the pair's song-writing skills). The early 1990's found Babyface balancing his solo career with cowriting for other established artists, including New Edition member Johnny Gill's "My, My, My," Whitney Houston's "I'll Be Your Baby Tonight" (and later "Queen of the Night" from the sound track for the film *The*

Babyface. (AP/Wide World Photos)

Bodyguard, 1992), plus harmony-heavy foursome Boyz II Men's "End of the Road" (which sat at the number-one spot for an astounding thirteen weeks).

For the Cool in You. By the time 1993's solo re-lease *For the Cool in You* hit stores, Babyface's hit-making was unstoppable, and he received the Best Male R&B Vocal Grammy Award for the acousti-cally slanted "When Can I See You." The stylistic shift also expanded Babyface's contributions out-side rhythm-and-blues contexts, quickly leading to writing and producing credits on Madonna's "Take a Bow" and Houston's "Exhale (Shoop Shoop)."

The Day. In 1996 Babyface again played both sides of the street, releasing his album *The Day* (fea-turing guests as diverse as Mariah Carey, Stevie Wonder, and Kenny G) and producing Eric Clap-ton's "Change the World" on the sound track for the movie *Phenomenon* (1996). Working with Clapton expanded Babyface's audience and earned him a Record of the Year Grammy Award. That coveted honor came in the midst of a three-year Producer of the Year Grammy streak.

Soul Food. Babyface and then wife Tracey Edmonds produced their first movie, the comedy *Soul Food*, in 1997. Its sound track boasted new songs by Boyz II Men and Dru Hill, with production and cowriting by Babyface. Additional diversity came courtesy of a television taping and subsequent release, *MTV Unplugged NYC 1997*, in which Babyface tapped into acoustic interests and produced stripped-down reworkings of "Whip Appeal," "Exhale (Shoop Shoop)," "End of the Road," and "Change the World."

Christmas with Babyface. During the late 1990's, Babyface slowed his recording, writing, and sound-track streak to concentrate on family life, though he maintained his presence across the board. In 1998 he issued *Christmas with Babyface*, featuring several traditional holiday favorites and the original song "You Were There."

Face2Face *and* **Grown and Sexy.** In 2001 Babyface switched to Arista Records, where Reid was an executive. His album *Face2Face* balanced a handful of ballads with songs rooted in soul-funk and spawned the singles "What If" and "There She Goes." In 2005 Babyface released *Grown and Sexy*, a testament to his personal growth and maturity.

Playlist. Despite his divorce, Babyface stayed active on the road, headlining and occasionally sharing the spotlight with Anita Baker. He also wrote the song "Not Going Nowhere" about staying close to his kids (even though split from their mother), which eventually surfaced on the 2007 album *Playlist* (his first for Mercury Records). Outside of that track and "The Soldier Song" (inspired by a family separated by war), the project covered several of Babyface's unexpected acoustic influences, including James Taylor, Dan Fogelberg, and Bob Dylan. Once again, the artist expanded his fan base, leaving listeners curious about the stylistic direction he would take in the future.

Musical Legacy

While Babyface is well regarded for his steady stream of singles and blockbuster album sales, versatility is his most enduring trait. His tenacity and unflinching dedication to the arts allowed him to progress from session man to solo star, songwriter, and producer. Babyface transcended style and culture lines, starting in the soul, rhythm-and-blues, and funk worlds and branching out to the pop and rock markets. His collaborations with such performers as Madonna and Eric Clapton refreshed their sounds and broke down sonic and racial stereotypes. Several like-minded stars—among them Jay-Z, Kanye West, and Timbaland—have followed Babyface's profitable formula of being simultaneously artist, writer, producer, and entrepreneur. An innovator in the late 1980's and early 1990's, Babyface continue to push the creative envelope and increasing his impact on almost every facet of music well into the twenty-first century.

Andy Argyrakis

Further Reading

Brackett, Nathan, and Christian Hoard, eds. *The New Rolling Stone Album Guide*. New York: Simon & Schuster, 2004. Though there are references to his work with other artists, this text also provides reviews and star ratings for Babyface's solo albums.

Collier, Aldore. "Babyface Explains the Inspiration for His Hot New Album, *Grown and Sexy*." *Jet*, August 1, 2005. Cover story featuring Babyface, discussing his career and the personal and professional maturity behind his *Grown and Sexy*.

_____. "Babyface: Singer/Songwriter." *Ebony* (April 1, 1996). Discusses Babyface's ongoing rotation between the worlds of solo singing and writing for other artists.

George-Warren, Holly, Patricia Romanowski, and Jon Pareles, eds. *The Rolling Stone Encyclopedia of Rock and Roll: Revised and Updated for the Twenty-first Century*. New York: Fireside, 2001. Entry relating to Babyface's musical contributions, tracking his pursuits on the front lines and behind the scenes.

Whitburn, Joel. *The Billboard Book of Top 40 Hits*. New York: *Billboard* Books, 2004. Given Babyface's wealth of singles across several genres, he appears often in this exhaustive analysis of *Billboard* charting hits.

See also: Blige, Mary J.; Clapton, Eric; Dylan, Bob; Madonna; Taylor, James; Wonder, Stevie.

Burt Bacharach

American pop vocalist, pianist, songwriter, film-score composer, and arranger

An innovative and prolific composer of popular music, Bacharach used new chord progressions, shifting meters, and irregular phrasing in his compositions, which captivated listeners and enticed top vocalists.

Born: May 12, 1928; Kansas City, Missouri

Principal works

FILM SCORES: *What's New Pussycat?*, 1965; *After the Fox*, 1966; *Alfie*, 1966; *Casino Royale*, 1967; *Butch Cassidy and the Sundance Kid*, 1969; *Lost Horizon*, 1973; *Arthur*, 1981; *Night Shift*, 1982; *Love Hurts*, 1991; *Isn't She Great?*, 2000.

MUSICAL THEATER (music): *Promises, Promises*, 1968 (lyrics by Hal David; libretto by Neil Simon; based on Billy Wilder's film *The Apartment*).

Principal recordings

ALBUMS: *Hit Maker! Burt Bacharach Plays His Hits*, 1965; *Reach Out*, 1967; *Make It Easy on Yourself*, 1969; *Burt Bacharach*, 1971; *Living Together*, 1973; *Futures*, 1977; *Painted from Memory*, 1998 (with Elvis Costello); *At This Time*, 2005.

The Life

Born in Kansas City, Missouri, to nationally syndicated newspaper columnist Bert Bacharach and his wife Irma Freeman, Burt Bacharach (BAK-uh-rak) grew up in Queens, New York, where his family moved when he was four. He did not show an early affinity for music; at age twelve his mother insisted he study piano. Bacharach dreamed of playing football, a dream he was not physically adapted to fulfill. It was jazz, however, that turned his musical talent to a passion. As an underage teen with a fake identification card, he sneaked into the Fifty-second Street jazz clubs to soak up the experimental rhythms and time signatures of Charlie Parker and Dizzy Gillespie. Bacharach reproduced those sounds in his high school band, which he joined at

the age of fifteen. Bacharach graduated from Forest Hills High School, and he went to McGill University in Montreal, where he studied music. Later he took classes in music theory and composition at the Berkshire Music Center and the New School of Social Research, where he studied composition with, among others, Darius Milhaud.

In 1950 Bacharach joined the Army, where his piano skills won him a comfortable billet as the featured entertainer at the officers' club on New York's Governors Island. The following year he was stationed in Germany, where he met the rising pop singing star Vic Damone. Upon his discharge in 1952, Bacharach toured with Damone as his accompanist. Tirelessly working at the nightclubs, Bacharach played for the big-name singers of the day. One young singer, named Paula Stewart, married Bacharach in 1953.

When Bacharach and Stewart divorced in 1958, the pianist, now becoming known in the music industry as a composer, joined film star and vocalist Marlene Dietrich as musical director for her world tour. He remained with Dietrich until 1962, by which time his songs were becoming popular hits for many singers. Over the next five years Bacharach wrote more than one hundred songs, many of which would continue to be performed for decades.

In 1966 he married film actress Angie Dickinson, who gave birth to their daughter Nikki later that year. Born prematurely, Nikki had fragile health, and she was later diagnosed with the autistic-spectrum disorder Asperger's Syndrome. Bacharach's instrumental composition "Nikki," which became the theme song for the ABC Movie of the Week in the 1970's, was written for his daughter.

Dickinson and Bacharach divorced in 1980, and Bacharach married lyricist Carole Bayer Sager, with whom he had written several songs. Their son Christopher was born in 1986. They divorced in 1991, and Bacharach married Jane Hanson in 1993, with whom he had a son and a daughter.

The Music

When Bacharach began writing music (he wrote his first song, "Night Plane to Heaven," while he was an undergraduate at McGill University), popular music was primarily three-chord progressions based on the twelve-bar blues structure. Bacharach's exploration of new chord progressions, shifting meters, and irregular phrasing was experimental; nevertheless, his music, accented with the heavy syncopation of jazz and pop standards, was popular. His compositions were so melodically interesting that talented vocalists favored Bacharach compositions to showcase their skill in phrasing.

Bacharach and David, 1957-1975. Bacharach paired with a number of talented lyricists over the years, but the Bacharach sound of the 1960's and 1970's was developed in collaboration with lyricist Hal David. The two met at the famous Brill Building in New York, which had been a magnet for songwriters since the 1930's. They landed immediately on the country charts with "The Story of My Life," which reached number one for Marty Robbins in 1957, and on the pop charts with "Magic Moments," which reached number four for Perry Como in 1958. At a recording session with the Drifters in 1961, one of the singers in the studio, Dionne Warwick, showed an unusual ability to articulate Bacharach's interesting chord and tempo progressions (probably because of her conservatory training), and Bacharach engaged her to record demos for the Bacharach-David songs that were accumulating. Thirty-eight of those would become popular recordings over the next decade, twenty-two of them Top 40 hits for Warwick. Almost every major singer of the late 1960's and early 1970's recorded Bacharach-David music, including the Beatles, Tom Jones, Dusty Springfield, Gene Pitney, the Carpenters, the Fifth Dimension, and Herb Alpert. A box-office, critical, and legal disaster with the Bacharach-David score for the 1973 film *Lost Horizon* caused the pair to split. They collaborated again in 1975, but they never equaled the success of their pre-*Lost Horizon* partnership.

Promises, Promises. In 1968 Broadway producer David Merrick hired Bacharach to work on a proposed adaptation of Billy Wilder's 1960 film *The Apartment*. Merrick had been impressed by the dramatic quality of Bacharach's music in film scores and by its commercial power in spinning off Top 40 radio hits, such as the title songs for *What's New Pussycat?* (a hit for Tom Jones,

reaching number five), *Alfie* (a hit for Cilla Black in England and winner of the Academy Award for Best Song), and *Casino Royale* (a hit for Herb Alpert, although Bacharach's "The Look of Love" from the same film was a bigger hit for Springfield). Bacharach's instrumental sound track for *Butch Cassidy and the Sundance Kid* had won an Academy Award and a Grammy Award, and the B. J. Thomas single "Raindrops Keep Fallin' on My Head" hit number one in 1967. Bacharach and David wrote sixteen musical numbers for Merrick's show, which ran for three years on Broadway, won a Tony Award for Best Musical, and a Drama Desk for Outstanding Music, and, as Merrick had hoped, produced two Top 20 hits for Warwick: the title song (on the charts for nine weeks and peaking at number nineteen) and "I'll Never Fall in Love Again," which hit number six on the *Billboard* Hot 100.

Burt Bacharach. (AP/Wide World Photos)

Bacharach and Bayer Sager. In the second half of the 1970's, Bacharach did not have a single Top 40 hit ("I Don't Need You Anymore" reached number eighty-six for Jackie DeShannon). However, Bacharach's first song with lyricist Bayer Sager, the title song for the 1981 film *Arthur*, reached number one for Christopher Cross, and it launched a series of hits for Bacharach and Bayer Sager. Their next film theme, "That's What Friends Are For," from *Night Shift* (1982), was a number-one hit for Warwick when she covered it for the Disney film *The Fox and the Hound*, and it was the top-selling single of 1986. "Heartlight," from *E.T.: The Extra-Terrestrial*, was a number-five hit for Neil Diamond in 1982. Bacharach and Bayer Sager also produced non-film hits for popular vocalists, such as Patti LaBelle's "On My Own," which spent twenty-three weeks on the *Billboard* Hot 100 in the summer of 1986, peaking at number one, and Roberta Flack's "Making Love," which reached the number-six spot on the *Billboard* adult contemporary chart in 1982.

Painted from Memory. In 1995 Bacharach worked with Elvis Costello on a song for the film *Grace of My Heart* (1996). When the result, "God Give Me Strength," was nominated for a Grammy Award, Costello asked Bacharach to continue writing with him, resulting in Costello's 1998 album *Painted from Memory*, with twelve Bacharach-Costello songs (including the film hit), and in a Costello-Bacharach tour. Popularity of the album and tour received a boost from the *Austin Powers* 1960's spy-film spoofs, which recognized Bacharach's contribution to the genre (1967's *Casino Royale*) with cameo appearances for Bacharach in three of the popular films, in 1997, 1998, and 2002.

New Music from an Old Friend. In 2007 Bacharach produced an album of original songs written with a variety of popular songwriters, including Kris Kristofferson, Paul Williams, Carole King, Willie Nelson, and Brian Wilson. For each of these long-established writers, this album marked the first collaboration with Bacharach.

Musical Legacy

With more than seventy Top 40 hits in a career spanning more than half a century, Bacharach has made an important contribution to American popular music. He was inducted into the Songwriters Hall of Fame in 1971, before he had composed some of his best work. Many top songwriters have acknowledged Bacharach's influence on their compositions, particularly Jimmy Webb and Tony Banks. Bacharach's jazz influences reasserted themselves late in his career, and Bacharach recorded jazz albums with pianist McCoy Tyner in 1997 and with vocalist Trijntje Oosterhuis in 2006. Several jazz artists, notably Stan Getz and Wes Montgomery, have recorded jazz interpretations of Bacharach songs, attracted by their jazz-inspired rhythmic versatility. An all-star tribute to Bacharach at London's Royal Albert Hall in 2000 included performances by Costello, Warwick, and Petula Clark. With his more than five hundred compositions, Bacharach has reached the Top 10 forty-eight times, with nine number-one hits. His music has won three Academy Awards and seven Grammy Awards. His 2005 Grammy Award for the album *At This Time* marked the first time Bacharach had written his own lyrics and the first time his songs offered political and social commentary. When TNT Cable Network launched its *TNT Masters Series* in 1998, it selected Bacharach to be the first featured artist. Though best known as a composer, Bacharach has since the mid-1960's recorded and performed his own music.

John R. Holmes

Further Reading

Brocken, Michael. *Bacharach: Maestro! The Life of a Pop Genius*. New Malden, England: Chrome Dreams, 2003. This critical biography includes an extensive bibliography and fourteen pages of photographs from every stage of Bacharach's career.

Dominic, Serene. *Burt Bacharach, Song by Song*. New York: Schirmer Books, 2003. True to its name, this volume is both a work of criticism and a reference book, commenting on every recorded Bacharach song at the time.

Kasha, Al, and Joel Hirschhorn. *Notes on Broadway: Conversations With the Great Songwriters*. Chicago: Contemporary Books, 1985. This book of interviews with a dozen top songwriters opens with Bacharach.

Lohof, Bruce. "Celebrity: The Rise and Fall of Burt Bacharach." In *American Commonplace: Essays on the Popular Culture of the United States*. Bowling Green, Ohio: Bowling Green State University Popular Press, 1982. An essay that is representative of the many premature announcements of the waning of Bacharach's career.

O'Brien, Geoffrey. "The Return of Burt Bacharach." In *Sonata for Jukebox: Pop Music, Memory, and the Imagined Life*. New York: Counterpoint, 2004. This essay celebrates the later career of the songwriter, and it is a corrective to the Lohof essay above.

Platts, Robin. *Burt Bacharach and Hal David: What the World Needs Now*. Burlington, Ont.: Collector's Guides, 2002. A thorough study of the famous collaboration, including commentary on most of the Bacharach-David hits.

See also: Alpert, Herb; Carpenter, Karen; Costello, Elvis; David, Hal; Dietrich, Marlene; Gillespie, Dizzy; Milhaud, Darius; Parker, Charlie; Warwick, Dionne.

Erykah Badu

American rhythm-and-blues vocalist

Badu drew from jazz and soul in her instrumentals and vocal delivery, and her lyrics were often driven by narrative, in the tradition of blues and folksingers. Expanding her musical vocabulary, she also embraced rap and hip-hop.

Born: February 26, 1971; Dallas, Texas
Also known as: Erica Abi Wright (birth name)

Principal recordings

ALBUMS: *Baduizm*, 1997; *Mama's Gun*, 2000; *Worldwide Underground*, 2003; *The Kabah*, 2007; *Badu*, 2007; *New Amerykah, Part One (Fourth World War)*, 2008.

The Life

Erykah Badu (EH-rihk-uh ba-DOO) was born in Dallas, Texas, in 1971. Her mother, Kolleen Wright, was an actor who encouraged her daughter's interest in performance, and Badu began performing at age four in her mother's theater company. Later, Badu landed a regular spot on a Dallas-area radio station, where she met future collaborator and trumpeter Roy Hargrove. Her early ambitions focused on dance, which was her concentration at both Booker T. Washington High School, a magnet arts school in Dallas, and Grambling State University, in Louisiana. Around this time, Badu changed her name from Erica Wright, in part to replace her slave name, Wright, and in part to demonstrate her Five Percenter convictions (showing her to be in the population group that is enlightened). Before completing her degree, she left Grambling to pursue a career in music.

After touring with her cousin Robert Bradford and circulating a demo called *Country Cousins*, Badu landed a record deal with Universal Records and released her debut album, *Baduizm*, in 1997. Badu took time off from her career to spend with her child, Seven, and in 2000 she returned with the release of *Mama's Gun. Worldwide Underground, The Kabah, Badu,* and *New Amerykah, Part One (Fourth World War)* were released between 2003 and 2008.

The Music

Badu's music features a blend of soul and funk instrumentals, and her albums have been mixed to produce a crisp, clean sound heavy in bass and sparse in higher registers. The themes of her albums progressed inward, with *Mama's Gun* presenting more intimate lyrics than *Baduizm*. She won four Grammy Awards: Best Rhythm and Blues album (*Baduizm*), Best Female Rhythm and Blues Vocal Performance ("On and On"), Best Rap Performance by a Duo or Group ("You Got Me," with the Roots featuring Erykah Badu, from *Things Fall Apart*), and Best Rhythm and Blues Song ("Love of My Life," from the *Brown Sugar* sound track).

"On and On." Badu's first commercial hit, "On and On" (from *Baduizm*), features her signature sound. The instrumental track is a simple combination of drum kit, bass, and guitar, mixed with a slight echo and a bass foreground that drives the song forward. The lyrics reflect Badu's worldview of enlightenment, including references to numerology.

"Love of My Life." Subtitled "Ode to Hip-Hop," the song "Love of My Life," which Badu performed with Common, is from the sound track for the 2002 film *Brown Sugar*. It extends a metaphor introduced by Common (with whom Badu was romantically involved) in his 1994 song "I Used to Love H.E.R.," in which he laments the fate of hip-hop, personifying the musical form as a woman who has been corrupted by worldly pleasure. The music video for "Love of My Life" traces the history of hip-hop through Badu's life, including scenes that feature famous rap artists. One scene cuts away from the progression of the song to show Badu rapping alongside MC Lyte, one of hip-hop's first commercially successful female rappers. The instrumental track marries Badu's usual soul sound with a more traditional drum sample.

"I Want You." On *Worldwide Underground*, each song tends to bleed into the next, and in the center is the extended "I Want You." Like most of Badu's songs, "I Want You" is driven by the bass line, which throbs along to the words "I" and "you," which are repeated seven times in each iteration of the chorus's line "I want you." The lyrics describe Badu's effort to ignore her urges, but the music builds toward a climax that finally wears itself out and gasps to a halt just before giving way to a futuristic guitar riff. The song ends with Badu singing almost inaudibly, "Just because I tell you I love you don't mean I do." The song's melody, reminiscent of "Love of My Life," joins with a heavy soul sound to suggest ambivalence about her former lover.

Erykah Badu. (AP/Wide World Photos)

Musical Legacy

Blending diverse black musical styles, Badu's work expresses the independent strength of rap and an overt yet closely guarded sexuality. Her musical development has served as a template for emerging soul and rhythm-and-blues singers.

Justin D. Burton

Further Reading

Emerson, Rana. "'Where My Girls At?' Negotiating Black Womanhood in Music Videos." *Gender and Society* 16, no. 1 (2002): 115-135. Emerson explores the ways in which black female musicians express their womanhood in music videos, discussing several examples of Badu's work.

McIver, Joel. *Erykah Badu: The First Lady of Neo-Soul*. London: Sanctuary, 2002. A biography of Badu through the early years of her career.

Perry, Imani. "'Who(se) Am I?' The Identity and Image of Women in Hip-Hop." In *Gender, Race,* *and Class in Media*, edited by Gail Dines and Jean McMahon Humez. Thousand Oaks, Calif.: Sage Publications, 2003. To explain the media's perception of Badu's identity and sexuality, Perry discusses her in relation to other hip-hop artists, such as Eve, Lil' Kim, and Lauryn Hill.

Stephens, Dionne, and April Few. "The Effects of Images of African American Women in Hip-Hop on Early Adolescents' Attitudes Toward Physical Attractiveness and Interpersonal Relationships." *Sex Roles* 56 (2007): 251-264. Presents research on sexual images, using adolescent reactions to several hip-hop artists, including Badu.

Thomas, Greg. "Queens of Consciousness and Sex Radicalism in Hip-Hop: On Erykah Badu and the Notorious K.I.M." *The Journal of Pan-African Studies* 1, no. 7 (2007): 23-37. Thomas compares the sexuality displayed by Badu and Lil' Kim.

See also: Holiday, Billie; Latifah, Queen.

Joan Baez

American folksinger and songwriter

An icon for the alienated generation of the 1960's, Baez used her considerable influence to promote peace, civil rights, human rights, and the environment. Her public performances spanned fifty years, and she released more than thirty albums. She is well known for her long relationship with Bob Dylan and for interpreting his work, as well as that of Paul Simon, the Rolling Stones, the Beatles, and many others.

Born: January 9, 1941; Staten Island, New York
Also known as: Joan Chandos Baez (full name)

Principal recordings

ALBUMS: *Joan Baez*, 1960; *Joan*, 1967; *Any Day Now*, 1968; *The First Ten Years*, 1970; *Blessed Are*, 1971; *Come from the Shadows*, 1972; *Where Are You Now, My Son?* 1973; *Gracias a la Vida*, 1974; *Diamonds and Rust*, 1975; *Speaking of Dreams*, 1989; *Play Me Backwards*, 1992; *Day After Tomorrow*, 2008.

WRITINGS OF INTEREST: *And a Voice to Sing With*, 1987; *Daybreak: An Intimate Journal*, 1968.

The Life

The second child of Albert Baez, a physics professor, and Joan Bridge Baez, a homemaker, Joan Chandos Baez (BI-ehz) moved around frequently with her family because of her father's work with UNESCO, the United Nations Educational, Scientific, and Cultural Organization. A key influence was the year she spent in Iran when she was ten, where she saw severe poverty and a great deal of public brutality. Another influence was her Quaker faith, to which her family converted when she was a child.

Baez attended high school in Palo Alto, California, and moved with her family in 1958 to Boston, then the center of the growing folk-music scene. She started singing locally in coffeehouses and clubs and attended the Fine Arts School of Drama at Boston University. She left the university to pursue her career at Club 47 in Cambridge, where she performed twice a week. She met the singer Bob Gib-

son, who invited Baez to perform with him at the 1959 Newport Jazz Festival. This performance generated a certain amount of publicity and led to Baez's signing with Vanguard Records the following year. In 1967, arrested for supporting the right to refuse military induction, Baez met David Harris in jail. They soon wed, but Harris was arrested for refusing induction in July, 1969, leaving his pregnant wife to appear at the Woodstock Festival and other events. Their son, Gabriel Harris, was born in December, 1969. On Harris's release the marriage began to fail, and the couple divorced in 1973. Baez never remarried.

In 1980 Baez received the Honorary Doctorate of Humane Letters from both Rutgers University and Antioch University for her political activism and the universal appeal of her music. She also helped with the 1985 Live Aid concert to help relieve famine in Africa and toured for many other humanitarian causes, including Amnesty International. In 1987 Baez traveled to the Middle East to sing songs of peace for Israelis and Palestinians, the same year that her autobiography, *And a Voice to Sing With*, appeared and became a *New York Times* best seller.

The Music

Early Works. Baez recorded her first album, *Joan Baez*, for Vanguard Records in 1960, a mix of blues, laments, and traditional folk ballads sung to her own guitar accompaniment. The album had moderate sales, but the following year her second release, titled *Joan Baez, Vol. 2*, was a big hit. During the next few years Baez emerged at the forefront of the American folk song revival, culminating her work at Vanguard with the Top 10 song, "The Night They Drove Old Dixie Down."

Where Are You Now, My Son? Baez switched to A&M records in 1972, where she stayed four years and recorded six albums. Among the notable ones were 1973's *Where Are You Now, My Son?*, which featured a twenty-three-minute title song that documented Baez's visit to Hanoi, North Vietnam, in December of 1972.

Diamonds and Rust. The political climate was beginning to change, and Baez began flirting with pop music and writing her own songs. In 1975 she released *Diamonds and Rust*, her first album that was not political. This album turned out to be the biggest seller of Baez's career. The title song, a senti-

Joan Baez. (National Archives)

mental piece about her relationship with Bob Dylan, became the second Top 10 hit of her career.

In 1983 Baez appeared on the Grammy Awards for the first time, where she sang Bob Dylan's hit "Blowin' in the Wind," a song she had first performed twenty years earlier. When her music career foundered during the 1980's, Baez acquired her first voice coach, Robert Bernard. Seeking therapy during these years, she divided her time between social activism and singing. She looked for a manager and settled on Mark Spector, who signed her with Virgin Records.

Gracias a la Vida. The title song of this Spanish-language album was written and first recorded by Chilean folksinger Violeta Para. Baez's album, released in 1974, was a success in both the United States and Latin America, a first for her. The success of Baez's album was cited by Linda Ronstadt as the inspiration to record her own Spanish-language album, 1987's *Canciones de Mi Padre*. In 2006, while participating in a tree sit-in on the property of

South Central Farm in Los Angeles, Baez sang several songs from *Gracias a la Vida* to an audience that included immigrant workers from South America, activists, and celebrities. The large group was protesting the imminent eviction of the community farmers. The songs included the title track and "No nos Moveron" ("We Shall Not Be Moved"), an anthem of the Civil Rights movement of the 1960's.

Play Me Backwards. This 1992 album, her first recording with Virgin Records, was Baez's first release with a major label in more than ten years. It was critically acclaimed, sold well, and marked a new path for her. The music was sophisticated and contemporary country rock, with acoustic guitar, electric bass, and percussion accompanying Baez singing songs by Janis Ian and Mary Chapin Carpenter. Carpenter's folk-rock ballad "Stones in the Road" is included in this album, and it gave Baez a musical opportunity to criticize the generation that followed her of being selfish materialists. Baez herself wrote several of the songs with her producers Wally Wilson and Kenny Greenberg, and her singing reached a new level of maturity and expressiveness. Virgin records was sold shortly afterward, however, and Baez switched record companies again, to Guardian.

Musical Legacy

Baez had a direct influence on such artists as Emmylou Harris, Judy Collins, Bonnie Raitt, and Joni Mitchell. In 2007 Baez's live album *Ring Them Bells* was rereleased by Proper, a European label, with a six-page booklet and five unreleased song tracks from the original recording sessions. Also, Baez was the recipient of 2007's Grammy Lifetime Achievement Award.

Sheila Golburgh Johnson

Further Reading

Baez, Joan. *And a Voice to Sing With: A Memoir*. New York: Summit Books, 1987. Personal account of the singer's slide from triumph with *Diamonds and Rust* to the difficulties of the 1980's.

———. *Daybreak: An Intimate Journal*. New York:

The Dial Press, 1968. Not many people publish an autobiography when they are twenty-six years old, but Baez had a strong sense of her own destiny and tells about it.

Hajdu, David. *Positively 4th Street: The Lives and Times of Joan Baez, Bob Dylan, Mimi Baez Fariña, and Richard Fariña.* New York: Farrar, Straus and Giroux, 2001. A detailed account of the love, rivalries, and jealousies among Baez, Dylan, singer-songwriter Richard Fariña, and Baez's sister Mimi, a singer and activist.

Nett, Bruno, and Helen Myers. *Folk Music in the United States.* Detroit: Wayne State University Press, 1976. The introduction gives a complete overview of folk music, culminating with Baez and Dylan.

See also: Collins, Judy; Dylan, Bob; Guthrie, Woody; Hopkins, Lightnin'; Mitchell, Joni; Odetta; Robertson, Robbie; Scruggs, Earl; Travis, Merle; Watson, Doc.

Samuel Barber

American classical composer

Barber's compositions are characterized by sweeping melodies and changing meters. Audiences love his music, in part, because it is direct and easy to understand. He is best known for his Adagio for Strings.

Born: March 9, 1910; West Chester, Pennsylvania
Died: January 23, 1981; New York, New York

Principal works

BALLET (music): *Medea*, 1946.
CHAMBER WORK: *Summer Music*, Op. 31, 1955 (for wind quintet).
CHORAL WORKS: *Prayers of Kierkegaard*, 1954.
OPERAS (music): *Vanessa*, Op. 32, 1958 (libretto by Gian Carlo Menotti); *A Hand of Bridge*, Op. 35, 1959 (libretto by Menotti); *Antony and Cleopatra*, Op. 40, 1966 (libretto by Franco Zeffirelli).
ORCHESTRAL WORKS: *Overture to "The School for Scandal,"* Op. 5, 1931; Adagio for Strings, 1936; Symphony No. 1, Op. 9, 1936; First Essay for

Orchestra, 1937; String Quartet, Op. 11, 1938; Violin Concerto, Op. 14, 1939; *Capricorn Concerto*, Op. 21, 1944; Piano Concerto, Op. 38, 1962.
PIANO WORKS: *Excursions*, Op. 20, 1942-1944; Sonata for Piano, Op. 26, 1949.
VOCAL WORKS: *Knoxville: Summer of 1915*, Op. 24, 1947; *Hermit Songs*, Op. 29, 1953; *Despite and Still*, Op. 41, 1969.

The Life

Samuel Barber grew up in West Chester, Pennsylvania, in what was once a Quaker neighborhood. He wrote his first piece at age seven and attempted his first opera at age ten. His father, a Presbyterian minister, did not encourage Barber's musical abilities. Undeterred, Barber continued his pursuit of composition, with the encouragement of his uncle, Sidney Homer. At fourteen Barber entered the Curtis Institute, where he studied voice, piano, composition, and conducting. While at Curtis, Barber met fellow composer Gian Carlo Menotti, who would write the librettos for Barber's Pulitzer Prize-winning operas *Vanessa* and *A Hand of Bridge*. Barber's work was championed by such world-renowned artists as pianist Vladimir Horowitz and conductor Arturo Toscanini. He received many awards and prizes during his career, including the American Prix de Rome, two Pulitzer Prizes, and election to the American Academy of Arts and Letters. Barber composed throughout his life, though his output diminished greatly after his opera *Antony and Cleopatra* failed to gain audience or critical acclaim. Barber died in 1981 with longtime friend Gian Carlo Menotti at his bedside.

The Music

Barber's musical style remained relatively unchanged throughout his life, and he was often criticized for this lack of experimentation. He did occasionally employ some twentieth century styles such as polytonality, but overall his works are quite tonal and neo-Romantic in style. Audiences find his accessible music appealing. Throughout his career, Barber showed a particular love of composing for voice. In total, Barber composed three operas, two ballets, more than one hundred songs, several choral works, various works for orchestra, and concerti for both piano and violin.

Adagio for Strings. Perhaps Barber's best known work, Adagio for Strings, originated in his String Quartet, Op. 11, composed in 1936 and premiered in 1938 by the NBC Symphony Orchestra under the baton of Arturo Toscanini. Considered by many America's national song of mourning, it was played after the deaths of Presidents Franklin Roosevelt and John Kennedy and following the attacks of September 11, 2001. Barber later used an arrangement of the Adagio for Strings in a choral composition on the text of the Agnus Dei from the Requiem Mass. The work pervades American culture: It has appeared in movies such as *Platoon* (1986) and *The Elephant Man* (1980), in television shows such as *The Simpsons*, and even in a video-game sequence.

Violin Concerto. Barber wrote his Violin Concerto when he was thirty years old, a commission for fellow Curtis Institute graduate Iso Briselli. Al-

though Briselli approved of the first two movements, he encouraged Barber to change the third movement, saying it did not match the sensibilities of the previous movements. Subsequently, Briselli did not play the premiere of the work. Instead, the concerto premiered later with the Philadelphia Orchestra. Though the third movement remains controversial to some virtuoso violinists, the work ranks as a favorite among American audiences and is one of the most frequently performed concerti in the modern repertoire.

Knoxville: Summer of 1915. This song cycle, based on the poetry of James Agee, tells the story of life in small-town America. The work mimics the simplicity of everyday activities and opens with the description of sitting on a porch swing in early evening. Within the work Barber moves freely among American music idioms—folk, jazz, and blues—and evokes nostalgia for early America. Eleanor Steber commissioned and premiered the work in 1948 with the Boston Symphony. Though often performed with voice and piano, the original score was for voice and orchestra, then later transcribed for voice and chamber orchestra. Its imagery and text make this perhaps Barber's most American composition.

Hermit Songs. This ten-song cycle uses texts found in the margins of manuscripts copied by Irish monks of the eighth to twelfth centuries. The poems range from boisterous to humorous to deeply religious, and, indicative of Barber's style, the pieces move freely between meters, always conforming to the rhythm of the texts. Each song is quite different in mood and style, but together they create one of the greatest song cycles of the twentieth century. It was first performed by American soprano Leontyne Price, then relatively unknown, with Barber at the piano. This collaboration led to a lifelong friendship, and later Barber composed for her the song cycle *Despite and Still*. She also starred in his last major work, the opera *Antony and Cleopatra*.

Vanessa. This 1958 opera earned Barber his first Pulitzer Prize. Neo-Romantic in style, it shows Barber's deft ability to move between meters and write melodies that conform to the speaking rhythm of the English language. With libretto by Gian Carlo Menotti, the opera is about Vanessa, a woman tortured by the memory of a past love. She is deter-

Samuel Barber. (Library of Congress)

mined to relive the past instead of accepting the reality of her unhappy situation. The characters in the opera are emotionally flawed, and Barber's music captures that mood expertly. Overwhelming sadness is especially evident in the beloved aria "Must the Winter Come So Soon." This haunting aria has become part of the standard repertoire for mezzo-sopranos. Though Barber originally conceived the role of Vanessa for Maria Callas, the role eventually went to Steber. The opera was a great success and led to a commission for the 1966 opening of the Lincoln Center.

Piano Concerto. The publishing company G. Schirmer commissioned Barber to write a piano concerto to commemorate its hundredth year. The work premiered on September 24, 1962, with pianist John Browning and the Philadelphia Orchestra. The concerto is in three movements, and though Barber completed the first two movements in 1960, Browning received the third movement just fifteen days before the premiere. The work was critically acclaimed, and for it Barber received the 1963 Pulitzer Prize (his second) and a Music Critics Circle Award in 1964.

Antony and Cleopatra. Riding the success of his second Pulitzer Prize, Barber accepted a commission from the Lincoln Center to celebrate the opening of the Metropolitan Opera's stage. Barber's opera opened on September 16, 1966, but failed to win the audience approval that *Vanessa* had, despite its all-star cast, including Price as Cleopatra. Though the opera exhibits some of his most dramatic writing, the production was marred by director Franco Zeffirelli's staging, which was too grand for Barber's sensitive musical style. This imbalance seems to have been its downfall. The failure of the opera greatly affected Barber, and although *Antony and Cleopatra* had some later success on smaller stages, the composer never regained the success he had prior to the premiere of *Vanessa*. He continued to compose, but his output was greatly diminished. He wrote a relatively small number of compositions between 1966 and his death from cancer in 1981.

Musical Legacy

Though Barber composed in the heart of the twentieth century, his style rarely reflected many of the trends of the era. Barber's music was always lyr-

ical and expressive and loved by audiences for beautiful melodies. Whether writing for strings, as in the famous Adagio for Strings, or for voice in his songs, Barber always displayed a refined taste. His music showed a love of lyricism and simplicity that wooed American audiences and made Barber one of the most beloved classical composers of the twentieth century. Though sometimes criticized for not being as experimental and forward-thinking as some of his contemporaries—namely Igor Stravinsky and Arnold Schoenberg—Barber remained committed to the composition of beautiful melodies. He received many awards for his music, including the American Prix de Rome Award, the Pulitzer Prize, a Guggenheim Fellowship, and election to the American Academy of Arts and Letters. His love of poetry created a legacy of melodic and lyrical writing.

Diane M. Ricks

Further Reading

Bredeson, Carmen, and Ralph Thibodeau. *Ten Great American Composers*. Berkeley Heights, N.J.: Enslow, 2002. A collection on American composers, with useful information on Barber and his contemporaries.

Felsenfeld, Daniel. *Britten and Barber: Their Lives and Their Music*. Pompton Plains, N.J.: Amadeus Press, 2005. Interesting comparison of English composer Benjamin Britten and American composer Samuel Barber.

Heyman, Barbara B. *Samuel Barber: The Composer and His Music*. New York: Oxford University Press, 1992. Most comprehensive book about Barber and his life, including anecdotes about his childhood and early aspirations to become a composer. Supplemented with articles, interviews, letters, and original manuscripts.

Lee, Douglas A. *Masterworks of Twentieth Century Music: The Modern Repertory of the Symphony Orchestra*. New York: Routledge, 2002. Discusses the standard repertoire of modern-day orchestras and considers Barber's rarely discussed contributions to orchestral repertoire.

Simmons, Walter. *Voices in the Wilderness: Six American Neo-romantic Composers*. Lanham, Md.: Scarecrow Press, 2006. Comprehensive assessments of composers who created significant, artistically meaningful bodies of work without abandoning traditional principles, forms, and procedures. Biographical overview, assessment of body of work and current place in the pantheon of American composers.

See also: Burton, Gary; Horowitz, Vladimir; Kander, John; Menotti, Gian Carlo; Price, Leontyne; Rota, Nino; Schoenberg, Arnold; Serkin, Rudolf; Solti, Sir Georg; Stravinsky, Igor; Toscanini, Arturo.

Daniel Barenboim

Argentine Israeli classical conductor and pianist

Pianist and conductor Barenboim became a fixture on world stages soon after his European debut in 1952, performing and recording most of the best-known works in the pianistic, operatic, and symphonic repertoire. Barenboim's passion for music and its power to unite people have also promoted peace by bringing young Israeli and Palestinian musicians together in concert.

Born: November 15, 1942; Buenos Aires, Argentina

Principal recordings

ALBUMS (as conductor): *Boulez: Notations 1-4/Rituel/Messagesquisse*, 1992; *Bruckner: Symphony 7*, 1995; *Franz Liszt: A Faust Symphony*, 1999; *Wagner: Overtures, Preludes, and Great Scenes*, 2000.

ALBUMS (as pianist): *Beethoven: Piano Sonatas*, 1990; *Mozart: Complete Piano Concertos*, 1990 (with English Chamber Orchestra); *Liszt: Dante Symphony*, 1994 (as pianist and conductor; with Berliner Philharmoniker); *Chopin: The Complete Nocturnes*, 1998; *Beethoven: Piano Concertos Nos. 1-5; Choral Fantasia*, 2002 (with New Philharmonia Orchestra).

WRITINGS OF INTEREST: *A Life in Music*, 1991.

The Life

Daniel Barenboim (BAHR-ehn-boym) began piano lessons at the age of five with his mother and continued his musical education with his father as his only teacher until he was seventeen. He gave his first public recital in Buenos Aires in 1950 at the age of seven. Barenboim's parents immigrated to Israel in 1952. Two years later the family traveled for the summer to Salzburg, where young Daniel took conducting lessons from Igor Markevitch. It was during this summer that Barenboim met the legendary conductor Wilhelm Furtwängler, whose letter stating that "the eleven-year-old Barenboim is a phenomenon" served as the young pianist's letter of introduction for the next twenty years.

In 1955 the family traveled to Paris, where Barenboim studied composition with Nadia Boulanger. By age sixteen, Barenboim could boast of an international career with annual concert tours in Europe and the United States. In 1967 he married the uniquely talented British cellist Jacqueline du Pré.

Few musicians can lay claim to the political importance that Barenboim's career continues to command. In 2001 he angered some Israelis by conducting the overture to Richard Wagner's *Tristan und Isolde* (1859) in Jerusalem; Wagner was and remains a controversial figure among Jews for his philosophy and the Nazis' use of his music to further their cause. Together with Edward Said, the famous Palestinian-American literary theorist and cultural critic, Barenboim founded the West-Eastern Divan Workshop, a program for young musicians from the Middle East that provides a forum on neutral ground for cultural exchange and mutual understanding through music and discussion.

Barenboim believes this unique arrangement will promote a peaceful future for both Israelis and Palestinians. He became the first Israeli citizen to receive honorary Palestinian citizenship, in 2008.

The Music

Few musicians have combined pianistic and conducting careers as successfully as Barenboim, and he has emerged in both areas as one of the most important performers of the late twentieth and early twenty-first centuries.

Paris Debut. Barenboim made his Paris debut playing Wolfgang Amadeus Mozart's *Jeunnehomme* piano concerto (Köchel listing 271) in 1955 and his New York debut with Sergei Prokofiev's Piano Concerto No. 1 (1912) in 1956. In 1960, he performed the complete cycle of Ludwig van Beethoven sonatas in Tel Aviv. His conducting debut took place in 1962 with the Israel Philharmonic Orchestra.

The English Chamber Orchestra and Bayreuth. In 1964, Barenboim initiated a long-lasting relationship with the English Chamber Orchestra during which he toured the world with the ensemble, performing both as a pianist and as a conductor. The Edinburgh Festival provided Barenboim his operatic conducting debut in 1973 with a performance of Mozart's *Don Giovanni* (1787). He first conducted the Bayreuth Festival in 1981 with Wagner's *Tristan und Isolde* and would return regularly thereafter, notably for a production of Wagner's *Der Ring des Nibelungen* (comprising *Das Rheingold*, 1869; *Die Walküre*, 1870; *Siegfried*, 1871; and *Götterdämmerung*, 1874), which ran from 1988 to 1992.

Conducting and Performing. In 1991, Barenboim officially succeeded George Solti as the music director of the Chicago Symphony and kept the post for fifteen years. He also accepted the position of music director at the Staatsoper in Berlin in 1992. Barenboim undertook the extraordinary feat of performing the complete cycles of Beethoven's piano sonatas and symphonies in London in 1998 and, two years later, in Vienna, Berlin, and New York.

Barenboim has performed and recorded much of the mainstream piano, symphonic, and operatic works and has had greater success than many musicians who have attempted dual careers in performing and conducting. Although he sometimes cedes the piano to another soloist and simply conducts a concerto, Barenboim more commonly leads the orchestra from the piano bench.

Musicianship. Barenboim is especially noted for his mastery of the German repertoire, for his sensitivity to musical structure, and for his interest in harmonic nuance. He shows little interest in the performance practice movement, which seeks fidelity, based on historical evidence, to particular instruments, dynamics, tempi, and other aspects of music as originally performed. He believes that the traditions of performance that grew around music are valid and interesting in their own right and that it is not necessary to imitate music as it might have been heard around the time it was composed.

Some critics have taken issue with Barenboim's "overly Romantic" phrasings, slow tempi, or his overuse of pedal in works by Johann Sebastian Bach, but he is far from radical in this regard, and many of these choices reflect a mainstream, early twentieth century tradition. Nevertheless, Barenboim's performances are always personalized, never dull or trite, and they generally provoke strong reactions, either positive or negative, from his listeners. Overall, Barenboim is widely viewed as a meticulous musician with sensitive instincts and a keen intelligence that is evident in his interpretations as a conductor and as a pianist.

Barenboim is an advocate of new music and does not limit himself to the standard repertoire. During his tenure at the Chicago Symphony he especially championed the music of Elliott Carter. Barenboim also conducted the premieres of works by Luciano Berio, Pierre Boulez, Alexander Goehr, and Hans Werner Henze and expanded his repertoire to include African American music, Argentinian tango, jazz, and Brazilian music.

Recordings. Throughout his career, Barenboim has recorded both as a conductor and a pianist for many labels including Westminster, EMI, Deutsche Grammophon, Decca, Philips, Sony Classical (CBS Masterworks), BMG, Erato Disques, and Teldec Classics International. He began recording in 1954, and he soon recorded complete cycles of the piano sonatas and concertos of Beethoven and Mozart. He signed an exclusive contract with Warner Classics International in 1992, which led to more than 130 discs. His recording of Wagner's *Tannhäuser* won a Grammy Award in 2002.

Musical Legacy

Performances by Daniel Barenboim are greeted with wild enthusiasm by his audiences, and his appearances have been known to evoke a response similar to that of a religious event. His acclaim as a "cultural messiah" is undoubtedly due in part to his musicianship but also to his role as an ambassador of peace who uses music as his means of communication.

In 2006, Barenboim accepted the title of Maestro Scaligero at the Teatro La Scala in Milan, and he was named conductor of the Vienna Philharmonic Orchestra's New Year's Day Concert for 2009. An active chamber musician, his recordings include collaborations with the best performers, such as Pinchas Zukerman, Isaac Stern, Yo-Yo Ma, Maxim Vengerov, and Dietrich Fischer-Dieskau. He won

Grammies for violin sonatas by Johannes Brahms performed with Itzhak Perlman (1990) and for his Mozart quintets (1994).

As one of the most influential and talented musicians of his time, Barenboim continues to move the world through his performances both on the podium and at the piano. His ability to bring music as an effective and universal language of peace to war-stricken countries has brought hope to musicians and audiences worldwide.

Lisa de Alwis

Further Reading

Barenboim, Daniel. *A Life in Music*. Rev. ed. New York: Arcade, 2002. Although it does not include much about his personal life, this autobiography covers Barenboim's career in his own words and includes both photographs and philosophical musings.

Barenboim, Daniel, and Edward Said. *Parallels and Paradoxes: Explorations in Music and Society*. New York: Pantheon Books, 2002. The best source in print for understanding Barenboim's views on music, culture, and politics. Said lends his thoughts on Barenboim and the "Wagner taboo" in Israel.

See also: Argerich, Martha; du Pré, Jacqueline; Perlman, Itzhak; Poulenc, Francis.

Ray Barretto

American Latin jazz percussionist, bandleader, and songwriter

Barretto was the first musician to integrate the African conga drum into jazz performances, and he is widely considered to be the most important and influential Latin percussionist in the history of jazz; he is also considered the "godfather" of Latin jazz in America.

Born: April 29, 1929; Brooklyn, New York
Died: February 17, 2006; Hackensack, New Jersey
Member of: The Fania All Stars; New World Spirit

Principal recordings

ALBUMS: *Barretto para bailar*, 1961; *Charanga moderna*, 1962; *Concinando suave*, 1962; *La moderna & el watussi*, 1962; *Pachanga*, 1962; *Latino!*, 1963; *On Fire Again (Encendido otra vez)*, 1963; *The Big Hits Latin Style*, 1963; *Guajira y guaguanco*, 1964; *Swing la moderna & los cueros*, 1964; *Viva watusi!*, 1965; *El Ray criollo*, 1966; *Señor 007*, 1966; *Alma alegre*, 1967; *Soul Drummer*, 1967; *Acid*, 1968; *Fiesta en el barrio*, 1968; *Hard Hands*, 1968; *Together*, 1970; *From the Beginning*, 1971; *Barretto Power*, 1972; *Carnaval*, 1972; *Concinando*, 1972; *Head Sounds*, 1972; *The Message*, 1972; *The Other Road*, 1973; *Barretto*, 1975; *Energy to Burn*, 1977; *Eye of the Beholder*, 1977; *Can You Feel It?*, 1978; *Gracias*, 1978; *La cuna*, 1979; *Rican/Struction*, 1979; *Giant Force*, 1980; *Que viva la musica*, 1982; *Rhythm of Life*, 1982; *Todo se va poder*, 1984; *Aqui se puede*, 1987; *Irresistible*, 1989; *Ray Barretto*, 1990; *Ritmo en el corazón*, 1990; *Handprints*, 1991; *Soy dichoso*, 1991; *Ancestral Messages*, 1992; *Latino con soul*, 1994; *Taboo*, 1994; *Descarga criolla*, 1995; *Moderna de siempre*, 1995; *My Summertime*, 1995; *Contact!*, 1997; *Portraits in Jazz and Clave*, 2000; *Trancedance*, 2001; *Bomba bomba*, 2002; *Homage to Art*, 2003; *Time Was—Time Is*, 2005; *Standards Rican-ditioned*, 2006.

The Life

Ray Barretto (bah-REHT-toh) was born in New York City of parents who were recent immigrants from Puerto Rico. His father left when Barretto was four years old, leading his mother to relocate Barretto and her two other children from Spanish Harlem to the South Bronx. While his mother worked and went to school, Barretto, an asthmatic, listened to radio broadcasts of the music of big bands led by Duke Ellington, Count Basie, Benny Goodman, and Glenn Miller. In 1946, at the age of seventeen, he joined the Army to escape the confines of school and the racial intolerance of the streets, and while stationed in Germany he was inspired by the album *Manteca*, by bebop trumpeter Dizzy Gillespie. Determined to become a jazz musician, Barretto chose percussion because, lacking previous musical training, he believed that he could master its technique most easily. Discharged from military service in 1949, Barretto returned to

New York and joined jam sessions in Harlem with established musicians; he went on to achieve recognition as a major artist in his own right, rising from the barrio to stardom in the world of jazz and Latin music.

In 1978 Barretto married Annette "Brandy" Rivera, with whom he had a son; an earlier marriage had produced three other children. After his death in 2006, Barretto's body was flown to Puerto Rico, where he was memorialized with official honors by the Institute of Puerto Rican Culture.

The Music

Barretto first learned to play drums in the style of the American swing and bebop bands, beginning his career working with jazz musicians in New York. Reconnecting with his roots in the New York Latin music of the same period, Barretto became an early crossover artist, fusing Afro-Caribbean rhythms with bebop's revolutionary improvisatory style.

"El Watusi." "El Watusi," from Barretto's *Charanga moderna* album, was his first and only major commercial hit. One of the earliest Latin songs to become a success in the United States, "El Watusi" featured the violins and flutes associated with charanga music but foregrounded the new boogaloo rhythm, an infectious blend of Caribbean rhythms and African American soul music that appealed to both Latin and rhythm-and-blues audiences. Written to accompany the popular Watusi dance of the day, the vocal featured an amusing *macho rodomontade* of street Spanish over a background of unbridled party sounds, clapping hands, and a catchy Latin beat. A high-spirited convergence of Cuban and Puerto Rican rhythms and African American soul, "El Watusi" remains a song that defined a cultural moment and introduced new energies into American music.

Acid. In 1967 Barretto joined Fania Records, the legendary New York record company synonymous with the blend of traditional Latin dance music and American jazz known as salsa. In 1968 he became a member of the Fania All Stars orchestra, composed

Ray Barretto. (AP/Wide World Photos)

of the leading Latin jazz artists of the day, eventually becoming its music director. He remained associated with the Fania All Stars for the rest of his life and is credited with helping form the group's musical identity as well as helping create the distinctive identity of the Fania label itself.

The move to Fania Records gave Barretto the opportunity to take his jazz-oriented percussive style beyond popular dance music into greater improvisation and more musically sophisticated compositions. He also began to infuse other musical currents into salsa and to experiment with electronic music and unusual instrumental combinations. The first example of Barretto's new musical direction was his highly successful 1968 album *Acid*, considered perhaps his most influential work. An innovative blend of soul, Latin, and jazz music, *Acid* has been praised as the best of all Latin jazz albums and was considered by Barretto himself a major advance, even a rebirth, of his musical identity.

Between 1968 and 1975, Barretto made eight more adventurous and eclectic albums for Fania, including *Carnaval*, *Rican/Struction*, and 1975's *Barretto*, his most popular album. His work during these years came to be considered the very life and soul of Latin jazz in America, Latin America, and the world.

New World Spirit. Throughout his career, Barretto played on recording sessions for many different kinds of musicians, especially major jazz musicians such as Sonny Stitt, Wes Montgomery, Kenny Burrell, Art Blakey, Cal Tjader, Lou Donaldson, Cannonball Adderly, and the musician who had first inspired him, Dizzy Gillespie. Barretto achieved the distinction of becoming the jazz world's most widely recorded conga player. Having always considered himself at heart a jazz musician, in 1992 Barretto turned from his salsa-based work to form the jazz sextet New World Spirit. This later period of Barretto's musical career produced such highly regarded albums as 1992's *Ancestral Messages* and 1994's *Taboo*, which blended Latin soul, salsa, and Afro-Cuban music with the genres with which Barretto most closely identified, hard bop and bebop.

Musical Legacy

Ray Barretto is considered one of the most influential Latin musicians of all time, not only a major presence in all of the developments in Latin music in the last half of the twentieth century but also a significant force in the integration of Latin music with such American idioms as bebop, rock, soul, funk, and dance music. His interpretive drumming pioneered the role of the conga in jazz, establishing its legitimacy as a jazz instrument. Instrumental in the flowering of fusion music such as boogaloo and salsa, Barretto fostered a multicultural cross-fertilization between American jazz and Latin American/Afro-Cuban music. With Puerto Rican roots but steeped in New York's bebop music, Barretto also made a major place for himself in the world of mainstream American jazz.

Barretto won many awards, including a Grammy for the album *Ritmo en el corazón* (with vocals by Cuban salsa legend Celia Cruz). He was inducted into the International Latin Music Hall of Fame in 1999, and in 2006, the National Endowment for the Arts gave Barretto its Jazz Masters Award for lifetime achievement.

Margaret Boe Birns

Further Reading

Alava, Silvio H. *Spanish Harlem's Musical Legacy, 1930-1980*. New York: Arcadia, 2007. Addresses Barretto's contributions to Spanish Harlem's musical development from the 1930's and 1980's in New York City.

Flores, Juan. *From Bomba to Hip-Hop*. New York: Columbia University Press, 2000. This examination of the progression of Puerto Rican culture in the United States over the past half century discusses Barretto among other artists.

Morales, Ed. *The Latin Beat: The Rhythms and Roots of Latin Music, from Bossa Nova to Salsa and Beyond*. New York: Da Capo Press, 2003. Includes a discussion of Barretto in the context of the roots of Latin music in Africa, Europe, and Latin America.

Roberts, John Storm. *The Latin Tinge: The Impact of Latin American Music on the United States*. New York: Oxford University Press, 1999. Includes Barretto in an examination of the role Latin American rhythms, musical forms, and musicians have played in shaping American culture.

Waxer, Lise. *Situating Salsa: Global Markets and Local Meanings in Latin Popular Music*. New York: Routledge, 2002. A comprehensive consideration of salsa music and its global social impact.

See also: Blades, Rubén; Cruz, Celia.

Béla Bartók
Hungarian classical composer and ethnomusicologist

Bartók was the first Western composer to scientifically collect folk music. His innovative composition style fused established Western techniques and rigorously organized formal patterns with traditional folklike structures. Bartók had an active career as a virtuoso pianist in both Europe and the United States and was a fervent advocate of new music.

Born: March 25, 1881; Nagyszentmiklós, Austro-Hungarian Empire (now in Sânnicolau Mare, Romania)
Died: September 26, 1945; New York, New York

Principal works

BALLETS (music): *A fából faragott királyfi*, 1917 (*The Wooden Prince*); *A csodálatos mandarin*, 1926 (*The Miraculous Mandarin*).

CHAMBER WORKS: String Quartet No. 1, 1910; String Quartet No. 2, 1918; Violin Sonata No. 1, 1921; Violin Sonata No. 2, 1922; String Quartet No. 3, 1929; String Quartet No. 4, 1929; String Quartet No. 5, 1935; Sonata for Two Pianos and Percussion, 1938; *Contrasts*, 1939 (for violin, clarinet, and piano); String Quartet No. 6, 1939; Sonata for Violin Solo, 1944.

OPERA (music): *A Kékszakállú herceg vára*, 1918 (*Bluebeard's Castle*; libretto by Béla Balázs).

ORCHESTRAL WORKS: *Kossuth*, 1904; Fourteen Bagatelles, Op. 6, 1908; Violin Concerto No. 1, 1908; *Románian kolinda-dallamok*, 1915 (*Romanian Christmas Songs*); *Román népi tánccock*, 1915 (*Romanian Folk Dances*); Suite, Op. 14, 1918; Four Orchestral Pieces, Op. 12, 1921; *Táncszit*, 1923 (*Dance Suite*); *Three Village Scenes*, 1926; String Quartet No. 3, 1927; Rhapsody No. 1, 1929 (for violin and orchestra); Rhapsody No. 2, 1929 (for violin and orchestra); Music for Strings, Percussion, and Celesta, 1937; Violin Concerto No. 2, 1939; *Divertimento*, 1940 (for strings); Concerto for Orchestra, 1944.

PIANO WORKS: *For Children*, 1910; *Improvisations on Hungarian Peasant Songs*, 1918; *Out of Doors*, 1926 (suite); Piano Sonata, 1926; *Mikrokosmos*, 1926-1939 (6 volumes); *Nine Small Piano Pieces*, 1926; Piano Concerto No. 1, 1926; Piano Concerto No. 2, 1931; Suite, Op. 4, 1941; Piano Concerto No. 3, 1945.

VOCAL WORK: *Cantata profana*, 1934.

WRITINGS OF INTEREST: "The Influence of Peasant Music on Modern Music," 1931 (essay).

The Life

Béla Bartók (BEH-lah BAHR-tok) was born to Béla and Paula in the small town of Nagyszentmiklós, Hungary (today's Sânnicolau Mare, Romania). After a series of short-term residencies in various areas of the Austro-Hungarian Empire, the family settled in 1894 in Bratislava, where the young Bartók frequented the Catholic Gymnasium. In 1899, upon being admitted to the Academy of Music in Budapest, he became the piano pupil of István Thóman, who had studied under Franz Liszt. Concurrently, he took composition with Hans Koessler.

Seen as a brilliant young pianist by his contemporaries, Bartók launched upon a concert career while still a student of the Academy, from which he graduated in 1903. Notable performances were those given in Spain and Portugal in the spring of 1906, when he had the opportunity to play a few Hungarian *czardas* at the request of the Spanish queen.

In the fall of the same year, he was appointed as a piano teacher at the Budapest Academy of Music. Although he was granted tenure in 1909 and occupied the position until 1934, he found composing, performing, and collecting folk music more rewarding than teaching. His didactic efforts materialized not so much in turning out a string of virtuoso pupils as in producing educational editions of Johann Sebastian Bach's *Well-Tempered Clavier*, Ludwig van Beethoven's piano sonatas, and Frédéric Chopin's waltzes and in composing original piano works of pedagogical scope, of which the most notable is the six-volume *Mikrokosmos*.

Bartók's career as a composer was intricately linked with his ethnomusicological activities, which required frequent travel. From 1906 through 1917 he devoted his summers to collecting, recording, transcribing, and analyzing folk music from Central and Eastern Europe as well as North Africa. His interest in this area led to his taking a position—which he occupied well into the mid-1920's—with the ethnographic section of the Hungarian National Museum. In 1909 he married Márta Ziegler, a former piano student who became his close assistant in the enormous task of transcribing and systematizing the collected folk material; their son Béla was born in 1910.

After World War II Bartók's concert career took off: Solo and chamber recitals and orchestral concerts, many of which promoted his own works, were scheduled between 1918 and 1938 in most European countries, including the Soviet Union. His first contact with the United States was occasioned by an extended lecture-recital and concert tour in 1927-1928 and was renewed in the spring of 1940.

By the autumn of that year, disgusted with the nazification of Europe in general and of Hungary in particular, and pained by the recent death of his mother, Bartók decided to emigrate: He left for New York in October, in the company of his second wife, Ditta Pásztory, an excellent pianist in her own

Béla Bartók. (Library of Congress)

right, whom Bartók had married in 1923 and with whom he had a son, Peter, born in 1924.

He spent the remaining years of his life in the United States, where he was awarded an honorary doctorate by Columbia University, whose collection of Serbo-Croatian music he had worked on in 1941-1942. In 1943 Harvard University engaged his expertise as an ethnomusicologist. Concurrently, he performed piano recitals across the country and completed work on his volumes of Romanian folk music. Suffering from leukemia and ailing rapidly during the American years, he died in New York in September, 1945.

The Music

In 1931 Bartók described his own music as stemming from three sources—Hungarian, Romanian, and Slovakian—and suggested that "it might be regarded as the embodiment of the very concept of integration so much emphasized in Hungary today."

Collecting Folk Songs. Field research begun in the summer of 1907 among the Székelys of the Eastern Transylvanian area of Csík led to the discovery of "examples of tunes which," Bartók wrote, "I had believed were now lost." These revealed that the most ancient layer of Hungarian folk music rested on pentatonic modes with no semitones and displayed characteristics of what Bartók termed the "old" style, free tempo (*parlando rubato*) and form, as opposed to the "new" style, possessed of rigorous tempo (*tempo giusto*) and clear formal structures.

In August, 1909, under the auspices of the Hungarian Ethnographic Museum, Bartók engaged in yet another collecting campaign among the Romanians of the Mezőség district. Writing enthusiastically about the "most exotic Wallachian (Romanian) songs" and their "striking melismas," he likened these melodies to "real coloratura arias." In a letter sent in 1910 to Romanian composer Dumitru G. Kiriac, Bartók put the total of the Romanian songs collected by then at six hundred. By January, 1912, he was again in Bihor to record and transcribe dances, ceremonial music, and instrumental performances. The following year, his book of Romanian folk songs from Bihor county was published under the auspices of the Romanian Academy.

Further field research was performed in 1913 on Arab and Berber music from Biskra in North Africa, where Bartók noticed the complicated rhythmic patterns executed on percussion instruments as well as the limited range of most songs and the "peculiar scales" of wind instruments. Bartók took his phonograph—a tool he had not used since his previous exploration of Romanian music in 1917—to Turkey in the fall of 1936. This was his last field trip; from then on he devoted his efforts to the systematic analysis of what he had already collected, meanwhile giving talks on the Budapest radio on the body of songs assembled in Anatolia.

A meticulously devised, original system of musical notation enabled Bartók to transcribe minuscule variations in pitch, tone, and vocal or instrumental color. By September, 1937, he had revised all the transcriptions from more than a thousand phonograph cylinders and had systematized, for comparative purposes, the song material collected from Bulgarians, Serbs, Croatians, Slovaks, Poles, and

Ukrainians. He anticipated 1940 as the date of completion for the colossal compendium of twelve thousand.

Style. In Bartók's youth, late Romanticism was the style of choice: In 1903 the composer detailed the project of a ten-part orchestral work inspired by Hungarian history; this was the symphonic poem *Kossuth*, with a program based on the figure of the national hero and the music influenced by Richard Strauss's *A Hero's Life*, which Bartók had earlier transcribed for piano.

By 1931 Bartók had for more than twenty years distilled, absorbed, and remolded the melodic contours, rhythms, and meters of folk songs into original compositions of increasing sophistication: thus a progression can be seen in his works from simple piano arrangements (*For Children*, on Slovak and Hungarian tunes) to overt use of pentatonic themes (the fourth movement of the Suite, Op. 4 for small orchestra; the final movement of the String Quartet No. 1, Op. 7); direct quotations from Hungarian and Slovak folk songs alongside a highly unorthodox treatment of the seventh as a consonance (Fourteen Bagatelles, Op. 6 for piano); characteristic melodic and rhythmic patterns of Romanian vocal *colinde* (*Romanian Christmas Songs* for piano) and instrumental music (*Romanian Folk Dances* for piano); elements of North African music (the inner movement of the String Quartet No. 2; the third movement of the Suite, Op. 14). Still from this period, *Allegro barbaro* for piano adopts a percussive, abrasive treatment of the instrument.

Debussy's influence on Bartók's music is quite obvious in the Four Orchestral Pieces, Op. 12, as well as the one-act opera *Bluebeard's Castle*, Op. 11; in addition, and alongside brilliant orchestration indebted to Strauss, the latter makes consistent use of a Wagnerian leitmotif (a device Bartók had already exploited in the incomplete "First" Violin Concerto dedicated to Stefi Geyer and reworked in 1908 as *Two Portraits*, Op. 5).

The overall formal design as well as more minute structural details employed in works from the second through the fourth decades of the century relied heavily on symmetry, especially of the mirror kind: For instance, the last section of the one-act ballet *The Wooden Prince*, Op. 13 is designed as a retrograde reiteration of thematic material from the first. Symmetry extends to encompass the spectrum of

modal relationships in the opening and closing of the *Cantata profana*, and that of key relationships among the movements of the Music for Strings, Percussion, and Celesta. In addition, it permeates the architecture of String Quartet No. 4 and String Quartet No. 5. In the latter, the first two and last two movements are strategically arranged with respect to the third, which provides the axis of symmetry. The five parts of Piano Concerto No. 2 display a similar formal outline.

Compositions of the 1920's involving subtly distilled folk-song traits were the orchestral *Dance Suite* (an assortment of structures invoking Arab chromaticism, as well as Hungarian and Romanian folk tunes) and the five-song cycle *Village Scenes* (on Slovak themes). In sharp contrast with these works, Bartók described his *Cantata profana* as "a setting to music of a Romanian *colinda* (Christmas song) text" whose music did not in involve imitation of folk music.

In the late 1920's and early 1930's the composer adopted an idiom that—within the general framework of Expressionism while preserving traces of tonal thinking and folk-derived structures—promoted a more overtly atonal language. Thus the pantomime *The Miraculous Mandarin*, Op. 19, the Piano Sonata, Piano Concerto No. 1, and String Quartet No. 3 involve the persistent use of dissonant layers to create harmonic tension that is never resolved.

A marked change in style is noticeable in works of the late 1930's; this is especially true about the Violin Concerto No. 2, dedicated to violinist Zoltán Székely, who gave it its 1939 world premiere in Amsterdam. Bartók's lyrical treatment of both the violin and orchestra has a Romantic quality foreign to his works of the previous decade, and while the concerto's second theme is based on a twelve-tone row, the whole movement revolves within a quasi-pentatonic, quasi-modal framework reminiscent of old Hungarian folk music. The composer's own description of such an approach as "polymodal chromaticism" is perhaps the best encapsulation of this newly found synthesis, arguably best represented in the modally derived, chromatic fugal theme employed in the opening of the Music for Strings, Percussion, and Celesta.

In a different vein, the 1930's were also devoted to the writing of piano pieces that would form the six-volume *Mikrokosmos*; these were arranged in increased order of difficulty and designed to cover a variety of technical skills. Concurrently, several of the 153 pieces involved both folk-based material and some of Bartók's preferred compositional devices, such as canon (a form of symmetry), variations, and ostinato.

Musical Legacy

More than once in his life Bartók expressed displeasure at the lack of receptivity of his music by Budapest audiences and performing ensembles, and so he vowed to keep his original works on his desk while dedicating all his energies to collecting folk music. Yet abroad he was revered as the quintessential Hungarian composer. His merits were recognized when, in 1930, he was elected to the International Committee of Cultural Cooperation of the League of Nations and was the recipient of the French government's Legion of Honor. Still, in 1930, the Hungarians did accord him the Corvin Wreath.

His legacy endures as one who skillfully forged a completely new musical style from traditions as different as ancient folk song, German and Italian Baroque counterpoint, nineteenth century Romantic lyricism, and twentieth century polytonality, chromaticism, and dissonance. Bartók did not initiate or lead a new, cohesive school of composition; rather, he traversed a variety of different styles and experimented with a variety of structures and techniques. His compositional excursions led to the complete artistic maturity achieved in works of the 1930's and influenced to a great extent the music of another prominent twentieth century composer, György Ligeti.

Luminita Florea

Further Reading

Bartók, Béla. *Letters*. Collected, selected, edited and annotated by János Demény. Translated by Péter Balabán and István Farkas. Revised by Elisabeth West and Colin Mason. New York: St. Martin's Press, 1971. Selection of letters by and to Bartók, representative of several significant periods in the composer's life. Includes correspondence penned during Bartók's years in the United States. List of works, bibliography, and general index.

Bartók, Péter. *My Father*. Homosassa, Fla.: Bartók Records, 2002. Bartók's second son's memoir, involving personal recollections and including hitherto unpublished letters written by his parents from the United States. Illustrations.

Bayley, Amanda, ed. *The Cambridge Companion to Bartók*. Cambridge, England: Cambridge University Press, 2001. Discusses works and their reception. Of special interest is the article on Bartók's recorded piano performances. Musical examples, five-page bibliography and index.

Frigeysi, Judit. *Béla Bartók and Turn-of-the-Century Budapest*. Berkeley: University of California Press, 1998. Explores Hungarian modernism and Bartók's own aesthetic system. Discusses *Bluebeard's Castle* from the perspective of its literary sources. Illustrations, musical examples, bibliography, index.

Laki, Peter, ed. *Bartók and His World*. Princeton, N.J.: Princeton University Press, 1995. Especially important are the articles originally published in Hungarian—now made accessible to the English-language reader—including interviews with the composer, as well as a selection of his travel letters from Europe, Asia, and North America.

Schneider, David E. *Bartók, Hungary, and the Renewal of Tradition: Case Studies in the Intersection of Modernity and Nationality*. Berkeley: University of California Press, 2006. With a focus on nationalism, examines the dynamics of tradition and innovation in works inspired from the "Hungarian style" of the nineteenth century and the style of peasant music.

See also: Argerich, Martha; Ashkenazy, Vladimir; Beecham, Sir Thomas; Berio, Luciano; Carter, Elliott; Chávez, Carlos; Chung, Kyung-Wha; Crumb, George; Debussy, Claude; Fleck, Béla; Glass, Philip; Goldsmith, Jerry; Golijov, Osvaldo; Grusin, Dave; Hindemith, Paul; Ives, Charles; Janáček, Leoš; Karajan, Herbert von; Kodály, Zoltán; Leonhardt, Gustav; Ligeti, György; Lutosławski, Witold; Menuhin, Sir Yehudi; Nielsen, Carl; Norman, Jessye; Parker, Charlie; Piazzolla, Astor; Rózsa, Miklós; Schnittke, Alfred; Shaw, Artie; Solti, Sir Georg; Strauss, Richard; Szigeti, Joseph; Watts, André; Williams, Mary Lou; Xenakis, Iannis; Zappa, Frank.

Count Basie

American jazz composer and pianist

As the leader of one of the most renowned jazz swing bands, Basie showed a graceful touch on piano, created blues-oriented compositions, demonstrated a perpetual sense of swing, and displayed the talent for developing great jazz musicians.

Born: August 21, 1904; Red Bank, New Jersey
Died: April 26, 1984; Hollywood, Florida
Also known as: William Basie (full name)
Member of: The Barons of Rhythm

Principal recordings

ALBUMS: *Dance Parade*, 1950; *Count Basie at the Piano*, 1950; *Dance Session*, 1952; *Count Basie and His Orchestra Collates*, 1952; *King of Swing*, 1953; *Basie*, 1954; *Basie Jazz*, 1954; *Blues Backstage*, 1954; *Count Basie Big Band*, 1954; *Count Basie Dance Session, Vol. 1*, 1954; *The Count Basie Sextet*, 1954; *April in Paris*, 1955; *Basie*, 1955; *Basie's Back in Town*, 1955; *Count Basie Dance Session, Vol. 2*, 1955; *Count Basie Swings—Joe Williams Sings*, 1955; *Jazz Royalty*, 1955; *Lester Leaps In*, 1955; *Let's Go to Prez*, 1955; *The Old Count and the New Count*, 1955; *Rock the Blues*, 1955; *The Band of Distinction*, 1956; *Basie Bash*, 1956; *Basie Rides Again*, 1956; *Basie Roars Again*, 1956; *The Count*, 1956; *Count Basie Sings Standards*, 1956; *The Swinging Count*, 1956; *Switzerland*, 1956; *Atomic Mr. Basie*, 1957; *Basie Plays Hefti*, 1958; *Basie Swings, Bennett Sings*, 1958; *Chairman of the Board*, 1958; *Memories Ad-Lib*, 1958; *One More Time*, 1958; *Sing Along with Basie*, 1958; *Basie and Eckstine, Inc.*, 1959; *Breakfast Dance and Barbecue*, 1959; *Dance with Basie*, 1959; *Every Day I Have the Blues*, 1959; *Hall of Fame*, 1959; *Strike up the Band*, 1959; *Benny Carter's Kansas City Suite*, 1960; *Count Basie and Sarah Vaughan*, 1960; *Easin' It*, 1960; *Just the Blues*, 1960; *Kansas City Suite*, 1960; *Not Now—I'll Tell You When*, 1960; *String Along with Basie*, 1960; *Back with Basie*, 1962; *Count Basie and the Kansas City 7*, 1962; *Lil' Ol' Groovemaker*, 1962; *On My Way and Shoutin' Again*, 1962; *Basie Land*, 1963; *Frankly Basie: Count Basie Plays the Hits of Frank Sinatra*, 1963; *Pop Goes the Basie*, 1964; *The World of Count Basie*, 1964; *Basie Meets Bond*, 1965; *Basie Picks the Winners*, 1965; *Basie's Beat*, 1965; *Basie's Beatle Bag*, 1966; *Basie's Swingin', Voices Singin'*, 1966; *Count Basie with Arthur Prysock*, 1966; *Inside Basie Outside*, 1966; *Showtime*, 1966; *Hollywood . . . Basie's Way*, 1967; *Straight Ahead*, 1967; *Basie's in the Bag*, 1968; *Basic Basie*, 1969; *Afrique*, 1970; *Basie on the Beatles*, 1970; *High Voltage*, 1970; *Have a Nice Day*, 1971; *Loose Walk*, 1972; *Basie Jam*, 1973; *The Bosses*, 1973; *For the First Time*, 1974; *Satch and Josh*, 1974; *Basie and Zoot*, 1975; *The Basie Big Band*, 1975; *For the Second Time*, 1975; *Basie Jam 2*, 1976; *Basie Jam 3*, 1976; *I Told You So*, 1976; *The Gifted Ones*, 1977; *Kansas City 5*, 1977; *Prime Time*, 1977; *Satch and Josh . . . Again*, 1977; *Big Bands, an Old Manuscript*, 1978; *Count Basie Meets Oscar Peterson*, 1978; *Milt Jackson and Count Basie and the Big Band, Vol. 1*, 1978; *Night Rider*, 1978; *The Timekeepers*, 1978; *Yessir, That's My Baby*, 1978; *Get Together*, 1979; *Milt Jackson and Count Basie and the Big Band, Vol. 2*, 1979; *On the Road*, 1979; *Kansas City Shout*, 1980; *Kansas City, Vol. 7*, 1980; *Kansas City Vol. 6*, 1981; *Warm Breeze*, 1981; *Farmer's Market Barbecue*, 1982; *88 Basie Street*, 1983; *Fancy Pants*, 1983; *Me and You*, 1983; *Mostly Blues . . . and Some Others*, 1983; *Long Live the Chief*, 1986; *Blues for Basie*, 1991; *Kansas City*, 1991; *Basie's Bag*, 1992; *Corner Pocket*, 1992; *Big Bank Basie*, 1995; *Count Basie Encounters Oscar Peterson*, 1998; *Swing Shift*, 1999; *Blue Skies*, 2002; *Good Time Blues*, 2004; *On the Sunny Side of the Street*, 2006.

SINGLES: "One o'Clock Jump," 1937; "Jumpin' at the Woodside," 1938; "Lester Leaps In," 1939; "Taxi War Dance," 1939; "Twelfth Street Rag," 1939.

The Life

William "Count" Basie (BAY-see) was born William Basie in 1904 to coachman Harvey Lee Basie and his wife Lillian Ann Childs, who were also musicians. Basie took piano lessons from an early age, and his knowledge of music was also influenced by the vaudeville shows, carnivals, and films he saw in New Jersey and in New York City. Basie did not attend high school, working at various jobs while developing his musical talents.

At about the age of twenty, he moved to Harlem, which was experiencing a musical renaissance. Pianists such as Willie "The Lion" Smith, James P. Johnson, and Fats Waller were developing the stride style of piano playing. Basie learned from them, receiving informal lessons from Waller and eventually replacing him as an accompanist in the vaudeville show Kate Crippen and Her Kids. As Basie traveled the country with various bands, he was accorded the nickname "Count." In 1928 he joined Walter Page's Blue Devils in Kansas City, and in 1929 he was invited to be the pianist with the Bennie Moten band. During this time, Basie briefly fronted his first big band, Count Basie and His Cherry Blossom Orchestra. After Moten died in 1935, Basie formed a big band composed largely of Moten's band musicians. The Basie band was one of the star performers in John Hammond's From Spirituals to Swing concerts in 1937, bringing the band national recognition. The Basie band played extended engagements in such famous New York venues as the Apollo Theater, the Roseland Ballroom, the Savoy Ballroom, and the Famous Door Nightclub. After a brief first marriage, Basie wed Catherine Morgan on August 21, 1942, and they moved to Queens, New York. They had a daughter, Diane.

With its popular recordings and its national tours, the Basie band became one of the most popular in the nation. Nevertheless, the postwar period saw the decline of big band and swing jazz, and Basie disbanded his band, and for several years he performed in small combos. In 1952 Basie reformed his big band, which would perform continually for the rest of his life. The Basie band became internationally famous, and many preeminent musicians passed through its ranks. Basie suffered a heart attack in 1979 that slowed but did not stop his performing career. His wife died in 1983, and the following year Basie died of pancreatic cancer in Hollywood, Florida.

The Music

Basie's characteristics as a musician were developed early in his life, and they remained remarkably consistent throughout his career. As a pianist, his style was noted for its spare, simple, understated technique. As a composer and bandleader, he was noted for blues-oriented, Kansas City-based rhythms, exemplifying an inimitable sense of swing.

Basie learned his piano style in New York City and his big band swing in Kansas City. In Harlem in the 1920's, Basie studied with the creators of the stride style, especially the inimitable Waller. The complexities of stride piano had evolved from ragtime music, and Basie further developed the technique in his own fashion. His piano playing was oriented toward accompaniment rather than soloing. Economical and light-fingered, his style emphasized only a few but absolutely critical notes.

In the Kansas City bands of Page and Moten, Basie learned the techniques of blues-inflected big band style. Jazz flourished in Kansas City in the 1920's in highly competitive jam and "cutting" sessions. Kansas City jazz was indebted to the new phrasing and rhythms pioneered by Louis Armstrong that had come to be called swing, and it added an infectious, fast-paced jumping meter originating in the rhythm section and echoing in the horns. That sound would be a trademark of the Count Basie Barons of Rhythm, formed from alumni

Count Basie at the piano. (AP/Wide World Photos)

of the Bennie Moten Band in 1935, and would continue through all the incarnations of the Count Basie bands. Characteristically, the Basie band based its music on "head" arrangements, in which the band would play a chorus of the main theme at the beginning and end of the song. The soloists would play extended improvisations, and the band sections would accompany with swinging riffs (repeated short, melodic variations of the head).

The first Basie band featured top-rate jazz musicians and vocalists, a trait that continued for all Basie bands. The rhythm section that provided the propulsive power of the Basie swing sound consisted of Jo Jones on drum, Freddie Greene on guitar, and Page on bass. Horn players included Herschel Evans and Lester Young on saxophone, Buster Smith and Earl Warren on alto saxophone, Buck Clayton and Harry "Sweets" Edison on trumpet, and Benny Morton and Dickie Wells on trombone. The extraordinary blues singer Jimmy Rushing was the vocalist, and Basie's piano provided contrapuntal accents for the soloists. The extraordinary quality of these musicians and the infectious "jumping" beat that Basie coaxed from them were noted by legendary jazz promoter John Hammond, who heard the Basie band on radio. Hammond arranged in the latter half of the 1930's for the Basie band to make its first recordings, for it to travel to New York to engage in a legendary January 16, 1938, swing showdown with the Chick Webb band, and for it to appear in the nationally known Carnegie Hall concerts From Spirituals to Swing.

"One o'Clock Jump." During this period the Basie band recorded such artistic gems as "Jumpin' at the Woodside," "Taxi War Dance," and "Lester Leaps In." The band's first national hit was Basie's composition, "One o'Clock Jump." The original July 7, 1937, recording featured a blues-oriented riff suggested by lead saxophonist Buster Smith, which was derived from Fats Waller's song "Six or Seven Times." Basie plays the opening riff, which is the head arrangement around which the soloists improvise, for eight bars followed by a two-chorus solo. Evans solos in the fourth chorus with his strong, large tone contrasting with the thinner trumpets and trombones. Young solos on the fifth chorus, his horizontal, lyrical, relaxed improvisation contrasting with that of Evans. Clayton provides an outstanding solo on the sixth chorus be-

fore Basie choruses in a restrained duet with bassist Page. "One o'Clock Jump," which would become the Basie band's theme song, perfectly illustrates the band's Kansas City swing style, with its alteration of creative solos and up-tempo ensemble riffs by the different sections of the band. The Basie band also recorded a live version of "One o'Clock Jump" at the From Spirituals to Swing concert of December 23, 1938.

The extraordinary quality of the Basie band continued in the 1940's, when such talented jazz musicians as saxophonists Don Byas, Buddy Tate, Illinois Jacquet, and Paul Gonzales played with the band, along with trumpeters Joe Newman and Emmett Berry and trombonist Vic Nickerson. Certainly the most influential of Basie musicians, however, was Young. (Acclaimed vocalist Billie Holiday sang with the Basie band only in the year 1937.) Young's light, airy, floating tenor saxophone sound is the typical cool sound in jazz; his influence on jazz saxophonists is exceeded only by that of Charlie Parker.

"Twelfth Street Rag." The classic "Twelfth Street Rag" was recorded by the Basie band on March 19, 1939. It exemplifies the flexibility with which Basie accompanied his musicians' solos as well as the opportunity his band provided a great musician such as Young to shine. The Basie band introduces the "Twelfth Street Rag" in an old-fashioned manner. However, the song is not arranged in a rag or in a stride format, which developed from ragtime, but in a classic four-beat Basie swing. Young and Edison solo, and Basie provides exquisite accompaniment, alternating between sharp treble chords over an ostinato bass and staccato patterns. Basie's solid support provides the perfect accompaniment for his stars to take extended improvisations. Here Young's imaginative solo exemplifies his linear, spacious style of saxophone play, which would have such a great influence on jazz.

The decline of big band swing forced Basie to disband his group in 1950 and to perform in smaller combos. Basie reformulated his big band in 1952, going on to new artistic and commercial success. The Basie band moved from an emphasis on the riff—the repetition of short, highly swinging phrases—for a newfound focus on precise ensemble playing, disciplined preparation, and arranged charts by such talented composers as Neal Hefti. Its best-known recordings include "April in Paris" (with multiple false endings), "Shiny Stockings," "L'il Darling," and "Corner Pocket." The tradition of great Basie vocalists continued with the versatile Helen Humes.

"Every Day I Have the Blues." Another talented Basie singer was Joe Williams, who, while not as profound a vocalist as Rushing or Holiday, was able to bring both a blues earthiness and a flexible, nimble styling. Williams's biggest hit with the Basie band was his March 17, 1955, recording of "Every Day I Have the Blues." Its commercial success brought an even wider audience to the reconstituted Basie band. Basie begins the song with a stride-like piano introduction, before the horns take over in a brassy Ernie Wilkins arrangement. Williams delivers a bold, brassy vocal of his own, bringing virtuosic blues inflections to key phrases of his lyric.

In the 1960's the Basie band had become a fixture of the international jazz scene. If no longer reaching the dazzling artistic heights of earlier years, the Basie band never lost the driving, beat-oriented sound that had made it famous. The Count Basie band appeared numerous times on television, and it recorded popular tunes in big band arrangements. Basie remained an inspiring bandleader, and his restrained, attenuated piano stylings remained as poignant and supportive as ever. Displaying his abilities as a piano soloist and as an accompanist, Basie made numerous well-received recordings with small groups and with famous jazz musicians and singers.

Musical Legacy

Basie left an outstanding legacy as both a pianist and a bandleader. The hallmark of both legacies is his simplicity, as Basie highlighted the essence of his music in a straightforward, rhythm-oriented manner. As a pianist, he was a minimalist, choosing the few notes that brought out the blues essence of his melodies and accentuated the excellent musicians he was accompanying. As a bandleader, he eschewed the complex orchestral arrangements increasingly popular in swing for the infectious, swinging rhythms of Kansas City, allowing for extended improvisations by band members. This blues-oriented style was organized around short,

melodic patterns known as riffs, played by the lead or head, and rhythmically repeated by the band, often in a call-and-response format. Basie's talent for accommodating and developing great talent made his band a progenitor of great jazz musicians. Certainly, Young and Holiday stand out at the top of the list, but other jazz musicians and singers were nourished by Basie's generous playing and his managerial effectiveness.

Howard Bromberg

Further Reading

Basie, Count, and Albert Murray. *Good Morning Blues: The Autobiography of Count Basie*. New York: Da Capo Press, 2002. This oral history is based on conversations with Basie.

Dance, Stanley. *The World of Count Basie*. New York: Da Capo Press, 1985. This resource features chapters on Basie, his band members, and other contemporaries.

Gridley, Mark. *Jazz Styles: History and Analysis*. Englewood Cliffs, N.J.: Prentice Hall, 1994. Informative textbook with numerous examples of Basie's music to illustrate blues-oriented swing music and the use of riffs.

Orgill, Roxanne. *Dream Lucky: When F.D.R. Was in the White House, Count Basie Was on the Radio, and Everyone Wore a Hat*. New York: HarperCollins, 2008. This book recounts the years 1936 to 1938, focusing on Basie's move from Kansas City to New York.

Schuller, Gunther. *The Swing Era: The Development of Jazz, 1930-1945*. New York: Oxford University Press, 1991. An in-depth and analytical jazz history, this second volume of Schuller's comprehensive coverage of jazz offers extensive treatment of Basie.

Williams, Martin. *Jazz Heritage*. New York: Oxford University Press, 1985. Various chapters on jazz musicians by an insightful musical critic explore the extraordinary jazz developments in Kansas City in the 1920's and 1930's and the changing course of the Basie band in the 1950's.

See also: Barretto, Ray; Bennett, Tony; Carter, Benny; Davis, Sammy, Jr.; Ellington, Duke; Fitzgerald, Ella; Garner, Erroll; Getz, Stan; Gillespie, Dizzy; Goodman, Benny; Hampton, Lionel; Holiday, Billie; Jones, Hank; Jones,

Quincy; Lee, Peggy; Lewis, John; Lucier, Alvin; Parker, Charlie; Peterson, Oscar; Reed, Jimmy; Sinatra, Frank; Tormé, Mel; Turner, Big Joe; Vaughan, Sarah; Waller, Fats; Wilson, Jackie; Young, Lester.

Amy Beach

American classical composer

Beach is credited with being the first American female to compose a symphony and a piano concerto and have her music performed by Boston's prestigious Handel and Haydn Society. Her music reflects the conservative European styles of the late Romantic era, the prevailing style in Boston at that time.

Born: September 5, 1867; Henniker, New Hampshire
Died: December 27, 1944; New York, New York

Principal works

CHAMBER WORKS: Sonata for Violin and Piano in A Minor, Op. 34, 1897.
CHORAL WORK: Mass in E-Flat, 1892.
OPERA (music): *Cabildo*, Op. 149, 1945 (libretto by Nan Bagby Stephens).
ORCHESTRAL WORKS: Symphony in E Minor, Op. 32, 1897 (*Gaelic Symphony*); *The Canticle of the Sun*, Op. 123, 1928.
PIANO WORKS: Piano Concerto in C-sharp Minor, 1900; Piano Quintet in F-sharp Minor, Op. 67, 1907; *The Hermit Thrush at Eve*, 1922; *The Hermit Thrush at Morning*, 1922; Piano Trio, Op. 150, 1939.

The Life

Amy Marcy Cheney was born into a musical family of some social status and as a youth took up the piano as a "socially acceptable" instrument for a young lady. She began playing the piano at age four and published her first musical composition at age thirteen: "The Rainy Day," a song based on Henry Wadsworth Longfellow's poem of the same name.

Her precocious talent propelled her through several concert appearances, including a debut with the Boston Symphony in 1885 at age eighteen, performing Frédéric Chopin's F Minor Concerto. In Victorian America, however, it was still a woman's role to be a wife, and so that year she married Dr. H. H. A. Beach, a respected Boston physician twenty-five years her senior. By most accounts this marriage was somewhat stifling to Beach, in part because her husband expected her to limit her public piano performances to one annual recital with proceeds given to charity, even though critics had been unanimous in praise for her pianism up to that point. She still managed to compose and perform in a curtailed manner until her husband died in 1910.

Her husband's curtailment of her active musical life can be seen both as a negative and a positive for Beach. While it temporarily stopped her public success as a pianist, it gave her more time to absorb the elements of compositional style and almost certainly enhanced her abilities as a composer, for which she is most remembered.

Following her husband's death, Beach scheduled a three-year tour of Europe as a performing pianist and returned to greater compositional activity as well, ultimately leaving behind a corpus of approximately three hundred compositions in the genres of song, solo piano pieces, sonatas, chamber music, symphony, choral music, and opera. Additionally, she became the first president of the Society of American Women Composers, and this role, combined with her compositional ability, established the almost heroic aura she held among women of her day. Beach retired in 1940 and died of heart disease in 1944.

The Music

Beach was largely self-taught, though in her youth she studied harmony for one year with composition teacher Junius W. Hill. Her musical education evolved in large part from her individual study of other composers' music and especially her translation of Hector Berlioz's *Treatise on the Art of Orchestration* (1843-1844). Social mores of her day dictated that she keep a lower profile and emphasize her role as a wife over music and career. It was a common belief at the end of the nineteenth century in New England that women made poor composers because they were too emotional and not cerebral enough. While Beach's music is emotive, it manifests great skill in structure, style and content, eas-

Amy Beach. (Library of Congress)

ily rising to or above that of her peers. Beach's first recognition as a composer may have come from her inclusion of several of her piano character pieces in adolescent recitals, but her Mass in E-Flat, performed by the Handel and Haydn Society of Boston in 1892, was her first unqualified success.

Gaelic Symphony. Beach began work on one of her most important instrumental works, her Symphony in E Minor, Op. 32—subtitled *Gaelic Symphony* because of its reliance on four Irish melodies as themes—in 1894 at age twenty-seven. She completed the work in 1896, when it received its premiere by the Boston Symphony, an orchestra with which she had had a long-standing affiliation. She embarked upon its composition in part as a response to a challenge issued by Antonìn Dvořák while he was in America from 1892 to 1895 that American composers turn to their folk music (by which he meant principally African American spirituals and slave music) as a source for their classical compositions, in much the same way that European composers from Modest Mussorgsky and Edvard Grieg to Bedřich Smetana and Dvořák himself used their

national folk melodies as the basis for many of their important compositions.

Beach took the challenge in a broader light. The immigrant folk population in Boston was mostly Irish, and so she turned toward Irish melodies for inspiration. In so doing, she placed herself in a large historical group of American composers (including Stephen Foster) who relied to some extent upon Irish tunes—going back to 1808, when Thomas Moore published the first American collection of Irish melodies.

Beach described the *Gaelic Symphony* in loosely programmatic terms, indicating that it represented multiple facets of the lives and struggles of the Irish—"the laments of a primitive people, their romance and their dreams"—who in the late nineteenth and early twentieth centuries were one of the largest immigrant groups in America and, especially on the East Coast, one of the most oppressed. Irish folk tunes from an 1841 collection can be found in the first three movements of this symphony. The fourth movement's melodies, though Irish in style, are original. Of the melodies themselves, she wrote:

> Their simple, rugged and unpretentious beauty led me . . . to develop their ideas in symphonic form. Most of the themes are actual quotations from this collection of folk music, and those which are original I have tried to keep in the same idiom and spirit.

The second movement's theme is a particularly lovely and lilting Irish melody entitled "The Little Field of Barley." It is presented first in the oboe but later heard in a rhythmically diminished variant at a faster tempo in the strings as the central section of the ternary movement.

This symphony follows a four-movement design Beach frequently used to advantage and demonstrates in part her reliance on instrumental models of such earlier composers as Felix Mendelssohn, Robert Schumann, and Grieg. Her Violin Sonata, also in four movements and similar in style to the symphony, represents another excellent alternative to the earlier European composers' music. It is well crafted, melodious, technically challenging, and in every way a worthy composition.

Cabildo. As she matured as a composer, Beach's style changed subtly, adding chromaticism, modulations by thirds, and increased use of secondary dominants and modal harmonies. She retained her nationalist leanings throughout her career, however, quoting later from Inuit melodies for her String Quartet and Creole melodies for her one-act opera *Cabildo*. Some of her last pieces verge on atonality and explore the complete nonresolution of chords, particularly dominant sevenths. Such a move was bold for her, yet in the context of history, her music still seems more tied to older models when compared to the music of Franz Liszt, then later Arnold Schoenberg, Igor Stravinsky, Aaron Copland, and others who were her contemporaries.

Cabildo, on a libretto by Nan Bagby Stephens, concerns pirate Pierre Lafitte, who was imprisoned at the Cabildo in New Orleans and mysteriously escaped. Beach composed it in 1932, yet it was not performed until 1945. It was revived in 1995 by the "Great Performers at Lincoln Center" in New York. Ransom Wilson, who organized its revival, stated that the opera exhibited "the same vocal graciousness and solid word setting" that Beach brought to her individual songs and shows clear unity with the use of motifs "which are largely derived from Creole folk tunes."

Piano Works. Two piano pieces, *The Hermit Thrush at Eve* and *The Hermit Thrush at Morning*, deserve mention. These character pieces have a quasi-improvisational mood evoking a personal experience with nature at both ends of the day. The harmonic language is largely tonal, but modal inflections bring a post-Impressionist aura to moments within the pieces. One hears references to Edward MacDowell's *Woodland Sketches* (1896) and the harmonic language of Charles Tomlinson Griffes.

Musical Legacy

Beach's greatest legacy remains her songs, of which she composed more than a hundred. Her larger works, including the *Gaelic Symphony*, Piano Concerto in C-sharp Minor, and the Violin Sonata, are experiencing a modest revival. In the year 2000 her name was added to the granite wall of the Hatch Shell in Boston alongside those of Johann Sebastian Bach, Ludwig van Beethoven, Frédéric Chopin,

and composers of similar musical stature. It remains the only female name on the wall.

Jonathan A. Sturm

Further Reading

Ammer, C. *Unsung: A History of Women in American Music*. Westport, Conn.: Greenwood Press, 1980. Textbook devoted to women in music, in which Beach is featured.

Block, Adrienne Fried. *Amy Beach, Passionate Victorian: The Life and Work of an American Composer, 1867-1944*. Oxford, England: Oxford University Press, 1998. A leading authority on Beach presents a thorough biography.

Brown, Jeanell Wise. *Amy Beach and Her Chamber Music: Biography, Documents. Style*. Metuchen, N.J.: Scarecrow Press, 1994. Within the context of a biography, Beach's chamber music is analyzed theoretically and discussed historically.

Jenkins, Walter S. *The Remarkable Mrs. Beach, American Composer: A Biographical Account Based on Her Diaries, Letters, Newspaper Clippings, and Personal Reminiscences*. Edited by John H. Baron. Warren, Mich.: Harmonie Park Press, 1994. Portrait of Beach from the vantage point of another composer, which includes primary sources for Beach, especially relating to her time at the MacDowell Colony.

Jezic, Diane Peacock. *Women Composers: The Lost Tradition Found*. 2d ed. New York: The Feminist Press, 1994. From a feminist perspective on many female composers, including Beach.

See also: Copland, Aaron; Schoenberg, Arnold; Stravinsky, Igor.

Sidney Bechet

American jazz composer, clarinetist, and saxophonist

Bechet was a jazz soloist with an expressive but forceful style, and his interpretations of repertoire from blues to ragtime and jazz to Tin Pan Alley were valued as stylistic benchmarks.

Born: May 14, 1897; New Orleans, Louisiana
Died: May 14, 1959; Paris, France

Principal recordings

ALBUMS: *Port of Harlem Jazzmen*, 1939; *Bechet, Bunk, and Boston*, 1945; *Jazz Nocturne, Vol. 1*, 1945; *Jazz Nocturne, Vol. 2*, 1945; *Jazz Nocturne, Vol. 3*, 1945; *Jazz Nocturne, Vol. 4*, 1945; *Jazz Nocturne, Vol. 5*, 1945; *Jazz Nocturne, Vol. 6*, 1945; *Jazz Nocturne, Vol. 7*, 1945; *Jazz Nocturne, Vol. 8*, 1945; *Jazz Nocturne, Vol. 9*, 1945; *Jazz Nocturne, Vol. 10*, 1945; *Jazz Nocturne, Vol. 11*, 1945; *Jazz Nocturne, Vol. 12*, 1945; *Masters of Jazz, Vol. 4*, 1945; *Giants of Jazz*, 1949; *We Dig Dixieland*, 1949; *Sidney Bechet's Blue Note Jazzmen*, 1950; *Days Beyond Recall*, 1951; *The Fabulous Sidney Bechet and His Hot Six*, 1951; *His Way*, 1951; *Sidney Bechet, Vol. 1*, 1951; *Sidney Bechet, Vol. 2*, 1951; *Immortal Performances*, 1952; *New Orleans Style, Old and New*, 1952; *Sidney Bechet Solos*, 1952; *Sidney Bechet*, 1952; *Wally Bishop's Orchestra*, 1952; *Dixie by the Famous Sidney Bechet*, 1953; *Jazz at Storyville*, 1953; *New Orleans Feetwarmers*, 1954; *Jazz á la Creole*, 1955; *King of the Soprano Saxophone*, 1955; *La Nuit est une sorcière*, 1955; *Back to Memphis*, 1956; *Creole Reeds*, 1956; *Grand Master of the Soprano Sax and Clarinet*, 1956; *Sidney Bechet Duets*, 1956; *Sidney Bechet with Sammy Price's Bluesicians*, 1956; *When a Soprano Meets a Piano*, 1957; *Young Ideas*, 1957; *Sammy Price and Sidney Bechet in Paris*, 1958; *The Fabulous Sidney Bechet*, 1958; *Parisian Encounter*, 1958; *Sidney Bechet and Friends*, 1972; *Perdido Street Blues*, 2002; *Sidney Bechet et Claude Luter*, 2007.

The Life

Sidney Bechet (beh-SHAY) was one of ten children born to Omar and Josephine Michel Bechet in New Orleans's Seventh Ward. As African American Creoles, the Bechets spoke French at home, and they had aspirations of social advancement, reflected in their love of music. Bechet's older brother Leonard was active as a trombonist, and he encouraged Bechet, who as a boy surreptitiously learned to play on Leonard's discarded clarinet.

After acquiring his own instrument, Bechet practiced diligently, although mostly without traditional instruction. Possessing a remarkable ear, he learned by listening to established clarinetists in the New Orleans idiom, such as Lorenzo Tio, Jr., and George Baquet. It was in the playing of Louis "Big Eye" Nelson, however, that Bechet found his inspiration. Nelson was also self-taught, and he played with a more bluesy, vocalized style than did other clarinetists. Bechet later recalled being influenced by music he heard during trips to the New Orleans Opera House and to the circus and from street bands.

Even as a youth, Bechet was considered influential. Clarinetists of his generation—such as Jimmie Noone, Albert Nicholas, and Barney Bigard—recalled being impressed with his development and paying attention to his style. At this time, Bechet began playing cornet, earning renown for his range and volume, although he shortly ceased playing the instrument. By the early 1910's, Bechet was playing in top-tier bands, and he was a fixture on the musical landscape of New Orleans. He also had developed a reputation for an explosive temper, hedonistic lifestyle, and disregard for authority.

Bechet began traveling in 1916, going first to Texas for a short tour. In 1917 he left home for good, going to Chicago to work with other New Orleans expatriates, including Joe Oliver and Freddie Keppard. By this time, New Orleans-style jazz had become tremendously popular across the country, largely because of the white Original Dixieland Jazz Band recordings and of the vaudeville tours by black groups such as the Creole Jazz Band. Bechet steadfastly refused to learn to read music, but his improvisational abilities were recognized, and he never wanted for work.

In June, 1919, Bechet was engaged by Will Marion Cook to go to England with his Southern Syncopated Orchestra. This large group, which played little jazz, was more along the lines of a pops orchestra. Following the breakup of the group in 1920, Bechet performed with a small band called the Jazz Kings. It was during this period that he bought his first soprano saxophone, although in New Orleans he had apparently experimented with a C-melody saxophone owned by a friend. Other than a short trip to Paris in 1921, Bechet remained in London until he was convicted of assault in November, 1922, and he was deported back to New York.

Once in New York, Bechet was almost immediately engaged to play and to act in a black stage show called *How Come?*, with which he toured until

April, 1923. Several other shows followed, suggesting Bechet was valued for his acting as well as his musical abilities. It was during this time that he began making recordings, mostly produced by New Orleans pianist Clarence Williams.

In September, 1925, Bechet sailed for Paris with the Revue Negre, and later he went to Russia, where he remained until May, 1926. Following this was an extended period of travel around Europe as a soloist. In Paris, Bechet again ran afoul of the law, and he was jailed after a gun battle in December, 1928. He stayed in prison for a year, moving to Berlin in December, 1929, to play and to appear in several films.

By the end of 1930, Bechet was back in New York, featured with Noble Sissle and His Orchestra. Sissle used him as a soloist on clarinet and soprano saxophone and as a member of the rhythm section, playing bass saxophone. In early 1932, Bechet decided to strike out on his own, and he played numerous freelance jobs throughout the New York area, including several weeks featured with Duke Ellington, before forming a sextet with former Sissle trumpeter Tommy Ladnier. Calling themselves the New Orleans Feetwarmers, they played for a few months and made several recordings before the lack of work and the realization that their New Orleans-styled music was out of fashion compelled them to disband. For an unsuccessful period the two ran a tailoring establishment, but Bechet returned to Sissle's band in May, 1934.

Bechet remained with Sissle until October, 1938, before deciding to become a leader himself. After a series of short engagements, he freelanced on numerous recordings, and he performed at various establishments in the New York and the Philadelphia area for the rest of the decade.

The 1940's represented more freelancing around New York, but often Bechet was called on to be a guest soloist with other bands. Bandleader Eddie Condon thought highly of him, using him frequently on his radio and early television broadcasts. Bechet was also a regular visitor to jazz clubs in both Philadelphia and Boston, and his efforts are well preserved by location recordings.

By the late 1940's, Bechet was looking beyond New York. In November, 1947, he began a long engagement as featured artist at Jazz Ltd. in Chicago, extending with some interruptions through January, 1949. He made a brief trip to Paris that May, and he resolved to return permanently. In this last phase of his career, Bechet found almost universal adulation among European jazz fans. Except for a few short visits to America in 1950 and 1951, he remained in Europe until his death, playing and recording as often as he wished.

Bechet's musical influence is his recorded legacy, which began in the 1920's. These early works announced his abilities to the public, and they served as influences for many musicians who were not able to hear him in person. While he had some success composing songs such as "Ghost of the Blues" and "Pleasure Mad," it was the application of his improvisational abilities to popular tunes of the day, blues, and jazz standards that gained him attention. The same was true in the 1930's and 1940's when he recorded frequently under his own name and as a sideman with various leaders. Although he recorded compositions of his own, such as "When the Sun Sets Down South" and "Blackstick" (and occasionally took credit for work composed by others), it was in his recordings for Blue Note (of Dixieland repertoire) and for Victor (of jazz tunes) from the 1920's that he became known.

After Bechet repatriated to France, he began featuring his own compositions more. Works such as "Les Oignons" and "Si tu vois ma mere" are tributes to the jazz style of his early years. During this time Bechet also experimented with composing longer forms. *La Colline du Delta* was a rhapsody for soprano sax and orchestra left incomplete at his death, and *La Nuit est une sorcière* was a ballet score that Bechet recorded featuring himself.

The Music

"Wild Cat Blues." Bechet's first appearance on record was "Wild Cat Blues," on *Clarence Williams's Blue Five*. From the first note, Bechet's passionate soprano dominates the record, pushing the cornet and the trombone into the background. While not containing any formal solo passages, this recording features numerous two-bar breaks, which Bechet carries off with a rhythmic security and flair for the dramatic usually associated with Louis Armstrong on his later pieces, such as "Cornet Chop Suey." This recording was made exactly one year before Armstrong appeared in New York to nationalize his reputation playing with Fletcher Henderson and His Orchestra.

"Maple Leaf Rag." "Maple Leaf Rag" probably began as a reminder of the repertoire Bechet had played in New Orleans in his youth. Eventually, it became an expression of his volcanic power with his soprano, again overwhelming the other members of the front line. Except for a short piano solo, the performance is driven by Bechet, culminating in a long, pulsating high note over an ensemble riff.

"Characteristic Blues." Of the many recordings Bechet made during his time with Sissle, "Characteristic Blues" is the closest example of straight-ahead jazz. Accompanied by only the rhythm section, Bechet (on clarinet) produces a passionate blues statement. Beginning at a languid tempo, the performance ends with Bechet quoting from the traditional "High Society" clarinet solo as the arrangement moves into double-time for the final chorus.

"Summertime." Although not released under his name, "Summertime" is one of Bechet's most famous recordings. The George Gershwin tune had previously been recorded by others, but here it found its definitive version. Bechet had been playing the number for some time, evolving a series of soprano variations that he featured for the rest of his life. His approach is both melodic and harmonic, the latter suggesting what Coleman Hawkins supposedly pioneered with his record of "Body and Soul" of nine months later. "Summertime" also marks the beginning of his association with Blue Note, which would continue for the next fourteen years.

"Egyptian Fantasy." Although credited to Bechet, this number was in fact "Egyptia," an Abe Olman tune featured by the Creole Jazz Band as early as 1914. Well adapted to Bechet's affection for exotic themes, "Egyptian Fantasy" features his low-register clarinet at its most atmospheric. This recording is representative of the higher degree of organization generally to be found on his Victor series, which ran concurrently with his Blue Note output in 1940 and 1941.

Musical Legacy

Swiss conductor Ernest Ansermet, who heard Bechet with the Southern Syncopated Orchestra in 1919, called him a "clarinet virtuoso" who "composed perfectly formed blues on the clarinet." It was through the blues that Bechet initially came to music, although his natural lyricism marked him as a melodist first and foremost. Numerous strands of influence combined within him to create, with Armstrong, the first prototype of the jazz soloist. During the 1920's, Bechet's influence on musicians was largely confined to New York. While he undoubtedly had his admirers in Europe, his circle there was limited, and so were his opportunities to play jazz. His American recordings and personal appearances advanced his fame, and so did his personal reputation. Ellington was generous in praising Bechet for helping to develop the "jungle" style of his early band, with which he played briefly in 1925. It was perhaps only his combative nature and his lack of reading ability (a key to playing popular music at the time) that kept Bechet's influence from being as pervasive as that of Armstrong.

Nevertheless, Bechet maintained a remarkable degree of consistency over the course of his career. He never ceased trying new techniques, new instruments, new repertoire, and new musical associates. His voice on clarinet and especially soprano saxophone was intensely personal, demonstrating a highly vocalized tone with a completely individual concept of sound and vibrato. Bechet's playing was imitated by scores of musicians, though his originality was not easily reproduced.

John L. Clark, Jr.

Further Reading

Bechet, Sidney. *Treat It Gentle: Sidney Bechet, an Autobiography.* New York: Da Capo Press, 1978. While this is a highly entertaining and anecdotal account of his life, this book is also self-serving and somewhat unreliable on dates and chronology.

Chilton, John. *Sidney Bechet: The Wizard of Jazz.* New York: Oxford University Press, 1987. This source is meticulously researched and presented. The early chapters are the most important contribution, while the post-1930's sections are overly dependent on recordings.

Lyttleton, Humphrey. *The Best of Jazz: Basin Street to Harlem.* New York: Penguin Books, 1980. The chapter devoted to Bechet is restricted to the 1920's, but it is valuable for its perspective from another performing jazz musician.

Williams, Martin. *Jazz Masters of New Orleans*. New York: Da Capo Press, 1979. The chapter on Bechet is a thorough examination of his career, with six pages being a transcribed interview with his student, Bob Wilber.

See also: Armstrong, Louis; Ellington, Duke; Gershwin, George; Hawkins, Coleman; Henderson, Fletcher; Hunter, Alberta; Kirk, Rahsaan Roland.

Beck

American rock singer, guitarist, and songwriter

Using influences from blues, hip-hop, country, and funk, Beck coupled his music with clever and witty lyrics to create a unique alternative rock sound.

Born: July 8, 1970; Los Angeles, California

Principal recordings

ALBUMS: *Mellow Gold*, 1994; *One Foot in the Grave*, 1994; *Stereopathetic Soul Manure*, 1994; *A Western Harvest Field by Moonlight*, 1995; *Odelay*, 1996; *Deadweight*, 1998; *Mutations*, 1998; *Midnite Vultures*, 1999; *Maximum Beck*, 2000; *Steve Threw Up*, 2001; *Sea Change*, 2002; *Guero*, 2005; *Guerolito*, 2005; *Remix EP #1*, 2005; *Venom Confection*, 2005; *The Information*, 2006; *Timebomb*, 2007.

The Life

Beck Hansen was born to David Campbell and Bibbe Hansen, who were living in downtown Los Angeles, where Campbell worked as a bluegrass street musician. His mother, once associated with Andy Warhol's Factory in New York, worked in an office. The family moved to a declining neighborhood in Hollywood, and thereafter Beck spent his childhood and adolescence staying with different members of his extended family. He spent time with his paternal grandparents in Kansas; he visited his maternal grandfather Al Hansen, an artist who lived in Europe; and, after his parents sepa-

rated, he lived in a Salvadoran neighborhood in the Los Angeles area. Beck dropped out of school, which was located in an unsavory area, in ninth grade to work as a busker, playing music for money on the streets. At age eighteen he took a bus trip from Los Angeles to New York, where he participated in the antifolk movement on the Lower East Side. A year later, tired of being cold and having no place to live, he moved back to Los Angeles. There he worked in a video store and played regularly in local punk dives.

In 1994 his song "Loser," released by Bong Load Custom Records, became an immediate success, making the Top 40 and getting continuous play on MTV. Two years later he experienced even greater success with the album *Odelay*, earning three Grammy nominations and winning two Grammy Awards. In 2004 he married Marissa Ribisi, and they had a son, Cosimo Henri. He and his wife became members of the Church of Scientology.

The Music

The places Beck spent his childhood influenced his music: Kansas, where he heard down-home church hymns; Los Angeles, where he experienced the 1980's punk culture; and Germany, where he was exposed to the artistic philosophy of his grandfather, Al Hansen, a member of the avant-garde Fluxus art movement. Often mislabeled as a spokesperson for the so-called slacker generation of the 1990's, Beck claimed he never had time to sit around and complain about being miserable. Instead, he produced music that was positive and life-affirming. Taking to heart the philosophy of his grandfather, who often created art out of disposable objects, Beck transformed musical ideas and styles of the past into something entirely new.

Early Works. At an early age, Beck was impressed by the blues music of Mississippi John Hurt, and Beck taught himself how to play Hurt's songs on an acoustic guitar he had found. Once he had mastered the music, he improvised lyrics and forced himself to perform on city buses in order to overcome the shyness he felt playing in public. After returning to Los Angeles from New York, Beck's talent was noticed by Tom Rothrock of Bong Load Custom Records. Rothrock saw potential in Beck as a recording artist and put him in touch with hip-hop producer Karl Stephenson. In

Stephenson's living room one afternoon, Beck improvised "Loser," with a looped slide-guitar riff over a hip-hop beat and rap lyrics in the style of Public Enemy that made fun of Beck's poor rapping skills. Bong Load Custom Records released only five hundred copies of "Loser," but soon radio stations everywhere were playing it. Although Beck was unhappy with the way people misinterpreted the song as a "slacker anthem," its success led to major record labels bidding for his services. He chose to work with David Geffen's DGC label, which gave him an unusual contract that allowed him to produce other records on independent labels. He made *Mellow Gold* for DGC Records in 1994, shortly followed by *One Foot in the Grave* and *Stereopathic Soul Manure* on independent labels.

Odelay. Beck's second release for DGC was produced in 1996 by the Dust Brothers. Making the *Billboard* Top 200, where it peaked at number sixteen, the album went platinum, selling a million units. Videos for its songs "Where It's At," "Devil's Haircut," and "The New Pollution" were staples on MTV's playlist. A fusion of hip-hop, rock, country-western, blues, reggae, punk, funk, and polka, the album had a remarkable continuity despite its many styles. Beck earned two Grammy Awards for this album: Best Alternative Music Performance and Best Male Vocal Performance for "Where It's At." Rolling Stone named *Odelay* its 1996 Album of the Year, and Beck was *Spin* magazine's Artist of the Year.

Guero. Released in March of 2005 by DGC Records and produced by the Dust Brothers, this album incorporates Brazilian pop influences and a healthy dose of the multiple styles featured on *Odelay*. Beck used new keyboard and percussion instruments that he would add to his regular repertoire. Noteworthy on this album is a forehead-slap solo by actress Christina Ricci on the song "Hell Yes." The album title refers to a Mexican slang term that Beck was called in his childhood, and it means a pale-skinned person, usually a white American. The album track "Qué Onda Guero" translates as "What's up, blond boy?"

Musical Legacy

Beck's genius lies in taking traditional music styles and melding them into something fresh. Seeking to perform for the pleasure of his audience

Beck. (AP/Wide World Photos)

rather than for self-glorification, he won the appreciation of lovers of all musical styles. His albums reflected a constant search for new ways to be creative.

Staci A. Spring

Further Reading

Beck, and Al Hansen. *Beck and Al Hansen: Playing with Matches.* Santa Monica, Calif.: Smart Art Press, 1998. A look at the personal and professional relationship between Beck and his grandfather, showing the influence of Hansen's artistic philosophy on Beck's music and artwork.

Jovanovic, Rob. *Beck! On a Backwards River: The Story of Beck.* London: Virgin, 2000. Full-length biography recounts Beck's early life and dedicates a chapter to each of the four major-label albums released up to the date of publication.

Kemp, Mark. "Beck." *Rolling Stone*, April 17, 1997, 58. Insightful interview with Beck after the success of his album *Odelay*. Includes comments on his professional history, family, lyrics, influences, and musical style.

Martell, Nevin. *Beck: The Art of Mutation*. New York: Pocket Books, 2001. This comprehensive portrait explores Beck's childhood, musical history, performances, and recording sessions. Includes complete discography, with listings of rare collaborations and appearances.

Palacios, Julian. *Beck: Beautiful Monstrosity*. London: Boxtree, 2000. In-depth look at Beck's music and his extraordinary life.

See also: Hurt, Mississippi John; Mitchell, Joni.

Jeff Beck

English rock guitarist and songwriter

Influenced by the sonic experimentations of guitarist Les Paul, Beck is noted for his use of distortion and controlled feedback, presaging the sounds of psychedelic rock and fusion.

Born: June 24, 1944; Wallington, Surrey, England
Member of: The Yardbirds; the Deltones

Principal recordings

ALBUMS (solo): *Truth*, 1968; *Beck-Ola*, 1969; *Rough and Ready*, 1971; *Jeff Beck Group*, 1972; *Shapes of Things*, 1972; *Beck, Bogert, and Appice*, 1973; *Blow by Blow*, 1975; *Wired*, 1976; *There and Back*, 1980; *Flash*, 1985; *Jeff Beck's Guitar Shop*, 1989; *Frankie's House*, 1992; *Crazy Legs*, 1993; *Up*, 1995; *Who Else!*, 1999; *You Had It Coming*, 2001; *Jeff*, 2003.

ALBUMS (with the Yardbirds): *For Your Love*, 1965; *Having a Rave Up*, 1965; *Roger the Engineer*, 1966; *Over Under Sideways Down*, 1966; *Blow-Up*, 1967; *Little Games*, 1967; *Birdland*, 2003; *Little Games*, 2003.

The Life

Jeff Beck began learning piano at age eight, and he later studied violin and cello before discovering rock and roll. At thirteen, he built his first electric guitar; at fifteen, he joined his first band, the Deltones. Beck was influenced by rock-and-roll guitarists of the late 1950's, and he discovered the

blues in 1962 after listening to recordings by Chicago bluesmen Otis Rush and Buddy Guy.

Beck briefly attended Wimbledon Art College before turning his attention full time to music. He was a sideman for Screaming Lord Sutch before joining the Tridents in 1963. While with the Tridents, Beck began to experiment with distortion and feedback. He joined the Yardbirds in 1965, replacing Eric Clapton as lead guitarist. Beck continued his sonic experiments with the Yardbirds and remained with that group until December, 1966.

Continuing Beck's quest for a new sound, the Jeff Beck Group was formed in 1967 with singer Rod Stewart and bassist Ronnie Wood. The group released two albums before Stewart and Wood left to join Faces. Beck reorganized the group in the early 1970's, and it released two albums before Beck dissolved that collaboration. In the process of forming a power trio with ex-Vanilla Fudge rhythm section Tim Bogert (bass) and Carmine Appice (drums), Beck was injured in a car accident that stalled his career for eighteen months. When he recovered, the trio released only one album, *Beck, Bogert, and Appice* (1973).

Drawn to the sounds of jazz fusion, Beck released the critically acclaimed albums *Blow by Blow* and *Wired*. His work with keyboardist Jan Hammer led to more experimentation with electronics. A fairly reclusive individual, Beck took lengthy sabbaticals throughout his career, releasing albums sporadically.

The Music

Beck's guitar style, while inspired by sonic experimentation with distortion and feedback, was not dependent on electronic devices. Instead, Beck preferred to work with the natural physics of the electric guitar. He plucked the strings with his fingers and nails and produced a variety of sounds on his Stratocaster. Along with the Stratocaster, Beck frequently played a Fender Telecaster and a Gibson Les Paul. He used the volume and tone control knobs to shape his notes and employed the vibrato (whammy) bar for extensive string bends. He was also one of the first to experiment with two-handed fretting, or tapping technique.

Early Influences. When first introduced to rock and roll, Beck was influenced by guitarists Hank Marvin of the Shadows; Cliff Gallup, the lead guitarist for Gene Vincent; and James Burton, lead guitarist for Ricky Nelson. Discovering the blues in the early 1960's, Beck was impressed by the guitar work of Chicago bluesmen Guy and Rush. He was also familiar with the overdubbing effects used by Paul. His exposure to Paul's sonic experiments led Beck, while a member of the Tridents, to try his hand at distortion and feedback. When he moved to the Yardbirds, he continued his experiments and defined what is perhaps the most successful period of the Yardbirds' career. Beck's use of fuzz tone, controlled feedback, the whammy bar, and other distortion devices can be heard on the songs "Heart Full of Soul" and "Shapes of Things" (later reworked in 1967 with a heavy psychedelic sound by the first Jeff Beck Group). For a brief time, the Yardbirds enjoyed a lead guitar duo: Beck and Jimmy Page (originally hired as bass player). Only two recordings with both guitarists were released: "Happenings Ten Years' Time Ago" and "Psycho Daisies."

Blow by Blow *and* Wired. After the breakup of the second Jeff Beck Group, Beck worked for a brief time in the early 1970's as a session guitarist for Stevie Wonder. Already inspired by the rhythmic quality of Bo Diddley's music, Beck found that his work with Wonder clarified the importance of a strong rhythmic groove for the guitarist. Particularly influential was the rhythm groove on "Superstition," a song originally composed for Beck and recorded with Bogert and Appice. In 1975, with the release of *Blow by Blow*, Beck began to fuse the sound of hard rock with the freedom of jazz improvisation. With this album and its follow-up, *Wired*, Beck opened the door for such rock instrumentalists as Steve Vai and Joe Satriani. *Wired* featured a solid approach to jazz, especially with the covers of jazz bassist Charles Mingus's "Goodbye Pork Pie Hat" and Narada Michael Walden's "Love Is Green." Beck's interest in electronics was enhanced by his collaboration with Hammer on these two albums and on *Live with the Jan Hammer Group* (1977).

Later Works. Following a brief hiatus, Beck returned to music in 1980 with the release of *There and Back*. This was followed by another hiatus, which Beck broke with the release of *Flash*. After another period of inactivity in the later 1980's, Beck released *Jeff Beck's Guitar Shop*. In the 1990's Beck recorded in the studio and composed sound-track music. He

created the sound track for BBC Television's film *Frankie's House* (1992) and performed on several sound tracks. He guested as a session guitarist for numerous performers. He released the solo albums *Crazy Legs*, *Jeff Beck Session Works*, *Who Else!*, *You Had It Coming*, and *Jeff*.

Musical Legacy

Beck influenced guitarists, particularly instrumental-oriented soloists, with his forays into jazz fusion. With the Yardbirds, Beck introduced several novel sounds to rock, including fuzz distortion and overdriving amplifiers, and he employed such devices as the wah-wah pedal and guitar knobs to control feedback. He earned Grammy Awards for Best Rock Instrumental for the songs "Escape" from *Flash* and "Dirty Mind" from *You Had It Coming* and Best Rock Instrumental for the album *Jeff Beck's Guitar Shop*. He was awarded *Guitar Player* magazine's Lifetime Achievement Award in 1995 and was inducted into the Rock and Roll Hall of Fame in 1992 as a member of the Yardbirds.

Stephen Valdez

Further Reading

Carson, Annette. *Jeff Beck: Crazy Fingers*. San Francisco: Backbeat Books, 2001. Although unauthorized, this biography is thoroughly researched and readable.

Clifford, Mike, ed. *The Harmony Illustrated Encyclopedia of Rock*. New York: Harmony Books, 1992. A brief entry on Beck contains a discography from the first Jeff Beck Group through 1989's *Jeff Beck's Guitar Shop*.

DeCurtis, Anthony, and James Henke with Holly George-Warren. *The Rolling Stone Illustrated History of Rock and Roll*. New York: Random House, 1992. Several articles mention Beck's career.

Hedges, Dan. *British Rock Guitar*. New York: Guitar Player Books, 1977. This book contains coverage of Beck drawn from articles previously published in *Guitar Player* magazine.

See also: Clapton, Eric; Diddley, Bo; Dixon, Willie; Eddy, Duane; Guy, Buddy; Howlin' Wolf; Mingus, Charles; Page, Jimmy; Paul, Les; Plant, Robert; Rush, Otis; Sibelius, Jean; Stewart, Rod; Sting; Van Halen, Eddie; Vaughan, Stevie Ray; Vincent, Gene.

Sir Thomas Beecham

English classical conductor and arranger

A leading conductor of classical music in Britain, Beecham promoted English composers within the classical repertoire.

Born: April 29, 1879; St. Helens, England
Died: March 8, 1961; London, England

Principal recordings

ALBUMS: *Atterberg: Symphony No. 6*, 1928; *Mozart: Symphony No. 34*, 1928; *Gounod's Faust*, 1929; *Chabrier's España*, 1932; *Mozart: Symphony No. 31 in D Major*, 1939; *Handel: The Faithful Shepherd Suite*, 1943; *Famous Overtures*, 1946; *Handel: Messiah*, 1947; *Handel: The Gods Go A-Begging*, 1947; *Sibelius: Symphony No. 2 in D Major, Op. 43*, 1947; *Sibelius: Symphony No. 6 in D Minor, Op. 104*, 1947; *Sibelius: Tapiola, Op. 112*, 1947; *Strauss: Ein Heldenleben*, 1947; *Sir Thomas Beecham Conducts Music from the Eighteenth Century*, 1948; *Delius: Brigg Fair: An English Rhapsody*, 1948; *Handel: The Great Elopement*, 1951; *Royal Festival Hall Concert*, 1959; *Handel: Love in Bath*, 1961; *Handel: Solomon*, 1969; *Sir Thomas Beecham Conducts Rossini*, 1979; *Beecham Plays Strauss*, 1980; *Sir Thomas Beecham Conducts Classical Symphonies*, 1981; *Thomas Beecham and the London Philharmonic Orchestra*, 1996; *Beecham Conducts*, 1997; *Beecham Conducts Sibelius*, 1998; *Sibelius: Symphony No. 4; Pelléas et Mélisande; Tapiola; Swanwhite; Symphony No. 7*, 2000.

WRITINGS OF INTEREST: *A Mingled Chime*, 1943 (autobiography); *Frederick Delius*, 1959.

The Life

Thomas Beecham (BEE-chuhm) came from a family that prized music as an avocation but did not practice it professionally. His father, Sir Joseph Beecham, a chemist and pill manufacturer, was made a baronet by Queen Victoria. Beecham grew up in Huyton, near Liverpool, but at the age of thirteen, he was sent to the newly founded Rossall School in Lancashire, a rigorous but experimental school that pioneered a modern approach to educa-tion. Beecham then attended Wadham College of the University of Oxford, from which he withdrew after a year to study music in Paris. Beecham studied music composition in England, with Irish composer Charles Wood, and in France, with exiled Polish-Jewish pianist Moritz Moszkowski. This combination of insular and Continental influences was a hallmark of Beecham's versatile and inclusive approach to the repertoire. Although Beecham had no formal training as a conductor, he founded his own symphony orchestra, named after himself, in 1909. He recruited young instrumentalists and used his verve and business acumen to put the fledgling orchestra on the musical map. He also became interested in conducting opera and ballet, performing frequently at Covent Garden in London as a prelude to founding his own opera company in 1915. This eventually became the British National Opera Company.

In 1903 Beecham married an American woman, Utica Wells; they had two children. In 1911 Beecham separated from his wife. When she refused to grant him a divorce, he had a widely publicized relationship with the noted socialite Maud Alice (Emerald) Cunard, and this brought him in touch with much of the British avant-garde and intelligentsia. As his children matured, Beecham was limited financially because his father, for reasons of spite, had cut off the flow of family money. His own idiosyncratic taste, which put his preferences ahead of the ticket-buying public's, rendered his musical ventures often short of cash.

In 1916, at the height of the carnage of World War I, he was knighted by King George V, becoming Sir Thomas. Ironically, he would have become that anyway later that year when his father died, bequeathing to Beecham the baronetcy (in which, unlike a knighthood, the title of Sir can be inherited). Beecham was particularly noted for his busy schedule during the war years, and he declined fees for many appearances. In the 1920's he became known as the man who brought serious music to England's provinces, especially the British industrial city of Manchester, for whose Hallé Orchestra he had made one of his first appearances. A cultured man who took the arts seriously, Beecham made it his mission to bring the best of classical music to the ordinary middle- and working-class Englishman, establishing him as a well-known and popular figure among a broad audience. Despite this fame and the considerable estate left to him by his wealthy father, Beecham faced fiscal problems, as his multiple commitments often left his financial affairs in a confusing tangle.

In the 1930's Beecham's interests once again focused on symphonic music. With funding from the prominent Courtauld family, he founded the London Philharmonic Orchestra in 1932 and returned to Covent Garden as principal opera conductor. Controversially, Beecham toured Nazi Germany in 1936, during which he played the works of the anti-Semitic opera composer Richard Wagner (to whose works Beecham became increasingly dedicated in the 1930's) while complying with a Nazi request not to play the Jewish German composer Felix Mendelssohn. However, after meeting Adolf Hitler, Beecham was repelled. His detestation of the Nazi leader nullified any attempt to use his visit as propaganda. The onset of war in 1939 and the heavy German bombing of England that started a year later hindered most London cultural institutions, so Beecham spent most of World War II in the United States, conducting the Metropolitan Opera in New York and spending time in Seattle, and even crossed the Pacific to Australia. He was not much criticized for choosing to leave England to pursue his career elsewhere during the war; indeed, his service in New York as a cultural ambassador, undertaken before the United States and Britain were allied in the war, was perceived as an important advertisement for Britain's cause in the war within the American cultural sphere. During these years Beecham's wife, Utica, finally agreed to divorce him. In 1943 he married the concert pianist Betty Thomas, who was born in 1900.

Beecham's energy was still undiminished in his sixties, and upon returning to London Beecham undertook the task of founding a new orchestra, the Royal Philharmonic. His relations with the London Philharmonic had cooled in his absence, during which the personnel had experienced more artistic independence and were then intolerant of Beecham's martinet-style management. In 1957 Queen Elizabeth II made him a Companion of Honour. Beecham made one last ambitious tour in 1958, conducting operas at the Teatro Colón in Buenos Aires, Argentina. That same year Betty died, and Beecham married his secretary, Shirley Hudson, the following year. He visited the United States and Canada the last time in 1959. Beecham was able to experience many tributes accorded him on his eightieth birthday before dying in 1961.

The Music

Beecham did not see music as merely a technical or virtuoso exercise—it was simply a part of culture. He lectured on music, making many public appearances that increased the visibility of classical music, and he championed such British composers as Charles Villiers Stanford, Ethel Smyth (a rare instance of a woman composer being widely performed in this era), Joseph Holbrooke, and especially Frederick Delius. As impresario and entrepreneur, Bee-

Sir Thomas Beecham. (AP/Wide World Photos)

cham was a pivotal figure in English culture whose erudition and high standards brought the grandeur of the nineteenth century in touch with the rigor and complexity of the twentieth.

Frederick Delius. Delius's lush, chromatic work depends crucially on tempo for its effects, and Beecham delighted in his interpretive role as its conductor. In the second movement of Delius's 1887 *Florida Suite*, "By the River," for example. Beecham used a persistent set of beats, about a second apart, to establish the natural and folk-culture milieu of the piece, and then accelerated the rhythm, leading to a thunderous clash of joy and release. Strongly programmatic, Delius's music depicted a specific scene or historical setting, and Beecham excelled at using it to paint pictures for the audience, achieving, more simplistically, the sort of total artistic effect aimed for by Wagnerian opera.

Beecham and Delius became close friends, both rooted in the north of England (Delius was from Yorkshire) but cosmopolitan with significant Continental influences and (unusually for cultured Englishmen of their generation save Winston Churchill) a great love of the United States. Beecham was far more sociable and business-minded than Delius and found surer footing in the salons of metropolitan London. It could be argued, however, that Delius's friendship strengthened Beecham's intellectual side. Delius influenced Beecham to read the works of Friedrich Nietzsche (whose *Also Sprach Zarathustra* provided the text for Delius's 1905 *A Mass of Life*).

Other Composers. Beecham's empathetic advocacy was not restricted to Delius. Such Continental composers as Mendelssohn and Camille Saint-Saëns were among his favorites, and he argued for the importance of less conspicuous French composers such as Vincent d'Indy, Emmanuel Chabrier, and André Gretry. Beecham also put effort into performing works by more renowned composers such as Ludwig van Beethoven, though his interpretations of Beethoven did not meet with universal praise. This was also true of his performances, castigated as too enthusiastic, of Finnish composer Jean Sibelius. More lauded were his performances of Hector Berlioz, whose Romanticism and intelligence found their perfect expositor in Beecham. Beecham was famed as a conductor of Mozart op-

eras and tried also to give the French opera tradition, as exemplified by comparative unknown Étienne Méhul, a beachhead among a generally unreceptive English audience.

An opera and ballet as well as a symphonic conductor, Beecham promoted a pioneering composer not necessarily associated with conventional ideas—Richard Strauss, whose major operas all received their British premieres under Beecham's direction. He also conducted the first British appearance of Serge Diaghilev's Ballets Russes, an important moment in legitimating modern approaches to the arts in the United Kingdom. He also sponsored the first British appearance of the Russian opera singer Feodor Chaliapin, one of the most iconic musical figures of the early twentieth century.

Beecham's musical tastes, however, were not ecumenical. He paid little or no attention to such giants as Igor Stravinsky, Arnold Schoenberg, and Béla Bartók, and Baroque music was not accorded much of his attention.

Conductor and Writer. Part of Beecham's success as a conductor lay in winning the loyalty, admiration, and, most of all, involvement of his musicians. His often capricious temperament was exacting, but Beecham's musicians found him challenging and provocative and worthy of their effort. This is all the more compelling given that Beecham's outsize ego—in many ways emblematic of nineteenth century musical tradition—had the potential to alienate people.

Beecham linked music to the other arts, especially literature, one of his great interests. He was more than just a student of literature; he was an author as well, although his memoir is not as colorful as his legendary hilarious aphorisms.

Musical Legacy

Beecham was so active and mercurial a force on the musical scene that inevitably his influence would fade with his death. His recordings are still listened to today, and his reintroduction of British music into the standard classical repertoire has had a permanent impact. Sir Thomas Beecham societies in the United States and the United Kingdom still pay tribute to and study the great conductor's achievements.

Nicholas Birns

Further Reading

Beecham, Sir Thomas. *A Mingled Chime*. New York: G. P. Putnam, 1943. Lacking the sparkle of his treasured aphorisms, Beecham's memoir is nonetheless a skillfully written and informative account of most of his career. Especially useful in establishing the contours of Beecham's musical tastes.

Cairns, David. "Sir Thomas Beecham: A Lifetime—and a Fortune—Devoted to Music." *Gramophone, the Classical Music Magazine* 78 (May, 2001): 8-11. Compact but informative overview of Beecham's career as a conductor and a philanthropist.

Fenby, Eric. *Delius as I Knew Him*. London: G. Bell and Sons, 1936. Memoir of Delius by his young amanuensis gives key details of the Beecham friendship.

Jefferson, Alan. *Sir Thomas Beecham: A Centenary Tribute*. London: Macdonald's and Jane, 1979. Full survey of Beecham's career, including copious illustrations and photographs.

Melior, David. "A Healthy Dose of Beecham." *The Mail on Sunday*, April 29, 2001, p. 75. A look at Beecham's contributions to musical culture.

Reid, Charles. *Thomas Beecham: An Independent Biography*. London: Gollancz, 1961. Published the year of his death, an objective and comprehensive study of Beecham.

See also: Björling, Jussi; Melchior, Lauritz; Schoenberg, Arnold; Strauss, Richard; Stravinsky, Igor.

Bix Beiderbecke

American jazz cornetist

Beiderbecke forged his own legend as an early and influential white jazz musician of the 1920's. His symphonic tone and melodic approach to improvisation were a precursor to the cool era of jazz.

Born: March 10, 1903; Davenport, Iowa
Died: August 6, 1931; New York, New York
Also known as: Leon Bismark Beiderbecke (full name)

Principal recordings

ALBUMS: *Bix Beiderbecke and the Chicago Cornets*, 1924; *Bix Beiderbecke and the Wolverines*, 1924; *Riverboat Shuffle*, 1924; *Davenport Blues*, 1925; *Bix Beiderbecke, Volume 1: Singin' the Blues*, 1927; *Bix Beiderbecke, Volume 2: At the Jazz Band Ball*, 1927; *Bixology*, 1927; *Jazz Me Blues*, 1927; *Bix Beiderbecke with Paul Whiteman, 1927-1928*, 1928.

The Life

Leon Bismark "Bix" Beiderbecke (BI-dur-behk) was born in Davenport, Iowa. His father, Bismark Herman Beiderbecke, supported the family by operating a fuel and lumber business. His mother, Agatha Jane Hilton, was an accomplished pianist who gave Beiderbecke piano lessons.

Although highly intelligent, Beiderbecke never applied himself in his high school studies, and consequently his parents enrolled him in Illinois's Lake Forest Academy. Because of poor grades, he was dismissed in 1922. From 1923 to 1925 he drifted from one orchestra to another, then enrolled at the University of Iowa in 1925 in an attempt to major in music. His college career lasted just eighteen days because he failed to comply with academic requirements.

Beiderbecke then traveled with various jazz bands around the country, ultimately joining the famous Paul Whiteman Orchestra in 1927. For two years he and his saxophonist friend Frankie "Tram" Trumbauer toured the country with small groups. Although his personal life was in disorder, he was enjoying increasing popularity. While playing college engagements, Bix met many notable jazz musicians, including Benny Goodman, Jimmy and Tommy Dorsey, Artie Shaw, and Gene Krupa. His last years were consumed with hospital stays because of his alcoholism and his deteriorating health. In August, 1931, an ailing Beiderbecke moved to Queens and died from his lifelong excess intake of bootleg liquor and pneumonia.

The Music

At a time when the rage was hot jazz with energetic tempi and forceful beat, Beiderbecke offered an alternative with his expressive tone and style based on European classical traditions. During a brief twelve-year career, he established a new sound in his improvisations, heavily influenced by composer Claude Debussy. Beiderbecke chose restraint, clean technique, and a mellow tone while still delivering powerful musical statements.

Hot Jazz. Beiderbecke's first exposure to jazz was a recording of "Tiger Rag" by the all-white Original Dixieland Jass (after 1917 spelled Jazz) Band. He was particularly influenced by trumpet player Nick La Rocca. By 1919 he owned his own Conn Victor cornet and was playing on a truck with his high school band at football games. Two years later he formed his first band, the Bix Beiderbecke Five.

The early 1920's was the era of hot jazz with a driving beat, featuring individual and collective improvised solos at incredibly quick tempi. Hot jazz ignited careers of such luminaries as Louis Armstrong and Jelly Roll Morton. The Benson Orchestra personified hot jazz, and in 1923 Beiderbecke performed with it professionally. A year later Beiderbecke became the featured soloist with the newly formed Wolverine Orchestra housed at the Stockton Club in Hamilton, Ohio. The Wolverines completed their first recordings in 1924 with "Fidgety Feet" on one side and the classic "Jazz Me Blues" on the other. Several more recordings followed, which further enhanced his reputation among jazz musicians.

Departing the Wolverines in 1924, Beiderbecke joined the Jean Goldkette Orchestra. His tenure with this group was a frustrating experience because this orchestra employed trained musicians who could read music, a skill in which Beiderbecke never gained proficiency. After two months he was fired and then remarkably rehired. Goldkette valued his improvised solos, and by then Beiderbecke had learned some of the music by memory.

On the Road. Beiderbecke then drifted around the country from one prominent orchestra to another, performing with Red Nichols and the Five Pennies, the California Ramblers, the Charlie Straight Orchestra, and the Breeze Blowers. In late 1926 Beiderbecke rejoined the Goldkette Orchestra, which now employed arranger Bill Challis. Challis's arrangements proved to be a catalyst for Beiderbecke because they provided space for his gifted improvisations, showcasing Beiderbecke's lyrical and mellow tone and his considerable technique tempered by subtlety.

In 1927, a productive period in his life, Beider-

Bix Beiderbecke. (AP/Wide World Photos)

becke performed in ballrooms, on radio broadcasts, and in recordings for the Victor Company. On February 4, Beiderbecke recorded the critically acclaimed "Singin' the Blues"; the other side featured the classic "Clarinet Marmalade," with his friend Tram. Another series of recordings followed, with different combinations of musicians producing "Way Down Yonder in New Orleans," "Riverboat Shuffle," "Royal Garden Blues," and "Jazz Me Blues."

The Goldkette Orchestra was in financial ruin by the middle of 1927 and disbanded. Beiderbecke briefly experimented with the New Yorkers, but after a few weeks that group disbanded as well. In October, Beiderbecke joined the famous Paul Whiteman Orchestra. Although Whiteman was nicknamed the King of Jazz, he was the leader of a commercial brand of jazz, far removed from the hot jazz so popular a few years earlier. (Whiteman was renowned for commissioning George Gershwin to compose and perform the epic *Rhapsody in Blue*.)

Beiderbecke achieved a significant milestone of his own when his composition for solo piano, "In a Mist," was recorded by the Okeh Record Company and performed with the Whiteman Orchestra at Carnegie Hall in October, 1928.

His body ravaged by alcohol, Beiderbecke was still able to perform with Whiteman on the Old Gold radio broadcasts and for a few more recordings. Fittingly, his last Whiteman recording in September, 1929, was "Waiting at the End of the Road," presaging Beiderbecke's death. His final endeavors were recording "I'll Be a Friend with Pleasure"—one of his best, according to critics, which also hinted at the emerging swing style of the 1930's—and copyrighting "Candlelights," "Flashes," and "In the Dark" with the Robbins Music Company in 1930 and 1931. They were published in 1938.

Musical Legacy

Some jazz historians maintain that Beiderbecke was the only cornet player ever to rival the proficiency and popularity of Louis Armstrong during the decade of the 1920's. Some even assert that Beiderbecke surpassed Armstrong. Comparisons are inevitable but unnecessary. Ultimately, a jazz musician's legacy is defined by influences, contributions, and innovations. Beiderbecke's improvisations provided a foundation for the cool movement in jazz, popularized in the 1950's, with its uncluttered textures and lighter approach.

Douglas D. Skinner

Further Reading

Berton, Ralph. *Remembering Bix: A Memoir of the Jazz Age.* New York: Harper and Row, 1974. The author met Bix as a boy. Berton's interpretive memoir includes photographs, bibliography, and discography.

Evans, Philip R., and Linda K. Evans. *Bix: The Leon Bix Beiderbecke Story.* New York: Prelike Press, 1998. An in-depth probe of his life, with numerous photographs and a collection of letters written by Beiderbecke.

James, Burnett. *Bix Beiderbecke.* London: Cassell, 1959. Biography of Beiderbecke and analysis of his jazz cornet style. Photographs and a short discography.

Sudhalter, Richard M., and Philip R. Evans. *Bix: Man and Legend.* New Rochelle, N.Y.: Arlington House, 1974. Photographs, diary, and discography. Nominated for a National Book Award.

Tirro, Frank. *Living with Jazz.* Orlando, Fla.: Harcourt Brace, 1996. A textbook for jazz history courses.

Wareing, Charles, and George Garlick. *Bugles for Beiderbecke.* London: Sidgwick and Jackson, 1958. Life and music of Beiderbecke in a biographical format with a discography.

See also: Armstrong, Louis; Debussy, Claude; Dorsey, Thomas A.; Goodman, Benny; Nichols, Red; Shaw, Artie; Whiteman, Paul.

Harry Belafonte

American calypso and folk vocalist, arranger, and songwriter

Belafonte popularized the integration of traditional folk melodies into the pop music lexicon when his 1956 album, Calypso, *sold a million copies and launched the craze for calypso music.*

Born: March 1, 1927; Harlem, New York
Also known as: Harold George Belafonte, Jr. (full name)

Principal recordings

ALBUMS: *Mark Twain and Other Folk Favorites*, 1955; *Three for Tonight*, 1955; *Belafonte*, 1956; *Calypso*, 1956; *Belafonte Sings of the Caribbean*, 1957; *Belafonte Sings the Blues*, 1958; *Presenting the Belafonte Singers*, 1958; *Belafonte at Carnegie Hall*, 1959; *Cheers: Drinking Songs Around the World*, 1959; *Love Is a Gentle Thing*, 1959; *Porgy and Bess*, 1959; *Belafonte Returns to Carnegie Hall*, 1960; *My Lord What a Mornin'*, 1960; *Swing Dat Hammer*, 1960; *At Home and Abroad*, 1961; *Jump Up Calypso*, 1961; *The Many Moods of Belafonte*, 1962; *The Midnight Special*, 1962; *To Wish You a Merry Christmas*, 1962; *Streets I Have Walked*, 1963; *Ballads, Blues, and Boasters*, 1964; *Calypso in Brass*, 1966; *In My Quiet Room*, 1966; *Belafonte on Campus*, 1967; *Belafonte Sings of Love*, 1968; *Homeward Bound*, 1969; *By Request*, 1970; *Calypso Carnival*, 1971; *The Warm Touch*, 1971;

Play Me, 1973; *Turn the World Around*, 1977; *Loving You Is Where I Belong*, 1981; *Paradise in Gazankulu*, 1988; *Belafonte '89*, 1989; *The Tradition of Christmas*, 1991; *American Wintertime*, 2006; *An Evening with Miriam Makeba*, 2006.

The Life

Harold George Belafonte, Jr. (behl-uh-FON-tee) was born in the Harlem section of New York City to immigrant parents. His father, Harold Belafonte, Sr., was a chef from Martinique, and his mother, Melvine, was a domestic from Jamaica. Because his parents were struggling to make ends meet, Belafonte went to live with his grandmother in Kingston, Jamaica, from 1935 to 1940. In 1943 Belafonte dropped out of high school to join the U.S. Navy and fight in World War II. Following his return from World War II in late 1945, Belafonte emulated the jazz crooning style of Frank Sinatra and the contemporary pop style of Perry Como. Belafonte spent the early part of his career surrounded by jazz musicians, often sharing the stage with Charlie Parker, Miles Davis, and Max Roach. Belafonte enrolled in acting classes at Erwin Piscator's famous dramatic workshops at the New School for Social Research. Belafonte honed his craft as an actor alongside such legendary figures as Marlon Brando, Sidney Poitier, Tony Curtis, and Walter Matthau, and he performed with the American Negro Theater. However, it was his success as a singer that catapulted Belafonte's career as an entertainer. In 1949 Belafonte signed with Jubilee Records, a relationship that yielded little success. Later that year Belafonte teamed with guitarist Millard Thomas, and they performed jazz-influenced pop tunes and folk music in many New York jazz clubs, including the Village Vanguard.

Belafonte debuted on the music scene with a successful engagement at the Royal Roost, a popular nightclub in New York. In his first singing engagements, the fledgling Belafonte was backed by jazz legends Parker, Roach, and Davis, and the young singer's early repertoire consisted primarily of jazz and pop standards. Between late 1949 and 1950 Belafonte became interested in tunes from the Archive of American Folk Song in the Library of Congress. Intrigued by African, Asian, American, and, most important, West Indian folk music,

Belafonte abandoned pop and jazz music to focus on hybrid versions of folk music. He secured a recording contract with RCA in 1952, and he enjoyed success with the single "Matilda," followed by bigger success with his album *Calypso* in 1956.

Belafonte's popularity on the music scene paved the way for lead roles in films and Broadway shows. His acting performance in *Island in the Sun* (1957) solidified his status as a viable leading man, and his 1959 television special, *Tonight with Belafonte*, earned him an Emmy Award, the first for an African American man. Throughout his life, Belafonte has been an outspoken activist, and he was deeply involved in the Civil Rights movement of the 1950's and 1960's.

The Music

Belafonte's career took off when he recorded the single "Matilda," so he began to focus on folk tunes, especially from the West Indies. His *Calypso* album,

Harry Belafonte. (Library of Congress)

which followed in 1956, combined the gentle, floating West Indian melodies of calypso patois with the infectious West Indian dance beats of limbo. Belafonte stripped the traditional expository song style from calypso as sung by Lord Kitchener and Mighty Sparrow, taming the lyrics. He delivered them in a smooth, crooning voice, in contrast to the percussive sound favored by most West Indians. Finding his niche, Belafonte made few changes to this style throughout the rest of his career, and his later albums of the 1970's and 1980's are similar in style to the ones of the 1950's.

Calypso Albums. Despite his early work singing jazz and pop standards from 1949 to 1951, Belafonte never felt truly comfortable in those styles. Although Belafonte had a string of engagements in 1951 as a balladeer singing British folk songs, winning acclaim from critics, he slowly began including "ditties," as he called them, which were calypsos and other up-tempo West Indian songs such as "Hold 'Em Joe."

Calypso. Building on the muscle of the RCA label following the success of "Matilda" and the self-titled album *Belafonte*, the singer collaborated with William Attaway on *Calypso*. The sound Belafonte created for this album would define his career and establish a musical phenomenon. Several songs on the album became instant classics, such as "Brown Skin Girl," "Jamaica Farewell," "Man Smart (Women Smarter)," and the ever-popular "Banana Boat Song (Day-O)," a West Indian version of the John Henry legend. Instead of driving steel, the black workmen toiled through the evening loading ships with fruit. Interestingly, only two songs from the album were traditional calypsos in form. However, the album's intense popularity led to any English-language Caribbean-influenced song being labeled a calypso. The *Calypso* album was on the *Billboard* Top 100 for ninety-nine weeks, spending thirty-one weeks at number one.

Musical Styles. Belafonte released several other calypso-flavored albums during the late 1950's and early 1960's. These included *Belafonte Sings of the Caribbean*, *Swing Dat Hammer*, and *Jump Up Calypso*, all stylistically similar to *Calypso*. However, during these years, Belafonte released several albums reflecting a broad and eclectic spectrum of blues, folk, pop, and gospel music influences, including *Bela-*fonte Sings the Blues*, *Porgy and Bess*, *The Midnight Special*, and *The Many Moods of Belafonte*. These albums paled in comparison to the commercial and critical success of two live concert recordings, *Belafonte at Carnegie Hall* and *Belafonte Returns to Carnegie Hall*.

Later Releases. After the decline of the calypso craze, Belafonte explored different musical projects, including extended collaborations and film and television sound tracks. During the late 1960's and 1970's, he collected songs recorded by various African American artists in order to produce *The Long Road to Freedom: An Anthology of Black Music*. The critically acclaimed packaged set was released in 2001.

Musical Legacy

By integrating traditional folk melodies with popular musical styles of the 1950's, Belafonte set a precedent for a new style of songwriting. He tapped his island musical heritage and created a popular genre. The cross-appeal of Belafonte's music to white audiences furthered the integration of African American music into American popular music. He received the National Medal of Arts, two Grammy Awards, and a Grammy Lifetime Achievement Award.

Andrew R. Martin

Further Reading

Attaway, William. *Hear America Singing*. New York: Lion Press, 1967. This book is a collection of lyrics and includes several songs made popular by Belafonte. Belafonte wrote the introduction.

Fogelson, Genia. *Harry Belafonte: Singer and Actor*. New York: Holloway House, 1997. Thorough coverage of Belafonte's career in the 1960's, including his work in film and television.

Funk, Ray, and Donald Hill. "Will Calypso Doom Rock and Roll?" In *Trinidad Carnival: The Cultural Politics of a Transnational Festival*, edited by Garth L. Green and Philip W. Scher. Bloomington: Indiana University Press, 2007. Traces the arrival of calypso music in the United States, showing how the genre reached into the American social fabric.

Shaw, Arnold. *Belafonte: An Unauthorized Biography*. Philadelphia: Chilton, 1960. This biography covers Belafonte's personal life, including details on two early marriages, and chronicles the rise and fall of the calypso craze.

Steirmen, Hy. *Harry Belafonte: His Complete Life Story*. New York: Hillman, 1957. This work tracks Belafonte's rise to stardom, leaving off at the release of the *Calypso* album.

See also: Davis, Miles; Fender, Freddy; Jordan, Louis; Lewis, John; Makeba, Miriam; Masekela, Hugh; Odetta; Parker, Charlie; Roach, Max; Seeger, Pete; Sinatra, Frank.

Tony Bennett

American vocalist

A popular singer of standard and jazz music, Bennett has entertained generations of listeners with his easy, down-to-earth style since the 1940's.

Born: August 13, 1926; Queens, New York
Also known as: Anthony Dominick Benedetto (birth name); Joe Bari

Principal recordings

ALBUMS: *The Beat of My Heart*, 1957; *Basie/Bennett*, 1958 (with Count Basie and His Orchestra); *Because of You*, 1959; *Blue Velvet*, 1959; *In Person!*, 1959; *A String of Harold Arlen*, 1960; *To My Wonderful One*, 1960; *I Left My Heart in San Francisco*, 1963; *I Wanna Be Around*, 1963; *When Lights Are Low*, 1964; *The Movie Song Album*, 1966; *Tony Sings the Great Hits of Today*, 1970; *The Rodgers and Hart Songbook*, 1973; *Life Is Beautiful*, 1975; *Tony Bennett with the McPartlands and Friends Make Magnificent Music*, 1977; *The Art of Excellence*, 1986; *Bennett/Berlin*, 1987; *Astoria*, 1990; *Perfectly Frank*, 1992; *Steppin' Out*, 1993; *MTV Unplugged*, 1994; *Here's to the Ladies*, 1995; *Isn't It Romantic?*, 1995; *My Romance*, 1995; *Tony Bennett on Holiday*, 1997; *The Playground*, 1998; *Bennett Sings Ellington: Hot and Cool*, 1999; *Playin' with My Friends: Bennett Sings the Blues*, 2001 (duets with others); *A Wonderful World*, 2002 (with K. D. Lang); *The Art of Romance*, 2004; *Duets: An American Classic*, 2006.

WRITINGS OF INTEREST: *The Good Life*, 1998 (autobiography).

The Life

Tony Bennett was born Anthony Dominick Benedetto, the son of Italian immigrants Giovanni and Anna Benedetto. Bennett's father, a grocer, died when he was ten years old, and his mother, Anna, took a job as a seamstress to support her children. Bennett attended New York City's School of Industrial Art (now known as the High School of Art and Design), where he trained as a painter. He dropped out of school at sixteen to help support his family by working a series of jobs, including as an elevator operator and a copyboy for the Associated Press. He did not last long at these jobs, and they only reinforced his desire to become a professional singer. He gave himself the stage name of Joe Bari and did whatever he could to start his career.

In 1944, at eighteen, Bennett was drafted into the Army and served in the infantry until the Germans surrendered to the Allies at the end of World War II. He found combat difficult and was glad to be reassigned to a division that provided entertainment for the troops. He performed with many talented musicians, singers, and arrangers, some of whom helped Bennett later in his career.

Bennett returned home from the military in 1946 determined to make it as a singer. He used his G.I. Bill benefits to go back to school, attending the American Theatre Wing. In 1952 Bennett married a young art student from Ohio named Patricia Beech. Together they had two sons, D'Andrea (Danny) and Daegal (Dae). The marriage suffered from Bennett's spending too much time on the road, and they separated in 1965. The divorce was made final in 1971.

While portraying the role of Hymie Kelly in the movie *The Oscar* in 1965, Bennett met Sandra Grant. Eventually they married and had two daughters, Joanna and Antonia. He moved the family to Hollywood, but the lifestyle began to takes its toll. He and Sandra fell behind in taxes, and the Internal Revenue Service (IRS) prepared to take away their home. Bennett's mother died, his own record label folded, and Bennett became depressed. A near-fatal drug overdose propelled him to reexamine his life and career. He called his sons, Danny and Dae, for help. In their twenties and familiar with the business side of the music industry, they came to Bennett's aid, Danny taking over as his manager. Unfortunately, Bennett and Sandra divorced.

This was a turning point for Bennett professionally and personally. With his second marriage over, he moved back to New York and revived his singing career. In addition to his musical success, Bennett gained acclaim as an artist. Painting under his birth name of Anthony Benedetto, he exhibited his works in art galleries across the country. He published an art book featuring many of his paintings, *Tony Bennett: What My Heart Has Seen* (1996).

The Music

Bennett's early years were spent listening to such greats as Al Jolson, Bing Crosby, and Maurice Chevalier. From these talented artists he learned a relaxed attitude that would appeal to every audience. At thirteen he developed a love for jazz, and at sixteen he dropped out of school to help support his family. He tried several jobs but ended up working as a singing waiter in an Italian restaurant, where he learned the standard songs from the other waiters and deduced what it took to be a performer.

During World War II Bennett served in the infantry, then was transferred to the 255th Regiment Band and the 314th Army Special Services Band of the European Theater, traveling around Germany entertaining the troops, often in the trenches. This experience provided Bennett with a great deal of artistic freedom since he could sing any song in any style, such as the new bebop. Many of the songs he performed in Germany—such as "Body and Soul" and "Sunny Side of the Street"—remained part of his repertoire for years.

After returning from the war, Bennett spent his days knocking on the doors of booking agents, club owners, and promoters. He received many rejections, which was a shock after the success he had experienced in the Army. At night he frequented clubs, singing for free and hoping someone would hear him. Performers such as Milton Berle and Jan Murray helped by arranging for him to sing when agents were in the audience.

"Boulevard of Dreams." Bennett's first demonstration disc featured "Crazy Rhythm" and "Boulevard of Dreams." The recording was not a huge success, but it attracted the attention of entertainment columnist Walter Winchell and singer Frank Sina-

tra. Mitch Miller of Columbia Records also found the disc interesting and offered Bennett a contract. Getting signed with a label was a positive step in Bennett's career. "Boulevard of Dreams" became his first Top 10 hit.

The songs recorded after "Boulevard of Dreams" were not as successful, and he was told that if he did not get a hit soon he would be dropped from the label. In 1951 he recorded "Because of You." It was not aired immediately on the radio, but it was a popular jukebox choice. Soon listeners from all over the country were calling their radio stations requesting the song. It was Bennett's first number-one hit on the *Billboard* pop chart, ultimately selling a million copies. It stayed on the chart for thirty-two weeks, ten at number one.

"Cold, Cold Heart." Bennett's second number-one hit was "Cold, Cold Heart," written by country singer Hank Williams. This was the first time a country song had crossed over to the Top 40 mainstream chart before becoming an international hit. Bennett was invited to perform it on the *Grand Ol' Opry* television show to pay tribute to Williams after his death.

Cloud 7. By 1955 Bennett had become dissatisfied with trying to beat the other pop singers for the number-one spot on the charts. He wanted to record a long-playing disc of jazz songs. Miller initially said no, but after the success of "Cold, Cold Heart," he finally agreed. *Cloud 7* was one of the first concept albums and one of Columbia's first twelve-inch long-playing discs. It featured jazz and classical inspiration, such as "My Reverie," based on classical composer Claude Debussy's *Reverie*. *Cloud 7* was not a smash hit, but it proved that Bennett was capable of doing something beyond singles and that he was ready for major changes in his career.

Mr. Broadway. The producers of the Broadway play *Kismet* asked Bennett to record "Stranger in Paradise" as a way to promote the play during a newspaper strike. It worked so well that several years later he was asked to record "Just in Time" from *Bells Are Ringing*. He eventually recorded enough songs for his 1962 album release *Mr. Broadway.*

"In the Middle of an Island." At first Bennett refused to record "In the Middle of an Island," which he did not like. He and Miller argued about it, but

Bennett finally gave in, managing to get through it in one take. Surprisingly, the song made the Top 10. Although the experience reinforced Bennett's belief that he should sing only songs that he liked in order to give the best he had to give to his listeners, giving in to Miller allowed him the freedom to record something more ambitious.

The Beat of My Heart. Bennett's next project was a compilation of standard songs using different kinds of rhythm, performed by all the great drummers Bennett could find. *The Beat of My Heart* attracted a whole new audience of jazz fans. With the success of the album, Bennett was allowed to make albums regularly.

"I Left My Heart in San Francisco." While preparing for his first concert in the city of San Francisco, Bennett's piano player, Ralph Sharon, handed him a song written by two unknown songwriters. Bennett liked the tune immediately, and so did audiences all over the country. It quickly became his signature song. The album of the same name was a Top 5 hit, and in 1962 the single won a Grammy Award for Record of the Year and Best Male Solo Vocal performance.

Tony Sings the Great Hits of Today. In 1967 rock and roll became the mainstay of most record labels. Columbia was no different and embraced the new sound, insisting all their artists record rock-and-roll tunes. Once again Bennett protested. He could not understand why he should sing songs that were definitely not his style. Bennett gave in again and recorded *Tony Sings the Great Hits of Today.* He was glad that his success in the 1950's had already established his career.

Improv. Bennett left Columbia in 1972 and signed with Polygram Records. His albums were released on the Philips label in England and on MGM/Verve in America. Two years later he started Tobill Enterprises and the record label Improv with Bill Hassett. Bennett produced four albums using different styles, something he would never have been able to do with a major label. The venture proved to be more difficult than they had expected, and it folded.

The Art of Excellence. Bennett's career began to slip in the 1970's. He was in debt from closing the record company and was having trouble with the IRS. He had been performing in Las Vegas but did not want to be labeled a Vegas act. He moved back to New York, and with Danny's help he refocused his career on a younger generation of music fans by booking shows at colleges and small theaters. The response was better than they had expected, without Bennett having to change his style of singing, his songs, or his trademark tuxedo. He re-signed with Columbia Records and recorded his first album with the label in fourteen years. *The Art of Excellence* was created with state-of-the-art digital equipment. A great album, it also attracted the attention of high-tech enthusiasts.

MTV Generation. Bennett and his son found another way to attract the attention of younger listeners. They convinced Columbia that he should do an MTV video. "Steppin' Out" was shot in black and white and featured all styles of dance with visual editing cut on the beat. Response to the video was so positive that Bennett was asked to co-present an award at that year's MTV Video Awards, and in 1994 he was invited to appear on *MTV Unplugged.* An album of the evening's performance became one of the top sellers of his career. With guest appearances by K. D. Lang and Elvis Costello, it won Grammy's Album of the Year in 1995.

Musical Legacy

By studying masterful entertainers, Bennett learned how to attract and maintain the public's interest. Keeping great songs alive and providing quality entertainment for all ages are significant parts of his legacy. As a representative of a beloved line of American vocalists, such as Frank Sinatra, Dean Martin, and Andy Williams, Bennett has preserved their art for a twenty-first century audience who revere him for his music and his enduring youthfulness.

Maryanne Barsotti

Further Reading

Bennett, Tony. *The Good Life*. New York: Pocket Books, 1998. Autobiographical account of Bennett's rise as one of the world's most enduring pop and jazz singers. Includes anecdotes, photographs, and discography.

Bennett, Tony, and Robert Sullivan. *Tony Bennett in the Studio: A Life of Art and Music.* New York: Sterling, 2007. A reflection of Bennett's careers as singer and painter. Includes memories, inspirations, and illustrations of his artwork.

Hoffman, Matthew. *Tony Bennett: The Best Is Yet to Come*. New York: MetroBooks, 1997. Describes Bennett's rise from singing waiter to international sensation. Includes photographs of Bennett at every stage of his career.

See also: Arlen, Harold; Basie, Count; Burke, Johnny; David, Hal; Ellington, Duke; Evans, Bill; Hart, Lorenz; Lang, K. D.; McFerrin, Bobby; Newley, Anthony; Rodgers, Richard; Streisand, Barbra; Webb, Jimmy; Williams, Hank.

Alban Berg

Austrian classical composer

Berg was one of the influential trio of Austrian composers known as the Second Viennese School. He artfully combined Romanticism with atonal and twelve-tone compositional techniques.

Born: February 9, 1885; Vienna, Austro-Hungarian Empire (now in Austria)
Died: December 24, 1935; Vienna, Austria

Principal works

CHAMBER WORKS: String Quartet, Op. 3, 1911; *Kammerkonzert*, 1925 (*Chamber Concerto*; for piano, violin, and thirteen wind instruments); *Lyrische Suite*, 1927 (*Lyric Suite*; for string quartet).

OPERAS (music): *Wozzeck*, Op. 7, 1924 (libretto by Berg; based on Georg Büchner's play *Woyzeck*); *Der Wein*, 1930 (libretto by Berg; based on Charles Beaudelaire's collection of poems translated by Stefan George, *Die Blumen des Bösen*); *Lulu*, 1937, revised and expanded 1979 (libretto by Berg; based on Frank Wedekind's play *Erdgeist*).

ORCHESTRAL WORKS: Piano Sonata, Op. 1, 1911; *Drei Orchesterstücke, Op. 6*, 1923 (*Three Orchestral Pieces*); Violin Concerto, 1936 (*To the Memory of an Angel*).

VOCAL WORKS: *Sieben Frühe Lieder*, 1908 (*Seven Early Songs*; for voice and piano, or orchestra); *Vier Lieder*, Op. 2, 1910 (*Four Songs*); *Fünf*

Orchesterlieder nach Ansichtkartentexten von Peter Altenberg, 1913 (*Five Songs on Picture Postcard Texts by Peter Altenberg*).

The Life

In his youth, Alban Berg (AL-bahn behrg), the third of four children in an affluent Viennese family, studied piano and, without formal training, composed songs. His father's death in 1900 caused a downturn in the family's fortunes, but an aunt assisted, permitting Alban to continue his education. Academic, health, and romantic difficulties (he had recently fathered an illegitimate child) led him to attempt suicide in 1903.

In 1904 Berg began compositional studies with Arnold Schoenberg, who was a respected leader of the Viennese avant-garde. Anton von Webern, a fellow student, was the third member of the triumvirate dubbed the Second Viennese School. The synergy among these three musicians was crucial to Berg's artistic life, and by the age of twenty-one he was devoting himself to composition full time.

By the time he composed his String Quartet, Op. 3, his music was completely atonal in nature. He dedicated the quartet to Helene Nahowski, whom he wed in 1911. Schoenberg left Vienna for Berlin shortly thereafter, and Berg inherited some of his master's students.

Berg's first work after the apprenticeship with Schoenberg was *Five Songs on Picture Postcard Texts by Peter Altenberg*, which demonstrated Berg's orchestrational prowess and at times hinted at twelve-tone techniques that were still a decade away. The 1913 Vienna premiere (conducted by Schoenberg) was marred by audience disruptions—not unlike the furor that would greet Igor Stravinsky's *The Rite of Spring* two months later—and only two of the five movements were attempted. Berg found the experience disheartening.

In 1914 Berg attended the Vienna premiere of Georg Büchner's play *Woyzeck*, about a hapless soldier brutalized to the point of madness. Compelled to create an operatic version of the story, Berg began to edit the script into a libretto.

After his own miserable military experiences in the Austrian army during World War I, he found new inspiration to complete *Wozzeck*, dedicating most of the next five years to the work. Premiered in Berlin in 1925, *Wozzeck* nearly caused a riot, but unlike the orchestral songs, the opera was soon recognized as a masterwork. With its condemnation of society and authority, *Wozzeck* was eventually banned by both the Nazis and the Communists but continued to receive regular performances in the West.

Following the success of *Wozzeck*, Berg completed his *Lyric Suite*, delving further into twelve-tone technique, first in a string-quartet version, then in one for string orchestra. The *Lyric Suite* was the first of several works to conceal cryptic references to Berg's love affair with Hanna Fuchs-Robettin.

In 1929 Berg began to develop the libretto for his second opera, *Lulu*, which dominated his efforts for the next six years (with a short break to fulfill a commission for a concert aria, *Der Wein*). In 1935 Berg again interrupted his work on *Lulu* for a commission—a violin concerto dedicated to the recently deceased daughter of Gustav Mahler's widow. With this inspiration, Berg wrote at an uncharacteristic rate of speed, creating the concerto (*To the Memory of an Angel*) in only four months. In the meantime, however, he failed to complete the orchestration of the third act of *Lulu*.

Only days after finishing the concerto, Berg suffered an insect bite that resulted in blood poisoning. Berg's health began a steady decline, and he died four months later, even before the premiere of the violin concerto and leaving *Lulu* incomplete. His widow refused to allow the completion of the third act during her lifetime, and so the full opera was not premiered until 1979, more than forty years after the composer's death.

The Music

Berg's compositions following the theories of the Second Viennese School are more accessible than Schoenberg's or Webern's and thus offer the listener a better window on these important aspects of twentieth century musical innovation. Nevertheless, some critics favor Schoenberg for his invention of the twelve-tone system and for *Sprechstimme* (the cross between singing and speech) and Webern for the miniaturization of form and the development of *Klangfarbenmelodie* (literally, tone-color-melody, a succession of notes characterized by rapid timbre changes). However, Berg's superior craftsmanship and attention to detail best demon-

Alban Berg. (Hulton Archive/Getty Images)

strate the potential of these techniques as expressive tools.

Early Works. Before his study with Schoenberg, Berg was primarily a songwriter in the style of Hugo Wolf. Berg's one-movement Piano Sonata, Op. 1, considered extremely mature for an initial offering, is occasionally performed. His *Three Orchestral Pieces*, Op. 6, combined the atonal compositional techniques of Schoenberg with the expansive orchestration and deep emotional expression of Mahler.

Wozzeck. Büchner's play *Woyzeck* (1836) was an account based on the true story of a beleaguered army private and his disintegration into madness. As father of an illegitimate child, as a harassed underling in the military, and as a troubled soul, Berg must have felt sympathy for the main character. Based on the atonal techniques Berg learned from Schoenberg, *Wozzeck* is the first opera to succeed without relying on tonality to organize the harmonic language.

The opera, in *aba* form, consists of three acts, each divided into five scenes and connected by instrumental interludes. The five character pieces forming act 1 demonstrate the relationships Wozzeck has with the other main characters. Act 2 is a symphony in five movements illustrating the deterioration of his relationship with Marie, his common-law wife and mother of his child. Act 3 consists of five variations on ostinatos, creating the climax of the opera. Berg's complex method of organizing the opera allowed him to create a unity and structure for an extended work without the use of tonal landmarks.

The opera uses three distinct vocal techniques to portray different aspects of the characters: dialogue underscored by the orchestra, direct song, and *Sprechstimme*. The range of musical styles is equally broad, including passages that sound post-Romantic and sections that are clearly atonal juxtaposed with folk elements and popular music. Berg even employed a honky-tonk piano to snatch the audience out of the mesmerizing "Invention on the Note B."

The opera's carefully devised structure employs fugal techniques, inventions, symphonic form, and passacaglias, but it was never Berg's intention that the formal organization be the focus. He wanted the music to underscore the dramatic themes in Büchner's text, and the results are indisputable. Despite initial criticism of the demanding score both in the theater and in the press, the power of the opera overcame the objections, and the revenue from performances of *Wozzeck* provided Berg with a comfortable income for the rest of his life.

Lulu. Berg first developed interest in the drama of Frank Wedekind in 1905. It was not until 1928, however, that Berg began combining two Wedekind scripts into the libretto of *Lulu*. After an interruption to compose *Der Wein*, Berg dedicated most of the next six years to writing this opera about the rise and fall of Lulu. Although he completed the libretto and a piano score through the end of the third act, the orchestration was completed only through the end of the second act at the time of Berg's death. Because of objections from his widow, the final section was not orchestrated until after her death in 1976.

In act 1 Lulu is entangled in affairs with every male character, and most of them meet ignominious ends. When Dr. Schön hands Lulu his gun and orders her to kill herself, she shoots him instead, precipitating her imprisonment—the climax and turning point of the opera. The entire work is a large palindrome and hinges on a remarkable scene. The director is instructed to prepare a silent film of Lulu's trial and incarceration. This scene is accompanied by two minutes of frighteningly expressionistic score, which then, at the peak of the palindrome, turns around and reverses upon itself. In the second half of the opera, double-casting brings back the actors who played Lulu's lovers in the first half, now as progressively more disturbing partners, until finally the actor who played Dr. Schön portrays Jack the Ripper and murders Lulu. The opera has come full circle.

The music of *Lulu* was created entirely by manipulation of the twelve-tone system. Experts debate the exact way the tone rows are used, and whether there are multiple rows or a single row. Berg's sketches for the opera suggest that, while he used Schoenberg's system as a departure point, he adapted it to his own purposes, employing it to create music that met his dramatic needs.

Violin Concerto: To the Memory of an Angel. In 1935, when he was struggling to complete *Lulu* despite continual health problems, Berg was approached by a young American violin virtuoso, Louis Krasner, to compose a concerto. Berg, who had turned down other commissions in his effort to complete *Lulu*, was reticent at first. Krasner suggested that Berg's lyricism might help overcome the impression that music created using the twelve-tone system was cerebral and dry. Progress was slow, however, until the emotional impetus arrived in a tragic fashion.

Berg and his wife, Helene, were good friends with Mahler's widow, Alma. Alma's daughter, Manon Gropius, had contracted polio and succumbed to the disease in April, 1935. Berg asked Alma's permission to dedicate the concerto "to the memory of an angel." Berg now had the inspiration to create an expressive twelve-tone violin concerto that would disprove any assumption that such music was without passion.

Berg worked feverishly on the concerto, putting aside his work on *Lulu*, creating a tone row that gave the music tonal references, using a series of triads followed by a fragment of the whole-tone scale.

When properly manipulated, the row allowed for inclusion of various tonal materials: the sound of the open strings of the violin, quotes from Viennese folk song, and passages from Johann Sebastian Bach's harmonization of the chorale *Es ist genug* (It is enough). The four-movement concerto shows the full range of emotion—sorrow, anger, resignation—achieving the purpose that Krasner had suggested to Berg and at the same time achieving Berg's purpose of memorializing Gropius. The result is a tour de force that many consider the most significant violin concerto of the twentieth century and a fitting tribute to Berg's masterful fusion of technique and art.

Musical Legacy

While several other works, like the *Chamber Concerto* and the *Lyric Suite*, are occasionally performed, the bulk of Berg's reputation rests on *Wozzeck*, *Lulu*, and his violin concerto *To the Memory of an Angel*. Clearly the most significant works of Berg's career, they are often performed and recorded. Berg demonstrated the lyrical and expressive possibilities inherent in the use of atonality and of Schoenberg's twelve-tone system in ways that neither Webern nor even Schoenberg himself was able to achieve. His music influenced generations of composers to come.

William S. Carson

Further Reading

Adorno, Theodor W. *Alban Berg: Master of the Smallest Link*. Translated by Juliane Brand and Christopher Hailey. Cambridge, England: Cambridge University Press, 1991. Adorno's study of his mentor is primary source material for those who wish to learn about the great composer and his music.

Hall, Patricia. *A View of Berg's Lulu Through the Autograph Sources*. Berkeley: University of California Press, 1996. Hall's scholarly volume, based primarily on Berg's sketches, analyzes the technical aspects of his second opera. Musical examples, bibliography.

Jarman, Douglas. *Alban Berg: Lulu*. Cambridge, England: Cambridge University Press, 1991. Historical, analytical, but not overly technical information about Berg's opera. Illustrations, bibliography.

_____. *Alban Berg: Wozzeck*. Cambridge, England: Cambridge University Press, 1989. Detailed introduction to *Wozzeck*, in accessible language. Illustrations, bibliography.

Pople, Anthony. *Berg: Violin Concerto*. Cambridge, England: Cambridge University Press, 1991. Like the Jarman studies (and part of the same series of Cambridge Music Handbooks), Pople's guide to the Violin Concerto introduces the work in language appropriate for concertgoers and students.

Simms, Bryan R. *Alban Berg: A Guide to Research*. New York: Garland, 1996. Thorough annotations aid the reader in locating and selecting materials.

See also: Babbitt, Milton; Berio, Luciano; Boulez, Pierre; Britten, Benjamin; Crumb, George; Fischer-Dieskau, Dietrich; Gould, Glenn; Hindemith, Paul; Mahler, Gustav; Nono, Luigi; Poulenc, Francis; Schoenberg, Arnold; Schreker, Franz; Solti, Sir Georg; Webern, Anton von.

Alan Bergman

American film and musical-theater composer/lyricist

In writing lyrics for stage and motion-picture songs, Bergman focused on drama, using the words to tell the story as well as depict the mood and the action.

Born: September 11, 1925; Brooklyn, New York

Principal works

MUSICAL THEATER (lyrics): *Something More!*, 1964 (with Marilyn Bergman; music by Sammy Fain; libretto by Nate Monaster); *Ballroom*, 1978 (with Marilyn Bergman; music by Billy Goldenberg; libretto by Jerome Kass).

Principal recordings

ALBUMS: *Lyrically, Alan Bergman*, 2007.
SONGS (lyrics; written with Marilyn Bergman): "Yellow Bird," 1966 (music and lyrics); "Bowlegged Polly," 1967; "In the Heat of the

Night," 1967; "It Sure Is Groovy," 1967; "The Windmills of Your Mind," 1968; "What Are You Doing for the Rest of Your Life?," 1970 (music and lyrics); Theme from *Maude*, 1972; "The Way We Were," 1973; Theme from *Good Times*, 1974; "You Don't Bring Me Flowers," 1977; "How Do You Keep the Music Playing?," 1982 (music and lyrics); "If We Were in Love," 1982 (music by John Williams); "It Might Be You," 1982 (music by David Grusin); "No Matter What Happens," 1983; "No Wonder," 1983; "Papa Can You Hear Me?," 1983; "A Piece of Sky," 1983; "This Is One of Those Moments," 1983; "Tomorrow Night," 1983; "The Way He Makes Me Feel," 1983; "Where Is It Written?," 1983; "Will Someone Ever Look at Me That Way?," 1983; "I Knew I Loved You," 1984 (music and lyrics).

The Life

Alan Bergman (BURG-man) began writing music at the age of eleven. His strongest musical influence was Johnny Mercer, who became his mentor. While in high school Bergman wrote shows that were original works or parodies. Later, Bergman studied music and theater at the University of North Carolina, Chapel Hill, and continued his studies at University of California, Los Angeles, where he met Mercer. They worked together for two years, and Bergman said this was the most significant part of his education. Mercer taught him to understand the craft of singing and how to use words to create specific images.

During World War II Bergman started writing and directing shows for the Army's Special Services, and from 1945 to 1953 he directed television shows for CBS in Philadelphia. During this time he wrote musical production numbers for singer Jo Stafford's shows as well as songs for Fred Astaire, for revues, and for nightclub acts.

In 1958 Bergman married Marilyn Keith, who became his career partner. Marilyn and Alan were born in the same hospital in Brooklyn and raised in the same neighborhood, but they did not meet until they both had relocated to Los Angeles.

The Music

Bergman's lyrics are connected to and drawn from the dramatic context for which he is writing.

As an exercise he would find specific scenes in short stories to illustrate with his lyrics. This prepared him for professional film work. Bergman would prefer to write the lyrics once the melody has been created, because lyrics are on the tip of the melody. While writing, he would always sing the lyrics aloud in order to diagnose problems in the text. He found it easier to write for someone with an established performance character, for example, Frank Sinatra.

"The Windmills of Your Mind." This was one of Bergman and his wife's first big successes. With music by Michel Legrand, it was written for the 1968 film *The Thomas Crown Affair*. The film's director, Norman Jewison, asked Legrand to write both the score and the theme song. Initially, Legrand approached composer-arranger Quincy Jones to write the lyrics to the song. Instead, Jones recommended a young couple, with whom he had just finished working. After meeting with Legrand and deciding on the style of the song, Bergman and his wife watched the motion picture with the director and discussed the point of the song as well as its function in the film. The crucial scene for the song was the protagonist flying in a glider as he plans the robbery. Jewison shot six minutes of the scene with only the sound of the wind, no dialogue and no sound effects. He did not want a song that would depict part of the plot or identify the character; rather, he wanted a stand-alone song that would enhance the character's restlessness. Initially, Legrand wrote six different melodies from which to choose, and the Bergmans, captivated by one, started the lyrics with just a line or phrase. The melody they chose had a circular quality, reflecting the action on the screen and portraying a mood with rhyming words, such as wheel and reel, spinning and running, sweeping and whirling. It earned the first Academy Award for the Bergmans and for Legrand.

"The Way We Were." In "The Way We Were," from the motion picture of the same title directed by Sydney Pollack, composer Marvin Hamlisch wanted to depict the life cycle of the main characters in the film: how they met, fell in love, started a life together, and finally separated. Following the story line, Hamlisch wanted to express a feeling of hope in what became a tragic development. Bergman and his wife were recommended to Hamlisch by film producer Ray Stark, and at this point the Bergmans already had a long-standing relationship with Barbra Streisand, who starred in the film and sang the theme song. When they initially presented the song to Streisand, Bergman suggested that he and his wife could improve it. Before the film was finished, Streisand and the Bergmans crafted a second version of the song, which the singer preferred. Pollack decided to put both songs on the sound track to compare them in the context of the scene. The original version seemed to work better, with its change in rhythm as it moves through three sections. The movement of the melody is enhanced by the text: On the chromatic change, Bergman sets the word color; in the B section, the stress of the words falls when the melody ascends. In 1973 Hamlisch and the Bergmans won the Academy Award for Best Song for "The Way We Were."

Musical Legacy

Bergman's career started rising as Broadway and Hollywood musicals were beginning their decline. His writing style belonged to a new generation of songwriters, whose roots were not set deeply in the Broadway musicals or the New York music scene. Bergman and his wife created a new school of writing lyrics and influenced a younger generation of composers of film music and of musicals.

In 1983 Bergman and his wife wrote an unprecedented three of the five songs that were nominated for an Academy Award for Best Song: "How Do You Keep the Music Playing?" (with Legrand, from the 1982 motion picture *Best Friends*); "It Might Be You" (with Dave Grusin, from the 1982 motion picture *Tootsie*); and "If We Were in Love" (with John Williams, from the 1982 motion picture *Yes, Giorgio*). Over the span of their careers, Bergman and his wife have been nominated for many Academy Awards. Among their main collaborators have been Legrand, Grusin, Hamlisch, Lew Spence, and Henry Mancini.

Bergman was inducted into Songwriters Hall of Fame in 1980, and in 1995 he was awarded an honorary doctorate from Berklee College of Music. In 2007 Bergman and the Berlin Big Band and Radio Orchestra recorded an album, *Lyrically, Alan Bergman*, featuring his and his wife's songs.

Daniela Candillari

Further Reading

Furia, Philip, and Michael Lasser. *America's Songs:. The Stories Behind the Songs of Broadway, Hollywood, and Tin Pan Alley*. New York: Routledge 2006. The book presents some of the most popular songs from 1910 to 1977 and provides a short history of each one. Featured are songs by Alan Bergman.

Hamlisch, Marvin, and Gerald Gardner. *The Way I Was*. New York: Charles Scribner's Sons, 1992. Hamlisch talks about his life and career, and he includes information about his main collaborators, Alan and Marilyn Bergman.

Pohly, Linda. *The Barbra Streisand Companion: A Guide to Her Vocal Style and Repertoire*. Westport, Conn.: Greenwood Press, 2000. A discussion of Streisand's interpretive style of singing, with references to songs by the Bergmans. Includes discography and bibliography.

See also: Fain, Sammy; Hamlisch, Marvin; Legrand, Michel; Mancini, Henry; Mercer, Johnny.

Luciano Berio

Italian classical composer

An important avant-garde and electronic composer, Berio is best known for the quotation, the deconstruction, and the transformation of preexisting musical materials.

Born: October 24, 1925; Imperia, Oneglia, Italy
Died: May 27, 2003; Rome, Italy

Principal works

BALLETS (music): *Linea*, 1974 (for two pianos, vibraphone, and marimba; choreography by Félix Blaska); *Per la dolce memoria di quel giorno*, 1974 (choreography by Maurice Bejart).

CHAMBER WORKS: *Toccata*, 1939 (for two pianos); *Divertimento*, 1946 (for string trio); *Tre pezzi*, 1947 (for three clarinets); *Différences*, 1959 (for flute, clarinet, harp, viola, cello, and tape); *Sincronie*, 1964 (for string quartet); *Memory*, 1970 (for electric piano and electric harpsichord); *Musica leggera*, 1974 (for flute, viola, and cello); *Duetti*, 1983 (thirty-four pieces for two violins); *Accordo*, 1981 (for four groups of wind instruments); *Voci*, 1984 (for viola and instrumental ensemble); *Call*, 1985 (for brass quintet); *Naturale*, 1986 (for viola, tam-tam, and tape); *Ricorrenze*, 1987 (for wind quartet); String Quartet No. 3, 1993 (*Notturno*).

OPERAS (music): *Mimusique No. 2*, 1955 (libretto by Roberto Leydi); *Allez-Hop!*, 1959 (libretto by Italo Calvino); *Esposizione*, 1963 (libretto by Edoardo Sanguineti); *Passaggio*, 1963 (libretto by Sanguineti); Opera, 1970 (libretto by Alban Berg); *Diario immaginario*, 1975 (radio opera for chorus, orchestra, and tape; libretto by Vittorio Sermonti); *Duo (teatro immaginario)*, 1982 (radio opera for baritone, two violins, choir, and orchestra; libretto by Calvino); *La vera storia*, 1982 (libretto by Calvino); *Un re in ascolto*, 1984 (libretto by Calvino); *Outis*, 1996 (libretto by Dario del Corno); *Cronaca del luogo*, 1999 (libretto by Talia Pecker-Berio).

ORCHESTRAL WORKS: *Preludio a una festa marina*, 1944; *Concertino*, 1949; *Nones*, 1954; *Variazioni*, 1954; *Allelujah I*, 1955; *Variazioni "Ein Mädchen oder Weibchen,"* 1956; *Serenata I*, 1957 (for flute and fourteen instruments); *Allelujah II*, 1958; *Sequenza* series, 1958-2002; *Tempi concertati*, 1959; *Quaderni I*, 1959; *Quaderni II*, 1961; *Quaderni III*, 1962; *Chemins I*, 1964; *Chemins II*, 1967; *Chemins III*, 1968; Concerto, 1973 (for two pianos and orchestra); *Still*, 1973; *Eindrücke*, 1974; *Points on the Curve to Find*, 1974; *Chemins IV*, 1975; *Corale on Sequenza VIII*, 1975 (for violin, two horns, and strings); *Il ritorno degli snovidenia*, 1977; *Encore*, 1978; *Chemins V*, 1980; *Fanfara*, 1982; *Requies*, 1985; *Formazioni*, 1987; Concerto II, 1989 (*Echoing Curves*); *Continuo*, 1989; *Festum*, 1989; *Rendering*, 1989; *Alternatim*, 1997 (for clarinet, viola, and orchestra); *SOLO*, 1999 (for trombone and orchestra).

PIANO WORKS: *Wasserklavier*, 1965; *Luftklavier*, 1985; *Feuerklavier*, 1989; *Brin*, 1990; *Leaf*, 1990; Sonata, 2001.

INSTRUMENTAL WORKS: *Gesti*, 1966 (for recorder); *Comma*, 1987 (for clarinet); *Psy*, 1989 (for double bass).

TAPE WORKS: *Mimusique No. 1*, 1953; *Ritratto di città*, 1954 (with Bruno Maderna; for one-track tape); *Mutazioni*, 1955 (for one-track tape); *Perspectives*, 1957 (for two-track tape); *Thema: Omaggio a Joyce*, 1958 (for two-track tape); *Momenti*, 1960 (for four-track tape); *Visage*, 1961 (for two-track tape); *A-Ronne*, 1975 (radio documentary for five actors; based on Edoardo Sanguineti's poem).

VOCAL WORKS: *O bone Jesu*, 1946 (for chorus); *Tre canzoni popolari*, 1947 (for female voice and piano); *Tre liriche greche*, 1948 (for solo voice and piano); *Due pezzi sacri*, 1949 (for two sopranos, piano, two harpsichords, timpani, and bells); *Magnificat*, 1949 (for two sopranos and orchestra); *Opus Number Zoo*, 1951 (for speakers, wind instruments, and French horn; lyrics by Rhoda Levine); *El mar la mar*, 1952 (for two sopranos and instruments; based on texts by Rafael Alberti); *Chamber Music*, 1953 (for female voice, cello, clarinet, and harp; based on James Joyce's poetry); *Circles*, 1960 (for female voice, harp, and percussion; based on texts by E. E. Cummings); *Epifanie*, 1961 (for female voice and orchestra; based on texts by Marcel Proust, James Joyce, Antonio Machado, Claude Simon, Bertolt Brecht, and Edoardo Sanguineti); *Folk Songs*, 1964 (for soprano and seven instruments); *Traces*, 1964 (for soprano, mezzo-soprano, two actors, chorus, and orchestra); *Laborintus II*, 1965 (for voices and orchestra; libretto by Sanguineti); *Rounds*, 1965 (for solo voice and harpsichord); *O King*, 1967 (for solo voice and instruments); *Air*, 1969 (for soprano and orchestra; libretto by Alessandro Striggio); *Questo vuol dire che*, 1969 (for three female voices, small chorus, instruments, and tape); *Sinfonia*, 1969 (for eight solo voices and orchestra); *Agnus*, 1971 (for two female voices, three clarinets, and a drone); *Bewegung*, 1971 (for baritone and orchestra); *E vo'*, 1972 (for soprano and instruments); *Recital I*, 1972 (for solo voice and instruments; libretto by Berio, Andrea Mosetti, and Sanguineti); *Folk Songs*, 1973 (for soprano and orchestra); *Calmo*, 1974 (for soprano and instruments; based on texts by Homer); *Cries of London*, 1974 (for six solo voices); *Chants parallèles*, 1975; *Coro*, 1976 (based on folk texts by Pablo Neruda); *Ofanim*, 1988 (for female voice, children's chorus, instruments, and electronics); *Canticum novissimi testamenti*, 1989 (for voices, four clarinets, and four saxophones).

The Life

Luciano Berio (lew-CHYAH-noh BEH-ree-oh) was born in Oneglia, Italy on October 24, 1925. His father and grandfather were organists, and Berio received both formal and informal music training. Studying piano, Berio performed in chamber settings from the age of nine, and though he began composing in his teens, he remained primarily a pianist until young adulthood. Forced into military service in Italian leader Benito Mussolini's army, Berio injured his hand in an explosion during his military training, ending his career prospects as a pianist.

After the war, Berio returned to study composition at the Milan Conservatory. Accompanying provided a small income for him, and it was while accompanying a voice class that he met Cathy Berberian, an American studying voice in Milan on a Fulbright Fellowship. They were married in 1950, and she was extremely influential on his compositional development, premiering several of his most important works in the 1960's.

After Berio returned from a trip to the United States in 1951, where he studied with Luigi Dallapiccola at the Berkshire Music Festival at Tanglewood, he took on work at RAI, an Italian radio and television network. In 1955, along with Bruno Maderna, he cofounded Studio Fonologia, and he invited important composers such as John Cage to work there. In 1960 Berio returned to the United States to teach at Tanglewood. Later he substituted for Darius Milhaud at Mills College in Oakland, California, and in 1965 he began teaching at the Juilliard School, where he remained until 1972. He was an important teacher, and his students included Louis Andriessen, Steve Reich, and Bernard Rands.

While teaching, Berio also maintained an active traveling schedule, attending premieres around the world. Divorced from Berberian, Berio married an American psychologist, Susan Oyama, in 1965, with whom he had two children. Eventually his busy traveling schedule caused him to stop teaching, and he returned to Italy in 1972. He was the director of IRCAM, the institute for the scientific study of music and sound, in Paris from 1974 to 1980, at the invitation of Pierre Boulez. Berio founded the Tempo Reale studio in Florence in 1987 after he and his third wife, the musicologist Talia Pecker, settled outside Siena. Though he served as the Distinguished Composer in Residence at Harvard University from 1994 until 2000, it was primarily at his Italian home that he composed until his death in 2003.

The Music

Berio actively composed from the 1950's until his death in 2003, and he remained intellectually curious throughout his life. Berio held a lifelong fascination with reinterpretation and transformation, both in individual pieces as well as between pieces. Parts of works reappear in later works, and many works were later revised, reorchestrated, or arranged for different performance mediums. Ideas or themes from electronic works influenced his acoustic ones and vice versa. He composed fourteen *Sequenzas* for solo instruments from 1958 through 2002. For each one he fastidiously studied the physical components and requirements of performance on each instrument. Thus, many embody the extreme possibilities of performance virtuosity.

Early Works. At the Milan Conservatory, Berio was a member of the composition class of Giorgio Federico Ghedini, an Italian composer who proved a major influence on him. Berio studied the works of Igor Stravinsky, Béla Bartók, Arnold Schoenberg, and Sergei Prokofiev, among others, and he experimented with serialism. As was the case for many other young Italian composers, Dallapiccola served as the model for serial composition. After Berio studied with him at Tanglewood, many of his works displayed Dallapiccola's influence. *Chamber Music* is the most well known of these. In the early 1950's, Berio also began to experiment with electronic music, and *Mimusique No. 1* for tape was his first electronic work. However, the three most important stylistic works from the 1950's are *Thema: Omaggio a Joyce* for tape, in which Berio electronically manipulated the words of James Joyce and Cathy Berberian's voice to provide an aural parallel to Joyce's textual world; *Sequenza No. 1* for flute and the first of fourteen *Sequenzas* for solo instruments; and *Différences* for flute, clarinet, harp, cello, and tape, in which Berio manipulated recordings of the instruments to merge the tape with the acoustic instruments rather than juxtaposing the two.

Circles. Written for Berberian in 1960, *Circles* takes its text from three poems by E. E. Cummings. Employing the same compositional techniques used two years earlier in the tape work *Thema: Omaggio a Joyce*, but using only acoustic instruments, Berio scored this for female voice, harp, and two percussionists. The work stands as a testament to Berio's fascination with cycles, symmetry, and intertextuality.

As the detailed performance notes specify, the singer is positioned at the front of the stage for the beginning of the piece, but, as the song cycle progresses, the singer gradually recedes into the ensemble. The vocalist is asked to play various percussion instruments, such as finger cymbals and claves, and the instrumentalists are asked to imitate the voice throughout, blurring the division between the singer and the players. As is found in later Berio works, the text is broken into phonemes that the singer is asked to sing, whisper, or speak. Eventually the line between poetry and music, singer and instrumentalist has been erased as the percussionists sing and the singer is simply a member of the ensemble.

Composed as an *abcb'a'* arch, the musical material is recycled throughout. When the second poem reappears, it is accompanied by fragments from the first song, and musical themes are interwoven. This type of intertextuality is an important aspect of Berio's style, a technique he used throughout his life. For example, the *Sequenzas* were recycled and transformed into another series, *Chemins*, and in his opera *La vera storia*, the text from one act is musically reinterpreted in another.

Sinfonia. Having established himself as an important composer through his work in the 1950's and 1960's, Berio received many commissions in the late 1960's. *Sinfonia* was commissioned by the New York Philharmonic on the occasion of its 125th anniversary, and it was dedicated to its conductor, Leonard Bernstein. The first four movements premiered on October 10, 1968, with the Swingle Singers, the New York Philharmonic, and Berio conducting. It was originally written in four movements, and a fifth movement was added in 1969.

Throughout the five movements, Berio quotes not only text but also music from earlier composers, such as Hector Berlioz, Ludwig van Beethoven, and Gustav Mahler, as well as Berio's contemporaries, such as Pierre Boulez and Karlheinz Stockhausen. The second movement is an earlier work, *O King*, written in 1967 in memory of Martin Luther King, Jr., and using the vowels and consonants from his name. *Sinfonia* is often called the first postmodern work because the most salient features of the piece are its references to preexisting musical sources rather than the resultant harmony or texture. The music of Arnold Schoenberg may be heard with text from the theorist Claude Levi-Strauss, and the singers sometimes seem to comment on the musical references themselves. Whereas Berio engages in textual deconstruction in *Circles* and the tape work *Visage*, here he deconstructs the music, creating not a pastiche or collage so much as a transformation of the

Luciano Berio. (© Christopher Felver/CORBIS)

sonic elements. In doing so, Berio calls into question the definition of an original musical work.

Points on the Curve to Find. With *Sinfonia*, Berio received unusually wide popularity for a contemporary composer. However, many of Berio's works from the 1970's emphasize less his deconstructionist techniques and more his interest in musical process and static harmonic fields. *Points on the Curve to Find* is scored for piano and twenty instruments. The title refers to a geometric curve, and in the work, the piano functions as the curve.

The piece lasts just more than eleven minutes, and the piano part features rapid thirty-second notes and other figures that Berio designates should be played as quickly as possible. The other instruments resonate aspects of the piano's curve, by doubling it in spots, echoing it in others, and frequently passing it back and forth among themselves. The piano part consists entirely of a ten-note musical sequence that cycles throughout. During each cycle, different pairs of the sequence are trilled, so that different harmonic fields are emphasized. What emerges is a constantly evolving, fanciful work, full of frenetic energy and ornamentation. It is often linked to other works from this period, such as *Linea*, for two pianos, vibraphone, and marimba, because of its emphasis on limited pitch material, musical process, and static harmonic fields. Berio remained committed to traditional formal structures, and this work exhibits a remarkable ability to fuse strict compositional methods with traditional dramatic formal shape.

Sequenzas I-XIV. Beginning in 1958 with *Sequenza I* for solo flute, Berio finished his last *Sequenza*, written for cello, in 2002. The fourteen *Sequenzas* provide a rare insight into the wide-ranging compositional interests and styles of the composer over an almost forty-five-year period. Each is intended as a study in what is possible on the instrument, and all require virtuosic performers. For each, Berio fastidiously studied the possibilities for performance. For *Sequenza III* for solo voice, Berio mapped out various resonant spots inside the mouth, and he requires the soloists to perform octave jumps, arpeggios, glissandi, and trills. *Sequenza XII* for bassoon solo requires circular breathing, among other extended techniques. The last cello *Sequenza* has a melancholy quality and folklike pizzicato rhythms.

Musical Legacy

Berio's intellectual curiosity led him in many stylistic directions over his career, but throughout he recognized the theatricality inherent in any musical performance. He sought to blur boundaries, using serialism if it suited the work, but he never prescribed to a specific orthodoxy. Credited with being hugely influential in electronic music, not only because of his work in founding his own electronic studios but also because of his employment of new electronic techniques to musical ends, he also influenced later generations of composers through his refusal to restrict his music to a singular style. Rather than capitalizing on the huge success of *Sinfonia* by continuing to write music that deconstructed the musical canon, he turned to more traditional compositional concerns, such as harmony and economy of musical means. Though he was the Italian representative of the Darmstadt School generation in the late 1950's, he was not part of the political infighting that characterized many composers from that period. He actively collaborated with other composers, and his work will forever be linked with his intellectual contemporaries in other fields, such as Bertolt Brecht, Levi-Strauss, and Umberto Eco.

Mary J. King

Further Reading

Berio, Luciano. *Remembering the Future*. Cambridge, Mass.: Harvard University Press, 2006. This short work provides Berio's insights into his works and the works of other composers.

Osmond-Smith, David. *Berio*. Oxford, England: Oxford University Press, 1991. A thorough overview of Berio's life and works, including a description of his musical language, his use of computers at IRCAM and Tempo Reale, the importance of folk music, and more.

See also: Babbitt, Milton; Barenboim, Daniel; Bartók, Béla; Berg, Alban; Bernstein, Leonard; Boulez, Pierre; Cage, John; Milhaud, Darius; Nono, Luigi; Reich, Steve; Schaeffer, Pierre; Schnittke, Alfred; Stockhausen, Karlheinz; Stravinsky, Igor; Watts, André.

Irving Berlin

Russian American musical-theater composer and lyricist

Composer of fifteen hundred songs, Berlin wrote in many styles—ragtime, swing, waltz, country, and classic Broadway—with an ear attuned to popular melody and lyrics and finding favor with generations of listeners.

Born: May 11, 1888; Mogilyov, Russia (now in Belarus)
Died: September 22, 1989; New York, New York
Also known as: Israel Baline (birth name)

Principal works

MUSICAL THEATER (music and lyrics): *Ziegfeld Follies of 1911*, 1911; *Watch Your Step*, 1914 (libretto by Harry B. Smith); *Stop! Look! Listen!*, 1915 (libretto by Smith); *The Century Girl*, 1916; *Yip, Yip, Yaphank*, 1918; *Ziegfeld Follies of 1919*, 1919; *Ziegfeld Follies of 1920*, 1920; *Music Box Revue of 1921*, 1921; *Music Box Revue of 1922*, 1922; *Music Box Revue of 1923*, 1923; *Music Box Revue of 1924*, 1924; *The Cocoanuts*, 1925 (libretto by George S. Kaufman); *Ziegfeld Follies of 1927*, 1927; *Face the Music*, 1932 (libretto by Moss Hart); *As Thousands Cheer*, 1933 (libretto by Hart); *Louisiana Purchase*, 1940 (libretto by Morrie Ryskind); *This Is the Army*, 1942; *Annie Get Your Gun*, 1946 (libretto by Herbert Fields and Dorothy Fields); *Miss Liberty*, 1949 (libretto by Robert E. Sherwood); *Call Me Madam*, 1950 (libretto by Howard Lindsay and Russell Crouse); *Mr. President*, 1962 (libretto by Lindsay and Crouse).

SONGS (music and lyrics): "Marie from Sunny Italy," 1907; "Alexander's Ragtime Band," 1911; "When I Lost You," 1913; "God Bless America," 1918; "Lazy," 1924; "Always," 1925; "Blue Skies," 1927; "Puttin' on the Ritz," 1929; "How Deep Is the Ocean (How High Is the Sky)," 1932; "Say It Isn't So," 1932; "Maybe It's Because I Love You Too Much," 1933; "Cheek to Cheek," 1935; "Top Hat, White Tie, and Tails," 1935; "I'm Putting All My Eggs in One Basket," 1936; "Let's Face the Music and Dance," 1936; "White Christmas," 1942; "Love and the Weather," 1947.

The Life

The youngest of eight children born to Moses and Leah Lipkin Baline in western Siberia, young Israel moved with his family to America in 1893 when their village was destroyed in a pogrom. Moses was unable to find work as a cantor, so he supported his large family as a kosher meat inspector and teacher. Life was hard in the shadow of the Manhattan Bridge and got worse when Moses died in 1901. Israel dropped out of school, left home, and supported himself as a street performer when he was just thirteen years old. With his innate musical talent, he was hired to be a singing waiter at Chinatown's Pelham Café. When the owner requested an Italian song, eighteen-year-old Israel Baline supplied the lyrics and house pianist Mike Nicholson the music in order to create "Marie from Sunny Italy." While the song was not a success—the lyricist earned thirty-seven cents—it was published and gave the wordsmith a new name: I. Berlin. The young songwriter embraced the Berlin typo and decided that the "I" would become Irving, replacing Israel and his nickname Izzy.

As songwriting clearly did not pay, Berlin returned to being a singing waiter, graduating to Jimmy Kelly's on Union Square in 1908. Publisher Ted Snyder was so impressed by Berlin's parodies of popular songs that in 1909 he signed the performer for twenty-five dollars a week as staff lyricist. Almost immediately, a Berlin/Snyder creation ("She Was a Dear Little Girl") was put into the Broadway musical *The Boys and Betty*. Berlin went from homeless street urchin to professional lyricist in only seven years, evidence of a fierce work ethic that was to serve him for the rest of his life.

After some success in popular music and on Broadway, Berlin had financial stability for the first time in his life. He married Dorothy Goetz in 1912, but she caught typhoid while on their honeymoon in Cuba and died five months after their wedding. Berlin channeled his grief into "When I Lost You," a heartrending ballad that went on to sell two million copies. Berlin was a private man, and this is the only lyric he ever acknowledged to have come from direct personal experience.

Plunging himself into work, Berlin became the

most prolific Broadway composer from 1914 to 1926. He allowed himself to be distracted when he met journalist Ellin Mackay in 1924. Ellin's Catholic father was not going to lose his daughter to a Jewish immigrant, Tin Pan Alley musician—albeit an amazingly successful one—so he shipped his daughter off to Europe. The two lovers were not deterred, however, and eloped on January 4, 1926. Enraged, Mackay cut his daughter out of his will; Berlin responded by signing over to his bride the copyright (and royalties) of his newly minted "Always," a song that made a small fortune. The loving couple had four children.

The 1920's were very good to Berlin personally and professionally, but with the death of his son, the looming Great Depression, and a growing insecurity about this own talent, he became depressed, a condition that would plague him for the rest of his life. It was in evidence much later, in the 1960's, when the relative failure of his last Broadway show, *Mr. President*, and Metro-Goldwyn-Mayer's cancellation of the film *Say It with Music* prompted Berlin to remark, "It was as if I owned a store, and people no longer wanted to buy what I had to sell." After singing "God Bless America" at the White House for prisoners of war returning from Vietnam in 1973, Berlin never made another public appearance. He kept in touch with friends and conducted business affairs by phone and lost his beloved wife Ellin in 1988, after sixty-two years of marriage. Berlin died in his sleep at his home in Beekman Place, New York City, a year later at the age of 101.

The Music

A chronic insomniac, Berlin wrote primarily at night. He set a personal goal of writing at least five songs a week, freely admitting that most were not good, estimating that only one song out of ten would be a success. This relentless motivation to work on his craft resulted in more than eight hundred high-quality songs copyrighted by Berlin. He never learned to read or write music, so he employed music secretaries to write down what he played (or sang to them over the phone).

Early Works. When ragtime was popular, Berlin turned out more than two dozen rags, including "That Mesmerizing Mendelssohn Tune," "Yiddle on Your Fiddle Play Some Rag Time," "That Beautiful Rag," "Everything in America Is Ragtime," and "That Revolutionary Rag." Ironically, his "Alexander's Ragtime Band" is not a rag but a song about ragtime. Nevertheless, with its syncopated rhythms and vernacular syntax, it was completely American in tone and became an international hit. It sold two million copies of sheet music in its first eighteen months, before the age of radio.

Influenced by his mentor and idol, George M. Cohan, Berlin set out to write songs that were accessible, succinct, and conversational in tone. His work added another Cohan dimension in 1918, when patriotism became a major theme in his lyrics. That year he was naturalized as a U.S. citizen,

Irving Berlin. (Library of Congress)

was drafted into the Army, and wrote the Army fund-raiser *Yip, Yip, Yaphank*. In the cast of three hundred servicemen (and one woman), Sergeant Berlin stopped the show every night with "Oh! How I Hate to Get Up in the Morning." During World War II, Berlin wrote a new fund-raiser, *This Is the Army* (for stage and film), which reprised "Oh! How I Hate to Get Up in the Morning" and introduced "I'm Getting Tired So I Can Sleep" and "I Left My Heart at the Stage Door Canteen." (The show's racially integrated cast of military personnel was the first such unit in World War II.) *This Is the Army* raised more than $15 million for the Army Relief Emergency Fund to aid wives and parents of U.S. servicemen.

Music Business. While most songwriters find managing their career to be the extent of their interest in business, Berlin established a music publishing firm, built and managed a theater, was a theatrical producer, and in 1914 helped establish the American Society of Composers, Authors, and Publishers (ASCAP).

From World War I to 1943, Berlin partnered with Saul Bornstein to create and run Irving Berlin, Inc., which published thousands of songs by others, including Buddy DeSylva, Lew Brown, Ray Henderson, and scores from early Disney films. The company was reorganized in 1943 to only publish songs by Berlin; the Berlin catalog was turned over to the Rodgers and Hammerstein Organization by his daughters after his death in 1989.

In 1921 Berlin (in conjunction with producer Sam Harris) built the Music Box Theatre on 45th Street in New York City. Elegant and intimate, this was the first theater built exclusively to showcase revues written by one composer. Even though there were only four editions of the *Music Box Revues*, these lavish, intricately crafted shows put the theater in the black within a year and yielded another collection of Berlin standards: "Say It with Music," "Lady of the Evening," "I'm Looking for Daddy Long Legs," "What'll I Do?," and "Don't Send Me Back to Petrograd." Before 1940 Berlin preferred the revue format over book musicals and revolutionized the form with *Face the Music* and *As Thousands Cheer*. The former introduced "Let's Have Another Cup of Coffee," while the latter showcased "Easter Parade" and three numbers for Ethel Waters: "Harlem on My Mind," "Supper Time," and "Heat Wave."

Berlin was involved as a producer with shows booked into his Music Box Theatre, and he also coproduced some of his own shows. As successful in business as he was in art, he made another fortune in this arena.

In publishing, the standard practice is that the lyricist gets 25 percent, the composer 25 percent, and the publisher 50 percent—so songs sold through Irving Berlin, Inc., collected 100 percent of their sales. He was also the first Hollywood songwriter to get a percentage of a film's gross.

Even though "Blue Skies" was written as a pop song, it soon found its way into the Broadway musical *Betsy* (the rest of the score was by Richard Rodgers and Lorenz Hart) and was sung by Al Jolson in the first sound film, *The Jazz Singer* (1927). Other independent blockbusters include "Lazy," "How Deep Is the Ocean (How High Is the Sky)," "Say It Isn't So," and "Love and the Weather." It had been originally written (but never used) for *Yip, Yip, Yaphank*, but Berlin rewrote "God Bless America" for Kate Smith in 1938. He gave the copyright of the country's "unofficial national anthem" to the Boy Scouts and Girl Scouts of America, who continue to benefit from its royalties ($500,000 in 2004). Celine Dion's recording of "God Bless America" reached number one in 2001.

Hollywood and Broadway. Berlin spent the bulk of the 1930's and 1940's in Hollywood, where "White Christmas" won the Academy Award. Bing Crosby's original recording of "White Christmas" became the best-selling single in history, and, encompassing all versions of the song, it has sold more than one hundred million units. Other standards written for the silver screen include "Puttin' on the Ritz," "Maybe It's Because I Love You Too Much," "Top Hat, White Tie, and Tails," "Cheek to Cheek," and "Let's Face the Music and Dance." Responding to the introduction of the integrated book Broadway musical, Berlin wrote *Louisiana Purchase*, *Annie Get Your Gun*, *Miss Liberty*, *Call Me Madam*, and *Mr. President*. Demonstrating that he could write for character and story, Berlin moved past Tin Pan Alley and proved he belonged in the golden age of American musical theater. Even though some critics were unimpressed with the production, *Annie Get Your Gun* surprised even the most dedicated of Berlin fans. Almost every song became a classic, and "There's No Business Like Show Business" is now the unofficial anthem of show business. Averaging 450 productions annually in the United States and Canada, the musical enjoyed a rousing Broadway revival in 1999 (with an altered book).

For a composer who worked hard to make a song sound simple, once in a while Berlin wrote a quodlibet or "double" song. "Play a Simple Melody" was his first polyphonic duet in which two melodies are introduced in separate stanzas, and then are sung together. Other counterpoint songs include "You're Just in Love," "Empty Pockets Filled with Love," and "An Old Fashioned Wedding," written for the 1966 Lincoln Center revival of *Annie Get Your Gun*. Berlin continued to copyright new songs until 1987, two years before his death.

Musical Legacy

The songwriter who personified Tin Pan Alley pop songs, helped define the Broadway musical and revue, and gave eighteen Hollywood film musicals many classic songs could not read or write music, could play in only one key at the piano, and yet knew the strength of his lyrics was appealing to emotions rather than intellect. In his twenty-one Broadway scores (books and revues), Berlin set out not to revolutionize the Broadway musical but to continue the trend started by Cohan, moving it away from its European roots and embracing the musical melting pot that was New York. Nearly three hundred of his songs—from Tin Pan Alley, Broadway, and Hollywood—made the Top 10 on the pop charts. The Berlin catalog earned seven million dollars in royalties in 2004. His songs have pleased the public for decades.

Showered with awards, Berlin received the Congressional Medal of Honor in 1954, a Grammy Lifetime Achievement Award in 1968, and the Medal of Freedom in 1977. Composer Jerome Kern commented that Berlin

> honestly absorbs the vibrations emanating from the people, manners, and life of his time and, in turn, gives these impressions back to the world—simplified, clarified, glorified. In short . . . Irving Berlin has no *place* in American music, he *is* American music.

Bud Coleman

Further Reading

Barrett, Mary Ellin Berlin. *Irving Berlin: A Daughter's Memoir*. New York: Simon & Schuster, 1994. Berlin's oldest child reveals her father's doubts, depressions, and nervous breakdowns, as well as celebrating the artist in him.

Berlin, Irving. *The Complete Lyrics of Irving Berlin*. Edited by Robert Kimball and Linda Emmet. New York: Alfred A. Knopf, 2001. Contains lyrics to twelve hundred Berlin songs written over eighty years, including four hundred songs never before published.

Gottlieb, Robert, and Robert Kimball. *Reading Lyrics*. New York: Pantheon Books, 2000. Brief appraisal of Berlin's career; includes lyrics to thirty-nine of his songs.

Hill, Tony L. "Irving Berlin." In *American Song Lyricists, 1920-1960*. Vol. 265 in *Dictionary of Literary Biography*, edited by Philip Furia. Detroit: Gale, 2002. Succinct chapter on Berlin the composer, lyricist, and businessman.

Hischak, Thomas S. *The American Musical Film Song Encyclopedia*. Westport, Conn.: Greenwood Press, 1999. Fifty-six of Berlin's songs are briefly described, including who originally sang them, which film they appeared in, and who subsequently recorded the song.

_____. "As Thousands Cheered: Irving Berlin." *Word Crazy: Broadway Lyricists from Cohan to Sondheim*. New York: Praeger, 1991. Concise chapter on Berlin the lyricist.

Leopold, David. *Irving Berlin's Show Business*. New York: Harry N. Abrams, 2005. Explores Berlin's influence on American popular culture.

Wilder, Alec. *American Popular Song: The Great Innovators, 1900-1950*. Edited by James T. Maher. New York: Oxford University Press, 1972. Thoroughly analyzes Berlin's work as a composer. Marveling at Berlin's endless inventiveness and lack of ego, Wilder argues that Berlin always put the integrity of the song first (its mood, its idea, its sound) rather than making his output recognizable by stylistic conformity.

See also: Arlen, Harold; Armstrong, Louis; Burke, Johnny; Cohan, George M.; Crosby, Bing; Fields, Dorothy; Fitzgerald, Ella; Goodman, Benny; Grappelli, Stéphane; Guthrie, Woody; Hammerstein, Oscar, II; Hart, Lorenz;

Henderson, Fletcher; Herbert, Victor; Kern, Jerome; Kreisler, Fritz; Lee, Peggy; Lerner, Alan Jay; Mercer, Johnny; Merman, Ethel; Newman, Alfred; Peterson, Oscar; Porter, Cole; Rodgers, Richard; Ronstadt, Linda; Smith, Kate; Steiner, Max; Tiomkin, Dimitri; Vaughan, Sarah; Whiteman, Paul; Williams, Mary Lou.

Elmer Bernstein

American film-score and musical-theater composer

One of Hollywood's most prolific and versatile composers, Bernstein wrote music for more than two hundred film and television productions, pioneering the use of jazz and electronic music.

Born: April 4, 1922; New York, New York
Died: August 18, 2004; Ojai, California

Principal works

FILM SCORES: *Saturday's Hero*, 1951; *Boots Malone*, 1952; *Sudden Fear*, 1952; *Cat-Women of the Moon*, 1953; *Robot Monster*, 1953; *The Man with the Golden Arm*, 1955; *The Ten Commandments*, 1956; *The Magnificent Seven*, 1960; *To Kill a Mockingbird*, 1962; *The Making of the President 1960*, 1963; *The Hallelujah Trail*, 1965; *Hawaii*, 1966; *Thoroughly Modern Millie*, 1967; *I Love You, Alice B. Toklas!*, 1968; *True Grit*, 1969; *Blind Terror*, 1971; *Cahill U.S. Marshal*, 1973; *From Noon Till Three*, 1976; *Animal House*, 1978; *Little Women*, 1978; *Airplane!*, 1980; *An American Werewolf in London*, 1981; *Stripes*, 1981; *Ghost Busters*, 1984; *¡Three Amigos!*, 1986; *The Good Mother*, 1988; *My Left Foot*, 1989; *The Grifters*, 1990; *Cape Fear*, 1991; *Rambling Rose*, 1991; *The Age of Innocence*, 1993; *Lost in Yonkers*, 1993; *Devil in a Blue Dress*, 1995; *The Rainmaker*, 1997; *Wild Wild West*, 1999; *Far from Heaven*, 2002; *The Rising of the Moon*, 2002.

MUSICAL THEATER: *How Now, Dow Jones*, 1967 (lyrics by Carol Leigh; libretto by Max Shulman); *Merlin*, 1983 (lyrics by Don Black; libretto by Richard Levinson).

The Life

Elmer Bernstein (BURN-steen) received encouragement from his family to pursue the arts. He performed as a professional dancer, won prizes for painting, and received a piano scholarship at age twelve. He represented the United States as a pianist and conductor from 1939 through 1950, performing in concerts throughout the world. During World War II, he did arrangements for American folk music and wrote dramatic scores for military-broadcast radio shows. This led to writing music for two United Nations radio shows, and Bernstein's compositions drew the interest of Sidney Buchman, a vice president at Columbia Pictures.

Buchman hired him to compose scores for *Saturday's Hero* and *Boots Malone*. His score for *Sudden Fear* in 1952 drew even more attention. Bernstein's career stalled, however, during the blacklisting of Hollywood celebrities by the supporters of U.S. Senator Joseph McCarthy, because Bernstein was identified with some left-wing causes. Consequently, Bernstein found himself reduced to scoring low-budget science-fiction films, although he set new trends in this capacity with his use of electronic music. Hired to compose dance music for Cecil B. DeMille's blockbuster *The Ten Commandments*, he ended up scoring the entire motion picture and went on to an award-winning career. He died of cancer in 2004.

The Music

The amazing variety of Bernstein's motion-picture scores makes him one of the most recognized composers of Hollywood's golden age. Nominated for fourteen Academy Awards plus many Emmy, Tony, Golden Globe, Western Heritage, and Grammy Awards, he had one of the longest careers of any composer in Hollywood history. He also helped establish many musical trends in film as he moved from one form to another. He was not related to composer Leonard Bernstein, but the two became known as "Bernstein West" (Elmer) and "Bernstein East" (Leonard).

Cat-Women of the Moon. Because he was swept up in the anti-Communist witch hunts of the early 1950's, Bernstein was blacklisted from scoring major motion pictures, and he was forced to find work on such films as this 3-D science-fiction adventure released in 1953. Despite the film's plot holes, the bad acting, and the low-budget production values, Bernstein's score generally gets high marks from critics. It helped meld science fiction with electronic music.

The Man with the Golden Arm. Once again, Bernstein's composing set a trend with this all-jazz score (utilized by other composers in many films that followed and in such television series in the late 1950's and early 1960's as *Peter Gunn*). The film, in which Frank Sinatra plays a heroin addict, received an Academy Award nomination in 1955 for Best Original Score.

The Ten Commandments. This score brought Bernstein back to the top rank of film composers. The 1956 epic was the last film directed by DeMille, who sought a composer who could achieve the Richard Wagner opera concept of blending action, setting, and dialogue through the background music. He hired Bernstein, who composed symphonic themes for each of the biblical events depicted.

The Magnificent Seven. If Bernstein had scored no other film, this 1960 Western would have assured his fame. One of the most recognized scores in cinema, it ranks in familiarity with the Lone Ranger, a popular radio and television cowboy, and his accompanying music, Gioacchino Rossini's overture to his opera *William Tell* (1829). For *The Magnificent Seven*, Bernstein was nominated for an Academy Award, and he won the Western Heritage Award for Best Original Score. The music was used in commercials for Marlboro cigarettes and Victoria Bitter beer, in three film sequels, and in a television series, further cementing its place in popular culture. Bernstein also scored the 1986 parody of this film, *¡Three Amigos!* He went on to score other popular Westerns, including many starring John Wayne, but he never eclipsed the popularity of the music from *The Magnificent Seven*.

Thoroughly Modern Millie. This 1967 musical comedy brought Bernstein an Academy Award for Best Original Score, even though he did not write all the music. This musical comedy featured tunes from other sources, such as *Jazz Baby* (1919), which had been acquired and adapted by General Mills to advertise the Wheaties breakfast cereal. However, the original scoring for the comedic and dramatic events of the story, ranging from love stories to white slavery kidnappings, is what earned the award.

Animal House. This raucous 1978 National Lampoon comedy gave Bernstein another challenge, composing musical themes reflecting the time in which the story is set (1962). One piece of background music begins like "A Summer Place" (the theme of the 1952 film of the same name), but then it goes off into a comedic spree. Bernstein used other sly musical tricks to punch up the goofiness that made the picture so popular.

Cape Fear. When the composer learned that director Martin Scorsese was going to do a remake of *Cape Fear*, Bernstein wanted to adapt Bernard Herrmann's score from the 1962 original for the 1991 version. Bernstein estimated that he wrote about six minutes of original music in this suspense thriller; the rest was a rearrangement of Herrmann's music to fit the revised script.

Musical Legacy

One of Hollywood's most innovative composers, Bernstein utilized all styles of music in his work, and his innovations often changed the direction of other composers' music. Even his scoring of low-budget science-fiction films helped pave the way for the genre's electronic-style music, just as his work in *Man with the Golden Arm* did for jazz scores. *The Magnificent Seven* score is one of the most famous Western films scores. Bernstein's half-century career, among Hollywood's longest running, covered many forms of music, ranging from the ballet music in the 1954 stage production of *Peter Pan* to the score for the 2002 drama of social taboos of the 1950's, *Far from Heaven*. That was his last film score, and it was nominated for the Academy Award and the Golden Globe for Best Original Score.

Paul Dellinger

Further Reading

Bernstein, Elmer. *Elmer Bernstein: An American Film Institute Seminar on His Work*. Glen Rock, N.J.: Microfilming Corporation of America, 1977. Presents views from various scholars of film music on Bernstein's work and his influence on cinema.

Faulner, Robert R. *Music on Demand: Composers and Careers in the Hollywood Film Industry*. Piscataway, N.J.: Transaction, 2003. An overview of the careers of various composers for motion pictures, including a discussion of Bernstein.

McGilligan, Patrick, and Paul Buhle. *Tender Comrades: A Backstory of the Hollywood Blacklist.* New York: St. Martin's Press, 1999. Collection of interviews with Hollywood figures affected by the proceedings of the 1947 House Un-American Activities Committee and its blacklist, which for a time included Bernstein.

Morgan, David. *Knowing the Score: Film Composers Talk About the Art, Craft, Blood, Sweat, and Tears of Writing for Cinema.* New York: HarperEntertainment, 2000. Interviews and discussions with well-known film composers, including Bernstein.

See also: Andrews, Dame Julie; Diamond, Neil; Green, Adolph, and Betty Comden; Grusin, Dave; Herrmann, Bernard; Mancini, Henry; Sinatra, Frank; Waxman, Franz.

Leonard Bernstein

American classical, musical-theater, and film-score composer and conductor

Conductor, composer, pianist, and educator, Bernstein was passionate about sharing his enthusiasm about music with all ages. He discussed music in terms people could easily understand and encouraged in young people an appreciation of music with a series of well-regarded televised concerts.

Born: August 25, 1918; Lawrence, Massachusetts
Died: October 14, 1990; New York, New York
Also known as: Lenny Bernstein

Principal works

BALLETS (music): *Fancy Free*, 1944; *Facsimile*, 1946; *Dybbuk*, 1974.

CHORAL WORKS: *Chichester Psalms*, 1965 (for boy soloist, chorus, and orchestra); *Songfest*, 1977 (for six singers and orchestra).

FILM SCORES: *On the Waterfront*, 1954.

MUSICAL THEATER (music): *On the Town*, 1944 (lyrics by Betty Comden and Adolph Green); *Peter Pan*, 1950 (music and lyrics by Bernstein; based on James M. Barrie's play); *Wonderful Town*, 1953 (lyrics by Comden and Green); *The Lark*, 1955 (incidental music; libretto by Lillian Hellman; based on Jean Anouilh's play *L'Alouette*); *West Side Story*, 1957 (lyrics by Stephen Sondheim; libretto by Arthur Laurents); *The Firstborn*, 1958 (incidental music; based on Christopher Fry's play); *Mass*, 1971 (lyrics by Bernstein and Stephen Schwartz); *1600 Pennsylvania Avenue*, 1976 (lyrics and libretto by Alan Jay Lerner); *The Madwoman of Central Park West*, 1979 (lyrics by various composers; libretto by Phyllis Newman and Laurents).

OPERAS (music): *Trouble in Tahiti*, 1952 (libretto by Bernstein); *Candide*, 1956 (lyrics by Richard Wilbur, John La Touche, Bernstein, Dorothy Parker, and Lillian Hellman; libretto by Hellman); *A Quiet Place*, 1983 (libretto by Stephen Wadsworth).

ORCHESTRAL WORKS: Symphony No. 1, 1942 (*Jeremiah*); Symphony No. 2, 1949 (*The Age of Anxiety*; based on W. H. Auden's poem); *Prelude, Fugue and Riffs*, 1949 (for solo clarinet and jazz ensemble); *Serenade*, 1954 (based on Plato's *Symposium*); *Fanfare I*, 1961; *Fanfare II*, 1961; Symphony No. 3, 1963 (*Kaddish*); *Slava! (A Political Overture)*, 1977; *Divertimento*, 1980; *A Musical Toast*, 1980; *Halil*, 1981; *Jubilee Games*, 1986; Concerto for Orchestra, 1989 (revision of *Jubilee Games*).

WRITINGS OF INTEREST: *The Joy of Music*, 1959; *Young People's Concerts*, 1962; *The Infinite Variety of Music*, 1966; *The Unanswered Question*, 1976.

The Life

On August 25, 1918, Louis Bernstein (BURN-stin) was born into a family of Russian immigrants. His parents, Samuel and Jesse Resnick Bernstein, had fled the anti-Semitism and pogroms that threatened Jews in Russia. One of three children, Bernstein was raised in a fervently religious, not notably musical family, although the family participated in the singing, clapping, and dancing that were part of the worship ceremonies at their synagogue. Bernstein, whose parents always called him Lenny, changed his name to Leonard at age sixteen.

His first exposure to music was accidental. His Aunt Clara was moving and needed a place to store her piano. The Bernsteins let her leave it with them.

Intrigued by this instrument, Bernstein immediately began to play it and soon got his parents to arrange piano lessons.

Although fascinated by music, Bernstein was expected to work at the family wholesale beauty-supply business when he finished high school rather than seek a career in music, which his father strongly opposed. By this time, the family had moved from Lawrence, Massachusetts, where Bernstein had been born, to Boston, where he entered the prestigious Boston Latin School. Upon graduation, he qualified for entrance to Harvard University, from which he graduated in 1939. He then went to Philadelphia, where he studied music with Frederick "Fritz" Reiner at the Curtis Institute of Music.

In 1940 Bernstein attended the Berkshire Music Festival at Tanglewood in Massachusetts, where he first met and favorably impressed legendary conductor Serge Koussevitzky, who recommended to music director Artur Rodzinski that he offer the young man a then-vacant post as assistant conductor for the New York Philharmonic Orchestra, an awesome position for one not yet twenty-five.

On November 14, 1943, conductor Bruno Walter, felled by influenza, was unable to conduct the orchestra, so Bernstein was brought in on short notice. Trembling from stage fright, Bernstein soon transfixed the audience with the virtuosity of his performance. The following day, a front-page account in *The New York Times* heaped lavish praise on his conducting. Such approbation led to Bernstein's receiving invitations from practically every major symphony orchestra in the United States to be guest conductor.

In 1957 Bernstein was appointed co-conductor with Dimitri Mitropoulos of the New York Philharmonic Orchestra; in 1958 he became its first full-fledged American conductor. He remained in this position until 1969, when, to the dismay of many, he resigned to devote more time to composing and engaging in work that would introduce young people to music. Bernstein remained fully engaged in musical activities for the rest of his life, conducting a concert at Tanglewood in August, 1990, just two

Leonard Bernstein. (AP/Wide World Photos)

months before he died in New York City on October 14.

The Music

Few musicians in the twentieth century possessed the versatility and enthusiasm that characterized Bernstein. An outstanding orchestral conductor, he was also a gifted and multifaceted composer, a pianist who sometimes played the piano portions in works he was conducting, and a musical educator who taught at such institutions as Harvard and Brandeis and wrote and performed for general audiences. Bernstein sought passionately to awaken in young people an appreciation for music and teach them the benefits of participating in and understanding it. Not only did he write books and compose musical pieces specifically directed at young people, but he also spent a great deal of time organizing and conducting a series of young people's concerts.

The Conductor. Bernstein started at the bottom rung of the musical ladder: as assistant conductor of the New York Philharmonic Orchestra, though the job had more to do with paperwork and organizational skills than with music making. Nevertheless, Bernstein persevered, realizing that the position could lead to the creative work he fervently yearned to do.

As an assistant, Bernstein knew that he could be called upon to fill in for the conductor on short notice. He took that responsibility seriously, renting an apartment directly above the concert hall so that he could be available almost instantly were he called upon to fill in for a scheduled conductor. He studied the scores that were slated for performance and went so far as to buy himself a tuxedo, prescribed conductor attire.

Finally, in November, 1943, twenty-five-year-old Leonard Bernstein was called upon to replace an ailing Bruno Walter in an intricate program at Carnegie Hall. He had less than twenty-four hours' notice.

Although Walter's special performance was to be broadcast all over the United States, there was not enough time for his replacement to rehearse the program. A nervous Bernstein was backstage, trembling and perspiring, when the audience was told that he was to replace the celebrated Walter.

Instead of being discouraged when the audience groaned, Bernstein was energized. Coming on stage determined to win the audience's adulation, he proceeded to do so. That performance established Bernstein as an outstanding talent and led to his being invited by almost every major orchestra in the United States to guest-conduct.

Despite his initial success, it was not until 1958, fifteen years later, that Bernstein was named musical director of the New York Philharmonic Orchestra, where he served as conductor until 1969, when he resigned to devote his energies to proselytizing for music among a broad range of audiences.

As conductor of the New York Philharmonic, Bernstein introduced new and imaginative concert programs to audiences. He catered to popular tastes, often to the dismay of more conservative concertgoers, but by doing so he attracted vast new audiences. He became the internationally acknowledged specialist on Gustav Mahler, bringing Mahler's major works before American audiences and reviving enthusiasm for his music all over the world.

The Composer. When he was just twenty-six, Leonard Bernstein wrote *On the Town*, his earliest musical-theater piece. He followed it with *Wonderful Town* in 1953 and *Candide* in 1956, which he revised in 1973. His first resounding hit, however, a Broadway production more successful than *Wonderful Town*, was his redaction of William Shakespeare's *Romeo and Juliet*, which Bernstein moved from Shakespeare's Verona, Italy, to the streets of New York, where the star-crossed lovers are not from noble families but involved with opposing street gangs.

West Side Story was remarkable for its ability to intermingle a modern musical genre such as jazz with serious opera and to deal simultaneously with such contrasting emotions as hatred and love. More than any other Bernstein production, this musical demonstrated how entertaining and moving such a marriage can be.

Bernstein's religious roots are found in many of his compositions, most notably in his Symphony No. 3 (titled *Kaddish*), the *Chichester Psalms*, and *Mass*. He also incorporated ballet into many of his compositions, including *Fancy Free*, *West Side Story*, and *Facsimile*. His incidental music for the film of *Peter Pan* (1953), which was made after Bernstein's stage production of the J. M. Barrie play, also capitalized on his understanding of dance.

His technical knowledge of opera is easily discernible in his short operas *Trouble in Tahiti* and *A Quiet Place*. Among his film scores, the incidental music for *Peter Pan* and the score for *On the Waterfront* are the most celebrated and reflect the scope of his musical knowledge.

The Performer and Educator. Bernstein dazzled audiences with his ability to perform in some of the concerts he conducted, leaving the podium to position himself at the keyboard and play piano in the work he was conducting. Although he is better known as a conductor, his performances were impressive. From the beginning of his musical career, however, Bernstein was most committed to sharing with others his enchantment with music. From the day he first struck the keys of his Aunt Clara's piano, this enchantment became a integral part of his being.

After he established himself as a notable in musical circles, Bernstein worked actively to spread his enthusiasm to diverse audiences of all ages. He was especially concerned with young people and reached out to them in seminars at Brandeis University from 1952 until 1957.

During this period, while still teaching at Tanglewood, he was preparing material for television programs he began offering in the mid-1950's and gathering material for his 1959 book, *Joy of Music*, which was directed at lay people. His liveliness and ability to discuss music in terms they could easily understand appealed to huge audiences, particularly in the Young People's Concerts he conducted around the country. A book that grew out of his television presentations, *The Infinite Variety of Music*, followed in 1966. In 1973 Bernstein delivered six Norton Lectures at Harvard University, which were gathered in a volume, *The Unanswered Question*, published in 1976.

Musical Legacy

Leonard Bernstein almost single-handedly democratized music in ways that increased its public acceptance. His early association with Koussevitzky, who brought music to the masses through the famed Boston Pops Concerts, made Bernstein realize the value of involving as many people as possible in musical adventures. Bernstein will probably be best remembered for his humanity and for his ability to reach audiences of every age. His musical compositions will also be long remembered for their versatility and breadth of impact, and his musical theater—particularly the timeless *West Side Story*—will endear him to young audiences always.

R. Baird Shuman

Further Reading

Burton, Humphrey. *Leonard Bernstein*. New York: Doubleday, 1994. Comprehensive study of Bernstein with valuable information gleaned from extended interviews with family and friends.

Ewen, David. *Leonard Bernstein*. London: W. H. Allen, 1967. Early consideration of Bernstein, his work, and his contributions to music.

Myers, Paul. *Leonard Bernstein*. London: Phaidon Press, 1998. Focuses on how he democratized music by adapting it for the masses.

Peress, Maurice. *Dvořák to Duke Ellington: A Conductor Explores America's Music and Its African American Roots*. New York: Oxford University Press, 2004. Chapter 9 offers a brief biographical sketch of Bernstein; chapter 14 provides a fifteen-page analysis of Bernstein's *Mass*.

Peyser, Joan. *Bernstein: A Biography*. Rev. and updated ed. New York: *Billboard* Books, 1998. Interesting psychological insights into Bernstein's relationship with his father who initially opposed his career in music.

Venezia, Mike. *Leonard Bernstein*. New York: Children's Press, 1997. This book, with pleasant illustrations, is directed toward young readers. Despite some unfortunate inaccuracies, it provides a readable starting point for youths unfamiliar with Bernstein and his work.

See also: Anderson, Leroy; Berio, Luciano; Bernstein, Elmer; Boulanger, Nadia; Copland, Aaron; Elliot, Cass; Gould, Glenn; Green, Adolph, and Betty Comden; Ives, Charles; Koussevitzky, Serge; Lerner, Alan Jay; Ma, Yo-Yo; McPartland, Marian; Mahler, Gustav; Messiaen, Olivier; Nielsen, Carl; Previn, Sir André; Rampal, Jean-Pierre; Rota, Nino; Shaw, Artie; Sondheim, Stephen; Stern, Isaac; Thomas, Michael Tilson; Tippett, Sir Michael; Watts, André; Weill, Kurt; Willson, Meredith.

Chuck Berry

American singer, guitarist, and songwriter

Berry is an early architect of the rock-and-roll sound. To the three-chord Delta blues on which he grew up, he ingeniously added the drive, rhythm, and spirit that have come to define rock and roll.

Born: October 18, 1926; St. Louis, Missouri
Also known as: Charles Edward Anderson Berry (birth name)

Principal recordings

ALBUMS: *After School Session*, 1958; *One Dozen Berrys*, 1958; *St. Louis to Liverpool*, 1964; *Chuck*

Berry in London, 1965; *From St. Louis to Frisco*, 1968; *San Francisco Dues*, 1971; *Bio*, 1973; *Chuck Berry '75*, 1975; *Rockit*, 1979.

WRITINGS OF INTEREST: *Chuck Berry: The Autobiography*, 1987.

The Life

Charles Edward Anderson Berry (BEH-ree) grew up in St. Louis, Missouri, spending most of his formative years attending school during the day and in his spare time working in his father's carpentry business. While still in junior high he developed a liking for the blues, eventually performing a racy but well-received version of Jay McShann's "Confessin' the Blues" for his classmates at a school assembly. Legend has it that from this point he was hooked on performing and quickly learned the ba-

Chuck Berry. (AP/Wide World Photos)

sic guitar chords and licks that would later propel him to international stardom.

Berry embarked on a long history of run-ins with authority when he was arrested and jailed for armed robbery while still a teenager. He served a three-year sentence, got married, and started a family within a year after his release.

In 1952 a St. Louis pianist invited Berry to perform at a New Year's Eve gig at a local nightspot, the Cosmopolitan Club. The gig led to a three-year stint at the popular St. Louis Club, which attracted hundreds of people excited to see Berry perform his unique hybrid of high-energy rhythm-and-blues and onstage antics such as the notorious "duck walk."

In 1955 Berry traveled to Chicago to watch his idol Muddy Waters perform. After the show, Berry asked Waters for advice on how to further his professional career. Waters told Berry to arrange an audition with Leonard and Phil Chess of the famous Chess Records. Impressed by Berry's youthful, original sound, the Chess brothers later that year released Berry's first hit, "Maybellene." By 1961 he had amassed ten more Top 10 hits and become one of the most popular and influential guitarists in rock and roll.

At the height of his popularity, Berry ran into legal trouble. Convicted in 1962 of taking an underage girl across state lines for immoral purposes under a statute known as the Mann Act, he spent the better part of 1962 and 1963 in prison in Springfield, Missouri. Berry publicly denied his incarceration for years. However, later he acknowledged it in his autobiography and claimed that he wrote some of his most memorable hits, including "Nadine" and "No Particular Place to Go," behind bars.

When Berry left prison and resumed his musical career, he was amused to find that younger artists were recording successful covers of his songs. Several American acts released Chuck Berry compositions in the early 1960's, earning him enormous recognition and lucrative songwriting royalties. During the British invasion of 1964 through 1967, major artists such as the Rolling Stones and the Beatles paid homage to their favorite American rock-and-roll artist by covering many of Berry's hits.

Berry continued to perform actively throughout the 1960's, 1970's, and 1980's. He had several hit albums during this period, and a number-one single,

"My Ding-a-Ling," in 1972. *Hail, Hail Rock 'n' Roll*, a documentary about his life and legacy, was released in 1987.

The Music

Chuck Berry's songs are characterized by a simple but relentlessly driving three-chord structure and insightful, witty lyrics. He developed his unique style by emulating the techniques of great Chicago bluesmen such as Howlin' Wolf and Muddy Waters, but substituting their woeful, ponderous approach with danceable, upbeat rhythms. Berry played the juke joints of St. Louis for nearly a decade for mere dollars a night honing the signature sound that the world would soon know as rock and roll.

"Maybellene." The first single Berry recorded for Chess Records in July, 1955, "Maybellene" was originally a country-flavored number entitled "Ida Red." The Chess brothers suggested the title change, along with a few minor alterations in instrumentation, and a rock-and-roll classic was born. The song laments the actions of an unfaithful lover, a theme that proved to be a staple for Berry throughout his career. A stripped-down but infectiously propulsive rhythm also defines the track.

"Roll Over, Beethoven!" This song, another signature Berry classic released by Chess in June, 1956, both commemorates and lampoons classical music. Initially its lyrics seem to deride the music of such sacred cows as Peter Ilich Tchaikovsky and Ludwig van Beethoven as hopelessly stuffy and obsolete, but a closer listening reveals that the song's incisive lyrics acknowledge the indisputable debt that rock and roll and other contemporary genres of music— including modern jazz and pop—owe to traditional classical music. This fresh and provocative message in the confines of a three-chord rock song makes "Roll Over, Beethoven!" an unforgettable standard.

"School Days (Ring! Ring! Goes the Bell)." When it comes to Berry's songwriting, his obvious strength is an uncanny ability to connect with his audience. Recognizing and commiserating with teens with such humor and verve as Berry does in "School Days (Ring! Ring! Goes the Bell)" made this tune one of his biggest early hits. Released in March, 1957, it depicts the typical day of high school as a bothersome, yet somehow worthwhile

series of obstacles. Its engaging rhythm and stellar guitar work contribute to its appeal.

"Sweet Little Sixteen." Unlike "Maybellene," "Sweet Little Sixteen" (released in January, 1958) presents a playful, tender, and at times rollicking view of young women. The heroine of its tongue-in-cheek lyrics worships two things above all else: rock-and-roll music and rock-and-roll musicians. The song is personal and anthemic, upbeat and tender, and one of the first of Berry's hits to appeal directly to the concerns of his target audience: American teenagers.

"Johnny B. Goode." Deemed by critics and musicians the world over as Berry's masterpiece, "Johnny B. Goode," released in April, 1958, with its memorable and often imitated opening guitar riff, is one of the most widely recognized rock-and-roll tunes ever written. Lyrically, the song narrates the tale of a young boy—implicitly modeled after Berry—whose talent for music brings him fame and fortune. Catchy and ebullient, "Johnny B. Goode" can be called a rock-and-roll classic.

"Almost Grown." Similar to "School Days," "Almost Grown" directs Berry's playful lyrics at a different teenage nemesis: parents. More than a one-dimensional rant against parental authority, the song depicts adulthood as a time of hope and promise.

"C'est la Vie." Although it may not have been intended as a sequel to "Almost Grown," "C'est la Vie" provides an affirmative view of the young adult world that is alluded to but never reached in "Almost Grown." In the song's endearing narrative, "Pierre" and his "mademoiselle" marry at a young age but, to the surprise of everyone, go on to lead an exceptionally happy married life. Granted, the lifestyle they pursue is fueled by a rock and jazz sound track, but Berry's lyrics suggest that the rock-and-roll generation can thrive and positively reshape tomorrow's world.

Musical Legacy

Fittingly, in 1986, Berry was one of the first musicians to be inducted into the Rock and Roll Hall of Fame. The unique shuffle rhythm and guitar hooks that characterize "Johnny B. Goode" and "Sweet Little Sixteen" made them some of the most popular rock-and-roll songs in history. Berry's innovative musicianship, lighthearted lyrics, and irresistible showmanship make him a giant of twentieth century pop. Although Berry's disdain for authority led him to several skirmishes with the law, this rebellious spirit enlivens his rock-and-roll lyrics. Echoes of his guitar style can be heard in the work of Eric Clapton, George Thorogood, Albert Lee, and scores of other guitarists. The vitality evoked in his lyrics is present in the songs of artists as diverse as the Beach Boys, the Beatles, the Clash, the Sex Pistols, and Green Day. Even today those who pick up a guitar to try their hand at rock and roll undoubtedly want to master Berry's arsenal of licks.

Gregory D. Horn

Further Reading

Berry, Chuck. *Chuck Berry: The Autobiography*. London: Faber & Faber, 2001. Filled with interesting anecdotes and facts about Chuck Berry's life—professional and otherwise—this book remains a primary source.

Collis, John. *Chuck Berry: The Biography (Illustrated)*. London: Aurum Press, 2002. Biography has lots of photographs and provides an informative and unbiased account of the major events of his musical career.

DeWitt, Howard. *Chuck Berry: Rock 'n' Roll Music*. 2d ed. Ann Arbor, Mich.: Pierian Press, 1985. A straightforward, readable biography of Berry, concentrating primarily on his musical career.

Pegg, Bruce. *Brown-Eyed Handsome Man: The Life and Hard Times of Chuck Berry*. London: Routledge, 2002. An unflinching and sometimes less-than-flattering portrait of Berry, this focuses primarily on the more unfortunate incidents—financial, social, and otherwise—that Berry experienced throughout his checkered career.

Ward, Ed, Geoffrey Stokes, and Ken Tucker. *Rock of Ages: The Rolling Stone History of Rock and Roll*. New York: Summit Books, 1986. Includes an extensive analysis of Berry's influence on the early development of the genre.

See also: Blackwell, Otis; Clapton, Eric; Diddley, Bo; Dixon, Willie; Domino, Fats; Eddy, Duane; Garcia, Jerry; Howlin' Wolf; Jagger, Sir Mick; James, Etta; Jett, Joan; Jordan, Louis; Lennon, John; McCartney, Sir Paul; Memphis Minnie; Neville, Aaron; Richards, Keith; Stanley, Ralph; Tosh, Peter; Van Halen, Eddie; Waters, Muddy; Wilson, Brian.

Jussi Björling

Swedish opera singer

As a singer gifted with a voice of unsurpassed beauty and impeccable technique, Björling set a high standard for operatic tenors.

Born: February 2, 1911; Stora Tuna, Sweden
Died: September 9, 1960; Siarö, near Stockholm, Sweden
Also known as: Johan Jonaton Björling (full name)

Principal works

CHORAL WORKS: Tenor soloist in *Requiem*, 1939 (by Giuseppe Verdi); tenor part in Ludwig van Beethoven's *Missa Solemnis*, 1940.

OPERATIC ROLES: Don Ottavio in Wolfgang Amadeus Mozart's *Don Giovanni*, 1930; Lamplighter in Giacomo Puccini's *Manon Lescaut*, 1930; Romeo in Charles Gounod's *Romeo et Juliette*, 1933; Duke of Mantua in Giuseppe Verdi's *Rigoletto*, 1937; Rodolfo in Puccini's *La Bohème*, 1938; Manrico in Verdi's *Il trovatore*, 1939; King Gustav III in Verdi's *Un ballo in maschera*, 1940; Don Carlo in Verdi's *Don Carlo*, 1950.

Principal recordings

ALBUMS: *Romeo et Juliette*, 1947; *Operatic Duets*, 1952; *Il Trovatore*, 1952 (with Zinka Milanov); *Cavalleria Rusticana*, 1953 (with Milanov); *Verdi: Aida*, 1955; *La Bohème*, 1956 (with Victoria de Los Angeles); *Verdi: Rigoletto*, 1956; *Tosca*, 1957; *Verdi's Requiem*, 1960 (with Leontyne Price and Giorgio Tozzi).

WRITINGS OF INTEREST: *Med bagaget i strupen*, 1945 (autobiography).

The Life

Johan Jonaton "Jussi" Björling (JUH-see BYUR-lihng) was born into a musical family in Sweden in 1911. His father, David, was a singer, and Björling's older brother, Olle, and his younger brother, Gosta, both pursued musical careers within their native Sweden. Baptized as Johan, Björling became known personally and professionally as Jussi. His voice can be heard in an early recording by the

Björling Male Quartet, and he made his first solo recordings in 1929. From then, until his premature death in 1960, he produced a steady stream of recordings of operatic arias, Swedish art songs and popular tunes, and complete operatic recordings with the finest international casts.

He made his stage debut in the small role of the Lamplighter in Giacomo Puccini's opera *Manon Lescaut* (1893), at the Swedish Royal Opera in 1930. His international operatic debuts came in swift succession in the mid-1930's: the Vienna Staatsoper in 1936, in New York and in Chicago in 1937, and at the Metropolitan Opera in 1938, in one of his signature roles, Rodolfo in Puccini's *La Bohème* (1896). He was awarded his first opening night at the Metropolitan Opera in 1940, when he portrayed King Gustav III in Giuseppe Verdi's *Un ballo in maschera* (1859), but then he returned to his native Sweden for the duration of World War II.

His choice of repertory was conservative, and even in an era of cautious and unimaginative stage productions he was known as a stolid stage performer. Nevertheless, he was a hardworking and conscientious performer, and he had fifty-five leading roles in his repertory. He most frequently appeared as Rodolfo in *La Bohème*, as title role in Charles Gounod's *Faust* (1859), and as Manrico in Verdi's *Il trovatore* (1853). He commanded an impressive one thousand dollars for a performance in the 1950-1951 season.

In 1957 Björling was diagnosed with serious heart problems, probably the result of his longtime chronic alcoholism, and he died suddenly of a massive heart attack during the summer of 1960, at age forty-nine. Despite his severe alcoholism, he was said never to have given a bad performance.

The Music

Among the great operatic tenors of his generation, including Richard Tucker, Jan Peerce, and Mario del Monaco, Björling was recognized for the purity of his vocal production, his thoroughness of technique, and his sheer beauty of voice. Anna-Lisa Björling, in her biography *Jussi* (1997), compares the sound of her husband's voice to "a silver bell struck by a crystal hammer," and enthusiasts of Björling's artistry, who often evoke the metaphors of silver and velvet, have always marveled at the purity of his technique.

Performance. His reputation for hard work is proven by his activities in November, 1950. He sang six performances, in New York and Philadelphia, of the title role of Verdi's *Don Carlos* (1867), in a spectacular new production at the Metropolitan Opera under the auspices of its new general director, Rudolf Bing; he sang at a memorial concert for the king of Sweden; and he appeared in a live television performance on *The Voice of Firestone*, a half-hour showcase for opera singers. On the television show, Björling sang Franz Schubert's "Was Ist Sylvia?" (1826), Georges Bizet's "Flower Song" from *Carmen* (1875), and a song by Victor Herbert, as well as the show's opening and closing maudlin theme songs, which show how uncomfortable he was singing in English. Björling shows effortless charm, as when he spontaneously awards the rose he held during the "Flower Song" to a woman in the chorus. As one of the relatively few visual records of Björling on stage, the videotape of this performance confirms Björling's astonishing vocal technique and personal appeal.

Recordings. Björling's most endearing album is probably a set of operatic duets with the American

Jussi Björling. (Hulton Archive/Getty Images)

baritone Robert Merrill; the duet from Bizet's *The Pearl Fishers* (1863) on that album still turns up in movies and television commercials. Björling's final complete operatic recording, of Puccini's *Turandot* (1926), with the Swedish soprano Birgit Nilsson (who was then at the beginning of a great international career), shows no diminution of the tenor's ability, except for an uncharacteristic avoidance of a couple of high C's.

Björling was comfortable singing in Italian, French, and German. He recorded one of his signature arias, known as "Lenski's Aria" from Peter Ilich Tchaikovsky's *Eugen Onegin* (1879), in Swedish rather than Russian. For some listeners, Björling's greatest musical legacy lies in his recordings of Swedish songs by such composers as Jean Sibelius, Hugo Alfven, Wilhelm Stenhammer, and Tűre Rangstrom.

Musical Legacy

Because of the great number of his recordings, Björling is widely cherished by opera enthusiasts, and his musical excellence sets a high standard for operatic tenors. His complete operatic recordings are his most enduring legacy. He recorded Puccini's *La Bohème* and *Madama Butterfly* (1904) with the Spanish soprano Victoria de Los Angeles, with Sir Thomas Beecham conducting. Both recordings retain their immense charm and youthful energy. This moving ardor is plentifully on display in Björling's live-performance recording in 1947 from the Metropolitan Opera Saturday broadcast of Gounod's *Romeo et Juliette* (1867), where he is partnered by the Brazilian soprano Bidu Sayão. Björling is a dashing Duke of Mantua, with Roberta Peters as Gilda, in a recording of Verdi's *Rigoletto* (1851). Best of all, perhaps, are the complete recordings of Verdi's *Il trovatore* and *Aida* (1871) with the Yugoslavian soprano (and Met mainstay of the 1950's) Zinka Milanov. The *Aida* boasts possibly the most impressive top-to-bottom cast of any operatic recording, with every singer at his or her peak: Milanov, Fedora Barbieri, Björling, Leonard Warren, and Boris Christoff. As Radamès, the doomed young Egyptian commander, Björling conveys the utter collapse into despair of his character in the pivotal third act, when he discovers the true identity of his lover, Aida, and the full extent of his inadvertent betrayal of his country.

Björling capitalized on the tradition set by an earlier generation of tenors, such as Enrico Caruso, John McCormack, and Leo Slezak, to record great operatic arias as well as popular songs and ballads. However, the latter have not retained much musical interest, although they are still worth hearing for the integrity of their performance. The greatest legacy of Björling lies in his recordings of complete operas, individual arias, and Swedish art songs. Few singers have ever matched the thoroughness of his vocal technique, and listeners continue to marvel at the purity of Björling's voice.

Byron Nelson

Further Reading

Bing, Rudolf. *Five Thousand Nights at the Opera.* Garden City, N.Y.: Doubleday, 1972. Filled with gossipy stories of life in the Metropolitan Opera of the 1950's.

Björling, Anna-Lisa, and Andrew Farkas. *Jussi.* Portland, Oreg.: Amadeus Press, 1997. Provides an insider's affectionate view of the Swedish tenor, although it is frank about Björling's shortcomings as a stage actor and about his difficult struggle with alcoholism.

Steane, J. B. *The Grand Tradition: Seventy Years of Singing on Record, 1900 to 1970.* London: Duckworth, 1974. Celebrates the splendor of Björling's voice, while showing less enthusiasm for his dramatic skills.

See also: Beecham, Sir Thomas; Caruso, Enrico; Herbert, Victor; Price, Leontyne; Puccini, Giacomo.

Otis Blackwell

American blues pianist, singer, and songwriter

A prolific songwriter during the early years of rock and roll, Blackwell wrote many classics, including Elvis Presley's "Don't Be Cruel" and Jerry Lee Lewis's "Great Balls of Fire."

Born: February 16, 1932; New York, New York
Died: May 6, 2002; Nashville, Tennessee

Principal recordings

ALBUMS: *Singin' the Blues*, 1956; *These Are My Songs*, 1978; *All Shook Up*, recorded 1976, released 1995; *They Called It Rock 'n' Roll*, 2003.

The Life

Otis Blackwell's introduction to music was gospel songs his family sang at home. While working as an usher in a Brooklyn motion-picture theater, Blackwell took an interest in the career of his favorite singer, Tex Ritter, a singing cowboy of the 1940's. Later, Blackwell won a talent contest at the legendary Apollo Theater in Harlem. While working as a presser in a Brooklyn tailor shop, he began singing, in New York clubs, songs that had been recorded by Larry Darnell and Chuck Willis. He was signed by RCA Victor in 1952, switching to Joe Davis's Jay-Dee label the following year and recording the hit "Daddy Rollin' Stone." Because Davis paid him only twenty-five dollars a week, Blackwell augmented his income by writing songs for other singers.

On December 24, 1955, Blackwell sold six songs for $150. When one, "Don't Be Cruel," became a hit for Elvis Presley in 1956, the demand for Blackwell's writing skills increased. Few of those who kept "Don't Be Cruel" and its flip side, Jerry Leiber and Mike Stoller's "Hound Dog," at number one on the pop charts for eleven weeks suspected that its creator was an African American.

Though the two never met because the songwriter feared their working relationship would collapse if he did not like Presley, Blackwell wrote for the popular singer such hits as "All Shook Up," "Paralyzed," and "Return to Sender." As stipulated in the contract, Presley received cowriting credit for those songs. Many of Blackwell's songs were written with others, and some were composed under pseudonyms, because of his contract with Jay-Dee, and that complicates compiling an accurate account of his work. One of his most lasting songs, "Fever," was cowritten with Eddie Cooley under the name John Davenport, after Blackwell's stepfather. In addition to Cooley, Blackwell collaborated with Jack Hammer and Winfield Scott.

Blackwell's other hits during the 1950's and early 1960's included "Great Balls of Fire" and "Breathless" for Jerry Lee Lewis, "Just Keep It Up" for Dee Clark, and "Handy Man" for Jimmy Jones.

He wrote Clark's "Hey Little Girl" for his childhood sweetheart, Josephine Peoples, who became his wife and the mother of his seven children.

Others who recorded Blackwell's songs included Pat Boone, Solomon Burke, the Coasters, Bobby Darin, Ben E. King, Clyde McPhatter, and Gene Vincent. Blackwell also produced recordings by Connie Francis and Mahalia Jackson, and he even gave actor Sal Mineo a hit song. When rock groups, inspired by the Beatles, began writing their own songs, Blackwell's influence diminished.

In 1976 Blackwell recorded *All Shook Up*, a collection of his hits, and toured. Because he recorded frequently in Nashville, he moved there in 1988, opened an office, and provided free advice for struggling songwriters. Shortly after marrying his second wife, Mamie Wiggins, in 1991, Blackwell suffered a stroke, leaving him paralyzed and having to communicate through a computer. He was inducted into the Songwriters Hall of Fame in 1991 and received a Pioneer Award from the Rhythm and Blues Foundation in 1994. Blackwell died of a heart attack in Nashville in 2002.

The Music

Blackwell combined elements of country music and rhythm and blues, particularly in the songs he wrote for Presley and Lewis, with driving tempi and simple, catchy lyrics. The songs were essentially more danceable variations of country songs.

"Don't Be Cruel." "Don't Be Cruel" was a perfect match for Presley's alternately snarling and smooth style. With a greater vocal range than most of the singers of Blackwell's songs, Presley easily shifted from a high pitch to a smooth baritone on "Don't Be Cruel." Blackwell's lyrics perfectly matched rock and roll, the music of youthful rebellion.

As was the practice of the day, Blackwell recorded demonstration versions of the songs he wrote for Presley, and some sources, such as Stoller, claim that Presley, as well as Lewis and others, copied the songwriter's vocal inflections. Blackwell said Presley had him record demos of songs written by others, such as "Teddy Bear," in order to imitate Blackwell's styling.

"All Shook Up." One of Presley's biggest hits, "All Shook Up," was a prime example of the rock and country merger known as rockabilly. In this song Presley constantly altered the tempo—speeding up, slowing down, and pausing—and mingled nonverbal sounds with the lyrics. The song's broad appeal resulted in its climbing to number one on the pop, country, and rhythm-and-blues charts. "All Shook Up" embodied both the physical gyrations made famous by Presley and the powerful emotional and sexual effect he had on his fans. Blackwell created a perfect song for the king of rock and roll.

"Great Balls of Fire." "Great Balls of Fire" is arguably Blackwell's greatest rock anthem. With Lewis's patented pumping piano style, "Great Balls of Fire" demonstrated that love songs had entered a new age. The sedate "moon" and "June" love-song lyrics were replaced by a rampaging passion, threatening, as with "All Shook Up," to consume the singer. Just as "All Shook Up" conveys the image of the hip-shaking Presley, "Great Balls of Fire" captures Lewis's hair-flopping, keyboard-pounding intensity.

"Handy Man." Blackwell's "Handy Man" was a hit three times: for Jimmy Jones in 1959, for Del Shannon in a raucous version in 1964, and for James Taylor as a tender ballad in 1977. Such style flexibility shows the genius of Blackwell's songwriting.

"Fever." Blackwell's most famous song is closer to jazz than rock and roll. "Fever" was first recorded by Little Willie John in 1956, hitting number one on the rhythm-and-blues charts. However, when Peggy Lee gave it her distinctive sultry spin two years later, the song became a pop classic. In the conservative 1950's, "Fever" was notable for its sexual suggestiveness.

Musical Legacy

By blending an array of influences, Blackwell enriched the burgeoning genre of rock and roll. Along with Chuck Berry and Sam Cooke, he was one of a handful of black songwriters who paved the way for such genres as soul and rap. Accepting an award in 1976, Stevie Wonder acknowledged his debt to Blackwell. The versatility of Blackwell's music is illustrated by the diverse performers who have recorded his songs: Michael Bublé, Cheap Trick, Rita Coolidge, Budd Guy, Billy Joel, Madonna, Dolly Parton, the Who, and Johnny Winter. A 1994 tribute to Blackwell, *Brace Yourself*, included new recordings by Dave Edmunds, Debbie

Harry, Chrissie Hynde, Kris Kristofferson, Graham Parker, Jon Spencer, Ronnie Spector, and others.

Michael Adams

Further Reading

Giddins, Gary. "Just How Much Did Elvis Learn from Otis Blackwell?" In *Riding on a Blue Note: Jazz and American Pop*. New York: Oxford University Press, 1981. Examines Presley's debt to Blackwell as songwriter and singer and explains how Blackwell's style grew out of the minstrel tradition. Includes an interview with Blackwell.

Strauss, Neil. "Otis Blackwell." *Rolling Stone* (June 20, 2002): 35. Overview of Blackwell's life, with a discussion on the origins of "All Shook Up."

Tosches, Nick. *Country: Living Legends and Dying Metaphors in America's Biggest Music*. New York: Charles Scribner's Sons, 1985. Brief assessment of Presley's debt to Blackwell.

See also: Berry, Chuck; Cooke, Sam; Lewis, Jerry Lee; Presley, Elvis; Ritter, Tex.

Rubén Blades

Panamanian Latin jazz and salsa guitarist, singer, and songwriter

Blades revolutionized salsa music by incorporating into his compositions new instrumentation, adventurous arrangements, other world music, and socially and politically relevant lyrics.

Born: July 16, 1948; Panama City, Panama

Also known as: Rubén Blades Bellido de Luna (full name)

Member of: Rubén Blades y Seis del Solar; Rubén Blades y Son del Solar

Principal recordings

ALBUMS (solo): *From Panama to New York*, 1970 (with Pete Rodriguez); *Bohemio y poeta*, 1979; *Maestra vida: Primera parte*, 1980; *Maestra vida: Segunda parte*, 1980; *Buscando América*, 1984; *Mucho mejor*, 1984; *Antecedente*, 1988; *Nothing but the Truth*, 1988; *Doble filo*, 1992; *El que la hace la paga*, 1992; *Rubén Blades with Strings*, 1992;

Joseph and His Brothers, 1993 (with Jorge Strunz and Ardeshir Farah); *Rosa de los vientos*, 1996; *Tiempos*, 1999; *Mundo*, 2002; *Salsa caliente de Nu York*, 2002; *Una década*, 2003; *O Melhor, Vol. 1*, 2004; *O Melhor, Vol. 2*, 2004.

ALBUMS (with Seis del Solar): *Escenas*, 1985; *Agua de luna*, 1986.

ALBUMS (with Son del Solar): *Caminando*, 1991; *Amor y control*, 1992.

ALBUMS (with Willie Colón): *Willie Colón Presents Rubén Blades*, 1977; *Siembra*, 1978; *Canciones del solar de los aburridos*, 1981; *The Last Fight*, 1992; *Sembra y otros favoritos salsa para siempre*, 2001.

The Life

Rubén Blades Bellido de Luna (rew-BEHN blaydz) was born in the barrio of San Felipe in Panama City, the second of five children in a family of immigrants. His mother, Anoland Bellido de Luna, was a Cuban singer and pianist, and his father, Rubén Blades, Sr., was a Colombian percussionist, basketball player, and detective. Blades's paternal grandfather was an English citizen from Saint Lucia who migrated to Panama to work on the canal. Although Blades and his family use the English pronunciation of their last name, the Spanish pronunciation (BLAH-dehs) is widely used.

His upbringing in a musical family proved fruitful for the development of Blades's skills and sensitivity, which were also nurtured by the diverse musical environment present in Panama City. While growing up, Blades lived through the height of rock and roll, listening not only to Elvis Presley and the Beatles but also to such jazz performers as Dizzy Gillespie and Duke Ellington. Blades was exposed to many popular Latin American musicians, such as Benny Moré, Perez Prado, Cheo Feliciano, and the Joe Cuba Sextet, all of whom proved influential to his career.

Blades performed onstage for the first time as a teenager, substituting for the vocalist in his brother's rock band, the Saints. The 1964 Panama Canal riots had an enduring effect on Blades, leading him to pursue his interests in politics and law over music. He decided to seek degrees in law and political science at the University of Panama, while singing with fellow university students in Los Salvajes del Ritmo (the rhythm savages) and working as a guest composer-singer for the professional Latin music group Bush y sus Magnificos (Bush and his magnificents). The University of Panama closed in 1969 because of political unrest, and Blades used this time to travel to New York, where he recorded his first album, *From Panama to New York*, with the popular orchestra of Pete Rodriguez. The album was a commercial failure, and, as soon as the University of Panama reopened, Blades returned to continue his studies, graduating in 1972.

After his father was accused by the Panamanian government of working as a spy for the Central Intelligence Agency (CIA), Blades's family moved to Miami in 1973. In 1973 and 1974 Blades worked as an attorney for the National Bank of Panama, but he became dissatisfied with his law career and moved to New York after visiting his family in Florida. In New York Blades worked for the Panamanian consulate and in the mail room of Fania, a salsa record label. There he auditioned as a singer and composer and began singing for the band of Ray Barretto, debuting at Madison Square Garden in 1974. After that, his musical career soared. He composed more hits for the Fania label and joined forces with trombone player, producer, and bandleader Willie Colón.

The collaboration of Blades and Colón was sensational, uniting Blades's compositional and poetical skills and Colón's amazing ear for arranging and producing albums. They began to compose *salsa conciente*, a type of salsa that communicated social and political issues through outspoken lyrics, stimulating both thought and dancing. Together, Blades and Colón recorded many albums for the Fania label, including *Siembra* (sow) and *Canciones del solar de los aburridos* (songs from the tenement of the bored).

During the early 1980's, Blades ended his artistic collaboration with Colón and went on to have a successful solo career as a musician and as an actor. He signed with Elektra Records, and in 1984 he released the album *Buscando América* (looking for America), which became a big hit. Blades's social activism, reflected in his lyrics, persevered throughout the 1980's. He continued his law career and earned a master's degree in international law from Harvard University in 1985.

Blades had a productive film career in the 1980's and 1990's. He appeared in Robert Redford's 1988 film *The Milagro Beanfield War*, and he collaborated

Rubén Blades. (AP/Wide World Photos)

on the sound track for Spike Lee's 1989 film *Do the Right Thing*. In 1994 Blades became a candidate for president of Panama. With 18 percent of the vote, he finished in third place. Continuing his successful career as a musician, Blades recorded albums through the 1990's and into the 2000's, including *Amor y control* (love and control) and *Mundo* (world). In 2004 Blades became Panama's minister of tourism.

The Music

Blades was a pioneer in blending intricate salsa arrangements with socially aware lyrics, creating *salsa conciente*. Addressing issues such as poverty, exploitation, sovereignty, and pan-Americanism, his music had much in common with Latin American *nueva canción* (new song, often protest songs). However, in contrast to *nueva canción* artists, who often perform solo, Blades used salsa orchestras or small Latin jazz ensembles to deliver his songs. Although he is largely an autodidact, Blades's compositions demonstrate great harmonic, melodic, and rhythmic understanding. Throughout his career he would tastefully incorporate a diverse palette of styles and genres into his compositions, including jazz, rumba, Cuban *son*, Puerto Rican bomba, bossa nova, reggae, and Celtic. Blades's independent and innovative spirit is evident in his music, which defies the limitations of genres by breaking with compositional and performance stereotypes.

"Plástico." An example of *salsa conciente*, "Plástico" (plastic) opened the best-selling album *Siembra*, and its inventive arrangement and lyrics reflect the multicultural environment present in 1970's New York. "Plástico" satirizes and condemns the vanity, materialism, racism, and superficiality that threaten to overpower the moral values of the Latin communities. In format and rhythm, the song presents the listener with surprises, beginning with an instrumental disco-funk section and switching to Afro-Cuban patterns and Puerto Rican bomba backing up Blades's verses. Typical of salsa, after the verses is a *coro y soneo* (chorus and lead singer) section, during which Blades improvises lyrics. The coda uses a bomba pattern, while Blades sends an outspoken pan-American message.

"Pedro Navaja." Also from *Siembra*, "Pedro Navaja" (Peter Pocketknife) became a top-selling salsa single. A subtle tribute to Bertolt Brecht's "Mack the Knife," this song is a masterpiece of narrative. With a tight arrangement by Luis Ortíz, "Pedro Navaja" uses studio effects (sirens and police radio) to support the story surrounding Navaja's death, the song portraying the life of the Latin barrios in New York and the Caribbean cities, where criminal activity is a constant threat. The song brilliantly balances tragedy and humor, while supporting the album's motto, "you reap what you sow." It was a huge hit that, seven and half minutes in length, defied radio format. After a full-orchestra introduction, the narrative starts with congas and voice, adding more instruments in subsequent stanzas, until all instruments join in the chorus and leader section. This song was a breakthrough for Blades as a singer and lyricist.

"Tiburón." With its expressed disapproval of U.S. intervention in Latin American affairs, "Tiburón" (shark) produced some enemies for Blades, especially in the community of Cuban exiles who approve U.S. efforts to stamp out communism. Nevertheless, "Tiburón" was a hit in many

Latin American countries and remains one of Blades's emblematic compositions. Opening the 1981 album *Canciones del solar de los aburridos*, "Tiburón" uses studio effects to its advantage. Blades sings over a traditional *guaguancó* pattern through the verses, while the chorus and leader section presents the usual salsa *son montuno* pattern, both examples of Afro-Cuban rhythms.

"El Padre Antonio y el Monaguillo Andrés." A song from the 1984 album *Buscando América*, "El Padre Antonio y el Monaguillo Andrés" (Father Anthony and altar boy Andrew) is another of Blades's great narrative songs. Based on the assassination of Oscar Romero, a priest in El Salvador, it tells the story of a government's repression of justice and the innocent casualties of civil war. Like the rest of the album, this song pushes the boundaries of salsa by using synthesizers in place of horns. The introduction and ending present an unusual musical pattern, reminiscent of Cuban *bembe* and Venezuelan *gaitas*, patterns rarely heard on salsa arrangements. With its adventurous instrumentation and arrangement, this innovative song hinted at the musical direction that Blades would follow for the next two decades.

"Primogenio." An experiment in world music, "Primogenio" (beginnings) successfully combined Celtic melodies played by Scottish pipes and fiddles with the sounds of a small Latin jazz ensemble. "Primogenio" appeared on *Mundo*, the album that won the Grammy Award for Best World Music Album in 2002. In it, Blades consolidates music from Brazil, North Africa, Spain, Great Britain, the United States, and the Caribbean. For "Primogenio" Blades uses the *tumbao*, the constant rhythmic relation between congas and bass typical of salsa. He also adds the Cuban rumba pattern in the middle and ending sections. Rumba patterns are often used to honor Cuban deities from the Yoruba pantheon, such as Eleguá, the deity Blades praises in "Primogenio." An impressive work of world-music juxtaposition, "Primogenio" serves as a great example of musical multiculturalism.

Musical Legacy

Following Blades's lead, many musicians in salsa and related genres, such as merengue, incorporated thought-provoking lyrics that address so-

cially relevant issues. This significantly expanded the audience for these genres, inviting both dancers and non-dancers alike to listen, think, and enjoy. Beyond the lyrics, the elegant and sometimes unusual compositions of Blades have influenced such musicians as Mark Anthony, Juan Luis Guerra, Gilberto Santa Rosa, and Ricky Martin. Beyond salsa, Blades's influence was seen in his varied collaborations with such musicians as Sting, Lou Reed, Los Fabulosos Cadillacs, Guerra, Maná, and Sun City.

After years of working under contract with record labels such as Fania and Elektra, Blades went independent, pioneering new ways to promote and sell records and encouraging younger generations of Latin musicians to follow his path. In the early 2000's Blades explored the idea of selling records on the Internet for a price determined by the listener-consumer, a practice later popularized by bands such as Radiohead.

Daniel Nuñez

Further Reading

Bordowitz, Hank. *Noise of the World: Non-Western Musicians in Their Own Words*. New York: Soft Skull Press, 2004. Contains a short section by Blades, offering insight into his background and his opinions about the music industry and salsa in general.

Cruz, Bárbara. *Rubén Blades: Salsa Singer and Social Activist*. Springfield, N.J.: Enslow, 1997. Biography of Blades up to 1997 written for a juvenile audience. It deals with Blades's life as a musician, actor, and politician.

Randel, Don Michael. "Crossing Over with Rubén Blades." *Journal of the American Musicological Society* 44, no. 2 (Summer, 1991): 301-323. An insightful musicological analysis of the innovative aspects of Blades's music and the source of his crossover appeal.

Wald, Elijah. *Global Minstrels: Voices of World Music*. New York: Routledge, 2007. A short chapter discusses Blades's character, ideas, and impact.

See also: Colón, Willie; Cruz, Celia; Ellington, Duke; Gillespie, Dizzy; Presley, Elvis; Price, Leontyne; Simon, Paul; Sting.

Eubie Blake

American jazz pianist and composer

A virtuoso ragtime pianist, Blake cowrote and produced in 1921 the all-black show Shuffle Along, *which helped establish the legitimacy of black actors on the Broadway stage.*

Born: February 7, 1887; Baltimore, Maryland
Died: February 12, 1983; New York, New York
Also known as: James Hubert Blake (full name)

Principal works

MUSICAL THEATER (music): *Shuffle Along*, 1921 (lyrics by Noble Sissle; libretto by Flournoy Miller and Aubrey L. Lyles); *Elsie*, 1923 (with Alma M. Sanders; lyrics by Sissle; libretto by Charles W. Bell); *The Chocolate Dandies*, 1924 (lyrics by Sissle; libretto by Sissle and Lew Payton); *Lew Leslie's Blackbirds*, 1930 (lyrics by Andy Razaf; libretto by Miller); *Swing It*, 1937 (with Milton Reddie; lyrics by Cecil Mack and Reddie; libretto by Mack); *Eubie!*, 1978 (lyrics by Sissle, Razaf, Johnny Brandon, Miller, and Jim Europe).

Principal recordings

ALBUMS: *Sissle and Blake: Early Rare Recordings, Vol. 1*, 1920 (with Noble Sissle); *Sissle and Blake: Early Rare Recordings, Vol. 2*, 1920 (with Sissle); *The Wizard of Ragtime Piano*, 1958; *The Marches I Played on the Old Ragtime Piano*, 1959; *Golden Reunion in Ragtime*, 1962; *The Eighty-six Years of Eubie Blake*, 1969; *Eubie Blake and His Friends*, 1973 (with others); *Eubie Blake Introducing Jim Hession*, 1973 (with Jim Hession); *Eubie Blake and His Protégés*, 1974 (with others); *Eubie Blake Song Hits*, 1976.

The Life

James Hubert "Eubie" (YEW-bee) Blake was born in Maryland to John and Emma Blake, one of eight children and the only one to survive to adulthood. His parents were freed slaves, and his father worked at the Baltimore docks, while his mother was a washerwoman. Blake manifested an early talent for music, and, after some early keyboard les-

sons from a neighbor, he began playing the piano at local brothels in Baltimore at age fifteen (first at Aggie Shelton's bordello and later at Annie Gilly's sporting house), gaining skill, repertoire, and a reputation as a keyboard wizard. In these positions, Blake listened to and was strongly influenced by other pianists, such as Jesse Pickett, C. Luckeyeth Roberts, and One Leg Willie.

Both of these jobs were done surreptitiously, without the knowledge of his parents. Blake recalled in interviews that he would typically go upstairs to bed, then sneak out his bedroom window, rent a pair of long pants from a man for twenty-five cents to cover the youthful shorts he wore, and play piano into the night for a small salary and generous tips. He also remembered that, one morning at his home, he was practicing the music he performed while his religious mother had left home for several hours. When she returned unexpectedly, she heard his music and threw him out of the house, stating, "Get that ragtime out of my house!" It was the first time he had heard the word ragtime.

Blake was married twice: first in 1910 at age twenty-three, to Avis Lee, who died in 1938; and second in 1945 to Marion Tyler. At age sixty-three, Blake enrolled in New York University's composition program, graduating in 1950 with a music degree. He continued to perform, to great adulation from audiences, until the 1980's. Suffering from pneumonia, Blake died in 1983.

The Music

Blake's musical career divides into three recognizable units—he began as a ragtime pianist, in his early twenties he became an important Broadway composer-producer, and he concluded his life as a musical legend.

Ragtime. Blake's music sprang from the sounds of the sporting house, or brothel. His energetic ragtime style, often approaching boogie-woogie—especially in the bass line patterns—was captivating to audiences, and it was impressive to other musicians. Blake's large hands could span the interval of a tenth, enabling voicing possibilities that other pianists could not manage. Additionally, he composed music with more complex harmonies than some of the less-inventive tonic-dominant-based rags, and his rhythms were buoyant and infectious. Improvisation was integral to the style and practice of ragtime in the early 1900's, and many rags were not written down at the moment of composition. Blake once stated that he composed his "Charleston Rag" in 1899, yet he wrote it down in 1915 when he had learned to write musical notation. Its original name was "Sounds of Africa," and it was renamed "Charleston Rag" in 1917 at its publication, four years before it became a staple number in *Shuffle Along*.

Broadway. When Blake met Noble Sissle (a lyricist and vocal performer who also conducted an early twentieth century dance orchestra) in 1915, his career shifted toward Broadway composing and producing for twelve years. Sissle and Blake first formed a vaudeville act called the Dixie Duo that initiated Blake's stage career, gave him a working knowledge of the stage, and created his first hit song: "It's All Your Fault." In 1921 Blake composed the songs (set to Sissle's lyrics) for *Shuffle Along*, a Broadway show for an all-black cast. *Shuffle Along* created such a sensation with its numerous hit songs (among them "I'm Just Wild About Harry," "Charleston Rag," "Bandana Days," and "Love Will Find a Way") that it required three touring companies to present it across the country. Its performance run extended to nearly five hundred nights, broke through racial barriers on the theater stages, presented the first love song between black characters in stage history, and helped establish the singing careers of Josephine Baker, Florence Mills, and Paul Robeson. *Shuffle Along* was successful in part because its infectious rhythms and melodies set it apart from the more traditional, stereotyped revues to which Broadway audiences were accustomed.

Sissle and Blake collaborated on several other shows, including *Elsie* and *The Chocolate Dandie*, and their work together continued until about 1927, when they parted ways. Blake composed for several shows without Sissle's involvement, including *Swing It, Lew Leslie's Blackbirds*, and *Eubie!* (a retrospective revue of his songs that premiered in 1978).

Legend. Blake retired from performing around 1946, but he returned to make an album in 1969 entitled *The Eighty-six Years of Eubie Blake*, a retrospective of his life. He toured the world following its release, talking about ragtime and his career. By the 1970's, he had become a musical legend, appearing in numerous concerts and as a guest on television,

on *The Tonight Show with Johnny Carson* several times and on *Saturday Night Live*.

Musical Legacy

Blake's life coincided with a time when ragtime was a national rage in music, and it lasted through two resurgences of interest in the style in the 1950's and 1970's. His name as a performer and composer is best known to aficionados of early jazz and Broadway history. In the broader spectrum of ragtime and jazz, his name is mentioned along with Fats Waller and Jelly Roll Morton. Blake's important legacy rests in his bold efforts in the 1920's to compose music for African American performers and audiences on African American topics and to create *Shuffle Along*, which broke the racial barrier on Broadway by moving black Americans and their music into the entertainment mainstream in New York.

For his musical accomplishments, he received an honorary doctorate from Brooklyn College in 1973,

Eubie Blake. (AP/Wide World Photos)

followed by honorary degrees from Dartmouth College, Rutgers University, the New England Conservatory, and the University of Maryland. He received the Presidential Medal of Freedom in 1981. He was inducted posthumously into the American Theater Hall of Fame, he had his likeness placed on a U.S. postage stamp, and he had his recording from 1969 entered in the Library of Congress National Recording Registry.

Jonathan A. Sturm

Further Reading

Kimball, Robert, and William Bolcom. *Reminiscing with Noble Sissle and Eubie Blake*. New York: Cooper Square Press, 2000. Extensive interviews with ragtime pianist Blake and his lyricist for *Shuffle Along*, Sissle. Includes photographs.

Rose, Al. *Eubie Blake*. New York: Schirmer Books, 1979. A comprehensive biography of Blake's personal life that puts him in context with the popular musicians of the early twentieth century. Includes photographs, discography, piano rollography, and filmography.

Southern, Eileen. "Blake, Eubie." *The New Grove Dictionary of Jazz*. 2d ed. Edited by Barry Kernfeld. London: Macmillan, 2002. A brief encyclopedia entry on Blake, with a few additional details and bibliography.

See also: Cole, Nat King; Goodman, Benny; Hunter, Alberta; Morton, Jelly Roll; Robeson, Paul; Still, William Grant; Waller, Fats.

Art Blakey

American jazz composer and drummer

A leading drummer of the modern jazz movement, Blakey was influential in developing the hard-bop style. His band, the Jazz Messengers, was a training ground for musicians, from Clifford Brown to Wynton Marsalis.

Born: October 11, 1919; Pittsburgh, Pennsylvania
Died: October 16, 1990; New York, New York
Member of: Art Blakey and the Jazz Messengers

Principal recordings

ALBUMS (with the Jazz Messengers): *Art Blakey and the Jazz Messengers*, 1953; *Art Blakey Quintet, Vol. 2*, 1954; *Blakey with the Jazz Messengers*, 1954; *Jazz Messengers*, 1954; *Art Blakey and the Jazz Messengers*, 1956; *Art Blakey with the Original Jazz Messengers*, 1956; *Drum Suite*, 1956; *Hard Bop*, 1956; *Hard Drive*, 1956; *The Jazz Messengers*, 1956; *Originally*, 1956; *Art Blakey and His Rhythm*, 1957; *Art Blakey Big Band*, 1957; *Art Blakey and the Jazz Messengers*, 1957; *Art Blakey/John Handy: Messages*, 1957; *Art Blakey's Jazz Messengers with Thelonious Monk*, 1957; *Cu-Bop*, 1957; *Dawn on the Desert*, 1957; *Jazz Messengers Play Lerner and Loewe*, 1957; *Midnight Session*, 1957; *Mirage*, 1957; *Night in Tunisia*, 1957; *Once Upon a Groove*, 1957; *Orgy in Rhythm, Vol. 1*, 1957; *Orgy in Rhythm, Vol. 2*, 1957; *Reflections on Buhania*, 1957; *Ritual: The Modern Jazz Messengers*, 1957; *Theory of Art*, 1957; *Second Edition*, 1957; *Art Blakey and the Jazz Messengers*, 1958; *Des femmes disparaissent*, 1958; *Drums Around the Corner*, 1958; *Holiday for Skins, Vol. 1*, 1958; *Moanin'*, 1958; *Africaine*, 1959; *Les Liaisons dangereuses*, 1959; *A Night in Tunisia*, 1960; *The Big Beat*, 1960; *Lausanne 1960, Pt. 1*, 1960; *Like Someone in Love*, 1960; *A Jazz Hour with Art Blakey's Jazz Messengers: Blues March*, 1961; *Art Blakey*, 1961; *Art Blakey!!!!! Jazz Messengers!!!!!*, 1961; *Buhaina's Delight*, 1961; *The Freedom Rider*, 1961; *Mosaic*, 1961; *Pisces*, 1961; *Roots and Herbs*, 1961; *The Witch Doctor*, 1961; *The African Beat*, 1962; *Caravan*, 1962; *Thermo*, 1962; *Three Blind Mice, Vol. 1*, 1962; *A Jazz Message*, 1963; *Selections from the Film Golden Boy*, 1963; *Blues Bag*, 1964; *Free for All*, 1964; *Indestructible*, 1964; *Kyoto*, 1964; *'S Make It*, 1964; *Soul Finger*, 1965; *Buttercorn Lady*, 1966; *Hold On, I'm Coming*, 1966; *Tough!*, 1966; *Art Blakey and the Jazz Messengers*, 1970; *For Minors Only*, 1971; *Anthenagin*, 1973; *Buhaina*, 1973; *Backgammon*, 1976; *Percussion Discussion*, 1976; *Gypsy Folk Tales: Art Blakey and the Jazz Messengers*, 1977; *In My Prime, Vol. 1*, 1977; *Reflections in Blue*, 1978; *A Night in Tunisia*, 1979; *One by One: Art Blakey and the Jazz Messengers*, 1979; *Album of the Year*, 1981; *Killer Joe: Art Blakey and George Kawaguchi*, 1981; *Straight Ahead*, 1981; *Art Blakey and the All Star*

Messengers, 1982; *Oh, by the Way*, 1982; *New York Scene*, 1984; *Blue Night*, 1985; *Buhaina: The Continuing Message*, 1985; *Farewell*, 1985; *Hard Champion: Art Blakey and the Jazz Messengers*, 1985; *Feeling Good*, 1986; *I Get a Kick out of Bu*, 1988; *Not Yet*, 1988; *Standards: Art Blakey and the Jazz Messengers*, 1988; *Feel the Wind*, 1989; *Art Blakey and Clifford Brown*, 1990; *Chippin' In*, 1990; *Jazz Messengers*, 1990; *One for All*, 1990; *Hot Licks: One by One*, 1993; *Are You Real*, 1995; *Art Blakey and the Jazz Messengers*, 1997; *Jazz in Paris: Jazz and Cinéma, Vol. 2*, 2002; *Recuerdo*, 2002; *Workshop*, 2002.

ALBUMS: *A Night at Birdland, Vols. 1-3*, 1954.

The Life

Art Blakey (BLAY-kee) was born in 1919 in Pittsburgh, Pennsylvania. His father had abandoned his mother before Blakey was born, and his mother died before his second birthday. At age fourteen, Blakey went to work in Pittsburgh's steel mills, and he played piano and led a jazz band in the evenings. The turning point in his musical life came when pianist Erroll Garner joined his band, which forced Blakey to switch to drums.

Blakey left Pittsburgh in 1939 to join Fletcher Henderson's band, and he played with Mary Lou Williams before returning to Henderson in 1943. In 1944 Blakey became the drummer for Billy Eckstine's big band, the incubator for the new bebop style. Dizzy Gillespie was the band's music director and trumpeter, and Eckstine's band included such future luminaries as Charlie Parker, Thelonious Monk, and Sarah Vaughan. With Gillespie's coaching, Blakey came of age as a bop drummer. When Eckstine's band dissolved in 1947, Blakey organized a rehearsal band called the Seventeen Messengers, and he recorded with an octet called the Messengers. When these groups proved unfeasible financially, Blakey traveled to Africa to study religion in 1948 and 1949.

In 1953 Blakey formed a cooperative group with pianist Horace Silver, saxophonist Hank Mobley, and trumpeter Kenny Dorham, and this group became the first Jazz Messengers. When Silver and the

Art Blakey. (AP/Wide World Photos)

other members left in 1956, Blakey retained the name and began the legacy of the Jazz Messengers as a training ground for young musicians. Highlights of Blakey's later career include the Jazz Messengers' first tour of Japan in 1961 and the drummer's involvement in the Giants of Jazz world tour in 1971. Blakey continued to lead and perform until just before his death from lung cancer in 1990.

The Music

In the mid-1950's, Blakey's collaborations with Silver resulted in a new style of jazz known as hard bop, which fused elements of bebop with rhythm and blues and black gospel. Its beginnings were inspired by artists such as Mahalia Jackson and Ray Charles, and it had a funky, earthy feel that was extremely popular and widely imitated. Throughout the thirty-five years he led the Jazz Messengers, Blakey remained faithful to the blues and to the swinging rhythms that defined hard bop.

Blakey's drumming was characterized by intense, driving rhythms and by his forceful and insistent two and four beat on the hi-hat. The influence of African drumming can be heard in Blakey's experimentations with altering the pitch of his drums and with complex polyrhythms. Blakey's best work was as leader of the Jazz Messengers, where he sought to teach and inspire through his strong leadership and tough playing.

A Night at Birdland. With *A Night at Birdland*, Blakey burst onto the jazz scene as a leader, and these recordings are still among the most favored by jazz fans. They were recorded live at the jazz nightclub Birdland in New York City on February 21, 1954, and they feature Blakey with Clifford Brown, trumpet; Lou Donaldson, alto saxophone; Silver, piano; and Curly Russell, bass. In addition to bop standards such as "A Night in Tunisia" and "Confirmation," *A Night at Birdland* includes several compositions by Silver. Highlights include Blakey's playing on "Quicksliver," the solos by Donaldson and Brown on "Wee-Dot," and Blakey's solo on "Mayreh."

At the Café Bohemia. These two volumes were made in Greenwich Village on November 23, 1955, and they feature the original group to take the name Jazz Messengers: Dorham, trumpet; Mobley, tenor saxophone; Silver, piano; Doug Watkins, bass; and Blakey, drums. The first volume features swinging tunes by Dorham, while the strength of the second volume is in its ballads. Throughout both volumes, Blakey is at his best, both as a drummer and as a leader. Notable is how Blakey perfectly complements and propels Dorham's solo on "Minor's Holiday," then explodes into a masterful solo of his own before the final chorus.

Moanin'. Considered by many to be Blakey's finest recording, *Moanin'* epitomizes characteristics of the Jazz Messengers that shaped the group for years to come: the hard-swinging, blues-based style, the intense solos, and the compositions by band members. The funky title track by pianist Bobby Timmons evokes gospel music, and it employs African American call-and-response refrains. Four of the five tracks of the album were composed by Messenger saxophonist Benny Golson; especially notable are his "Along Came Betty" and "Blues March." In addition to Blakey, Golson, and Timmons, the recording features Lee Morgan, trumpet, and Jymie Merritt, bass.

A Night in Tunisia. This album features one of the finest configurations of the Jazz Messengers, with Blakey joined by Lee Morgan, trumpet; Wayne Shorter, tenor saxophone; Timmons, piano; and Merritt, bass. The title track begins with Blakey accompanied by other band members on auxiliary percussion before the other instruments gradually join to state the tune. Blazing solos by Shorter and Morgan are supported by fabulous playing by Blakey, Timmons, and Merritt. After Merritt and then Blakey solo, the auxiliary percussion joins again to lead into the closing statement of the tune. The Jazz Messengers, however, are not yet done with "A Night in Tunisia": The piece continues with spectacular unaccompanied interludes first by Morgan and then by Shorter before the band joins for the closing. The remainder of this outstanding album features compositions by band members Shorter, Timmons, and Morgan.

Musical Legacy

Blakey left decades of outstanding jazz performances, many of which survive in recordings, and a long line of outstanding musicians. The list of Blakey's more than 150 Jazz Messengers sidemen reads like a "who's who" of jazz, and it includes such stars as trumpeters Brown, Dorham, Morgan, Freddie Hubbard, Chuck Mangione, Wynton Marsalis, and Terence Blanchard; saxophonists Mobley, Jackie McLean, Golson, Shorter, Bobby Watson, and Branford Marsalis; trombonist Curtis Fuller; pianists Silver, Timmons, Cedar Walton, JoAnne Brackeen, Mulgrew Miller, and Benny Green; and bassists Watkins, Merritt, and Lonnie Plaxico.

Mark A. Peters

Further Reading

Goldberg, Joe. "Art Blakey." In *Jazz Masters of the Fifties*. New York: Da Capo, 1965. This chapter describes Blakey's many accomplishments in the 1950's, and it gives an accurate picture of Blakey as man and musician.

Goldsher, Alan. *Hard Bop Academy: The Sidemen of Art Blakey and the Jazz Messengers*. Milwaukee, Wis.: Hal Leonard, 2002. An upbeat tribute to Blakey and the Jazz Messengers, with brief vignettes on many of the sidemen for the Jazz Messengers.

Gourse, Leslie. *Art Blakey: Jazz Messenger*. New

York: Schirmer Books, 2002. Jazz biographer Gourse presents a study of Blakey's life.

Korall, Burt. *Drummin' Men: The Heartbeat of Jazz—The Bebop Years*. Oxford, England: Oxford University Press, 2002. Detailed story of Blakey's life and music, with quotations about Blakey from numerous interviews conducted by the author.

Rosenthal, David H. "The Big Beat! Conversation with Art Blakey." *The Black Perspective in Music* 14 (1986): 267-289. In this conversation Blakey comments on a wide range of topics, including his life, his music, and the Jazz Messengers.

See also: Adderley, Cannonball; Barretto, Ray; Brown, Clifford; Charles, Ray; Garner, Erroll; Gillespie, Dizzy; Gordon, Dexter; Hancock, Herbie; Henderson, Fletcher; Jackson, Mahalia; Jarrett, Keith; Jones, Hank; Marsalis, Wynton; Monk, Thelonious; Parker, Charlie; Rollins, Sonny; Shorter, Wayne; Vaughan, Sarah.

Mary J. Blige

American rhythm-and-blues singer

A noted singer and songwriter, Blige combined rap and hip-hop in her empowering songs that center on self-esteem.

Born: January 11, 1971; Bronx, New York

Also known as: Mary Jane Blige (full name); Queen of Hip-Hop Soul

Principal recordings

ALBUMS: *What's the 411?*, 1992; *What's the 411? Remix*, 1992; *My Life*, 1994; *Share My World*, 1997; *Mary*, 1999; *No More Drama*, 2001; *Dance for Me*, 2002; *Love and Life*, 2003; *The Breakthrough*, 2005; *Growing Pains*, 2007.

The Life

Born in the Bronx, Mary Jane Blige (blij) spent her early years in Savannah, Georgia, where she had her first singing experiences in church. Soon she moved back to New York with her mother and sister, residing in a housing project since her broken family's budget was strained. Music was a positive influence in Blige's underprivileged life, though she dropped out of high school by junior year, a decision she regretted later. On a trip to a local mall, Blige recorded a cover of Anita Baker's "Caught Up in the Rapture" at a karaoke station. When that tape reached a local music industry executive, she got work as a background vocalist and a record deal with Uptown Records. Later, she was discovered by Sean "Puffy" Combs, who produced Blige's 1992 debut disc *What's the 411?* on Uptown/MCA. While her music career was launching, her personal life was making headlines—for several romantic relationships, including a tumultuous one with Cedric "K-Ci" Hailey (singer for soul group Jodeci), and for her abuse of drugs and alcohol. In 2000 she met music industry executive Martin Kendu Isaacs, and he helped free her from addictions. They married in 2003 in a private ceremony.

Blige has had success in other pursuits. She has acted, appearing in the television series *The Jamie Foxx Show*, in the independent film *Prison Song* (2001), and in the Off-Broadway play *The Exonerated* (2004). In addition, she started a record label, Matriarch Records, and she invested in the Carol's Daughter line of beauty products.

The Music

Early in her career, Blige was described as a combination of Aretha Franklin, Chaka Khan, and Patti LaBelle. In fact, Blige evolved from rhythm-and-blues and soul styles to rap and hip-hop.

Early Works. Thanks to the diverse sound offered in her debut *What's the 411?*, Blige attracted many listeners. The album featured the production talents of Combs, and it introduced her singular blend of hip-hop and soul, resulting in a wide array of sounds (including the danceable "Real Love" and a streetwise cover of "Sweet Thing," originally by Khan's group Rufus). Its widespread popularity paved the way for *My Life*, inspired in part by her stormy personal relationships, and it sold more than three million copies. Momentum continued with "Not Gon' Cry" on the sound track for *Waiting to Exhale* (1995) and a duet with Method Man on "I'll Be There for You/You're All I Need to Get By," for which she won her first Grammy Award for Best Rap Performance by a Duo or Group.

Share My World. On *Share My World*, Blige worked with such prominent producers as Jimmy Jam, Terry Lewis, R. Kelly, and Babyface Edmonds.

The project ran the stylistic gamut from rhythm and blues to hip-hop, and it included collaborators as diverse as the soulful Kelly, rapper Nas, and jazz artist George Benson. The album sold five million copies, and it won an American Music Award for Favorite Soul/Rhythm & Blues Music. The project also propelled Blige onto the concert circuit, which in 1998 resulted in another album, the sound track *The Tour*.

Mary. In 1999 Blige interjected pop into her urban sound, simultaneously expanding her fan base without alienating her core fans. On *Mary*, Blige sampled from or had direct contributions from Elton John, Aretha Franklin, Eric Clapton, and Lauryn Hill. This album showcased her vocal talents beyond the rap and hip-hop style.

No More Drama. Though Blige was never shy about sharing her personal emotions or admitting her faults (such as struggles with alcohol and in relationships), *No More Drama* is arguably her most forthright lyrical project. In it she sings about dismissing the harmful forces and relationships in her life, and its empowering songs (such as the title cut) became anthems for self-esteem. Besides debuting at number two on the *Billboard* album charts, it had a number-one single, "Family Affair." It sold more than three million copies in the United States.

Love and Life. As the title implies, this project centers on happy themes. With the involvement of producer Combs, the album reached back to her early sound stylings. She also reunited with Method Man on "Love @ 1st Sight"—which, along with the other singles, "Ooh!," "It's a Wrap," and "Not Today" (with Eve)—led to a chart-topping debut on the *Billboard* 200.

The Breakthrough. *The Breakthrough*, which found a top spot on the album charts, had several contributors, including urban superstars Jay-Z, 50 Cent, and the Game. Blige broke new ground by teaming up with U2, covering its hit single "One," recording it with the band, and trading vocal lines with front man Bono. It had eight nominations for Grammy Awards, and it won three, including Best Female Rhythm and Blues Vocal Performance, Best Rhythm and Blues Song, and Best Rhythm and Blues album.

Reflections: A Retrospective. After such a consistent and prolific album streak, the performer was due for a break, while her fans requested a career-spanning singles collection. Outside of radio hits such as "Real Love," "Not Gon' Cry," "No More Drama," and "Family Affair," it included four new tracks (including a duet with John Legend called "King and Queen").

Growing Pains. Blige returned in late 2007 with a thematic continuation of her prior two studio albums. *Growing Pains* discusses her lifelong struggles, and it showcases the spiritual realizations that led to her healing. The tone is old-school soul and rhythm and blues, with an occasional hip-hop and rap undercurrent. The lead single "Just Fine" was another of her odes to self-esteem. The collection was followed by an extensive concert tour with Jay-Z, which sold out several arenas across the United States.

Musical Legacy

Whether in rap, hip-hop, soul, rhythm-and-blues, or pop style, Blige's impassioned vocals are unmistakable. Her versatility has allowed her to cross over on a variety of charts. She is an inspiration to artists performing in all those styles, and she has successfully reached the success of her models, Chaka Khan and Patti LaBelle. Blige rose above her underprivileged roots and her troubles with addictions, chronicling her struggles in her songs.

Andy Argyrakis

Further Reading

Brackett, Nathan, and Christian Hoard, eds. *The New Rolling Stone Album Guide*. New York: Simon & Schuster, 2004. A definitive guide to Blige's many albums until 2004 includes background information on her rise to fame.

Brown, Terrell. *Mary J. Blige*. Broomall, Pa.: Mason Crest, 2008. In a series for juvenile readers about the hip-hop genre, the author places Blige in context and chronicles her rise to become the Queen of Hip-Hop Soul.

Hardy, Ernest. "Mary J. Blige Has Something to Tell You About Fighting AIDS, Creating a Hot New Album, and Doing the Hard Work of Living with Joy." *The Advocate*, December 4, 2007. A cover story interview in which Blige addresses issues for the gay community, along with anecdotes about her album *Growing Pains*.

Torres, Jennifer. *Blue Banner Biography: Mary J. Blige*. Hockessin, Del.: Mitchell Lane, 2007. A short but detailed account, tracing Blige's early struggles at home through her professional discovery and eventual international success.

Waldron, Clarence. "Mary J. Blige Roars Back with Hit CD *The Breakthrough* and Testifies 'You Can't Hold a Good Woman Down.'" *Jet* (January 23, 2006): 54-55. Timed for the release of *The Breakthrough*, this cover story discusses Blige's personal struggles and how she rose above her underprivileged background.

See also: Babyface; Bono; Clapton, Eric; Combs, Sean; Elliott, Missy; 50 Cent; Franklin, Aretha; Jay-Z; John, Sir Elton; LaBelle, Patti; Simone, Nina; Sting.

Kurtis Blow

American rap singer, songwriter, and keyboard player

One of the creators of the rap genre, Blow distinguished himself as a disc jockey and emcee. He was the first rapper to sign a deal with a major record label and the first rapper to have a gold record.

Born: August 9, 1959; Harlem, New York
Also known as: Curtis Walker (birth name); Kool DJ Kurt

Principal recordings

ALBUMS: *Kurtis Blow*, 1980; *Deuce*, 1981; *Tough*, 1982; *Ego Trip*, 1984; *Rapper in Town*, 1984; *America*, 1985; *Kingdom Blow*, 1986; *Back by Popular Demand*, 1988; *Only the Strong Survive*, 1988.

SINGLES: "The Breaks," 1979; "Christmas Rappin'," 1979; "Party Time?," 1983; "The Breaks 94," 1994; "Freak Rock Til the Break of Dawn," 1995.

The Life

Kurtis Blow was born as Curtis Walker in Harlem in 1959. As a teen, he attended New York's High School of Music and Art, although he was expelled for poor attendance. At his next school he was caught selling drugs, and the dean suggested that Blow skip high school and enroll in college. Blow entered the City College of New York to study

vocal performance and started programming at the radio station there. He was also working block parties as a break dancer and disc jockey, going by the name Kool DJ Kurt. Around this time he met Russell Simmons, future rap entrepreneur and cofounder of Def Jam Recordings, who persuaded him to move to Queens, another section of New York City, and change his name to Kurtis Blow.

Blow released a number of albums in the 1980's, but after his initial hits, his star waned and he began producing other rappers, such as the Fearless Four and the Fat Boys. In the early 1990's he moved to California with his wife and three children in order to pursue an acting career. However, he found success as a radio disc jockey, hosting an old-school rap show. Later he joined Sirius Satellite Radio, and he created a hip-hop ministry featuring Christian-themed rap.

The Music

When Blow first began performing as a disc jockey and emcee in the 1970's, rap was an underground genre. It was mostly heard at block parties in Harlem and Brooklyn and was traded on cassette tapes or recorded on independent labels for extremely limited release. Major record companies believed rap would be a passing fad and were not interested in adding rappers to their rosters. Surprised by the success of Sugarhill Gang's "Rapper's Delight," which became a crossover hit in 1980, Mercury Records discovered Blow's independently produced "Christmas Rappin'." It signed him, making Blow the first rapper with a major record deal. His first album sold well, but his popularity declined as the artists for whom he paved the way came up with more successful innovations in the genre. Blow's work swiftly lost its fresh sound, as rap became faster, edgier, wittier, and more rhythmically complex.

"Christmas Rappin'." Blow cowrote this song with Robert Ford, a writer from *Billboard* magazine, and released it independently in 1979. An urban retelling of *The Night Before Christmas*, the song was an underground success. Mercury Records signed Blow for two singles, agreeing that if these did well, it would release a full-length album. "Christmas Rappin'" tells the story of Santa Claus showing up to deliver gifts at a house where a Christmas Eve party is taking place and pausing there to flirt and dance with the girls before continuing on his way. The bass line mimics the one used in Queen's "Another One Bites the Dust." Slow, innocent, and comical, the single eventually went gold. Blow's career was launched on the basis of this sweet and idiosyncratic modern Christmas carol.

"The Breaks." This 1979 follow-up single clocked in at seven minutes and forty-three seconds, and it was one of the first singles to be released on a twelve-inch record. It reached the Top 5 on the *Billboard* rhythm-and-blues chart, and it marked a defining moment in rap. Using the kind of wordplay that would become common in 1980's rap, "The Breaks" refers to good and bad luck as well as break-dancing moves.

Kurtis Blow. In 1980 Blow released his first album, *Kurtis Blow*. It included "The Breaks"; "Rappin' Blow, Part Two," a sequel to "Christmas Rappin'"; and the sociopolitically themed "Hard Times." "Hard Times" presaged the political commentary that became a characteristic of later rap artists, such as Furious Five and Public Enemy. Indicating that rap had not found its foothold and that record labels were struggling to define the genre, the album contained a surprisingly ill-conceived cover of Bachman-Turner Overdrive's arena rock anthem, "Taking Care of Business."

Musical Legacy

Blow crossed paths with a surprising array of musicians during his heyday. In 1980 he opened for Bob Marley and the Wailing Wailers at Madison Square Garden in New York City. At various points he opened for the Commodores and the Clash. Bob Dylan contributed vocals to a cut on 1986's *Kingdom Blow*. When Blow's musical career went into decline, he supported other rappers' careers, helping the Fat Boys get a record deal and producing most of their albums. He had a role in the rap-themed 1985 film *Krush Groove*. Blow's hits are classics of the old-school genre, and his song "Basketball" is frequently heard at National Basketball Association games. Blow was ordained a minister, and he claims that he never in his entire career recorded a curse word. In collaboration with the National Association for the Advancement of Colored People (NAACP), he crusaded to clean up the language on contemporary hip-hop albums.

Lacy Schutz

Further Reading

Blow, Kurtis. "The Ministry of Hip-Hop: Interview with Kurtis Blow." Interview by Scotty Ballard and Javonne Stewart. *Jet*, August 28, 2006. In this interview, Blow talks about Hip Hop Church, which he founded and which uses music to attract teens and young adults to Christian services.

Forman, Murray, and Mark Anthony Neal, eds. *That's the Joint! The Hip-Hop Studies Reader*. Oxford, England: Routledge, 2004. This anthology compiles twenty-five years of scholarship on rap and hip-hop.

Fricke, Jim, and Charlie Ahearn. *Yes Yes Y'All: The Experience Music Project Oral History of Hip-Hop's First Decade*. New York: Da Capo Press, 2002. Produced by Seattle's Experience Music Project for its Hip-Hop Nation exhibit, this extensively illustrated compilation traces hip-hop's early days.

George, Nelson. *Hip-Hop America*. New York: Penguin, 2005. A journalist who has been writing about rap since the 1970's looks at the cultural milieu into which hip-hop was born.

Rockwell, John. "The New 'Rapping' Style in Pop." *The New York Times*, October 12, 1980. An early mainstream assessment of the then-new genre of rap.

See also: Dylan, Bob; LL Cool J; Marley, Bob; Simmons, Joseph "Run."

Bono

Irish rock singer and songwriter

Bono, lead vocalist and principal lyricist of the Irish rock group U2, is noted for his distinct voice and pointed lyrics about religion, politics, and human rights.

Born: May 10, 1960; Dublin, Ireland
Also known as: Paul David Hewson (birth name); Bono Vox
Member of: U2

Principal recordings

ALBUMS (solo): *God's Favorite Son*, 2004.

ALBUMS (with U2): *Boy*, 1980; *October*, 1981; *War*, 1983; *The Unforgettable Fire*, 1984; *The Joshua Tree*, 1987; *Rattle and Hum*, 1988; *Achtung Baby*, 1991; *Zooropa*, 1993; *Pop*, 1997; *All That You Can't Leave Behind*, 2000; *How to Dismantle an Atomic Bomb*, 2004; *No Line on the Horizon*, 2009.

SINGLES (with U2): "New Year's Day," 1983; "Sunday Bloody Sunday," 1983; "Pride (In the Name of Love)," 1984; "I Still Haven't Found What I'm Looking For," 1987; "Where the Streets Have No Name," 1987; "With or Without You," 1987.

WRITINGS OF INTEREST: *On the Move*, 2006.

The Life

Paul David Hewson was born in Dublin, Ireland, to Robert and Iris Hewson, and, with his older brother Norman, he was raised in the Protestant religion. He attended the Protestant-run Mount Temple Comprehensive School, where he met his future U2 bandmates and his wife, Ali. In his street-gang youth, Hewson had several nicknames, including Bono (BAH-noh), an abbreviation of a loose Latin translation of bonavox (good voice) taken from a Dublin hearing aid store, and he has been known as Bono, publicly and privately, ever since.

In 1976 Bono responded to Larry Mullen's school bulletin board advertisement for musicians to form a band. Almost two years later, U2 won a talent show in Limerick, Ireland, and the prize included funding for a demo release. In May, 1978, Paul McGuinness became U2's manager, and the band—with Bono on guitar, Mullen on drums, David Evans (The Edge) on guitar and keyboards, and Adam Clayton on bass—began its long and extremely successful musical career.

Aside from his work with U2, Bono collaborated with other artists, made several profitable financial investments, wrote poetry, and participated in numerous humanitarian efforts to help those suffering in Africa and from AIDS. To support his charities, he established EDUN, described as a socially conscious clothing line. He met with President George

Bono. (AP/Wide World Photos)

W. Bush at the National Prayer Breakfast in Washington, D.C., in 2006. Among Bono's numerous achievements are British knighthood and nominations for the Nobel Prize and Academy, Golden Globe, and Grammy Awards.

The Music

Bono is best recognized as a rock musician, specifically as lead vocalist and principal lyricist of the Irish rock group U2. U2's consistent popularity can be linked to its willingness to experiment sonically, while maintaining its distinctive sound, and the broad range of subjects in its songs' lyrics.

Early Works. In 1976, after an inauspicious beginning in Mullen's kitchen, U2 garnered some attention when it released a demo that gained the notice of Island Records, which signed the band in 1980. U2's first major release, *Boy*, received positive reviews, and that was followed by a less-successful second album, *October*. Both albums' lyrics reveal a strong emphasis on the band's Christian faith, with *October* earning a spot on *Contemporary Christian Music Magazine*'s list of top Christian albums of all time. U2's third album, *War*, retained some of the band's earlier Christian themes, but it was more politically charged. The Daniel Lanois-Brian Eno-engineered fourth release, *The Unforgettable Fire*, was a marked change from previous albums, with its experimental, impressionistic, and improvisatory music.

The Joshua Tree *and* Rattle and Hum. The band's exploration of indigenous American musical genres helped shape its fifth album, *The Joshua Tree*, which quickly rose to the top of international charts and which some consider one of the best rock albums of all time. The American-influenced recording also won U2 its first two Grammy Awards and is a consistent best-seller. The next album and its accompanying documentary, *Rattle and Hum*, contained a mixture of new material and live recordings; however, it received mixed reviews from critics.

Achtung Baby. Taking a break from *Rattle and Hum*, U2 released its seventh album in 1991 to rave reviews and reception. The band starting arguing while they were recording the album, because Bono and the Edge wanted to incorporate more techno-electronic and dancelike sounds, while Mullen and Clayton wanted to maintain U2's rock-and-roll feel. The conflict threatened to break apart the band, but the members eventually came together to write the mega-hit "One."

Later Works. Following the outstanding success of *Achtung Baby*, U2's next two albums, *Zooropa* and *Pop*, utilized the band's interest in experimental music and techniques and were not as commercially successful as previous albums. After a brief hiatus from recording, U2's 2000 release, *All That You Can't Leave Behind*, signaled a return to the band's traditional roots in rock. That album and the next, *How to Dismantle an Atomic Bomb*, were extremely successful, garnering more Grammy Awards for the band. In 2005 U2 was inducted into the Rock and Roll Hall of Fame.

Musical Legacy

As principal lyricist and lead singer of the rock group U2, Bono became a rock-and-roll legend. U2's distinct sound is largely credited to Bono's unique vocals, which range from impassioned and throaty to falsetto. Lyrically, Bono has been inspired by his Christian faith, his mother's untimely death, political concerns, social justice, and humanitarian work. Despite the public's fickle taste in popular music, U2 has maintained its popularity, with its forays into various musical sounds, from gospel to techno. Bono cites as his influences the Clash, the Beatles, and the Who. U2, in turn, has influenced Coldplay, the Killers, Snow Patrol, and many more.

Anastasia Pike

Further Reading

Bordowitz, Hank. *U2 Reader*. Milwaukee, Wis.: Hal Leonard, 2003. An excellent resource documents the band from professional and personal perspectives. Includes notable newspaper interviews and objective analysis.

Cashman, Lola. *Inside the Zoo with U2: My Life with the World's Biggest Rock Band*. London: John Blake, 2003. U2's first stylist gives an interesting, highly subjective, and controversial glimpse into U2's image.

De la Parra, Pimm Jal. *U2 Live: A Concert Documentary*. London: Omnibus Press, 2003. Extensive documentation of all U2 concerts through part of the PopMart tour. Contains details from set lists to pizza-delivery orders.

Scharen, Christian. *One Step Closer: Why U2 Matters to Those Seeking God*. Ada, Mich.: Brazos Press, 2006. Written by a Yale Divinity School faculty member and Lutheran minister, the book explores the seeming dichotomy between U2's Christian lyrics and the rock-and-roll lifestyle.

U2, and Neil McCormick. *U2 by U2*. New York: HarperCollins, 2006. The band's autobiography includes stunning photography and personal insights from each member.

See also: Blige, Mary J.; Jones, Quincy; Lennon, John; McCartney, Sir Paul; Morrison, Van; Orbison, Roy; Pavarotti, Luciano; Prokofiev, Sergei; Strummer, Joe.

Nadia Boulanger

French classical composer, conductor, and teacher

Known as Mademoiselle to her legions of students, Boulanger taught numerous performers and composers, among them Aaron Copland, Darius Milhaud, and Leonard Bernstein, the intricacies of musicianship.

Born: September 16, 1887; Paris, France
Died: October 22, 1979; Paris, France
Also known as: Nadia Juliette Boulanger (full name)

Principal works

CHAMBER WORKS: *Trois Pièces*, 1911 (for organ); *Trois Pièces*, 1914 (for voice); *Pièce for orgue sur des airs populaires flamands*, 1915; *Vers la vie nouvelle*, 1917.

CHORAL WORKS: *Allons voir sur le lac d'argent*, 1905; *Les Sirènes*, 1905; *À l'aube*, 1906; *Selma*, 1907; *À l'hirondelle*, 1908; *La Sirène*, 1908; *Roussalka*, 1909; *Soir d'été*, 1909.

ORCHESTRAL WORKS: *Allegro*, 1905; *Fantaisie variée*, 1912.

The Life

Nadia Juliette Boulanger (NAH-dyah zhoo-LYEHT boo-lahn-ZHAY), born in 1887, was the daughter of Raïssa Mychestsky, singer, and Henri Alexandre Ernest Boulanger, composer, vocal professor, conductor, and pianist. An older and younger sister died in infancy, and Boulanger's surviving sister, Marie-Juliette Olga (Lili) Boulanger, became a well-known composer.

Boulanger began to show an interest in music at the age of five. Her father, a man she respected throughout her life, was her first teacher; he taught her aesthetics, art, and music. Her mother instructed her in reading, geography, and French and German. The strong work ethic instilled by her mother remained with Boulanger all her life.

Boulanger entered the Paris Conservatory when she was nine years old, although she had been auditing classes since she was seven. She continued private lessons, studying piano and organ with Louis Vierne. She eventually studied with Paul Vidal, Alexandre Guilmant, and Auguste Chapuis. Boulanger's intense focus on her lessons resulted in numerous first-place awards from the Paris Conservatory, which did not give out diplomas but instead awarded prizes indicating that a student had mastered the information.

Four years after her father's death in 1900, the family moved to an apartment on rue Ballu in Paris, and this was Boulanger's home for the rest of her life. It also functioned as her studio and salon, where she entertained the notable musicians, artists, and writers of the era. At this time, Boulanger, her mother, and her sister purchased a home in Gargenville, France, where they retreated during the hot summer months.

Boulanger met pianist Raoul Pugno in 1904 during her last exam, the accompagnement au piano, at the Paris Conservatory. He acted as her adviser until his death in 1914. Together they collaborated on *Les Heures claire*, a series of songs, and *La Ville morte*, an opera that was never performed.

When Boulanger completed her studies, she began her professional career in order to support her family. She played the organ; she worked as an assistant to Henri Dallier at the Church of the Madeleine; she accompanied such performers as Paul Franz, Marthe Chenal, and Suzanne Balguerie; and she performed as a pianist and conductor in concerts with Pugno. One concert featured her *Fantaisie variée* for piano and orchestra.

Just seventeen when she began teaching, Boulanger wore austere clothing—low-heeled shoes, long black skirts with white shirts, dark bow ties, black jackets, and spectacles—and pulled her hair back into a chignon to project an air of maturity. (Only when visiting Gargenville did she relax her style.) Her first students were her sister Lili and young ladies from wealthy families, including Annette Dieudonné, who became her companion in later life. In the rue Ballu apartment, Boulanger instructed her students using one of the two Pleyel grand pianos or the full-sized Cavaillé-Coll-Mutin organ with fourteen ranks of pipes. Lessons included performance, sight reading, sight singing, harmony, composition, counterpoint, accompaniment, and music history. Later, Wednesday-afternoon salons at Boulanger's apartment were regarded as significant, and only students who showed promise were invited to mingle there with the reigning composers of the day, such as Igor Stravinsky, Maurice Ravel, and Francis Poulenc.

In addition to being active in the musical world, Boulanger participated in such civic activities as writing letters to soldiers and arranging music for them throughout World War I. At the end of the war, Boulanger performed a concert to benefit the orphans. When World War II erupted, she moved to the United States at the request of her students, but she continued to be active in raising money for French musicians and soldiers.

In 1918 Lili died at the age of twenty-four, a death that deeply affected Boulanger, who pledged to devote herself to preserving her sister's memory. She accomplished this by promoting Lili's musical compositions and assisting Walter Damrosch, conductor of the New York Symphony, when he programmed Lili's *Faust et Hélène*.

In 1920 Boulanger replaced Paul Dukas in teaching music history at the École Normale de Musique in Paris, the first woman to hold this position. In addition, she taught organ, harmony, counterpoint, and composition there until 1939. In 1921 Damrosch persuaded Boulanger to join the faculty at the newly created summer American Conservatory in Fontainebleau, where she taught harmony, composition, and counterpoint, and at one point she was appointed director of the school. Boulanger also took a position in the Conservatoire Femina-Musica, and she received an appointment to teach at the Paris Conservatory. During World War II, while she lived in the United States, she was a visiting professor at the Longy School of Music in Cambridge, Massachusetts, and she taught at Radcliffe College in Boston, Massachusetts; at Wellesley College in Wellesley, Massachusetts; at Juilliard School of Music in New York City; and at the Dominican Convent in Santa Clara, Wisconsin.

After a lifetime of teaching music, Boulanger died in her home in Paris in 1979. She left the majority of her papers, including family documents, musical scores, personal compositions, honorary degrees, correspondence, and more, to the Boulanger archives in the Bibliothèque Nationale in Paris.

The Music

Boulanger's strict musical education resulted in first prizes in organ, accompagnement au piano,

and fugue from the Paris Conservatory. Following her father's death, her goal was to support her family by writing music, giving lessons, and performing. Her lessons continued outside the Paris Conservatory with Alphonse Duvernoy, Charles Widor, Paul Vidal, and Gabriel Fauré.

La Sirène. In 1908 Boulanger won the second prize in the prestigious Prix de Rome competition for her cantata *La Sirène*, although there was some controversy. There was an allegation that Boulanger, in the early stage of the competition, had composed the fugue for string quartet instead of for vocalists. This almost caused her to be disqualified from the competition, because the composition was required to be written for at least four voices.

Monteverdi. As an accomplished conductor and music historian, Boulanger organized numerous concerts of music from the medieval, Renaissance, and Baroque style periods featuring her vocal ensemble of talented amateur and professional singers in both live and recorded sessions. In 1937 Boulanger and her vocal ensemble produced five recordings of the madrigals of Claudio Monteverdi, one of the first times Monteverdi's music had been recorded.

Conductor. Although Boulanger was a composer and arranger, she renounced composition two years after her sister Lili's death. She continued to perform as an accomplished organist and conductor, the first woman to lead such renowned orchestras as the Royal Philharmonic Orchestra of London, the New York Philharmonic Orchestra, the Philadelphia Orchestra, and the Boston Symphony Orchestra.

Musical Legacy

Boulanger's musical legacy is her students, with whom she shared her vast knowledge of music, including composition, theory, harmony, and history, and in whom she stimulated interests in various types and styles of music. Boulanger witnessed the changes in music from the teachings of her father, who focused on late 1800's works, through the experimentation of Stravinsky and the serialism of Arnold Schoenberg. In fact, all music was valuable to her. She was fascinated by the polyrhythms found in American jazz.

Boulanger taught her students to recognize the significance of a composition by Johann Sebastian

Bach and by Monteverdi. Her composition and her performing students were encouraged to find "la grande ligne" to accentuate the flow of the music throughout the piece. In addition, she encouraged them to understand all the musical elements and their function in the composition and the place that the composition held in musical history.

History and technique were just two of the gifts Boulanger gave her students: In addition, she championed her students' musical abilities. Former students stayed in touch with Boulanger and sent her their compositions for review, which she promoted to other musicians. For example, she commissioned Aaron Copland to compose Symphony for Organ and Orchestra. She performed the work with Damrosch and the New York Symphony Orchestra and then with Serge Koussevitzky and the Boston Symphony.

Roberta L. Lindsey

Further Reading

Campbell, Don G. *Master Teacher: Nadia Boulanger.* Washington, D.C.: Pastoral Press, 1984. A biography, with writings by Boulanger and quotations from her students. Includes illustrations.

Kendall, Alan. *The Tender Tyrant: Nadia Boulanger, a Life Devoted to Music.* Wilton, Conn.: Lyceum Books, 1976. A student of Boulanger examines her teaching techniques and incredible knowledge of music. Includes illustrations.

Monsaingeon, Bruno, and Nadia Boulanger. *Mademoiselle: Conversations with Nadia Boulanger.* Boston: Northeastern University Press, 1988. This intriguing book provides mock interviews with Boulanger, the author sculpting Boulanger's words to his imagined questions. Includes illustrations.

Rosenstiel, Léonie. *Nadia Boulanger: A Life in Music.* New York: W. W. Norton, 1982. Violinist, student, and family friend of Boulanger presents a thorough biography of the composer-teacher. Includes illustrations.

Spycket, Jérôme. *Nadia Boulanger.* Translated by M. M. Shriver. Stuyvesant, N.Y.: Pendragon Press, 1992. Originally written in French, this book won a prize for literature from the Académie des Beaux-Arts. Spycket, a musician, artist, and writer, portrays Boulanger in a fair and balanced manner. Includes illustrations and bibliography.

See also: Barenboim, Daniel; Carter, Elliott; Copland, Aaron; Glass, Philip; Koussevitzky, Serge; Legrand, Michel; Piazzolla, Astor; Poulenc, Francis; Ravel, Maurice; Schoenberg, Arnold; Stravinsky, Igor; Thomson, Virgil; Xenakis, Iannis.

Pierre Boulez

French classical composer and conductor

A prominent composer, conductor, and director of the avant-garde in the postwar era, Boulez broke with past musical traditions by developing and promoting music characterized by integral serialism, pointillism, and indeterminacy. As the director of the Institut de Recherche et Coordination Acoustique/Musique (IRCAM), he influenced the direction of electroacoustic music.

Born: March 26, 1925; Montbrison, France

Principal works

CHAMBER WORKS: Sonatina for Flute and Piano, 1947; *Polyphonie X*, 1951 (for eighteen instruments); *Le Marteau sans maître*, 1955; *Livre pour quatour*, 1955; *Éclat*, 1965; *Domaines*, 1968; *Explosante-fixe*, 1972; *Répons*, 1981.

ORCHESTRAL WORKS: *Le Soleil des eaux*, 1950 (for voice and orchestra); *Le Visage nuptial*, 1957; *Doubles*, 1958; *Poésie pour pouvoir*, 1958; *Pli selon pli*, 1960; *Livre pour cordes*, 1968; *Rituel*, 1975; *Notations*, 1980.

PIANO WORKS: *Notations*, 1945; Piano Sonata No. 1, 1946; Piano Sonata No. 2, 1950; *Structures*, 1952, completed 1953, revised 1961; Piano Sonata No. 3, 1957.

WRITINGS OF INTEREST: *Pierre Boulez: Conversations with Celestin Deliege*, 1985; *Orientations: Collected Writings*, 1990.

Principal recordings

ALBUMS (as conductor): *Schönberg: Das Chorwek*, 1990; *Debussy: Pelléas et Mélisande*, 1991; *Richard Wagner: Overtures and Preludes*, 1995; *Mahler: Symphony No. 4*, 2000; *Bartók: Piano Concertos*

Nos. 1 and 3, 2003; *Stravinsky: The Firebird Suite*, 2005; *Wagner: Der Ring des Nibelungen*, 2006.

The Life

Pierre Boulez (pyehr boo-LEHZ) was born in 1925 during the peace between the two world wars. He showed an aptitude for music and math, both important for his professional development. After a conflict with his father, who wanted him to pursue engineering, Boulez moved to Paris in 1942 to enroll in the Paris Conservatory. For the next three years, in German-occupied Paris, Boulez received his musical training from teachers such as Olivier Messiaen (harmony and analysis), René Leibowitz (serial techniques), and Andrée Vaurabourg (counterpoint). By the end of the war in 1945, Boulez had completed his formal studies.

As a composer, Boulez rose to prominence while still at the Paris Conservatory, having won a first prize in harmony before leaving in 1945. From the beginning of his career, he produced works in an avant-garde style and aesthetic, consciously avoiding formal structures and idioms from the past. From 1945 through 1952, he experimented with integral serialism. Throughout the 1950's, he also experimented with indeterminacy, producing some of his most famous works. Gradually, throughout the 1950's and early 1960's, his compositional output decreased, with Boulez shifting his energies to teaching and to conducting.

As an educator, Boulez taught composition at the Darmstadt International Summer Courses for New Music, at the Basle Musik-Akademie, and at Harvard. Many of his lectures and writings related to his teaching career during the 1950's and 1960's have been published, and they are a valuable source to understanding his music as well as the overall direction of postwar contemporary music.

As a director, Boulez began his successful career with a position as director of the Compagnie Renaud-Barrault, a new company formed in Paris in 1946. Although he was only twenty-one years old at the time, Boulez already showed an aptitude for management in the music industry. In 1954, less than ten years later, he established the Domaine Musical concert series, providing a venue for the performance of new music. He continued to influence the direction of musical life in Paris, becoming the president of the Paris Musicians' Union in 1965.

In 1969 he accepted a position as chief conductor of London's BBC Symphony Orchestra. In 1970 he became the director of the New York Philharmonic, serving in that capacity until 1977. In that year, the Institut de Recherche et Coordination Acoustique/Musique (IRCAM) opened in Paris. Boulez became its first director, remaining in that position until 1992.

The Music

Boulez wrote his first works under the influence of Olivier Messiaen. Boulez was attracted to the idea of rhythm as an extension, rather than a division, of time, as well as to his precompositional, objective, logical, and serial determinations of the various elements of music.

Additionally, the composers known as the Second Viennese School—Arnold Schoenberg, Alban Berg, and especially Anton von Webern—influenced Boulez's early experiments with serial techniques. Not satisfied with the classical and Romantic idioms still existing in Arnold Schoenberg's and Alban Berg's music, Boulez moved toward integral serialism. The strictest compositions in this style were analogous to the pointillist technique of painting in art. By 1952, after the composition of *Structures* for two pianos, his own style emerged.

In addition to serial techniques, Boulez experimented with open forms that allowed for a certain amount of indeterminacy in performance. He allowed performers to choose the order of defined sections within larger works. Although his works were not as freely determined by chance as were the aleatory works of John Cage, with whom he was in frequent communication, Boulez remained an important figure in this area. Throughout his career, Boulez's compositional method has included reworking older pieces. For this reason, his oeuvre is characterized by numerous versions and revisions of the same work, a number of which remain unpublished.

Early Works. From 1945 until about 1950, Boulez produced works that had been heavily influenced by his formal training and his teachers. Although he experimented with unconventional instruments such as the ondes martenot, he wrote largely for works that included the piano. In Sonatina for Flute and Piano, Boulez consciously departed from the prevailing French neoclassic style, choosing rather the style of Schoenberg's tone rows and Messiaen's rhythmic cells. This piece, for which Boulez received a public review, marked his debut as an important composer. Piano Sonata No. 1 and Piano Sonata No. 2 were also composed during this time, a further attempt to integrate serial techniques into all areas of the music and to eliminate large formal structures.

Le Visage nuptial. Originally written in 1946 and based on five poems by René Char, *Le Visage nuptial* can be seen as an early work, although it is an example of many of Boulez's works that have undergone reworking. The first version was scored for solo soprano along with a small group of instruments that included two ondes martenot. The 1951 revised work is for women's chorus and full orchestra. The music shows further experimentation with precompositional serial processes that give a non-sentimental objectivity, an expressionistic, and a highly charged tension to the music. Instead of the classical structures of song, strophic, refrain, variation, and other text-based forms, Boulez created a structure based on symmetry and retrogradable rhythmic phrases found entirely in the music.

Structures. Written for two pianos, this first of two works with the title *Structures* is considered to be the textbook example of total serialism. Boulez's inspiration for this work was Messiaen's "Mode de valeurs et d'intensités," the starting point for *Structures*. This work is governed by a series of twelve factors in each of four elements of music—pitch, duration, attack, and dynamics—although Boulez achieves variety through transposition, inversion, and retrograde applications. Whereas these elements are determined rigidly by the rows and their manipulations, some choice is evident in assignments to register and density. The result is a disjunctive, pointillistic texture of seemingly random and unrelated pitches, sounding in a wide variety of dynamic levels and attacks. The series is the underlying order to the work, although it is not easily apparent to the listener.

Le Marteau sans maître. In 1953 Boulez began work on *Le Marteau sans maître* (the hammer without a master), a vocal work in nine movements again based on poetry by Char. The composition is based on serialism, but it is one that grows by extending variations and multiplications of the basic series in order to sustain coherence in a large work. It also explores unusual sonorities of various groupings of instruments in each of the movements, reminiscent of Schoenberg's *Pierrot lunaire* (1912).

Pli selon pli. Inspired by the poetry of Stéphane Mallarmé, *Pli selon pli* (fold upon fold), composed for soprano and orchestra, is one of Boulez's most famous works. The five movements—"Don," three interior "Improvisations sur Mallarmé," and "Tombeau"—are a tribute to the life and death of the poet. While continuing to employ serial techniques and rhythmic ideas that constantly avoid the establishment of a regular beat, Boulez experiments with a limited degree of indeterminacy, in which some choices in performance are given to either the conductor or the performer.

Piano Sonata No. 3. Reaching the height of Boulez's exploration of indeterminacy, Piano So-

Pierre Boulez. (Library of Congress)

nata No. 3 incorporates freedom in choosing the order in performance of given sections of the music. Rather than having movements, the five major parts of the work are called "formants," because they are always in flux within a given set of parameters. In this sense, the music follows combinatorial procedures that allow for a range of performance possibilities. The first formant, "Antiphonie," is composed with two independent structures that have several possible orderings in performance together. Within each of the formants, there is a specified formula for changing the order and sequence of the sections. In the overall work, the formants themselves may be performed in an order allowing for some limited choices. "Antiphonie," for example, may be performed first, second, or last, but "Constellation" and "Constellation-miroir," the middle formant, must remain at the center of the piece.

Musical Legacy

Boulez has been one of the most influential composers and conductors of the latter half of the twentieth century. His work to eradicate every element from past traditions in the Western style and to create compositions that explored new ways of thinking about and composing music became an ideal for other composers. His continual reworking of his own compositions is evidence of a mind that continually seeks to incorporate new ideas. His thinking has advanced with musical innovation, from his early experiments in serialism to his excursions into quarter tones, indeterminacy, and electronic music. Although his compositional output decreased as he devoted more time to conducting and directing, all of his works can be found at the forefront of the avant-garde.

Because Boulez was a prolific writer, his legacy extends to his written work. He continues to influence musicians and composers through his philosophy, his attitude, his technical explanations, his views of other composers, and his analyses of the works of others and of his own.

In terms of his work as a promoter of new music through his positions as directors of large orchestras in Europe as well as in the United States, he has taken an active role in bringing new works to stages that had hitherto resisted modernization. His work as director of IRCAM has furthermore placed him in a prominent position to foster new avenues for creative research in music.

Sandra S. Yang

Further Reading

Born, Georgina. *Rationalizing Culture: IRCAM, Boulez, and the Institutionalization of the Musical Avant-Garde*. Berkeley: University of California Press, 1995. This is a study of the organization of IRCAM, the sociology of its composers and employees, and its importance in understanding the culture and economy of government-funded avant-garde music production. Born is an anthropologist who spent time participating in the activities at IRCAM.

Boulez, Pierre. *Orientations: Collected Writings*. Edited by Jean-Jacques Nattiez and translated by Martin Cooper. Cambridge, Mass.: Harvard University Press, 1986. This complete collection of writings by the composer is divided into three major sections: one that explains Boulez's own compositional processes and aesthetic, one that comments on other composers, and one of reflections.

Boulez, Pierre, and John Cage. *The Boulez-Cage Correspondence*. Edited by Jean-Jacques Nattiez and translated and edited by Robert Samuels. Cambridge, England: Cambridge University Press, 1993. This valuable source contains the letters of the two great composers, often with detailed theoretical and analytical notes regarding new works. A valuable source for understanding parallel developments in avant-garde music in Europe and in the United States.

Gable, David. "Boulez's Two Cultures: The Postwar European Synthesis and Tradition." *Journal of the American Musicological Society* 43 (1990): 426-456. This article analyzes Boulez's work and the extent to which he was able to cast off the Western traditions he had inherited.

Glock, William, ed. *Pierre Boulez: A Symposium*. London: Eulenburg Books, 1986. This detailed biography of Boulez is written by a variety of scholars, all knowledgeable in the life and work of the composer. The book systematically discusses Boulez's contributions over the span of his career.

Vermeil, Jean. *Conversations with Boulez: Thoughts on Conducting*. Translated by Camille Nash. Portland, Oreg.: Amadeus Press, 1989. This valuable work in the format of an interview contains a famous treatise on conducting by Boulez.

See also: Babbitt, Milton; Barenboim, Daniel; Berg, Alban; Berio, Luciano; Cage, John; Carter, Elliott; Honegger, Arthur; Messiaen, Olivier; Nono, Luigi; Rampal, Jean-Pierre; Ravel, Maurice; Schoenberg, Arnold; Stockhausen, Karlheinz; Varèse, Edgard; Webern, Anton von.

David Bowie

English rock-pop singer and songwriter

Throughout his career, Bowie has presented completely new stage personas and fresh compositional styles—encompassing folk, glam rock, psychedelic, soul, disco, heavy metal, hip-hop, avant-garde, electronic, and other subgenres.

Born: January 8, 1947; London, England
Also known as: David Robert Jones (birth name); Ziggy Stardust; Thin White Duke

Principal recordings

ALBUMS: *David Bowie*, 1967; *Space Oddity*, 1969; *Hunky Dory*, 1971; *The Man Who Sold the World*, 1971; *The Rise and Fall of Ziggy Stardust and the Spiders from Mars*, 1972; *Aladdin Sane*, 1973; *Pin Ups*, 1973; *Diamond Dogs*, 1974; *Young Americans*, 1975; *Station to Station*, 1976; *Heroes*, 1977; *Low*, 1977; *Lodger*, 1979; *Scary Monsters (and Super Creeps)*, 1980; *Let's Dance*, 1983; *Oddity*, 1984; *Tonight*, 1984; *Never Let Me Down*, 1987; *Sound and Vision*, 1989; *Black Tie, White Noise*, 1993; *Outside*, 1995; *Earthling*, 1997; *Hours*, 1999; *London Boy*, 2001; *Heathen*, 2002; *Reality*, 2003.

The Life

Born David Robert Jones on January 8, 1947, in London, England, David Bowie (BOH-ee) was the son of Heywood Stenton Jones and Margret Burns, who married in September, 1947. Bowie grew up with a half sister, Annette, and a stepbrother, Terry.

As a youngster, he learned to play saxophone. In Bromley, Kent, he attended a technical boys' high school, where a fistfight with a classmate left him with a permanently dilated left pupil.

Leaving school at age sixteen, Bowie worked briefly as a commercial artist. He meanwhile performed with a succession of bands: the Kon-rads, King-Bees, Manish Boys, Lower Third, and Riot Squad. By 1966, to avoid being mistaken for Davy Jones of the Monkees, he changed his name to David Bowie.

Bowie released his debut self-titled album in 1967, the first of more than twenty recordings, most of which have charted well in England. Bowie added acting to his repertoire with the lead role in the film *The Man Who Fell to Earth* (1976), and he has appeared in other films, such as *The Hunger* (1983), *Merry Christmas, Mister Lawrence* (1983), *Labyrinth* (1986), *The Last Temptation of Christ* (1988), and *The Prestige* (2006), and he has appeared on Broadway in *The Elephant Man* (1979). Bowie also served as producer on acclaimed albums from Iggy Pop, Lou Reed, and others. Ever the innovator, in the late 1990's, he launched BowieNet, an Internet service provider.

An androgynous, highly visible, controversial figure, Bowie in the early 1970's publicly declared his bisexuality, but he later admitted it was a temporary lifestyle choice. He married his first wife, Angela Barnett, in 1970, and they had a son, Duncan Zowie Heywood Jones, born in 1971, before they divorced in 1980. After extended periods of drug abuse during the 1970's and 1980's, Bowie married for a second time, to Somali supermodel Iman (Abdulmajid) in 1992, and they had a daughter, Alexandria Zahra Jones, in 2000. The family divides time between homes in New York and London. After recuperation from an angioplasty in 2004, Bowie resumed a restrained tour schedule, and he is involved in a variety of other activities, including writing the sound track for a video game and contributing to other musicians' albums.

The Music

The lyrics of an early Bowie single, "Changes," encapsulate his entire musical career. Extreme change—in the form of wildly different onstage personas and musical styles—has characterized

Bowie's work since he began writing and performing in the 1960's.

Early Works. Bowie began with little clear musical direction. His self-titled debut album mixed pop songs, psychedelic-influenced tunes, and novelty numbers, and it drew scant attention. He injected theatrical elements into his performances, and he began creating characters to lend visual interest to his music. His first hit, the single "Space Oddity," released in 1969 to coincide with the Apollo moon landing, rocketed to the top of the charts in England.

Glam Rock. After moderately successful heavy rock (*The Man Who Sold the World*) and acoustic (*Hunky Dory*) albums, Bowie made a major impact with *The Rise and Fall of Ziggy Stardust and the Spiders from Mars*, a glam rock concept album that produced hits such as "Moonage Daydream," "Starman," and "Suffragette City." Adopting the title character's persona, Bowie toured in support of the album, sporting a wild mane of red hair and outrageous costumes. At the same time, Bowie established Main Man Productions, which produced breakthrough albums for Lou Reed and the Stooges.

Bowie's follow-up album, *Aladdin Sane*, added to his star allure, rising to number one on charts in England and yielding such hits as "The Jean Genie" and "Drive-in Saturday." *Pin Ups*, featuring Bowie's covers of 1960's standards, also hit number one in England. In 1974 Bowie switched to pop-oriented music, releasing the rhythm-and-blues- and disco-heavy *Diamond Dogs*. The album claimed the top spot on British charts, and it reached number five in the United States, with hit singles such as the title cut and "Rebel Rebel." The funky, soulful *Young Americans* album solidified Bowie's foothold in the United States with the hit single "Fame."

The Thin White Duke. By the release of the U.S. number-three-ranked *Station to Station*, in which the soul theme, though choppy and disjointed, was still prominent, Bowie—now in the alter ego of the Thin White Duke—was a star in America. Nevertheless, at the peak of his popularity, Bowie moved to West Berlin to combat his cocaine addiction. During a four-year sojourn, he discovered electronics and minimalism, producing three experimental albums that incorporated world-beat rhythms—*Low*, *Heroes*, and *Lodger*—but yielded no major hits.

In 1980 Bowie released the hard-edged *Scary Monsters (and Super Creeps)*, which generated a top single, "Ashes to Ashes." *Let's Dance* built upon that momentum with the hits "Modern Love" and "China Girl," as did a second dance album, *Never Let Me Down*. Following a two-year stint with Tin Machine, a new band that did little to enhance his reputation, Bowie changed direction with *Black Tie, White Noise*, focusing on soul, jazz, and hip-hop.

Later Work. After veering into alternative and electronic music with *Outside*, Bowie returned to an emphasis on live instrumentation and on a softer, introspective sound with *Hours*. *Heathen*, featuring darker material, charted well with singles such as "Slow Burn" and "I've Been Waiting for You."

Musical Legacy

An original, much-emulated, gender-bending theatrical stage presence, Bowie has demonstrated an uncanny ability to anticipate and capitalize on trends. Performing in an amazing range of genres, he has remained at the cutting edge of music, and he has produced well-received performances on film and stage, and he has demonstrated excellent skills as a sound and video producer.

Bowie has received many honors during his lifetime: Grammy Awards (in 1984 for Best Video Short Form and in 2006 for lifetime achievement), BRIT Awards (in 1984 for best British Male Solo Artist and in 1996 for outstanding contributions to music), and Webby Awards (in 2007 for outstanding contributions to music). Bowie was inducted into the Rock and Roll Hall of Fame in 1996. He refused knighthood in 2003.

Jack Ewing

Further Reading

Bowie, Angela. *Backstage Passes: Life on the Wild Side with David Bowie*. New York: Cooper Square Press, 2000. Written by Bowie's former wife, this behind-the-scenes personal memoir focuses on the singer's bizarre behavior.

Buckley, David. *Strange Fascination: David Bowie: The Definitive Story*. London: Virgin Books, 2001. An in-depth biography of Bowie, illustrated with photographs, emphasizes the singer as an artist.

Pegg, Nicholas. *The Complete David Bowie*. Richmond, England: Reynolds & Hearn, 2006. This comprehensive and illustrated look at Bowie features analyses of albums, production histories, and live show documentation.

Waldrep, Shelton. *The Aesthetics of Self-Invention: Oscar Wilde to David Bowie*. Minneapolis: University of Minnesota Press, 2004. This scholarly work examines various personalities, among them Bowie, who created images for public consumption.

Welch, Chris. *Davie Bowie: We Could Be Heroes: The Stories Behind Every David Bowie Song*. New York: Thunder's Mouth Press, 1999. This is a song-by-song examination of the inspiration for Bowie's lyrics and music.

See also: Brel, Jacques; Eno, Brian; Glass, Philip; Latifah, Queen; Newley, Anthony; Prokofiev, Sergei; Reed, Jimmy; Reich, Steve; Simone, Nina; Vaughan, Stevie Ray.

Jacques Brel

Belgian cabaret and pop vocalist, songwriter, and film-score composer

A major figure in the French chanson tradition of the 1950's and 1960's, Brel wrote and performed songs that were musically rich and varied and were noted for their masterful and expressive lyrics.

Born: April 8, 1929; Brussels, Belgium
Died: October 9, 1978; Bobigny, France
Also known as: Jacques Romain Georges Brel (full name)

Principal works

FILM SCORES: *Un Roi sans divertissement*, 1963; *La Bande à bonnot*, 1969; *Mon oncle Benjamin*, 1969; *Le Bar de la Fourche*, 1972; *L'Emmerdeur*, 1973.

Principal recordings

ALBUMS: *Jacques Brel et ses chansons*, 1955; *Jacques Brel Vol. 2*, 1957; *Jacques Brel Vol. 3*, 1958; *American Début*, 1959; *Jacques Brel Vol. 4*, 1959; *Jacques Brel (1962)*, 1962; *Jacques Brel accompagne pas François Rauber et son orchestra*, 1963; *Jacques Brel Vol. 5*, 1964; *Jacques Brel Vol. 6*, 1964; *Jacques Brel*, 1965; *Encore*, 1966; *Jacques Brel*, 1966; *J'arrive*, 1968; *Jacques Brel*, 1968; *Brel*, 1977; *Infiniment*, 2004.

The Life

Jacques Romain Georges Brel (jahk brehl) was born to Romain and Élisabeth Brel. Although at first Brel worked in his father's cardboard factory, he displayed little interest in continuing in that line of work, focusing instead on culture. He began acting and singing after joining the Franche Cordée, a Catholic humanist youth organization. It was there that he met his wife, Thérèse Michielsen, whom he married in 1950.

In 1953 Brel quit his job in Belgium and moved to Paris to pursue a singing career. He performed in the city's cabarets and music halls, and he wrote music. By the late 1950's Brel was being recognized in France and beyond, thanks to his albums and to his performance schedule of nearly three hundred shows a year. With the assistance of his friend Georges Pasquier and pianists Gérard Jouannest and François Rauber, Brel found his songs attaining new depth as he explored the grim sides of life, love, death, and society.

Inspired by a visit to Broadway during a trip to the United States in 1967, Brel translated *L'Homme de le Mancha* (*Man of La Mancha*) into French, and he directed and starred in the musical in France. In the late 1960's Brel appeared frequently as an actor and director in films such as *L'emmerdeur* and *Mon oncle Benjamin*. In 1974 Brel embarked on a cruise around the world, and upon reaching the Canary Islands, he was diagnosed with lung cancer. After spending his final years in Paris and the Marquesas Islands, Brel died in 1978. He is buried in Calvary Cemetery in the Marquesas Islands.

The Music

Along with Georges Brassens, Brel stands as one of the most significant composers of French popular chanson. Brel's chanson is varied and innovative, responding sensitively to the mood and meaning of the text, with recitativelike vocal lines that favor declamation over melody. Brel's initial performances in the 1950's consisted solely of voice and guitar; later, in collaboration with his arranger, pianist Rauber, his songs used extensive orchestral

Jacques Brel. (Hulton Archive/Getty Images)

accompaniments, often featuring the skills of pianist Jouannest.

"Ne me quitte pas." Although Brel composed nearly forty songs before 1959, his Parisian experiences led to more complex and diverse themes. "Ne me quitte pas" (1959) is among the most well-known of Brel's songs. Inspired by an ill-fated affair with fellow singer Suzanne Gabriello, "Ne me quitte pas," typically accompanied by piano, strings, and flute, is characterized by gradually descending vocal lines of minimal breadth in a recitative style.

"Les Bourgeois." Brel's songs were also notable for their social criticisms. The lyrics of "Les Bourgeois" (1962) comment on society, quite a different theme from Brel's somber love ballads. While not as penetrating or caustic as Brel's other songs dealing with society ("Les Singes," 1961, and "Jaures," 1977), "Les Bourgeois" is a gently mocking piece set

in a waltzlike triple meter with an abundance of dotted rhythms. Accordion, harpsichord, percussion, and brass instruments showcase Brel's increasing forays into larger and more colorful accompaniments. A substantial number of Brel's songs portray either people ("Mathilde," 1964; "Les Flamandes," 1959) or places ("Le Plat Pays," 1962; "Bruxelles," 1962).

"Amsterdam." One of the most notable aspects of Brel's craftsmanship was his ability to create striking verbal portraits. He did not shy away from depicting the unsavory side of society; alcoholics, drifters, drug addicts, and prostitutes are given insightful and compassionate portraits in "Jef" (1964), "La Chanson de Jacky" (1965), and "Amsterdam" (1964). "Amsterdam," which he recorded multiple times with a full orchestral arrangement, displays Brel at his most caustic, with the harsh criticism of society implicit in the song's text mirrored by an ever-rising and frenzied vocal line and accompaniment.

"Jojo." The late 1960's and 1970's saw a decrease in Brel's chanson output as he focused instead on musical theater and his growing film career. The songs of Brel's final years are intensely personal and reflective ("Avec élégance," 1977, and "L'Amour est mort," 1977), and the primary example of this is "Jojo" (1977). In 1974, shortly after embarking on his trip around the world, Brel received word that his friend Pasquier ("Jojo") had passed away. With only guitar for accompaniment, "Jojo" shows Brel at his most intimate as he reflects on the significance of his friendship with Pasquier and Brel's own impending death.

Musical Legacy

Although Brel's music is not widely known outside of French-speaking countries, it has had a remarkable influence on artists and performers worldwide. In the English-speaking world, despite the difference in genres, he is often seen as a forebear of Bob Dylan and Leonard Cohen, whose lyrics, similarly, delved into personal, sometimes dark, subjects with unflinching seriousness.

English translations of Brel's songs have been recorded by artists worldwide, including David Bowie, Frank Sinatra, and Shirley Bassey. "Ne me quitte pas" has been translated into numerous languages (Marlene Dietrich's "Bitte geh nicht fort" and Rod McKuen's "If You Go Away" are two of the most well known) and recorded in the original French by artists ranging from Nina Simone to Sting.

In 1968 the Off-Broadway musical *Jacques Brel Is Alive and Well and Living in Paris* was introduced to the American public with great success. Although some criticized the English translations of Brel's lyrics, the musical brought Brel's brand of energetic, introspective, romantic, touching, hopeful, and humorous songs to a wide audience.

Ryan Scott Ebright

Further Reading

Blau, Eric. *Jacques Brel Is Alive and Well and Living in Paris*. New York: E. P. Dutton, 1971. A narrative of the creation of the Off-Broadway musical, with biographical details about Brel and the French lyrics and corresponding English translations of songs used in the musical.

Clayson, Alan. *Jacques Brel: The Biography*. London: Sanctuary Publishing, 1996. A brief biography of Brel's career, one of the few resources in English.

Tinker, Chris. *Georges Brassens and Jacques Brel: Personal and Social Narratives in Post-war Chanson*. London: Liverpool University Press, 2005. An interesting study that examines the mix of personal and social personas developed in the songs of Brassens and Brel.

See also: Cohen, Leonard; Collins, Judy; Dietrich, Marlene; Dylan, Bob; Simone, Nina; Sting.

Benjamin Britten

English classical composer

Britten resurrected the British operatic tradition dormant since the time of Henry Purcell in the seventeenth century.

Born: November 22, 1913; Lowestoft, Suffolk, England
Died: December 4, 1976; Aldeburgh, Suffolk, England
Also known as: Edward Benjamin Britten (full name); Baron Britten of Aldeburgh

Principal works

BALLET (music): *The Prince of the Pagodas*, 1957 (choreography by John Cranko).

CHAMBER WORKS: *Lachrymae*, Op. 48, 1950 (for viola and piano); *Metamorphoses*, Op. 49, 1951 (for solo oboe; based on texts by Ovid); Suite No. 1, Op. 72, 1964 (for cello); Suite No. 2, Op. 80, 1967 (for cello); Suite No. 3, Op. 87, 1971 (for cello).

CHORAL WORK: *A Boy Was Born*, 1934.

CHORAL WORKS: *Ceremony of Carols*, Op. 28, 1942; *Hymn to St. Cecilia*, Op. 27, 1942 (based on texts by W. H. Auden); *Rejoice in the Lamb*, Op. 30, 1943 (festival cantata for trumpet, soloists, chorus, and organ); *Missa Brevis*, Op. 63, 1959 (for boys' voices); *War Requiem*, Op. 66, 1962 (for choirs, orchestra, chamber orchestra, and organ).

OPERAS (music): *Paul Bunyan*, Op. 17, 1941 (libretto by W. H. Auden); *Peter Grimes*, Op. 33, 1945 (libretto by Montague Slater; based on George Crabbe's poem "The Borough"); *The Rape of Lucretia*, Op. 37, 1946 (libretto by Ronald Duncan; based on André Obey's play *Le Viol de Lucrèce*); *Albert Herring*, Op. 39, 1947 (libretto by Eric Crozier; based on Guy de Maupassant's story "Le Rosier de Madame Husson"); *The Beggar's Opera*, Op. 43, 1948 (based on John Gay's opera); *The Little Sweep*, Op. 45, 1949 (libretto by Crozier); *Billy Budd*, Op. 50, 1951 (libretto by E. M. Forster and Crozier; based on Herman Melville's novel); *Dido and Aeneas*, 1951 (libretto by Nahum Tate; based on Henry Purcell's opera); *Gloriana*, Op. 53, 1953 (libretto by William Plomer); *The Turn of the Screw*, Op. 54, 1954 (libretto by Myfanwy Piper; based on Henry James's novel); *Noye's Fludde*, Op. 59, 1958 (based on Alfred W. Pollard's edition of the Chester Mystery Cycle); *A Midsummer Night's Dream*, Op. 64, 1960 (libretto by Britten and Peter Pears; based on William Shakespeare's play); *Curlew River*, Op. 71, 1964 (libretto by Plomer); *The Burning Fiery Furnace*, Op. 77, 1966 (libretto by Plomer); *The Golden Vanity*, Op. 78, 1967 (libretto by Colin Graham; based on the old English ballad); *The Prodigal Son*, Op. 81, 1968 (libretto by Plomer); *Owen Wingrave*, Op. 85, 1971 (libretto by Piper; based on James's novel); *Death in Venice*, Op. 88, 1973 (libretto by Piper).

ORCHESTRAL WORKS: *Simple Symphony*, Op. 4, 1934 (for string orchestra); *Variations on a Theme by Frank Bridge*, Op. 10, 1937 (for strings); Piano Concerto, Op. 13, 1938; Violin Concerto in D Minor, Op. 15, 1939; *Sinfonia da Requiem*, Op. 20, 1940; *Young Person's Guide to the Orchestra*, Op. 34, 1946 (based on a theme from Henry Purcell's suite *Abdelazar*); Cello Symphony, Op. 68, 1963.

VOCAL WORKS: *Our Hunting Fathers*, Op. 8, 1936 (for soprano or tenor and orchestra); *On This Island*, Op. 11, 1937 (for high voice and piano); *Les Illuminations*, Op. 18, 1939 (for high voice and strings); *Seven Sonnets of Michelangelo*, Op. 22, 1940 (for tenor and piano); *Serenade*, Op. 31, 1943 (for tenor, horn, and strings).

WRITINGS OF INTEREST: *The Story of Music*, 1958 (with Imogen Holst; reprinted as *The Wonderful World of Music*, 1968).

The Life

Born on November 22, the day that honors Saint Cecilia, patron saint of music, Edward Benjamin Britten (BRIH-tuhn) displayed from the earliest age a rare musical fluency. He was encouraged in composition by his dominating, musical mother, Edith, who predicted he would be "the fourth B"—after Johann Sebastian Bach, Ludwig van Beethoven, and Johannes Brahms. At age fourteen, Britten learned rigorous professional technique from composer Frank Bridge, who encouraged musical expression of what Britten found within himself, including the pacifism that remained a lifelong concern. Well ahead of his peers, Britten worked out his frustrations at the Royal College of Music from 1930 to 1933 by composing for the innovative documentaries of the General Post Office Film Unit (working alongside the poet W. H. Auden) and honing his dramatic skills.

In Britten's concert music the 1936 song cycle *Our Hunting Fathers* marks the formative influence of Auden, who wrote the text during a time when Britten was moving away from his mother's institutional Christian religion. This period of philosophical and sexual change is reflected in a series of diverse works further developing his strong interest in international styles and literature. In 1939, after the death of his father, his mother, and Bridge, Britten followed Auden to America and there cemented his relationship with his lifelong partner, the tenor Peter Pears, for whom he wrote much of his music. Returning to England in 1942 after the critical (but not public) failure of his Auden operetta, *Paul Bunyan*, Britten achieved international recognition at the end of the war with his opera *Peter Grimes* (title role created by Pears). Basing himself and Pears in Snape and Aldeburgh, a few miles down the coast from his birthplace, Britten produced a series of operas and concert works that enabled the establishment of the Aldeburgh Festival in 1948. He regularly accompanied Pears in recitals around the world, and their 1956 tour of Asia proved decisive for his compositional language. In 1967 Queen Elizabeth II officially opened the Snape Maltings Concert Hall, built on Britten's vision. Britten suffered ill health throughout his life and in 1973 underwent heart surgery from which he never fully recovered.

The Music

A Boy Was Born. Britten's early period, consisting of much more music than the opus numbers indicate, culminates in his set of choral variations *A Boy Was Born*, Op. 3. Britten's motivic mastery, developed through his early love of Beethoven, Arnold Schoenberg, and the German school, is matched by a choral mastery, juxtaposing "experienced" adult voices with those of "innocent" children. The work points toward Britten's future preferences both for text setting and for the theme of corrupted innocence, which is a reflection of his own nature.

Our Hunting Fathers. Britten's musical language underwent a decisive evolutionary climax in his symphonic song cycle *Our Hunting Fathers*, Op. 8, first performed at the Norwich Festival. W. H. Auden selected three central medieval poems—"Rats Away," "Messalina," and "Dance of Death: Hawking the Partridge"—and framed them with his original poems "Prologue" and "Epilogue: Our Hunting Fathers." The cycle charts a spiritual crisis that ends in death—of the individual and of a culture. Britten's letters imply that the work is a commentary on the contemporary Spanish Civil War.

Sinfonia da Requiem. Written and performed in New York in the immediate aftermath of his union with Pears, and dedicated to the memory of his parents, the *Sinfonia da Requiem*, Op. 20, reinscribes the themes of *Our Hunting Fathers* in climactically personal and purely orchestral terms. This is a summation of his technical training under Bridge in "music as self-revelation," and his debt to Gustav Mahler and Alban Berg is evident. The technical and spiritual clarifications made in the *Sinfonia* are so significant for Britten's mature style that his later *War Requiem* is a texted expansion of them.

Peter Grimes. *Peter Grimes*, Op. 33, was written to a libretto by Montagu Slater after George Crabbe and first performed at London's Sadler's Wells theater. Its references to private (Pears, who created the title role) and international (World War II) sources give the opera a raw, visceral power that contributes to its continued success in repertory. *Peter Grimes* deals with issues of alienation caused by the rebellion of the ego—on the personal level, symbolized by Grimes, and at the public level, symbolized by the character of the Borough in which he lives (Aldeburgh). The fusion of music and water (specifically the sea) as narrator of spiritual truth is seminal. Grimes's drowning at sea is as symbolic of the aesthetic purpose of the opera as it is a baptism into hell for both Grimes and the religiously hypocritical Borough.

War Requiem. Britten's *War Requiem*, Op. 66, can be considered a "second summation" after *Peter Grimes*, whose public popularity it rivals. Britten's radical, tropelike setting of Wilfred Owen's poetry in the context of the liturgy is spatially illuminated by the separation of adult choir, soprano soloist, and symphony orchestra (liturgy) from tenor and baritone soloists with chamber orchestra (Owen settings) and boy's choir and organ (liturgy). The alienation of these forces culminates in the Pyrrhic final tutti as the two soldiers sleep together, offset by the repetition of the tritone that pervades the work and the distant, haunting sound of innocent boys' voices.

Curlew River. Britten's "First Parable for Church Performance" (libretto by William Plomer), *Curlew River*, Op. 71, marks his final evolutionary stage. The mixing of medieval Eastern (Japanese No play) and Western (sung liturgical drama)

Benjamin Britten. (Library of Congress)

musico-dramatic forms, presented by an all-male cast and a handful of unconducted instrumentalists, radically refocused Britten's compositional language. The heterophonic suspension of pitches derived from and returning to plainsong results in surprisingly new dissonances—blending modality, tonality, and modern atonalism—befitting the intensely ritualized nature of the unfolding dramaturgy concerning a Madwoman seeking her abducted son. The second and third Parables, *The Burning Fiery Furnace*, Op. 77, and *The Prodigal Son*, Op. 81, contribute a unique trilogy to the genre of twentieth century music-theater.

Death in Venice. Britten's final opera, *Death in Venice*, Op. 88—which should ideally be experienced after *Owen Wingrave*, Op. 85, to which it is related by librettos by Myfanwy Piper after Thomas Mann and Henry James, respectively—is not only a final summation to his operatic oeuvre but also a retroactive philosophical key to Britten's entire output. The composer's psychodramatic attempt to make peace between Western- and Eastern-inspired musical ideas embodied by the antihero writer and Britten surrogate Gustav von Aschenbach (Western) and the object of his erotic desire, the boy Tadzio (Eastern), is a culmination of Britten's entire aesthetic quest. He arrays the full weight of his compositional achievement behind a philosophical position at odds with the Christianity of his idealized youth and the part of the conscience he kept alive and in tension with his adult self. That Britten was able to bring such musical beauty from a fatal dualistic philosophical flaw (that is, Aschenbach's spiritual as well as physical death in Venice) is not only the key to Britten's own output but also a commentary on the Western compositional tradition embodied in the city where Aschenbach expires.

Musical Legacy

Britten's re-creation of a British operatic tradition (resulting in the operas of Sir Michael Tippett, Sir Peter Maxwell Davies, Sir Harrison Birtwistle, Mark-Anthony Turnage, and Thomas Adès) and that on the international landscape (such as the operas of Hans Werner Henze and music of Arvo Pärt) is seminal. The absolute integrity of his music for children is a significant part of his legacy. The international Aldeburgh Festival, for which Britten wrote most of his mature music, has been a model for many new summer festivals in England and around the world. The steady release of archival recordings of Britten's work as a conductor and performer, especially of Wolfgang Amadeus Mozart, has achieved special acclaim. Recordings by Pears and Britten of his work are considered peerless.

Britten's genius in manipulating his modal and tonal heritage to highly personal, expressive ends during a period of derision of such reactionary practice finds parallel with the work of his friend Dmitri Shostakovich. Their shared ability to transform the language and psycho-dramatic themes of Gustav Mahler and Alban Berg to different ends—Britten's to private and social, Shostakovich's to political—is indicative of their development of musical tradition in a way that increasingly eclipses the avant-garde in the mainstream repertory. In Britten's case this has led to a scholastic industry devoted to issues of gender and sexuality and, more recently, investigation into the religious and spiritual implications of his legacy.

Stephen Arthur Allen

Further Reading

Allen, Stephen Arthur. "*Billy Budd*: Temporary Salvation and the Faustian Pact." *Journal of Musicological Research* 26 (January, 2006): 43-73. A close reading and musical analysis of the religious tensions at the core of Britten's seminal opera.

_____. "Christianity and Homosexuality in the Operas of Benjamin Britten." *The International Journal of the Humanities* 2 (2005): 817-824. An essential, nontechnical overview of Britten's religious tensions.

Brett, Philip. *Music and Sexuality in Britten: Selected Essays*. Edited by George E. Haggerty. Berkeley: University of California Press, 2006. Groundbreaking investigation into the connection between sexuality and gender and the culture of Britten's music.

Britten, Benjamin. *Britten on Music*. Edited by Paul Kildea. Oxford, England: Oxford University Press, 2003. An indispensable collection of Britten's writings about his own music and that of others, edited by a major Britten scholar.

_____. *Letters from a Life: Selected Letters and Diaries*. 2 vols. Edited by Donald Mitchell and Philip Reed. London: Faber & Faber, 1991. A mine of information in Britten's own words, covering 1923 to 1951.

_____. *Selected Letters*. Edited by Donald Mitchell, Philip Reed, and Mervyn Cooke. London: Faber & Faber, 2004. Letters place Britten in the context of the British and continental musical scene of the period, focusing on the period 1946 to 1951.

Carpenter, Humphrey. *Benjamin Britten: A Biography*. London: Faber & Faber, 1992. Authorized, no-holds-barred biography, but fair and insightful in spite of superficial musicological analysis.

Cooke, Mervyn. *Britten and the Far East Asian Influences in the Music of Benjamin Britten*. Aldeburgh Studies in Music 4. Woodbridge, Suffolk, England: Boydell Press, 1998. A comprehensive account and analysis of Britten's relationship to the music and culture of Asia.

_____, ed. *The Cambridge Companion to Benjamin Britten*. Cambridge, England: Cambridge University Press, 1999. Provocative essays charting the trends of current musicology.

Evans, Peter. *The Music of Benjamin Britten*. Oxford: Clarendon Press, 1996. The standard positivist analysis of Britten's entire work.

Rupprecht, Philip. *Britten's Musical Language*. Cambridge, England: Cambridge University Press, 2001. Invaluable insights into the nature of Britten's music.

See also: Berg, Alban; Elgar, Sir Edward; Fischer-Dieskau, Dietrich; Mahler, Gustav; Menotti, Gian Carlo; Pärt, Arvo; Previn, Sir André; Rostropovich, Mstislav; Rutter, John; Schoenberg, Arnold; Shostakovich, Dmitri; Solti, Sir Georg; Sutherland, Dame Joan; Tippett, Sir Michael; Vaughan Williams, Ralph; Walton, Sir William.

Garth Brooks

American country singer-songwriter and guitarist

Country-music singer-songwriter Brooks promoted his crossover approach by performing his music in 1970's-style rock shows. His enormous popularity resulted largely from his accessibility to his fans and humble, Everyman image. He is renowned as the best-selling solo artist in American history, with several multiplatinum albums and sales of more than 123 million units.

Born: February 7, 1962; Tulsa, Oklahoma
Also known as: Troyal Garth Brooks (full name)

Principal recordings

ALBUMS: *Garth Brooks*, 1989; *No Fences*, 1990; *Ropin' the Wind*, 1991; *Beyond the Season*, 1992; *The Chase*, 1992; *In Pieces*, 1993; *Fresh Horses*, 1995; *Sevens*, 1997; *In the Life of Chris Gaines*, 1999; *Garth Brooks and the Magic of Christmas*, 1999; *The Magic of Christmas: Songs from Call Me Clause*, 2001; *Scarecrow*, 2001.

The Life

Troyal Garth Brooks was born in Tulsa, Oklahoma, to Troyal Raymond Brooks, an oil company draftsman, and Colleen Carroll Brooks, a country singer who had recorded with Capitol Records during the 1950's. As a student at Oklahoma State University, Brooks performed with lead guitarist Ty

England in a club band. Brooks graduated with a degree in marketing and headed to Nashville to begin a career as a performer. Soon, however, he returned to Oklahoma. Brooks married his college girlfriend, Sandy Mahr, in 1987, and they returned to Nashville, where he signed with Capitol Records.

For the next three years, Brooks's career skyrocketed, and he was inducted into the Grand Ole Opry in October, 1990. In 1993, however, his image began to take a downturn when, against the wishes of his management, he positioned himself as an activist for world peace. In August, 1997, Brooks performed an enormously successful concert in Manhattan's Central Park that was attended by hundreds of thousands of fans and broadcast live by Home Box Office. This concert provided a well-timed boost of Brooks's image and career, effectively promoting the release of a new album.

Unfortunately, the glow of this success faded with his brief, unsuccessful foray into the film industry. Brooks and his wife divorced in 2000. He then went into retirement until, in 2005, he released a DVD that included a duet with singer Trisha Yearwood, whom he married in 2006.

The Music

Brooks introduced pop-rock influences to country music by combining the country styles of George Strait and George Jones, the folk-rock approach of James Taylor, and the pop-rock musical styles of Elton John, Dan Fogelberg, and the bands Kiss, Styx, and Boston. In so doing, he brought a whole new audience to country music. His stadium-arena spectaculars were customarily attended by tens of thousands of people, for whom Brooks intentionally kept the ticket prices low. He further engaged his audiences by wearing a headset microphone, facilitating his active and energetic movement around the stage while breaking away from the previous tradition in country music whereby singers had performed in a stationary position behind a microphone.

Garth Brooks. In 1989, Brooks released his self-titled first album to immediate success. Its style combined a nod to traditional country in the single "Much Too Young (to Feel This Damn Old)" with the sensitivity of "If Tomorrow Never Comes." This album catapulted Brooks's crossover reputation from country into pop, particularly with the release of "The Dance," the single that effectively tripled album sales, making *Garth Brooks* the best-selling country album of the 1980's.

No Fences. Brooks's second album was released to great acclaim in 1990, selling 700,000 copies within its first ten days and staying at the top of the country charts for twenty-three weeks. As a result of *Billboard*'s new method of tallying sales through SoundScan, *No Fences* moved from number sixteen to number three on the pop charts. The first single, "Friends in Low Places," had been unofficially released to a local radio station, spurring the enormous popularity of the album through its rollicking, honky-tonk, humorous music and lyrics. Another hit, "Unanswered Prayers," again demonstrated Brooks's talent for sensitive reflection.

The album's most controversial song, "The Thunder Rolls," turned out to be the greatest asset to the sales of the album because the accompanying video generated media interest in the depiction of spousal violence and was briefly taken off the air by Country Music Television (CMT) and The Nashville Network (TNN). Since the song's subject matter was familiar to many, the video was returned to the airwaves and gained great popularity. By 1993, *No Fences* had sold in excess of ten million copies. As of 2006, it was certified as multiplatinum, at 17 million sales, by the Recording Industry Association of America (RIAA).

Ropin' the Wind. Released in 1991, this was the first country album to debut at number one on both the country and pop charts, with an unprecedented four million prerelease orders. Unlike the hit singles "What She's Doing Now" and "Shameless" (originally written and recorded by Billy Joel), which continued Brooks's themes of love and conflict between a man and a woman, the popularity of "The River" stemmed from its positive lyrics, urging people to risk believing in themselves. The combination of Brooks's abilities as a consummate performer and his album sales in the tens of millions garnered superstar status for Brooks with the release of this album. Courted by the mass media, he was featured on the covers of major magazines such as *Time*, *Forbes*, and *Entertainment Weekly*.

The Chase. *The Chase* debuted in 1992, but it only sold five million copies and did not rise above number twelve on the charts, a level of performance much lower than that of his previous works. Brooks received particularly negative criticism for "We Shall Be Free," as it was perceived to incorporate a moralistic, gospel style through its music and lyrics urging racial tolerance and suggesting homosexual tolerance as well.

Fresh Horses. Although *Fresh Horses*, released in 1995, topped at quadruple platinum, like *The Chase* it did not meet with Brooks's previous successes. This slump in his album sales reflected a negative change in Brooks's personality, as he became increasingly arrogant toward the media. The single entitled "The Change" shows this development; its lyrics, unlike his previously inspiring messages, came across instead as cynical and defensive.

Musical Legacy

Brooks drew from his own background as a suburban American who grew up listening to 1970's pop and rock but developed a desire to return to country, a sentiment shared by millions of baby-boomer Americans between the late 1980's and early 1990's. A high-energy performer, he became completely interactive with his audience in concerts, even to the point of crowd-surfing while singing. As a result of Brooks's success in bringing country music to a huge new audience, he lent enormous support to the country-music scene and industry.

Brooks has received numerous awards, including the Country Music Association Horizon Award (1990), two Grammys (1991, 1997), and the following Academy of Country Music awards: Entertainer of the Year (1990, 1991, 1992, 1993, 1997, 1998), Artist of the Decade (1998), and the first Crystal Milestone Award (2008).

Laurie R. Semmes

Further Reading

Appell, Glenn, and David Hemphill. *American Popular Music: A Multicultural History*. Belmont, Calif.: Thomson Higher Education, 2006. Places the various styles of country music in historical and cultural context.

Feiler, Bruce. *Dreaming Out Loud: Garth Brooks, Wynonna Judd, Wade Hayes, and the Changing Face of Nashville*. New York: Avon Books, 1998. Based on the author's three-year period of fieldwork with the artists in Nashville, Tennessee.

Kingsbury, Paul, Alan Axelrod, and Susan Costello, eds. *Country: The Music and the Musicians— From the Beginnings to the Nineties.* New York: Abbeville Press, 1994. A history that is amply illustrated with archive photographs.

Millard, Bob. *Country Music: Seventy Years of America's Favorite Music.* New York: HarperPerennial, 1993. Combination of year-by-year list of events with prose. Brief foreword by Garth Brooks.

Starr, Larry, and Christopher Waterman. *American Popular Music: The Rock Years.* New York: Oxford University Press, 2006. Briefly mentions country music's intersection with rock in Brooks's generation.

See also: Campbell, Glen; Jones, George; Strait, George.

Clifford Brown

American jazz trumpeter and composer

Talent, perseverance, and diligence made Brown one of the most creative jazz trumpeters-improvisers of the twentieth century. He combined flawless instrumentalism with the lyricism, rhythm, and harmony of bebop language.

Born: October 30, 1930; Wilmington, Delaware
Died: June 26, 1956; Pennsylvania
Also known as: Clifford Benjamin Brown (full name); Brownie

Principal recordings

ALBUMS: *The Beginning and the End,* 1952; *Alternate Takes,* 1953; *Clifford Brown and Art Farmer,* 1953; *The Clifford Brown Sextet in Paris,* 1953; *Memorial Album,* 1953; *New Star on the Horizon,* 1953; *Clifford Brown,* 1954; *Clifford Brown All Stars,* 1954; *Clifford Brown and Max Roach, Vol. 1,* 1954; *Daahoud,* 1954; *Jazz Immortal,* 1954; *Clifford Brown with Strings,* 1955; *More Study in Brown,* 1955; *Study in Brown,* 1955; *At Basin Street,* 1956.

The Life

Clifford Benjamin Brown, youngest of the eight children of Joe Brown and Estella Hackett, was born on October 30, 1930, in Wilmington, Delaware. Driven with desire to possess a shiny new trumpet, which he saw in his father's collection, Brown enrolled in the school band at the age of nine. By twelve he was provided with private trumpet lessons on a regular basis.

From 1943 to 1946 Brown was exposed to the fundamentals of trumpet performance, music theory, ear-training, arranging, piano, jazz music, and improvisation. His instructors were Robert "Boysie" Lowery and Harry Andrews. Performing with the Little Dukes, a band that played rearranged popular big band repertoire at dance parties, was Brown's first professional job.

From 1946 to 1950 Brown was introduced to progressive music of Charlie "Yardbird" Parker and Dizzy Gillespie. Brown visited Philadelphia and its big jazz scene, participated in jam sessions, met Parker and Gillespie, and impressed them with his exceptional instrumental abilities, creativity, and talent.

With Gillespie's encouragement to pursue a career as a performing musician, Brown transferred to Maryland State College as a music major. At the same time he was mentored by Theodore "Fats" Navarro, whose style became a model for Brown's musical expression.

In 1950 Brown was seriously injured in a car accident, resulting in postponement of his artistic dreams for a year. In 1951 he joined the touring band Chris Powell and the Blue Flames, performing rhythm and blues, soul, calypso, and mambo with slight modern-jazz elements. By 1952 Brown had established himself on the New York and Philadelphia jazz scenes. He appeared alongside such jazz modernists as James Louis "J. J." Johnson, Lou Donaldson, Elmo Hope, Philly Joe Jones, and Percy Heath on the Blue Note label and with Tad Dameron's ensemble on Prestige label's recording sessions. Brown's musicianship, improvisational style, and maturity earned him the admiration of colleagues and critics.

During 1953-1954 Brown cut his first album as a leader for Blue Note label, signed a contract with Lionel Hampton's band, toured Europe, and managed to record with European jazz artists. Upon his return to the United States, he moved to New York City, joining Art Blakey and the Jazz Messengers. With this group he recorded for the Blue Note label.

Clifford Brown. (Hulton Archive/Getty Images)

In 1954 Brown relocated to Los Angeles, California, to collaborate with drummer Max Roach (Brown and Roach, Inc.). They signed a record contract with the EmArcy label, although Brown recorded for other labels as well. The same year, Brown won *Down Beat* critics' New Star of the Year poll. On June 26, 1954, Brown married Larue Anderson, and their son, Clifford Brown, Jr., was born the following year. For Brown, 1955 and 1956 were years of recording and extensive touring on the East and West Coasts. He actively composed and tirelessly continued to shape his mastery.

On the night of June 26, 1956, his second wedding anniversary, Brown's life was cut short in a tragic automobile accident.

The Music

Brown's music is characterized by flawless sound and technique and fluid inventiveness. Though his improvisations were a symbiosis of his primary influences—Navarro, mixed with inspirations of Parker, Gillespie, and Earl "Bud" Powell—his accomplished musicianship and constant search

for improvement allowed Brown's artistic individuality to blossom. His approach to arranging, composition, and bandleading made him one of the most prominent figures of hard bop in jazz history.

Early Records. Brown's solo debut album as a leader, *Brownie's Eyes* (later renamed *Memorial Album*), was recorded on August 28, 1953. This record presented his strong arranging and compositional skills. However, it was on Ray Noble's "Cherokee"—a Parker signature piece—that Brown's full mastery became apparent. Brown was the first trumpeter in jazz history to improvise over the chord progressions of "Cherokee" with a fluidity equal to Parker's technical, emotional, and intellectual levels, implementing a saxophone-piano approach to his trumpet style.

Live at Birdland. A role of featured star in Art Blakey and the Jazz Messengers reinforced Brown's artistic potential. Five volumes of live recording sessions entitled *Live at Birdland*, made on February 21, 1954, for the Blue Note record label, allowed Brown's creativity to stretch out.

Study in Brown *and* More Study in Brown. These two prominent records came out as a result of sessions recorded on August 3, 1954, and February 23-25, 1955, for the EmArcy label: a coleadership between Brown and drummer Roach, then an established star in the jazz world. Both records were considered classics among jazz musicians, fans, and critics. Marked by his intricate and smoothly harmonized melodies, Brown's originals "Daahoud," "Joy Spring," "Blues Walk," and "Sandu" became jazz hits and standards often performed by other musicians. Brown's phenomenal progress, achieved in the short period of two years, was confirmed by the new version of Noble's "Cherokee" that put him on the pedestal of renowned sensations of bebop trumpet.

Musical Legacy

Brown's relatively large recording archives, produced in a short span of five years, showcase his consistent high-quality performance and serve as a practice manual for every jazz trumpeter. Stylistic echoes of Brown can be heard in records of such jazz trumpet giants as Booker Little, Louis Smith, Joe Gordon, Donald Byrd, Wilbur Harden, and Johnny Coles. Brown's bright talent made him a jazz icon.

Gregory Rivkin

Further Reading

Ahlfors, Elizabeth. "Sweet Clifford Brown." *Delaware Today*, May 20, 1996. Short musical biography of Brown spiced with interesting quotations from his peers, colleagues, widow, and former instructor.

Catalano, Nick. *Clifford Brown: The Life and Art of the Legendary Jazz Trumpeter*. New York: Oxford University Press, 2001. Professor of music and literature presents a biographic sketch of Brown's life.

Hentoff, Nat. "Blindfold Test: Brownie Digs Only Modern Jazz." *Down Beat*, February 22, 1956. Informative article about Brown's musical taste.

_____. "Brown and Roach Inc., Dealers in Jazz." *Down Beat*, May, 1955. Brown and Roach talk about their partnership, their band, and their career steps.

_____. "Clifford Brown: The New Dizzy." *Down Beat* 72 (2005). Reissued interview from April 7, 1954. Brown speaks about his music and what it takes to maintain a career as a jazz musician.

See also: Blakey, Art; Gillespie, Dizzy; Lovett, Lyle; Navarro, Fats; Parker, Charlie; Powell, Bud; Roach, Max; Rollins, Sonny; Vaughan, Sarah.

James Brown

American rhythm-and-blues singer, pianist, and songwriter

Brown validated the cultural significance of African Americans in the arts, placing more than a hundred song hits on the best-selling charts during his five-decade career.

Born: May 3, 1933; Barnwell, South Carolina
Died: December 25, 2006; Atlanta, Georgia

Also known as: James Joseph Brown (full name)

Principal recordings

ALBUMS: *Please Please Please*, 1959; *Try Me*, 1959; *Think*, 1960; *The Amazing James Brown*, 1961; *James Brown Presents His Band and Five Other Great Artists*, 1961; *Night Train*, 1961; *Jump Around*, 1962; *Shout and Shimmy*, 1962; *Tour the U.S.A.*, 1962; *Live at the Apollo*, 1963; *Prisoner of Love*, 1963; *Grits and Soul*, 1964; *Out of Sight*, 1964; *Showtime*, 1964; *James Brown Plays James Brown: Yesterday and Today*, 1965; *Papa's Got a Brand New Bag*, 1965; *Handful of Soul*, 1966; *I Got You (I Feel Good)*, 1966; *It's a Man's Man's Man's World*, 1966; *James Brown and His Famous Flames Sing Christmas Songs*, 1966; *James Brown Plays New Breed*, 1966; *Mighty Instrumentals*, 1966; *Cold Sweat*, 1967; *James Brown Plays the Real Thing*, 1967; *James Brown Sings Raw Soul*, 1967; *I Can't Stand Myself When You Touch Me*, 1968; *I Got the Feelin'*, 1968; *James Brown Plays Nothing but Soul*, 1968; *James Brown Sings out of Sight*, 1968; *James Brown Presents His Show of Tomorrow*, 1968; *A Soulful Christmas*, 1968; *Soul Party*, 1968; *A Thinking About Little Willie/A Few Nice Things*, 1968; *Gettin' Down to It*, 1969; *It's a Mother*, 1969; *The Popcorn*, 1969; *Say It Loud—I'm Black and I'm Proud*, 1969; *Ain't It Funky*, 1970; *Hey America*, 1970; *It's a New Day—So Let a Man Come In*, 1970; *Sex Machine*, 1970; *Soul on Top*, 1970; *Hot Pants*, 1971; *Sho Is Funky Down Here*, 1971; *Soul Brother No. 1*, 1971; *Super Bad*, 1971; *Get on the Good Foot*, 1972; *There It Is*, 1972; *Black Caesar*, 1973; *The Payback*, 1973; *Slaughter's Big Rip Off*, 1973; *Hell*, 1974; *Reality*, 1974; *Everybody's Doin' the Hustle and Dead on the Double Bump*, 1975; *Sex Machine Today*, 1975; *Bodyheat*, 1976; *Get Up Offa That Thing*, 1976; *Hot*, 1976; *Mutha's Nature*, 1977; *Strangers*, 1977; *Jam/1980's*, 1978; *Take a Look at Those Cakes*, 1978; *The Original Disco Man*, 1979; *People*, 1980; *Soul Syndrome*, 1980; *Nonstop!*, 1981; *Special*, 1981; *The Third Coming*, 1981; *Bring It On!*, 1983; *Gravity*, 1986; *I'm Real*, 1988; *Love Over-Due*, 1991; *Universal James*, 1992; *James Brown*, 1994; *Bodyheat*, 1995; *I'm Back*, 1998; *The Merry Christmas Album*, 1999; *Funky Christmas*, 2001; *Feel So Good*, 2002; *Give It Up or Turn It Loose*, 2004.

The Life

James Joseph Brown was born to Joseph Gardner and Susie Brown in the rural South in the extreme poverty of the Great Depression. When his mother abruptly left home, six-year-old "Junior" was sent to live with his aunt in her bordello in Augusta, Georgia. As a child he worked the streets of Augusta as a shoeshine boy and danced for tips. As a teenager, Brown drifted into petty theft, was caught, was convicted, and at sixteen was sent to a juvenile detention center. Singing gospel music in prison, Brown was heard by Bobby Byrd, who persuaded the authorities to release Brown under his cognizance in order to perform under Byrd's tutelage. In time, Brown joined Byrd's group just as Byrd was shifting its musical identity to secular rhythm and blues. With this new orientation, the

Avons, as they had been known, became the Flames, and Brown was their front man.

With the release of his first hit single, Brown faced his life as a touring musician and recording artist with a newfound self-possession. Determined to overcome the insults and discrimination he endured as a black American during the civil rights era, he refused the bookers and theater owners who had slighted him earlier. Brown fought with his label, King Records, for control of production and design of his albums and singles. As Brown continued in his efforts to broaden his appeal to wider audiences, he began a new production company, Fair Deal, intending to create instrumental albums and singles for Mercury Records' subsidiary Smash Records. Brown believed that his contract with King Records covered only vocal

James Brown (right). (Library of Congress)

work, but the record label objected, and during the legal battle between Smash Records and King Records, Brown was unable to record vocals for a year.

With the wealth delivered by his success, Brown in 1967 purchased a Knoxville, Tennessee, radio station, renaming it WJBE. By the end of the decade he had purchased several radio stations, including Augusta's WRDW, in front of which he once shined shoes.

By 1970 Brown's new backing band was known as the J. B.'s. In 1971 Brown began recording for Polydor Records and later completed the sound track for *Black Caesar*. During the 1970's, Brown also recorded a number of songs with sociopolitical topics, such as "Don't Be a Drop-Out" and "Papa Don't Take No Mess." The end of the 1970's—with the advent of disco and hip-hop—rendered Brown a figure of the cultural past, even though both popular idioms had first been developed by him. At that time, Brown had largely limited his work to the occasional film or television appearance, along with the reissuing of his older recordings, though his live appearances continued to sell many tickets.

In 1988 Brown was arrested following a high-speed police chase. He was convicted for various drug, driving, and assault offenses, and he was not released until 1991. In the last fifteen years of his life, Brown was repeatedly arrested on charges of domestic violence. He continued to tour until the year of his death, and a number of his late performances were before record-breaking crowds.

The Music

Brown's music derived from several sources. As a teenager Brown heard Louis Jordan and resolved to become a popular singer. While at reform school Brown began a gospel group and perfected his gospel-inflected style and striking vocal delivery. Last, Brown was influenced by Frank Sinatra, whose independent image Brown admired.

Early Works. Brown's recordings for Federal Records are proscribed somewhat by the conventions of the day, the songs being regular rhythm-and-blues fare. While the Flames largely played Southern venues, the group succeeded in signing a contract with Federal Records and in 1956 released their first single, a million-seller entitled "Please, Please, Please." In this work the Brown sound arrived, fully formed. The textual content is severely

thin, entire verses given over to permutations of one word. Brown shrieks in his high voice, then instantly drops to a soothing, enveloping baritone. "Please, Please, Please" was the template upon which Brown's future vocal style was based.

Live at the Apollo. In 1963, in opposition to King Records owner Syd Nathan, Brown self-financed the production of a live album entitled *Live at the Apollo*, which proved to be a tremendous commercial success, enjoying substantial sales to white listeners, as Brown had intended. At the time, the music industry was singles-oriented, so *Live at the Apollo*, intended to reproduce the concert experience, was pioneering. The concert repertory heard here demonstrates Brown's range of musical ideas, including such up-tempo rockers as "I'll Go Crazy," followed immediately by the slower and more sensitive "Try Me." Fairly simple chord changes are the rule, with creative arrangements of horn and electric guitar, all designed as a backdrop for Brown's impassioned vocals. *Live at the Apollo* represents a forward-looking attempt to utilize the long-playing (LP) format to offer the excitement of a live concert to the listener.

"Papa's Got a Brand New Bag" *and* **"I Got You (I Feel Good)."** In 1965 two important Brown songs appeared to worldwide acclaim. "Papa's Got a Brand New Bag" and "I Got You (I Feel Good)" overwhelmed the sales charts, making Brown arguably the most successful African American in the public eye. The former features a blues-based chord change, with Brown singing more melodically, the band switching from the blues chord to a static pulse, then back again for the next verse. "I Got You" is similar, although its bridge section involves more elaborate horn changes. Lyrics are delivered in a comprehensible manner, with dramatic vocal signatures saved for line endings. Both songs have an ear for dance, and for years the discotheques of the world resounded with these pieces.

"Super Bad." On the original album, this song, approximately fifteen minutes long, has a relentless, propulsive, rhythmic drive. With the inclusion of the J. B.'s, the shift from older soul styles to the newer funk sound that Brown had been developing through the late 1960's was complete. There is only one chord change, for the bridges, which are forcefully presaged by Brown's vocals and which bracket a fierce sax solo by Maceo Parker. The band drops and then rises back in intensity, and the horns function in close order with the rhythm section. In this performance Brown reaches an expressive peak in which the rhythmic force supports his immense vocals.

"Sex Machine." This song was first released as a single, then was made the featured work on an album of the same name. Structured in fashion similar to "Super Bad," it is a prolonged funk exercise in D, with an occasional bridge. One difference in the arrangement is the use of a secondary voice in place of horns to ornament the rhythmic pulse. In this recording Brown leads his band in a recounting of the towns in which they have performed, handled much like a Southern religious service. Again, Brown's vigorous, staunchly male persona infuses the work with meaning, lending drama to the seemingly never-ending rhythmic propulsion.

Musical Legacy

Brown remains at the pinnacle of the African American musical experience. From his beginnings as the lead singer for the Flames, he devised performance techniques far beyond what other rhythm-and-blues singers of the time could offer. The soul sound of black American popular music prevalent in the 1960's was, with its gutsy and forceful yet vulnerable singers, largely created by Brown's example. The funk that supplanted soul to a great degree in the 1970's is principally Brown's invention, showcased in such works as "Super Bad" and "Sex Machine." Even the disco craze of the late 1970's, which supposedly caught Brown by surprise, owes much of its rhythmic component to Brown's dance music first performed in the 1960's.

The musical idiom of hip-hop reflects Brown's influence in its intensely rhythmic vocal delivery. Brown's recordings are one of the most popular sampling sources in the digital age. His influence on five decades of popular music cannot be overestimated, and his stylistic innovations and irresistible recordings remain part of the contemporary musical arena.

Jeffrey Daniel Jones

Further Reading

Brown, James. *I Feel Good: A Memoir of a Life of Soul*. New York: New American Library, 2005. Brown intersperses biographical information with pro-

nouncements on what ails America. The introduction by Marc Eliot is a helpful biographical summary.

Brown, James, with Bruce Tucker. *James Brown: The Godfather of Soul*. Glasgow: Fontana/Collins, 1986. Brown's first attempt at a memoir. While the story line is autobiographical, the written dialogues are too precise to be verbatim. Nonetheless, many stories in this memoir are not found in the other.

Guralnick, Peter. *Sweet Soul Music: Rhythm and Blues and the Southern Dream of Freedom*. New York: Back Bay Books, 1986. Fascinating details on Brown during the 1950's and 1960's, the years of his meteoric rise.

Vincent, Rickey. *Funk: The Music, the People, and the Rhythm of the One*. New York: St. Martin's Griffin, 1996. Describes funk, the propulsive musical style of the 1970's. Includes an excellent biographical chapter on Brown, concentrating on his development of the funk style in the late 1960's and early 1970's.

See also: Costello, Elvis; Ice Cube; Ice-T; Jackson, Michael; Jordan, Louis; LL Cool J; Pickett, Wilson; Redding, Otis; Seger, Bob; Sinatra, Frank; Wilson, Jackie; Wolfe, Julia.

Roy Brown

American rhythm-and-blues singer-songwriter

Brown, an important figure in the post-World War II rhythm-and-blues scene of the late 1940's, introduced gospel-inspired vocal stylizations.

Born: September 10, 1925; New Orleans, Louisiana
Died: May 25, 1981; San Fernando, California

Principal recordings

ALBUMS: *Roy Brown and Wynonie Harris*, 1959; *Hard Times*, 1968; *The Blues Are Brown*, 1968; *Cheapest Price in Town*, 1979; *Courage*, 1995; *Saturday Nite*, 1999.

SINGLES: "Let the Four Winds Blow," 1957; "Party Doll," 1957.

The Life

Born to True Love and Yancy Brown, a conservative, religious couple, Roy Brown was encouraged toward musicality as a child by his mother, the organist and choir director at her church. Upon his mother's death when he was fourteen, Brown followed his father to Houston, Texas, and then Los Angeles.

By 1946 Brown had become a professional singer and relocated to Galveston, Texas, where he composed his first hit, "Good Rockin' Tonight." By the following year Brown was back in New Orleans, where he tried, unsuccessfully, to sell his song to blues shouter Wynonie Harris. However, Brown was able to sell his own performance of "Good Rockin' Tonight" to Jules Braun of DeLuxe Records. Upon noting the good sales of Brown's version, Harris changed his mind and decided to record and release the song, ending up with a greater hit than its composer had.

During the period 1948-1951 Brown recorded a number of hits for the DeLuxe label, but in subsequent years the popularity of his recordings declined. During the rock-and-roll boom of the mid-1950's, Brown was unable to capitalize on the explosion of a sound that he had helped to create, and his recordings for King Records sold inadequately. His record sales did improve when he signed with Imperial Records in 1957, releasing "Let the Four Winds Blow" and a version of "Party Doll" to placement on the national sales charts.

The 1960's were lean years for Brown, whose musical style seemed archaic for that decade. In 1970, remembered by fellow bandleader Johnny Otis, Brown was contracted to close Otis's show at the Monterey Jazz Festival, and he did it to great acclaim. That performance was dramatic enough to gain Brown a contract with Mercury Records, which released "Love for Sale," Brown's first hit record in nearly fifteen years. In the later 1970's the Scandinavians discovered Brown, releasing a compilation album of his older work and welcoming him in a successful tour of the region. By 1980 Brown was enjoying a resurgence in popularity, performing at the Whisky a Go Go in Hollywood and in 1981 headlining the New Orleans Jazz & Heritage Festival. This resurgence of Brown's musical prominence was cut short by his death from a heart attack in May of that year.

The Music

Brown's early years of singing in church provided good training for his vocal technique, honing his ability to sing melismatically, with multiple notes per syllable of text. This gave his voice a flexibility and tunefulness not typical of the blues shouters of the era and made his music distinctive and desirable, thus eminently salable to rhythm-and-blues audiences. Also, unlike many singers who simply bought songs to perform, Brown wrote and recorded his own material, making him one of the earliest in the category singer-songwriter.

"Good Rockin' Tonight." Brown's first big hit record was from his initial recording session upon reaching New Orleans in July, 1947. A classic rhythm-and-blues tune, it describes the pleasures to be had meeting with one's lover in the evening. The remarkable aspect of the performance is Brown's voice, light and elegant (a contrast to Harris's strident, shouting vocal style). The song enjoyed even greater popularity when it was sung by Elvis Presley in 1954 for Sun Records and sold two years later to RCA.

"Hard Luck Blues." This song was produced for King Records around 1953, but it did not achieve the healthy sales of Brown's recordings for DeLuxe. The hot up-tempo rocker shows Brown coming close to the standard rhythm-and-blues shouting style. His confident tenor voice traces melodic lines and high notes that would have defeated many of his contemporaries in rhythm and blues. Also notable is the arrangement, featuring a larger, more elaborate sound of horns and guitar than found in his earlier recordings.

"Let the Four Winds Blow." Recorded on January 22, 1957, this was Brown's big hit for Imperial Records and a second chance to demonstrate the salability of his music. The song reflects the changes in the popular-music scene that had occurred since Brown's previous time on the charts. His higher, tuneful vocals were successful at matching the newer, lighter sound aimed at the teenage buyer. After several years of struggling, Brown had once again written a piece perfect for its day, showing his mastery of rock and roll.

"Love for Sale." After appearing at the Monterey Jazz Festival as part of Johnny Otis's show, Brown was sought out by Mercury Records to record "Love for Sale." Here Brown returns to slow blues, singing with passion and feeling. The melismatic flexibility of his voice is apparent, and the lighter, tuneful sound is undiminished. Brown rerecorded this song for a late 1970's album, and it is heard in a live recording made near the end of his life.

Musical Legacy

Brown's appearance in the late 1940's was timely. His smooth, romantic style proved to be highly desirable to the record-buying public and for a few years made him a top-selling performer. Brown helped steer the rhythm-and-blues style of his era toward the rock-and-roll sound of the mid-1950's, and elements from his performance style were appropriated by many singers of succeeding decades, such as Sam Cooke, Al Green, and Whitney Houston.

Jeffrey Daniel Jones

Further Reading

Broven, John. *Rhythm and Blues in New Orleans.* Gretna, La.: Pelican Publishing, 1978. Short biography of Brown's life and career and a good description of the New Orleans rhythm-and-blues scene from which he emerged.

_____. "Roy Brown Part 1: Good Rockin' Tonight." *Blues Unlimited* 123 (January/February, 1977).

_____. "Roy Brown Part 2: Hard Luck Blues." *Blues Unlimited* 124 (March/June, 1977). Two-part article consists of an interview with Brown in the late 1970's and covers facts about and personal impressions of Brown through the years.

Harris, Sheldon. "Roy Brown, 1925-1981." *Living Blues,* no. 52 (Spring, 1982). Obituary and sympathetic summation of Brown's career, with interesting details not found in other sources.

Santelli, Robert. *The Big Book of Blues: A Biographical Encyclopedia.* New York: Penguin Books, 2001. Includes a brief but insightful entry on Brown.

Tosches, Nick. *Unsung Heroes of Rock 'n' Roll.* New York: Da Capo Press, 1999. A book on the early singers and musicians who invented the rock-and-roll style in the late 1940's and early 1950's. Includes an interesting chapter on Brown, discussing the ups and downs of his career.

See also: Cooke, Sam; Green, Al; Otis, Johnny; Presley, Elvis.

Jackson Browne

American rock singer, songwriter, guitarist, pianist, and keyboard player

A literate, poetic songwriter, Browne has exhibited versatility in writing love ballads, protest songs, cynical self-explorations, and tunes that incorporate a multitude of world-beat styles. An evocative vocalist and a superb musician on guitar and piano, Browne has turned out a string of hits that illustrate his ability to blend significant lyrics with memorable music.

Born: October 9, 1948; Heidelberg, Germany
Also known as: Clyde Jackson Browne (full name)

Principal recordings

ALBUMS: *Jackson Browne,* 1972; *For Everyman,* 1973; *Late for the Sky,* 1974; *The Pretender,* 1976; *Running on Empty,* 1977; *Hold Out,* 1980; *Lawyers in Love,* 1983; *Lives in the Balance,* 1986; *World in Motion,* 1989; *I'm Alive,* 1993; *Everywhere I Go,* 1994; *Looking East,* 1996; *The Naked Ride Home,* 2002; *Solo, Acoustic, Vol. 1,* 2005; *Solo Acoustic, Vol. 2,* 2008; *Time the Conqueror,* 2008.

SINGLES: "Running on Empty," 1978; "Doctor My Eyes," 1991; "Sky Blue and Black," 1994; "About My Imagination," 2003.

The Life

The son of an American father stationed in Germany and his American wife, Clyde Jackson Browne was born in Heidelberg, Germany. The family returned to the United States in 1951, settling in Los Angeles, where Browne learned to play keyboards and guitar. After graduating from high school, Jackson joined the Nitty Gritty Dirt Band. Under contract, he also wrote and published songs for Nina Music. Following a short stint with Tim Buckley's band in Greenwich Village, New York, Browne released the first of more than a dozen well-received albums. Initially known for poignant lyrics and sensitive songs of personal angst, Browne later became a social activist. He cofounded the antinuclear organization Musicians United for Safe Energy (MUSE) in 1979. He has performed at benefits supporting Farm Aid, Amnesty International, the Children's Defense Fund, and other causes, especially Democratic political candidates.

In 1975 Browne married actress and model Phyllis Major, two years after the birth of their son Ethan Zane. Phyllis committed suicide in 1976 at the age of thirty. Browne married again in 1981, to Australian model Lynne Sweeney, and their son Ryan Daniel was born in 1982. The couple divorced in 1983, following Browne's highly publicized affair with actress Daryl Hannah. Browne began a relationship with artist Dianna Cohen in the mid-1990's.

The Music

Browne's musical career can generally be divided into three phases. From the beginning to the middle of the 1970's, he was an introspective, truth-seeking confessional artist. His tuneful, folk-rock songs, delivered in a plaintive tenor, focused on romance and the meaning of life, incorporating heartfelt, literary lyrics. From the middle to the late 1970's, Browne produced more up-tempo, mainstream material that brought him a broader audience. From the late 1970's to the early 1990's, he was actively committed to a variety of political and social causes. In the early 1990's—during which time he released only three new albums, plus several compilations—Browne's output began to blend elements from all three phases and new themes, including celebrations of world diversity and homage to Southern California. Regardless of the period, several characteristics are common to Browne's work: clear vocals, accessible melodies, strong production values, and virtuosity on guitar and keyboard.

Jackson Browne. Also known as *Saturate Before Using*, this album established Browne as a thoughtful, versatile force to be reckoned with. Ably assisted by singer David Crosby, bassist Leland Sklar, drummer Russ Kunkel, and others, the singer-songwriter produced the bouncy "Doctor My Eyes," a Top 10 single, and hard-driving tunes such as "Rock Me on the Water" and "Jamaica Say You Will" that received considerable airplay.

Late for the Sky. This solidified Browne's reputation as a powerful music maker, capable of bending allegory to his will. Here, he focused on the search for love in a troubled world through such

classics as the title tune and in the apocalyptic "Before the Deluge." *Late for the Sky* charted in the Top 20 among pop albums.

The Pretender. Browne's first album after the suicide of his wife, unsurprisingly, deals with the subject of death. One track, "Here Come Those Tears Again," was co-written with Nancy Farnsworth, his late wife's mother. Though dark in tone—especially in "Sleep's Dark and Silent Gate"—the album features a broad mix of styles, from flamenco ("Linda Paloma") to country ("Your Bright Baby Blues"). The cynical title tune helped propel *The Pretender* to number five on the pop album charts.

Running on Empty. A concept album recorded live, *Running on Empty* gives behind-the-scenes glimpses of touring and performing. Ten cuts deal with everything from setting up and tearing down gear ("The Load-Out") to the boredom of long bus rides ("Running on Empty") to the drug use endemic to rock and roll ("Cocaine"). The album pro-

Jackson Browne. (AP/Wide World Photos)

duced two Top 20 hits and rose to number three on pop album charts.

Lives in the Balance. An overtly political album, *Lives in the Balance* took direct aim at U.S. foreign policy under president Ronald Reagan. Particular targets were American-sponsored conflicts in Guatemala, El Salvador, and Nicaragua in such songs as "Soldier of Plenty," "For America," and the title track. Though tempered by such diversions as the reggae-flavored "Till I Go Down" and a love ballad, "In the Shape of a Heart," this angry album sets up Browne's even more outspoken polemical follow-up, *World in Motion*.

Musical Legacy

With unflinching honesty, Browne has examined the complexities of relationships, agonized over self-discovery, and searched for truth and justice, not just in himself but also in the world at large. Originally known as a balladeer, Browne over the course of his career has expanded his repertoire to encompass diverse traditions across the musical spectrum. He has produced a body of work that ranges from soft folk to bitter protest, including more than twenty hit singles that continue to receive frequent radio airplay. For his compositional skills, Browne was inducted into the Rock and Roll Hall of Fame in 2004. For his environmental and social contributions, he received the John Steinbeck Award in 2002.

Jack Ewing

Further Reading

Bego, Mark. *Jackson Browne: His Life and Music.* New York: Citadel, 2005. An illustrated biography with a general overview of the artist's musical output.

Hoskyns, Barney. *Hotel California: The True-Life Adventures of Crosby, Stills, Nash, Young, Mitchell, Taylor, Browne, Ronstadt, Geffen, the Eagles, and Their Many Friends.* Hoboken, N.J.: Wiley, 2007. An informative look at the 1960's-1970's Los Angeles musical scene, the book explores the complex relationships among the top artists of the place and time.

Marcus, Greil, ed. *Stranded: Rock and Roll for a Desert Island.* 2d ed. Cambridge, Mass.: Da Capo Press, 2007. Answering a question about what single album one would want to have on a desert island, these essays by leading rock critics include the Jackson Browne-Glenn Frey song "Take It Easy."

Waterman, J. Douglas, ed. *Song: The World's Best Songwriters on Creating the Music That Moves Us.* Cincinnati, Ohio: Writer's Digest Books, 2007. Interviews compiled from *American Songwriter* in which artists, including Jackson Browne, discuss why and how they write songs.

Wiseman, Rich. *Jackson Browne: The Story of a Hold Out.* New York: Doubleday, 1982. Early review of Browne's life that delves deeply into family history and emphasizes the stories behind his music.

See also: Crosby, David; Raitt, Bonnie; Rush, Tom; Staples, Pops; Taylor, James; Vaughan, Stevie Ray; Young, Neil.

Dave Brubeck

American jazz composer and pianist

As a composer, pianist, and leader of an influential quartet, Brubeck introduced unusual time signatures, polyrhythms, and polytonalities to the jazz world.

Born: December 6, 1920; Concord, California
Also known as: David Warren Brubeck (full name)
Member of: The Dave Brubeck Quartet

Principal recordings

ALBUMS: *Brubeck Trio with Cal Tjader, Vol. 1*, 1949; *Brubeck Trio with Cal Tjader, Vol. 2*, 1949; *Brubeck/Desmond*, 1951; *Dave Brubeck Quartet*, 1951; *Stardust*, 1951; *Dave Brubeck/Paul Desmond*, 1952; *Dave Brubeck and Paul Desmond at Wilshire-Ebell*, 1953; *Jazz at Oberlin*, 1953; *Brubeck Time*, 1954; *Jazz Goes to College*, 1954; *Paul and Dave's Jazz Interwoven*, 1954; *Brubeck Plays Brubeck*, 1956; *Distinctive Rhythm Instrumentals*, 1956; *Jazz Impressions of the U.S.A.*, 1956; *Dave Digs Disney*, 1957; *Jazz Goes to Junior College,*1957; *Plays and Plays and . . .*, 1957; *Reunion*, 1957; *Dave Brubeck Plays Solo*, 1958; *Gone with the Wind*, 1959; *The Riddle*, 1959;

Southern Scene, 1959; *Time Out*, 1959; *Brubeck a La Mode*, 1960; *Brubeck and Rushing*, 1960; *Brubeck Plays Bernstein Plays Brubeck*, 1960; *Tonight Only*, 1960; *Brandenburg Gate: Revisited*, 1961; *Near-Myth*, 1961; *Real Ambassadors*, 1961; *Time Further Out*, 1961; *Angel Eyes*, 1962; *Bossa Nova USA*, 1962; *Countdown: Time in Outer Space*, 1962; *Gold and Fizdale Play Dave Brubeck's Jazz Ballet*, 1962; *Music from West Side Story*, 1962; *Time Changes*, 1963; *Jazz Impressions of Japan*, 1964; *Jazz Impressions of New York*, 1964; *Anything Goes: The Music of Cole Porter*, 1965; *Time In*, 1965; *Jackpot!*, 1966; *My Favorite Things*, 1966; *Compadres*, 1967; *Blues Roots*, 1968; *The Light in the Wilderness: An Oratorio for Today*, 1968; *The Gates of Justice*, 1969; *The Dave Brubeck Trio with Gerry Mulligan and the Cincinnati Symphony Orchestra*, 1970; *Elementals for Jazzcombo, Orchestra, and Baritone-Solo*, 1970; *Adventures in Time*, 1972; *We're All Together Again (For the First Time)*, 1972; *All the Things We Are*, 1973; *Truth Is Fallen*, 1973; *Two Generations of Brubeck*, 1973; *Brother, the Great Spirit Made Us All*, 1974; *1975: The Duets*, 1975; *La fiesta de la posada (Festival of the Inn)*, 1976; *A Cut Above*, 1978; *Back Home*, 1979; *Tritonis*, 1980; *Paper Moon*, 1981; *Concord on a Summer Night*, 1982; *For Iola*, 1984; *Reflections*, 1985; *Blue Rondo*, 1986; *Moscow Night*, 1987; *New Wine*, 1987; *Quiet as the Moon*, 1988; *Sound of Jazz*, 1988; *Once When I Was Young*, 1991; *Trio Brubeck*, 1993; *In Their Own Sweet Way*, 1994; *Jazz Sonatas*, 1994; *Just You, Just Me*, 1994; *Young Lions and Old Tigers*, 1994; *A Dave Brubeck Christmas*, 1996; *To Hope! A Celebration*, 1996; *One Alone*, 1997; *So What's New*, 1998; *The Crossing*, 2000; *On Time*, 2001; *I Hear a Rhapsody*, 2002; *V and J*, 2002; *Brubeck in Chattanooga*, 2003; *Classical Brubeck*, 2003; *Private Brubeck Remembers*, 2004; *London Flat, London Sharp*, 2005; *Songs*, 2005; *Brubeck Piano Compositions*, 2006; *Rondo*, 2006; *Indian Summer*, 2007.

SINGLES: "Old Sound from San Francisco," 1954.

The Life

Born in 1920 in Concord, California, David Warren Brubeck (BREW-behk) was attracted to music at an early age, influenced by his mother, a piano teacher. His childhood ambition was to be a cattle

Dave Brubeck. (Library of Congress)

rancher, emulating his father, who owned a forty-five-thousand-acre ranch in the Sierra Nevada foothills. Brubeck combined his daily ranch chores with playing the piano in local dance bands. Persuaded by his parents, Brubeck enrolled as a veterinary student in the College of the Pacific. However, a year later, he was majoring in music. He married Iola Marie Whitlock, the host of a weekly campus radio show.

Following college graduation in 1942, Brubeck was drafted into the Army, and he spent World War II playing piano to entertain the troops. After his discharge, Brubeck enrolled at Mills College to study with Darius Milhaud, the renowned French composer. At Mills College, he studied polytonality, counterpoint, and other classical-music topics. Nevertheless, he retained his fascination with jazz, which was encouraged by Milhaud.

In 1947 Brubeck began his professional jazz career in a San Francisco nightclub, the Geary Cellar, with an octet. At that time a serious swimming accident forced him to interrupt his career for several months. After his recovery, Brubeck formed his first quartet, with saxophonist Paul Desmond, drummer Joe Dodge, and bassist Bob Bates. The quartet played a series of nightclub and college engagements and recorded albums for a few years, gaining great notoriety. In 1954 Brubeck was featured on the cover of *Time*. Joe Morello, a highly regarded drummer, replaced Dodge in 1956. Eugene Wright replaced Bates on bass soon thereafter. One acclaimed album after another was released from the mid-1950's through the mid-1960's.

Despite the success in recordings and appearances, Brubeck dissolved the quartet in 1967. He began to compose in other idioms, such as ballets, liturgical music, and symphonic works.

Brubeck performed for Presidents John Kennedy, Lyndon Johnson, Ronald Reagan, and Bill Clinton. He received the Lifetime Achievement Award from the National Academy of Recording Arts and Sciences and a National Medal of the Arts. He was inducted into the *Down Beat* Hall of Fame, and he was granted honorary doctorate degrees from six universities.

The Music

Brubeck's early career coincided with the gradual decline of the big band era and the development of bop. Following a different path, Brubeck used his training in classical music and composition to develop a jazz piano style that was suitable for small combo settings.

Early Years. Advised by his Mills College mentor, Milhaud, to pursue jazz, Brubeck assembled an octet with other Milhaud disciples. Among them were Cal Tjader (vibraphone) and Desmond (alto saxophone), who would later become iconic figures in jazz. The octet gave way to a trio, which won the *Down Beat* Best Small Combo Award in 1949. The trio expanded to a quartet with the addition of Desmond in 1951. The contrasting improvisations of Brubeck and Desmond proved to be a winning blend.

Jazz at College. The early edition of the Dave Brubeck Quartet employed various bassists and drummers, but Desmond was a fixture. With a steady engagement at the Blackhawk in San Francisco, the quartet was able to expand to other performance venues. Brubeck's wife, Iola, wrote to colleges across the United States, soliciting invitations for the quartet to appear on campus. The effort paid

off. It was estimated that during one college tour the quartet performed sixty "one-nighters" in a row. The campus concerts produced steady income and broad exposure, and, importantly, they introduced jazz to a new generation. College students demonstrated their support by faithfully buying the quartet's recordings: *Jazz at Oberlin*, *Jazz Goes to College*, and *Jazz Goes to Junior College*, among others. The college-concert period set the stage for Brubeck's innovative and experimental ideas.

The Classic Quartet. The addition of Morello on drums and Wright on bass solidified the quartet. Instead of a homogeneous group of musicians with similar personalities, tastes, and styles, the Dave Brubeck Quartet comprised four individualistic musicians, unafraid to take risks. Brubeck could easily shift from powerful chords to subtle nuances as the music demanded. Desmond's silky, feathery alto tone provided lyrical melodies, even in improvisational solos. Wright on bass was a steadying influence, playing in a traditional style reminiscent of earlier jazz eras. Morello possessed a keen ability to play in difficult meter signatures and still maintain a strong swing feel. Together, they complemented as well as inspired each other.

"Take Five." Brubeck first encountered odd meters when traveling to Turkey and Africa, and he realized their potential for use in American-style jazz. The landmark album *Time Out* proved to be a turning point in jazz history: It included the jazz classics "Take Five" in 5/4 time and "Blue Rondo à la Turk" with a mixture of meter signatures, including 9/8 time. The management of Columbia Records and the producer of the album were fearful this innovative music style strayed too far from the standards on the successful college albums. The quartet, however, refused to compromise. *Time Out* went gold, "Take Five" was a gigantic hit, and Columbia relented. *Time Further Out*, *Countdown: Time in Outer Space*, and similar albums followed.

Polyrhythm and Polytonality. Besides experimenting with odd meters, Brubeck infused polyrhythm and polytonality into the quartet's music. Polyrhythm involves multiple rhythms being played simultaneously. The ideal drum-set artist, Morello could play four different rhythms at once, using hands and feet separately, and at the same time he could synchronize the various rhythms throughout the composition.

The use of polytonalities was another step in the quartet's evolution. The standard procedure for a composer is to write a tune in a major or minor key, and musicians perform it in the original key or transpose it to another. However, the melody remains in one key at a time. Brubeck's polytonal approach was to layer his compositions so that two or three different keys were employed together. Traditionalists rejected such unconventional techniques, but Brubeck never wavered in his determination to compose and perform music his way.

West Coast Jazz. Some viewed Brubeck as a member of the West Coast, or cool, jazz style because he was based in California when West Coast jazz flourished. In reality, Brubeck played the piano in a heavy, aggressive style, atypical of ethereal and lyrical cool jazz. With Desmond applying the lighter touch, Brubeck was free to provide the contrast that the quartet utilized so successfully.

Indian Summer. In 2007 Brubeck produced this retrospective solo piano recording. The album featured new Brubeck compositions along with a collection of standards and ballads, performed with sensitivity and restraint. Full of nostalgia, *Indian Summer* showed Brubeck coming full circle, back to his roots.

Musical Legacy

During his long and successful career, Brubeck created a wide audience for jazz and endeared himself to fans. His body of work is sophisticated and pioneering as well as voluminous, and his signature piece, "Take Five," is familiar to even the most casual jazz, and nonjazz, listeners. Brubeck's alma mater honors his legacy in the Brubeck Institute of the University of the Pacific, established in recognition of Brubeck and his wife, Iola. It preserves Brubeck's educational and creative musical contributions and perpetuates his interests in environmental issues, social issues, and international relations. The institute manages the Brubeck archives and sponsors a jazz festival, an outreach program, a fellowship program, and a summer jazz colony.

Douglas D. Skinner

Further Reading

Hall, Fred. *It's About Time*. Fayetteville: University of Arkansas Press, 1996. Written by a radio broadcaster, this book traces Brubeck from boy-hood to experienced jazzman. Includes interviews and stories of life on the road.

Martin, Henry. *Enjoying Jazz*. New York: Schirmer Books, 1986. A compendium of jazz styles and jazz artists that contains an in-depth analysis of Brubeck's "Blue Rondo à la Turk."

Megill, David W., and Paul O. W. Tanner. *Jazz Issues: A Critical History*. Madison, Wis.: Brown and Benchmark, 1995. This text for jazz history places Brubeck at strategic points in jazz history. Provides listening recommendations.

Ostransky, Leroy. *Understanding Jazz*. Englewood Cliffs, N.J.: Prentice-Hall, 1977. An overview of jazz origins written by a jazz educator. Brubeck's influences and importance to jazz are detailed.

Taylor, Billy. *Jazz Piano: History and Development*. Dubuque, Iowa: W. C. Brown, 1982. Eminent jazz pianist Billy Taylor describes Brubeck's piano style.

See also: Armstrong, Louis; Desmond, Paul; Hancock, Herbie; Milhaud, Darius; Waller, Fats.

Jimmy Buffett

American rock singer, songwriter, and guitarist

With a musical style best described as an amalgam of country-western, rock, and reggae, Buffett created a roster of appealing, lighthearted story songs that celebrate coastal towns, libations, and carefree lifestyles.

Born: December 25, 1946; Pascagoula, Mississippi
Also known as: James William Buffett (full name)

Principal recordings

ALBUMS: *Down to Earth*, 1970; *A White Sport Coat and a Pink Carnation*, 1973; *A-1-A*, 1974; *Living and Dying in 3/4 Time*, 1974; *Rancho Deluxe*, 1975; *Havana Daydreamin'*, 1976; *High Cumberland Jubilee* (1972), 1976; *Changes in Latitudes, Changes in Attitudes*, 1977; *Son of a Son of a Sailor*, 1978; *You Had to Be There*, 1978; *Volcano*, 1979; *Coconut Telegraph*, 1981;

Somewhere over China, 1982; *One Particular Harbour*, 1983; *Riddles in the Sand*, 1984; *Last Mango in Paris*, 1985; *Floridays*, 1986; *Hot Water*, 1988; *Off to See the Lizard*, 1989; *Feeding Frenzy*, 1990; *Fruitcakes*, 1994; *Barometer Soup*, 1995; *Banana Wind*, 1996; *Christmas Island*, 1996; *Don't Stop the Carnival*, 1998; *Beach House on the Moon*, 1999; *Captain American*, 2002; *Far Side of the World*, 2002; *License to Chill*, 2004.

The Life

James William Buffett (BUH-fet) was born in Mississippi, but he grew up in Mobile, Alabama. He attended a Catholic elementary school and an all-male high school. He studied at Auburn University in Alabama and at Pearl River Community College in Mississippi before transferring to the University of Southern Mississippi, where he earned a bachelor of science degree in history and journalism in 1969. That year he married Margie Washichek, moved to Nashville, Tennessee, and worked as a freelance journalist for *Billboard*. He performed locally in Nashville and recorded two albums that met with limited success.

In the early 1970's he divorced and moved to Florida, where his musical career flourished. He worked with country-music singer Jerry Jeff Walker and started a long and fruitful collaboration with the Coral Reefer Band. He met Jane Slagsvol; they married and had three children.

In addition to being a singer and a songwriter, Buffett was an airplane pilot, a record producer, a film producer, a sound-track composer, a conservationist, and an entrepreneur. Notably, he was one of a few authors to have a *New York Times* best seller in both the fiction and nonfiction categories. Although his most popular songs were written in the 1970's, his concert tours kept his music vital. His devoted fans are called Parrot Heads.

The Music

Buffett composes humorous and sentimental ballads and sings them over a simple accompaniment. His music does not fit one genre; it samples several, such as country-western, rock, and reggae. Supported by a marimba, a ship's bell, an electronic piano, an organ, an acoustic guitar, conga drums, and other percussion instruments, Buffett unspools his first-person tales in lyrics that revolve around themes of sailing, drinking, and living freely.

Backed by the Coral Reefer Band, Buffett released several albums in the 1970's, including the immensely successful *Changes in Latitudes, Changes in Attitudes* and *Son of a Son of a Sailor*. His duet with Alan Jackson, "It's Five o'Clock Somewhere," was a country hit in 2003, and in 2004 his album *License to Chill* was his first to be ranked number one on the *Billboard* chart.

"Come Monday." Buffett's first nationally successful song, "Come Monday," appeared on the *Billboard* singles chart under the pop, country, and adult contemporary headings. This slow ballad, which features a steel guitar, a string section, and tender lyrics about being separated from a loved one, has a definite country sound. "Come Monday" was the only hit song from the album *Living and Dying in 3/4 Time*.

"Margaritaville." "Margaritaville" was a surprise hit when it was released in 1977 on Buffett's album *Changes in Latitudes, Changes in Attitudes*. The singer's persona relates the story of his return to Margaritaville (evidently a tropical tourist destination) and the inebriation that he initially blames on a woman but admits is "my own damned fault." The combination of guitar, marimba, conga drums, electronic keyboard, and Buffett's tranquil voice became the quintessential elements of his sound. "Margaritaville" ranked in the Top 15 on the *Billboard* charts in the pop, country, and adult contemporary categories. Even after the album was certified platinum later that year, no one suspected just how big the song would become outside the music arena. In addition to the restaurant chain Jimmy Buffett's Margaritaville and the satellite radio station Radio Margaritaville, a Margaritaville brand of tequila, a margarita mix, footwear, and frozen shrimp products were created. One Buffett biography was titled *Jimmy Buffett: The Man from Margaritaville Revealed*; a two-disc collection of Buffett's songs was called *Meet Me in Margaritaville*. When Buffett released an album of his greatest hits in 1985, its title made subtle reference to the enormity of the song's success: *Songs You Know by Heart: Jimmy Buffett's Greatest Hit(s)*.

"Cheeseburger in Paradise." "Cheeseburger in Paradise" was released in 1978 on the album *Son of a Son of a Sailor*. This song is the story of Buffett's failed attempt to become a vegetarian, and his ultimate desire to consume an elaborate, perfect cheeseburger. In addition to his standard use of guitar, drums, and vocals, this song features an electric organ, hand clapping, harmonica, and a female chorus. In *The Parrot Head: Handbook*, Buffett wrote that the inspiration for this song was a cheeseburger he imagined while he was lost on the Caribbean Sea. He landed on an island and, to his surprise, found a restaurant that served cheeseburgers. He ordered the cheeseburger he imagined, he was served something rather different, but he was pleased, nonetheless, to be fed and back on dry land. In addition, a restaurant chain was built around this song.

Musical Legacy

Although Buffett's music is distinctive for its leisurely attitude, Buffett himself is tireless. He performed on concert tours for decades, he composed and recorded music for numerous albums, he wrote several books, and he traveled extensively. He is noted for his involvement in multiple business ventures and conservationist organizations. He collaborated with other musicians, such as James Taylor, Merle Haggard, Waylon Jennings, Jim Croce, and Alan Jackson. He and his fans contributed "parrot head," "phlock," and "parrot hedonism" to the lexicon.

Joseph R. Matson

Further Reading

Buffett, Jimmy. *The Parrot Head: Handbook*. Universal City, Calif.: MCI Records, 1992. A general account of the culture surrounding Buffett's concerts and background stories from the author himself. Photographs, discography, and facsimiles of his notebooks.

_____. *A Pirate Looks at Fifty*. New York: Random House, 1998. Short stories chronicle Buffett's life and travels.

Corcoran, Tom. *Jimmy Buffett: The Key West Years*. Marathon, Fla.: Ketch & Yawl Press, 2006. Short chapters explain Buffett's early years in Florida, with photographs.

Eng, Steve. *Jimmy Buffett: The Man from Margaritaville Revealed*. New York: St. Martin's Press, 1996. Although written without the participation of Buffett, this is a thorough biography. Features an extensive discography, a bibliography, and an index.

Quigley, Jackson, with Jerry Gontang. *Jimmy dotcom: The Evolution of a Phan*. Lake Forest, Calif.: St. Somewhere Press, 2000. A humorous account of Buffett's impact on his fans, including more than a thousand photographs.

Thomas, Ryan. *The Parrot Head Companion: An Insider's Guide to Jimmy Buffett*. Secaucus, N.J.: Carol, 1998. A history of Buffett's professional career, including reviews of his albums and books up to 1998.

See also: Haggard, Merle; Jennings, Waylon; Taylor, James.

Johnny Burke

American musical-theater composer and lyricist

One of the most popular lyricists of the 1930's and 1940's, Burke wrote primarily for film musicals, many featuring Bing Crosby. His fanciful lyrics mentioned moonbeams, stars, dreams, and cottages built of lilacs and laughter, balm for Depression-era Americans.

Born: October 3, 1908; Antioch, California
Died: February 25, 1964; New York, New York
Also known as: John Francis Burke (full name)

Principal works

MUSICAL THEATER: *Nellie Bly*, 1946 (lyrics; music by Jimmy Van Heusen); *Carnival in Flanders*, 1953 (lyrics; music by Van Heusen); *Donnybrook!*, 1961.

SONGS (lyrics; music by Rudolf Friml): "Bon Jour," 1956; "Comparisons," 1956; "This Same Heart," 1956; "Vive la You," 1956; "Watch out for the Devil," 1956.

SONG (lyrics; music by Erroll Garner): "Misty," 1955.

SONGS (lyrics; music by Arthur Johnston; from *Pennies from Heaven*): "Pennies from Heaven," 1936; "All You Want to Do Is Dance," 1937; "Double or Nothing," 1937; "The Moon Got in

My Eyes," 1937; "One, Two, Button Your Shoe," 1937.

SONGS (lyrics; music by James Monaco): "I've Got a Pocketful of Dreams," 1938; "Sing a Song of Sunbeams," 1939; "Ain't It a Shame About Mame?," 1940; "Only Forever," 1940; "Sweet Potato Piper," 1940 (from *The Road to Singapore*); "Too Romantic" 1940 (from *The Road to Singapore*).

SONGS (lyrics; music by Harold Spina): "Shadows on the Swanee," 1932; "Annie Doesn't Live Here Anymore," 1933; "My Very Good Friend the Milkman," 1934; "You're Not the Only Oyster in the Stew," 1934.

SONGS (lyrics; music by Jimmy Van Heusen): "Imagination," 1942 (from *The Road to Morocco*); "Moonlight Becomes You," 1942 (from *The Road to Morocco*); "Polka Dots and Moonbeams," 1942 (from *The Road to Morocco*); "Sunday, Monday, or Always," 1943 (from *Dixie*); "Going My Way," 1944 (from *Going My Way*); "It Could Happen to You," 1944 (from *Going My Way*); "Swinging on a Star," 1944 (from *Going My Way*).

The Life

Born in California, John Francis Burke grew up in Chicago, where his father was in the construction business and his mother taught school. Although he had a classical music education—he played piano in the University of Wisconsin orchestra—it was in popular music where Burke made his name. The talented youngster got a job as staff pianist, selling songs, in the Chicago office of the Irving Berlin Music Corporation after he graduated from the University of Wisconsin in 1927. At the same time, he was playing piano in dance bands and for vaudeville.

After a transfer to the New York office of the Irving Berlin Music Corporation, Burke began writing lyrics for composer Harold Spina, and in short order they wrote some minor hits, enough to attract the attention of Hollywood. In 1939, Burke signed a contract with Paramount Pictures, where he stayed for the rest of his career. Personable and gregarious, Burke enjoyed the parties and the golf games that Southern California had to offer. However, his heavy drinking was a detriment to his health, and he died at the age of fifty-five of a heart attack in his

sleep in 1964. Married four times, Burke had four children with Bess Patterson, to whom he was married from 1939 to 1955.

The Music

Burke wrote the lyrics to more than 550 published songs, most of which appeared in forty-two motion pictures and three Broadway musicals. When Burke started at Paramount Pictures, he was first paired with composer Arthur Johnston, and he was given an assignment that would change his life: to write a song for Bing Crosby.

Ballads for Bing. "Pennies from Heaven" was a big hit for Crosby, and the crooner and the studio liked the song (which was nominated for an Academy Award) so much that it became the title of the film. The song also began a relationship between Burke and Crosby that produced a string of popular songs. Burke's lyrics reinforced and helped establish Crosby's signature troubadour style. The lyricist downplayed his accomplishment, saying he simply listened to Crosby talk and either took phrases directly from him or patterned some after Crosby's way of putting phrases together. Crosby was more direct: "One of the best things that's happened to me is a 145-pound Irish leprechaun named Johnny Burke." For the next seventeen years, in 120 personally tailored songs in twenty-three films, Burke largely created the Crosby song persona. Burke was one of Crosby's closest friends, and the singer nicknamed Burke "the poet."

Collaborations with Van Heusen. When Johnston left Paramount for Twentieth Century-Fox, Burke teamed with James Monaco, and he continued writing hits for Crosby, including "I've Got a Pocketful of Dreams," "Sing a Song of Sunbeams," "Only Forever" (nominated for an Academy Award), "Ain't It a Shame About Mame?," and "Too Romantic." The team wrote songs for the first of the "road pictures" starring Crosby, Bob Hope, and Dorothy Lamour, *The Road to Singapore* (1940).

When Burke changed to composer Jimmy Van Heusen, he found his ideal collaborator, and they produced hit after hit for the next fifteen years. Writing songs for sixteen more Crosby films, the team also wrote material for others, including Frank Sinatra ("Polka Dots and Moonbeams") and the Glenn Miller Orchestra ("Imagination").

Written for *The Road to Morocco* (1942), "Moon-

Johnny Burke. (AP/Wide World Photos)

light Becomes You" was another hit from Burke and Van Heusen, which prompted Crosby to dub them his Gold Dust Twins. Crosby insisted that the songwriting team be paid $150,000 a year at Paramount Pictures, the highest salary of any studio songwriting team. Burke and Van Heusen made good on this investment, winning the Academy Award for Best Song for "Swinging on a Star," written for *Going My Way* (1944). The song was inducted in the Grammy Hall of Fame in 2002. In 1944 the duo created Burke and Van Heusen, Inc., a music publishing firm, with backing from Crosby, Sidney Kornheiser, and Edwin H. Morris.

The box office magic that Burke and Van Heusen inspired in film audiences, however, did not work on Broadway theatergoers. Their first stage musical, *Nellie Bly*, ran just two weeks, despite the presence of two great stars, Victor Moore and William Gaxton. While *Carnival in Flanders* ran only six performances, it did yield the team's greatest torch song: Sammy Cahn listed "Here's That Rainy Day" as one of the ten best songs ever written, and Rosemary Clooney called it "the most evocative song I've ever sung."

Solo Work. Burke and Van Heusen's partnership was increasingly strained because of Burke's heavy drinking, so Van Heusen began to look for a new writing partner, eventually finding one in Cahn. Now alone, Burke set lyrics in 1955 to a well-known jazz instrumental, "Misty," by Erroll Garner. "Misty" became Sarah Vaughan's signature song, and it was included in the Grammy Hall of Fame in 2002. He wrote new lyrics to Rudolf Friml melodies for *The Vagabond King* (1956). Burke's last major work was the Broadway musical *Donnybrook!*, which was based on the film *The Quiet Man* (1952), for which he wrote lyrics and music. Burke was heartbroken that it lasted only sixty-eight performances.

Musical Legacy

In addition to providing Crosby with numerous popular hits, Burke produced lyrics that were recorded by other great vocalists, such as Tony Bennett, Rosemary Clooney, Nat King Cole, Perry Como, Harry Connick, Jr., Doris Day, Lena Horne, Betty Hutton, Johnny Mathis, Linda Ronstadt, Frank Sinatra, and Mel Tormé. Burke was among the few lyricists who had seventeen songs selected to appear on *Your Hit Parade*, and he was one of the first songwriters to be inducted into the Songwriters Hall of Fame. Thirty-one years after his death, the Broadway musical revue *Swinging on a Star: The Johnny Burke Musical* (1995) introduced his genius to another generation of music lovers.

Bud Coleman

Further Reading

Furia, Philip, and Michael Lasser. *America's Songs: The Stories Behind the Songs of Broadway, Hollywood, and Tin Pan Alley*. New York: Routledge, 2006. Furia and Lasser comment on the historical importance of Burke's writing.

Giddins, Gary. *Bing Crosby—A Pocketful of Dreams: The Early Years, 1903-1940*. New York: Little, Brown, 2001. Giddins credits a great deal of Crosby's success to Burke's skill as a lyricist.

Gottlieb, Robert, and Robert Kimball. *Reading Lyrics*. New York: Pantheon Books, 2000. This source offers a brief appraisal of Burke's career and includes lyrics to nineteen of his songs.

Hischak, Thomas S. *The American Musical Film Song Encyclopedia*. Westport, Conn.: Greenwood Press,

1999. Sixty-four of Burke's songs are briefly described, including who originally sang them, in which film they appeared, and who subsequently recorded the song.

Nolan, Frederick. "Johnny Burke." In *Dictionary of Literary Biography: American Song Lyricists, 1920-1960*. Detroit: Gale, 2002. An extensive source of information about Burke.

See also: Bennett, Tony; Cole, Nat King; Crosby, Bing; Ronstadt, Linda; Sinatra, Frank; Tormé, Mel; Van Heusen, Jimmy; Vaughan, Sarah.

Solomon Burke

American rhythm-and-blues singer and songwriter

With a stylistic depth and considerable vocal range, Burke ranked as one of the most versatile early singers of soul music.

Born: March 21, 1940; Philadelphia, Pennsylvania

Principal recordings

ALBUMS: *Solomon Burke*, 1962; *Rock 'n' Soul*, 1964; *The Rest of Solomon Burke*, 1965; *I Wish I Knew*, 1968; *King Solomon*, 1968; *Proud Mary*, 1969; *Electronic Magnetism*, 1972; *King Heavy*, 1972; *I Have a Dream*, 1974; *Back to My Roots*, 1975; *Music to Make Love By*, 1975; *Lord We Need a Miracle*, 1979; *Sidewalks, Fences, and Walls*, 1979; *King of Rock 'n' Soul*, 1981; *Lord I Need a Miracle Man*, 1982; *Soul Alive*, 1984; *A Change Is Gonna Come*, 1986; *Homeland*, 1990; *Into My Life You Came*, 1990; *This Is His*, 1990; *Soul of the Blues*, 1993; *The Definition of Soul*, 1997; *We Need a Miracle*, 1998; *Not by Water but Fire This Time*, 1999; *Don't Give Up on Me*, 2002; *The Incredible Solomon Burke at His Best*, 2002; *Soulman*, 2002; *The Apollo Album*, 2003; *Make Do with What You Got*, 2005; *Nashville*, 2006; *Soul Lucky*, 2006; *Like a Fire*, 2008.

SINGLES: "None of Us Are Free," 2003; "Rhino Hi-Fives: Solomon Burke," 2005; "Tomorrow Is Forever," 2007.

The Life

Solomon Burke was born on March 21, 1940, in Philadelphia. The oldest of seven children, he began singing in the church founded by his grandmother, becoming a soloist when he was nine. At twelve he had a radio program, *Solomon's Temple*, during which he sang and preached. In 1955 Kae Williams, a Philadelphia disc jockey, helped Burke contact record companies, and he signed with Apollo Records, issuing his first single, "Christmas Gifts from Heaven."

When his gospel tunes sold poorly, Burke became disenchanted with the recording industry. He became a funeral director, opening a chain of mortuaries later operated by two of his sons. Eventually, Paul Ackerman of *Billboard* persuaded him to give music another chance, and in December, 1960, he signed with Atlantic Records, where legendary producer Jerry Wexler helped Burke to develop a soulful, secular singing style that would reach wider audiences. However, when Atlantic Records did not renew Burke's contract in 1968, he blamed Wexler for allowing his career to stall.

In the 1970's Burke frequently changed labels. While at MGM he recorded songs for the sound track of *Cool Breeze* (1972). When the songs he recorded for Chess Records in 1975 did not meet expectations, Burke, already an ordained minister, began devoting his energies to leading his Philadelphia church and recording gospel music for Savoy Records. In 1984 Rounder Records released *Soul Alive*, a live album of Burke's 1960's and 1970's hits and some soul classics.

In 1995 Jim Fifield, head of EMI Music, helped Burke sign with Point Blank Records, which resulted in *The Definition of Soul*. The album reunited Burke with Wexler on "Your Turn to Cry," the only tune not cowritten by Burke, and "Everybody's Got a Game," a duet with Little Richard, which revitalized Burke's career.

The father of fourteen daughters and seven sons, the three-hundred-pound Burke acted occasionally; he had a prominent role as a crime boss opposite Dennis Quaid and Ellen Barkin in *The Big Easy* (1987). Burke received a Pioneer Award from the Rhythm and Blues Foundation in 1993. Because of Burke's longtime relationship with the Catholic Church, he performed at the Vatican for Pope John Paul II and Pope Benedict XVI.

The Music

Burke's singing was influenced by artists as diverse as Gene Autry, Nat King Cole, Big Joe Turner, and Muddy Waters. Before Ray Charles made it acceptable for black performers to record country-western songs, Burke scored a hit at Atlantic Records with "Just Out of Reach (Of My Two Empty Arms)," originally recorded by Faron Young. A blend of country, gospel, and rhythm and blues, "Down in the Valley," featuring King Curtis on saxophone and Bucky Pizzarelli on guitar, demonstrated Burke's ability as a singer and songwriter to merge genres. As he related in the blues concert documentary *Lightning in a Bottle* (2004), Burke was invited to perform at a Ku Klux Klan event, whose organizers thought he was a white country singer.

Songwriter. Burke wrote or cowrote most of his hits during his years with Atlantic Records, including the infectious dance tune "Everybody Needs Somebody to Love." A rousing version appeared on 1965's *The Rolling Stones Now!*, and forty years later, Burke was the Rolling Stones' opening act on some stops of their *A Bigger Bang* tour. His biggest soul hit, "Cry to Me," was recorded by the Rolling Stones and other artists, such as Tom Petty. It also can be heard on the sound track for *Dirty Dancing* (1987), one of several films to feature Burke's songs.

Despite Burke's inspirational leanings, his secular songs always had a sensual, though not explicitly erotic, quality, as with "Tonight's the Night." Throughout his career, Burke's music had a raw, spontaneous spirit, never sounding overproduced. He was more melodic and less a shouter than many other soul singers. Music historians considered him a pioneer, along with Charles, for injecting the vocal motifs of African American religious music into pop music.

Although he had six songs on the rhythm-and-blues charts during the period 1961-1965, Burke, unlike his contemporaries Charles, Sam Cooke, Percy Sledge, and Otis Redding, never had a major hit on the pop charts, an odd occurrence given the crossover appeal of his music. "Just Out of Reach (Of My Two Empty Arms)," "Got to Get You off My Mind," "Tonight's the Night," and "If You Need Me" were all Top 40 hits, though none placed higher than number twenty-two.

The Next Phase. A group of Burke's admirers wrote songs for *Don't Give Up on Me*, which was nominated for a Grammy Award as Best Contemporary Blues album. Burke took music composed by famous singer-songwriters and made it his own, although retaining the style of its creator. Elvis Costello's almost operatic "The Judgement" tested the strength of Burke's powerful voice. Van Morrison's "Fast Train" and "Only a Dream" were tributes to Burke's gospel roots. Bob Dylan's "Stepchild" featured the odd, demanding rhythms of the legend's late composing style. Nick Lowe, Tom Waits, and Brian Wilson also contributed songs to the album, arguably Burke's best.

Following the similar *Make Do with What You Got*, with songs by Dylan, Morrison, Mick Jagger, Keith Richards, and Dr. John, Burke recorded his first completely country album. *Nashville* included solo efforts, including Bruce Springsteen's "Ain't Got You," as well as duets with Patty Griffin, Emmylou Harris, Patty Loveless, Dolly Parton, and Gillian Welch. Unlike other such collaborations, the songs in *Nashville* are heartfelt and never strained, a distinguishing characteristic of Burke's music.

Solomon Burke. (AP/Wide World Photos)

Musical Legacy

Burke was described as one of the founders of soul, building upon the contributions of Charles and Cooke and paving the way for Aretha Franklin, Wilson Pickett, and Redding. Waits praised him as one of the architects of American music, and both Wexler and Ahmet Ertegun, cofounder of Atlantic Records, considered him the greatest soul singer. While Burke never achieved widespread popularity, he was a role model for dozens of singers and songwriters.

Michael Adams

Further Reading

Ertegun, Ahmet, and Perry Richardson. *"What'd I Say?" The Atlantic Story: Fifty Years of Music.* New York: Welcome Rain, 2001. A look at Burke's years at Atlantic Records.

Guralnick, Peter. *Sweet Soul Music: Rhythm and Blues and the Southern Dream of Freedom.* New York: Harper & Row, 1986. Burke's achievements examined in the context of the history of African American music.

Light, Alan. "Song of Solomon." *Gentlemen's Quarterly* 72 (August, 2002): 86-90. Analysis of Burke's impact on popular music and his legacy. In an interview, the singer explains the nature of soul.

Newman, Melinda. "Point Blank Goes Regional with Soul Legend Burke." *Billboard* 109 (January 25, 1997): 13. Burke discusses the making of *Definition of Soul* and his relationship with Wexler.

See also: Blackwell, Otis; Charles, Ray; Franklin, Aretha; Jagger, Sir Mick; Redding, Otis; Turner, Big Joe; Waters, Muddy.

Gary Burton

American jazz songwriter, vibraphone player, and marimba player

A major figure in jazz, Burton revolutionized vibraphone performance by playing with four mallets instead of two.

Born: January 23, 1943; Anderson, Indiana

Principal recordings

ALBUMS: *New Vibe Man in Town*, 1961; *Who Is Gary Burton?*, 1962; *Three in Jazz*, 1963; *Artist's Choice*, 1963; *Something's Coming*, 1963; *The Groovy Sound of Music*, 1964; *Tennessee Firebird*, 1966; *The Time Machine*, 1966; *Duster*, 1967; *A Genuine Tong Funeral* (with Carla Bley), 1967; *Lofty Fake Anagram*, 1967; *Country Roads and Other Places*, 1968; *Good Vibes*, 1969; *Paris Encounter*, 1969; *Throb*, 1969; *Alone at Last*, 1971; *Gary Burton and Keith Jarrett* (with Keith Jarrett), 1971; *Crystal Silence* (with Chick Corea), 1972; *Works*, 1972; *The New Quartet*, 1973; *Seven Songs for Quartet and Chamber Orchestra*, 1973; *Hotel Hello* (with Steve Swallow), 1974; *Matchbook* (with Ralph Towner), 1974; *Ring* (with Eberhard Weber), 1974; *Dreams So Real*, 1975; *Passengers*, 1976; *Times Square*, 1978; *Duet* (with Corea), 1979; *Easy as Pie*, 1980; *In Concert, Zurich* (with Corea), 1980; *Picture This*, 1982; *Real Life Hits*, 1984; *Gary Burton and the Berklee All Stars*, 1985; *Slide Show* (with Towner), 1986; *Whiz Kids*, 1986; *Times Like These*, 1988; *Reunion* (with other performers), 1989; *Right Time, Right Place*, 1990; *Cool Nights*, 1991; *Six Pack*, 1992; *It's Another Day*, 1993; *Face to Face*, 1994; *Astor Piazzolla Reunion: A Tango Excursion*, 1996; *Departure*, 1997; *Like Minds* (with other performers), 1998; *Libertango: The Music of Astor Piazzolla*, 2000; *For Hamp, Red, Bags, and Cal*, 2001; *Virtuosi*, 2002; *Music of Duke Ellington*, 2003; *Generations*, 2004; *Next Generation*, 2005.

The Life

Gary Burton was born January 23, 1943, in Anderson, Indiana. He taught himself to play the marimba at the age of six and the vibraphone at the age of eight. He was joined by his sister on the piano and his brother on clarinet and bass. The family group's repertoire included classical pieces, Dixieland tunes, and novelty numbers. At their peak, the siblings played about a hundred performances a year. At age thirteen Burton discovered jazz and lost interest in the family group.

When he was seventeen, Burton made his first recordings for RCA Records with country guitarist Hank Garland. After Burton graduated from high school, he spent the summer in Nashville, playing with Garland. Burton then moved to Boston to study at the Berklee School of Music for two years, during which time he recorded as a bandleader for RCA Records. In 1962 Burton moved to New York, and in 1963 he joined George Shearing's quintet. He then rose to prominence as a member of Stan Getz's quartet (1964-1966), winning the *Down Beat* Talent Deserving of Wider Recognition Award in 1965. In 1967 he formed his own quartet with Larry Coryell, Steve Swallow, and Bob Moses, a group whose style was influenced by rock music. *Down Beat* awarded Burton its Jazzman of the Year award in 1968, and his 1971 album *Alone at Last* (a solo vibraphone concert recorded at the 1971 Montreux Jazz Festival) was honored with a Grammy Award.

Gary Burton. (Reuters/Landov)

Burton moved back to Boston to teach percussion and improvisation in the fall of 1971, and in 1985 he was named dean of curriculum and later executive vice president of the Berklee College of Music. In 2003 he retired and moved to Fort Lauderdale, Florida.

The Music

A virtuoso vibraphonist, Burton developed an original style of improvisation distinct from his famous predecessors, Lionel Hampton and Milt Jackson. In the early 1960's Burton departed from the two-mallet playing style and always held four mallets. At the time, Burton was one of the few modern jazz improvisers not to have drawn substantially on the melodic conceptions of the bebop pioneers Charlie Parker and Dizzy Gillespie. Instead, Burton's musical vocabulary emphasized classical, country, and rock styles. He frequently employed accompanying vamps and pedal points made possible by his consistent use of four mallets.

Duster. In the late 1960's Burton's recordings featuring a mixture of jazz, country, and rock styles were among the earliest of the fusion sound that would later become mainstream with Miles Davis's *Bitches Brew* (1969). With Burton's quartet record-

ing of *Duster*, the electric guitar became a leading instrument in jazz, and rock elements were first introduced into virtuosic jazz. This and other RCA Records recordings Burton did in the late 1960's with guitarist Coryell created a new jazz-rock sound, and the Gary Burton Quartet was invited to play at concert performances with such well-known rock groups as the Electric Flag and Cream at the Fillmore West in San Francisco in 1967.

A Genuine Tong Funeral. Burton's recording of Carla Bley's wordless opera *A Genuine Tong Funeral* is a musical portrait of the emotions surrounding death. Bley originally intended this work for staging with costumes. In *A Genuine Tong Funeral* Burton's quartet is augmented by five horn players, with Bley on piano and organ. The themes are derived from American jazz, European cabaret styles, and Chinese processional music. *A Genuine Tong Funeral* is unique in Burton's oeuvre, since he rarely recorded large-scale works.

Crystal Silence. *Crystal Silence* marks the beginning of Burton's recordings for the ECM label and the start of his collaboration with pianist Chick Corea. Burton's late 1960's fusion style was replaced in the early 1970's by virtuosic acoustic jazz. The performances on *Crystal Silence* demonstrate the precision and accuracy of Burton's and Corea's tight improvisatory imitations. Avoiding blues and bebop clichés, Burton and Corea focused on modern melodies. Their duets resulted in several noteworthy ECM recordings, including the Grammy Award-winning *Duet* and *In Concert, Zurich*.

Libertango. Burton's recordings of Astor Piazzolla's tangos transformed Burton's work. Unlike the expanded solos in his traditional jazz playing, Burton shifts smoothly back and forth between written parts and short improvisations.

Virtuosi. Burton's *Virtuosi* includes performances of classical repertoire and improvisations with pianist Makoto Ozone. *Virtuosi* includes works by Maurice Ravel, Sergei Rachmaninoff, George Gershwin, Alessandro Scarlatti, Johannes Brahms, Léo Delibes, and Ozone. Some pieces, such as Samuel Barber's *Excursions* (1945), flow seamlessly from composed to improvised and back; other pieces show clear distinctions between the composed and improvised sections.

Musical Legacy

Among Burton's many recorded performances, those with a lasting historical significance are the fusion recordings from the late 1960's. Burton produced several of the earliest jazz-rock fusion and country-jazz fusion recordings with guitarist Coryell. The influence of the Burton Quartet's interactions with rock groups such as Cream is evident in the adoption of extended improvisations in rock music of the late 1960's. Burton transformed the jazz vibraphone technique with an innovative four-mallet grip that was adopted by jazz vibraphonists worldwide. His technique became widely used on orchestral keyboard percussion instruments, such as the marimba, the xylophone, and orchestra bells.

David Steffens

Further Reading

Kart, Larry. "Gary Burton." In *Jazz in Search of Itself*. New Haven, Conn.: Yale University Press, 2004. Burton discusses his career and his development as a vibraphonist and a bandleader.

Mattingly, Rick. "Gary Burton: The Innovator of the Vibraphone." *Percussive Notes* 37, no. 5 (October, 1999): 8-14. Mattingly interviews Burton about his early career, the history of the vibraphone, and the influences of Red Norvo, Jackson, and Hampton.

Petercsak, Jim. "A Profile of Gary Burton: The Man and His Music, Part One." *Percussive Notes* 12, no. 2 (Winter, 1974). Petercsak interviews Burton about his youth, his musical training, his approach to improvisation, and his recordings.

Scott, Craig. "Gary Burton's Solo on 'Bud Powell.'" *Percussive Notes* 33, no. 6 (December, 1995): 52-56. A complete transcription of Burton's solo on "Bud Powell" from a live performance with Chick Corea in Munich, 1979.

Wanamaker, Jay. "A Profile of Gary Burton: The Man and His Music, Part Two." *Percussive Notes* 18, no. 1 (Fall, 1979). Wanamaker interviews Burton about his ECM recordings, his improvisations, and his use of electronics with the vibraphone.

See also: Corea, Chick; Getz, Stan; Hampton, Lionel; Jarrett, Keith; Metheny, Pat; Piazzolla, Astor.

Adolf Busch
German violinist

Busch was hailed as a great violinist in the German tradition, and his interpretations in performances and recordings (especially of Beethoven's late string quartets) were described as masterpieces that elucidated the complex architecture of violin works.

Born: August 8, 1891; Siegen, Westphalia, Prussia (now in Germany)

Died: June 9, 1952; Guilford, Vermont

Also known as: Adolf Georg Wilhelm Busch (full name)

Member of: The Busch Quartet; the Busch Chamber Players

Principal recordings

ALBUMS: *Schubert: String Quartets 14 and 15*, 1932 (with the Busch Quartet); *Brandenburg Concertos*, 1936 (with the Busch Chamber Players); *Beethoven's String Quartet No. 13 in B-Flat, Op. 130*, 1941 (with the Busch Quartet).

The Life

Adolf Georg Wilhelm Busch (boosh) was born into a musical family that included his father, his older brother Fritz (who became a well-respected conductor), and his younger brother Hermann (who became the cellist for the Busch Quartet). He began violin lessons at the age of three with his father, who had reputedly been a pupil of the great German virtuoso violinist, opera composer, and violin pedagogue Louis Spohr. Busch entered the Cologne Conservatory at the age of eleven, where he continued his studies with violinists Willy Hess and Bram Eldering, both of whom had been pupils of the nineteenth century virtuoso Joseph Joachim. When he was fifteen, Busch turned pages at a performance in Bonn by Joachim's string quartet, with Ernst von Dohnanyi at the piano, an influential experience for the youthful musician.

Busch's education was rooted in an exclusively Germanic line of musicians, so his mature style stood in contrast to such soloists as Jascha Heifetz, Mischa Elman, and Nathan Milstein, who had been trained by Leopold Auer in the Russian school. In 1907 Busch met composer Max Reger, and they maintained a strong friendship until Reger's death in 1916. Busch frequently performed Reger's violin concerto and solo works, and he adopted Reger's style in his own compositions, which number more than two hundred and include symphonies, concerti, choral works, chamber music, and solo pieces. Busch's original compositions, however, have faded in the light of his greater accomplishments as a performer.

In 1913 Busch married Frieda Grüters, the daughter of Hugo Grüters, his composition professor, and they had a daughter. Busch left Germany as the Nazi regime expanded its power and influence, and he settled first in Basel, Switzerland, in 1927, adopting Swiss citizenship. In 1939 he emigrated to the United States. His professional life centered around his performances as a concerto soloist, as the first violinist of his string quartet, and as the founding member of the Busch Chamber Players.

Shortly after Frieda died in 1946, Busch married Hedwig Vischer, and they had two sons. In 1950 and 1951 he founded, along with Rudolf Serkin and Marcel Moyse, the Marlboro Music Festival in Vermont, which is among the greatest chamber music festivals in the United States, and is a proving ground for aspiring chamber musicians. Busch performed for most of his life on a Stradivarius violin known as the Wiener Strad. He died in 1952 at the age of sixty.

The Music

Busch's professional career began in 1910, when he performed Reger's violin concerto in Berlin, with the composer conducting the orchestra. In 1912 he assumed the position of concertmaster of the Konzertverein Orchestra in Vienna. It was in this position that Busch founded his first quartet, the Vienna Konzertverein Quartet, composed of principals from the orchestra. The quartet disbanded during World War I. He also taught for a time at the Musikhochschule in Berlin beginning in 1916.

The Busch Quartet. Following World War I, Busch regrouped with three colleagues to form the Busch Quartet. Its original membership consisted of Busch as first violin, Karl Reitz as second violin, Emil Bohnke on viola, and Paul Grümmer on cello. Later, Gösta Andreasson became the second violinist and Karl Doktor became the violist. With these musicians (and again later in 1930, when the younger Hermann Busch replaced Grümmer on cello), the Busch Quartet garnered international acclaim, especially for its interpretations of the music of the works of Ludwig van Beethoven, Franz Schubert, and Johannes Brahms, much of which they also recorded. The quartet's style was reminiscent of the Joachim Quartet's interpretations a generation earlier, emphasizing clarity of musical architecture through honest adherence to the printed score.

The Busch Chamber Players. The Busch Chamber Players came into being, according to one source, as a result of a request from the city of Florence to perform as a part of its May Festival in 1935. In order to bring the Florentine audience a performance of Johann Sebastian Bach's Brandenburg concerti at an artistic level Busch felt acceptable, nearly seventy hours of rehearsal were required. The Busch Chamber Players continued giving concerts for many years, ultimately including Serkin, who became Busch's son-in-law.

A review of many of Busch's concert programs shows how often he was featured performing either Beethoven's Violin Concerto in D Major (which he performed in 1927—the Beethoven Centenary—

more than one hundred times), Brahms's or Reger's concerti, or Wolfgang Amadeus Mozart's Violin Concerto in D Major. These were among his favorites and formed his basic repertoire. Similarly, his recital programs frequently presented Bach's solo sonatas and partitas, along with sonatas by Beethoven, Brahms, and Reger. Busch was close friends with many of the greatest musicians of his day, including Arturo Toscanini, Yehudi Menuhin, Efrem Zimbalist, Vladimir Horowitz, George Szell, and Bruno Walter.

Musical Legacy

Busch was hailed in his lifetime as the greatest violinist of the German school, continuing the tradition established by Spohr and Joachim. He was influential on the musical world of the mid-twentieth century for his performances (as a soloist and as the first violinist of the Busch Quartet), for his teaching (among his students was Menuhin), and for his founding in 1950 of the Marlboro Music Festival in Vermont.

Busch concertized extensively, principally in Europe and America, and he recorded the major concerti, from those of Bach to Brahms, and a considerable number of string quartets and chamber music with the Busch Quartet and the Busch Chamber Players (which included his brother and son-in-law Serkin, among others).

During the height of his career, Busch was avidly sought as a soloist and chamber musician. His concert schedule was full, and his letters from the time reveal what he termed a "hectic lifestyle." His emphasis on clarity of form and structure, and his faithful adherence to the composer's intent were perhaps more in line with the styles of a generation later.

Jonathan A. Sturm

Further Reading

Busch, Adolf. *Adolf Busch: Letters, Pictures, Memories*. Edited by Irene Busch Serkin, translated into English by Russell Stockman. Walpole, N.H.: Arts and Letters Press, 1991. This two-volume set collects primary source material on Busch, including letters, pictures, drawings, and more, presenting a comprehensive portrait.

Potter, Tully. *Adolf Busch: The Life of an Honest Man*. Lancaster, England: Toccata Press, 1986. Subjec-

tive and narrative in tone, this brief book nevertheless contains valuable information, including repertoire lists, composition lists, and recording data.

See also: Horowitz, Vladimir; Menuhin, Sir Yehudi; Serkin, Rudolf; Toscanini, Arturo; Walter, Bruno.

Ferruccio Busoni

Italian classical composer and conductor

A virtuoso concert pianist who championed Johann Sebastian Bach, Busoni urged other composers to take up bold, new musical experiments. His own compositions owe much to his personal study of Bach's music and demand great technical prowess from performers.

Born: April 1, 1866; Empoli, Italy
Died: July 27, 1924; Berlin, Germany
Also known as: Dante Michelangelo Benvenuto Ferruccio Busoni (full name)

Principal works

ORCHESTRAL WORKS: Piano Concerto, Op. 39, 1904; *Turandot Suite*, Op. 41, 1905; *Die Brautwahl*, 1911; *Sonatina seconda*, 1912 (for piano); *Turandot*, 1917 (based on Carlo Gozzi's play); *Arlecchino*, 1917; Piano Sonatina No. 6, 1920 (*Fantasia da camera super Carmen*); *Fantasia contrappuntistica*, 1921 (for two pianos); *Doktor Faust*, 1923.

PIANO WORKS: *An die Jugend*, 1909; *Fantasia nach J. S. Bach*, 1909.

Principal recordings

ALBUMS: *Chorale Prelude "Nun freut euch liebe Christen,"* 1922 (by Johann Sebastian Bach); *Ecossaisen*, 1922 (by Ludwig van Beethoven); *Étude, Op. 10, No. 5*, 1922 (by Frédéric Chopin); *Étude, Op. 25, No. 5*, 1922 (by Chopin); *Hungarian Rhapsody No. 13*, 1922 (by Franz Liszt); *Nocturne, Op. 15, No. 2*, 1922 (by Chopin); *Prelude and Fugue No. 1*, 1922 (by Bach); *Prelude, Op. 28, No. 7 and Étude, Op. 10, No. 5*, 1922 (by Chopin).

The Life

Dante Michelangelo Benvenuto Ferruccio Busoni (fehr-REW-chyoh boo-SOH-nee) was born to musical parents: His father, Ferdinando, was a virtuoso clarinetist, and his mother, Anna Weiss, was a concert pianist. Busoni received his early musical education from his parents and was introduced to the music of Johann Sebastian Bach by his father. With the help of money from a wealthy patron, Busoni began studies at the Vienna Conservatory when he was nine years old. Unsatisfied with the curriculum, the family moved to Graz, Austria, where Busoni studied composition with Wilhelm Mayer. In 1886 Busoni moved to Leipzig, Germany, where he made a living through performing, teaching, and publishing transcriptions and original compositions. There he developed friendships with composers Edvard Grieg and Frederick Delius as well as the young Egon Petri, who would become one of Busoni's most famous piano students. Busoni also contributed to *Neue Zeitschrift für Musik*, an important musical journal.

In 1888, at the age of twenty-two, Busoni accepted a post as professor of piano at the conservatory in Helsinki, Finland. While in Finland, he cultivated a friendship with composer Jean Sibelius (only a few years his elder). Busoni entered the Anton Rubinstein Competition in St. Petersburg, Russia, taking first place for his *Concert Piece* for piano and orchestra. His success opened new professional opportunities, and in 1890 Busoni left Helsinki to accept a teaching post at the Moscow Imperial Conservatory. While in Moscow, he married Gerda Sjöstrand, the daughter of Swedish sculptor Carl Aeneas Sjöstrand. After only one year, Busoni left for the United States to teach piano and composition in the graduate department of the New England Conservatory of Music in Boston. While in Boston, their first son, Benvenuto ("Benni"), was born. Disappointed with the limitations and restrictions of his academic appointments, Busoni began to support his family primarily through his performing and compositional activity.

The family returned to Europe in 1894, taking up permanent residence in Berlin, Germany. A second son, Rafaello ("Lello"), was born in 1900. Busoni focused his beliefs on the future of music and artistic expression in the essay "Entwurf einer neuen Ästhetik der Tonkunst" (1907, revised in 1916; "Outline of a New Aesthetic of Music," 1911). The events of World War I drove the family to leave Berlin. They resided in the United States for a short time and eventually moved to Zurich, Switzerland. While in Zurich from 1915 to 1920, Busoni turned increasingly to operatic composition. His operas *Arlecchino* and *Turandot* both premiered to great critical success in 1917.

Busoni returned to Berlin in 1920. Increasingly ill, he gave his final public piano performance on May 29, 1922. He continued to teach a small number of composition students, including Kurt Weill. He spent his last years working on his opera *Doktor Faust*, leaving two scenes unfinished at the time of his death in 1924 from heart failure and kidney disease.

The Music

Busoni the Pianist. Technique came easily to Busoni, even in his youth; however, he despised the notion of technique as an end in itself. While he was

Ferruccio Busoni. (Library of Congress)

a clear descendant of the Romantic piano tradition, Busoni's approach to playing was cerebral and analytical. He experimented boldly with the instrument, especially with the pedals, to achieve new effects in tone production.

Busoni had a prodigious memory and his repertoire was vast, but the music of Bach and Franz Liszt remained the cornerstone of his programming. The piano concerti of Wolfgang Amadeus Mozart were also greatly admired by Busoni. He performed them frequently, with original cadenzas that reflected modern compositional trends rather than Mozartian conventions. Busoni also programmed the works of Frédéric Chopin, though his performances were criticized for being perfunctory and abstract. Busoni would often take liberties with the music of other composers, adding notes and recomposing in a manner unheard of today. While he performed his own compositions, he rarely performed modern works.

During his lifetime, Busoni made only a few recordings. He disliked the process greatly, given that the works often had to be distorted to fit time constraints. Of the recordings that were eventually released, only about a half hour's worth of music exists. These include performances of Liszt's *Hungarian Rhapsody*, No. 13; a Bach prelude; an ecossaise by Beethoven; a handful of pieces by Chopin; and Busoni's own arrangement of a Bach chorale prelude.

Busoni the Philosopher. Busoni's musical and compositional contributions are augmented by his writings. He was a prolific letter writer and essayist, and his "Outline of a New Aesthetic of Music" reached a wide readership at its revised publication in 1916. In the essay Busoni advocated the attributes of absolute music over program music, arguing that the latter is often trivial and of little depth. He outlined his beliefs for music theater, condemning the trend of realism in favor of more psychological or spiritual representations. For Busoni, the artist should not be bound by laws and prescribed forms but rather should seek to cultivate new modes of expression. Near the end of the essay, he proposed exploring further subdivisions of the octave beyond its traditional twelve tones, a technique known as microtonalism. His criticisms of the German musical traditions created a backlash, most notably in the writings of Hans Pfitzner; at the

same time, Busoni stirred up support, especially among the younger set of artists in Berlin.

Bach and Busoni. Busoni was introduced to the music of Bach at a young age; as an adult, he paved the way for the development of a pianistic approach to Bach's music, which was originally conceived for the harpsichord, clavichord, and organ.

Busoni's earliest transcription of Bach's works dates from the Leipzig years. After hearing a performance of Bach's Prelude and Fugue in D Major played at St. Thomas Church in Leipzig, Busoni quickly produced a piano transcription. Other transcriptions followed, including his now-famous piano transcriptions of the Chaconne for Violin in D Minor and ten of Bach's organ chorale preludes. He prepared a complete edition of Bach's two volumes of *The Well-Tempered Clavier* (vol. 1, 1894; vol. 2, 1916). These editions are heavily edited and annotated but reveal an insight into Busoni's understanding of this music as both a pianist and a composer. Busoni's editions are still in print and consulted frequently by students, teachers, and performers.

The study of Bach left an indelible imprint on Busoni's original compositions. His *An die Jungend* for piano features a movement in which Busoni combines themes from Bach's Prelude and Fugue in D Major in a contrapuntal tour de force. In the same year, Busoni wrote the haunting *Fantasia nach J. S. Bach*, dedicated to the memory of his deceased father. His most monumental work in the tradition of Bach is the *Fantasia contrappuntistica*, which takes its inspiration and material from Bach's *The Art of Fugue*, the German chorale *All Glory Be to God on High*, and Bach's own musical signature: the pitches B-flat, A, C, and B-natural (H, in German).

Late Operas. Busoni spent the last decade of his life composing opera. His one-act opera *Arlecchino* (with a libretto by the composer) is based on characters and situations from Italian commedia dell'arte. Busoni's work is dark and satirical, exploring themes of fidelity and human cruelty. Busoni's *Turandot* premiered in the same year as *Arlecchino* and in fact was considered a possible companion piece. For *Turandot*, Busoni constructed a libretto based on the play by Carlo Gozzi. (Giacomo Puccini used the same source material for his opera of the same name.) However, these music-theater pieces were only preludes to the major project of his last years, *Doktor Faust*. In fact most of Busoni's compositions written after 1918 were studies for a grand musical-theater piece that he had been planning since his teenage years. Conductor Antony Beaumont refers to twenty-three "satellite pieces" that provided Busoni with the musical material for *Doktor Faust*. The opera, which remained unfinished at the time of Busoni's death, has been completed in at least two versions: one by composer Philipp Jarnach (performed in Dresden, Germany, in 1925) and another by Beaumont (performed in Bologna, Italy, in 1985).

Musical Legacy

Busoni left little in terms of recorded performance. His pianistic legacy lives on largely through the playing and teaching of his students (Egon Petri the most influential among them) and his writings on the subject. Busoni invigorated a tradition of playing the keyboard music of Bach on the piano in public. He developed a technical and stylistic approach to the Bach repertoire (albeit one that runs counter to current trends of historically informed performance) and disseminated his interpretations through his editions and transcriptions. His formidable piano technique is legendary; he inspired generations of pianists to experiment boldly with sound (especially through the use of the instrument's pedals). Despite his vibrant presence in recital, Busoni promoted the music over the performer, abhorring the cult of the superstar virtuoso.

Busoni advanced some daring musical ideas in his writings, including the use of electronics and microtonalism. His ideas had direct influence on such composers as Edgard Varèse and members of the Italian Futurist movement, including Luigi Russolo.

Although Busoni's editions and transcriptions of Bach's works have been widely available since his death, his own works are complex and often difficult to perform. His piano concerto takes more than an hour and requires a men's chorus in addition to the orchestra and soloist. Nevertheless, his music, noted for its depth and richness, is drawing an ever-growing audience.

Joseph A. Bognar

Further Reading

Beaumont, Antony. *Busoni the Composer*. Bloomington: Indiana University Press, 1985. A chronological study of the life of the composer as seen through his musical works. Includes photographs, facsimiles, and a catalog of works.

Brendel, Alfred. "Busoni." In *Musical Thoughts and Afterthoughts*. Suffolk, England: Robson Books, 1998. Brendel reflects on the legacy and pianism of Busoni.

Busoni, Ferruccio. *The Essence of Music and Other Papers*. Translated by Rosamond Ley. New York: Dover, 1957. A collection of Busoni's short essays, letters, notes, and aphorisms.

_____. *Letters to His Wife*. Translated by Rosamond Ley. London: E. Arnold, 1938. A look at the personal life of Busoni, told through correspondence with his wife.

_____. *Selected Letters*. Translated and edited by Antony Beaumont. Boston: Faber & Faber, 1987. Letters give insight into Busoni and his music.

_____. "Sketch of a New Esthetic of Music." In *Source Readings in Music History*, edited by Oliver Strunk and Leo Treitler, translated by Robert P. Morgan. New York: W. W. Norton, 1998. Excerpts from Busoni's treatise in English translation, including Busoni's outline for the use of microtonal divisions of the octave.

Couling, Della. *Ferruccio Busoni: "A Musical Ishmael."* Lanham, Md.: Scarecrow Press, 2005. A detailed yet readable biographical account of Busoni's life, using letters and other source material.

Schonberg, Harold C. "Dr. Faust at the Keyboard." *The Great Pianists: From Mozart to the Present*. Rev. ed. New York: Simon & Schuster, 1987. The longtime music critic of *The New York Times* discusses Busoni's pianism and his small recorded output.

Sitsky, Larry. *Busoni and the Piano*. New York: Greenwood, 1986. Second-generation Busoni student gives comprehensive analysis of the piano works. Includes a discography and bibliography.

See also: Argerich, Martha; Feldman, Morton; Grainger, Percy Aldridge; Schnabel, Artur; Segovia, Andrés; Sibelius, Jean; Tiomkin, Dimitri; Watts, André; Weill, Kurt.

Paul Butterfield

American blues singer and harmonica player

Butterfield was a major figure in the emergence of white blues bands in the 1960's, bringing an overlooked, indigenous American music to a new audience.

Born: December 17, 1942; Chicago, Illinois
Died: May 4, 1987; Los Angeles, California
Member of: The Paul Butterfield Blues Band

Principal recordings

ALBUMS (solo): *Put It in Your Ear*, 1976; *North-South*, 1981; *The Legendary Paul Butterfield Rides Again*, 1986.

ALBUMS (with Better Days): *Better Days*, 1973; *It All Comes Back*, 1973; *Live at Winterland '73*, 1999.

ALBUMS (with the Paul Butterfield Blues Band): *The Paul Butterfield Blues Band*, 1965; *East-West*, 1966; *The Resurrection of Pigboy Crabshaw*, 1967; *In My Own Dream*, 1968; *Keep on Moving*, 1969; *Sometimes I Just Feel Like Smilin'*, 1971; *The Original Lost Elektra Sessions*, 1995; *East-West Live*, 1996; *Strawberry Jam*, 1996.

The Life

Paul Butterfield was born in Chicago, and he grew up in the affluent area of Hyde Park. His father was a successful lawyer, and his mother was a painter, and they encouraged their son's musical studies on the flute, which continued into high school. As a teenager, Butterfield starred on the high school track team, and it was also during this time that his older brother and a friend, Nick Gravenites (later a successful musician), pushed Butterfield to investigate the urban blues they heard on the radio. Chicago's South Side hosted such African American blues greats as Muddy Waters, Howlin' Wolf, and Marion "Little" Walter Jacobs.

Butterfield and Gravenites began frequenting the black-only blues clubs, and before long Butterfield assembled the Paul Butterfield Blues Band, which played for about five years. Butterfield continued to form other bands with different players until 1976, when he embarked on a solo career, releasing a few poorly received albums and working as a session player for other musicians. Butterfield developed peritonitis from heavy drinking, and he died in 1987 of a heroin overdose.

The Music

Once he saw Little Walter play an amplified harmonica, Butterfield became an avid fan of the instrument, and he quickly formed a band with Elvin Bishop, a guitarist from Oklahoma studying at the University of Chicago. They recruited two players from Muddy Waters's band—drummer Sam Lay and bassist Jerome Arnold—and by 1963 they had become the house band at Big John's, a folk music club. The group became so popular that it was the first electric band signed to the folk label Elektra Records.

The Paul Butterfield Blues Band. The group's eponymously titled first record, released in 1965, was a hard-edged sampler of urban blues that challenged the dominance of the British and American pop songs that saturated radio airwaves. The album opens with the band's signature song, "Born in Chicago," which Butterfield sings with his trademark raw intensity, while belting out powerful harp licks. The band featured two guitarists, Bishop and Michael Bernard Bloomfield, as well as keyboardist Mark Naftalin, a player recruited for these sessions who remained with the band for several years. The album is a heady mix of traditional blues songs—"Shake Your Money Maker," "Blues With a Feeling," "I Got My Mojo Working," "Mellow Down Easy," among others—and original compositions, such as the loose jam "Thank You Mr. Poobah," Bloomfield's guitar workout, "Screamin'," and "Our Love Is Drifting." The album immediately became popular with a predominantly rock audience, and the band was launched.

East-West. The following year, *East-West*, the band's second release, continued with traditional blues numbers, such as "Walkin' Blues" and "Never Say No," as well contemporary offerings, such as Allen Toussaint's "Get Out of My Life, Woman" and a reinterpreted Monkees' song, "Mary, Mary." The album also featured two lengthy instrumentals, "Work Song" and "East-West," a rock raga homage to Ravi Shankar.

Un-Banded. By the next year, half of the members of the band had left, including Bloomfield, and Butterfield reconfigured the band to include a horn section. In 1967 he released *The Resurrection of Pigboy Crabshaw*, an album featuring fewer traditional blues numbers and less of Butterfield's signature harp work. *In My Own Dream*, the band's fourth album, released in 1968, continued in a similar, though far less satisfying, vein. The last original members had left the band, and each successive release was inconsistent in quality. *Keep on Moving* and *Sometimes I Just Feel Like Smilin'* were disappointing, and in their wake Butterfield broke up the band.

In 1972 Butterfield had modest success with a new band, Better Days, releasing two records, *Better Days* and *It All Comes Back*, and he then pursued a solo career. Releases such as *Put It in Your Ear*, *North-South*, and *The Legendary Paul Butterfield Rides Again* were uneven or simply embarrassing. The harmonica was now largely absent as Butterfield ranged through rhythm and blues, jazzy arrangements, or synthesized music.

Rereleases. A decade later, *The Original Lost Elektra Sessions*, the first recordings of the original band, appeared from tapes once considered lost and inferior. The performances are not as polished as later studio offerings, but the power of the first band is clearly evident. *Strawberry Jam*, a collection of live performances, was released, along with *East-West Live*, a disk that provides a fascinating view of the evolution of that seminal song. Tapes of a stellar performance of the Better Days band, *Live at Winterland '73*, was issued in 1999, and they reveal how accomplished that collection of musicians was. *An Anthology: The Elektra Years* (1998) collects some of the best early material by Butterfield.

Musical Legacy

Though some rock journalists and historians dismiss Butterfield's contributions as merely derivative, that assessment is contradicted by his contemporaries, among them Bloomfield, Corky Siegel, Levon Helm, and Muddy Waters. Butterfield revered the blues, and he never corrupted the genre for commercial purposes.

His principal contribution was bringing the blues to a white rock-and-roll audience, paving the way for other white musicians to play and build upon the traditions of the blues masters. He was so successful that in 1965 his band was invited to play at the historic Newport Folk Festival, which had never before featured electric music. At that same festival, members of Butterfield's band backed up Bob Dylan when he switched from acoustic to electric music.

Butterfield's best albums reveal a musicologist's broad knowledge of sources and an impassioned playing. *East-West* is a tour-de-force, with its mixtures of styles and astounding virtuosity, and "East-West" is an audacious musical experiment, with its emulation of Eastern modalities and its pure inventiveness.

David W. Madden

Further Reading

Butterfield, Paul, and Happy Traum. *Paul Butterfield Teaches Blues Harmonica Master Class: Sessions with a Legendary Player.* Woodstock, N.Y.: Homespun Tapes, 1997. This book and accompanying compact disc offer detailed instructions on the playing of blues harmonica.

Ellis, Tom, III. "The Real World of Paul Butterfield." *Blues Access* 23 (Fall, 1995): 11-19; "The

Paul Butterfield. (AP/Wide World Photos)

Glory Years: The Maturation of an Idea." *Blues Access* 25 (Spring, 1996): 22-35; "Building a New Tradition: Butterfield Gets the Blues Back in Touch with Jazz." *Blues Access* 27 (Fall, 1996): 28-40; "The Woodstock Years." *Blues Access* 29 (Spring, 1997): 20-36; "Paul Butterfield: The Final Years." *Blues Access* 31 (Fall, 1997): 13-25. A detailed and comprehensive assessment of Butterfield is contained in this series of articles from *Blues Access* magazine. Ellis traces Butterfield's career, with its high and low points.

Sebastian, John, and Paul Butterfield. *Blues Harmonica*. Woodstock, N.Y.: Homespun Tapes, 2005. Originally released as a collection of tapes, the book offers advice from two musicians on playing the harmonica, and it includes observations on the blues and the great musicians who have mastered this instrument.

Wolkin, Jan Mark, Bill Keenom, Michael Bloomfield. *Michael Bloomfield—If You Love These Blues: An Oral History*. San Francisco: Miller Freeman Books, 2000. In this memoir, Bloomfield reflects on his bandmates and his career. Butterfield figures prominently in reminiscences.

See also: Cotton, James; Dylan, Bob; Howlin' Wolf; Shankar, Ravi; Van Ronk, Dave; Waters, Muddy.

David Byrne

American rock guitarist, singer, and songwriter

As singer and principal songwriter for the Talking Heads, Byrne was an influential figure in the post-punk new wave movement of the late 1970's and early 1980's. His prodigious talent as a musical and visual artist made him an exciting and memorable front man.

Born: May 14, 1952; Dumbarton, Scotland
Member of: The Talking Heads

Principal recordings

ALBUMS (solo): *The Catherine Wheel*, 1981; *The Knee Plays*, 1985; *Rei Momo*, 1989; *The Forest*, 1991; *Uh-Oh*, 1992; *David Byrne*, 1994; *Feelings*, 1997; *In Spite of Wishing and Wanting*, 1999; *Look into the Eyeballs*, 2001; *Lead Us Not into Temptation*, 2003; *Grown Backwards*, 2004.

ALBUMS (with Brian Eno): *My Life in the Bush of Ghosts*, 1981; *Everything That Happens Will Happen Today*, 2008.

ALBUMS (with the Talking Heads): *Talking Heads: 77*, 1977; *More Songs About Buildings and Food*, 1978; *Fear of Music*, 1979; *Remain in Light*, 1980; *Speaking in Tongues*, 1983; *Little Creatures*, 1985; *Sounds from True Stories*, 1986; *True Stories*, 1986; *Naked*, 1988.

SINGLES (with the Talking Heads): "Houses in Motion," 1981; "Re-Mixes," 1983; "Take Me to the River," 1983; "Once in a Lifetime," 1984; "And She Was," 1985; "Lady Don't Mind," 1985; "Road to Nowhere," 1985; "Blind," 1988; "Burning Down the House," 1989; "Lifetime Piling Up," 1992; "Love for Sale," 2006; "(Nothing but) Flowers," 2006.

The Life

Although born in Scotland, David Byrne (burn) grew up in North America. He spent most of his childhood in the suburbs of Hamilton, Ontario, and Baltimore, Maryland, and their innocuous middle-class landscapes later played a role in many of his songs. He was the son of a respected scientist, whose work brought the family across the Atlantic while Byrne was a toddler. However, Byrne's keen aesthetic sensibilities took him in a career direction quite different from his father's. After high school, Byrne was accepted at the prestigious Rhode Island School of Design (RISD) in 1970. He stayed at RISD for only a year, dismissing art schools as overpriced and unnecessary. While in art school, he met drummer Chris Franz and bassist Tina Weymouth, and their musical collaboration resulted in the formation of the Talking Heads, one of new wave's most vital and influential bands. After playing sporadically in Boston and New York, in 1975 the Talking Heads added guitarist-keyboardist Jerry Harrison (formerly of Jonathan Richman's band the Modern Lovers) and landed regular gigs at Hilly Kristal's music club CBGB. Because it was one of the few clubs at the time to feature such cutting-edge bands as the Ramones, Television, Blondie, and the Talking Heads, this small but important Manhattan venue came to be recognized as the birthplace of the fledgling punk, new wave scene of the mid- to late 1970's.

By 1979 Byrne and the Talking Heads were the undisputed darlings of the new wave scene, having chalked up two popular albums and an appearance as musical guests on NBC television's *Saturday Night Live*. As lead singer and principal lyricist, Byrne garnered considerable attention. His intense, frenetic stage persona made him a charismatic, exciting performer, and his astute but accessible lyrics delighted both mainstream fans and avant-garde purists. The Talking Heads' *Remain in Light* made several critics' Top 10 lists for 1980, and the album was widely heralded as a groundbreaking fusion of pop, disco, funk, and experimental music. Having penned most of the album's tracks, Byrne rapidly earned the attention of the worldwide rock press. Offers for Byrne to participate in a number of projects poured in.

By the early 1990's Byrne had toured the world as a rock performer, scored films and ballets, appeared in hit music videos and a full-length concert film, shown his paintings and mixed-media installations in gallery exhibitions, and published books. In 1991 the Talking Heads officially broke up. Even though the band's working relationship had been dysfunctional since the release of *Naked* in 1988, greater interest in side and solo projects on the part of Byrne and the other band members compelled them to go their separate ways.

Byrne was an ambitious and prolific artist, working in a staggering variety of genres. Beginning in 1981 he released several solo albums and collaborated on recordings with other musicians. He established a record label, Luaka Bop, in the early 1990's, focusing primarily on African and other world-music performers. He displayed numerous works, from drawings and paintings to photographs and furnishings, in prestigious art galleries. In the late 1990's he hosted the public television show *Sessions at West 54th* and later appeared in other television series, including *The Simpsons* and *Inside the Actors Studio*.

The Music

Byrne worked in several musical styles, running the gamut from the Talking Heads' jaunty early minimalism to the group's later lush, radio-friendly productions. As a solo artist, Byrne released projects that include experimental, African-influenced, and acoustic works. An open mind and a penchant for eclecticism typified his music, and his lyrics were characterized by plain phrasing and wide-eyed optimism.

Talking Heads: 77. Falling somewhere between punk and new wave, the Talking Heads' debut album features a fresh combination of stark instrumentation and quirky lyrics. The popular single "Psycho Killer" combines a brooding, infectious bass line with ponderous lyrics written from a serial murderer's point of view. Byrne delivers the song's vocal in a terse, nervy staccato that punctuates the song's message. In thematic terms, however, "Psycho Killer" is atypical of the album, which features several songs—particularly "Love Comes to Town" and "Don't Worry About the Government"—with brazenly enthusiastic, sometimes even kitschy lyrics. Byrne's distinctive vocal style, simultaneously shrill and sincere, gives these tracks the irony-laden, painfully self-conscious flavor that defines new wave.

Remain in Light. By 1980 the Talking Heads had abandoned the minimalism of its early albums for a more complex sound. *Remain in Light* is generally regarded as their artistic breakthrough, a work that masterfully combines African rhythms and dense, emotive musical landscapes with some of Byrne's most perceptive lyrics. The album features "Once in a Lifetime," which spawned a video that made the Talking Heads one of MTV's earliest stars. "Life During Wartime" and "This Must Be the Place," also thematic centerpieces of the album, show Byrne's depth as a lyricist and remain among the band's most respected recordings.

My Life in the Bush of Ghosts. In 1980 avant-garde musician Brian Eno produced *Remain in Light*, and that collaboration between Eno and Byrne spawned 1981's *My Life in the Bush of Ghosts*. Acclaimed for its distinctive sound, at turns dreamy and ominous and always unpredictable, the work is perhaps best known for its use of samples—digitally manipulated and reinterpreted fragments of other recordings—as a central part of its sound.

The Catherine Wheel. In the early 1980's Byrne expanded his musical scope to include scores, his first being for modernist choreographer Twyla

Tharp's ballet *The Catherine Wheel*. Byrne wrote, produced, and performed the music for the ballet, which is considered one of the most important works of contemporary American dance.

Little Creatures. *Little Creatures* was markedly devoid of the dense, sample-laden funk soundscapes that had characterized the Talking Heads' previous albums. The clean, stripped-down songs—especially the Talking Heads' classics "Road to Nowhere" and "Stay Up Late"—brought Byrne's refreshingly innocent, joyous lyrics to the forefront in a way that had not been heard since the band's debut.

Naked. Although a critical and commercial success, *Naked* was the Talking Heads' last album. During the album's production, the band was rife with internal struggles, but the result was a remarkably cohesive album, in both sound and theme. Several songs, particularly Byrne's, lament the alienation caused by modern mechanization. Tracks such as "Blind" and "(Nothing but) Flowers" point out the intellectual and spiritual sterility to which unbridled technological development has given birth. Author Bret Easton Ellis used lyrics from "(Nothing but) Flowers" as the epigraph for his nihilistic novel *American Psycho* (1990).

Grown Backwards. Byrne's 2004 solo effort, released by the folk-jazz label Nonesuch Records, signaled another musical departure. *Grown Backwards* includes the heavy use of orchestral string arrangements as well as two operatic arias. Following the release of the album, Byrne toured North America and Australia with the renowned Tosca Strings, performing selections from the release.

Musical Legacy

One of the most recognizable faces from MTV, Byrne was also familiar to those who attend art galleries and theaters. For his contributions to the development of punk and new wave music, Byrne's status in musical history was secure. However, his contributions to the visual and theatrical arts distinguished Byrne as one of the most dynamic figures in contemporary popular culture. His many prestigious accolades included Grammy Awards for his recordings with the Talking Heads and a score of gold and platinum albums commemorating his commercial triumphs. Talking Heads was inducted into the Rock and Roll Hall of Fame in 2002.

Gregory D. Horn

Further Reading

Bowman, David. *This Must Be the Place: The Adventures of Talking Heads in the Twentieth Century*. New York: HarperCollins, 2001. A biography of the band focuses on the internal conflicts that led to the group's breakup and highlights the aesthetic differences between Byrne and Weymouth. Includes black and white photographs, a bibliography, a discography, and a filmography.

Gans, David. *Talking Heads: The Band and Their Music*. London: Omnibus Press, 1986. Overview of the Talking Heads that explores their work at its artistic and commercial apex.

Howell, John. *American Originals: David Byrne*. Berkeley, Calif.: Publishers Group West, 1992. A biography of Byrne that covers his work with the Talking Heads and his significant endeavors outside the band. Includes an insightful discussion of Byrne's creative process in music and art. Also provides extensive insights into Byrne's artistic collaborations, particularly with choreographer Tharp and musicians Laurie Anderson, Robert Wilson, and Eno.

Olinsky, Frank, and Talking Heads. *What the Songs Look Like*. New York: Perennial Library, 1987. Through a pastiche of paintings, sculptures, photographs, and drawings, artists capture the visual essence of the Talking Heads' songs. Included are lyrics and biographies of the artists.

Reese, Krista. *The Name of This Book Is Talking Heads*. Saline, Mich.: Proteus Publishing, 1982. Unique insights into the band's formative years, with noteworthy comments from CBGB's owner Kristal, guitarist Adrian Belew, and singer Nona Hendryx.

See also: Eno, Brian; Glass, Philip; Puente, Tito; Smith, Mamie.

C

John Cage

American classical composer

Cage is a significant contributor to the avant-garde music of increasing openness and vitality in which chance and improvisation play a central role.

Born: September 5, 1912; Los Angeles, California
Died: August 12, 1992; New York, New York

Principal works

CHAMBER WORKS: *First Construction (In Metal)*, 1939 (for six percussionists); *Second Construction*, 1940 (for four percussionists); *Third Construction*, 1941 (for four percussionists); *Two*, 1987 (for flute and piano).

EXPERIMENTAL WORKS: *Imaginary Landscape No. 1*, 1939 (for two variable-speed turntables, frequency records, muted piano, and cymbal); *4'33"*, 1952 (for any ensemble or number of players); *Fontana Mix*, 1958 (for four-channel tape); *Variations I*, 1958; *Music for . . .*, 1984 (any combination of one to seventeen instrumental parts).

KEYBOARD WORKS: *Bacchanale*, 1940 (for prepared piano); *The Perilous Night*, 1944 (for prepared piano); *A Valentine out of Season*, 1944 (for prepared piano); *Music for Marcel Duchamp*, 1947 (for prepared piano); *Dream*, 1948 (for piano); *Experiences No. 1*, 1948 (for two pianos); *In a Landscape*, 1948 (for piano or harp); *Sonatas and Interludes*, 1948 (for prepared piano); *Suite for Toy Piano*, 1948; *Music of Changes*, 1951 (for piano); *Cheap Imitation*, 1969.

ORCHESTRAL WORKS: *Concerto*, 1951 (for piano and chamber orchestra); *Atlas Eclipticalis*, 1961 (for orchestra; parts for eighty-six musicians).

VOCAL WORKS: *The Wonderful Widow of Eighteen Springs*, 1942 (for voice and closed piano); *Aria*, 1958 (for solo voice); *Roaratorio: An Irish Circus on Finnegan's Wake*, 1979 (for voice, tape, and combination of instrumental parts); *Ryoanji*,

1983-1985 (for voice, flute, oboe, trombone, contrabass, percussion, and chamber orchestra).

The Life

In 1930 John Cage left college to roam in Europe and to decide what course to take for his professional life. Settling on music, he returned to America and began serious study in composition. His studies led him to the experimental composer Henry Cowell and later to Arnold Schoenberg.

Cage prided himself on his wise choice of teachers. From Cowell, Cage learned to value unexpected sound sources and radical methods. From Schoenberg, Cage learned a systematic approach to composition. In 1937 Cage began working as an accompanist for dancers, and this led him to an appointment to the Cornish School of the Arts in Seattle, Washington, where he met choreographer Merce Cunningham. Working with Cunningham and other dancers, Cage produced a body of innovative work that used recurring patterns of durations as a central organizing principle. For one of his collaborations with Cunningham, he found the theater too small for his percussion ensemble to play his music. He solved his problem in a creative manner emblematic of his early career: He inserted foreign objects, such as nuts and bolts, into the strings of the piano, effectively transforming their pitch and timbre to simulate the instruments of his percussion ensemble. He returned often to this instrument, which he called the prepared piano.

Eventually, his work brought him to New York City, where he taught at the New School for Social Research. Cage's interest in Eastern philosophy (especially Zen Buddhism) and his contact with the Abstract Expressionist movement in the visual arts combined to lead him in a more radical direction, creating a series of works configured in part to erase the individual desires of the composer from the composition while functioning to "sober and quiet the mind, thus making it susceptible to divine influences." His music from this point forward em-

John Cage. (AP/Wide World Photos)

braced elements of chance in the creation and execution of the work.

During the 1950's he allied himself with piano virtuoso David Tudor; likeminded composers Morton Feldman, Christian Wolff, and Earle Brown; and minimalist La Monte Young to promote avantgarde music. In 1961 Cage's compositions started to be published by C. F. Peters Editions, granting his ideas worldwide reach. His book, *Silence: Lectures and Writings*, published that same year by Wesleyan University Press, became required reading for artists and intellectuals drawn to his ideas of open music based on principles of chance and improvisation. From 1961 onward, Cage was in such high demand for new compositions and speaking and teaching engagements that he was forced to turn down many offers.

His winsome public persona and unusual lecture practices made him a celebrity at universities. As a guest lecturer, he prepared in advance an-

swers to questions often posed by audience members, and then, while on stage, he would roll dice to randomly select an answer, trusting that chance would lead to answers of greater use to the questioner. He also on occasion recorded himself giving lectures, and then he would play the recordings while he lectured. He added lengthy pauses so that there would be many moments when there was only one Cage speaking. The resulting theater of a man competing with his mechanically recorded self made a wonderful impact on audiences. Of course, some were offended by his unwillingness to conform to the conventions of public speaking. However, their displeasure added to the amusement of his delighted fans and made him popular on the lecture circuit.

In the last five years of his life, his productivity as a composer soared, and he produced forty-three works. When he died of a stroke in 1992, Cage was an internationally celebrated artist and thinker.

The Music

First Construction (In Metal). Using the idea of structuring a work around recurring patterns of durations, this piece for six percussionists typifies the composer's early output. In it, Cage enriches the timbral options available by introducing diverse objects not usually considered musical instruments (such as brake drums), utilizing instruments previously unused in classical composition (such as a Yavapai rattle), and addressing traditional percussion in new ways (such as a submerged gong drawn from water during the performance). This piece, like many he composed in the 1930's and 1940's, was meant for use in conjunction with dance.

Bacchanale. This was Cage's first work for his invention, the prepared piano. He later created more celebrated compositions for this instrument.

Sonatas and Interludes. This large-scale work constitutes his most ambitious solo work for prepared piano. In this musical meditation on seven permanent emotions described in Hindi aesthetics (erotic, heroic, odious, angry, mirthful, sorrowful, and wondrous), each emotion is treated in a distinct sonata. In keeping with the Hindi origins, these emotions tend toward stasis, which Cage presents in the diffuse interludes. The piece prompted *Time* magazine to declare Cage "America's most promising composer," and the success of the piece earned him the Guggenheim Prize. Nevertheless, this work marks the end of a phase—using a durational system, as he did in *First Construction (In Metal)*—in his compositional output. After this, Cage favored chance operations to determine the content of his compositions.

Music of Changes. Taking its name from the Chinese *I Ching* (or Book of Changes), an ancient book used for divining wisdom, this work for solo piano in four sections presents an early attempt to efface the composer's desires from the composition. Creating a matrix of possible events that constantly changes and consulting a Chinese system of random number generation rooted in the use of the *I Ching*, Cage used chance to determine the specific events of this work. The result is not a true effacement, since the matrixes exemplify a musical style drawn from Cage's desires. Nevertheless, the work did initiate his lengthy search for methods that might detach his compositions from his musical desires, with the purpose of creating pieces of "sound come into its own."

4'33". This work calls for the performer or performers to make no sounds for the titular duration of the piece. First presented at a concert featuring David Tudor in Woodstock, New York, it became one of Cage's most celebrated pieces. This so-called silent piece is not completely silent; it comprises all the accidental and ambient sounds in the performance room, including the respiration of the audience members. Cage's ambitious effort to rethink the act of composition is often misunderstood, and the piece sparked challenges to his credentials as a composer.

Variations I. Cage composed several works over several decades titled *Variations*, and these pieces constitute some of his most radical compositions. These scores contain no specific instructions to performers on what pitches or rhythms to execute. Instead, Cage regulates the duration of the work, and he guides performers in choosing how dense the materials might be. These materials can be made up of anything the performers may select. The only limitation Cage composed into his score is the density of material, not the material itself.

Cheap Imitation. This work comprises fragments of Erik Satie's work *Socrate*. For it, Cage uses chance to reorganize Satie's ambling harmonic and melodic work into a less goal-oriented composition. Despite its self-deprecating title, it was an act of sincere homage for a composer who inspired Cage for his quiet and simple audacity.

Two. Like many works from Cage's later life, this finds small amounts of material isolated in pools of silence. This work calls for flute and piano, and it allows for careful, studious listening to modest quantities of sound.

Musical Legacy

Cage's influence continues in the innumerable performances his compositions receive worldwide each year. Diverse composers have creatively explored the ideas presented by the avant-garde composer, and the members of the alternative rock bands Sonic Youth and Radiohead acknowledge Cage's influence. Performance artists, such as Brenda Hutchinson and Scot Jenerik, draw from Cage's innovations. While his impact outside of music history may be little felt in the music academies, Cage and his techniques are studied for their practical applications to aesthetic theories in dance and fine art.

Michael Lee

Further Reading

Cage, John. *Empty Words*. Middletown, Conn.: Wesleyan University Press, 1979. In this volume of lectures and essays covering the bulk of the 1970's, Cage reveals his evolving musical sensibility, and he shares insights into his methods and aims.

_____. *Silence: Lectures and Writings*. Middletown, Conn.: Wesleyan University Press, 1961. Cage's collection of essays and anecdotes is full of humor and insight into the avant-garde art and music of the 1960's.

Duckworth, William. *Talking Music*. New York: Da Capo Press, 1999. Among the excellent interviews with experimental composers is one with Cage, which forms a thorough introduction to his art and ideas. Cage comments on the seeming contradiction of continuing to compose in the wake of *4'33"*.

Kostelanetz, Richard. *Conversing with Cage*. New York: Kindle Editions, 2007. Kostelanetz takes snippets from dozens of Cage's interviews to construct a book-length insight into the composer.

Nyman, Michael. *Experimental Music: Cage and Beyond*. New York: Da Capo Press, 1999. This important volume identifies Cage as the catalyst for an international movement in music toward greater experimentation. The author, an important composer, provides a penetrating first attempt at writing the history of a movement as it is unfolding. The book is especially remarkable in linking Cage with the minimalist movement.

Pritchett, James. *The Music of John Cage*. Cambridge, England: Cambridge University Press, 1993. This exemplary scholarly work is a comprehensive effort to take stock of Cage's career. Cage's important works are discussed in vivid terms that will enlighten both professional musicologists and the curious.

See also: Adams, John; Berio, Luciano; Boulez, Pierre; Cowell, Henry; Crumb, George; Eno, Brian; Feldman, Morton; Janáček, Leoš; Lucier, Alvin; Lutosławski, Witold; Satie, Erik; Schaeffer, Pierre; Schoenberg, Arnold; Seeger, Ruth Crawford; Stockhausen, Karlheinz; Takemitsu, Tōru; Tan Dun; Varèse, Edgard; Zappa, Frank.

Sammy Cahn

American musical-theater lyricist

Cahn had a considerable impact on films, since many of his songs, by becoming popular hits, helped increase the box office.

Born: June 18, 1913; New York, New York
Died: January 15, 1993; Los Angeles, California
Also known as: Samuel Cohen (birth name)

Principal works

MUSICAL THEATER: *High Button Shoes*, 1947 (music and lyrics with Jule Styne); *Skyscraper*, 1965 (lyrics; music by Jimmy Van Heusen); *Walking Happy*, 1966 (lyrics; music by Van Heusen; *Thoroughly Modern Millie*, 1967 (lyrics; music by Van Heusen); *Look to the Lilies*, 1970 (lyrics; music by Styne).

SONGS (lyrics; music by Nicholas Brodszky): "Be My Love," 1950; "Wonder Why," 1951; "Because You're Mine," 1952.

SONGS (lyrics; music by Saul Chaplin): "Shake Your Head from Side to Side," 1933; "Rhythm Is Our Business," 1935; "Shoe Shine Boy," 1936; "Until the Real Thing Comes Along," 1936; "Bei mir bist du schoen," 1937; "If You Ever Should Leave," 1937; "Please Be Kind," 1938.

SONG (lyrics; music by Gene de Paul): "Teach Me Tonight," 1953.

SONGS (lyrics; music by Axel Stordahl and Paul Weston): "I Should Care," 1945; "Day by Day," 1946.

SONGS (lyrics; music by Jule Styne): "I've Heard That Song Before," 1942; "Victory Polka," 1943; "I'll Walk Alone," 1944; "Let It Snow, Let It Snow, Let It Snow," 1945; "Five Minutes More," 1946; "The Things We Did Last Summer," 1946; "Time After Time," 1947; "It's Magic," 1948; "Saturday Night Is the Loneliest Night of the Week," 1952; "Three Coins in the Fountain," 1954.

SONGS (lyrics; music by Jimmy Van Heusen): "Love and Marriage," 1955; "The Tender Trap," 1955; "All the Way," 1957; "Come Fly with Me," 1957; "High Hopes," 1959; "The Second Time Around," 1960; "Call Me Irresponsible," 1963; "My Kind of Town," 1964.

WRITINGS OF INTEREST: *I Should Care: The Sammy Cahn Story*, 1974 (autobiography).

The Life

Sammy Cahn, born Samuel Cohen, the only son of Abraham and Elka Riss Cohen, had four sisters. His parents were Jews from Galicia, Poland, who had emigrated about 1905. Cahn was not a good student, and he claimed to hold the truancy record at P.S. 147. He frequented pool rooms, attended the Windsor motion picture theater, and saw many vaudeville performers, including future pal Milton Berle, at Loew's Delancey. When he was eighteen, he got his first job at the United Dressed Beef Corporation, although he was also a violinist with the Pals of Harmony, a Dixieland group. After writing songs for two-reel shorts for Warner Bros.' Vitaphone Corporation, they were sent to Hollywood in 1940, eventually getting jobs with Republic Pictures.

Sammy Cahn. (AP/Wide World Photos)

In California, Cahn became close friends with Frank Sinatra, at whose house he met his future wife, Gloria Delson. They married September 5, 1945, and they had two children: Steven, born in 1947, and Laurie, born two years later. After eighteen years of marriage, the couple, who had been drifting apart and who had separated for a time, divorced in 1964.

Shortly before the divorce, Cahn was operated on for his ulcers, which had troubled him since he was thirteen. Although he barely survived the operation, he continued to write songs for the Broadway stage and for films. On August 2, 1970, he married Tita Basile Curtis, to whom he had proposed after a visit with Nancy Sinatra, who had served as matchmaker for his first marriage.

In 1974 Cahn appeared in *Words and Music,* a show featuring his songs, and he toured with the show for many years. That year his autobiography was published. In his later years he served as a goodwill ambassador for the perfume house Fabergé. Cahn died of congestive heart failure in 1993.

The Music

Cahn's musical career began in 1927, when he played the violin for the Pals of Harmony. He wrote his first song, "Shake Your Head from Side to Side," and with pianist Saul Chaplin he began writing specialty songs for vaudeville acts. The pair changed the name Pals of Harmony to Cahn and Chaplin, and they played the summer season in the Catskills, a Jewish resort area in New York. Cahn progressed to writing songs for such big band singers as Ella Fitzgerald in the 1930's, including her big hit "If You Should Ever Leave." When in 1937 he translated the Yiddish lyrics of the song "Bei mir bist du schoen" into English, he had a small success.

Music for Film. While working for Vitaphone Studios in the late 1930's, Cahn and Chaplin wrote "Please Be Kind" for one of the studio's short subjects; the song was the first of its kind to make the hit parade. After a futile trip to Warner Bros. studios in Hollywood, they returned to New York. Nevertheless, they went back to California and got jobs with Republic Pictures, writing the story, the screenplay, and the score for *Rookies on Parade* (1941). After Cahn and Chaplin split up in 1941, he joined Jule Styne, in what turned out to be a successful and longtime collaboration. Their song "Three Coins in the Fountain" won an Academy Award in 1954. "I'll Walk Alone," another of their hits, sold one million copies as sheet music. He and Styne went on to write many songs for Columbia Pictures, headed by Harry Cohn. Some of the more memorable Cahn-Styne songs were "I've Heard That Song Before" and "I'll Walk Alone," both of which were nominated for Academy Awards, and "Five Minutes More," "Saturday Night Is the Loneliest Night of the Week," and "Time After Time."

Meeting Sinatra. Cahn's meeting with Sinatra resulted in another fruitful collaboration, this one with Jimmy Van Heusen in the 1940's. The pair won three Academy Awards: for "All the Way" in *The Joker Is Wild* (1957) and "High Hopes" in *A Hole in the Head* (1959), both of which were sung by Sinatra, and for "Call Me Irresponsible" in *Papa's Delicate Condition* (1963). They also wrote "Love and Marriage" and "Come Fly with Me." Cahn's collaboration with Nicholas Brodszky also produced memorable tunes, including "Be My Love" and "Because You're Mine." In addition to his film work, he wrote the popular "Love and Marriage" for the television production of *Our Town* (1938); "Love and Marriage" became the theme song for the television series *Married with Children*, a satiric look at marriage and family life.

Music for the Stage. Cahn also wrote for the stage, beginning with *High Button Shoes* (with Styne), and, twenty years later, *Skyscraper* and *Walking Happy* (both with Van Heusen). *Look to the Lilies* was a collaboration with Styne in 1970. Those experiences may have encouraged Cahn to produce and act in his *Words and Music*, in which he sang his own songs. He toured with that show until a few years before his death.

Musical Legacy

During his career, Cahn was nominated for thirty-one Academy Awards and five Golden Globe awards. His songs, regardless of his collaborator, were upbeat and romantic, featuring optimism and high hopes. (In fact, he established the High Hopes Fund at the Joslin Diabetes Center in Boston.)

Thomas L. Erskine

Further Reading

Cahn, Sammy. *I Should Care: The Sammy Cahn Story*. New York: Arbor House, 1974. Breezy account of Cahn's relationships with collaborators, film stars, and friends. Includes the stories behind the writing of the songs, the lyrics of the most popular songs, a "songography," and recipes for matzot brei and Hawaiian chicken barbecue.

_____. *The New Sammy Cahn Songbook*. New York: Cherry Lane Music, 2003. Music for ninety-nine of Cahn's compositions. Includes an introduction that quotes Sinatra as saying, "Sammy's words fit my mouth the best of all the writers."

_____. *Sammy Cahn's Rhyming Dictionary*. New York: Cherry Lane Music, 2002. Cahn arranged fifty thousand words phonetically, not alphabetically, because he was interested in the sound of the words, not their spellings. Includes thirty-two-page introduction by Cahn, who relates stories about his songs and their contexts.

Ewen, David. *American Songwriters: An H. G. Wilson Biographical Dictionary*. New York: H. G. Wilson, 1987. Entry for Cahn focuses on his songs written for film.

Taylor, Theodore. *Jule: The Story of Composer Jule Styne*. New York: Random House, 1979. Recounts stories about the Styne-Cahn collaboration, from the beginning to their eventual breakup.

See also: Burke, Johnny; Ronstadt, Linda; Sinatra, Frank; Styne, Jule; Van Heusen, Jimmy; Webb, Jimmy.

Maria Callas
American opera singer

Opera diva Callas revived the classical bel canto repertoire with her dramatic, versatile, and lyrical singing. Her powerful performances and recordings of the whole range of repertoire captivated audiences and transformed opera.

Born: December 2, 1923; New York, New York
Died: September 16, 1977; Paris, France
Also known as: Maria Cecilia Sophia Anna Kalogeropoulos (birth name)

Principal works

OPERATIC ROLES: Santuzza in Pietro Mascagni's *Cavalleria rusticana*, 1939; Beatrice in Franz von Suppé's *Boccaccio*, 1940; Tosca in Giacomo Puccini's *Tosca*, 1942; La Gioconda in Amilcare Ponchielli's *La Gioconda*, 1947; Norma in Bellini's *Norma*, 1948; Brünnhilde in Richard Wagner's *Die Walküre*, 1949; Elvira in Vincenzo Bellini's *I puritani*, 1949; Turandot in Puccini's *Turandot*, 1949; Eurydice/Genio in Joseph Haydn's *L'anima del filosofo*, 1951; Lucia in Gaetano Donizetti's *Lucia di Lammermoor*, 1952; Anna in Donizetti's *Anna Bolena*, 1957; Aida in Giuseppe Verdi's *Aida*, 1959.

Principal recordings

ALBUMS: *Verdi: Nabucco*, 1949; *Verdi: Il Trovatore*, 1950; *Verdi: Aida*, 1951; *Bellini: Norma*, 1952; *Verdi: Macbeth*, 1952; *Bellini: I Puritani*, 1953; *Cherubini: Medea*, 1953; *Mascagni: Cavalleria*

Rusticana, 1953; *Puccini: Tosca*, 1953; *Leoncavallo: Pagliacci*, 1954; *Spontini: La Vestale*, 1954; *Bellini: Norma*, 1955; *Donizetti: Lucia di Lammermoor*, 1955; *Verdi: La Traviata*, 1955; *Verdi: Rigoletto*, 1955; *Puccini: La Bohème*, 1956; *Verdi: Un Ballo in Maschera*, 1956; *Verdi: Il Trovatore*, 1956; *Bellini: La Sonnambula*, 1957; *Donizetti: Anna Bolena*, 1957; *Rossini: Barber of Seville*, 1957; *Verdi: Un Ballo in Maschera*, 1957; *Mad Scenes and Bel Canto Arias*, 1958; *Verdi: La Traviata*, 1958; *Ponchielli: La Gioconda*, 1959; *Bizet: Carmen*, 1964; *Puccini: Tosca*, 1964.

The Life

Maria Cecilia Sophia Anna Kalogeropoulos (kah-lah-geh-ROH-pew-lohs) was born to George and Evangelia Kalogeropoulos, who had emigrated from Greece to New York in 1923. She had an older sister Jackie and a brother Vassilis, who died in 1922. Her father was a pharmacist, and he changed the family name to Callas (KA-las) for easier pronunciation. Callas's mother recognized her daughter as a child prodigy and encouraged her talent. By the age of five Callas was singing arias along with recordings of famous operas. In 1932 Callas began piano lessons, and by the age of eleven she was entering children's talent contests and singing on radio programs.

Faced with financial difficulties and a deteriorating marriage, Callas's parents separated in 1937, and Callas moved back to Greece with her mother and sister. In 1938 Callas entered the National Conservatory in Athens, where she studied with Maria Trivella. On April 11, 1938, she performed with fellow students in her first public recital, a duet from Giacomo Puccini's *Tosca*. On April 2, 1939, Callas made her stage debut as Santuzza in a student production of Pietro Mascagni's *Cavalleria rusticana* at the Olympia Theatre.

The following fall Callas enrolled at the Athens Conservatory, where she studied with Elvira de Hidalgo, the famous Spanish coloratura soprano. Later, Callas would acknowledge de Hidalgo's great influence on her artistic development. In 1940 Callas made her professional operatic debut, appearing as Beatrice in Franz von Suppé's *Boccaccio* at the National Lyric Theater. During World War II, she continued to perform in small opera productions.

After the war, she returned to New York but found no desirable major roles. Finally, in 1947, she made her Italian debut singing Amilcare Ponchielli's *La Gioconda* at the Arena in Verona. She met Giovanni Battista Meneghini, a wealthy businessman thirty years her senior. He became her agent and patron. They married in 1949 and separated in 1959.

A celebrated diva during the 1950's, she performed in the world's major opera houses. Callas revived the nineteenth century bel canto repertoire, including works by Gioacchino Rossini, Vincenzo Bellini, and Gaetano Donizetti. She often gave fifty performances a year, but by 1959 she was experiencing vocal problems, and she retired from singing after 1965. She acted in an unsuccessful film adaptation of *Medea* in 1969.

In 1957 Callas met Greek shipping magnate Aristotle Onassis, and their love affair received much publicity. In 1968 Onassis abruptly ended their relationship to marry president John F. Kennedy's widow Jacqueline Kennedy. Callas died at the age of fifty-three in Paris in 1977.

The Music

Callas was perceived to have three voices, with her exceptionally broad range just short of three octaves, from F-sharp below middle C to E-natural above high C. Although she could perform trills in every register, the high register was sometimes undependable and shrilly. The middle voice could be velvety and beautifully haunting. The lower voice could sound either rich or edgy.

Her teacher de Hidalgo had encouraged her to concentrate on light bel canto roles to strengthen the three registers and to take advantage of her voice's flexibility. Unlike most other sopranos, Callas maximized every gesture, facial expression, and movement onstage. She overcame vocal limitations by using subtle tonal accents, shadings, and inflections to make every word and phrase meaningful and dramatic.

Stardom. During her Italian debut in Verona in 1947, conductor Tullio Serafin was impressed with Callas's talent. He became her mentor and arranged for her to sing Isolde in Richard Wagner's *Tristan und Isolde* and Turandot in Puccini's *Turandot*.

The turning point in Callas's career occurred in 1949 in Venice. She had just sung Brünnhilde in

Wagner's *Die Walküre*, and Serafin insisted she replace the ailing Margherita Carosio in the florid bel canto role of Elvira in Bellini's *I puritani*. Such versatility in one person was unheard of, and Callas's reputation soared. In 1950 Callas sang Giuseppe Verdi's *Aida* in her debut at La Scala in Milan, which during the next decade became the scene of some of her greatest performances in a wide range of roles. She also would restore bel canto operas to the standard opera repertoire.

Bel Canto. Bel canto (beautiful singing) originated in Italy in the late seventeenth century and reached its peak during the first half of the nineteenth century with the operas of Donizetti, Bellini, and Rossini. Characteristics of these operas included rich melodies and florid ornamentation or embellishment, with fast cadenzas and scales. They also featured legato or smoothly connected notes in sustained passages, a continuity of tone and lyric timbre, and a light upper register. Emphasis was on technique rather than volume.

Maria Callas. (AP/Wide World Photos)

Lucia di Lammermoor. Donizetti's masterpiece, this opera premiered in 1835 and is full of beautiful melodies for solo and ensemble. In the plot Lucia secretly loves Edgardo, whose Ravenswood family is feuding with Lucia's Lammermoor family, but Lucia's brother tricks her into marrying Arturo. The third act contains the famous "mad scene," in which a crazed Lucia, who has just murdered her new husband, appears with a bloody knife. Lucia's long and demanding coloratura aria "Il dolce suono" (the sweet sound), with its high notes and unique interplay of flute and voice, perfectly showcased Callas's technical and dramatic abilities. She first appeared in *Lucia di Lammermoor* in 1952 in Italy, and this would become one of her most frequently performed roles. *Lucia di Lammermoor* was also her first commercial recording for EMI in 1953. Callas sang *Lucia di Lammermoor* in her Berlin debut in 1955 and her Vienna debut in 1956.

Anna Bolena. Callas also revived another Donizetti opera, *Anna Bolena*, which was the composer's first success when it premiered in Milan in 1830. It is based on the story of King Henry VIII and his second wife, Anne Boleyn, and the final scene with Boleyn in the Tower of London awaiting execution features a beautiful soprano aria, "Al dolce guidami castel natio," a plea to be led to the dear castle where she was born. Callas's successful productions of *Anna Bolena* in 1957 and 1958 made this opera popular again.

Norma. Vincenzo Bellini's *Norma* was Callas's signature role, one she sang more often than any other. She first performed it in Florence in 1948, at her London debut in 1952, her American debut in Chicago in 1954, and her New York Metropolitan Opera debut in 1956. Her final performance in *Norma* was in 1965.

First produced in 1831, *Norma* takes place in Gaul in 50 B.C.E. during the Roman occupation. The heroine is a Druid priestess who has broken her vow of chastity for the Roman pro-consul Pollione. The role of Norma is extremely challenging, requiring a coloratura soprano with a dramatic, flexible, and intense voice. "Casta diva" was one of Callas's best arias.

Tosca. As the complex beauty Floria Tosca in *Tosca*, Callas was ideal—powerful and impassioned but also tender and vulnerable. She performed this role more than fifty times between 1942 and 1965, often to standing ovations. In one of opera's great dramatic scenes, Tosca stabs the sinister Scarpia, chief of police, who had imprisoned Tosca's lover and wanted to seduce her in exchange for her lover's life. Callas's renditions of the aria "Vissi d'arte" (music and love) delighted audiences.

Medea. Callas's intense performances in Luigi Cherubini's *Medea* were considered haunting and thrilling. In Greek mythology, Medea was the enraged wife who killed her own children when her husband Jason abandoned her for another woman.

Later Years. In the 1960's, as Callas experienced increasing vocal problems, she gradually withdrew from the stage. Her final operatic performance was as Tosca at Covent Garden on July 5, 1965. In 1971-1972 Callas gave twenty-three master classes at the Juilliard School of Music in New York. She then reunited with the famous tenor Giuseppe di Stefano, with whom she had performed and recorded frequently. In 1973 they began an international recital tour to raise money for his daughter's medical treatments. Panned by the critics, they ended their tour with a final concert in Sapporo, Japan, on November 11, 1974. This was Callas's last public performance. During her career, Callas recorded more than twenty complete operas and performed more than forty different roles.

Musical Legacy

Callas had a profound influence on opera and subsequent generations of singers. She revitalized opera by making it exciting theater as well as music. She was a passionate actress and vocal artist who mesmerized audiences with her intense dramatic character portrayals.

She also revived the bel canto operas through her musicianship and compelling performances of this neglected repertoire, creating a new generation of bel canto opera stars, including Joan Sutherland, June Anderson, Beverly Sills, and Marilyn Horne.

Callas's master classes at Juilliard provided future generations of vocalists and teachers with her personal insights and lessons on technique and expression. John Ardoin transcribed tapes of the classses and published them as a book to help pass along this valuable musical tradition. These classes also inspired Terrence McNally's historical drama, *Master Class*, in 1995. Off the stage, the Callas persona and her newsworthy personal life also changed the world of opera. She was a classical music superstar, much like popular rock or film stars whose lives are always in the limelight.

Fascination with Callas persisted after her death. Biographies, journal articles, international fan clubs, Web sites, and other tributes continued the Callas legend. In 2007 pop singer Celine Dion dedicated to Callas the song "La Diva" on Dion's French album *D'elle*.

Alice Myers

Further Reading

Ardoin, John. *Callas at Juilliard: The Master Classes*. Portland, Oreg.: Amadeus Press, 2003. From 1971 to 1972, Callas taught twenty-three two-hour opera master classes at Juilliard. The author, a preeminent Callas scholar, has transcribed and arranged the tapes of the classes into a valuable volume, including Callas's suggestions for the expressive use of cadenzas, word accents, consonants, and ornaments. Illustrated.

_____. *The Callas Legacy: The Complete Guide to Her Recordings on Compact Disc*. Milwaukee, Wis.: Hal Leonard Corporation, 2003. Thorough guide to all Callas compact disc recordings, with detailed commentary on each recording. Illustrated, with bibliography and index.

Edwards, Anne. *Maria Callas: An Intimate Portrait*. New York: St. Martin's Press, 2001. Well-researched and revealing portrait that provides insight into Callas's personal and professional life, including her relationships, her "mystery child" with Aristotle Onassis, her rise to fame, and the circumstances surrounding her death. Illustrated, with bibliography and index.

Huffington, Arianna Stassinopoulos. *Maria Callas: The Woman Behind the Legend*. New York: Cooper Square Press, 2002. Comprehensive biography, based on extensive interviews and research. Illustrated, with bibliography and index.

Levine, Robert. *Maria Callas: A Musical Biography*. New York: Black Dog & Leventhal, 2003. Artistic biography focusing on Callas's voice, musical development, and performances. The accompanying compact discs and expert commentary feature Callas's major performances. Illustrated, with rare photographs. Includes discography, videography, index, and two sound discs.

Petsalis-Diomidis, Nicholas. *The Unknown Callas: The Greek Years*. Portland, Oreg.: Amadeus Press, 2001. An intimate portrait covering the crucial formative years from 1937 to 1945. Based on Athenian archives and more than two hundred interviews, this book won Greece's National Biography Award in 1999. Extensive bibliography, notes, and index.

Stancioff, Nadia. *Maria Callas Remembered: An Intimate Portrait of the Private Callas*. Boulder, Colo.: De Capo Press, 2000. Intimate account of the private Callas by a close friend, who knew Callas from 1969 until her death. Based on the author's own memories and interviews with Callas's sister Jackie, friends, and colleagues. Illustrated.

See also: Barber, Samuel; Sills, Beverly; Sutherland, Dame Joan; Tebaldi, Renata.

Glen Campbell

American country singer and guitarist

A respected session player for artists from Elvis Presley to the Beach Boys, Campbell became a country singer that crossed over successfully to a pop career.

Born: April 22, 1936; Billstown, Arkansas
Also known as: Glen Travis Campbell (full name)

Principal recordings

ALBUMS: *The Astounding Twelve-String Guitar of Glen Campbell*, 1964; *By the Time I Get to Phoenix*, 1967; *Gentle on My Mind*, 1967; *Oh Happy Day*, 1968; *Wichita Lineman*, 1968; *Galveston*, 1969; *Bobbie Gentry and Glen Campbell*, 1970; *Try a Little Kindness*, 1970; *The Last Time I Saw Her*, 1971; *Glen Campbell*, 1973; *I Knew Jesus (Before He Was a Star)*, 1973; *Houston (I'm Comin' to See You)*, 1974; *Reunion: The Songs of Jimmy Webb*, 1974; *Arkansas*, 1975; *Rhinestone Cowboy*, 1975; *Bloodline*, 1976; *Southern Nights*, 1977; *It's Just a Matter of Time*, 1986; *Still Within the Sound of My Voice*, 1988; *Meet Glen Campbell*, 2008.

The Life

Glen Travis Campbell was born to Wes and Carrie Campbell, one of twelve children in a family of poor farmers. Taught to play a five-dollar Sears and Roebuck guitar by his uncle Boo, Campbell quickly became well known among local musicians by the time he was eight years old. Remarkably proficient with the twelve- and six-string guitar, Campbell became adept at playing everything from jazz standards to country and pop tunes. Never a dedicated student, Campbell dropped out of school at the age of fourteen to tour with two of his uncles and their band of musicians. In 1955, at the age of nineteen, he married Diane Kirk. The marriage, which lasted four years, produced a daughter, Debra Kay, from whom Campbell remained estranged until the 1980's.

Campbell eventually outgrew playing with his uncles on the circuit of proms, weddings, dance halls, and local radio shows, and he moved to California in the late 1950's. He met and married Billie Jean Nunley, with whom he had another daughter, Kelli Glen, and a son, William Travis. Campbell's solo recording career took off in the late 1960's, but it was his 1968-1972 television variety show, *The Glen Campbell Goodtime Hour*, that made him an international star. Campbell's television success led to a brief stint in Hollywood, where he costarred with John Wayne in the Western *True Grit* (1970). Success had a downside, however, as drugs and alcohol contributed to the end of Campbell's marriage to Nunley as well as to a much-publicized affair with and a brief marriage to Sarah Davis, wife of country-pop star Mac Davis, in 1975. In the late 1970's, Campbell and rising teen country singer Tanya Tucker began a tumultuous affair. In 1982 Campbell married Kim Woolen, who helped lead him to sobriety and stability, though he suffered a relapse in 2004 when he was arrested for drunk driving and sentenced to ten days in jail. Nonetheless, the marriage to Woolen survived this episode. Campbell performs regularly at the Glen Campbell Goodtime Theatre in Branson, Missouri.

The Music

In 1960 Campbell joined Dash Croft and Jimmy Seals in the revamped pop band the Champs, which had already hit a peak with the Top 40 instrumental single "Tequila." A year later, Campbell became a staff writer for American Music, and he cowrote, with Jerry Capehart, "Turn Around, Look at Me." Campbell recorded and released this song as his first solo effort on Capehart's Crest label, but it would be a new vocal group, the Vogues, fashioned after the Lettermen, who turned the song into a smash hit seven years later.

Session Work. While he continued to write songs and to play in a variety of bands, Campbell supplemented his income by becoming an in-demand session guitarist and vocalist. He played guitar and occasionally bass, and he supplied background vocals on hundreds of studio recording sessions for some of the most important pop stars of the 1950's and 1960's, including Jan and Dean, the Crystals, Ricky Nelson, Bobby Darin, Wayne Newton, the Kingston Trio, Elvis Presley, Dean Martin, Nat King Cole, Jack Jones, and Frank Sinatra.

Campbell's most famous early association, however, was with the Beach Boys. Having already played and sung on several Beach Boys recordings, Campbell was asked to fill in for Brian Wilson in 1964 when the increasingly reclusive pop songwriter refused to tour with the group. In 1965 the group asked Campbell to become a permanent member but he declined. He was ready to devote all his energy to his fledgling solo career.

Songs by Webb. After releasing several unsuccessful singles in the mid-1960's Campbell was immensely successful with a release of John Hartford's folk song "Gentle on My Mind," though his most successful partnership would be with pop songwriter Jimmy Webb. His recordings of two classics by Webb—"By the Time I Get to Phoenix" (1967) and "Wichita Lineman" (1968)—sealed the connection between the two in the public mind. Both songs dominated the pop, country, and easy-listening charts. Webb's unique blend of down-home lyricism, urbane melodies, and slightly psychedelic arrangements (such as the organ flourishes at the end of "Wichita Lineman") satisfied the upscale ambitions of Campbell's traditional country audience while attracting new recruits from both the pop and rock audiences.

In 1969 Campbell hit it big again with two more Webb songs, "Galveston" and "Where's the Play-

Glen Campbell. (AP/Wide World Photos)

ground, Susie?" In 1970 he recorded Webb's "Honey Come Back," a song that had only moderate success on the country charts. Campbell, who once called Webb the "best songwriter ever born in America," would eventually record more than thirty Webb songs. Although Campbell's recording career faded as he entered the 1980's, he still achieved Top 10 country radio hits as late as 1987 with "The Hand That Rocks the Cradle" and Webb's "Still Within the Sound of My Voice."

Rhinestone Cowboy. Campbell's biggest-selling single (and only number-one hit) is 1976's "Rhinestone Cowboy." This song, and the follow-up hit, "Country Boy (You've Got Your Feet in L.A.)," seemed to be based on Campbell's image as a pop singer who had abandoned his country roots. "Rhinestone Cowboy" tells the tale of a country singer resigned to acting out a role to make a living, while "Country Boy (You've Got Your Feet in L.A.)" is critical of that compromise. Both songs were smash hits, selling millions of copies, making them Campbell's biggest-selling records.

Musical Legacy

Despite his significant performances as a session guitarist in the late 1950's and early 1960's, Campbell will likely be remembered as the singer of the Webb classics "By the Time I Get to Phoenix," "Wichita Lineman," and "Galveston." His contributions to country music are unparalleled. He was one of the first major country artists to successfully cross over and dominate the country and pop charts. Significantly, he introduced many country artists of the late 1960's to a larger audience by insisting that they be regular guests on his successful CBS television variety show, *The Glen Campbell Goodtime Hour*. His promotion of country-music performers paved the way for the "new country" explosion of the 1980's and 1990's. Through his efforts, the careers of Vince Gill, Garth Brooks, and Alan Jackson (whom Campbell discovered) were made possible.

Tyrone Williams

Further Reading

Campbell, Glen, with Tom Carter. *Rhinestone Cowboy*. New York: Villard, 1994. In this frank autobiography, Campbell gives the details of his life. He recounts the poverty of his youth, his life as an adolescent on the road with his uncles in the Southwest, his recording sessions as a guitarist with some of the best singers and bands of the early 1960's, his affairs with Davis and Tucker, and his redemption as a Christian.

Eng, Monica. "Glen Campbell's Redemption: Star Talks of Life, New Beginnings." *Chicago Tribune*, July 26, 2005. Eng interviews Campbell shortly after he moved from Phoenix, where he was arrested and jailed for drunk driving, to Malibu, California. Campbell reports that he is sober and enjoying clean living.

Flippo, Chet. "Glen Campbell Sounds Off on Country Music, Bryan White, Down Under." *Billboard* 18, no. 32 (August 10, 1996): 29. Campbell criticizes the glitzy new Nashville sound and performers, though he singles out some, such as White, for praise.

See also: Cole, Nat King; Hopkins, Lightnin'; Nelson, Ricky; Sinatra, Frank; Webb, Jimmy; Wilson, Brian.

Mariah Carey

American pop singer and songwriter

With her spectacular five-octave range, Carey has inspired a generation of female pop and soul singers.

Born: March 27, 1970; Huntington, Long Island, New York

Principal recordings

ALBUMS: *Mariah Carey*, 1990; *Emotions*, 1991; *Music Box*, 1993; *Merry Christmas*, 1994; *Daydream*, 1995; *Butterfly*, 1997; *Rainbow*, 1999; *Glitter*, 2001; *Charmbracelet*, 2002; *The Emancipation of Mimi*, 2005; *Maximum Mariah Carey*, 2005; $E = MC^2$, 2008.

The Life

Mariah Carey (mah-RI-ah KEH-ree) was born to an opera-singer mother (whose heritage was Irish and American) and an aeronautical-engineer father (whose heritage was Venezuelan and African American). Her first name came from the song "They Call the Wind Mariah" from the Tony Award-winning musical *Paint Your Wagon* (1951).

The youngest of three siblings, Carey did not have a happy home. Her sister Alison turned to drugs and prostitution at fifteen, got pregnant, and contracted HIV. Her brother Morgan was diagnosed as a child with cerebral palsy. Her parents went through a bitter divorce when Carey was three, leaving her mother to raise the three children single-handedly. She supported the household with a work schedule that meant Carey was alone at home for extended periods.

Carey turned to music as an escape, listening to New York's rhythm-and-blues station WBLS-FM and to her mother's Minnie Riperton records. Carey started singing almost as soon as she began talking, and she used music as a way to deal with her insecurity about being biracial. At seventeen, right out of high school, Carey moved to New York City to pursue music, and she supported herself with backup singing jobs and with being a waitress.

She befriended singer Brenda K. Starr, who reportedly gave Carey's demo tape to business mogul and Columbia Records head Tommy Mottola. Mottola was smitten with the voice and the person behind it, signing Carey to a record deal that resulted in her 1990 debut release. A Columbia Records artist at the time relates a memo Mottola sent to the promotional staff at Columbia: "Make Mariah Carey a star, or it's your job."

Mottola left his wife of twenty years and married Carey, almost twenty years his junior. Together they bought a ten-million-dollar home, but quickly the marriage began to deteriorate. Carey believed Mottola was manipulative and controlling, and she called her home with Mottola "Sing Sing" (referring to the prison and to what was expected of her). The couple divorced in 1997, and in 2001 Carey left Mottola's label to sign a contract with Virgin Records.

That same year, a live studio audience of MTV's *Total Request Live* witnessed Carey's erratic behavior on stage, and shortly thereafter the singer checked in to a Connecticut clinic, taking a break from public performances. Her film *Glitter* (2001) was a box-office failure, and in 2002 Virgin Records ended her eighty-million-dollar contract (the largest ever at the time) with a twenty-eight-million-dollar buyout.

Nevertheless, Carey overcame her personal struggles, rising again to prominence. She signed a contract with Island Records in 2002, and she established a record label, MonarC Music. With the success of later albums, Carey ranks among the largest-selling female artists of all time and the first to hit number one consecutively for every year in the 1990's. In May, 2008, Carey married Nick Cannon, an actor and a rap artist.

The Music

"Visions of Love." Carey quickly achieved fame with four number-one singles from her debut album, *Mariah Carey*, including "Visions of Love." In 1991 she won two Grammy Awards, for Best New Artist and Best Female Vocalist. In a performance on the television show *MTV Unplugged*, Carey proved that her vocal talents were real, not created in a studio.

Music Box. Despite the fact that critics panned her second album, *Emotions*, Carey's third album, *Music Box*, sold twenty-five million copies, launching her to worldwide popularity. *Billboard* hailed

the album as "heart-piercing." She continued to top the charts, releasing several solo albums: *Merry Christmas*, *Daydream*, *Butterfly*, *Rainbow*, *Glitter*, and *Charmbracelet*. Her two compilations, *MTV Unplugged EP* and *#1's*, went platinum or better.

The Emancipation of Mimi. In 2005 the thirty-five-year-old singer released an album that delivered her back to her rhythm-and-blues roots and to the top of the charts. *The Emancipation of Mimi* hit number one on the *Billboard* Top 100, along with its tracks "It's Like That" and "We Belong Together." The album garnered commercial and industry acclaim, and Carey earned another Grammy Award. The video for its track "We Belong Together" shows Carey jilting an older fiancé at the wedding, in order to pursue a younger lover. Carey wore her own twenty-five-thousand-dollar Vera Wang wedding dress for the shoot.

$E = MC^2$. In this release from 2008, Carey plays on Einstein's famous formula, declaring that "Emancipation equals Mariah Carey to the second power." Debuting at number one, the album garnered Carey the largest opening-week sales of her career and featured the hit single "Touch My Body."

Musical Legacy

Carey has won five Grammy Awards, and several of her albums have achieved platinum sales. As a singer, she has utilized her voice, with its substantial vocal range and power, to great effect on hit singles. Carey evolved in her musical career to include songwriting and record-producing, and she has overcome personal and professional hardships with a remarkable resilience. In April, 2008, Carey appeared as a mentor on the television show *American Idol*, coaching the contestants in her singing style.

Louis R. Carlozo, Madeleine Kuhns,
and LeeAnn Maton

Further Reading

Nickson, Chris. *Mariah Carey Revisited: Her Story*. New York: St. Martin's Griffin, 1998. This exploration of Carey's life and music as of 1998 provides a snapshot of the singer at the height of her 1990's popularity.
Parker, Judy. *Mariah Carey*. New York: Children's Press, 2001. Appealing to her younger fans, this

biography for juvenile readers chronicles the singer's rise to fame.

Shapiro, Marc. *Mariah Carey: The Unauthorized Biography*. Toronto, Ont.: ECW Press, 2001. Using behind-the-scenes information, Shapiro describes the personal struggles and triumphs behind Carey's musical career.

See also: Babyface; Combs, Sean; Elliott, Missy; Franklin, Aretha; Seeger, Peggy; Snoop Dogg; Summer, Donna.

Wendy Carlos

American composer, arranger, keyboardist, and synthesizer player

A pioneering electronic music artist, Carlos popularized the Moog synthesizer and legitimized its use as a medium for classical-music composition and performance. Her techniques of electronic orchestration—which depend on a thorough knowledge of classical models, the synthesizer, and the possibilities and limitations of stereo sound recording—surpassed those of her contemporaries and remain vital today.

Born: November 14, 1939; Pawtucket, Rhode Island

Also known as: Walter Carlos (birth name)

Principal works

FILM SCORES: *Timesteps*, 1970; *A Clockwork Orange*, 1972; *Tron*, 1982.

Principal recordings

ALBUMS: *Switched-On Bach*, 1968; *Switched-On Brandenburgs, Vol. 1*, 1969; *The Well-Tempered Synthesizer*, 1969; *Sonic Seasonings*, 1972; *Digital Moonscapes*, 1984; *Beauty in the Beast*, 1986; *Secrets of Synthesis*, 1990; *Switched-On Bach 2000*, 1995; *Tales of Heaven and Hell*, 1998; *Switched-On Bach II*, 2001; *Switched-On Brandenburgs*, 2001; *By Request*, 2003.

The Life

Born Walter Carlos, the composer felt she was female from the time she was five years old. She be-

gan the process resulting in her sex reassignment in 1967, after her career had already been established. Carlos began studying the piano at the age of six but was also attracted to science and visual art. She pursued undergraduate studies in physics and music at Brown University and in 1965 earned a master's degree in composition from Columbia University, where her teachers included Jack Beeson, Otto Luening, and Vladimir Ussachevsky. In 1964 she collaborated with Robert Moog on the development of his Moog synthesizer; after graduation, she continued consulting with him and worked as a recording engineer. Around the same time she met Rachel Elkind, who became an important companion and artistic collaborator. Elkind convinced her to work on an album of Bach compositions realized for the synthesizer; the album, *Switched-On Bach*, was produced by Elkind and released on Columbia Records in 1968. It became the first platinum-selling classical album. Elkind and Carlos's important collaboration continued until 1980, resulting in a series of crossover albums containing both original work and additional realizations of others' music. Carlos, who received the Society for Electro-Acoustic Music in the United States' SEAMUS Lifetime Achievement Award in 2005, continues to compose. In addition to electronic music, she has written a concerto for string quartet and orchestra, commissioned by the Kronos Quartet, and excerpts from her *Digital Moonscapes* have been performed by orchestras in Berkeley, California, and Boston under the direction of Kent Nagano.

The Music

Carlos's early works include *Dialogues for Piano and Two Loudspeakers* and *Episodes for Piano and Electronic Sound*. The two works are episodic and largely atonal but depend on a remarkable and carefully crafted relationship between the solo instrument and the electronic sounds. In particular, both tape and piano parts contain presentations of similar recognizable melodic, rhythmic material.

The Well-Tempered Synthesizer. The follow-up to *Switched-On Bach* was released in 1969 and contained realizations of Bach's Brandenburg Concerto No. 4 and four sonatas of Domenico Scarlatti, as well as realized excerpts from George Frideric Handel's *Water Music* and Claudio Monteverdi's *L'Orfeo*. In this album Carlos refined basic elements of her electronic orchestrations, including the selective doubling of certain parts and the rapid shifting of parts from one side of the stereo image to the other. Her realizations of Scarlatti's Sonatas in G Major and D Major and the final movement of the Brandenburg Concerto are stunning in this regard.

Sonic Seasonings. This work, first released in 1972, is a large-scale suite of four movements depicting the four seasons. The music explores a wide expressive range and includes recordings of natural sounds as well as a haunting vocalise—a vocal exercise without words—by Elkind in the final movement. As Carlos later observed, *Sonic Seasonings* anticipated the development of what came to be called ambient music.

Timesteps. *Timesteps* was originally designed to ease listeners into an electronic realization of excerpts from Ludwig van Beethoven's Ninth Symphony. However, her reading of Anthony Burgess's novel *A Clockwork Orange* around the same time helped *Timesteps* evolve into what Carlos called "an autonomous work with an uncanny affinity for *Clockwork*." *Timesteps* was her first original work to use the same techniques of orchestration she had developed in *The Well-Tempered Synthesizer* and also included her pioneering use of the vocoder, a speech analyzer and synthesizer, to produce electronically altered vocal sounds. As in many of her works, the musical material includes textures and gestures that could be produced only by electronic instruments as well as many ideas that suggest music for conventional instruments. Examples include a lyrical episode with electronic birdsong, church bells, and the crashing of waves. The penultimate section initially combines a minimalist ostinato with ominous vocoder textures and ultimately superimposes musical ideas from the work's beginning in a manner best accomplished through the technology of the studio.

Beauty in the Beast. In this suite of evocative character pieces, Carlos experimented with a number of alternative tuning systems, although there is no loss of melodic grace or accessibility. The title track is a particularly fine example. A gentle theme is harmonized by triads, but the tuning system prevents the triads from agreeing with each other. A central section includes a menacing, stepwise theme and a sudden explosion of maniacal circus

music, after which the theme returns and brings the piece to a mysterious, tentative close.

Musical Legacy

By emphasizing recognizable melody, harmony, and rhythm in her electronic music, Carlos influenced both her contemporaries and younger composers to use synthesizers for the creation and performance of new but more accessible music. Mother Mallard's Portable Masterpiece Co., founded by David Borden in 1969, was the first performing group to use Moog synthesizers in its performances; the better known Philip Glass Ensemble began to replace electric organs with synthesizers in the 1980's. Unlike Borden or Glass, however, Carlos rarely sought to have her work performed in concert settings. Her concentration on studio electronic music and the emotional difficulties she experienced before and after her sex reassignment—as well as her tendency toward reclusiveness—also made it difficult for her to cultivate a more extensive career as a composer for the concert hall. Nevertheless, her best music has wit, charm, and considerable sophistication and is deserving of more widespread acclaim.

Rob Haskins

Further Reading

Bakan, Michael B., Wanda Bryant, and Guangming Li. "Demystifying and Classifying Electronic Music Instruments." *Selected Reports in Ethnomusicology* 8 (1990): 37-64. Modifies and extends the Hornbostel/Sachs instrument classification system to include electronic instruments. Includes a description of *Switched-On Bach*.

Carlos, Wendy. "Tuning: At the Crossroads." *Computer Music Journal* 11, no. 1 (Spring, 1987): 29-43. A comprehensive discussion of various tuning systems available via digitally controlled music synthesis.

Darter, Tom, comp. *The Art of Electronic Music: The Instruments, Designers, and Musicians Behind the Artistic and Popular Explosion of Electronic Music.* New York: William Morrow, 1984. A compendium of articles originally published in *Keyboard* from 1975 to 1983, this book includes an interview with Carlos.

Doerschuk, Robert L. "Wendy Carlos: The Magic in the Machine—Reflections from the First Great

Modern Synthesist." *Keyboard* 21, no. 8 (August, 1995): 50-63. Short but informative introduction to Carlos's work and aesthetics.

Pinch, Trevor, and Frank Trocco. *Analog Days: The Invention and Impact of the Moog Synthesizer*. Cambridge, Mass.: Harvard University Press, 2002. Critical history that includes a chapter on *Switched-On Bach*.

See also: Babbitt, Milton; Glass, Philip.

Karen Carpenter

American singer

As female vocalist and drummer in the brother-sister act the Carpenters, Carpenter scored a series of hit singles and albums throughout the 1970's, demonstrating that "easy-listening" and "middle-of-the-road" music could still break into the Billboard *Hot 100. Her close harmonies with brother Richard and their knack for choosing great material made them one of the most influential recording groups of the decade.*

Born: March 2, 1950; New Haven, Connecticut
Died: February 4, 1983; Downey, California
Also known as: Karen Anne Carpenter (full name)
Member of: The Carpenters

Principal recordings

ALBUMS (with the Carpenters): *Offering*, 1969; *Close to You*, 1970; *The Carpenters*, 1971; *A Song for You*, 1972; *Now and Then*, 1973; *Horizon*, 1975; *A Kind of Hush*, 1976; *Passage*, 1977; *Christmas Portrait*, 1978; *Made in America*, 1981; *Voice of the Heart*, 1983; *An Old-Fashioned Christmas*, 1984.

The Life

Karen Anne Carpenter was the second child of Harold and Agnes Carpenter. Their first child, Richard, four years older, was a prodigy on the piano, and in 1963 the family moved to Downey, California, to aid Richard's career by being close to the recording industry. At Downey High School, Ka-

ren played drums in the marching band and for the first time discovered her own musical talent. At fifteen she joined her brother's jazz group, the Richard Carpenter Trio, on the drums. In 1969 she and her brother signed with A&M Records as The Carpenters, releasing *Ticket to Ride*, which barely scratched the *Billboard* Hot 100 (the title song peaked at number fifty-four). The next album began a decade of Top 40 hits. She and her brother were, as their hit single put it, "On Top of the World." By the middle of the decade, however, it became evident that Karen was battling anorexia nervosa, a then little-known eating disorder. She married real-estate developer Tom Burris in August, 1980; the couple separated the following November. In 1982 she received treatment for anorexia, but the strain on her heart from the disorder led to her death a few months later in 1983.

The Music

Karen spent her teen years in the shadow of her brother Richard, though she did not seem to resent it: Even as a part of his musical groups, she remained one of her brother's staunchest fans. In the Richard Carpenter Trio and the more pop-oriented Spectrum, Karen played drums so well that Herb Alpert of A&M Records noticed her and signed the duo to his label. (Jazz drumming legend Buddy Rich, *Modern Drummer* magazine, and the *Playboy* jazz poll would later join Alpert in praising Karen's work.) Their first album, *Ticket to Ride*, did not have a song in the Top 40, but their second album had two.

Close to You. The second Carpenters album collected twelve songs that sounded great alone and worked well together, including three original songs by Richard and one of his guitarists from Spectrum, John Bettis. Karen began a career-long association with Burt Bacharach by including two of his songs: the title track and "I'll Never Fall in Love Again" from the Broadway show *Promises, Promises*. The latter was overshadowed by Dionne Warwick's version, which hit number six, but "Close to You" hit number one, stayed at the top for four weeks, and remained on the charts for fifteen. Their second gold single from the album, "We've Only Just Begun," demonstrated the Carpenters' ear for good material. Composed by Paul Williams for a local bank commercial in California, it struck the Carpenters as a potential hit, and it became one:

Karen Carpenter. (CBS/Landov)

number two on the *Billboard* Hot 100 and for six weeks number one in the *Billboard* adult contemporary category. Karen's contralto vocals on both hits became key to the duo's success. In 2003 *Rolling Stone* listed this album in the Top 500 of all time at number 175.

The Carpenters. Richard and Karen followed their success with "We've Only Just Begun" by cutting another Paul Williams composition, "Rainy Days and Mondays," again with Karen singing lead. It, too, soared on the charts. It was their third gold record. The B side of the album was unified by a six-song Burt Bacharach-Hal David medley. "Superstar," which had been successful for both Joe Cocker and Bette Midler, again capitalized on Karen's solo voice against a contrasting bass line. The song did not quite fit the group's wholesome image, but Richard changed the line "I can hardly wait to sleep with you again" to "I can hardly wait to see you again." Once again, the Carpenters went to

number-two pop, number-one adult contemporary, and a gold single.

A Song for You. With the highest concentration of hit singles—six—ever for the Carpenters, their fourth album saw four songs reach the Top 12. "Top of the World" became their second number one. The album made Cash Box's Top 100 for 1972 at number twenty-six.

Now and Then. When Ricky Nelson's song "Garden Party" prompted an interest in "oldies" music, the Carpenters responded with their first concept album (though Richard had originally conceived their previous album that way). The B side was a medley of hit songs from the early 1960's, with Karen and Richard duplicating the arrangements and vocal styles of the originals. Their guitarist, Tony Peluso, played a DJ weaving the songs together, and the whole side was introduced with the Richard Carpenter-Bettis nostalgic original "Yesterday Once More" (which became another number-two pop, number-one adult contemporary hit). From the A side, "Sing," which advisers warned would not overcome its association with the children's television show *Sesame Street*, became a gold single and peaked at number-one adult contemporary.

Musical Legacy

Though Karen died before the compact-disc medium became standard, her hits continue to be packaged on compilation compact discs—including her 1979 solo album, which was not released in its entirety until 1996. Karen's success on drums has proven an inspiration for female aspirants to one of the last male-dominated instruments in pop music. Her clear and strong contralto became a trademark. Her homey image helps to make the Carpenters' two Christmas albums, *Christmas Portrait* and *An Old-Fashioned Christmas*, continue to sell, and her vocal leads on "The Christmas Song" and "Merry Christmas, Darling" remain radio and Muzak perennials during the holiday season. Although Karen attempted to shed her clean-cut image in her solo album, there is no doubt she primarily will be remembered as the smiling girl next door on the Carpenters' album covers. Seven months after Karen's death, the Carpenters received a star on the Hollywood Walk of Fame.

John R. Holmes

Further Reading

Coleman, Ray. *The Carpenters: The Untold Story. An Authorized Biography*. Boston: HarperCollins, 1994. The author had access to Carpenter family records and memories.

Garcia, Ronald. *Close to You: The Story of Richard and Karen Carpenter*. Chicago: The Good Reading Company, 1995. Well-written basic coverage, mostly of the years of the Carpenters' success, 1970-1982.

Schmidt, Randy. *Yesterday Once More: Memories of The Carpenters and Their Music*. New York: Tiny Ripple Books, 2000. Music-oriented biography, a good source for commentary on individual songs and albums.

Stockdale, Tom. *Karen Carpenter*. Philadelphia: Chelsea House, 2000. Brief biography, with a good selection of photographs from all stages of Karen's short life.

See also: Alpert, Herb; Anderson, Leroy; Aznavour, Charles; Warwick, Dionne.

Benny Carter

American jazz saxophonist

Carter mastered all phases of jazz music from the 1920's until the end of the twentieth century. To study his career is to review major jazz developments over a span of seventy years.

Born: August 8, 1907; New York, New York
Died: July 12, 2003; Los Angeles, California
Also known as: Bennett Lester Carter (full name)

Principal recordings

ALBUMS: *Symphony in Riffs*, 1930; *Alto Saxes*, 1954; *Benny Carter Plays Pretty*, 1954; *Jazz Giant*, 1957; *Aspects*, 1958; *Further Definitions*, 1961; *The King*, 1977; *A Gentleman and His Music*, 1985; *Benny Carter Meets Oscar Peterson*, 1986; *Central City Sketches*, 1987; *In the Mood for Swing*, 1987; *My Man Benny, My Man Phil*, 1989; *Harlem Renaissance*, 1992; *Elegy in Blue*, 1994; *Another Time, Another Place*, 1996; *Songbook*, 1996.

The Life

Bennett Lester Carter was born in New York City on August 8, 1907, the son of Norrell and Sadie Carter. He was called Bennett, his mother's maiden name, in the family but soon became Benny to others. He was the youngest of three children and the only boy.

Music was important in the Carter household. His father was a self-taught guitarist, and his mother played the organ and piano. Although Carter did not complete the seventh grade and his musical training consisted only of early instruction on the piano, he learned a great deal from reading about music and the world in general, becoming highly articulate. Music was always his passion, but he did pay marked attention to the origin and usage of the English language and sought to express his thoughts as clearly and effectively as he did his music.

Carter had an active social life and made many friends around the world, but interviewers had considerable difficulty eliciting personal information from him. He was more interested in discussing the present than the past. Well informed about politics and international affairs, he generally restricted his activities to matters pertaining to music; for instance, as a man who had known and performed with white musicians most of his life, he worked at integrating local musicians' unions. He taught part time at a number of schools and colleges, and students found him helpful and always interested in their work if they displayed devotion to music, even if their talents were decidedly limited.

Carter married five times. His first marriage ended with his wife's early death; three others were terminated by divorce. He had one daughter, Joyce. Carter met Hilma Arons in 1940, when she visited the Savoy Ballroom in New York to hear his orchestra play. In 1979, when he was in his seventies and she in her late fifties, they married. A graduate of Barnard College, she managed many of his business details and also advised him when he was writing lyrics for the songs he composed. She and his daughter survived him when he died a few weeks short of his ninety-sixth birthday.

The Music

Carter's contributions to jazz were so many that it is difficult to specify the greatest. Probably most admired as an instrumentalist, he ranks among the most talented of reed players and also received much acclaim as a trumpeter. In addition, he played the piano and trombone professionally. Carter disagreed strongly with critics who thought that the differences in the mouthpieces and embouchure (use of facial muscles and shaping of the lips around the mouthpiece) of reed instruments and trumpets prevented a musician from excelling at both. All that was needed, he insisted, was sufficient practice. He also was convinced that his various musical activities, such as being able to compose a work and play or direct it, enhanced one another.

Benny Carter. (AP/Wide World Photos)

Early Jazz Achievements. In the late 1920's and early 1930's Carter played in several jazz organizations populated by important young musicians. He performed in the orchestras of Charlie Johnson, Fletcher Henderson, Chick Webb, and the group known as McKinney's Cotton Pickers, and he arranged for most of them. In 1931 he composed one of his best-known songs, "Blues in My Heart." From 1932 to 1934 he recorded with his own orchestra. By this time he was incorporating trumpet solos as well as those for clarinet and saxophone. Maintaining a fourteen-piece orchestra in the Depression was difficult, and although several of the performers later ranked Carter's first orchestra as one of the best they had ever been in, he had to disband in 1934.

Carter in Europe. Like many other American jazz musicians, Carter spent several years in Europe, from 1935 to 1938, recording with various orchestras and chamber groups in such places as London, Copenhagen, Stockholm, The Hague, and Paris. A highlight occurred on April 18, 1937, when Carter was set to record with an orchestra led by the great tenor saxophonist Coleman Hawkins. Carter arrived in Paris without having prepared arrangements that he had agreed to prepare for the date, but he then quickly arranged Fats Waller's "Honeysuckle Rose" and Roger Wolfe Kahn and Joseph Meyer's "Crazy Rhythm." The former featured

Hawkins, but Carter's solo on the latter is still regarded as one of his finest. He also contributed a notable thirty-two-bar solo on the trumpet in "Out of Nowhere." For many of these foreign performances, the orchestra was an international one, in this instance including two of France's best reed players.

"When Lights Are Low." Carter introduced his best-known song, "When Lights Are Low," in Europe, but the most important of several of his recordings of it came on September 11, 1939, in New York with Lionel Hampton's orchestra. No fewer than three top tenor saxophonists—Hawkins, Ben Webster, and Leon "Chu" Berry—can be heard on this recording. The session was also important because twenty-one-year-old Dizzy Gillespie was asked to replace the unavailable lead trumpeter. Hampton later described Gillespie's performance during another number at this session as the first time he had ever heard bebop played on a trumpet. Both Carter's arrangement and his solo on "When Lights Are Low" stand high among his achievements, and Hampton's vibraharp solo on the second take, which was not released for many years (perhaps because of some mistakes by the then-inexperienced Gillespie), is another high point.

During this period Carter was busy arranging for Benny Goodman, Glenn Miller, Teddy Wilson, Artie Shaw, and Count Basie. However, World War II and a 1942 ban on recording imposed by the

American Federation of Musicians brought an end to the period called the Swing Era.

Motion-Picture Work. From 1942 to 1946 Carter headed another orchestra, which arrived in California for engagements near the end of 1942. A few weeks later he was invited to work on the film *Stormy Weather*, which had a talented all-black cast. Carter's arrangements impressed the music supervisor, Alfred Newman, who allowed him many more contributions to the film, including one of Carter's own compositions, "Moppin' and Boppin'." He played trumpet on two songs in a septet led by Fats Waller, arranged for and played in the large studio orchestra, soloed on the saxophone, and arranged the title song for Lena Horne. However, even in this film populated by black performers, he neither appeared on screen nor was given any screen credits.

Carter's later Hollywood experiences were also mixed. He resigned from one all-black film because the musical director claimed that his arrangements were "too good," beyond the capacity of early black bands, despite Carter's insistence that he had been in such bands and that they were better than the current ones. Later, he not only wrote and arranged music for films but also appeared in some of them, including *An American in Paris* (1951), for which he arranged several George Gershwin tunes.

Two Later Performances. Two of Carter's finest performances are *Further Definitions*, an album recorded in New York on November 15, 1961, and his July 13, 1977, concert at the Montreux Jazz Festival in Switzerland. In the former he was reunited with Hawkins, along with two younger reed players and a rhythm group. *Further Definitions* includes two of his best (but not especially well-known) songs, "Doozy" and "Blue Star." In his Montreux performance, he worked as part of a quartet that included pianist Ray Bryant, one of many much younger musicians with whom Carter played in his later years. There were seven songs; on five Carter played alto saxophone and on two both saxophone and trumpet, once muted and once open bell.

Critics raved about Carter's appearance at Montreux in his seventies and later performances, but he wished to be judged by his playing, not his age. Carter did not give up his instruments until he was in his nineties, when he decided that his playing was no longer up to his own standards.

Songbook. In 1996 MusicMasters Records issued *Songbook.* Carter wrote hundreds of songs but did not often have his own orchestras play them and generally seemed to disdain promoting them. Although he worked on this project, he did not, at the age of eighty-eight, take part in its promotion. The performers included such well-known singers as Joe Williams, Peggy Lee, Bobby Short, and cornetist Warren Vaché. The project brought a selection of his songs together for the first time. Although praised by reviewers, it was not a commercial success, but it brought together for the first time fifteen of Carter's best songs, including his only hit song, "Cow-Cow Boogie."

Musical Legacy

Carter played with a pure tone, dexterity, dynamic shading, and an ease in all registers. His early work was in chamber and orchestral jazz, but he contributed to the swing music of the late 1930's as performer and arranger. In the early 1940's he employed many of the young men who would establish a new era in jazz a few years later: Gillespie, J. J. Johnson, Max Roach, Art Pepper, and Miles Davis. Although Carter's roots were in more traditional jazz, he learned from these men and incorporated later jazz developments in his own playing and composing. Carter's capacity for adapting musical ideas from later musicians is one of his most striking achievements.

In his later years he was involved in educational work. A self-educated man, he began teaching during the 1970's at Princeton University and other institutions of higher learning and supported the development of an important jazz research and education center at Rutgers University.

Carter made many trips to Europe and also performed in South America, Africa, the Middle East, and Japan, even when he was well up in his eighties. He won numerous awards, including the National Medal of Arts, conferred by President Bill Clinton on December 20, 2000.

Robert P. Ellis

Further Reading
Berger, Monroe, Edward Berger, and James Patrick. *Benny Carter: A Life in American Music.* 2d ed. 2 vols. Rutgers, N.J.: Institute of Jazz Studies, 2002. Definitive work on Carter's musical legacy, in-

cluding biography, discography, filmography, and bibliography.

Gioia, Ted. *The History of Jazz.* New York: Oxford University Press, 1997. Jazz historian stresses Carter's songwriting, particularly his expertise as a composer of ballads.

Schuller, Gunther. *Early Jazz: Its Roots and Development.* New York: Oxford University Press, 1968. Schuller includes musical excerpts from Carter's arrangements for Fletcher Henderson's orchestra beginning in the late 1920's.

_____. *The Swing Era: The Development of Jazz, 1930-1945.* New York: Oxford University Press, 1989. A discussion of Carter's strengths and weaknesses, with an emphasis on Carter's versatility and his unusual success as a performer in his later years.

Stewart, Rex. *Jazz Masters of the Thirties.* New York: Macmillan, 1972. One of the musicians who played with Carter offers an extensive account of his influence.

See also: Basie, Count; Gershwin, George; Gillespie, Dizzy; Hampton, Lionel; Hawkins, Coleman; Henderson, Fletcher; Lee, Peggy; McPartland, Marian; Peterson, Oscar; Tatum, Art; Waller, Fats; Webster, Ben.

Elliott Carter

American classical composer

Carter's influence extended beyond the sphere typically occupied by modernist composers. His innovations in expressive character and rhythm inspired not only those who shared his stylistic bent but also those striking out in different musical directions. Prolific for more than five decades, he inspired postwar composers around the world.

Born: December 11, 1908; New York, New York
Also known as: Elliott Cook Carter, Jr. (full name)

Principal works

BALLETS (music): *Pocahontas*, 1936; *The Minotaur*, 1947.

CHAMBER WORKS: Eight Études and a Fantasy for Wind Quartet, 1949; String Quartet No. 1, 1951; String Quartet No. 2, 1959; String Quartet No. 3, 1971; *Triple Duo*, 1983 (for wind, string, and percussion instruments); *Penthode*, 1985 (for five groups of four instruments); String Quartet No. 4, 1986; String Quartet No. 5, 1995; *Mosaic for Harp and Ensemble*, 2004; *Réflexions for Ensemble*, 2004.

INSTRUMENTAL WORKS: Eight Pieces for Four Timpani, 1949; *Night Fantasies*, 1980 (for piano); *Changes*, 1983 (for guitar); *Intermittences*, 2005 (for piano); *Catenaires*, 2006 (for piano).

OPERA (music): *What Next?*, 1998 (libretto by Paul Griffiths).

ORCHESTRAL WORKS: Symphony No. 1, 1942; *Holiday Overture*, 1944; Piano Sonata, 1946; Cello Sonata, 1948; *Variations for Orchestra*, 1955; Double Concerto, 1961 (for piano, harpsichord, and two chamber orchestras); Piano Concerto, 1964; Concerto for Orchestra, 1969; *A Symphony of Three Orchestras*, 1976; Oboe Concerto, 1987; *Three Occasions*, 1989; Violin Concerto, 1990; Clarinet Concerto, 1996; *Symphonia: Sum Fluxae Pretium Spei*, 1996 (*I Am the Prize of Flowing Hope*); ASKO Concerto, 2000; Cello Concerto, 2001; *Boston Concerto*, 2002; *Dialogues*, 2003 (for piano and orchestra); *Three Illusions*, 2004 (in three parts: "Micomicón," "Fons Juventatis," and "More's Utopia"); *Soundings*, 2005 (for piano and orchestra); Horn Concerto, 2007; *Interventions*, 2007 (for piano and orchestra).

VOCAL WORKS: *Three Poems of Robert Frost*, 1942 (for baritone and ensemble); *A Mirror on Which to Dwell*, 1975 (for soprano and ensemble); *Syringa*, 1978 (for mezzo-soprano, bass-baritone, guitar, and ensemble); *In Sleep, in Thunder*, 1981 (for tenor and ensemble); *Of Challenge and of Love*, 1994 (for soprano and piano); *In the Distances of Sleep*, 2006 (for voice and ensemble).

WRITINGS OF INTEREST: *The Writings of Elliott Carter: An American Composer Looks at Modern Music*, 1977; *The New Worlds of Edgard Varèse: A Symposium*, 1979 (papers by Carter, Chou Wen-Chung, Robert P. Morgan, and Sherman van Solkema).

The Life

Elliott Cook Carter, Jr. was born in New York but spent a lot of time in Europe; his father was a wealthy importer and his family traveled frequently. In particular, he spent a great deal of time in France, learning French at a young age. He started piano lessons early, but his musical development was impacted less by his family than by the encouragement he received from Charles Ives, whom he met in 1924 and with whom he attended many concerts. Carter had a broad range of musical interests, stylistically speaking. He was interested in many of the modernists of the early twentieth century, such as Henry Cowell, Edgard Varèse, and Roger Sessions, even though Carter's early works seem to belie this influence.

In 1926 Carter began to study at Harvard but felt that the music department was too conservative. Instead, he turned to studying Greek and English literature. He maintained some musical studies, in solfeggio and piano, and ultimately earned a master's degree in music in 1932. Among his primary teachers were Gustav Holst and Walter Piston. Like many American composers of his generation, he studied in Paris with Nadia Boulanger, first privately and then at the École Normale de Musique. His move to Europe was at least in part because of the enjoyable experiences he had during his travels in his youth. Upon completion of his studies in 1935, he returned to New York to devote his time to composing. He assumed the directorship of Ballet Caravan. The music he composed for this group was typical of neoclassicism of the time—most clearly displaying the influence of his studies with Boulanger.

Carter's later works (after 1948) established him as one of the foremost innovators in the twentieth century. He held a number of teaching posts on the East Coast, primarily in the New York area, where he taught at Columbia University, Queens College, with his longest stint at the Juilliard School from 1964 to 1984. Carter received the Pulitzer Prize twice, once in 1960 and then again in 1973. In 1987 the Paul Sacher Foundation arranged to acquire all of Carter's manuscripts, assuring their place alongside the papers of such other twentieth century masters as Igor Stravinsky, Pierre Boulez, Béla Bartók, Paul Hindemith, and Richard Strauss.

The Music

Early Works. Carter's early works bear a strong resemblance to his neoclassical contemporaries, many of whom also studied with Boulanger in Paris. Two compositions in particular, *Pocahontas* and *The Minotaur*, suggest that Carter's compositional output was following a path similar to that of his friend Aaron Copland. The former was written for the Ballet Caravan and the latter for the Ballet Society (the precursor of the New York City Ballet). Style and timing help explain why Carter's career did not flourish in quite the same manner as that of his contemporaries at the time. *Pocahontas* is rather similar to Copland's style and had its premiere on the same night as Copland's *Billy the Kid*. It is also interesting to note that the works deal with American and Native American subjects, respectively. *The Minotaur*

Elliott Carter. (AP/Wide World Photos)

combines Copland-like strains with a healthy dose of Stravinsky. It shared a number of other similarities with *Orpheus*, a work by Stravinsky to which it is often compared. *Orpheus* was produced by George Balanchine, and Carter collaborated with the legendary choreographer on *The Minotaur*. Both are based on Greek myths, and both were premiered by the Ballet Society. While these early works did take strides away from neoclassicism, particularly in their dramatic expression, they did not compare favorably to the works of Carter's more established colleagues. Radical stylistic change was, however, on the horizon.

Sonata for Cello. In 1948, the year after *The Minotaur* was completed, Carter composed a work that pinpoints when he left the path of the mainstream, populist composers he seemed to be emulating. Carter was looking for new rhythmic structures not found in traditional Western art music. He found his inspiration in the music of Africa, Arabia, and Southeast Asia. Initially, Carter composed the second movement, the only one that utilizes key signatures. The tonality and jazzy sounds in this movement were identified by Carter as a parody of the work of his American colleagues at the time. It is interesting to note that after attending concerts together, Carter and Ives would often rush to a piano to play parodies of the various composers they had heard; perhaps that game was the genesis of this movement. The other movements, however, foreshadow Carter's later works in their simple form and modernist language.

This work displays some of the devices that would pervade Carter's later compositions. It shows his penchant for assigning different characteristics to different instruments. In this case, the cello begins with a free, legato melody, while the piano's clocklike percussion contrasts sharply. The characteristics of each instrument shift dramatically and between movements seem to trade such elements as melody and tempo. In this work Carter also establishes his method of "metric modulation," a technique that owes a debt to the composer's exploration of the rhythms of other cultures. The music shifts through proportionally related tempi rather quickly, the rhythmic analogue of modulation between keys in a tonal system. It was not originally well received—in Carter's own words, "Everybody hated it."

String Quartet No. 2. The change in compositional philosophy in the Sonata for Cello led to a period of exploration and discovery, involving increasingly complex polyrhythms and bearing the influence of his friend Ives, along with that of Conlon Nancarrow and Béla Bartók. His String Quartet No. 1 and the *Variations for Orchestra* combined these influences and expanded his ideas while achieving the critical success that the Cello Sonata did not. The String Quartet No. 2 represents the next step in the evolution of Carter's compositional language. Much more dissonant and angular than his earlier pieces, this work divides the ensemble into four characters, each identified by varying intervals, rhythms, tempi, and dynamics. Also, the members of the quartet are instructed how to sit: in pairs, with violin and viola seated across from violin and cello and as far apart as possible, so that it seems as if they are playing two distinct pieces. Carter won his first Pulitzer Prize in 1960 for this work.

Later Works. Carter remained prolific throughout his long career, and the concepts and devices created in the Cello Sonata and String Quartet No. 2 were expanded upon in the works that followed, establishing him as one of the true innovators of the twentieth century. Among these devices are chords whose notes exhibit all possible intervals (all-interval chords), increasingly complex polyrhythms, a circular time plan, and opposing forces and characters in his chamber and orchestral works. These, along with an increasing expressiveness, are shown in the String Quartet No. 3 (for which he won his second Pulitzer Prize), *A Mirror on Which to Dwell* for soprano and chamber ensemble, *Triple Duo*, and the Oboe Concerto. While the evolution of his musical language was rapid and sharp in the late 1940's, Carter never disavowed his earlier works and seemed quite comfortable with their place in his oeuvre.

Musical Legacy

Carter never belonged to one group or symbolized one movement. He is usually described as a modernist, but this label does not tell the whole story. While his works show tremendous compositional control and a highly chromatic character, he never explicitly utilizes the serial system, as did most of the composers who are often mentioned in the same breath, such as Milton Babbitt, Pierre Boulez, or Karlheinz Stockhausen. Carter's influence has been felt on both sides of the Atlantic, and his innovations, particularly in rhythm, have impressed composers whose styles and philosophies range far beyond the circle of modernism. Carter described his compositional goal as follows: "I want to invent something I haven't heard before."

David J. Weisberg

Further Reading

Carter, Elliott. *Elliott Carter: Collected Essays and Lectures, 1937-1995.* Edited by Jonathan W. Bernard. Rochester, N.Y.: University of Rochester Press, 1998. Includes writings and talks by Carter. Many are nontechnical, dealing with his influences, experiences, and compositional goals.

_____. *Harmony Book.* Edited by Nicholas Hopkins and John F. Link. New York: Carl Fischer Music, 2002. A comprehensive catalog Carter kept during his compositional processes of the harmonies he derived. Includes an interview with the composer and examples from the works with detailed explanations.

Link, John F. *Elliott Carter: A Guide to Research.* New York: Routledge, 2000. Comprehensive guide to sources. Includes list of compositions (published and unpublished), interviews with the composer, and articles about the composer.

Rosen, Charles. "Elliott Carter." In *Dictionary of Contemporary Music,* edited by John Vinton. New York: E. P. Dutton, 1974. Reference article about Carter, including biography and insightful descriptions of works.

Schiff, David. *The Music of Elliott Carter.* 2d ed. Ithaca, N.Y.: Cornell University Press, 1998. Complete examination of the composer and his body of work by a former compositional student. Includes essays by the composer, full-length interviews, and anecdotes. Combines historical background of the various works with discussions of the composer's techniques.

See also: Barenboim, Daniel; Boulanger, Nadia; Copland, Aaron; Cowell, Henry; Dodge, Charles; Holst, Gustav; Ives, Charles; Levine, James; Ma, Yo-Yo; Nancarrow, Conlon; Seeger, Ruth Crawford; Solti, Sir Georg; Stravinsky, Igor.

Maybelle Carter

American country guitarist

As part of the musical Carter family, Carter helped create modern commercial country music, familial ties giving early country music its musical flavor as well as its stage presence.

Born: May 10, 1909; Nickelsville, Virginia
Died: October 23, 1978; Nashville, Tennessee
Also known as: Maybelle Addington (birth name); Mother Maybelle
Member of: The Carter Family; the Carter Sisters and Mother Maybelle

Principal recordings

ALBUMS: *Mother Maybelle Carter,* 1951; *Queen of the Autoharp,* 1964; *Living Legend,* 1965; *An Historic Reunion: Sara and Maybelle, the Original Carters,* 1967 (with Sara Carter and Joe Carter); *Will the Circle Be Unbroken,* 1972 (with the Nitty Gritty Dirt Band); *Wildwood Pickin',* 1997.

The Life

Maybelle Addington was born on May 10, 1909, in Nickelsville, Virginia, in the small Appalachian community of Rich Valley in Scott County. Of the many valleys created by the five mountain ridges that ran through the county, the neighboring one, Poor Valley, more accurately described conditions there. Isolated and sparsely populated, with no more than twenty thousand residents, the county was home to farmers and coal miners. For these people, life was mostly a struggle. However, they took consolation in their faith, and the church was the most important community institution in both Poor Valley and Rich Valley. In church, people found another comfort, music. Gospel singing with the congregation on Sundays and fiddle music and square dances on Saturday were the main diversions from hard lives. What we know today as country music was born in this environment.

Although Maybelle and her cousin, Sara Dougherty, grew up within a quarter mile of each other in Rich Valley, they were not especially close as children. Their lives became entwined later, when they married brothers from Poor Valley, Ezra and Alvin Pleasant (A. P.) Carter.

The Music

A. P. Carter held a variety of jobs before he met and married Dougherty in 1915. It was a love of music and Sara's beautiful alto voice that brought them together. In 1926 they were joined by Maybelle (around the time she married Ezra, or "Eck"), and they unsuccessfully played before a Brunswick Records talent scout. The following year, however, they recorded six sides for three hundred dollars—a significant sum when the average American wage was seven hundred dollars a year—for Victor executive Ralph Peer at an audition twenty-six miles away in Bristol, Tennessee (a day's drive from Poor Valley, an especially trying summer journey for Maybelle, who was eight months pregnant).

The Bristol Sessions. The so-called Bristol sessions have often been called the starting point of country music, and Peer discovered a wealth of talent—including Jimmie Rodgers—during his ten-day stay. Peer was one of the first New York record executives to realize the commercial potential in Southern rural music. Besides finding good acts, he also was looking for material that could be copyrighted, and song collector A. P. Carter was happy to help.

A. P. Carter's special genius was taking lyrics and melodies from old traditional mountain songs and "working them up" (as he called it) with Maybelle and Sara into something marketable. Several further recording sessions with Peer followed, with significant sales—more than seven hundred thousand records—until the stock market crash in 1929 threw the country into the Great Depression. This hurt sales and prevented the Carters from doing radio tours and from touring the vaudeville circuit. As Maybelle and Sara began to devote more attention to their children and families, the Carter Family got together mainly for recording records.

The Carter Style. The music the Carters were making—focusing on hard times, personal tragedies, and the rewards offered in heaven—was just the mix American listeners wanted to hear, especially as the Dust Bowl winds and drought punished the South and Midwest. In the early 1930's, Sara lost patience with A. P. Carter's temper and his

sullen ways, and she fell in love with another man. She divorced A. P. Carter in 1936. Though estranged, the trio still performed professionally. Oddly, the divorce bound the group together more tightly (more work meant more royalties, which allowed A. P. Carter to pay off his settlement to Sara more quickly).

By 1938 the Carter Family was broadcasting on XERA, a five hundred-kilowatt radio station in Mexico across the border at Del Rio, Texas. These transmissions were so powerful, they could be heard all over North America. The two years the Carter Family performed on XERA increased their record sales and their audience significantly. The station closed when the United States and Mexico signed a broadcast agreement in 1941. Though they performed off and on as a group on a North Carolina radio show, the original Carter Family effectively was finished by 1943. A. P. Carter retired to a country store in Poor Valley, and Sara and her second husband moved to California.

After the Breakup. Maybelle and her daughters Helen, June, and Anita then went on to form the group the Carter Sisters and Mother Maybelle, and they played for three years, from 1943 to 1946, at radio station WRNL in Richmond, Virginia. For the rest of the 1940's, they played on various barn dance radio shows throughout the South. June was a natural salesperson, and she was committed to becoming a professional musician as well as a comedian. In 1950 Maybelle and the Carter Sisters, along with fledging guitar giant Chet Atkins, went to the Grand Ole Opry, the mecca of country-music venues. Television appearances throughout the early 1950's followed, including a tour with Elvis Presley in 1955 (during which Anita and Presley had a brief flirtation). Meanwhile, from 1952 to 1956, A. P. Carter and his ex-wife Sara and their children performed and recorded locally with little fanfare. When A. P. Carter died in 1960, the Carter Sisters and Mother Maybelle took back the Carter Family name.

With the rise of rock and roll and sanitized Nashville-produced popular country music, interest by the public in older traditional and hillbilly sounds waned. However, with the folk music revival in the 1960's, Maybelle was in great demand once again as a solo performer on the college and festival circuit. There was a renewed interest in Carter Family materials, and artists as diverse as Presley and the Kingston Trio covered their songs. Maybelle reunited with Sara to perform at the famous Newport Folk Festival in 1967 (and a few more times before Sara died in 1979). In 1968 June married Johnny Cash, and they became stars of their television show in the 1970's. Mother Maybelle and daughters Helen and Anita appeared on many of these weekly shows. Before her death in 1978, Maybelle went on to do some important recordings, especially on the Nitty Gritty Dirt Band's seminal album, *Will the Circle Be Unbroken* (a title based on a Carter song).

Musical Legacy

The Carter Family is the "first family" of country music, and Mother Maybelle is the matriarch. While the original trio broke up in the early days of World War II, Maybelle kept alive the traditions and songs for nearly another four decades. The original Carter Family recorded 287 sides (all are still available), and half of them are part of the modern country-music canon. In 2004 a tribute compact disc titled *The Unbroken Circle: The Musical Heritage of the Carter Family* was released. The contributors included the most noted country and crossover artists, including Willie Nelson, Johnny Cash, Sheryl Crow, Shawn Colvin, and John Prine.

Maybelle never learned to read music, but her way of playing the guitar—often called a Carter run or a Carter scratch—changed the way country musicians approached the instrument. A largely self-taught guitar virtuoso, Maybelle picked parts of the melody line while strumming chords. This distinctive way of blending melody on the bass strings with harmony on the treble strings while forming a partial chord has affected three generations of players, from country to rock. The Grateful Dead's Jerry Garcia, the Rolling Stones' Keith Richards, Atkins, and Doc Watson are just a few of the many guitarists who have publicly acknowledged their musical debt to Mother Maybelle.

The Carter Family was inducted into the Country Music Hall of Fame in 1970, the first group so honored. However, the Carter Family's influence was not bound by country music. Many songs, such as "Will the Circle Be Unbroken," painted a portrait of a United States mired in an economic depression and poised at the bring of war. Most of the music

from the film *O Brother, Where Art Thou?* (2001) were songs that A. P. Carter gathered, arranged, and played with Maybelle and Sara. The dozens of family acts and groups of relatives that perform at country and bluegrass venues can trace that heritage to the Carter Family. In the last years of her life, Maybelle was recognized as the mother of country music.

James Stanlaw

Further Reading

Bufwack, Mary. "Carter Sisters." In *The Encyclopedia of Country Music: The Ultimate Guide to the Music.* New York: Oxford University Press, 1998. A general article on the group Maybelle formed with her daughters in 1943.

Carr, Patrick. *The Illustrated History of Country Music.* New York: Random House, 1995. An accessible thematic overview of the development of the country-music genre, with hundreds of photographs from the magazine's archives. Provides a good description of the growth and development of country music during the Great Depression, when the Carter Family was just beginning.

Dorman, Katie. "Something Old, Something New: The Carter Family's Bristol Sessions Recordings." In *The Bristol Sessions: Writings About the Big Bang of Country Music,* edited by Charles Wolfe and Ted Olson. Jefferson, N.C.: McFarland, 2005. A definitive account of what went right and wrong for the Carter Family at the birth of country music in 1927.

McCloud, Barry. "Carter Family (a.k.a. the Carter Sisters)" and "Mother Maybelle Carter." In *Definitive Country: The Ultimate Encyclopedia of Country Music and Its Performers,* edited by Barry McCloud. New York: Perigee, 1995. Succinct but informative articles on Maybelle's life and on her career after the original Carter Family trio broke up.

Malone, Bill. *Country Music USA.* Rev. 2d ed. Austin: University of Texas Press, 1985. An excellent single-volume history of the genre through the 1970's. Good material on the commercialization of hillbilly music.

Stambler, Irwin, and Grelun Landon. "Carter, Mother Maybelle." In *The Encyclopedia of Folk, Country, and Western Music.* 2d ed. New York: St. Martin's Press, 1984. An article devoted only to

Maybelle, a rarity among the standard country-music encyclopedias.

Zwonitzer, Mark, and Charles Hirshberg. *Will You Miss Me When I Am Gone? The Carter Family and Their Legacy in American Music.* New York: Simon & Schuster, 2004. The first biography of the Carter Family and their musical influence. Largely based on oral histories and on recollections of relatives and friends, the book has no bibliography or source notes.

See also: Atkins, Chet; Cash, Johnny; Cobain, Kurt; Nelson, Willie; Presley, Elvis; Richards, Keith; Scruggs, Earl; Seeger, Mike; Watson, Doc.

Enrico Caruso

Italian opera singer

Caruso, possessed of a magnificent, expressive, tenor voice, combined with classic technique, was a leading operatic star, and he was the first singer to be heard by millions of people through the newly invented gramophone.

Born: February 25, 1873; Naples, Italy
Died: August 2, 1921; Naples, Italy

Principal works

OPERATIC ROLES: Enzo Grimaldo in Amilcare Ponchielli's *La gioconda*, 1895; Edgardo Ravenswood in Gaetano Donizetti's *Lucia di Lammermoor*, 1895; Duke in Giuseppe Verdi's *Rigoletto*, 1895; Don José in Georges Bizet's *Carmen*, 1896; Rodolfo in Giacomo Puccini's *La Bohème*, 1896; Canio in Ruggero Leoncavallo's *Pagliacci*, 1897; Loris in Umberto Giordano's *Fedora*, 1898; Radamès in Verdi's *Aida*, 1900; Mario Cavaradossi in Puccini's *Tosca*, 1900; Nemorino in Donizetti's *L'elisir d'amore*, 1901; B. F. Pinkerton in Puccini's *Madama Butterfly*, 1906; Lyonel in Friedrich von Flotow's *Martha*, 1906; Prince of Urgel in Verdi's *Il Trovatore*, 1908; Dick Johnson in Puccini's *La fanciulla del west*, 1910; Don Alvaro in Verdi's *La forza del destino*, 1918; Eléazar in Fromental Halévy's *La Juive*, 1919.

Principal recordings

ALBUMS: *Cielo e mar aria from Ponchielli's Gioconda*, 1902; *E lucevan le stelle Puccini's Tosca*, 1902; *Non t'amo pui aria*, 1902; *Pagliacci vesti la giubba*, 1902; *Il songo manon*, 1904; *Rigoletto la donna è mobile*, 1904; *Tiempo antico*, 1916; *Vesti la giubba*, 1920.

The Life

Enrico Caruso (kah-ROO-soh), born in 1873 in Naples, Italy, to Marcellino and Anna Baldini Caruso, was the third of seven children; his two older brothers died in infancy. A mechanic, Caruso's father earned barely enough money to supply his family with the necessities. Although an unruly student, Caruso developed a great love of singing. At eleven, he became the lead soloist of his school's choir, earning enough money to pay for private voice lessons. At thirteen, he left school to work at a factory, although he continued to train with Naples's talented musical teachers. Caruso was drafted into the Italian army, but he was a lackluster soldier. Discharged at the age of twenty, he supported himself by singing at various Neapolitan events and eventually at the opera.

Caruso's star rose quickly, and he soon developed an international reputation. On July 2, 1898, Caruso and his longtime mistress, opera singer Ada Giachetti, had a son, Rodolpho. On September 7, 1904, Caruso and Giachetti had a second son, Enrico. Meanwhile, Caruso was starring at the New York Metropolitan Opera and recording operatic and popular songs, which made him world famous and brought him great wealth and a lavish lifestyle.

In 1907 relations between Caruso and Ada became strained after he had an affair with Ada's sister, Rina. Caruso purchased the opulent Villa Bellosguardo estate outside Florence, where he relaxed by drawing outstanding caricatures. In 1908 Ada scandalously left Caruso for their chauffeur, and Caruso acquired a new mistress, Mildred Meffert. On August 20, 1918, Caruso married a young American aristocrat, Dorothy Park Benjamin. Their daughter, Gloria, was born on December 18, 1919. In December, 1920, Caruso, taxed by overwork, contracted pleurisy, a disease of the lungs. The illness fatal, he returned to Naples in 1921, where he died.

The Music

When he perfected his singing technique, Caruso rose meteorically in the world of opera. A tenor, Caruso debuted at Naples's Teatro Nuovo in 1894. He was approved by the composer Giacomo Puccini to sing the role of Rodolfo in *La Bohème* in the 1897 summer opera season at Livorno. The next year Caruso performed for Czar Nicholas II in St. Petersburg and at the Teatro La Opera in Buenos Aires. In 1900 Caruso began performing regularly at La Scala opera house in Milan. Caruso debuted in Covent Garden in London in 1902 and at the Metropolitan Opera in New York in 1903, where for the next seventeen seasons, until his death, he would star as the lead tenor. Caruso received $960 for each performance at the Metropolitan Opera, which in a few years reached three thousand dollars. For singing engagements, Caruso received as much as fifteen thousand dollars. He was paid a hundred thousand dollars for each of his two motion-picture appearances in 1919, in *My Cousin* and *The Splendid Romance*.

Enrico Caruso. (Library of Congress)

Gramophone Recordings. On April 11, 1902, Caruso made his first recording for the newly invented gramophone. In 1904 Caruso entered a long-term contract with Victor Talking Machine Company. The strength of his voice and his technical control were perfectly suited to phonographic technology, and his records were an incredible success. During his career he would make more than two hundred 78-rpm records, which sold millions of copies, earning Caruso as much as five million dollars, prompting some to ask, "Did Caruso make the gramophone or did the gramophone make Caruso?"

As can be heard on these recordings, despite their primitive technology, Caruso had a beautiful voice, often described as lyrical, velvety, and lustrous. Although a tenor, Caruso retained some of the rich timbre and lower register of a baritone. His voice was noble and bold, and yet it contained a disarming warmth and sweetness at its core. A practiced professional, Caruso had near-perfect control of his pitch, tone, and range. His intonation was flawless, his high notes clarion, his lower register dark and vibrant. He was capable of precise phrasing, with a mastery of portamento and legato. Caruso had tremendous lung and chest capacity, with disciplined breath and diaphragm control. His voice was flexible, and he adapted it with precision to every role. Excelling in the older bel canto style, Caruso had a lively, masculine voice that was also well suited to the newer realistic verismo style. He was unabashed in exhibiting passionate, emotional singing. In addition to opera, Caruso's concert and recording repertoire included famous Neapolitan love songs, such as "Santa Lucia" and "O sole mio."

Vesti la Giubba. Caruso first sung the role of Canio in Ruggero Leoncavallo's *Pagliacci* in 1897. It would become Caruso's most famous role, and he sang it in seventy-eight major productions. His versatility and passion were put to great effect as Canio, the head of a troupe of traveling comic players, who sings with ironic laughter, pathos, and rage. Caruso's rendition of Canio's final aria, "Vesti la giubba" (put on the costume), with its heart-rending plea of "Ridi Pagliacco" (laugh, clown) and sobbing conclusion, overpowered listeners. In 1907

Caruso's recording of "Vesti la giubba" was the first record to sell more than a million copies.

"Over There." With his colorful personality, generosity, and Italian mannerisms, Caruso was an appealing celebrity to millions of Americans. He returned America's affection, despite a 1906 conviction for pinching a woman at the Central Park Zoo. Caruso raised money for the Allied effort in World War I, adopting George M. Cohan's patriotic war song, "Over There," which he sang at Liberty Bond rallies throughout the country. On September 19, 1918, he sang "Over There" before a huge audience in New York's Central Park, and his heroic recording of the song in 1918 in English and French is thrilling, expressing the martial spirit of the song with great energy.

Musical Legacy

Caruso is one of the great opera tenors of all time, in a celebrated tradition dating from eighteenth century star Luigi Bassi to twentieth century star Luciano Pavarotti. Caruso's fame coincided with the rise of the phonograph, and as such Caruso became the first international celebrity of singing, whose mellifluous voice was heard by vast audiences. His recordings had the widest influence, loved by millions of people who knew little about opera. Caruso changed the world of opera, reestablishing the celebrated role of male tenor, perfecting verismo style, and bringing operatic sensibilities to a wide populace.

Howard Bromberg

Further Reading

Caruso, Dorothy. *Enrico Caruso: His Life and Death.* New York: Simon & Schuster, 1945. These memoirs by Caruso's last wife served as the basis for the 1956 film *The Great Caruso,* starring Mario Lanza.

Caruso, Enrico, Jr., and Andrew Farkas. *Enrico Caruso: My Father and My Family.* Portland, Oreg.: Amadeus Press, 1990. Caruso's youngest son relates firsthand information about his father, and he focuses on his and his siblings' chaotic lives as the children of Caruso.

Marafioti, P. M. *Caruso's Method of Voice Production.* Mineola, N.Y.: Dover Publications, 1981. This describes Caruso's scientific and methodical approach to voice control.

Scott, Michael. *The Great Caruso.* Boston: Northeastern University Press, 1989. This comprehensive biography offers a critical assessment of Caruso's phonographic career. Includes detailed discography.

See also: Björling, Jussi; Cohan, George M.; Dodge, Charles; Melba, Dame Nellie; Pavarotti, Luciano; Puccini, Giacomo; Puente, Tito.

Henri Casadesus

French classical composer and arranger

A member of an illustrious French family of musicians, Casadesus founded the Société des Instruments Anciens, dedicated to the performance and dissemination of early music. He was a notable advocate of the viola d'amore, reviving the instrument's popularity.

Born: September 30, 1879; Paris, France
Died: May 31, 1947; Paris, France

Principal works

OPERETTA (music): *Le Rosier,* 1923 (libretto by Maurice Devilliers).

ORCHESTRAL WORKS: Concerto for Viola and Orchestra in B Minor, 1924; Twenty-four Preludes for Viola d'Amore and Harp, 1931; Concerto for Viola in C Minor, 1947.

VOCAL WORKS: *La Sommeilleuse,* 1949; *Sur les jolis ponts de Paris,* 1949.

Principal recordings

ALBUM (as arranger): *Maurice Maréchal Book 3,* 1998.

The Life

Henri Casadesus (kas-ah-DEE-sus) was the son of Louis Casadesus, an amateur violinist and guitarist. Seven of Louis's children became professional musicians, including Francis, founder and director of the American Conservatory at Fontainebleau, and Robert, a pianist and composer. Casadesus was educated at the Paris Conservatory, where he studied music history with Albert Lavignac and viola with Théophile Laforge.

Between 1910 and 1917, Casadesus was violist for the Capet Quartet. He also served as director of the Théâtre de la Gaîté-Lyrique in Paris and the opera theater of Liège, Belgium. With bassist Edouard Nanny, Casadesus performed concerts of early music, leading to the formation of the Société des Instruments Anciens Casadesus in 1901. Camille Saint-Saëns was named honorary president.

The group's membership included, at various times, Casadesus's brothers Marcel and Marius on viola da gamba and pardessus de viole and his sister, Regina Patorni-Casadesus, on harpsichord. Another brother, Francis, occasionally conducted the group. Their repertoire included "rediscovered" works of old masters and lesser known composers such as François Franccœur and Jean-Joseph Mouret. Many of these works were likely composed by Casadesus and other members of the group. Casadesus amassed a large collection of musical instruments, some of which he sold to the Boston Symphony Orchestra in 1926.

The Music

Casadesus's notable works are those that he wrote and attributed to early composers, such as George Frideric Handel and Carl Philipp Emanuel Bach. In this sense, he was much like his contemporary Fritz Kreisler, the great violinist, who also composed works in the style of other composers and did not acknowledge who had created them. Casadesus also wrote operettas, ballet music, film scores, songs, and a method for viola d'amore. In general he was a master of late-Baroque styles, but his music, forged and otherwise, recounts these historical genres from a nineteenth century perspective. His operettas are derivative of the works of Jacques Offenbach but possess a classical bent with clear textures and lyric content.

Le Rosier. Set to a libretto by Maurice Devilliers, a member of the Société des Instruments Anciens, the work premiered in 1923 at the Liège Opera and later, in Paris, at the Théâtre des Folies-Dramatiques in 1925. The operetta was one of several similar works composed by Casadesus after World War I, likely to raise money for the financially strapped musician. Set in three acts with an obligatory ballet, the work is well crafted if not de-

rivative. Stylistically, *Le Rosier* recalls nineteenth century opéra bouffe, including a cancan and alternating vocal combinations with ensembles. Casadesus employs chromaticism and nonharmonic tones strategically throughout but never at the expense of tonal clarity and lyrical melodies.

Concerto for Viola and Orchestra in B Minor. Originally published in 1924 as a work by Handel, subsequent analysis has determined that it is a work by Casadesus in the style of Handel. Written for viola and orchestra, the work has been transcribed for a number of other instruments, and its popularity is evidenced by performances by the famous violist William Primrose and by its appearance in the Suzuki-method canon. The work enjoyed significant fame as a Handel concerto until its true origins were discovered in the 1950's, and it demonstrates that Casadesus had a masterly command of the Handel compositional style.

Set in three movements, the concerto possesses the virtuosic, the expressive, and the rhythmic vitality inherent in many works of its kind. In typical Baroque concerto fashion, the first movement is built on rapid sixteenth-note figures weaving in and out of closely related tonalities. The second movement is slow and expressively lyrical, with a simple but emotionally rich melody. The last movement is lively and playful, with continuous motion throughout.

Twenty-four Preludes for Viola d'Amore and Harp. Published in 1931 as part of the *Technique de la viole d'amour*, an instructional method for the instrument, the preludes span the gamut of Baroque compositional styles. Though the music is historically derived, the works are well crafted and musically charming, highlighting Casadesus's unique compositional abilities.

Concerto for Viola in C Minor. This concerto was performed by the Société des Instruments Anciens and eventually published in 1947. It was attributed to Johann Christian Bach until further stylistic research led to the conclusion that it was written by Casadesus. The work is characterized less by the gallant style that one might expect from Bach and more by rich Romantic textures.

The first and last movements are characterized by rapid rhythmic figurations, and the middle movement is slower and more lyrical. The opening allegro has a vibrant and dramatic theme shared by orchestra and solo, accompanied by richly textured harmonies. The slow adagio is expressive, with a highly ornamented melody. The last movement is in the style of a gigue, with a solo voice performing energetic arpeggiations capped with a climactic cadenza.

Musical Legacy

Although his performance style was embedded in a Romantic conception of early music, Casadesus was an important figure in the historic performance movement of the first half of the twentieth century. As leader of the Société des Instruments Anciens, he brought the music of early composers to audiences around the world. He played a significant role in the rebirth of the viola d'amore by promoting it as an expressive musical instrument and not merely a museum piece. His compositions for the instrument reflected an impressive creative gift and musicality. Casadesus's uncanny talent for mimicry assured his legacy as a first-rate musical forger. He mastered the style of the late Baroque and presented his own work as that of older masters. His contributions to operetta demonstrated a high level of craftsmanship and command of this entertaining genre.

Brian Doherty

Further Reading

Haskell, Harry. *The Early Music Revival: A History.* London: Thames & Hudson, 1988. Examines Casadesus's role in the evolution of the early music movement.

IBM Gallery of Science and Art. *The Casadesus Collection of Old Musical Instruments.* New York: IBM Gallery of Science and Art, 1964. A detailed description of the portion of Casadesus's instrument collection sold to the Boston Symphony Orchestra in 1926. Includes background information on how Casadesus assembled the collection.

See also: Kreisler, Fritz; Suzuki, Shin'ichi.

Pablo Casals

Spanish classical cellist, composer, and conductor

Casals transformed cello technique and brought recognition to the cello as a solo instrument, contributing greatly to a reinvigoration of the music of Johann Sebastian Bach.

Born: December 29, 1876; El Vendrell, Catalonia, Spain
Died: October 22, 1973; San Juan, Puerto Rico
Also known as: Pau Carlos Salvador Casals y Defilló (full name)

Principal works

CHORAL WORKS: *El pessebre*, 1960; *Hymn for the United Nations*, 1971.

ORCHESTRAL WORKS: *Revérie*, 1896 (for cello and piano); *La Sardana*, 1926; Sonata, 1972 (for violin and piano).

Principal recordings

ALBUMS: *A Concert at the White House, November 13, 1961*, 1961; *The Art of Pablo Casals*, 1964; *Pablo Casals at Montserrat*, 1968; *Casals Conducts Mozart*, 1970; *Pablo Casals in Concert*, 1972; *Pablo Casals Conducts Beethoven*, 1975; *Bach: Suites for Cello*, 1988; *Pablo Casals Plays Works for Cello and Orchestra*, 1989; *Beethoven: Cello Sonatas*, 1990; *Casals Festivals at Prades, Vols. 1 and 2*, 1991; *Early Recordings, 1925-1928*, 1994.

The Life

Pau Carlos Salvador Casals y Defilló, who would come to be known as Pablo Casals (kah-SAHLZ), was the third of eleven children born to Pilar Defilló i Amiguet and Carlos Casals i Riba. The couple resided in El Vendrell, Spain, a small Catalonian town to the southwest of Barcelona, where Carlos, a talented pianist and vocalist, served as organist at the local church, led a men's chorus, and gave private instruction in piano and voice. Thus the young Casals was immediately immersed in music. Soon after Pablo, or Pau, as he was known in Catalan, began piano studies at age four, his father permitted him to join the church choir, and by six or seven the child was composing short pieces for the piano. Pablo first heard a violoncello at the concert of a professional chamber trio in 1888, and at once he became enamored of the instrument. His father managed to obtain a small cello for his son, and Pablo, at twelve, began preliminary instruction. Within the same year, Pablo and his mother traveled to Barcelona, so that he could begin serious musical study at the Municipal School of Music.

As a student in Barcelona, Casals performed regularly with a trio at a local café and with several local orchestras. Wherever the young cellist went, his playing was well received and his talent widely recognized, perhaps most importantly by Isaac Albéniz, Spain's foremost pianist at the time. With Albéniz's recommendation, Casals came under the patronage of Count Guillermo Morphy y Férriz de Guzmán, private secretary to María Cristina, the queen regent of Spain. The count tutored Casals in a broad range of subjects, both academic and musical, and María Cristina, a pianist and enthusiastic patron of the arts, awarded Casals a stipend, enabling him to study at the Madrid Conservatory. After an unsuccessful attempt to transfer to the Brussels Conservatory and a short and disastrous stint as a professional musician in Paris, Casals returned to Barcelona in 1896. His reputation now well established within Spain, he performed in chamber concerts, in recitals, and as a soloist with the Madrid Symphony Orchestra.

Three years later Casals made his first major European solo debuts, most notably in London and Paris. He toured extensively from 1899 through 1906, quickly achieving an international fame unrivaled by any cellist up until that time. He made his North American debut in 1901, he toured South America in 1903, and he performed in Russia for the first time in 1905. Success as a soloist created opportunities to perform chamber music with outstanding musicians of the day. In late 1905 or early 1906 Casals formed a chamber trio with the pianist Alfred Cortot and the violinist Jacques Thibaud, two talented French musicians who were accomplished soloists. The superstar trio performed together for almost thirty years and left several recordings as testament to their brilliant musicianship.

By the age of thirty, Casals had achieved international stardom, which in turn brought considerable

wealth. For a time, he found romance with a Portuguese cellist, Guilhermina Suggia, who lived with him in Paris for several years. Later, after an extremely brief courtship, he married an American soprano, Susan Scott Metcalfe, in April of 1914. However, the couple separated in 1927, eventually divorcing in 1957 so that Casals could marry his dying companion, Franchisca Vidal de Capdevila, a former student who had accompanied him into exile at the end of the Spanish Civil War.

By 1920, realizing the cello did not completely satisfy his musical creativity, Casals mounted the conductor's podium. That year he formed the Orquestra Pau Casals, which he conducted from its base in Barcelona until 1936, the year that marked the beginning of the conflict in Spain between the elected republican government and the Fascist opposition led by General Francisco Franco. When Franco assumed power in 1939, Casals, an ardent republican, was forced into exile. He relocated to Prades, France, and resided there during World War II, performing only sporadically and always to benefit victims of the European conflict and Franco's tyranny.

Casals's opposition to Franco was so vehement that Casals publicly declared his intent never to perform in countries that recognized the Fascist state of Spain. His music making continued, a tool he utilized to promote global peace and democracy. Casals spoke and performed several times at the United Nations, and he was a candidate for the Nobel Peace Prize in 1958. A year earlier he had set up residence in Puerto Rico, the birthplace of his mother and the home of his soon-to-be-bride, Marta Montañez, a cello student sixty years his junior.

In the last twenty years of his long life, Casals appeared as a cellist, a conductor, and a pedagogue at festivals in Prades and Puerto Rico. At the age of ninety-four, Casals performed for the last time at the United Nations, once again calling attention to the plight of his homeland, Catalonia, a region whose existence was being threatened by Franco's nationalist policies. Casals died in 1973, at the age of ninety-six, in San Juan, Puerto Rico, surrounded by friends, family, and the music of Bach.

The Music

New Cello Technique. Casals began to revolutionize the technique of playing cello before he was fifteen. Nineteenth century conventions dictated that the cellist hold the bow arm close to the body, thus forcing the right wrist to be crooked and, in Casals's view, creating unnecessary tension. José García, Casals's cello teacher, instructed his students to practice with a book held under the right arm in order to ensure proximity between the arm and the body. However, Casals chose to practice without the book, which enabled greater freedom of movement and permitted a more expressive variety of sounds to be produced. García also taught that the fingers of the left hand should be kept close to one another, requiring the cellist to shift the hand position in order to traverse the lengthy cello fingerboard and creating unwanted interruptions in the musical line. Casals instead played with his left hand in an open position, permitting him to extend his fingers to reach notes, decreasing the number of hand shifts, and preserving musical continuity. His technical innovations arose from his need for a particular musical result from the cello.

Pablo Casals. (Library of Congress)

Musical Interpretation. Under the influence of French philosopher Henri-Louis Bergson, Casals believed that music was a creative life force common to all humanity. Because he considered human life to be dynamic, he aspired to create a similar dynamism in his music. Casals described music as a "succession of rainbows"; in other words, music is constantly in oscillation, and each note or phrase comes in the context of a musical ebb and flow. For example, the pitches of a melody go higher or lower, and the tempo of the music slows or accelerates. The task of the interpreter is to bring these changes to the fore. When Casals played, long notes or repeated notes never slumped into monotony. Such notes were growing or subsiding, creating direction and sustaining vitality.

Casals often dropped the fingers of his left hand onto the fingerboard in a percussive manner, sometimes even plucking the string with his left hand, to set the string in vibration prior to the playing of a note, which created a robust, clean sound. He colored the tone by portamento (sliding the left hand's fingers on the strings), by varying the speed of his vibrato, and by experimenting with the strings' sonorities. Intonation was an expressive tool for Casals. Unlike the pianist, the string player can raise or lower the pitch by small increments, and Casals applied this technique in order to emphasize harmonic relationships between a succession of notes or those within a chord.

Casals and Bach. Casals's technical ingenuity was astounding, but his ultimate aim was to reveal the beauty of the composer's score. For Casals, the greatest composer was Johann Sebastian Bach. Casals discovered Bach's Six Suites for Unaccompanied Cello when he was thirteen, at a time when the German Baroque composer was largely neglected. Though it was relatively unheard of to perform more than a movement or two of a suite, twelve years later Casals would often include an entire suite in his recital programs. He revered Bach, and the Six Suites for Unaccompanied Cello were an integral part of his daily life. Casals actively promoted the composer throughout his lifetime, bringing new recognition to the forgotten genius. Bach was born again in Casals's lively and deep interpretations.

In Bach's brilliant polyphonic writing, Casals perceived a vast emotional spectrum, ranging from playfulness to pathos. He conveyed the various moods embedded in the music through a calculated use of rubato (the stretching or compression of the rhythmic pulse), applied in a manner that did not upset the dancelike quality of the movements. For this and other reasons—one being Casals's occasional use of portamento—his interpretations have been criticized by some musical purists who insist upon a strict adherence to the stylistic conventions of the composer's time. Casals contended, however, that the studied application of technical and stylistic innovations would facilitate musical expression and elucidate timeless and profound meaning. Believing in the inevitability of new musical insights and the potential for multitudes of valid interpretations, he chose never to edit a published manuscript of the Six Suites for Unaccompanied Cello.

Musical Legacy

Largely ignored by eighteenth century and Romantic composers, the cello rarely rated a concerto setting. However, with a virtuosic technique, an impeccable intonation, a powerfully beautiful sound, and an assured and profound musicality, Casals convinced the world of the cello's worth as a solo instrument. Memorable cello concerti by composers Edward Elgar and Dmitri Shostakovich perhaps attest to Casals's elevation of the instrument. As a cellist, Casals achieved international renown and paved the way for such great twentieth century cellists as Gregor Piatigorsky, Jacqueline du Pré, and Mstislav Rostropovich and such twenty-first century cellists as Yo-Yo Ma and Mischa Maisky.

Joshua Addison

Further Reading

Baldock, Robert. *Pablo Casals*. Boston: Northeastern University Press, 1992. Compact yet comprehensive biography with photographs and a discography.

Blum, David. *Casals and the Art of Interpretation*. Los Angeles: University of California Press, 1977. Details Casals's philosophy of musical interpretation, with a chapter on the music of Johann Sebastian Bach, for whom the cellist exhibited a lifelong affinity.

Corredor, Josep M. *Conversations with Casals*. Translated by André Mangeot. New York: E. P. Dutton, 1956. A series of interviews with Casals provides valuable insights into the mind and the convictions of the maestro.

Henle, Fritz. *Casals*. Garden City, N.Y.: American Photographic, 1975. Casals's words of wisdom juxtaposed with a series of photographs taken in 1972, when Casals was ninety-five.

Kahn, Albert E. *Joys and Sorrows: Reflections by Pablo Casals*. New York: Simon & Schuster, 1970. Casals's autobiography, as told to Kahn, which reveals the cellist's musical philosophy and political convictions.

See also: du Pré, Jacqueline; Hawkins, Coleman; Rostropovich, Mstislav; Rubinstein, Artur; Segovia, Andrés; Shostakovich, Dmitri.

Johnny Cash
American country singer, guitarist, and songwriter

Singing of the trials and tribulations of the common man, Cash sold more than fifty million albums during his lifetime.

Born: February 26, 1932; Kingsland, Arkansas
Died: September 12, 2003; Nashville, Tennessee
Also known as: J. R. Cash (full name); the Man in Black
Member of: Johnny Cash and the Tennessee Two; Johnny Cash and the Tennessee Three; the Highwaymen

Principal works

MUSICAL THEATER: *Return to the Promised Land*, 1992 (music and lyrics with June Cash).

Principal recordings

ALBUMS: *Johnny Cash with His Hot and Blue Guitar*, 1957; *The Fabulous Johnny Cash*, 1958; *Hymns*, 1959; *Songs of Our Soil*, 1959; *Ride This Train*, 1960; *Blood, Sweat, and Tears*, 1963; *Ring of Fire*,

1963; *Bitter Tears: Ballads of the American Indian*, 1964; *I Walk the Line*, 1964; *Keep on the Sunny Side*, 1964 (with June Carter); *Johnny Cash Sings the Ballads of the True West*, 1965; *Orange Blossom Special*, 1965; *Mean as Hell*, 1966; *Carryin' on with Johnny Cash and June Carter*, 1967; *Johnny Cash at Folsom Prison*, 1968; *The Holy Land*, 1969; *Johnny Cash at San Quentin*, 1969; *Story Songs of the Trains and Rivers*, 1969 (with the Tennessee Two); *Hello, I'm Johnny Cash*, 1970; *Little Fauss and Big Halsy*, 1970 (with Carl Perkins and Bob Dylan); *Singing Storyteller*, 1970 (with the Tennessee Two); *The World of Johnny Cash*, 1970; *Johnny Cash and Jerry Lee Lewis Sing Hank Williams*, 1971; *The Man in Black*, 1971; *America*, 1972; *Folsom Prison Blues*, 1972; *Give My Love to Rose*, 1972 (with June Carter Cash); *A Thing Called Love*, 1972; *Any Old Wind That Blows*, 1973; *Johnny Cash and His Woman*, 1973 (with June Carter Cash); *Five Feet High and Rising*, 1974; *The Junkie and the Juicehead Minus Me*, 1974; *Ragged Old Flag*, 1974; *Johnny Cash Sings Precious Memories*, 1975; *Destination Victoria Station*, 1976; *One Piece at a Time*, 1976; *Strawberry Cake*, 1976; *Last Gunfighter Ballad*, 1977; *The Rambler*, 1977; *Gone Girl*, 1978; *Silver*, 1979; *A Believer Sings the Truth*, 1980; *Rockabilly Blues*, 1980; *The Baron*, 1981; *The Adventures of Johnny Cash*, 1982; *Highwayman*, 1985 (with the Highwaymen); *Rainbow*, 1985; *Believe in Him*, 1986; *Class of '55 (Memphis Rock and Roll Homecoming)*, 1986 (with Roy Orbison, Jerry Lee Lewis, and Carl Perkins); *Heroes*, 1986 (with Waylon Jennings); *Johnny Cash Is Coming to Town*, 1987; *Water from the Wells of Home*, 1988; *Highwayman 2*, 1990 (with the Highwaymen); *The Mystery of Life*, 1991; *American Recordings*, 1994; *The Road Goes on Forever*, 1995 (with the Highwaymen); *Unchained*, 1996; *American III: Solitary Man*, 2000; *American IV: The Man Comes Around*, 2002.

WRITINGS OF INTEREST: *Man in Black: His Own Story in His Own Words*, 1975 (autobiography); *Cash: The Autobiography*, 1997 (with Patrick Carr).

The Life

Johnny Cash, born J. R. Cash, was the son of Ray and Carrie Cash, both of Scottish descent. His par-ents were involved in the New Deal farm program and settled on land in Dyess Colony in northeast Arkansas. When he was young, he joined his family in picking cotton on the farm and sang with them while they worked. A flood that devastated the family farm inspired a song he wrote many years later called "Five Feet High and Rising." When Cash was twelve years old, his older brother, Jack, died in an accident involving a table saw, an incident that Cash suggested may have provided the dark edge to his music.

Gospel and radio music permeated his childhood, and he started to write songs as a boy. He sang on a radio station in high school and later enlisted in the U.S. Air Force as a radio operator. He was assigned to a U.S. Air Force Security Service unit in Landsberg, Germany, where he bought his first guitar and started a band. After his service in the Air Force ended in 1954, he married Vivian Liberto, whom he had met during technical training at Brooks Air Force Base in San Antonio, Texas. Their first child, Rosanne Cash, was born in 1955. That year the family moved to Nashville, where Cash sold appliances while he studied to be a radio announcer.

His musical career took off in the 1960's, but Cash started to drink heavily and became addicted to amphetamines, using "uppers" to stay awake during tours. Despite the fact that he and Vivian had four daughters, their marriage did not survive Cash's constant touring and drug abuse. Vivian and Cash divorced in 1966.

By the mid-1960's, Cash's singing partner, June Carter, had helped him overcome his addiction. Carter was a member of one of the most influential singing groups in country music, the Carter Family. Although Carter and Cash were married to other people when they met, they fell in love and were married in 1968.

By the end of the 1960's, many people considered Cash the hottest recording artist, outselling The Beatles. From 1969 to 1971 *The Johnny Cash Show* ran on ABC, featuring such diverse guests as Louis Armstrong, Neil Young, Merle Haggard, and Bob Dylan. The Statler Brothers opened every show for him.

In the mid-1970's, Cash's singing career started to decline, but at the same time his Christian faith grew. With his friend, the Reverend Billy Graham,

Johnny Cash. (AP/Wide World Photos)

work. Although it is not easy for country artists to cross over to a different genre, during his long career Cash successfully recorded folk, rockabilly, blues, rock and roll, gospel, and popular music. He was inducted into the Nashville Songwriters Hall of Fame as well as the Country Music Hall of Fame, at forty-eight the youngest living inductee. He received the Kennedy Center Honors in 1996. His songs were about love, humor, those down and out, and prisoners; later in his life, his themes were moral tribulation and redemption.

Early Works. Cash signed with the Sun Records label in the mid-1950's, and in 1956 he became a full-time musician after his two-sided hit, "So Doggone Lonesome" and "Folsom Prison Blues," jumped to number five on the *Billboard* country chart. A draft of "Folsom Prison Blues" had been written earlier, when Cash was in the service in West Germany and saw the movie *Inside the Walls of Folsom Prison*. He had great sympathy for prisoners and began performing prison concerts starting in the late 1950's. These concerts produced two successful albums issued in the late 1960's: *Johnny Cash at Folsom Prison*, introduced by his moving rendition of "Folsom Prison Blues," and *Johnny Cash at San Quentin*. "Folsom Prison Blues" became one of his signature songs and was followed by "I Walk the Line," Cash's first number-one country hit and entry on the popular Top 20 chart. "I Walk the Line" is a love song attesting to his fidelity by keeping "a close watch on this heart of mine." By 1958, with more than six million records sold, Cash felt constrained by Sun's small label and signed with Columbia Records.

"Ring of Fire." This song was written by Carter and Merle Kilgore, who eventually became a manager for other recording artists. Although Carter was married to another man when she wrote the lyrics, the words came to her while she was driving down a highway early one morning, thinking about the dangers of falling in love with Cash. She was frightened by his drug abuse, and it came to her that loving him was like a ring of fire. When the

he cowrote and narrated a film about the life of Jesus titled *The Gospel Road*. He also continued to appear in televised Christmas specials and with June Carter on the television series *Little House on the Prairie*.

During the 1980's, Cash appeared as an actor in several television films. He also suffered a severe abdominal injury and underwent heart bypass surgery in 1988. After Columbia Records dropped Cash's recording contract, he had an unsuccessful partnership with Mercury Records and in the early 1990's signed with the American Recordings label. In 1997 Cash was diagnosed with autonomic neuropathy associated with diabetes. A year later he was hospitalized with severe pneumonia, which damaged his lungs.

Carter died during heart-valve surgery on May 15, 2003. While hospitalized at Baptist Hospital in Nashville, Tennessee, Cash followed her in death on September 12, 2003.

The Music

Known for his distinctive baritone, the sound of his backup band, and his black clothes, Cash had perhaps the most recognized voice in country music. With his sold-out tours and more than fifteen hundred recordings, he left an impressive body of song was completed, Carter's sister Anita recorded it to little notice for her 1962 album of the same name. However, a year later, using mariachi-style horns, Cash recorded "Ring of Fire," and it became the biggest hit of his career, remaining number one on the charts for seven weeks. Since then, numerous versions of the song have been produced. In 1990, twenty-seven years after Cash released it, Social Distortion recorded it to great commercial success.

"A Boy Named Sue." Written by Shel Silverstein, a songwriter and author best known for his whimsical children's books, the song was inspired by humorist Jean Shepherd, a friend of Silverstein who was teased as a child for his first name. Cash first heard "A Boy Named Sue" at an informal gathering of musicians in Nashville where Silverstein sang his song. Carter thought it would be a great song for Cash, and later, when they left to record *Live at San Quentin*, they took it along. Cash sang the song unrehearsed for the first time in front of the prison audience. The recording became a hit, rising to number one on the country charts and to number two on the pop charts. It also became Cash's first hit in England and Ireland. "A Boy Named Sue" tells the unlikely story of a boy who grows up resentful of his father, both for leaving him and for giving him a girl's name. Later the boy, now grown, meets his father in a bar and finally understands that the father gave him the name "Sue" to make him tough.

Musical Legacy

Cash was legendary for the longevity of his career. His signature tune, "Folsom Prison Blues," was recorded and became a hit in 1956, and his video *Hurt* won an MTV Video Music Award forty-seven years later. Although his career experienced slumps, especially in the mid-1960's when he became addicted to drugs, by the end of that decade he was the voice of country music. Again, in the 1980's, his recording career and connections with the Nashville establishment sank to an all-time low. In the 1990's his career was rejuvenated, and he became popular all over again with a new generation of young people who were admirers of rock and hip-hop. He continued to earn industry awards and enjoyed remarkable commercial success.

Cash influenced numerous artists and was the first to record the songs of Kris Kristofferson and Bob Dylan, who later became popular artists in their own right. He had a long friendship with Dylan, who cited Cash as a major influence on his own work. Cash welcomed Ray Charles to Nashville when Charles came to record his first country song there and became his lifelong friend. Cash was a pioneer in the rockabilly sound and early rock and roll, and for his contributions he was recognized by the Rockabilly Hall of Fame and the Rock and Roll Hall of Fame. An Academy Award-winning film biography of Cash, *Walk the Line*, was released in 2005 to both commercial and critical success.

Sheila Golburgh Johnson

Further Reading

Cash, Johnny, with Patrick Carr. *Cash: The Autobiography*. New York: HarperCollins, 1997. Cash attributes his life, health, and success to Carter.

Streissguth, Michael. *Johnny Cash at Folsom Prison: The Making of a Masterpiece*. Cambridge, Mass.: Da Capo Press, 2004. Examines in depth the legendary concert at Folsom Prison and the live album, placing the concert in the greater context of Cash's career and the music of the times.

_____. *Johnny Cash: The Biography*. Cambridge, Mass.: Da Capo Press, 2006. Relying on interviews with family members such as Cash's daughter, Rosanne, this book paints a fairly objective picture of Cash and illustrates the influence of his family members while he was growing up.

Turner, Steve. *The Man Called Cash: The Life, Love, and Faith of an American Legend*. Nashville: Thomas Nelson, 2004. This authorized biography, which deals fairly and honestly with Cash's personal issues, was published in time for the first anniversary of the singer's death and relies heavily on interviews with such Cash fans as Larry Gatlin and Kris Kristofferson.

Urbanski, Dave. *The Man Comes Around: The Spiritual Journey of Johnny Cash*. New York: Relevant Books, 2003. A spiritual chronicle of Cash's life explores in detail the highs and lows and the failures and successes. His faith became more important to him as he grew older.

See also: Axton, Hoyt; Carter, Maybelle; Charles, Ray; Diamond, Neil; Dorsey, Thomas A.;

Dylan, Bob; Harris, Emmylou; Howlin' Wolf; Jennings, Waylon; Kristofferson, Kris; Leadbelly; Lewis, Jerry Lee; Monroe, Bill; Nelson, Ricky; Nelson, Willie; Orbison, Roy; Perkins, Carl; Ritchie, Jean; Strummer, Joe; Tubb, Ernest.

Ray Charles

American rhythm-and-blues pianist, singer, and songwriter

Charles helped shape the sound of rhythm and blues and soul, and he was one of the first musicians to own his master recordings.

Born: September 23, 1930; Albany, Georgia
Died: June 10, 2004; Beverly Hills, California
Also known as: Ray Charles Robinson (birth name)

Principal recordings

ALBUMS: *Confession Blues*, 1954; *The Great Ray Charles*, 1957; *Ray Charles*, 1957; *Soul Brothers*, 1958 (with Milt Jackson); *Yes, Indeed!!*, 1958; *The Genius of Ray Charles*, 1959; *Genius + Soul = Jazz*, 1960; *The Genius Hits the Road*, 1960; *Ray Charles in Person*, 1960; *Ray Charles Sextet*, 1960; *Dedicated to You*, 1961; *Do the Twist with Ray Charles!*, 1961; *The Genius After Hours*, 1961; *The Genius Sings the Blues*, 1961; *Ray Charles and Betty Carter*, 1961 (with Betty Carter); *Soul Meeting*, 1961 (with Jackson); *Hallelujah I Love Her So!*, 1962; *Modern Sounds in Country and Western Music*, 1962; *Modern Sounds in Country and Western Music, Vol. 2*, 1962; *Spotlight on Ray Charles*, 1962; *Ingredients in a Recipe for Soul*, 1963; *Have a Smile with Me*, 1964; *Sweet and Sour Tears*, 1964; *Country and Western Meets Rhythm and Blues*, 1965; *Crying Time*, 1966; *Ray's Moods*, 1966; *A Man and His Soul*, 1967; *Ray Charles Invites You to Listen*, 1967; *Doing His Best*, 1969; *I'm All Yours, Baby!*, 1969; *Love Country Style*, 1970; *My Kind of Jazz*, 1970; *Volcanic Action of My Soul*, 1971; *A Message from the People*, 1972; *Presents the Raelettes*, 1972; *Through the Eyes of Love*, 1972; *My Kind of Jazz, Number 2*, 1973; *My Kind of Jazz, Pt. 3*, 1975; *Renaissance*, 1975; *World of Ray Charles, Vol. 2*, 1975; *True to Life*, 1977; *Love and Peace*, 1978; *Ain't It So*, 1979; *Brother Ray Is at It Again*, 1980; *Wish You Were Here Tonight*, 1983; *Do I Ever Cross Your Mind*, 1984; *Friendship*, 1984; *The Spirit of Christmas*, 1985; *From the Pages of My Heart*, 1986; *Just Between Us*, 1988; *What Would You Believe*, 1990; *My World*, 1993; *Strong Love Affair*, 1996; *I Wonder Who's Kissing Her Now*, 1997; *Blues*, 1999; *Thanks for Bringing Love Around Again*, 2002; *Portrait*, 2003; *Ray Charles Portrait*, 2003; *Genius Loves Company*, 2004; *At Newport*, 2005; *Genius and Friends*, 2005; *With the Voice of Jubilation Choir*, 2006.

SINGLES: "Basin Street Blues," 1960; "Baby It's Cold Outside," 1961 (with Betty Carter); "Hit the Road Jack," 1962; "I Can't Stop Loving You," 1963; "Ballad of Ray Charles," 1964; "Ballad Style of Ray Charles," 1965; "Ray Charles Sings," 1965; "Swinging Style," 1965; "Take These Chains," 1965; "Busted," 1966; "What'd I Say," 1975; "Seven Spanish Angels," 1988; "I'll Take Care of You," 1990; "Fresh Out of Tears," 1991; "Living Without You," 1991; "Song for You," 1993; "Ellie My Love," 2004; "Here We Go Again," 2005.

The Life

Ray Charles was born to impoverished parents Aretha Williams, who stacked boards in a sawmill, and Bailey Robinson, a railroad repairman, mechanic, and handyman. His parents were not married, and when Charles was an infant, the family moved to Greenville, Florida. Bailey, who had three other families, later abandoned Aretha with her two sons, and she raised her children on her own.

When Charles was five, he witnessed his younger brother George drown in his mother's portable laundry tub. At the age of six, Charles suffered from glaucoma, and he began to lose his sight. By age seven, he was totally blind. His mother sent him to the St. Augustine School for the Deaf and the Blind in St. Augustine, Florida, and she died two years later. At the school, Charles received a formal musical education, learning to read, to write, to arrange music in Braille, and to score for big bands. In addition, he learned how to play piano, organ, saxophone, clarinet, and trumpet.

Charles moved to Seattle in 1947 and formed a trio, which emulated the style of Nat King Cole and Charles Brown. At this time, to avoid being confused with boxer Sugar Ray Robinson, Charles dropped the Robinson from his name. In 1952 Atlantic Records signed him to a contract, and during the next year he enjoyed his first commercial success. Charles began using heroin during this time, and in 1965 he was arrested for possession of heroin and marijuana. At the time, he revealed that he had been addicted for nearly two decades. Although this was his third arrest, he was allowed to check in to a clinic in Los Angeles to recover and to avoid jail time. By 1966 he had completely recovered from his long-standing heroin addiction.

During the 1960's and 1970's, Charles released several hits, but as his music became increasingly sentimental, it fell from popularity. During the 1980's and 1990's, he became recognizable among younger audiences with his appearances in films, such as *Blues Brothers* (1980), and television shows, such as *The Cosby Show* and *The Super Dave Osbourne Show*.

Although he was exceptionally successful as a musician, Charles had a complicated private life. He was divorced twice, and he had twelve children, both in and outside his marriages. He was married to Eileen Williams for one year, between 1951 and 1952. Later, in 1955, he married Della Beatrice Howard, and they divorced in 1977.

In 2004, even though he was suffering from liver disease, Charles worked on a recording project of duets (*Genius Loves Company*) with musicians Willie Nelson, Bonnie Raitt, B. B. King, Elton John, and Norah Jones. He died from acute liver disease in 2004 at the age of seventy-three.

The Music

Charles's works reflect a broad array of music genres, including country, jazz, blues, funk, and pop. As an artist, he was as comfortable working in rock and roll as in the songs of George Gershwin. His career spanned fifty-eight years, and his music appeared on more than 250 albums, most of which have been top sellers in different musical genres.

Gospel. Charles brought a new perspective to gospel music, bringing it from the African American church tradition and making it popular among white audiences. Although he was highly criticized

for this, he never stepped back. Charles was a pioneer in mixing gospel, jazz, blues, and rock and roll, opening new doors for musical artists. His highly developed and controlled technique as a performer made him greatly admired by audiences and other artists; singer Frank Sinatra called Charles "the only genius in the business."

"I Got a Woman." Charles's first rhythm-and-blues album was *Confession Blues* with Atlantic Records. A career-defining song from this album was "I Got a Woman," which was released as a single in December, 1954. Some believe that this song, a combination of gospel and rhythm, led to soul music. "I Got a Woman" was Charles's first number-one rhythm-and-blues hit, and it was later ranked number 235 in the list of the 500 Greatest Songs of All Time in *Rolling Stone*. The song utilized vocal techniques (moans and grunts) common in African American church music and applied them to explicitly sexual material. Charles withstood criticism for this, continuing to make this part of his performing style.

Ray Charles. (AP/Wide World Photos)

"I Can't Stop Loving You." This song was composed by country singer and songwriter Don Gibson and recorded in 1957. Charles recorded it in 1962, for his *Modern Sounds in Country and Western Music* album. His cover version features a string arrangement and a gospel choir. This love song about heartbreak peaked on the *Billboard* Hot 100 and the rhythm-and-blues and adult contemporary charts. It ranked number forty-nine on Country Music Television's 100 Greatest Songs in Country Music and number 161 on *Rolling Stone*'s list of the 500 Greatest Songs of All Time.

"Hit the Road Jack." Charles's good friend Percy Mayfield wrote this song as a tribute to Jack Kerouac's novel *On the Road* (1957). "Hit the Road Jack" was on the *Billboard* Hot 100 chart at number one for two weeks in 1961, and it won the Grammy Award for Best Male Rhythm and Blues Recording in 1961. The jazzy song—about a woman asking her lover to leave—launched Charles to international stardom. It is played at sports events, for example, when a hockey player is sent to the penalty box or a basketball player is taken out of the game.

"Busted." Written by Nashville songwriter Harlan Howard and originally recorded by Johnny Cash in 1962, this song won for Charles the 1963 Grammy Award for Best Rhythm and Blues Recording. "Busted" is a country-style song about a farmer who is broke and has no hope in life. The single features brass arrangements and Charles's vocals.

"Georgia on My Mind." This song, with lyrics by Stuart Gorrell and music by Hoagy Carmichael, became the official state song of Georgia. However, it is not clear whether Gorrell's lyrics refer to Carmichael's sister, Georgia, or to the state of Georgia. Carmichael's autobiography, *Sometimes I Wonder* (1965), indicates that a friend suggested to Gorrell that he write a song about Georgia because you cannot go wrong writing about the South. Charles recorded the song for his album *The Genius Hits the Road*. On March 7, 1979, he performed the song before the Georgia General Assembly, and later, on April 24, 1979, the Assembly adopted it as the state song. The song is played on Georgia public television late Sunday nights when it goes off the air. It was also used as the theme song for the television situation comedy *Designing Women*. "Georgia on My Mind" has a string arrangement, female back vocals, and Charles's vocals and piano.

"Unchain My Heart." This song was written by Bobby Sharp, who sold it to Teddy Powell for fifty dollars in order to buy drugs. Charles's rendition became extremely popular, and later Powell demanded half the songwriting credit. Sharp fought for the rights to his song successfully, renewing the copyright for his publishing company (B. Sharp Music) in 1987.

When Charles released the single in 1961, it reached number one on the rhythm-and-blues chart and reached the Top 10 on the pop singles chart. "Unchain My Heart" was also the working title of the biographical film *Ray* (2004).

The song—about a man who wants to be free from a woman—features Charles accompanied by his female vocal group, the Raelettes, his longtime saxophonist David "Fathead" Newman, and other members of Charles's band, with brass and percussion. In 1987 Joe Cocker covered the song, popularizing it even further.

Musical Legacy

Charles inspired many blind musicians, such as Ronnie Milsap and Terri Gibbs, to be successful in the business. He brought a new singing style to country music with his landmark album *Modern Sounds in Country and Western Music*, and *Genius Loves Company*, a duet album, won eight Grammy Awards, including Album of the Year and Record of the Year. Charles was inducted into the Blues Foundation's Hall of Fame in 1982 and the Rock and Roll Hall of Fame in its first year, 1986. He received the prestigious President's Merit Award from the Grammy organization. In his long career, Charles won twelve Grammy Awards and three Emmy nominations. He also received the Kennedy Center Honors, the Grammy Lifetime Achievement Award, and the National Medal of Arts. *Rolling Stone* ranked Charles at number ten on its list of the 100 Greatest Artists of All Time in 2004. He also received eight honorary doctorates, including one in 2003 from Dillard University in New Orleans. In October, 2004, a feature film based on his life story, *Ray*, opened to great success. The Ray Charles Robinson Foundation was established in 1987 to assist the hearing impaired. It has been rated one of the top five most competent nonprofit organizations, serving nearly 150 charities.

Dilek Göktürk

Further Reading

Charles, Ray, and David Ritz. *Brother Ray: Ray Charles' Own Story*. New York: Da Capo Press, 2004. Charles tells the story of his life (until 1978) in his own words. Written in a conversational style, this book is especially helpful in understanding the singer's early life.

Duggleby, John. *Uh Huh! The Story of Ray Charles*. New York: Morgan Reynolds, 2005. This excellent biography builds a convincing case for the significant contributions Charles made to twentieth century music, influencing the Beatles, Presley, and other musical icons. Includes color photographs.

Evans, Mike. *Ray Charles and the Birth of Soul*. London: Omnibus Press, 2007. Evans, who has written books on the Beatles and Presley, uses interviews with Charles to tell his life story. Since it was published after his death, the book covers Charles's entire life. Includes discography.

Lydon, Michael. *Ray Charles: Man and Music*. New York: Routledge, 2004. A veteran music journalist adds fresh details to Charles's life story, covering the performer as well as the offstage man. Includes photographs and bibliography.

See also: Blakey, Art; Burke, Solomon; Cash, Johnny; Cole, Nat King; Costello, Elvis; James, Etta; John, Sir Elton; Jones, Quincy; Jordan, Louis; King, B. B.; Morrison, Van; Nelson, Willie; Pickett, Wilson; Presley, Elvis; Rush, Otis; Sinatra, Frank.

Carlos Chávez

Mexican classical composer

Chávez's music balances traditional forms with intense chromaticism, nonrepetitive development, polyrhythms, contrapuntal textures, and a characteristic Mexican sound. He held significant government positions in the arts.

Born: June 13, 1899; Mexico City, Mexico
Died: August 2, 1978; Mexico City, Mexico
Also known as: Carlos Antonio de Padua Chávez y Ramírez (full name)

Principal works

BALLETS (music and libretto): *El fuego nuevo*, unstaged; written 1921 (*The New Fire*); *Caballos de vapor*, 1932 (*Horsepower*); *La hija de Cólquide*, 1946 (*Dark Meadow*; libretto by Martha Graham); *Los cuatro soles*, 1951.

CHAMBER WORKS: Sonatina, 1924 (for cello and piano); *Energía*, 1925; Sonata No. 3, 1930 (for four horns); *Soli I*, 1933; *Toccata*, 1941 (for six percussionists); *Xochipilli: An Imagined Aztec Music*, 1941 (for wind and percussion instruments); Violin Concerto, 1950; *Invention*, 1960 (for strings); *Soli II*, 1961 (for wind quintet); *Soli IV*, 1966.

CHORAL WORKS: *Imágen Mexicana*, 1923; *El Sol*, 1934 (*The Sun*); *Ah! Freedome*, 1942; *Prometheus Bound*, 1956.

OPERA (music): *Panfilo and Lauretta*, 1957 (libretto by Chester Kallman; based on Giovanni Boccaccio's *Fiammetta*; revised as *The Visitors*, 1973).

ORCHESTRAL WORKS: Symphony No. 1, 1933 (*Sinfonía de Antígona*); *Chapultepec*, 1935 (for a band); Symphony No. 2, 1935 (*Sinfonía India*); Concerto for Piano with Orchestra, 1938; *Toccata para orquesta*, 1947; Symphony No. 4, 1953 (*Sinfonía romántica*); Symphony No. 3, 1954; Symphony No. 5, 1953 (for string orchestra); Symphony No. 6, 1961; *Resonancias*, 1964; *Soli III*, 1965; *Pirámide*, 1968; *Mañanas mexicanas*, 1974 (for a band); *Tzintzuntzan*, 1974 (for a band); *Zandunga Serenade*, 1976 (for a band).

PIANO WORKS: Sonata No. 1, 1917 (*Fantasia*); Sonata No. 2, 1919; Ten Preludes, 1937; Sonata No. 4, 1941; *Miniatura: Homenaje a Carl Deis*, 1942; *Danza de la pluma*, 1943; Sonata No. 5, 1960; Sonata No. 6, 1961.

WRITINGS OF INTEREST: *Toward a New Music: Music and Electricity*, 1937; *Musical Thought*, 1961.

The Life

Carlos Antonio de Padua Chávez y Ramírez (CHAH-vehz ee rah-MIH-rehz) was born to Juvencia Ramírez, the principal of a school for young women, and Agustín Chávez, an inventor who died in 1904. His youth was framed by the Mexican Revolution (1910-1920), a period of intense political and social turmoil. When Chávez was around nine years old, he started studying piano with his brother Manuel and later with Asunción Parra. Between 1910 and 1914, he received piano lessons from the famous composer Manuel María Ponce, and between 1915 and 1920, he received piano lessons from Pedro Luis Ogazón. Chávez started composing for the piano by the age of ten, and he took lessons in harmony from Juan B. Fuentes. A determined autodidact, Chávez decided not to seek the instruction of a composition teacher; instead, he studied on his own the works of Ludwig van Beethoven, Richard Wagner, and Claude Debussy. Significant during his formative years were his family's frequent trips to Tlaxcala, where he came in contact with indigenous Native American music.

Chávez married the pianist Otilia Ortiz on September 1, 1922, and soon after they left to tour Europe for seven months. In Germany, the firm Bote und Bock accepted two of his piano pieces for publication, and in France the composer Paul Dukas encouraged him to continue incorporating popular music in his compositions. Back in North America, he traveled to New York, where he met Edgard Varèse, at the time one of the most visible proponents of musical modernism. Varèse commissioned him to write a chamber work, *Energía*, which he finished in 1925.

Back in Mexico, Chávez organized a series of concerts of new music between 1924 and 1926, featuring compositions by Béla Bartók, Arnold Schoenberg, Igor Stravinsky, and Edgard Varèse. Around this time, he finished the ballet *Los cuatro soles*, which dealt with Aztec mythology. Avoiding dependence on indigenous themes, the piece presented Native American sonorities, and it included indigenous percussion instruments in the orchestra. In 1926 Chávez traveled again to New York, where he worked in collaboration with muralist Diego Rivera on another ballet, *Horsepower*.

When Chávez returned to Mexico in 1928, the Musicians' Union asked him to direct the new Orquesta Sinfónica de México. Chávez was able to establish the first long-standing orchestra in the country, remaining its musical director for twenty-one seasons. In addition, in 1928 Chávez was appointed director of the National Conservatory of Music, where he reformed what he saw as an old-fashioned education. He developed courses in free composition, and among his students were Candelario Huizar and Silvestre Revueltas, as well as the Grupo de los Cuatro: Daniel Ayala, Blas Galindo, Salvador Contreras, and José Pablo Moncayo. Chávez also created in the conservatory the Academy of Investigation to collect and catalog indigenous music from Mexico, and he started the music journal *Música, revista mexicana*. In 1932 Chávez visited the RCA Victor studios in New Jersey and the Bell Telephone Laboratories in New York, and this gave birth to his book *Toward a New Music: Music and Electricity*.

In 1933 Chávez accepted the position of chief of the department of fine arts at the Secretariat of Public Education, where he oversaw programs in music, dance, and the arts, and he promoted interest in popular and indigenous Mexican culture. By 1940 Chávez's visibility in the United States led Nelson Rockefeller, at the time coordinator of the Office of Inter-American Affairs for the U.S. State Department, to invite Chávez to organize a series of concerts for an exhibit at the Museum of Modern Art in New York. At his request for a piece incorporating indigenous instruments Chávez composed *Xochipilli: An Imagined Aztec Music* for six percussion instruments and four wind instruments.

Carlos Chávez. (Library of Congress)

Chávez was inducted in the prestigious Colegio Nacional in 1943, and this provided him unprecedented governmental support. Together with other Mexican and expatriate Spanish composers, Chávez created the journal *Nuestra Música* and the publishing house Ediciones Mexicanas de Música. In 1947 the newly elected president of Mexico, Miguel Alemán, appointed Chávez to direct a new administrative body for the arts, the Instituto Nacional de Bellas Artes (INBA). Within the INBA, Chávez created a new orchestra, the Orquesta Sinfónica Nacional, which he guest conducted until 1971. His administrative duties slowed down Chávez's compositional production, although he finished his Violin Concerto before his retirement in 1952.

The years between 1953 and 1961 were quite prolific for Chávez, both as a composer and as a teacher. During this period he finished the last four of his six symphonies and several other pieces. During this time, he gave summer courses at Tanglewood in 1953, he had a lectureship at the University of Buffalo, and he held the Charles Eliot Norton Poetic Chair at Harvard University between 1958 and 1959. The lectures given at Harvard were eventually published in 1961 as *Musical Thought*.

In 1959 Chávez started a series of composition workshops in the National Conservatory. Among his most prominent students were Eduardo Mata, Hector Quintanar, and Mario Lavista. As the 1960's advanced, Chávez's compositions moved toward the progressive and even experimental. Works such as *Resonancias* for orchestra and *Soli III*, for bassoon, trumpet, viola, timpani and orchestra, present high chromaticism, atonality, and they exemplify what he called nonrepetitive procedures.

Always a critic of tradition-bound education, Chávez lectured in 1969 regarding the substandard teaching of the National Conservatory and the poor direction of the Orquesta Sinfónica Nacional. Following this criticism, President Luis Echeverría appointed Chávez in 1971 to develop a national plan for music. Chávez assumed the position of head of the music department at INBA and the direction of the Orquesta Sinfónica Nacional. A strike by orchestra members who did not agree with Chávez's policies and the lack of support from the government that had appointed him caused his resignation from both positions. During the 1970's, Chávez continued composing and revising earlier works,

and his indefatigable interest in teaching continued with lectureships in several universities and colleges in the United States and England. Weakened during the last couple of years of his life, Chávez died of cancer on August 2, 1978.

The Music

Chávez's music helped define Mexican nationalist art music in the mid-twentieth century, although his compositions were strongly embedded in the classical and Romantic traditions of Western Europe. His traditional forms and intense polyphonic textures that privilege counterpoint over harmonic constructions show a highly intellectual compositional process. At the same time, although his music adopts elements from Mexican indigenous and popular music sources, he avoids the common cliché of quoting folkloric melodies. The nationalistic tendency in Chávez's compositional output peaks in the early 1930's. Compositions such as *El Sol*, *Chapultepec*, and the successful *Sinfonía India* show nationalist topics, musical materials, and texts deriving from both Native American and revolutionary Mexican sources. Nevertheless, Chávez's creative output was not only confined to nationalistic pieces. Works such as his *Sinfonía de Antígona*, *Soli I*, the Concerto for Piano with Orchestra, and even the *Sinfonía India* show a particular alignment to the neoclassicism of Paul Hindemith, Stravinsky and Aaron Copland.

El fuego nuevo. Chávez's earliest compositions were for piano and piano and voice, and by 1920 several of them had been published by A. Wagner and Levien in Mexico City. These pieces combined European models from the eighteenth and nineteenth centuries and settings of revolutionary and traditional Mexican songs. In 1921 Chávez received a commission for a ballet with an indigenous theme from the Minister of Public Education José Vasconcelos, a key figure in the post-revolutionary revitalization of Mexico's arts. Chávez's ballet *El fuego nuevo*, based on an Aztec legend, was scored for orchestra, women's chorus, and large percussion section, and it included flutes from Mexican Native Americans. Chávez evoked a particular indigenous character without directly quoting from indigenous tunes through his invention of neoprimitive pentatonic melodies and harmonies built on fourths and fifths.

Horsepower. During Chávez's stay in New York in 1926, he collaborated with muralist Rivera in the creation of a ballet symphony titled *Horsepower*, a hard-edged composition depicting the age of the machine and its implications in the contemporary Mexican social context. In this sense, the piece has been compared to compositions such as Arthur Honnegger's *Pacific 231* (1924). The piece superimposes harsh sounds representing machines, Mexican dances, and rhythms such as the huapango and the zandunga.

Sinfonía India. Of Chávez's six symphonies, *Sinfonía India* is the most popular. Premiered by the CBS Symphony Orchestra under the composer's baton, the piece consists of only one movement for orchestra, and it features several indigenous percussion instruments. Characteristic of *Sinfonía India* and present in most of Chávez's music with nationalistic tendencies are the motor rhythms and the use of the sesquialtera, a superimposition of 3/4 and 6/8, common in popular musics of Latin America. The *Sinfonía India* is one of the few cases in which Mexican indigenous melodies are present, taken from music of the Cora, Yaqui, Sonora, and Seri Indians.

***Soli* chamber works.** Between 1933 and 1966 Chávez wrote four pieces: *Soli I*, *Soli II*, and *Soli IV* are for small wind groups, and *Soli III* is for orchestra with four soloists. In them, a soloist is given prominence in each movement of the works. They reveal a progressive and experimental facet of Chávez, with strong dissonances, high chromaticism, angular melodies, polyrhythmic figures, and, most important, the nonrepetition of materials. As shown by scholar Robert Parker, Chávez's music after the 1950's moved toward a continuous flow void of repetition, in which each new material was generated by the previous one, in a self-perpetuating cycle.

Musical Legacy

Latin American composers during the twentieth century fluctuated between nationalistic and universalistic approaches to music composition. These tendencies were commonly seen as opposed, but they frequently were interpreted lightly, resulting in mannerism and false objectivity. Chávez, together with Heitor Villa-Lobos and Alberto Ginastera, is a part of a generation of Latin American composers whose work attempts to synthesize nationalistic and universalistic trends. Chávez integrates through his music characteristics from the Western European musical tradition and his own personal perception of what constitutes an authentic Mexican music derived from indigenous and popular cultures.

Chávez became a key figure in the post-revolutionary formation of governmental institutions involving the arts, creating a structure of support unequaled in other Latin American countries. This structure, however, was highly hierarchical, and it paralleled the one-party rule that the Mexican revolution left as a legacy for more than seventy years. In 1969, when Chávez had withdrawn somewhat from official positions of power, he gave a lecture titled "The Lyre of Orpheus." In it, he posed the question: "What are the guardians of culture going to do?" He pointed out that nobody was yet carrying the leadership of Mexico's musical life, as he had done in the previous decades.

Eduardo Herrera

Further Reading

Carmona, Gloria. *Epistolario selecto de Carlos Chávez*. México: Fondo de Cultura Económica, 1989. An extensive collection of letters exchanged between Chávez and important artistic and political figures.

Chávez, Carlos. *Musical Thought*. Cambridge, England: Harvard University Press, 1961. A compilation of the lectures given by Chávez at Harvard in 1958 and 1959. It includes essays on being a Latin American composer, art as communication, form in music, enjoyment of music, and repetition in music.

_____. *Toward a New Music: Music and Electricity*. New York: W. W. Norton, 1937. This report following Chávez's visit to the RCA Victor Studios and the Bell Telephone Laboratories discusses possibilities provided by electricity, especially radio, recording, film, and electric instruments.

Parker, Robert. *Carlos Chávez: A Guide to Research*. New York: Garland, 1998. A bibliographical annotated guide to the literature on Chávez. Includes a biography and a list of works.

_____. *Carlos Chávez: Mexico's Modern-Day Orpheus*. Boston: Twayne, 1983. In this resource, a leading Chávez scholar discusses a large number of representative compositions. It includes a list of works, discography, a list of orchestras Chávez conducted, and a selected bibliography.

See also: Bartók, Béla; Copland, Aaron; Hindemith, Paul; Honegger, Arthur; Revueltas, Silvestre; Schoenberg, Arnold; Stravinsky, Igor; Varèse, Edgard.

Maurice Chevalier

French pop and show tune singer

A cultural ambassador for France, Chevalier brought to Hollywood in the 1930's the image of the cavalier French playboy. In the late 1940's Chevalier's sunny French-jazz style influenced many singers until rock and roll took hold in the late 1950's.

Born: September 12, 1888; Ménilmontant, France
Died: January 1, 1972; Paris, France
Also known as: Maurice Auguste Chevalier (full name)

Principal recordings

ALBUMS: *Encore Maurice!*, 1982; *No Business Like Show Business*, 1994; *Fourteen Songs*, 1995; *Ma pomme y d' la joie*, 1996; *Moi avec une chanson*, 1998; *The Romance of Paris*, 2000; *Valentine*, 2002; *Inoubliable*, 2002.

WRITINGS OF INTEREST: *With Love*, 1960; *I Remember It Well*, 1970.

The Life

Born in 1888, Maurice Auguste Chevalier (mah-REES sheh-VAHL-yay) established his reputation as a singer and dancer when his career as an acrobat came to an abrupt end after an accident. While in the military, he was wounded and captured by the Germans in World War I. After a two-year incarceration, during which he learned English from a fellow prisoner, Chevalier returned to Paris, where he discovered jazz and became a huge star.

Chevalier began making short French films in 1908. He was called to Hollywood in 1928; two years later he was nominated for two Academy Awards as Best Actor. Two films with Jeanette MacDonald, *One Hour with You* and *Love Me Tonight*, were smash hits in 1932 and helped create the craze for Hollywood musicals. Audiences loved Chevalier's naughty double entendres and insouciant characters.

Chevalier spent World War II in France and protected his Jewish wife, Nita Ray. He performed at the German prisoner of war camp where he had been interned in World War I, but he refused to sing on German radio. After the war, Chevalier was accused of collaborating with France's enemies, and he was marked for death by the French Resistance. Later, he was cleared of the charges.

Chevalier reestablished his American film career in the 1950's with Cole Porter's *Can-Can* (1960), Billy Wilder's *Love in the Afternoon* (1957), and most notably Alan Jay Lerner and Frederick Loewe's *Gigi* (1958). He received a special Academy Award for his lifetime of work in 1958. Chevalier continued to tour and made a few minor films in the 1960's and early 1970's. He died in Paris after a brief illness at age eighty-three.

The Music

A charming, smiling fellow in his trademark tuxedo and straw hat, Chevalier was the embodiment of Gallic charm. Chevalier knew the limitations of his voice, which was a natural rather than a well-trained one. His sunny performances helped audiences momentarily forget the difficult times they were enduring. He was everyone's favorite bachelor uncle or perhaps secret French lover.

Early Works. In many of his songs (such as "Mimi" and "Louise"), Chevalier spoke the middle section, which allowed him to act out instead of merely singing the song. In his work as a music-hall entertainer, Chevalier had to project a song to the last row of seats, so he developed impeccable diction. His recorded voice was so precise that listeners with little knowledge of French could understand some of the words. "Paris sera toujours Paris" (Paris, stay the same) was one of Chevalier's most popular songs during World War II, tolerated by the occupying Germans.

Love Me Tonight. Marcel Orphül's documentary on the French Occupation, when Germany occupied France during World War II, *Le Chagrin et le pitié* (1971; the sorrow and the pity) famously ends

Maurice Chevalier. (AP/Wide World Photos)

Jourdan's bachelor uncle who gives his nephew romantic advice gleaned from his years of romancing beautiful women. This is one of Chevalier's best dramatic performances. His semispoken rendition of "I Remember It Well" blends beautifully with the character of his former lover, Hermione Gingold, who was not a singer and primarily spoke her lyrics. His jaunty "I'm Glad I'm Not Young Anymore" charms audiences once again with his smiling, boulevardier manner.

Musical Legacy

Chevalier was one of the best-loved performers in France and America for more than half a century. His early work in Hollywood helped establish the musical motion picture as a popular genre. Singers of a later generation, such as Frank Sinatra and Dean Martin, modeled their stage personas as happy-go-lucky ladies' men on Chevalier, and their light, jazzy singing styles paid homage to his. Even three decades after Chevalier's death, Harry Connick, Jr., demonstrated his debt to Chevalier in sunny but sophisticated performances.

David E. Anderson

with Chevalier singing "Sweepin' the Clouds Away" from his Hollywood debut *Paramount on Parade* (1930). However, it was 1932's *Love Me Tonight*, with songs by Richard Rodgers and Lorenz Hart, that elevated Chevalier to stardom in a long string of motion-picture musicals in the 1930's and 1940's.

Love Me Tonight introduced two Chevalier standards, "Isn't It Romantic?" and "Mimi." Chevalier displays his suave, man-about-town side in "Isn't It Romantic?" as the verses of the song pass from person to person, locale to locale, until they reach MacDonald in her chateau. In "Mimi," which does not advance the plot, Chevalier flirts suggestively with MacDonald, in his trademark singsong and talky delivery. This song later bounces from character to character in the chateau.

Gigi. This 1958 film adaptation of Collette's story—about a young girl who, despite being groomed to be a rich man's plaything, finds true love—introduced Chevalier to a younger generation. Chevalier plays to type as actor Louis

Further Reading

Behr, Edward. *The Good Frenchman: The True Story of the Life and Times of Maurice Chevalier*. New York: Villard, 1993. Behr captures the shadow beneath Chevalier's sunny smile: problems maintaining romantic relationships, fears of returning to the poverty of his youth, and feelings of inadequacy.

Bret, David. *Maurice Chevalier: On Top of a Rainbow*. London: Robson Books, 1993. Fully authorized biography of Chevalier details the accusations against Chevalier for collaborating with the Germans and the French Resistance marking him for death.

Chevalier, Maurice. *I Remember It Well*. New York: Macmillan, 1970. Chevalier's recollection of his life's events should be balanced with other biographies.

Chevalier, Maurice, Eileen Pollock, and Robert Mason Pollock. *With Love*. Boston: Little, Brown, 1960. Lively, personal account of Chevalier's life.

Vals, François. *Maurice Chevalier*. Paris: Didier Carpentier, 2002. Chevalier's right-hand man for the last twenty years of his career shares his insights. Vals had access to Chevalier's personal material.

See also: Bennett, Tony; Connick, Harry, Jr.; Fain, Sammy; Hart, Lorenz; Legrand, Michel; Lerner, Alan Jay; Loewe, Frederick; Piaf, Édith; Porter, Cole; Rodgers, Richard; Sinatra, Frank.

Charlie Christian

American jazz guitarist and songwriter

With his virtuosic, swinging solos featuring sustained notes and volume levels comparable to wind instruments, Christian expanded the guitar's role beyond mere accompaniment and popularized the electric guitar.

Born: July 29, 1916; Bonham, Texas
Died: March 2, 1942; New York, New York
Also known as: Charles Henry Christian (full name)
Member of: The Benny Goodman Sextet

Principal recordings

ALBUMS (solo): *Live Sessions at Minton's Playhouse*, 1941; *Jazz Gallery/C. Christian*, 1999.

ALBUM (with Benny Goodman Sextet): *Slipped Disc, 1945-1946*, 1946.

The Life

Charles Henry Christian grew up in a supportive African American family, surrounded by music. Both of his parents were involved with music; although his blind father passed away before Christian started playing the guitar seriously, it had been one of his father's favorite instruments. The family moved to Oklahoma City when Christian was young, and there he was exposed to musical acts that traveled through the important trade hub. Because of segregation, many opportunities were closed to Christian and his friends, but they enthusiastically participated in baseball as well as music. He was encouraged in music by his older brother and other musicians, such as guitarist Ralph Ham-

ilton, who invited Christian to participate in a jam session with touring musicians. That public performance, in which Christian improvised long melodic variations on acoustic guitar, was well received. As his reputation grew into the late 1930's, he began playing an amplified guitar. When John Hammond of Columbia Records heard Christian play in 1939, Hammond arranged for the guitarist to meet Benny Goodman. During the next two years, Christian became internationally famous, playing and recording with Goodman's sextet as well as with other musicians, such as Lionel Hampton, and with some of the creators of the bebop style. Christian played incessantly, often going from one engagement to the next in the same evening. Often he would work with Goodman and then travel to a marathon jam session at a small club in Harlem. In the summer of 1941, he was diagnosed with tuberculosis and was hospitalized. Tragically, Christian died just a few months later.

The Music

From the beginning, Christian preferred playing melodic lines rather than focusing on the strummed chord melodies that were popular at the time. Long before adopting the electric guitar, he developed a strong, energetic technique. Christian created a musical style cultivated by midwestern jazz musicians in the 1930's, including a driving rhythm with a light chordal texture; an emphasis on extended, competitive solo improvisation over strict rhythmic cycles; and the use of repeated melodic figures (riffs) to build arrangements. Although Christian was aware of the work of his predecessors on acoustic guitar (including Django Reinhardt), his melodic style was more deeply influenced by wind-instrument players, such as tenor saxophonist Lester Young, whom Christian first met when Young was touring in the Midwest with the Blue Devils.

Benny Goodman. Most of Christian's recorded solos are associated with Goodman's groups from 1939 to 1941. Although he occasionally played with Goodman's orchestra, Christian's most influential solos were recorded with the smaller ensembles: the sextet and septet. In these recordings, the clarity of the thinner textures allowed the tone of the electric guitar to contrast more clearly with the sounds of the vibraphone, the piano, and the other instruments. Along with adding to the midwestern stylistic features of the ensemble as a whole (which are more prominent in the later recordings), Christian introduced dissonant melodic patterns that would become characteristic of modern jazz. He took advantage of the guitar's natural qualities in adopting leaps of perfect fourths, made easier on the guitar by the instrument's standard tuning, and also chromatic double neighbor tones, which are facilitated by the guitar's chromatic fingerboard. In terms of accompaniment, he also changed the rhythmic role of the guitar, which was no longer bound to reinforce the double bass's steady stream of quarter notes.

Live Sessions at Minton's Playhouse. While in New York with Goodman, Christian worked frequently with the musicians who created the bebop style, including trumpeter Dizzy Gillespie and pianist Thelonious Monk. Most of the musicians played into the morning hours at Minton's Playhouse and other places in Harlem. Recordings of these early noncommercial experiments are rare, but it is clear that Christian contributed to the development of the genre, especially considering the melodic characteristics of his recorded solos. Fortunately, Jerry Newman, a jazz fan, brought portable recording equipment to Minton's and captured a few of Christian's jam sessions with drummer Kenny Clarke, tenor saxophonist Don Byas, and others. Associates remember that Christian was constantly refining and perfecting his style.

Musical Legacy

In the decades following Christian's recordings, the electric guitar evolved from an obscure oddity to become the dominant sound of popular music. The first major player of the instrument, Christian extended his influence far beyond his own brilliance as a jazz musician. Ironically, the newer, louder genres eclipsed the music that Christian loved, at least in terms of popularity. Within the jazz world, several generations of the best guitarists point to him as a source of style and inspiration. Wes Montgomery, hailed by many as his successor, began by learning Christian's solos note for note. In addition, Christian played an important role in the development of bebop, the first aggressively modern genre to appear in jazz.

John Myers

Further Reading

Alexander, Charles. *Masters of Jazz Guitar: The Story of the Players and Their Music.* San Francisco: Backbeat, 2002. Includes a chapter on Christian.

Broadbent, Peter. *Charlie Christian: Solo Flight, the Seminal Electric Guitarist.* Blaydon on Tyne: Ashley Mark, 2003. Coverage of Christian's career, including interviews with musicians and personal accounts of the guitarist, discography, photographs, and appendixes.

Christian, Charlie. *Charlie Christian, the Definitive Collection.* Milwaukee, Wis.: Hal Leonard, 2003. By Pete Billmann, Jeff Jacobson, and Wolf Marshall, transcriptions, chord symbols, and staff notation and tablature of Christian's most famous recorded solos.

Ellison, Ralph, and Robert G. O'Meally. *Living with Music: Ralph Ellison's Jazz Writings.* New York: Modern Library, 2001. Includes a chapter on Christian, setting him in cultural context.

Goins, Wayne E., and Craig R. McKinney. *A Biography of Charlie Christian, Jazz Guitar's King of Swing.* Lewiston, N.Y.: Edwin Mellen Press, 2005. Detailed account of Christian's life, including commentary on music. With illustrations, bibliography, and index.

See also: Gillespie, Dizzy; Goodman, Benny; Hampton, Lionel; Johnson, Lonnie; Monk, Thelonious; Montgomery, Wes; Parker, Charlie; Powell, Bud; Reinhardt, Django; Walker, T-Bone; Williams, Mary Lou; Young, Lester.

Chuck D
American rap vocalist and songwriter

As a member of Public Enemy, Chuck D crafted direct, sometimes confrontational rap. His lyrics incorporated Black Power ideology and highlighted the social and political double standard that marginalizes African Americans.

Born: August 1, 1960; Long Island, New York
Also known as: Carlton Douglas Ridenhour (birth name); Chuckie D; Mista Chuck

Musicians and Composers of the 20th Century

Member of: Public Enemy; Spectrum City; Confrontation Camp; Fine Arts Militia

Principal recordings

ALBUMS (solo): *Autobiography of Mistachuck*, 1996; *Tribb to JB*, 2007.

ALBUMS (with Confrontation Camp): *Objects in the Mirror Are Closer than They Appear*, 2000.

ALBUMS (with Fine Arts Militia): *We Are Gathered Here*, 2003.

ALBUMS (with Public Enemy): *Yo! Bum Rush the Show*, 1987; *It Takes a Nation of Millions to Hold Us Back*, 1988; *Fear of a Black Planet*, 1990; *Apocalypse 91 . . . The Enemy Strikes Black*, 1991; *Muse Sick-N-Hour Mess Age*, 1994; *He Got Game*, 1998; *There's a Poison Goin' On*, 1999; *Revolverlution*, 2002; *New Whirl Odor*, 2005; *Beats and Places*, 2005; *Rebirth of a Nation*, 2006; *How You Sell Soul to a Soulless People Who Sold Their Soul?*, 2007.

ALBUMS (with Spectrum City): *Check out the Radio*, 1984; *Lies*, 1984.

The Life

Chuck D was born Carlton Douglas Ridenhour in Roosevelt, New York, a suburb in Long Island's Black Belt. This was a string of communities across the island that became primarily black after white flight short-circuited school integration efforts. Chuck's experience with the racial double standard of the suburbs, combined with his parents' political activism, left an indelible impression that was reflected in his lyrics.

Chuck attended Adelphi University to study graphic design, and there he met most of the future members of Public Enemy, including William Drayton (Flavor Flav), Hank "Shocklee" Boxley, Norman Rogers (Terminator X), and Richard Griffin (Professor Griff). Though he had built a considerable reputation as a capable emcee while at Adelphi, Chuck did not immediately consider hip-hop a viable career. Def Jam Recordings hired Bill Stephney, who had given Chuck and Boxley a radio show on Adelphi's WBAU when the three were in college, to persuade Chuck to sign a contract. Public Enemy's first album, *Yo! Bum Rush the Show*, was a moderate success. However, it was the next three—*It Takes a Nation of Millions to Hold Us Back*, *Fear of a Black Planet*, and *Apocalypse 91 . . . The Enemy*

Strikes Black—that certified Public Enemy as an important rap group.

Chuck D served as rapper, producer, and media liaison for Public Enemy. He also appeared as a commentator on news and political programs and hosted two political and cultural talk shows on Air America Radio: *Unfiltered* and *On the Real*.

The Music

For Public Enemy, Chuck D was involved in rapping, production, media, and security. Though he was not directly responsible for the group's sound, he served as its touchstone.

"Don't Believe the Hype." From *It Takes a Nation of Millions to Hold Us Back*, "Don't Believe the Hype" is a straightforward combination of a funk guitar sample and looping drums. The soundscape features a sampled instrument screech reminiscent of a scream that invades the last beat and a half of each measure. The scream is appropriate, as Chuck addresses the critics who have marked him as a social threat, a reverse racist who espouses Black Power and Nation of Islam antiwhite rhetoric. Here, Chuck walks a thin line: bluntly stating his position while discrediting the worried wails of those who fear him.

"Rebel Without a Pause." From *It Takes a Nation of Millions to Hold Us Back*, this was recorded just after the release of Rakim's "I Know You Got Soul." "Rebel Without a Pause" features Chuck asserting himself as both a conscientious voice and a stylistic force to rival Rakim. Chuck's lyrics are rapped over a beat that is a sample of Robert McCollough's saxophone squeal, tweaked until it sounds like a tea kettle. Hip-hop, Chuck tells us, has reached a boiling point, and he is determined to move it into a new, more visible position.

"Fear of a Black Planet." From the album of the same name, this song shows Chuck toying with the notion of the black man as sexual predator, out to seduce or steal women of all colors from their mates. His critique of the racial-purity ideal sounds among a chorus of samples of the word "fear" that jump from left to right speaker and complete the musical track.

"Fight the Power." From *Fear*, "Fight the Power" is Public Enemy's signature song and was featured in the opening credits of Spike Lee's *Do the Right Thing* (1989), a coupling that launched the director and Chuck into the mainstream. The instrumental track is a typical blending of funk guitar samples and drum sounds, and its militant hook solidified Chuck and Public Enemy as the antiestablishment vanguard.

"By the Time I Get to Arizona." From *Apocalypse 91 . . . The Enemy Strikes Black*, this piece is a response to Evan Mecham's first act as governor of Arizona: overturning the Martin Luther King, Jr., holiday. Chuck raps atop a slow, funky track that includes gospel choir swells and a guitar sample that features a ripping chainsaw in each measure. The song's title was meant to be threatening, and the accompanying video depicted the poisoning of a senator, the assassination of Mecham, and other gunplay.

Musical Legacy

Public Enemy's early sound featured an endless stream of samples that had been cut, processed, and pasted together by the Bomb Squad, the group's production team that included Boxley, to form a backdrop for Chuck and Drayton's flow. The hyper-sampled sound complemented the group's lyrical message, as both words and music commented upon the culture. The act of signifying through sampling marked much message rap until stricter copyright guidelines forced producers to pay expensive royalties for samples or abandon the practice altogether.

Chuck D's uncompromising lyrics and persona made him a role model for message rap artists. Along with William Michael Griffin, Jr. (Rakim), Chuck reclaimed the substantive messages that marked hip-hop of the early 1980's and cleared a space for explicitly socially conscious rappers to exist alongside the gangsta scene in the 1990's.

Justin D. Burton

Further Reading

Chang, Jeff. "What We Got to Say" and "Follow for Now." In *Can't Stop, Won't Stop: A History of the Hip-Hop Generation*. New York: St. Martin's Press, 2005. A hip-hop journalist weaves Public Enemy's story into the larger tapestry of hip-hop history.

Chuck D, and Yusuf Jah. *Lyrics of a Rap Revolutionary*. New York: Offda Books, 2007. Chuck ex-plores the political ramifications and possibilities of hip-hop beyond the social scene.

Chuck D, Yusuf Jah, and Spike Lee. *Fight the Power: Rap, Race, and Reality*. New York: Delta, 1997. Chuck's book addresses many of the same issues that his music does, especially racial inequality in America.

Friskics-Warren, Bill. "Fight the Power: Spearheads, the Mekons, and Public Enemy." In *I'll Take You There: Pop Music and the Urge for Transcendence*. New York: Continuum, 2005. An overview of Public Enemy's heyday, exploring the ways in which Chuck's lyrics aimed at transcendence.

Walser, Robert. "Rhythm, Rhyme, and Rhetoric in the Music of Public Enemy." *Ethnomusicology* 39, no. 2 (1995): 193-217. Walser explores the rhetoric of Public Enemy's music with an analysis of "Fight the Power."

Watkins, S. Craig. "The Digital Underground." In *Hip-Hop Matters: Politics, Pop Culture, and the Struggle for the Soul of a Movement*. Boston: Beacon Press, 2005. Overview of a legal struggle concerning digital music files, with Chuck D as a central character.

See also: Badu, Erykah; Simmons, Joseph "Run"; Snoop Dogg.

Kyung-Wha Chung
Korean classical violinist

Chung's success as violinist ushered in a new era for accomplished Asian musicians playing classical Western music. Her style combines elegance, perfection, and passion.

Born: March 26, 1948; Seoul, South Korea

Principal recordings

ALBUMS: *Tchaikovsky, Sibelius: Violin Concertos*, 1970; *Beethoven: Violin Concertos*, 1982; *Berg and Bartók: Violin Concertos*, 1984; *Béla Bartók: Violin Concerto No. 2 and Rhapsodies 1 and 2*, 1988; *Mendelssohn: Concerto for Violin in E Minor*, 1990; *Bach: Concerto in E/Trio Sonata Nos. 2 and*

4/ Suite No. 2, 1991; *Tchaikovsky: Piano Concertos Nos. 1-3; Violin Concerto*, 1996; *Brahms: Violin Sonatas Nos. 1-3*, 1998; *Celibidache Conducts Strauss and Resphigi Violin Sonatas*, 2000; *Vivaldi: The Four Seasons*, 2001; *Wagner's Ring*, 2001; *Beethoven Piano Trios Nos. 1, 4, 5, and 7*, 2007.

The Life

Kyung-Wha Chung (kyuhng wah chuhng) was born on March 26, 1948, in Seoul, South Korea, daughter of businessman Won Sook Lee Chung and his wife Chun Chai Chung. Kyung's parents loved music, and they educated their nine children in a variety of Western instruments. Kyung settled on playing the violin at six. By nine, she performed with the Seoul Philharmonic Orchestra.

In 1961, at thirteen, Chung moved to New York City to study at the Juilliard School under Ivan Galamian. Her first triumph occurred in 1967, when she was cowinner of the Edgar Leventritt Competition, and her breakthrough came in 1970, when she impressed a London audience with her performance. In 1972 she was awarded the Republic of Korea's Medal of Merit.

Throughout the 1970's and early 1980's, Chung recorded successful albums, and she performed with most of the major orchestras of Western Europe, the United States, South Korea, and Japan. At her peak, she gave 120 performances each season.

In 1984 Chung married British businessman Geoffrey Leggett, with whom she had two sons, Frederick and Eugene. To balance her personal and professional life, she cut her performance schedule in half. In 1988 she won her first Gramophone Award, and in 2000 she won her second Gramophone Award.

The Music

Chung developed a musical style as a concert violinist that combined fireworks with elegance and intelligence with exuberance. Performing with the leading conductors of her era, Chung established herself as a world-class violinist with successful recordings, and she paved the way for other Asian classical music performers, especially Asian women. Her ability to bring genteel refinement to passionate playing and to work with a variety of international symphony orchestras solidified her reputa-

Kyung-Wha Chung. (Hulton Archive/Getty Images)

tion as one of the Western world's outstanding violinists.

The Leventritt Competition. At nineteen, Chung entered the prestigious Edgar Leventritt Competition, despite the fact that her teacher, Galamian, tried to dissuade her from competing with another of his protégés, Pinchas Zukerman. Chung's impressive performance of works by Max Bruch, Wolfgang Amadeus Mozart, Ludwig van Beethoven, and Camille Saint-Saëns created a problem for the judges, who could not decide between her and Zukerman as first-place winner. When a second competitive round failed to settle the issue, for the first time in twenty-seven years the Leventritt jury split the first prize between Chung and Zukerman. Chung's performance, characterized by sensitivity, grit, and passion, became her trademark style. That win set Chung on a successful trajectory. She performed at the inauguration of President Richard Nixon in 1969, and she was invited to play with the Chicago Symphony Orchestra and the New York Philharmonic.

Tchaikovsky Violin Concerto. Chung replaced an ailing Itzhak Perlman at the 1970 Royal Festival Hall performance of Peter Ilich Tchaikovsky's Violin Concerto with conductor André Previn and the London Symphony Orchestra. Her surprise performance brought out the fire in Tchaikovsky's composition and exposed the cool mastery of his score. A rave review in London's *Financial Times* opened the doors to solo engagements with major symphonies in Japan, in West Germany, and in the United States.

Tchaikovsky, Sibelius: Violin Concertos. In 1970 Decca Records in London asked Chung to record violin concerti by Tchaikovsky and Jean Sibelius, with the orchestra conducted by Previn. Her album met an appreciative audience who took to her vigorous, yet elegant interpretation of the works. In 2007 Decca released a remastered compact disc of the recording, with the fervor of her performance engrossing both new and old listeners.

Bartók's Violin Concerto No. 2. The Free World was Chung's stage for much of the 1970's, the 1980's, and the 1990's. While communists shunned her for her South Korean heritage, audiences elsewhere took enthusiastically to her mix of fire and restraint. Her performance of Béla Bartók's Violin Concerto No. 2 became the hallmark of her talent and style. Its 1988 recording with Sir Simon Rattle and the City of Birmingham Symphony Orchestra became an instant classic. In the same year, she formed the Chung Trio with her cellist sister Myung Wha and her pianist brother Myung Whun, both accomplished musicians.

Violin Sonatas. In 2000 Chung's passionate, sensitive, and refined rendition of select violin sonatas by Richard Strauss and Ottorino Respighi, as conducted by Krystian Zimmerman, earned her another Gramophone Award. Her shining evocation of these works brought to the fore a master violinist at the height of her craft.

The Four Seasons. In February, 2001, Chung released a recording of Antonio Vivaldi's *The Four Seasons*, which confirmed the belief of critics and audiences that Chung was a rare talent who could render old favorites with new charm. Performing with St. Luke's Chamber Ensemble, Chung gave a majestic and passionate performance.

Beethoven and Brahms. Chung's November, 2001, release of her solo performance in Beetho-ven's Symphony No. 5 and Johannes Brahms's Violin Concerto in D Major, Op. 77 with Sir Simon Rattle and the Vienna Philharmonic Orchestra gave a fresh accent to popular works. Critics lauded her mix of fire and elegance, acuity and tenderness. Her May, 2003, performance in New York City of the Brahms Violin Concerto with André Previn, conductor at her breakthrough in 1970, closed a personal circle.

Musical Legacy

Through her passionate mastery of Tchaikovsky and Bartók, Chung demonstrated that performers from all over the world could give new meaning and musical freshness to classical European music. As a woman Asian violinist, Chung paved the way for later stars, such as Midori, and she matched talents with other great violinists of her time. Chung's combination of fire and elegance, passion and restraint, exuberance and technical artistry, gave her performances a special poignancy and appeal. Proving her teacher Galamian wrong, Chung succeeded both in the musical profession and in having a fulfilling family life.

R. C. Lutz

Further Reading

Althouse, Paul. "Guide to Records: Beethoven." *American Record Guide* 65, no. 2 (March/April, 2002): 70. Glowing review of Chung's album of Beethoven's Symphony No. 5 and Brahms's Violin Concerto, with praise for an excellent performance of uncommon breadth and beauty.

Homfray, Tim, and Joanne Talbot. "A Balance of Friendship." *Strad* 113, no. 1348 (August, 2002): 828. The article discusses Chung's love for her favorite violin bow, a Grand Adam, she has used since the late 1960's.

Kurzbauer, Heather. "The Art of Balance." *Strad* 110, no. 1314 (October, 1999): 1030. Thorough portrait of Chung at fifty, with a focus on her balance of art and family. Includes photographs.

Sand, Barbara. "The Prodigy Returns." *American Record Guide* 62, no. 1 (January/February, 1999): 5. Sympathetic profile of Chung, with details on her relationship with her teacher Galamian, her work-life balance, and her linkage of concert and recording engagements. Includes photograph.

Time. "Cookie and Pinky Come Through." May 26, 1967. Contemporary account of Chung's co-winning first prize in the Leventritt competition with Zukerman.

See also: Perlman, Itzhak; Previn, Sir André; Szigeti, Joseph.

Eric Clapton

English blues/rock singer, guitarist, and songwriter

As lead guitarist for the Yardbirds and Cream, and as a solo artist, Clapton pioneered virtuosic technique and controlled distortion in rock music.

Born: March 30, 1945; Ripley, England
Also known as: Eric Patrick Clapp (birth name); Slowhand
Member of: Yardbirds; John Mayall and the Bluesbreakers; the Glands; Blind Faith; Cream; Derek and the Dominos

Principal recordings

ALBUMS (solo): *Eric Clapton*, 1970; *Eric Clapton's Rainbow Concert*, 1973; *461 Ocean Boulevard*, 1974; *E.C. Was Here*, 1975; *There's One in Every Crowd*, 1975; *No Reason to Cry*, 1976; *Slowhand*, 1977; *Backless*, 1978; *Another Ticket*, 1981; *Money and Cigarettes*, 1983; *Behind the Sun*, 1985; *August*, 1986; *Crossroads*, 1988; *Journeyman*, 1989; *Twenty-four Nights*, 1991; *The Magic of Eric Clapton*, 1993; *From the Cradle*, 1994; *Pilgrim*, 1998; *Riding with the King*, 2000; *Reptile*, 2001; *Me and Mr. Johnson*, 2004; *Back Home*, 2005.

ALBUMS (with Blind Faith): *Blind Faith*, 1969.

ALBUMS (with Cream): *Fresh Cream*, 1966; *Disraeli Gears*, 1967; *Wheels of Fire*, 1968; *Goodbye*, 1969.

ALBUMS (with Delaney and Bonnie): *Delaney and Bonnie and Friends*, 1970.

ALBUMS (with Derek and the Dominos): *Layla and Other Assorted Love Songs*, 1970.

ALBUMS (with John Mayall and the Bluesbreakers): *John Mayall and the Bluesbreakers*, 1966.

ALBUMS (with the Yardbirds): *Five Live*, 1964; *Sonny Boy Williamson and the Yardbirds*, 1964; *For Your Love*, 1965.

WRITINGS OF INTEREST: *Clapton: The Autobiography*, 2007.

The Life

Born at the home of his maternal grandparents, Eric Clapton was the son of Patricia Clapton and Edward Fryer, a Canadian airman stationed in England. He was raised by his grandparents, and they gave him his first guitar when he turned fifteen. Immediately drawn to American blues, Clapton was strongly influenced by the recordings of Big Bill Broonzy, Ramblin' Jack Elliott, and Blind Boy Fuller. He was later attracted to the sound of Chicago blues and the recordings of Muddy Waters and Howlin' Wolf. He was also inspired by the recordings of Mississippi blues legend Robert Johnson, who would be an influence throughout Clapton's career.

He joined his first band as lead guitarist; it was a London-based rhythm-and-blues group known as the Roosters, whose membership also included future Rolling Stones guitarist Brian Jones and future Manfred Mann singer Paul Pond (Paul Jones). Clapton left the Roosters to play lead guitar for the group Casey Jones and the Engineers; he remained with this group for two weeks before replacing Anthony "Top" Topham as lead guitarist for the Yardbirds. Other group members were Keith Relf (vocals, harmonica), Chris Dreja (rhythm guitar), Paul Samwell-Smith (bass), and Jim McCarty (drums).

The Yardbirds played mostly rhythm-and-blues and blues covers, along with a few original songs. While performing with the Yardbirds, Clapton helped develop the rave-up, an extended improvisation based on the twelve-bar blues progression. The rave-up was an integral part of the Yardbirds' live performances and became an important aspect of Clapton's later group Cream. Clapton remained with the Yardbirds until March, 1965, when he left because of artistic differences.

After a brief retirement to the country, Clapton was hired by British blues performer John Mayall to play in the Bluesbreakers. The Bluesbreakers with Clapton, consisting of Clapton (guitar, vocals), Mayall (keyboards, vocals), John McVie (bass), and Hughie Flint (drums), recorded only one album, but *John Mayall and the Bluesbreakers* is considered to be one of the top British blues albums. Upon leaving the Bluesbreakers, Clapton played in a small blues group called the Glands in 1966; later that year he formed the Powerhouse with Steve Winwood (formerly with the Spencer Davis Group), with whom he would later form the group Blind Faith. In late 1966 Clapton began rehearsing with fellow Bluesbreakers alumni Peter "Ginger" Baker and Jack Bruce, forming the first power trio and supergroup Cream.

Cream was an international success, one of Clapton's most successful groups. However, artistic differences among the members led to their breakup in 1968. At this point Clapton formed another supergroup with Baker and Winwood, Blind Faith. After one album and an unsuccessful U.S. tour, Clapton found himself looking for a new band. He found this in 1969 with a U.S. group, Delaney and Bonnie and Friends. Clapton became a touring member of the group and simultaneously embarked on a solo career, releasing his first solo album, *Eric Clapton*, with the hit "After Midnight." Drawing on Delaney and Bonnie's rhythm section—Carl Radle (bass), Bobby Whitlock (keyboards, vocals), and Jim Gordon (drums)—Clapton next formed Derek and the Dominos. The Dominos is best described as a talented but drug-troubled blues-based rock group. After recording sessions began, the group was augmented by the slide-guitar sounds of Southern rocker Duane Allman. After releasing two albums, *Layla and Other Assorted Love Songs* and a live album, the Dominos disbanded in 1971. During 1972 Clapton retired, dealing with his major heroin problem. Eventually, several friends, led by the Who's Pete Townshend, coaxed Clapton into cleaning himself up so he could return to playing. The result was an all-star Rainbow Concert, featuring Clapton, Townshend, Winwood, Ron Wood, and other Clapton friends and bandmates.

At that point Clapton resumed a successful career, releasing several albums. Besides albums with a pop-rock sound such as *461 Ocean Boulevard*, *Slowhand*, and *Reptile*, Clapton remained true to his blues roots with releases such as *From the Cradle*, *Riding with the King* (a collaboration with venerated bluesman B. B. King), and *Me and Mr. Johnson* (a tribute to Mississippi bluesman Robert Johnson).

The Music

Although Clapton found a strong voice as a singer and songwriter, he was revered for his guitar technique. His earliest recordings with the Yardbirds were originally released as singles and demonstrated the beginnings of his blues technique. Songs such as "Baby What's Wrong" and "Good Morning Little School Girl" featured Clapton as a lead soloist, imitating his Chicago blues influences. His playing featured frequent slides and discrete bent strings as well as a prevalent use of descending minor pentatonic scales. The smoothness of his finger slides led his fans to call him Slowhand.

As he moved on to the Bluesbreakers, his melodic approach became smoother and cleaner, as demonstrated on his solo on "All Your Love." Here, Clapton retained his fluid technique, adding an even, slow vibrato on long-held notes. This vibrato and his ability to bend strings almost to the point of feedback are trademarks of Clapton's guitar style.

Cream. In his performances with Cream, Clapton was influenced by the psychedelic guitar sounds of acid rock and especially the grand technique of Jimi Hendrix. With Cream, Clapton explored the possibilities of sound distortion, with effects such as wah-wah, fuzz tone, and natural feedback. Though Clapton usually preferred the sound of the solid-body Fender Stratocaster, with Cream he often soloed on his Gibson Les Paul guitar for a more biting sound. Exemplary solos during this period included the minor blues performance on "Sunshine of Your Love" from *Disraeli Gears*, the live "Crossroads" on *Wheels of Fire*, and his uncredited guest spot on "While My Guitar Gently Weeps" on the Beatles' *White Album*. One of the most notable aspects of Cream's sound was the juxtaposition of Bruce's jazz-influenced bass lines, Baker's busy but clear jazz-based drumming, and Clapton's raw-edged, psychedelic-distorted blues-based guitar sound.

Blind Faith. Beginning with his days with Blind Faith, Clapton more frequently employed an acoustic guitar on his recordings, played with a folklike fingerpicking style as on "Can't Find My Way Back Home." While he recorded primarily on electric instruments, Clapton also used his acoustic guitar to change mood. Other notable acoustic guitar performances included "Tears in Heaven," a tribute written after the tragic death of his four-year-old son in 1991; his performance on MTV's *Unplugged* series, which featured an excellent acoustic reconstruction of "Layla"; and a rare acoustic guitar duet with B. B. King on Broonzy's "Key to the Highway" on the album *Riding with the King*.

Derek and the Dominos. For the heavily blues-influenced *Layla and Other Assorted Love Songs* with Derek and the Dominos, Clapton returned to his favorite Stratocaster sound. Sharing solos with slide guitarist Allman, Clapton reverted to a clean sound with less distortion and more blues techniques, such as finger slides and string bends. Particularly effective were the solos traded between Clapton and Allman on "Key to the Highway." Although primarily a blues album, there were some raw, rough-edged rock solos heard on their cover of Hendrix's "Little Wing," the title cut "Layla," and the song "Why Does Love Got to Be So Sad?"

Later Works. After his drug rehabilitation, Clapton's playing became as smooth and tasteful as a fine cognac. He had successful radio singles along the way, such as "I Shot the Sheriff" from *461 Ocean Boulevard* and "Lay Down Sally" and "Wonderful Tonight" from *Slowhand*. In the mid-1970's, Clapton shifted to a low profile, releasing an occasional Top 20 single and recording relaxed albums of pop-rock material. He composed and performed on a number of film sound tracks, including *Lethal Weapon* (1987), *Lethal Weapon 2* (1989), *Lethal Weapon 3* (1992), *Edge of Darkness* (1985), and *Rush* (1991). He was a guest artist on several albums, ranging from classical guitarist Leona Boyd's *Persona* (1986), to spots on rock albums by George Harrison, Sting, Leon Russell, and the Rolling Stones, to blues collaborations with blues guitarists Buddy Guy, Howlin' Wolf, and B. B. King.

Through it all, Clapton's guitar style was based in the Chicago blues with a smooth melodic sensibility, expressive string bends, and evenly paced vibrato. He no longer depended on sound distortion, either with natural feedback or with distortion devices. Instead, Clapton's playing featured clear and precise note placement seasoned with his blues techniques.

Musical Legacy

Clapton was one of the first musicians in the rock era to gain a strong following based on his instrumental technique rather than his singing or his looks. His fans during the Yardbirds era were so enthralled with his technique they began to spray-paint graffiti around London that read "Clapton is God." While many of his original songs became rock classics, particularly his output with Cream, Blind Faith, Derek and the Dominos, and some of his solo material, Clapton remained faithful to his blues roots. He was inducted into the Rock and Roll Hall of Fame on three separate occasions for his work with the Yardbirds (1992) and Cream (1993) as well as for his solo endeavors (2000). He was awarded six Grammy Awards for his *Unplugged* album in 1993, including Album of the Year and Best Song (for "Tears in Heaven"). In 1998 Clapton founded the Crossroads Centre in Antigua, West Indies, a clinic for rehabilitation of drug and alcohol abusers.

Stephen Valdez

Further Reading

Clapton, Eric. *Clapton: The Autobiography*. New York: Broadway Books, 2007. The complete and authoritative story of his life from Clapton.

Clifford, Mike, ed. *The Harmony Illustrated Encyclopedia of Rock*. 7th ed. New York: Harmony Books, 1992. Brief articles on Clapton and the groups of which he was a member. Includes a selective discography of Clapton's career to the early 1990's.

Roberty, Marc. *Eric Clapton: The Complete Recording Sessions, 1963-1992*. New York: St. Martin's Press, 1993. Exhaustively researched, this book lists all of the recording sessions in which Clapton took part, from the Yardbirds to his solo releases and guest sessions, to 1992. Includes a complete discography and videography and lists the instruments Clapton used in each session.

Schumacher, Michael. *Crossroads: The Life and Music of Eric Clapton*. New York: Hyperion, 1995. Well-written biography of the musician through 1994, including a selective discography of Clapton's career from the Yardbirds to his solo works, including bootlegs, and a discography of other artists for whom Clapton played guitar in the studio and in concert. Includes complete listing of groups and personnel with whom Clapton played from his first group (the Roosters) to his solo albums and concerts.

Shapiro, Harry. *Eric Clapton: Lost in the Blues*. New York: Da Capo Press, 1993. Good biography of Clapton, though not as complete as Schumacher's *Crossroads* or Clapton's autobiography. Contains a thorough discography and an appendix on the technical aspects of Clapton's guitars and equipment.

See also: Babyface; Beck, Jeff; Berry, Chuck; Blige, Mary J.; Eddy, Duane; Fogerty, John; Fuller, Blind Boy; Guy, Buddy; Hendrix, Jimi; Howlin' Wolf; James, Elmore; Johnson, Robert; King, Albert; King, B. B.; Marley, Bob; Page, Jimmy; Paul, Les; Reed, Jimmy; Robertson, Robbie; Rush, Otis; Santana, Carlos; Stills, Stephen; Sting; Tosh, Peter; Townshend, Pete; Van Halen, Eddie; Vaughan, Stevie Ray; Waters, Muddy; Waters, Roger; Williamson, Sonny Boy, I.

James Cleveland

American gospel pianist, trombonist, and choral director

A leading star in gospel music for four decades, Cleveland was known for his gruff voice, dynamic showmanship, and innovative work directing gospel choirs. The Gospel Music Workshop of America, founded by Cleveland, became the most significant force in shaping choral music in modern gospel.

Born: December 5, 1932; Chicago, Illinois
Died: February 9, 1991; Culver City, California
Also known as: Reverend Dr. James Cleveland; Crown Prince of Gospel
Member of: Angelic Choir; the Charles Fold Singers; the Southern California Community Choir; the Cleveland Singers; Voices of the Tabernacle

Principal recordings

ALBUMS (solo): *This Sunday in Person*, 1962 (with the Angelic Choir); *James Cleveland and the Angelic Choir*, 1962 (with the Angelic Choir); *Peace Be Still*, 1963 (with the Angelic Choir); *I Stood on the Banks of the Jordan*, 1964 (with the Angelic Choir); *Lord, Let Me Be an Instrument*, 1966 (with the Charles Fold Singers); *I Told Jesus to Change My Name*, 1974 (with the Southern California Community Choir); *In the Ghetto*, 1974 (with the Southern California Community Choir); *Trust in God*, 1975 (with the Gospel Girls); *James Cleveland and the Charles Fold Singers, Vol. II*, 1977; *James Cleveland and Ruth Schofield Edition*, 1978; *James Cleveland and the Charles Fold Singers, Vol. III: Is There Any Hope for Tomorrow*, 1978; *James Cleveland and the Southern California Community Choir*, 1978; *Reunion*, 1979 (with Alberta Walker); *The Promise*, 1980 (with the Philadelphia Mass Choir); *A Praying Spirit*, 1982 (with the Cornerstone Choir); *Twentieth Anniversary Album*, 1982 (with the World's Greatest Choirs); *Amazing Grace*, 1990 (with the Southern California Community Choir); *For the Prize*, 1990 (with the Houston Mass Choir); *Give Me My Flowers*, 1990 (with the Angelic Choir); *Hallelujah 'Tis Done*, 1990 (with Cassietta George); *Having Church*, 1990 (with the Southern California Community Choir); *His Name Is Wonderful*, 1990 (with the Angelic Choir); *I Don't Feel Noways Tired*, 1990 (with the Salem Inspirational Choir); *I Know He Can*, 1990 (with Alberta Walker); *James Cleveland Sings with the Great Gospel Star Parade*, 1990; *This Too Will Pass*, 1990 (with the Charles Fold Singers); *James Cleveland and the Angelic Choir*, 1991; *Merry Christmas*, 1991 (with the Angelic Choir).

ALBUMS (with the Cleveland Singers): *In the Beginning*, 1978; *At the Cross*, 1990; *Especially for You*, 1990; *God's Promises*, 1990; *His Eye Is Sparrow*, 1990; *I Love to Tell*, 1990; *I'm Giving My Love*, 1990; *Inspired*, 1990; *Lord Help Me to Hold Out*, 1990; *Love of God*, 1990; *The One and Only*, 1990; *Pilgrim of Sorrow*, 1990; *Praise 88*, 1990; *Rev. James Cleveland and the Cleveland Singers*, 1990; *Sun Will Shine Afterwards*, 1990; *To the Glory of God*, 1990; *Tomorrow*, 1990; *Touch Me*, 1990; *Where Is Your Faith*, 1990; *Down Memory Lane*, 1991; *Out on a Hill*, 1991; *Songs My Mother Taught Me*, 1991; *Victory Shall Be Mine*, 1991.

The Life

James Cleveland was born to Benjamin and Rosie Lee Cleveland. Benjamin worked for the Works Progress Administration. Young James attended Pilgrim Baptist Church with his family, and his exceptional singing talent was quickly noticed. Thomas A. Dorsey, who is considered the father of gospel music, was the choir director at Pilgrim Baptist Church and mentored James as well as writing a composition for him. The famous gospel music pianist and composer Roberta Martin played keyboards for the choir and helped develop James's skills on the piano. She also published Cleveland's first composition, "I Want to See Jesus."

As a young man, Cleveland moved to Philadelphia, where he helped form the gospel group the Gospelaires. During the 1950's he lived in Philadelphia, New York, Detroit, and Chicago; served as music minister and assistant pastor in several churches; sang in various gospel groups; and established his reputation as a singer, pianist, and arranger.

In the 1960's, Cleveland was ordained and moved to Los Angeles to pastor the New Greater Harvest Baptist Church. In 1968, he organized the Gospel Workshop of America to teach, improve, and spread gospel music. In 1970, he founded the Cornerstone Baptist Church, featuring an internationally known choir. He had a daughter, LaShone.

Cleveland was awarded an honorary doctorate from Trinity Bible College. After his death in 1991, allegations of financial and other improprieties were leveled against him, some by his foster son, Christopher Harris. However, his legacy as the father of modern gospel choir music has continued to grow.

The Music

For the Reverend Cleveland, his life as a church minister and his work as a gospel singer were entwined. He developed his singing talent as a boy under the tutelage of the famous gospel musicians Thomas A. Dorsey and Roberta Martin. As a young adult, he served as music minister and choir leader in various churches, founding his first group in 1959. Much of his early prominence as a singer came from his performances with the legendary gospel group the Caravans. In 1963, he formed the James Cleveland Singers. During his adult career, he took as his mission the forging of gospel choirs into a modern musical force, capable of assimilating the more sophisticated influences and harmonies of jazz, blues, soul, and even classical music.

"The Love of God." While at the Prayer Tabernacle in Detroit, Michigan, Cleveland helped form the Voices of the Tabernacle choir. In 1959, he recorded his first solo hit, "The Love of God" with this group. After a light piano introduction, Cleveland's entry is dramatic. He croons variations of the refrain "Love of God" with his trademark bullfrog timbre. The choir sighs, moans, and swells in the background. Cleveland's singing combines preaching, pop balladry, and soulful glissandi.

"Peace Be Still." In the early 1960's, Cleveland recorded three long-playing (LP) albums for the

James Cleveland. (Hulton Archive/Getty Images)

Savoy label with the Angelic Choir, featuring Billy Preston at the organ. Volume I, recorded in 1962 and titled *This Sunday in Person*, was apparently the first live gospel session to be recorded. The second volume, 1962's *James Cleveland and the Angelic Choir*, featured Cleveland's hit recording of the gospel standard "How Great Thou Art."

The third volume, *Peace Be Still*, recorded live and released in 1963, was the first gospel LP to sell move than fifty thousand albums; by 2008, it had more than one million. It featured Cleveland's greatest hit, "Peace Be Still," derived from a little-known eighteenth century madrigal. The recording features Cleveland's trademark arrangement: a large choir, rhythms heavily influenced by blues and jazz, and swaying organ and percussion accompaniment. Cleveland's rough-hewn vocals alternate theatrically with the smooth-sounding, swelling choir. Perhaps most notable about the recording is the rousing chorus that assumes prominence in the second half of the performance, as the choir rhythmically and intricately chants "Peace Be Still."

Cleveland performed with the Southern California Community Choir, which he formed when he founded the Cornerstone Baptist Church. The Southern California Community Choir sang behind him on his two Grammy Award LP albums *Live at Carnegie Hall* and *In the Ghetto*.

"I Don't Feel No Ways Tired." Cleveland's version of the gospel standard "I Don't Feel No Ways Tired," available on the album of the same name, illustrates his complex interplay of lead voice and choir. Cleveland's gruff lead contrasts starkly with the harmonic chants of the choir. Cleveland pauses to exhort, to preach, and to allow the choral rhythms to emerge. He delivers ecstatic variations on the sung word "believe." Likewise, the choir's varied arrangements of the refrain "I believe he brought me this far" exemplify the sophistication and elegance of Cleveland's choral compositions.

Musical Legacy

Cleveland became the leading modern exponent of the gospel choir. As a choral director, he was innovative as well as instructive, influencing many generations of singers. He performed with most of the leading gospel choirs, including the Voices of the Tabernacle, the Angelic Gospel Choir, and the Southern California Community Choir. The concerts of the Gospel Music Workshop of America, which he founded, featured choirs of as many as three thousand singers. He brought influences from contemporary secular and popular music into the traditional gospel choir. Whereas previous arrangements in gospel were often spontaneous, basic, and emotional, Cleveland arranged choral music with complex rhythms, varied tempi, and sophisticated harmonies. His annual Gospel Singers Workshop Convention spread gospel to thousands of singers and other musicians. Cleveland himself wrote more than four hundred songs and released more than one hundred albums of gospel music, winning four Grammy Awards.

For his contributions to gospel music, vocals, composition, and performance, Cleveland has been called the Crown Prince of Gospel. He was an exciting vocalist—with a hoarse, gritty quality to his voice, in striking contrast to the sweet-toned, imploring choir that accompanied him. The "foghorn" quality of his vocals has been likened to that of Louis Armstrong, and his preaching lyrics were heartfelt and gripping. Cleveland also sang with or accompanied such gospel stars as Clara Ward and had a strong influence on Aretha Franklin.

Howard Bromberg

Further Reading

Boyer, Horace Clarence. *How Sweet the Sound: The Golden Age of Gospel*. Washington, D.C.: Elliott and Clark, 1995. A conversational history of gospel music told biographically and geographically by a gospel musician and scholar.

Broughton, Viv. *Too Close to Heaven: The Illustrated History of Gospel Music*. London: Midnight Books, 1996. An updated history of gospel music that served as the basis for a British television documentary.

Carpenter, Bil. *Uncloudy Days: The Gospel Music Encyclopedia*. New York: Hal Leonard Books, 2007. Based on more than one hundred interviews, this comprehensive reference work reveals both the highlights and the low points in gospel music history.

Cusic, Don. *The Sound of Light: A History of Gospel Music*. Bowling Green, Ohio: Bowling Green State University Popular Press, 1990. Relates the story of gospel music in the broader context of religious musical history and contemporary musical forms.

Darden, Robert. *People Get Ready: A New History of Black Gospel Music*. New York: Continuum International, 2005. Roots gospel in spirituals, holiness churches, and blues evangelists such as the remarkable Blind Willie Johnson ("Dark was the Night . . . Cold Was the Ground").

See also: Crouch, Andraé; Dorsey, Thomas A.; Franklin, Aretha; Grant, Amy; Jackson, Mahalia; Smith, Michael W.; Staples, Pops; Ward, Clara.

Van Cliburn

American classical pianist

An important figure in the cultural landscape of the Cold War, Cliburn won the 1958 International Tchaikovsky Competition in Moscow two months after the Soviet Union launched the satellite Sputnik, reviving American pride and launching his performing career. His performances of Romantic piano works were notable for their warm, spontaneous sound, and his ability to connect with an audience brought new fans to classical music.

Born: July 12, 1934; Shreveport, Louisiana
Also known as: Harvey Lavan Cliburn, Jr. (full name)

Principal recordings

ALBUMS: *Tchaikovsky: Concerto No. 1/Rachmaninoff: Concerto No. 2*, 1958; *Brahms: Concerto No. 2/ MacDowell: Concerto No. 2*, 1961; *My Favorite Chopin*, 1962; *Beethoven: Concerto Nos. 4 and 5*, 1988; *Beethoven Sonatas*, 1989; *Beethoven: Piano Concerto No. 3; Brahms: Rhapsodies; Intermezzo*, 1992; *Chopin: Sonatas for Piano No. 2; Liszt: Années de Pèlerinage, 2nd Year*, 1992; *Beethoven: Concerto No. 5/Rachmaninoff: Concerto No. 2*, 1994; *Schumann: Piano Concerto; Prokofiev: Piano Concerto No. 3*, 1995; *Tchaikovsky: Piano Concerto No. 1*, 2003; *Piano Concertos by Beethoven and Schumann*, 2007.

The Life

The mother of Harvey Lavan Cliburn, Jr., Rildia Bee, was an aspiring concert pianist who studied with Arthur Friedheim. She immediately recognized her three-year-old son's musical talent when she discovered him playing by ear a waltz that one of her students had just practiced. She began teaching Cliburn piano immediately, and she remained his principal teacher until he went to college.

The results of his mother's tutelage were quickly apparent. Cliburn debuted when he was four years old, playing the Prelude in C Major from the first book of Johann Sebastian Bach's *Well-Tempered Clavier*. Through the Texas Federation of Music Clubs, the twelve-year-old Cliburn won an appearance with the Houston Symphony Orchestra, performing Peter Ilich Tchaikovsky's Piano Concerto No. 1, a work that became identified with him. On March 12, 1948, he debuted at Carnegie Hall in New York for a National Music Festival Award. He began spending summers in New York City with his mother, and in 1951 he gained admittance to Juilliard and the piano class of Rosina Lhévinne, the Russian-born teacher of John Browning, Garrick Ohlsson, Misha Dichter, and James Levine.

Lhévinne put finishing touches on her student's formidable technique, and, from 1952 to 1958, Cliburn enjoyed an unprecedented winning streak, taking top honors in every piano competition he entered. In 1952 he won the Dealey Memorial Award and the Kosciuszko Foundation's Chopin prize. In 1953 he won the Juilliard concerto competition. Significantly, in 1954 Cliburn won the Leventritt Award, the first time that honor had been bestowed since 1951. In the intervening years, no entrant was deemed worthy.

Upon graduation, Cliburn was poised for a performing career, debuting with the New York Philharmonic on November 14, 1954, and even appearing on the *Tonight Show* with television host Steve Allen. However, in 1957, his draft number was called, and he had to report for military service, canceling his performing dates. Cliburn was not accepted into the Army, so he returned home to Kilgore, Texas, to take care of his parents and run his mother's piano studio. In 1958, encouraged by his teacher, Cliburn entered the first Tchaikovsky International Piano Competition in Moscow, winning first prize.

For the next sixteen years, Cliburn enjoyed a career both as a performing musician and as a cultural embassador. He signed with RCA Victor and made more than fifteen records. In 1961 he embarked on a U.S. State Department-sponsored tour of Mexico, the first of many such tours. In 1962 the first Van Cliburn International Piano Competition was held in Fort Worth, Texas, offering the largest amount of prize money of any competition.

Then, in 1974, his father and his manager died within two months of each other. Realizing he wanted to spend more time with friends and family, he stopped securing concert dates, and on September 29, 1978, he gave his final performance. Cliburn's retirement lasted until 1987 when the White House invited him to perform at a state dinner in honor of Soviet leader Mikhail Gorbachev. Offers poured in after that concert, and Cliburn has performed a few times a year, usually at important events.

Van Cliburn. (Hulton Archive/Getty Images)

The Music

The American Sputnik. On October 4, 1957, a spherical satellite named Sputnik was launched into space by the Soviet Union, a feat at the time that the United States could not match. Two months later, the Soviet Union announced the first Tchaikovsky International Piano Competition. Upon hearing of the competition, Lhévinne urged Cliburn to enter. Cliburn eagerly complied, and on April 2, 1958, the six-foot-four Texan took the stage in Moscow and caused a sensation. By the final round, in which he played Tchaikovsky's Piano Concerto No. 1, Dmitri Kabalevsky's Rondo (written for the competition), and Sergei Rachmaninoff's Piano Concerto No. 2, even the judges gave Cliburn a standing ovation. After securing Soviet Premier Nikita Khrushchev's permission, the jury awarded him first prize, and Cliburn returned to the United States a hero, greeted with a ticker-tape parade in New York (the first one ever given for a classical musician). A performance at the White House for President Dwight Eisenhower and numerous television appearances followed. He was hailed as the American Sputnik.

Cliburn is associated with the concerti he played in the Tchaikovsky competition: Tchaikovsky's Piano Concerto No. 1 and Rachmininoff's Piano Concerto No. 2. His recordings of those works on the RCA label made in the years following his win stand as two of the best of their kind, and the Tchaikovsky recording was the first classical record certified platinum.

The Repertoire. Other notable concerti Cliburn frequently performed were Edward MacDowell's Concerto No. 2, Ludwig van Beethoven's Concerto No. 5 ("Emperor"), and Sergei Prokofiev's Concerto No. 3. In the solo repertoire, Cliburn's rendition of Franz Liszt's *Hungarian Rhapsody* No. 12 was noted as moving beyond technical virtuosity to plumb the work's pathos, and his performances of Wolfgang Amadeus Mozart's Piano Sonata in C Major stand out for their original approach to Mozart's style. Finally, when Cliburn returned to the stage at the White House, he did so with Johannes Brahms's *Intermezzo*, Rachmaninoff's *Étude Tableau*, Liszt's transcription of Robert Schumann's lied "Widmung," and Claude Debussy's "L'isle joyeuse," displaying the melodic focus and the singing tone he always cultivated in his playing.

Musical Legacy

By the time of his retirement in 1978, Cliburn was receiving harsh critical evaluations. Some critics maintained that Cliburn had a limited repertoire and that he lacked musical curiosity, causing his career to stall. Nevertheless, Cliburn never apologized for his focus on the Romantic repertoire, and he enjoyed an active performance career that continually sold out houses as long as he desired it.

His greatest legacy to American musical culture rests in two areas. First, he brought the rich, full, and idiosyncratic Russian style of playing (which originated with Anton Rubinstein) to American pianism and the wider public. Second, as a wholesome American pianist, Cliburn, in winning a Soviet competition in Moscow, reassured a country nervous about Sputnik's implications. Although the pianist had an enviable warmth of tone and expressive power, making him a classical-music celebrity, it was his role as cultural hero that brought him fame and honor. It was this role that brought him in 2001 the Kennedy Center Honors and in 2003 the Presidential Medal of Freedom and the Grammy Lifetime Achievement Award. His warm personality and genuine love of his audience made him popular throughout the world, particularly in Russia, where in 2004 he was awarded the Order of Friendship, the country's highest civilian award. Cliburn was committed to his belief in music's power to bridge divides and to speak universally.

S. Andrew Granade

Further Reading

Horowitz, Joseph. *The Ivory Trade: Music and the Business of Music at the Van Cliburn International Piano Competition.* New York: Summit Books, 1990. An unbiased look at the competition's history and Cliburn's role in American culture.

Kenneson, Claude. *Musical Prodigies: Perilous Journeys, Remarkable Lives.* Portland, Oreg.: Amadeus, 1998. A fascinating look at the childhood lives of numerous musical prodigies, among them Cliburn.

Reich, Howard. *Van Cliburn.* Nashville, Tenn.: Thomas Nelson, 1993. A full-length biography of Cliburn, this book is musically knowledgeable and features a useful annotated discography.

See also: Debussy, Claude; Prokofiev, Sergei; Rachmaninoff, Sergei; Rubinstein, Artur.

Jimmy Cliff
Jamaican reggae singer and songwriter

A major figure in the ska music of the 1960's and in the reggae of the 1970's, Cliff has been influenced by a variety of styles, including pop, African, and South American.

Born: April 1, 1948; St. Catherine, Jamaica
Also known as: James Chambers (birth name)

Principal recordings

ALBUMS: *Hard Road*, 1967; *Give Thanx*, 1969; *Jimmy Cliff*, 1969; *Wonderful World, Beautiful People*, 1970; *Another Cycle*, 1971; *The Harder They Come*, 1972; *Struggling Man*, 1973; *Music Maker*, 1974; *Brave Warrior*, 1975; *Follow My Mind*, 1976; *Unlimited*, 1977; *Oh Jamaica*, 1979; *I Am the Living*, 1980; *Give the People What They Want*, 1981; *House of Exile*, 1981; *Special*, 1982; *Power and the Glory*, 1983; *Can't Get Enough of It*, 1984; *Cliff Hanger*, 1985; *Sense of Direction*, 1985; *Fundamental Reggae*, 1987; *Hanging Fire*, 1987; *Shout for Freedom*, 1987; *Images*, 1990; *Breakout*, 1992; *Jimmy Cliff, Vol. 2*, 1995; *Many Rivers to Cross*, 1995; *Higher and Higher*, 1998; *Humanitarian*, 1999; *Journey of a Lifetime*, 2001; *Fantastic Plastic People*, 2002; *Sunshine in the Music*, 2003; *Black Magic*, 2004.

SINGLES: "Hurricane Hattie," 1962; "King of Kings," 1962; "Pride and Passion," 1962; "I Can See Clearly Now," 1993.

The Life

Jimmy Cliff was born James Chambers in a small village in Jamaica to working-class parents of Pentecostal origins. By age thirteen, the ambitious Cliff had changed his name and moved to Kingston. In 1962 he recorded his first ska-influenced hit, "Hurricane Hattie," with producer Leslie Kong.

Beginning in 1964, Cliff spent four years in England, working for Chris Blackwell of Island Records. This was a difficult and confusing time for Cliff, who had to alter his Jamaican patois toward the cosmopolitan ambitions of the label.

After a six-month stay in South America, Cliff released his first international hit, "Wonderful

World, Beautiful People." In 1972 director Perry Henzel approached Cliff to play the title role in Jamaica's first feature film, *The Harder They Come*. The sound track, coproduced by Cliff, was one of the most successful reggae albums ever.

To capitalize on the success of this sound track, Cliff toured and recorded constantly, although the U.S. market was especially elusive, and his career has remained more popular outside the United States. During the 1970's, Cliff traveled to Africa to seek a deeper understanding of his Muslim faith, and he continued to pursue his interests in film, in both music and acting. This led to roles in *Bongo Man* (1980) and *Club Paradise* (1986) and to a hit single with "I Can See Clearly Now" for the film *Cool Runnings* (1993). Cliff moved to Paris, and from this base he has continued to tour worldwide.

The Music

Cliff began his recording career in the early 1960's, during the high point of Jamaica's ska period, a precursor to reggae. His time in England and South America was fertile, because he was introduced to samba and rock, and he honed his songwriting abilities to adapt to the more universal style of soul. With the release of *The Harder They Come*, Cliff's early reggae style, for which he would become recognized, was celebrated.

Toward the end of the 1970's, despite commercial pressure to remain with his roots, Cliff embraced the influences of artists outside Jamaica, redefining his style. In fact, his three Grammy Award nominations came for work that was collaborative with artists outside the field of reggae: two lush, party pop albums with Kool and the Gang in the mid-1980's, *Power and the Glory* and *Cliff Hanger* (which won a Grammy Award for best reggae album), and *Black Magic*, a compilation record produced by Dave Stewart, with guest artists Annie Lennox, Sting, Wyclef Jean, Kool and the Gang, Yannick Noah, and Joe Strummer (in one of his last recordings).

Wonderful World, Beautiful People. This album from 1970 is among Cliff's finest, showing great musical diversity and emotional depth. Well known is the deeply moving "Many Rivers to Cross," which was written during Cliff's troubled period in England and which is sung in a simple, spiritual gospel style. It tells of being lost and

"washed up for years," with only pride to hold on to. A devastating protest song, "Vietnam" has a deceptively easy arrangement that serves to underline the terror of the theme: a letter telling a mother about the death of her son. Both Paul Simon and Bob Dylan hold this work in great esteem. There is, however, light among the grim themes, particularly in the title track, which manages to have an island quality with lush symphonic additions. The buoyant opening track, "Time Will Tell," with its prominent and active bass guitar, preaches timeless Cliff themes of patience, strong will, and hope for the future.

The Harder They Come. This compilation album put reggae and Cliff on the international stage. Among the eighteen tracks by artists such as Toots and the Maytals and Desmond Dekker, Cliff contributes five, including "The Harder They Come," "You Can Get It If You Really Want It," and "Sitting in Limbo." The title song is one of Cliff's best. Its energy lies between Cliff's soaring vocals and the no-nonsense arrangement of crisp double-time riffs between bass and organ. This film, about an impoverished young man who travels to the ghettos of Trenchtown to try to make it in the exploitive Jamaican music industry, was quoted in the Clash song "Guns of Brixton," and it remains a popular underground film in the United States.

Jimmy Cliff: Anthology. There are quite a few Cliff anthology records, but many are incomplete because Cliff recorded with so many different labels. This double album includes works from the 1960's, with three early ska works from Cliff's days with Kong, through 1993. This compilation features the major hits as well as the Brazilian hit from 1969, "Waterfall," the title song from the film *Club Paradise* (1986), the Johnny Nash cover "I Can See Clearly Now." The cover of Cat Stevens's "Wild World," however, is not the wonderful live version from the brilliant 1976 album *In Concert*. The infectious "Reggae Nights," which was a huge hit in Europe, is also missing.

Musical Legacy

With the release of *The Harder They Come* in 1972, Cliff was responsible for introducing reggae to an international audience and for paving the way for Bob Marley and others. Cliff, however, would never achieve the prominence of Marley. This is perhaps because he transitioned through many record labels, or because he decided not to adopt Rastafarianism, or because he made music with a crossover nature. Nevertheless, Cliff has continued to tour throughout his career, and he has found much popularity beyond the United States, especially in Africa, South America, and Europe (France and Scandinavia). He and his music are held in high esteem by other artists, as evidenced by the collaborators on his album *Black Magic*, and he helped make reggae appealing to pop and rock audiences.

Sonya Mason

Further Reading

Brown-Martin, Graham. "Black Magic Man." *Air Jamaica: SkyWritings* 153 (July/August, 2004): 38. An interview with Cliff about his album *Black Magic*, with his thoughts on faith and his connection to reggae roots.

Chang, Kevin O'Brien, and Wayne Chen. *Reggae Routes*. Jamaica: Ian Randle, 1998. The source presents the history of reggae from a Jamaican point of view. Includes song lists, artists, and rankings.

Davis, Stephen. *Reggae Bloodlines: In Search of the Music and Culture of Jamaica*. New York: Da Capo Press, 1992. This resource focuses on reggae during its developmental period in the 1970's. Includes an insightful interview with Cliff and photographs by Peter Simon.

Larkin, Colin, ed. *The Virgin Encyclopedia of 70's Music*. London: Virgin Books, 2002. The entry on Cliff gives detailed information on his time in England and a list of album ratings.

Thompson, Dave. *Reggae and Caribbean Music*. San Francisco: Backbeat Books, 2002. In this comprehensive history of reggae and Caribbean music, the profile of Cliff looks at his life before and after the 1970's. Includes artist profiles and lists of leading Jamaican producers, singles, and albums.

See also: Dylan, Bob; Gil, Gilberto; Marley, Bob; Simon, Paul; Stevens, Cat; Sting; Strummer, Joe; Tosh, Peter.

Patsy Cline

American country singer

One of the first artists to achieve success in country and in popular music, Cline combined her country sensibility with her sophisticated, throaty voice and pop arrangements to make her music accessible to and loved by both audiences.

Born: September 8, 1932; Winchester, Virginia
Died: March 5, 1963; Camden, Tennessee
Also known as: Virginia Patterson Hensley (birth name)

Principal recordings

ALBUMS: *Patsy Cline*, 1957; *Showcase*, 1961 (with the Jordanaires); *Sentimentally Yours*, 1962.

SINGLES: "A Church, a Courtroom, and Then Goodbye," 1955; "I Loved and Lost Again," 1956; "Pick Me Up on Your Way Down," 1956; "Stop, Look, and Listen," 1956; "Fingerprints," 1957; "A Stranger in My Arms," 1957; "Walkin' After Midnight," 1957; "Crazy," 1961; "I Fall to Pieces," 1961; "Imagine That," 1962; "She's Got You," 1962; "So Wrong," 1962; "When I Get Thru With You," 1962; "Sweet Dreams," 1963.

The Life

Patsy Cline was born Virginia Patterson Hensley, one of three children of Samuel Lawrence Hensley, a blacksmith, and Hilda Patterson Hensley, a seamstress. The Clines moved nearly twenty times before finally settling in Winchester, Virginia, when Cline was in the eighth grade. When Cline was fifteen, her parents divorced, reportedly because of her father's heavy drinking. This forced Cline to quit high school to help her mother support the family, and she worked as a waitress and as a soda jerk.

Cline had been interested in music since the age of eight, when her mother gave her a piano for her birthday, which she learned to play by ear. At thirteen, she had a serious bout with rheumatic fever, which she later credited as giving her the deep, throaty quality of her voice. Cline began singing in the Baptist church choir and then on local radio shows and at dances. In 1952 she met and married

Gerald Cline, but in 1956 the couple separated. A year later, she married Charles Dick. She gave birth to a daughter, Julie, in 1958, and a son, Randy, in 1961. Cline received her first national recognition on *Arthur Godfrey's Talent Scouts* in 1957, and she achieved the peak of her career in 1961. Cline was involved in a near-fatal automobile accident in 1961, and in 1963 she died in a plane crash, along with Cowboy Copas and Hawkshaw Hawkins, on a flight from a benefit concert in Kansas City to Nashville.

The Music

Early Works. Cline achieved a measure of local fame as a country singer in the Virginia-Maryland area through appearances on radio and especially as a regular on Connie B. Gay's *Town and Country* television show, which also featured country singer Jimmy Dean, broadcast out of Washington, D.C. In 1955 she signed with Four Star Records, with the stipulation that she record only songs by Four Star writers. Between 1955 and 1957, she recorded fifty-

Patsy Cline. (AP/Wide World Photos)

one songs with Four Star; none of them achieved any notable success. All of the Four Star material was country, honky-tonk, and rockabilly style, including "Fingerprints," "Pick Me Up on Your Way Down," and "A Stranger in My Arms." During this period, Cline made several appearances at the Grand Ole Opry.

Country-Pop Crossover. At the insistence of her record label, Cline recorded "Walkin' After Midnight," by Don Hecht and Alan Block, for her first album. The song proved so popular with the audience of the Godfrey show that it was released as the first single on her first album, *Patsy Cline.* The song was a hit on both the country and pop charts, reaching number two on the country charts and number twelve on the pop charts. Cline became one of the first country artists to achieve crossover success.

In 1959 Cline began to work with a new manager, Randy Hughes, and in 1960 she signed a contract with Decca Records, working under the direction of producer Owen Bradley. With his use of arrangements and instruments more sophisticated than those previously found on country records, Bradley helped create, together with RCA's Chet Atkins, what became known as the Nashville Sound. This sound replaced the prevailing honky-tonk style of country music with a smoother sound. Although Cline never liked the fact that she was singing pop rather than country material, she achieved her greatest success in these crossover recordings.

Cline's first recording for Decca, "I Fall to Pieces," released in 1961 and written by Hank Cochran and Harlan Howard, was her first number-one hit on the country charts, and it reached number twelve on the pop charts. The tremendous success of "I Fall to Pieces" and the national fame that it brought were followed by a serious car accident. However, after a month in the hospital, Cline came back stronger than ever, recording Willie Nelson's "Crazy." Although she initially balked at recording it, "Crazy" became her signature song and a huge hit, landing in the Top 10 of the pop charts. Cline's unprecedented success as a crossover artist continued with "She's Got You," written by Cochran, released in 1962, which became her second number-one hit on the country charts. This was followed by the minor hits "When I Get Thru with You," "Imagine That," and "So Wrong."

Musical Legacy

Cline was one of the most popular female country singers in recording history and one of the first performers to find success in both the country and pop music worlds. She was a pioneer of the Nashville Sound, and she paved the way for such crossover artists as Loretta Lynn and Dolly Parton. Cline was also the first female country artist to headline her own show and to be inducted into the Country Music Hall of Fame. She opened doors for female country artists, who previously had been sidelined in the music business. Cline enjoyed more popularity after her death than she did during her life.

Mary Virginia Davis

Further Reading

Brown, Stuart E., Jr., and Lorraine F. Meyers. *Patsy Cline: Singing Girl of the Shenandoah Valley.* Berryville, Va.: Virginia, 1996. This source offers rare photographs, stories from Cline's early years, and information on her family history.

Hazen, Cindy, and Mike Freeman. *Love Always, Patsy: Patsy Cline's Letters to a Friend.* New York: Berkley Books, 1999. A collection of letters written between 1955 and 1959 by Cline to the president of her fan club.

Jones, Margaret. *Patsy: The Life and Times of Patsy Cline.* New York: HarperCollins, 1994. A sympathetic and detailed biography, based on extensive interviews with several country artists. Includes photographs, discography, and index.

Mansfield, Brian. *Remembering Patsy.* Nashville, Tenn.: Thomas Nelson, 2003. An extensive collection of photographs of Cline features recollections of those who knew her. A companion to an MCA compact-disc tribute to Cline.

Nassour, Ellis. *Honky Tonk Angel: The Intimate Story of Patsy Cline.* New York: St. Martin's Press, 1993. This much revised version of Nassour's 1981 *Patsy Cline* biography includes several new interviews and insights. Includes discography and index.

See also: Everly, Don and Phil; Haggard, Merle; Lang, K. D.; Lynn, Loretta; Presley, Elvis; Williams, Hank.

Kurt Cobain

American rock guitarist, singer, and songwriter

A major figure in the alternative rock movement, Cobain was lead singer, songwriter, and guitarist for the Seattle-based grunge-rock band Nirvana. With his angst-filled lyrics, his guttural singing voice, his distorted guitar technique, and his high-energy live music performances, he became the voice for Generation X.

Born: February 20, 1967; Hoquiam, Washington
Died: April 5, 1994; Seattle, Washington
Also known as: Kurt Donald Cobain (full name)
Member of: Nirvana

Principal recordings

ALBUMS (solo): *Collector's Box*, 2006.
ALBUMS (with Nirvana): *Bleach*, 1989; *Nevermind*, 1991; *In Utero*, 1993; *MTV Unplugged in New York*, 1994; *The Classic Interviews*, 2005; *A Golden Legacy*, 2006.
SINGLES (with Nirvana): "Smells Like Teen Spirit," 1991; "Come as You Are," 1992; "In Bloom," 1992; "Lithium," 1992; "All Apologies," 1993; "Heart Shaped Box," 1993.
WRITINGS OF INTEREST: *Journals*, 2003.

The Life

Kurt Donald Cobain (koh-BAYN) was born to Donald and Wendy Cobain on February 20, 1967. Cobain's parents divorced when he was seven years old, and as a result he was shuffled among family and friends' homes. Growing up, Cobain showed a keen interest in art and music, and he was given a guitar for his fourteenth birthday.

In high school, Cobain immersed himself in art classes and, realizing that he was short on class credits, decided to drop out of high school two weeks before graduation. In the following years Cobain held a number of part-time jobs and experienced brief periods of homelessness. Nonetheless, during this time he spent a great deal of energy writing songs and developing his guitar playing.

In 1985 Cobain formed his first band, Fecal Matter, with other local Seattle musicians. The band was short lived and self-recorded only one sixteen-song demo tape, *Illiteracy Will Prevail*. Upon hearing *Illiteracy Will Prevail*, Cobain's friend Krist Novoselic saw promise in the budding songwriter and agreed to form a band with him. With the addition of drummer Chad Channing, the highly influential rock band Nirvana was formed.

Nirvana's first album, *Bleach*, was released in 1989 on a Seattle independent record label, Sub Pop Records, and met with moderate success. The band toured on several occasions and generated a significant amount of attention among the major record labels. In 1990 drummer Channing was replaced by Dave Grohl, and the band signed with David Geffen of Geffen Records.

While recording Nirvana's 1991 major label debut *Nevermind*, Cobain was introduced to singer Courtney Love, and the two developed a romantic relationship. On February 20, 1992, they were married in Hawaii; in August, Love gave birth to their daughter, Frances Bean.

Throughout much of his life, Cobain was plagued with chronic stomach ailments. Despite many attempts to solve the medical problem, he was unable to remedy the persistent pain. Because of this, Cobain turned to self-medication in the form of heroin, claiming it was the only drug that could alleviate his stomach pains. Accordingly, he developed a severe heroin addiction.

Nirvana returned to the studio in 1993 to record its third full-length album, *In Utero*. It was a huge success, and the band went back on tour with a significant amount of media attention, specifically focused on Cobain and Love's personal life. Cobain became increasingly uncomfortable with the media spotlight and increased his drug abuse.

During a European tour in 1994, Cobain was hospitalized for a drug overdose, involving alcohol and insomnia medication. The tour was canceled, and Cobain returned to Seattle. Back in the United States, Love and other friends staged an intervention, and with some persuasion Cobain entered a drug-rehabilitation center in Los Angeles. After a few days, Cobain fled the rehabilitation center and, unbeknown to friends and family, returned to the Seattle area. Love and others mounted a search for the missing singer.

On April 8, 1994, Cobain's body and suicide note were found by a local electric company field technician in Cobain's Lake Washington home. The coroner's report indicated that Cobain died from a self-inflicted shotgun wound to the head on April 5, 1994.

The Music

Cobain's musical interests were diverse. Early influences were such bands as the Beatles and the Monkees. Later his interests progressed to such rock bands as Kiss, Black Sabbath, the Meat Puppets, the Sex

Kurt Cobain. (AP/Wide World Photos)

Pistols, and the Clash. Cobain's guitar solos at live performances consisted of extended periods of ad lib, guitar-amp feedback, and noise.

"Smells Like Teen Spirit." When one of Cobain's friends spray-painted "Kurt Smells Like Teen Spirit" on a wall, Cobain was inspired to compose the successful song "Smells Like Teen Spirit." With only a few weeks before recording *Nevermind*, the band's major-record-label debut, Cobain played the song. It was not an immediate band favorite. Cobain played the guitar part for nearly an hour and a half before someone suggested that the song be slowed down in tempo. At a slower pace, the song fell into place, and it became a hugely popular anthem for Generation X. The song sold more than a million copies, and it was nominated for two Grammy Awards. Despite the song's success, Nirvana attempted to distance itself from "Smells Like Teen Spirit," claiming it had become a parody.

"Come as You Are." "Come as You Are" was the second most popular song on Nirvana's *Nevermind* album, and it helped catapult the band to the top of rock charts again. After Cobain died in 1994, "Come as You Are" was the subject of speculation and controversy. Eerily, the original music video for the song depicted a gun being fired at Cobain, followed by him dying in slow motion. In 1994 Nirvana released an acoustic version of the song on the album *MTV Unplugged in New York*. Cobain's hometown of Aberdeen, Washington, elected to use the title as the town's motto: Aberdeen, Washington: Come as You Are.

"Heart Shaped Box." "Heart Shaped Box" was the first single from Nirvana's third album, *In Utero*, written between 1992 and 1993. The song was inspired by American writer and feminist social critic Camille Paglia, who explored the role of female sex organs and their depiction in society. In addition, Love had sent Cobain a heart-shaped box during the early stages of their courtship, and Cobain and Love collected numerous heart-shaped boxes, displaying them prominently in their Seattle home. "Heart Shaped Box" spent three weeks at number one on the *Billboard* modern rock charts. Its music video garnered Nirvana two MTV Music Video Awards for Best Art Direction and Best Alternative Video. The awards ceremony was conducted after Cobain's death, and the awards were accepted by the remaining members of Nirvana.

Musical Legacy

Cobain's music, with its simplified melodic and harmonic compositional styling, was noted for its raw, unpolished sound. His unique styling marked a dramatic shift in mainstream musical taste away from the highly complex, aurally perfect sound of glam rock and dance music of the late 1980's to the simplicity of alternative rock. Despite having a short life, Cobain influenced mainstream rock music and various subgenres, such as punk, grunge, and independent rock. Cobain's music was labeled the music of Generation X, his contemporaries born in the 1960's and 1970's, and they helped make him one of the highest-grossing musicians of all time.

Delbert S. Bowers

Further Reading

Azerrad, Michael. *Come as You Are: The Story of Nirvana*. New York: Main Street Books, 1993. Written before Cobain's death in 1994, a snapshot-in-time look at Nirvana's place in rock history, including the band's beginnings and its significance in rock.

Cobain, Kurt. *Journals*. New York: Riverhead Books, 2003. Contains entries from more than twenty journals Cobain wrote from the late 1980's until his death, providing a strikingly personal look into Cobain's deepest thoughts.

Crisafulli, Chuck. *Nirvana: The Stories Behind Every Song*. New York: Thunder's Mouth Press, 2006. Lists every Nirvana song written, recorded, and performed, tracing its origins, story, and meaning.

Cross, Charles C. *Heavier than Heaven: A Biography of Kurt Cobain*. New York: Hyperion, 2002. An indepth look at Cobain's personal and public life, using details from hundreds of interviews and articles.

Peterson, Charles. *Screaming Life: A Chronicle of the Seattle Music Scene*. New York: HarperCollins, 1995. A book of photographs from Seattle's grunge-music scene during the early and post-Nirvana years, illustrating the energy that produced some of the most popular bands of the 1990's.

See also: Lennon, John; McCartney, Sir Paul; Strummer, Joe.

George M. Cohan

American musical-theater composer

Cohan was lauded during his lifetime as a song-and-dance man, but it is as a lyricist and librettist that he made a lasting impact. He "Americanized" the Broadway musical by writing about American characters using American popular music.

Born: July 3, 1878; Providence, Rhode Island
Died: November 5, 1942; New York, New York
Also known as: George Michael Cohan (full name)

Principal works

MUSICAL THEATER (music, lyrics, and libretto unless otherwise stated): *The Governor's Son*, 1901; *Running for Office*, 1903; *Little Johnny Jones*, 1904; *Forty-five Minutes from Broadway*, 1906; *George Washington, Jr.*, 1906; *The Honeymooners*, 1907; *The Talk of New York*, 1907; *The American Idea*, 1908; *The Cohan and Harris Minstrels*, 1908; *Fifty Miles from Boston*, 1908; *The Yankee Prince*, 1908; *The Man Who Owns Broadway*, 1909; *The Little Millionaire*, 1911; *Hello, Broadway*, 1914; *Cohan and Harris*, 1916; *The Cohan Revue of 1916*, 1916; *The Cohan Revue of 1918*, 1918; *The Voice of McConnell*, 1918 (music with Ernest R. Ball, Chauncey Alcott, Monte Carlo, and Alma M. Sanders; lyrics with Rida Johnson Young and Richard W. Pascoe); *Little Nellie Kelly*, 1922; *The Rise of Rosie O'Reilly*, 1923; *The Song and Dance Man*, 1923; *The Merry Malones*, 1927; *Billie*, 1928.

SONG: "Over There," 1917.

The Life

George Michael Cohan (KOH-han) was born in the proverbial trunk to traveling vaudevillians, who took their infant son on stage as a prop. Soon, the Four Cohans—Jeremiah (Jerry) and Helen (Nellie), and children Josephine (Josie) and George—were touring the circuit, winning enough acclaim to be booked into New York City in 1893. With almost no formal education, Cohan found his schoolroom to be the theater, and he was a good student in this nontraditional venue. By the age of

nine, he had his first speaking role, and by the age of eleven he was writing sketches for his family to perform. Publishing songs by sixteen, he wrote his first hit song, "Venus, My Shining Love," in 1893.

While the Four Cohans were earning a thousand dollars a week—a tremendous amount of money at the time—Cohan married actress Ethel Levy in 1899, and she joined the troupe. On August 26, 1900, the couple had a daughter, Georgette.

Tension grew between Ethel and Cohan's sister, so in 1904 Josie and her new husband signed on to their own production, breaking up the Four Cohans. The newly configured Four Cohans (Jerry, Nellie, George, and Ethel) was disrupted when Ethel left the cast in December, 1906, during the run of *George Washington, Jr*. Cohan had fallen in love with a chorus girl from *Little Johnny Jones*, and he married Agnes Mary Nolan on June 29, 1907. They had three children: Mary, Helen, and George, Jr.

Jerry and Nellie decided to retire from the stage at the conclusion of the run of Cohan's comedy *Broadway Jones*, and their thirty-five-year-old son said he would do the same. Performing since he was seven, Cohan told the press that his other ventures demanded more of his time. Even though he professed to wanting "to write an American play that will live," he returned to acting ten months later. His last appearance in New York, however, proved to be a disappointment, when his *The Return of the Vagabond* (1940) lasted only one week.

In 1941 Cohan was diagnosed with intestinal cancer, which killed him the following year at the age of sixty-four. His funeral was held in St. Patrick's Cathedral in New York City.

The Music

Although the Four Cohans were a hit on the vaudeville circuit, Cohan longed to be on Broadway in legitimate houses, not in musical revues or vaudeville. Since performers rarely transitioned from vaudeville to Broadway, twenty-two-year-old Cohan made a bargain with producer Louis Behman. He could book the Four Cohans for a year on his vaudeville circuit if he would produce them in their first musical on Broadway, *The Governor's Son*.

A modest success in New York, Cohan took the show on the road where he continued to refine the material.

Little Johnny Jones. By his third musical, *Little Johnny Jones*, Cohan had created that magical blend of song, dance, plot, and character that all raced to a climactic finish. This musical introduced "Yankee Doodle Dandy" and "Give My Regards to Broadway," and the latter was used in the opening montage in Hollywood's first musical film, *The Broadway Melody* (1929).

Little Johnny Jones does not feature harmonic breadth; indeed, in all of his compositions, Cohan relied on the four chords he could play using only the black keys on the piano. While based on the life of famous American jockey Tod Sloan, *Little Johnny Jones* is more about Cohan than about Sloan. With its naive sentimentality and its poetic justice, the musical permitted Cohan to turn the story of an American jockey unjustly accused of throwing a race in England into a tap-dancing tour de force. While he was born on July 3, Cohan always said he was born on July 4. Since telling reporters was not sufficient, he made it into a lyric: "I'm a Yankee Doodle dandy,/ A Yankee Doodle, do or die;/ A real live nephew of my Uncle Sam,/ Born on the Fourth of July."

On Broadway. Cohan became an established star on Broadway, a position he sustained for the next thirty years. While most of his early shows were written to showcase his family (and wife Ethel), the first Cohan musical that did not feature the author as a performer was *Forty-five Minutes from Broadway*, which introduced another set of standard tunes ("Mary's a Grand Old Name" and "So Long, Mary"). Fay Templeton and up-and-coming talent Victor Moore proved that Cohan's material did not require his stage presence to make it popular; *Forty-five Minutes from Broadway* is arguably Cohan's strongest libretto.

Many of Cohan's twenty-two musicals contain similar themes: America vs. Europe, Cinderella plots, stock characters (stage Yankee, plucky ingenues, daft old ladies), endings ruled by poetic justice, and lots of patriotic American flag waving, such as in his songs "You're a Grand Old Flag," "Any Place the Old Flag Flies," "For the Flag, for the Home, for the Family." Cohan idolized the American dream and Yankee ingenuity, and so his stage character was always a winner.

Cohan returned to writing for his family with *George Washington, Jr.* Despite a preposterous plot, the show was a success, no doubt buoyed by such hit songs as "You're a Grand Old Flag" (the first song written for a musical which sold more than a million copies of sheet music) and the rousing showstopper, "I Was Born in Virginia."

Reared in vaudeville, Cohan was uniquely situated to excel in the episodic nature of the musical revue. *Hello, Broadway*—called "A Musical Crazy Quilt Patched and Threaded Together with Words and Music and Staged by George M. Cohan"—and two editions of *The Cohan Revue* in 1916 and 1918 were well received.

The Show Doctor. Many of the plays and musicals produced by Cohan were rewritten and/or restaged by him, and in doing so he made another name for himself as a well-respected "show doctor," who could rectify weaknesses in a musical production. He did not always publicize these projects, but the Anselm Goetzl-William Cary Duncan operetta *The Royal Vagabond* became a hit once Cohan worked it over, and it was billed as a "Cohanized Opera Comique."

George M. Cohan. (Library of Congress)

Cohan's celebratory, positive librettos not only gave shape to American musical theater, they almost single-handedly elevated the stage Irishman from his role as a low comic and second-class citizen. With shows such as *Little Nellie Kelly* (at 276 performances, the longest run in Cohan's career), *The Rise of Rosie O'Reilly*, and *The Merry Malones*, and songs such as "Harrigan" and "Ring to the Name of Rosie," Cohan redeemed an ethnic group long derided in the press and on the stage.

During the peak of Cohan's artistic accomplishments, he was indeed *The Man Who Owns Broadway* (1909); in 1920 he had three productions running simultaneously on Broadway. By the 1920's, the swagger of Cohan's homespun songs was being eclipsed by younger writers: Irving Berlin, Jerome Kern, Noël Coward, and George and Ira Gershwin. Although Berlin acknowledged he was the songwriting heir of Cohan, the son eclipsed the father in terms of technical skill, versatility, and longevity. Cohan's last musicals sounded like period pieces, even though they were new. While Cohan revolutionized the Broadway musical with well-structured librettos, high-energy, and fast pacing, his work did not evolve with the times. In the late 1920's, his musical *Billie* contained none of the innovations ushered in by *Show Boat* (1927). After *Billie*, Cohan concentrated on writing nonmusical plays.

Cohan and Hollywood. Cohan rarely ventured into film, but he did appear in the Hollywood film *The Phantom President* (1932), with six songs by Richard Rodgers and Lorenz Hart. Cohan took the part, assuming he would write his own songs; resigned to singing someone else's material, Cohan generally made himself quite disagreeable during the filming. Much more successful was his work as an actor in Eugene O'Neill's *Ah, Wilderness!* (1933) on Broadway. Against their wishes, Rodgers and Hart were reunited with Cohan when he was signed to perform the lead in *I'd Rather Be Right* (1937).

Cohan the Playwright. The restless Cohan was not content to master vaudeville and the Broadway musical, he wanted to excel as a playwright as well. His first attempt at a nonmusical play, *Popularity* (1907), was not well-received, but *Broadway Jones* (1912) was a hit. Classic melodramas, *Seven Keys to Baldpate* (1913) and *The Tavern* (1920), have enjoyed

success as revivals. Cohan ultimately penned twenty nonmusical plays.

Cohan the Businessman. Frustrated by the lack of success of his first two book musicals and his constant rejections from music publishers, Cohan teamed up with another artist, Sam Harris, thwarted by the Broadway establishment. Cohan and Harris's first joint venture was coproducing *Little Johnny Jones*, and it marked the beginning of one of the most successful producing firms on Broadway; in fifteen years, they produced twenty-two productions. In 1908 they started the Cohan & Harris Publishing Company. In 1911, proof of their success as producers, Cohan and Harris had six hit Broadway shows and controlled seven theaters. Other ventures included opening the George M. Cohan Theater in 1911, which was located in the heart of Broadway (at Broadway and Forty-third Street). With murals celebrating the career of the Four Cohans, the theater became a film house in 1932, and in 1938 it was demolished.

Cohan's multiple responsibilities in the theater came into conflict when Actor's Equity Association called for its first strike in 1919. As an actor, he could certainly see the need to protect actors from unscrupulous producers. As a businessman, he aligned himself with producers, only to see himself mocked and criticized by fellow actors. The experience so soured him that he announced his retirement from the stage, he dissolved his partnership with Harris, and he even resigned from the Lambs, the Players, and the Friar's Club. When the Actors' Equity Association signed with the Producer's Management Association, Cohan refused to join the union. For the next twenty-two years, even though he continued to act, it was always by special arrangement.

Musical Legacy

Almost every one of Cohan's five hundred songs reflects his individual performing style. Self-taught, he was not insecure about his lack of training; rather, he celebrated his limited musical and lyrical vocabulary. He once wrote he preferred "a Sousa strain/ Instead of a Wagner pain" (from "I Want to Hear a Yankee Doodle Tune," 1911). His music may have been naive, but his melodies are unforgettable. As a lyricist, Cohan was accused of being "unpoetic," but he was a master at shaping the colloquial into lyrics so that they sounded natural and conversational. Examples of this skill include "Life's a Funny Proposition After All" (1904), "When a Fellow's on the Level with a Girl That's on the Square" (1907), and "We Do All the Dirty Work" (1911). Leaving majestic Romantic rhetoric to the nineteenth century and witty Ivy-league patter to Hart and Cole Porter, Cohan embraced slang and short phrases so that his lyrics sounded up to date. Oscar Hammerstein II acknowledged this skill, noting "Cohan's genius was to say simply what everybody else was subconsciously feeling."

Cohan's single biggest hit song did not come from one of his shows: "Over There" was written about World War I. Initially selling more than two million copies, Cohan donated its royalties to war charities. Brought back into popularity during World War II, Congress approved a special Medal of Honor for Cohan in 1940, the first time a songwriter had ever been so decorated.

Cohan lived long enough to see himself wonderfully (though inaccurately) immortalized on film by James Cagney in *Yankee Doodle Dandy* (1942), for which Cagney won the Academy Award for Best Actor.

Using Cohan's life and songs, the musical biography *George M!* (1968)—book by Michael Stewart, John Pascal, and Francine Pascal—introduced a new generation to this brash, rich, arrogant, cantankerous, self-opinionated, egocentric, and talented showman.

In 1981 the Goodspeed Opera House in East Haddam, Connecticut, produced a rousing entertainment when they mounted *Little Johnny Jones* (albeit with a radically altered libretto by Alfred Uhry). While Cohan's musical and nonmusical plays are not often revived, his music lives on. He created a personality for the Broadway musical, one with a signature blend of grit, brashness, and inexhaustible energy, that has surfaced repeatedly in such later projects as *Of Thee I Sing* (1931), *Annie Get Your Gun* (1946), *The Pajama Game* (1954), *Fiorello!* (1959), *The Music Man* (1957), *Guys and Dolls* (1950), *Barnum* (1980), *Annie* (1976), and *Hairspray* (2002).

Seventeen years after his death, a statue of Cohan was erected at Broadway and Forty-seventh Street, so that once again, Cohan could survey the Great White Way. In the 1970's, the American Guild of Variety Artists named their annual awards the "Georgie," and the U.S. Postal Service released a stamp in Cohan's honor in 1978 to commemorate the centennial of his birth. While Cohan was followed on Broadway by many multifaceted artists, he was singular in performing so many aspects of theater: as a lyricist, a composer, librettist, a playwright, a theater owner, a performer, a director, a choreographer, a publisher, and a producer.

Bud Coleman

Further Reading

Cohan, George M. *Twenty Years on Broadway and the Years It Took to Get There; The True Story of a Trouper's Life from the Cradle to the "Closed Shop."* New York: Harper & Brother, 1925. Cohan's autobiography focuses only on the Four Cohans in vaudeville and his career up to 1900, so spends little or no time on his marriage to Ethel, his children, the Actor's Equity strike, or the dissolution of the Cohan-Harris partnership.

Fisher, James. "George M. Cohan." In *Dictionary of Literary Biography, Volume 249: Twentieth-Century American Dramatists*, edited by Christopher Wheatley. New York: The Gale Group, 2001. This analysis of Cohan's contribution to the formation of American musical comedy stresses that the musical-comedy texts and songs Cohan wrote were fresh and new in style.

Gottlieb, Robert, and Robert Kimball. *Reading Lyrics*. New York: Pantheon Books, 2000. This resource contains a brief biography of Cohan and reprints the lyrics to sixteen of Cohan's songs. The authors celebrate his "spunky, Irish-American patriotic swagger."

Hischak, Thomas S. *Boy Loses Girl: Broadway's Librettists*. Lanham, Md.: Scarecrow Press, 2002. The author notes Cohan's innovations, which led to a uniquely American shape and tone of the musical-theater libretto with "better stories, believable characters, and efficient staging."

_____. *Word Crazy: Broadway Lyricists from Cohan to Sondheim*. New York: Praeger, 1991. The author claims that Cohan's biggest achievement is the quality of his lyrics and that Cohan and Stephen Foster created an American song vernacular that distinguished itself from contemporary European models.

McCabe, John. *George M. Cohan: The Man Who*

Owned Broadway. Garden City, N.Y.: Doubleday, 1973. This excellent biography uses information from many individuals who worked with Cohan.

Morehouse, Ward. *George M. Cohan, Prince of the American Theatre*. Philadelphia, Pa.: J. B. Lippincott, 1943. This *New York Sun* theater critic met Cohan in 1931 and published his first biography. Focusing on Cohan's life, the book contains little analysis of his art.

See also: Berlin, Irving; Caruso, Enrico; Coward, Sir Noël; Gershwin, George; Gershwin, Ira; Hammerstein, Oscar, II; Hart, Lorenz; Kern, Jerome; Porter, Cole; Rodgers, Richard.

Leonard Cohen

Canadian singer and songwriter

Established as a poet and novelist before embarking on a career as a folksinger, Cohen wrote lyrics of literary depth and emotional sophistication. Although his own albums have sold modestly, his songs remain among those most recorded by other performers.

Born: September 21, 1934; Montreal, Quebec, Canada

Also known as: Leonard Norman Cohen (full name)

Principal recordings

ALBUMS: *Songs of Leonard Cohen*, 1967; *Songs from a Room*, 1969; *Songs of Love and Hate*, 1971; *New Skin for the Old Ceremony*, 1974; *Death of a Ladies' Man*, 1977; *Recent Songs*, 1979; *Various Positions*, 1985; *I'm Your Man*, 1988; *The Future*, 1992; *Ten New Songs*, 2001; *Dear Heather*, 2004.

The Life

Leonard Norman Cohen (KOH-uhn) was born into one of Montreal's most prominent Jewish families. From his mother Masha, the daughter of a scholarly rabbi, he inherited a love of the literary arts. From his father, a successful clothier who died when Cohen was nine, he inherited a trust fund that provided him sufficient income to devote himself to his literary and musical interests. Although he

had begun playing the guitar and performing country music while a teenager, it was as a poet that Cohen first distinguished himself, publishing his first book, *Let Us Compare Mythologies*, in 1956 under the auspices of the Canadian modernist poet Louis Dudek, five years after enrolling at Montreal's McGill University.

Let Us Compare Mythologies made Cohen a local celebrity and led to his first recordings: readings of his poetry for an album released by Folkways Records. His second volume of poetry, *The Spice-Box of the Earth*, followed in 1961, strengthening and spreading Cohen's reputation. By this time Cohen had moved to the Greek island of Hydra, where he would live and work for several years.

His next work was the semiautobiographical novel *The Favorite Game* (1963), in which Cohen, thinly disguised as protagonist Lawrence Breavman, traced his life and coming of age. After another book of poems, *Flowers for Hitler* (1964), Cohen wrote and published what would become his best-known prose work, the ambitiously experimental and controversially explicit *Beautiful Losers* (1966). His fourth volume of poems, *Parasites of Heaven*, appeared shortly thereafter.

By the publication of his *Selected Poems, 1956-1968*, Cohen had been discovered as a songwriter and performer by the folksinger Judy Collins, who recorded his "Suzanne" (a poem from *Parasites of Heaven* set to music) to considerable acclaim on her 1966 album, *In My Life*.

From 1969 to 2004, Cohen was prolific, releasing several albums and books, and he was the subject of two video documentaries. He also advanced the career of his occasional background singer Jennifer Warnes, whose critically well-received recording, *Famous Blue Raincoat: The Songs of Leonard Cohen*, appeared in 1987.

During the 1990's he practiced meditation at the Mount Baldy Zen Center in California and was ordained a Buddhist monk in 1996. In 2006 he oversaw the recording of *Blue Alert*, an album of unpublished Cohen lyrics, by Anjani Thomas, a singer with whom he was romantically involved.

The Music

Although popular musicians have occasionally been known to publish books of poetry or fiction, Cohen is the among the few poets and novelists to have successfully made the transition from a literary career to a musical one. Likewise, although popular musicians have been known to undergo religious conversions and in turn reflect these conversions in their work, Cohen is notable for so consistently, thoroughly, and unabashedly integrating the traditions, language, and sensibility of his faith into his music. It is this combination of highly developed literary and religious sensitivities, even more than Cohen's nearly obsessive exploration of the spiritual dimensions of romantic despair, that sets his work apart from that of other serious, verbally gifted performers and that, along with his preference for fashion-defying instrumental settings, gives it a uniquely timeless quality.

Songs of Leonard Cohen. Released in December, 1967, at a time when pop music was becoming increasingly ornate, Cohen's debut album exhibited a hauntingly stark acoustic mood that set the tone for his first four albums and resulted in his being categorized, along with Neil Young and Joni Mitchell, as part of a new folk movement. Although "Suzanne," which had been previously covered by Collins, was the album's best-known track, three others ("Sisters of Mercy," "So Long, Marianne," and "Hey, That's No Way to Say Goodbye") would become fixtures in the Cohen canon.

Songs from a Room. Even more sparse sounding than *Songs of Leonard Cohen*, Cohen's second album (1969) became a cult classic as much for its unrelenting bleakness as for its inclusion of "Bird on a Wire," a song that would become another Cohen favorite after "Suzanne" and that, like "Suzanne," had previously been recorded by Collins.

Songs of Love and Hate. Released in 1971 and similar in mood to *Songs from a Room*, *Songs of Love and Hate* is noted for its concluding track, "Joan of Arc," which joined "Suzanne" and "Bird on a Wire" as archetypes of Cohen finding erotic epiphanies in traditionally religious subject matter and vice versa.

Live Songs. Unlike most live albums of its time, this 1973 collection of Cohen's 1970 and 1972 performances in London, Paris, Berlin, Brussels, Tennessee, and the Isle of Wight was not padded with jams and drum solos, enhanced with postproduction studio overdubs, or marketed as a surrogate "greatest hits." Instead, it captured the extent to which an audience could bring out the performer in

Leonard Cohen. (AP/Wide World Photos)

Cohen and help transform his songs from solitary meditations into a kind of communal liturgy.

The Best of Leonard Cohen. For almost thirty years, this 1975 sampling of Cohen's first four studio albums was the only remotely comprehensive Cohen compilation. It remains his best-selling title to date.

Death of a Ladies' Man. Following as it did the canon-defining *The Best of Leonard Cohen*, this 1977 album was scrutinized for indications of the new directions, if any, that Cohen would take during his next phase. Instead it was an anomaly. With the legendary "Wall of Sound" producer Phil Spector at the controls, the album was out of synch with the spare, hushed intensity that had characterized Cohen's previous recordings.

Various Positions. Because Columbia, unconvinced of its commercial potential, refused to release this album, it suffered from the underpromotion inevitable from being released by the independent Passport Records. In retrospect, its combination of bare-bones electronics and Cohen's seductively sinister whisper-singing indicated that he had discovered a sound that would both honor his past and allow him to age gracefully. The album's fifth track, "Hallelujah," would be recorded by more performers than any other post-1970 Cohen composition. Along with "If It Be Your Will," it imbued the album with a devotionally religious mood and made it a sound track of sorts to Cohen's 1984 literary collection, *Book of Mercy*.

I'm Your Man. Stylistically similar to *Various Positions*, this 1988 recording became Cohen's most celebrated and best-selling album in more than a decade, with the video to "First We Take Manhattan" transforming the reclusive Cohen into a presence on MTV.

The Future. In the wake of the renewed interest in Cohen created by *Various Positions* and *I'm Your Man*, this ambitiously diverse and (for Cohen) uncommonly topical and political 1992 album found an eager audience among the public in general and Hollywood film directors Oliver Stone, Curtis Hanson, and Alan Parker in particular, who included music from *The Future* in the sound tracks to *Natural Born Killers*, *Wonder Boys*, and *The Life of David Gale* respectively.

Ten New Songs. This is a 2001 collaboration with the American singer-songwriter and former Cohen background vocalist Sharon Robinson, who also produced the album.

Dear Heather. Like *Ten New Songs*, this 2004 album found Cohen again collaborating with Robinson. Unlike *Ten New Songs*, it found Cohen also collaborating with Thomas and covering or setting to music everything from "Tennessee Waltz" to the poetry of Lord Byron and Francis Reginald Scott, opening Cohen to charges that, at seventy, he was finally running out of ideas and perhaps energy.

The Essential Leonard Cohen. This two-disc 2002 compilation judiciously (and democratically) covered the highlights of every Cohen studio album from his debut through *Ten New Songs*.

Musical Legacy

The power of Cohen's music arises in large part from his ignoring traditional boundaries. Whether as a poet who wrote novels, a novelist who wrote songs, a Jew who mastered Zen Buddhism, or a religious man committed to the exploration of erotic love, he defied conventions and the expectations of his various audiences at every turn, discovering in the process a method for perpetually renewing the timelessness and sacramental appeal of humankind's most enduring archetypes. By choosing music as the medium most hospitable to his carefully crafted words, he imbued his notoriously dark meditations with a fragile buoyancy.

He also defied the notion that popular music was the exclusive domain of the young or that success was best measured in terms of airplay and album sales. Already thirty-three years old at the time of his first album's release, he was from the beginning a forceful if quiet voice of maturity and reflection in a genre usually identified with prolonged adolescence. Without ever placing a single on the *Billboard* Top 40 or selling a million copies of any one of his albums, he created an immensely influential body of work. From 1971 to 2007 his songs were used in the sound tracks of more than twenty films, and the roster of performers who have recorded his songs, which includes Sting, Elton John, the Neville brothers, and U2, is as varied as it is stellar.

Arsenio Orteza

Further Reading

Cohen, Leonard. *Beautiful Losers*. New York: Vintage, 1966. The better known of Cohen's two novels, notorious at the time of its publication for its explicit depiction of the seamier details of a love triangle among "losers" obsessed with the seventeenth century saint, Catherine Tekakwitha.

_____. *Book of Longing*. New York: HarperCollins, 2006. Drawings and song lyrics from the *Ten Songs* and *Dear Heather* albums, along with poems, most of which were composed during Cohen's residence at a Buddhist monastery in the 1990's.

_____. *Book of Mercy*. Toronto: McClelland & Stuart, 1984. Contemporary psalms and poems in the mystically biblical vein of the lyrics comprising Cohen's *Various Positions* album.

_____. *The Spice-Box of the Earth*. Toronto: McClelland & Stuart, 1961. The second and best known of the four volumes of poetry that Cohen published before beginning his career as a recording artist.

Green, Roger. *Hydra and the Bananas of Leonard Co-hen: A Mid-life Crisis in the Sun.* New York: Basic Books, 2003. A quixotic multifaceted memoir by a British poet obsessed with Cohen's life on the Greek island of Hydra and the music that he composed there.

Nadel, Ira Bruce. *Various Positions: A Life of Leonard Cohen.* Austin: University of Texas Press, 2007. The latest version of this most thorough of the Cohen biographies takes into account his record-ings through 2006 and benefits from the author's access to Cohen and his unpublished writings.

Sheppard, David. *Leonard Cohen.* New York: Da Capo Press, 2000. An examination of the com-plex intersection of the religious and the roman-tic in Cohen's work.

See also: Brel, Jacques; Collins, Judy; Diamond, Neil; Glass, Philip; John, Sir Elton; Kristofferson, Kris; Mitchell, Joni; Spector, Phil; Sting; Vega, Suzanne; Young, Neil.

Nat King Cole

American singer, jazz pianist, and songwriter

An innovative jazz pianist and one of the top vo-calists in any musical genre in the 1950's, Cole proved that rock and roll was not the only music that would sell in the Elvis Presley era.

Born: March 17, 1919; Montgomery, Alabama
Died: February 15, 1965; Santa Monica, California
Also known as: Nathaniel Adams Coles (birth name)
Member of: The Nat King Cole Trio

Principal recordings

ALBUMS (solo): *Nat King Cole at the Piano*, 1950; *Penthouse Serenade*, 1952; *Top Pops*, 1952; *Nat King Cole Sings for Two in Love*, 1954; *Unforgettable*, 1954; *Tenth Anniversary Album*, 1955; *Vocal Classics*, 1955; *Ballads of the Day*, 1956; *In the Beginning*, 1956; *The Piano Style of Nat King Cole*, 1956; *After Midnight*, 1957; *Just One of Those Things*, 1957; *Love Is the Thing*,
1957; *This Is Nat King Cole*, 1957; *Cole Español*, 1958; *St. Louis Blues*, 1958; *To Whom It May Concern*, 1958; *The Very Thought of You*, 1958; *A Mis Amigos*, 1959; *Welcome to the Club*, 1959; *Every Time I Feel the Spirit*, 1960; *The Magic of Christmas*, 1960; *Tell Me All About Yourself*, 1960; *Wild Is Love*, 1960 (lyrics by Dotty Wayne and Ray Rasch); *The Nat Cole Story*, 1961; *The Touch of Your Lips*, 1961; *Dear Lonely Hearts*, 1962; *More Cole Español*, 1962; *Nat King Cole Sings, George Shearing Plays*, 1962; *Ramblin' Rose*, 1962; *Nat King Cole Sings My Fair Lady*, 1963; *Those Lazy-Hazy-Crazy Days of Summer*, 1963; *Where Did Everyone Go?*, 1963; *I Don't Want to Hurt Anymore*, 1964; *Let's Face the Music*, 1964; *Nat King Cole Sings His Songs from Cat Ballou and Other Motion Pictures*, 1965; *The Unreleased Nat King Cole*, 1987; *Night Lights*, 2001.

ALBUMS (with the Nat King Cole Trio): *Jumpin' at Capitol*, 1943; *The King Cole Trio*, 1944; *The King Cole Trio, Vol. 2*, 1946; *King Cole for Kids*, 1948; *The King Cole Trio, Vol. 3*, 1948; *The King Cole Trio, Vol. 4*, 1949.

The Life

Nathaniel Adams Coles was born in Montgom-ery, Alabama, but his family soon relocated to Chi-cago when his father, Ed Coles, a deacon in the Bap-tist church, found a church of his own. His mother Perlina was the church organist, and Cole learned keyboards at her side. He had a natural talent, and he made his first public performance at age four. When he was twelve, his parents sent him for for-mal lessons, wanting him to learn classical music, but at night he sneaked out to absorb the new sounds of jazz in nightclubs, where he heard the trumpet of Louis Armstrong and the piano of Earl Hines.

Imitating Hines's style, Cole began playing pi-ano in clubs in the mid-1930's. His older brother, Eddie Coles, had success as a bassist, and the two teamed up, recording under the name Eddie Cole's Solid Swingers for Decca Records in 1936. On the strength of those recordings, Cole was hired to play for the touring company of a revival of Eubie Blake's all-black musical *Shuffle Along* (1921). Cole fell in love with a dancer in the company, Nadine Robinson, and when the company disbanded in Los Angeles, Cole and Nadine stayed in Southern

California, where they were married. In 1937 Bob Lewis asked Cole to lead the hotel band at his Hollywood nightclub the Swanee Inn, with just piano, guitar, and bass. Trios were a novelty in the big band era, so the King Cole Trio was a hit. Recording and touring with Lionel Hampton in 1939 led to recording sessions with Decca Records for the trio in 1940 and 1941, but it was their long-term contract with Columbia Records in 1943 that really launched Cole as a recording artist.

In the late 1940's, Cole began recording for a wider popular audience. In the midst of this rise to stardom, Cole and Nadine quietly divorced, and Cole married singer Maria Hawkins Ellington in 1948. Cole and Maria had five children, the eldest of which, Natalie, also became a pop singer.

In the 1950's, Cole was one of Columbia Records's top stars, and he had his own television variety show in 1956. That year he was assaulted on stage by members of the White Citizens Council during a concert in Birmingham, Alabama. He quietly continued the concert. He continued making hit records through the rock-and-roll era, until his death from lung cancer in 1965.

The Music

Cole, who dropped the final "s" from his surname when he turned professional, was still in his teens when he first recorded his Hines-influenced jazz piano with his brother Eddie in 1936. His early sound was distinctive and energetic, and these early recordings remind us that, before he had ever sung a recorded note, Cole was a talented jazz pianist.

"Sweet Lorraine." Trios with the combination Cole invented—piano, guitar, and bass (no drums)—became so common in the World War II years that it is hard for today's jazz listener to appreciate how innovative it was in 1940. The development of the electric guitar, played in the trio by Oscar Moore, made possible a fuller sound with just three instruments. With Cole on piano and Wesley Prince on bass, the trio signed a contract with Decca

Nat King Cole. (AP/Wide World Photos)

Records (after a disappointing session the year before with a smaller studio), and they recorded eight sides in the winter of 1940-1941. It was in this session that Cole emerged as a solo singer. In their gigs at the Swanee Inn at that time, the trio was mostly playing instrumentals, when a patron asked to hear the 1928 jazz song "Sweet Lorraine." Cole loved the song (he had heard Louis Armstrong sing it), but he refused the request, insisting he was a pianist and not a singer. Nevertheless, because the patron was a regular and a big spender, owner Lewis pressured Cole to sing. He did, and it was such an immediate hit that the trio was obliged to include it in their sets from then on. The version recorded for Decca in 1940 was a hint of things to come. Cole's delicate piano opening in F major leads directly into the mellow vocals that would become familiar to listeners for the next two and a half decades.

"Straighten Up and Fly Right." After the Decca recordings, bassist Prince left, and he was replaced by Johnny Miller. This new version of the King Cole Trio signed with Capitol Records, and it went into the studio in 1943, for the first time recording Cole's own compositions. One of his songs became Cole's biggest seller of the war years, "Straighten Up and Fly Right," which sold half a million copies (a super hit by wartime standards). The song was partly a tribute to Cole's father and to his African American heritage. It was based on an African American folk tale his father had related in a sermon, about a buzzard who tried to trick a monkey into flying with him, thinking the monkey would be helpless in the air. The monkey got a choke hold on the buzzard, forcing him to "Straighten Up and Fly Right." While most white listeners interpreted this as a fable about justice, black audiences recognized it as a parable of how intertwined the fates of black and white Americans were. Any injustice on the part of the buzzard (representing white America) would be as fatal to him as to his passenger. The song set the tone for the low-key way in which Cole would oppose racism in his career.

Unforgettable. By the late 1940's, Cole had abandoned the trio, and he recorded with full orchestra supporting his vocals. Many jazz fans were disturbed that Cole had sold out to acquire a mainstream audience. The packaging of records had changed, too; as early as 1944 Columbia had been putting Cole's music on long-playing disks slowed down to fit several songs per side. His first ten-inch single without the trio was *Nat King Cole at the Piano. Unforgettable* would prove his most enduring album. It was released three times: first in the ten-inch long-playing format; then again in 1955 as a twelve-inch long-play (LP); rereleased a decade later when Cole's death caused a surge in sales of his records. The title song, which Cole had recorded as a single in 1951, with a rich Nelson Riddle orchestration, would hit the charts again forty years later, when Cole's daughter, Natalie Cole, remixed it so that she could sing a duet with her late father. The result was a hit on the *Billboard* charts. The song won seven Grammy Awards for Natalie and, posthumously, for her father.

St. Louis Blues. In 1958 Cole starred in a Paramount Pictures film about the life of composer W. C. Handy. Columbia Records took the opportunity to release an album of Handy songs from the film, performed by Cole and arranged by Nelson Riddle, who had written some of the film's soundtrack music. The film and the album were a perfect opportunity for Cole to return to his jazz and blues roots, since many jazz fans had accused him of turning his back on the genre of music that had produced his initial success in the music industry. (Cole had recorded an all-jazz album, *After Midnight*, only two years earlier in 1956.) The *St. Louis Blues* album proved so popular that Columbia reissued it in 1962 under the title *Nat King Cole Sings the Blues*.

Musical Legacy

A number of jazz pianists, including Charles Brown and Ray Charles, were influenced by Cole's distinctive keyboard style, and Cole's guitar-piano-bass formula for the trio was emulated by Oscar Peterson and Art Tatum. His unforgettable voice is inimitable. His daughter Natalie gave him a hit twenty-six years after his death. In 2001 an album Cole recorded in 1956 but never released was issued as *Night Lights*. In 1983 an archivist for Capitol Records' Dutch subsidiary discovered master tapes for an unreleased album of Cole singing in other languages—mostly Spanish, but also Japanese. It came out later as *The Unreleased Nat King Cole*. Cole's popularity was international: In 1958 he went to Havana to record an album in Spanish (*Cole Español*). Central and South American audiences already buying his English-language records responded favorably to this album and to two sequels, *A Mis Amigos* and *More Cole Español*. Cole is also remembered, though inaccurately, as the first black star of a network television variety show in America. That distinction belongs to another jazz pianist, Hazel Scott, whose 1950 variety show predated Cole's by seven years. From November, 1957, to December, 1958, Cole appeared each week with other singers as guests. However, the show failed to find a national sponsor willing to risk Southern boycotts for supporting the show.

John R. Holmes

Further Reading

Cole, Maria. *Nat King Cole: An Intimate Biography*. New York: William Morrow, 1971. Cole's wife provides intimate details about her husband's life and career in music. Includes photographs and discography.

Haskins, James, with Kathleen Benson. *Nat King Cole: A Personal and Professional Biography*. Chelsea, Mich.: Scarborough House, 1990. Interviews with family members, friends, and other musicians illuminate this biography of Cole.

Lees, Gene. *You Can't Steal a Gift: Dizzy, Clark, Milt, and Nat*. New Haven, Conn.: Yale University Press, 2001. The author chronicles the effect of racism on the careers of Dizzy Gillespie, Clark Terry, Milt Hinton, and Cole.

See also: Armstrong, Louis; Blake, Eubie; Burke, Johnny; Burke, Solomon; Campbell, Glen; Charles, Ray; Davis, Sammy, Jr.; Gaye, Marvin; Gordon, Dexter; Hampton, Lionel; Handy, W. C.; Jones, Hank; Leadbelly; Otis, Johnny; Peterson, Oscar; Ronstadt, Linda; Strayhorn, Billy; Tatum, Art; Tormé, Mel; Young, Lester.

Cy Coleman

American musical-theater composer and pianist

Though he began as a classical pianist who turned to jazz, Coleman is noted for his work in musical theater and popular song.

Born: June 14, 1929; New York, New York
Died: November 18, 2004; New York, New York
Also known as: Seymour Kaufman (birth name)

Principal works

MUSICAL THEATER (music): *John Murray Anderson's Almanac*, 1953 (music with Richard Adler and Jerry Ross; lyrics by Adler and Ross); *Compulsion*, 1957 (incidental music; lyrics by Carolyn Leigh); *Wildcat*, 1960 (lyrics by Leigh; libretto by Nathaniel Richard Nash); *Little Me*, 1962 (lyrics by Leigh; libretto by Neil Simon); *Sweet Charity*, 1966 (lyrics by Leigh; libretto by Simon); *Seesaw*, 1973 (lyrics by Dorothy Fields; libretto by Michael Bennett); *Straws in the Wind*, 1975 (lyrics and libretto by Betty Comden and Adolph Green); *Hellzapoppin'!*, 1976 (music by Coleman, Jule Styne, and Hank Beebe; lyrics by Leigh and Bill Heyer; libretto by Abe Burrows, Heyer, and Beebe); *I Love My Wife*, 1977 (lyrics by Michael Stewart; based on Luis Rego's play); *On the Twentieth Century*, 1978 (lyrics and libretto by Comden and Green); *Home Again, Home Again*, 1979 (lyrics by Barbara Fried; libretto by Russell Baker); *Barnum*, 1980 (lyrics by Stewart; libretto by Mark Bramble); *Thirteen Days to Broadway*, 1983 (lyrics by Fried; libretto by Baker); *Let 'Em Rot*, 1988 (lyrics by Coleman and A. E. Hotchner; libretto by Hotchner); *City of Angels*, 1989 (lyrics by David Zippel; libretto by Larry Gelbart); *Welcome to the Club*, 1989 (lyrics by Coleman and Hotchner; libretto by Hotchner); *The Will Rogers Follies*, 1991 (lyrics by Comden and Green; libretto by Peter Stone); *The Life*, 1997 (lyrics by Ira Gasman; libretto by David Newman, Gasman, and Coleman); *Exactly Like You*, 1998 (lyrics by Hotchner and Coleman; libretto by Hotchner).

SONGS (music; lyrics by Carolyn Leigh): "A Moment of Madness," 1957; "My, How the Times Goes By," 1957; "Witchcraft," 1957; "Firefly," 1958; "It Amazes Me," 1958; "Rules of the Road," 1961; "The Best Is Yet to Come," 1959; "Pass Me By," 1964; "When in Rome," 1964.

The Life

Cy Coleman (si KOHL-muhn) was born Seymour Kaufman, the son of Russian immigrants Max and Ida Kaufman. Coleman began playing the piano when one was left in their building by a family who moved out without paying the rent. A child prodigy, he played a recital at Steinway Hall at the age of six and at Carnegie Hall at the age of seven. At New York City's High School for the Performing Arts, Coleman focused on classical piano, composition, and conducting. However, his love for jazz would send him in a different musical direction. He changed his name to Cy Coleman at the age of sixteen when he began to write with lyricist Joseph A. McCarthy, Jr.; at the age of seventeen he was playing Manhattan clubs with the Cy Coleman Trio. Unusual for a Broadway composer, Coleman was an accomplished jazz pianist who loved to perform. He appeared occasionally in nightclubs for the rest of his life.

A longtime bachelor, Coleman married Shelby Brown in 1997, and they had a daughter, Lily Cye, in 2000. He died of heart failure at the age of seventy-five in 2004, leaving behind several unfinished projects, including *Pamela's First Musical*, with a libretto by Wendy Wasserstein.

The Music

The year he graduated from high school, Coleman began writing music for television shows, and in 1952 he had his first hit single, with lyricist McCarthy, "Why Try to Change Me Now," recorded by Frank Sinatra. Coleman and McCarthy's music first appeared on Broadway in the musical revue *John Murray Anderson's Almanac* ("Tin Pan Alley," 1953). When McCarthy's drinking began to get in the way, Coleman looked for a new lyricist.

Collaborations with Leigh. Even though their disagreements were legendary, the partnership between Coleman and Carolyn Leigh created two Broadway musicals (*Wildcat* and *Little Me*) and a string of some of the biggest nonrock hits of the 1950's and 1960's: "A Moment of Madness" (recorded by Sammy Davis, Jr.), "My, How the Time Goes By," "Witchcraft" (recorded by Sinatra), "Firefly," "It Amazes Me," "Rules of the Road," and "The Best Is Yet to Come." Their last successful pop songs were released in 1964: "When in Rome" (recorded by Barbra Streisand) and "Pass Me By" (recorded by Peggy Lee).

Lucille Ball's only Broadway show, *Wildcat*, closed when its star became ill, leaving behind the wonderful "You've Come Home" and "Hey, Look Me Over!" Another star vehicle, *Little Me*, featured Sid Caesar in 1962 and Martin Short in 1998, and it contains "I've Got Your Number" and "Le Grand Boom-Boom." For a 1982 revival, the Coleman-Leigh collaboration, which had ended twenty years before, was temporarily renewed when they contributed two new songs to the score.

Coleman's five-year collaboration with Leigh was particularly productive: approximately twenty popular songs (many of them hits), scores for two Broadway shows, and several numbers for motion pictures. Their wry, sophisticated songs became favorites of discriminating cabaret singers, such as Mabel Mercer. Following the team's acrimonious split after *Little Me*, Coleman wrote almost exclusively for musical theater.

Collaborations with Fields. Dorothy Fields thought her career was over by the late 1950's. Mu-

sical styles had changed, and she was reeling from the deaths of her brother and husband. When Coleman approached her at a party with an invitation to write together, however, she leaped at the opportunity. Joining the team of Coleman, librettist Neil Simon, and director-choreographer Bob Fosse, Fields was twenty-five years older than her collaborators, but together they created the steamy, edgy, sassy *Sweet Charity*. Instant classics from the score include "Hey, Big Spender," "If My Friends Could See Me Now," and "There's Gotta Be Something Better than This."

While they abandoned a project about Eleanor Roosevelt, Coleman and Fields did complete the romantic comedy *Seesaw*, working with director-choreographer Michael Bennett. "It's Not Where You Start (It's Where You Finish)" became a star turn for Tommy Tune. When Fields died in 1974, Coleman was once again without a lyricist.

Later Works. After writing four musicals with female lyricists, Coleman wrote his first Broadway musical with a male lyricist, Michael Stewart. Together they created *I Love My Wife*, undoubtedly the first musical about wife swapping in New Jersey. Coleman turned again to lyricist Stewart to pen the musical biography *Barnum* (1980), a lavish spectacle which ran for 854 performances.

The mock operetta *On the Twentieth Century* was the product of a new collaboration for Coleman, working with the lyric-writing team of Betty Comden and Adolph Green. Both *I Love My Wife* and *On the Twentieth Century* were financially successful, but *Home Again, Home Again* closed out-of-town in 1979. Working with his fourth female lyricist, Coleman teamed up with Barbara Fried on this epic story of a male protagonist's fifty-year search for life's meaning.

In 1989 Coleman opened two musicals on Broadway: *Welcome to the Club* and *City of Angels*. The former, with lyrics by Coleman and A. E. Hotchner, ran only twelve performances. *City of Angels*, on the other hand, won six Tony Awards, including Best Musical and Best Score, and it ran for 878 performances. With a book by Larry Gelbart and lyrics by David Zippel, *City of Angels* is set in 1940's Hollywood. (Many consider this jazz-infused score to be Coleman's best.) Two years later, Coleman was back on Broadway with *The Will Rogers Follies*, teaming again with Comden and Green. This show marked Coleman's return to musicalizing the biography of a show business personality, and for it he won his third Tony Award for Best Musical.

Musical Legacy

In an age when composing for musical theater was almost completely a male reserve, Coleman worked with nearly all the female lyricists of his generation: Comden, Fields, Fried, and Leigh. These were fortunate choices, because so many of Coleman's most memorable and heartfelt characters have been women, even when they are not the leads. Without a woman on his creative team, Coleman often found his shows taking on a decidedly misogynistic tone, especially *Welcome to the Club* with A. E. Hotchner (rewritten as *Exactly Like You*, 1999) and *The Life*, with lyrics by Ira Gasman.

Coleman won three Tony Awards for Best Score, three Emmy Awards, two Grammy Awards, an Academy Award nomination, and he was inducted into the Songwriters Hall of Fame in 1981. Although he may not be as well known as some of his contemporary songwriters, he has contributed to the stage some popular showstoppers: "It's Not Where You Start (It's Where You Finish)," "Hey, Look Me Over!," "If My Friends Could See Me Now," "Nobody Does It Like Me," and more.

Coleman's music has always been influenced by the stylistic flair and the energy of his collaborators. With Leigh, his music tended to be feisty and brittle, like her lyrics. Fields's verses were world-weary and wry, so Coleman gave her music for those colors in a way he did not for Hotchner (*Welcome to the Club*) or Ira Gasman (*The Life*), whose lyrics can be crass but funny. Comden and Green brought Coleman flamboyant, educated lyrics, and he responded with the zest of *On the Twentieth Century* and *The Will Rogers Follies*. Zippel (*City of Angels*) and Stewart (*I Love My Wife*) wrote lyrics that were quick and smart, reflected in Coleman's music.

Bud Coleman

Further Reading

Sheed, Wilfrid. *The House That George Built: With a Little Help from Irving, Cole, and a Crew of About Fifty*. New York: Random House, 2007. One of the few book-length histories of musical theater that celebrates the work of Coleman.

Suskin, Steven. *Show Tunes, 1905-1985: The Songs, Shows, and Careers of Broadway's Major Composers*. New York: Dodd, Mead, 1986. Suskin does a brief analysis of Coleman's work, suggesting that it peaked with *Sweet Charity*.

Vallance, Tom. "Obituary: Cy Coleman." *The London Independent* (November 22, 2004). Overview of Coleman's life, with references to his many musicals.

Viagas, Robert, ed. *The Alchemy of Theatre: The Divine Science*. New York: Playbill Books, 2006. Contains a brief interview with Coleman, who talks about his collaborators.

See also: Fields, Dorothy; Green, Adolph, and Betty Comden; Lee, Peggy; Sinatra, Frank; Streisand, Barbra; Styne, Jule.

Ornette Coleman

American jazz saxophonist and composer

Saxophonist Coleman, a leader of the avant-garde of the 1960's, pioneered new approaches to improvisation that expanded the boundaries of jazz.

Born: March 19, 1930; Fort Worth, Texas
Member of: Prime Time

Principal recordings

ALBUMS: *Something Else!!!! The Music of Ornette Coleman*, 1958; *Change of the Century*, 1959; *The Shape of Jazz to Come*, 1959; *Tomorrow Is the Question!*, 1959; *Free Jazz*, 1960; *Jazz Abstractions*, 1960; *This Is Our Music*, 1960; *The Art of the Improvisers*, 1961; *Beauty Is a Rare Thing*, 1961; *Ornette!*, 1961; *Ornette on Tenor*, 1961; *Twins*, 1961; *Town Hall*, 1962; *Chappaqua Suite*, 1965; *An Evening with Ornette Coleman*, 1965; *Who's Crazy, Vol. 1*, 1965; *Who's Crazy, Vol. 2*, 1965; *The Empty Foxhole*, 1966; *The Music of Ornette Coleman: Forms and Sounds*, 1967; *Saints and Soldiers*, 1967; *Love Call*, 1968; *New York Is Now*, 1968; *Ornette at Twelve*, 1968; *The Unprecedented Music of Ornette Coleman*, 1968; *Crisis*, 1969; *Friends and Neighbors*, 1970; *Science*

Fiction, 1971; *J for Jazz Presents O.C. Broadcasts*, 1972; *Skies of America*, 1972; *Body Meta*, 1976; *Dancing in Your Head*, 1976; *Soapsuds*, 1977; *Of Human Feelings*, 1979; *Ornette and Prime Time: Opening the Caravan of Dreams*, 1983; *Prime Time/Time Design*, 1983; *Song X*, 1985 (with Pat Metheny); *In All Languages*, 1987; *Virgin Beauty*, 1988; *Naked Lunch*, 1991; *Sound Museum: Hidden Man*, 1994; *Sound Museum: Three Women*, 1994; *Tone Dialing*, 1995; *Sound Grammar*, 2006.

The Life

Ornette Coleman was born and raised in Fort Worth, Texas. His father died when he was seven, and his seamstress mother raised him. He received his first saxophone, an alto, at age fourteen, and he began playing in local rhythm-and-blues bands shortly thereafter. He switched to tenor sax in his high school band, and local saxophonist Red Connors initiated Coleman into bebop. In 1949 Coleman began traveling the South with carnival and rhythm-and-blues bands. Stranded in New Orleans, he switched back to alto saxophone, and he solidified his personal style playing with drummer Edward Blackwell, with whom he would later record.

Coleman moved to Los Angeles in the early 1950's, and he began sitting in with jazz musicians, who widely rejected his radical style of playing. In 1954 he married Jayne Cortez, who later established an important career as a poet, and in 1956 their son Denardo was born. Cortez introduced Coleman to her friends in the Los Angeles jazz community, and by 1957 Coleman was rehearsing his original music with a group that included trumpeter Don Cherry. In 1958 Coleman secured a record contract with Los Angeles-based Contemporary Records. Although there remained some hostility toward his style of playing, Coleman had a small coterie of supporters, eventually including members of the Modern Jazz Quartet, who helped him gain a recording contract with Atlantic Records in 1959, yielding six albums over the next several years.

The New York debut of Coleman's quartet in 1959 was an important event in jazz history, sparking great controversy over the validity of his music. At age twenty-nine, with significant record label support, a steady gig in New York playing to curious crowds every night, and intense press cover-

age, Coleman achieved instant notoriety. For the next two years his group played steadily, gradually moving up the pay scale, commanding salaries that approached the more mainstream jazz groups.

At the end of 1962 Coleman dropped out of recording and public performance, apparently pricing himself out of the business. In the interim, he taught himself violin and trumpet, and he added those instruments to his performances and recordings when he began touring with his new group in 1965. He toured Europe through the 1960's, and he received Guggenheim Fellowships for composition in 1967 and 1974.

Coleman's interest in composing music for string and wind ensembles, recorded throughout the 1960's, had its most ambitious showing when his *Skies of America* debuted at the 1972 Newport Jazz Festival. Columbia Records issued a recording of it with the London Symphony Orchestra later that year. In 1975 Coleman unveiled his new group, Prime Time, which, with two electric guitars and an electric bass, moved him in the direction of the electric dance music of the time. Coleman continued touring and recording with Prime Time through the 1980's and 1990's, while also playing with versions of his 1960's groups.

Coleman's stature continued to grow in his sixties and seventies. In 1994 he received the prestigious MacArthur Fellowship; in 1997 he was featured for four consecutive nights at Lincoln Center (including a New York Philharmonic performance of *Skies of America*); and in 2007 he received a Pulitzer Prize for his album *Sound Grammar*, and a Grammy Lifetime Achievement Award.

The Music

From his initial recordings, Coleman's compositional and improvisational radicalism were evident, intertwined with his highly personal sound and his sense of melodic invention, uniquely accented by his use of a plastic, rather than a brass, alto saxophone. His most intense creative impact stems from his six albums on the Atlantic label recorded between 1959 and 1961, where his concept of small-group improvisation came to full fruition. Shortly thereafter, Coleman branched out and began writing for classically based string and wind ensembles. His Prime Time ensemble moved him toward a more rock-based and accessible style. In the 1980's he returned to his original format, occasionally adding a second bassist, a guitarist, a drummer, or a pianist. Throughout his career Coleman rarely abandoned a steady beat in his small ensembles, with the notable exception of slow ballads, wherein the melody was often through-composed. Even when his later ensembles tended toward nonmetric playing, Coleman's solo implied a steady tempo, if not an overriding meter.

Something Else!!!! _and_ **Tomorrow Is the Question.** _Something Else!!!! The Music of Ornette Coleman_ and _Tomorrow Is the Question,_ Coleman's first two albums (on the Contemporary label), established him as a creative new compositional voice with an unusual sound. His compositions typically had surprising melodic turns and odd numbers of measures in their structure, although they were typically rounded out to twelve-bar blues and thirty-two-bar _aaba_ forms during the solos. His soloing appeared to be unfettered by the looming influence of alto saxophonist Charlie Parker, although it was clear that he had absorbed the lessons of Parker. Despite the apparent freedom in the soloing, however, his band maintained the steady recurring cyclic structure that characterized jazz up to that point.

The Shape of Jazz to Come. Coleman's third album, _The Shape of Jazz to Come_ (on the Atlantic label), established him as a controversial artist in jazz and the visible leader of the growing avant-garde movement. Both in performance and on records, the soloists (Coleman and trumpeter Cherry) and the rhythm section (bassist Charlie Haden and drummer Billy Higgins) would expand or contract the recurring cyclic form and at times even abandon it. This was a radical new development in jazz, with only Cecil Taylor and his group exploring the same territory. The pianoless quartet featured uncanny start-and-stop unison melody statements by Coleman and Cherry and extended trio improvising (one of the horns with bass and drums), in which the bass player could either retain the form of the composition ("Chronology" and "Peace") or follow Coleman and temporarily abandon the form ("Congeniality"). "Lonely Woman" represented a subgenre in the repertory, in which a long rubato melody would be played outside of any single governing beat; both Coleman and Cherry played the melody in unison, but the bass and drums appeared to be in their own separate meters.

Free Jazz. Coleman's Atlantic album _Free Jazz_ not only gave its name to a musical movement and style but also opened the door to large ensemble improvisation. Performed by a double quartet (two groups, each containing bass, drums, trumpet, and bass clarinet or saxophone), the thirty-seven-minute recording took up both sides of the album, giving space for all eight of the musicians to solo. Still not abandoning a steady beat, "Free Jazz" (the title of the single piece on the album) featured composed unison melodies played by the horns alternating with one of the four horns soloing over the two bassists and two drummers. Occasionally other horns would join the soloist, providing the model for large group improvisation that developed later in the decade.

Skies of America. While the circumstances of rehearsing and recording a full symphony orchestra were not at all congenial for Coleman, _Skies of America,_ a single piece more than forty minutes long in

Ornette Coleman. (AP/Wide World Photos)

twenty-one movements taking up both sides of an album, represented the most ambitious recording project of Coleman's career. Although he had had his compositions recorded by string and wind chamber ensembles, those did not approach the large scale of *Skies of America*. The writing is reminiscent of Charles Ives's music, with its folklike, yet dense melodies. The solo phrases that Coleman plays on the saxophone over the orchestra throughout the piece are not novel in his repertory, but the juxtaposition of his soaring playing over the sometimes dense arrangements of his melodies represented something new.

Dancing in Your Head *and* **Body Meta.** With his new band, Prime Time, Coleman issued two albums, *Dancing in Your Head* (which also featured a short track of Coleman playing with Moroccan musicians in Jajouka, Morocco) and *Body Meta*. Prime Time was a dramatic departure for Coleman, consisting of two electric guitarists, an electric bassist, and a drummer. The Prime Time pieces on *Dancing in Your Head*, "Theme from a Symphony, Variations 1 and 2," were each more than ten minutes long and featured extended guitar-based dance grooves over which Coleman soloed. While Coleman's foray into non-Western music was a rare event in his career, Prime Time was his major focus for the next two decades. The ensemble's sound became more dense when Coleman later added a second bassist and drummer.

Sound Museum. Coleman released two extraordinary companion albums, both titled *Sound Museum*, but with the subtitle *Hidden Man* for one and *Three Women* for the other. The albums were extraordinary in two ways: Coleman rarely performed with a pianist (perhaps never recording with one in a quartet setting), and the two albums contained alternate takes of the same pieces. The pianist (Geri Allen) added a new dimension to Coleman's sound, avoiding the chord patterns that Coleman rejected early on and providing polyphonic lines, clusters, and harmonically ambiguous chords. The alternate takes ranged from close variants ("Home Grown") to dramatically different arrangements ("Mob Job").

Sound Grammar. In the 1980's and 1990's, Coleman collaborated with his colleagues from the 1960's (such as Haden, Higgins, and Dewy Redman), and he also made new partnerships (such as guitarist Pat Metheny and pianist Allen). *Sound Grammar* features him as soloist backed by two upright bass players and his son Denardo on drums. Coleman, in his mid-seventies, sounds fresh and inventive, yet he retains much of the blues and rhythm-and-blues melody and phrasing, which first brought him to great notoriety and acclaim in the late 1950's. "Turnaround," first recorded by Coleman more than forty-five years earlier, has all the familiar Coleman trademark phrases, floating over a rhythm section that suspends time in uncanny ways.

Musical Legacy

Coleman's most enduring contribution to twentieth century music stems from his live performances in the late 1950's and early 1960's and from his early albums on the Atlantic label. His performances and recordings revealed a highly original compositional voice combined with an improvisational spontaneity and freedom from harmonic constraint that inspired generations of musicians. Coleman's phrasing was often unencumbered by bar lines and chord changes, yet his compelling statements challenged conventional improvisational styles. He steadfastly adhered to his musical style in the face of criticism, even ridicule. Although he lacked formal training, Coleman's musical genius was evident in his system of improvisation based on an intuitive understanding of melody and harmony.

Eric Charry

Further Reading

Jost, Ekkehard. *Free Jazz*. New York: Da Capo Press, 1981. This is a classic text focusing on musical analysis and providing a capsule history of the new movement in jazz in the 1960's. One chapter is devoted to Coleman.

Litweiler, John. *Ornette Coleman: A Harmolodic Life*. New York: Da Capo Press, 1994. Extensive biography of Coleman, giving full coverage of his life and career through the late 1980's.

Mandel, Howard. *Miles, Ornette, Cecil: Jazz Beyond Jazz*. New York: Routledge, 2008. A personal appreciation of Coleman's place in twentieth century American music written by a veteran jazz journalist.

Spellman, A. B. *Four Lives in the Bebop Business*. Ann

Arbor: University of Michigan Press, 2004. Spellman, a perceptive African American jazz writer, provides a chapter on Coleman with a wealth of biographical material and a sympathetic analysis of Coleman's place in American music.

Wild, David, and Michael Cuscuna. *Ornette Coleman, 1958-1979: A Discography*. Ann Arbor, Mich.: Wildmusic, 1980. An excellent discography and sessionography of Coleman's career through the late 1970's, accompanied by finely detailed coverage of his life and music.

Wilmer, Valerie. *As Serious as Your Life: John Coltrane and Beyond*. London: Serpent's Tail, 1992. An excellent, intimate portrait of the movement that Coleman helped initiate in jazz, covering the 1960's and 1970's.

See also: Coltrane, John; Dolphy, Eric; Ives, Charles; Jones, Elvin; Metheny, Pat; Parker, Charlie; Taylor, Cecil.

Judy Collins

American singer and songwriter

With her pure voice, her appreciation of socially conscious lyrics, and her ear for good melodies, Collins was at the forefront of the urban folk revival movement of the 1960's.

Born: May 1, 1939; Seattle, Washington
Also known as: Judith Marjorie Collins (full name)

Principal recordings

ALBUMS: *A Maid of Constant Sorrow*, 1961; *Golden Apples of the Sun*, 1962; *Judy Collins #3*, 1963; *The Judy Collins Concert*, 1964; *In My Life*, 1966; *Wildflowers*, 1967; *Who Knows Where the Time Goes*, 1968; *Whales and Nightingales*, 1970; *True Stories and Other Dreams*, 1973; *Judith*, 1975; *Bread and Roses*, 1976; *Hard Time for Lovers*, 1979; *Running for My Life*, 1980; *The Times of Our Lives*, 1982; *Home Again*, 1984; *Trust Your Heart*, 1987; *Sanity and Grace*, 1989; *Baby's Bedtime*, 1990; *Baby's Morningtime*, 1990; *Fires of Eden*, 1990; *Judy Sings Dylan . . . Just like a Woman*, 1993; *Come Rejoice! A Judy Collins Christmas*, 1994; *Shameless*, 1994; *Voices*, 1995; *Christmas at the Biltmore Estate*, 1997; *All on a Wintry Night*, 2000; *Judy Collins Sings Leonard Cohen*, 2004; *Portrait of an American Girl*, 2005; *Judy Collins Sings Lennon and McCartney*, 2007.

WRITINGS OF INTEREST: *Trust Your Heart*, 1987 (autobiography).

The Life

Judith Marjorie Collins was born in Seattle, where her father, a professional singer, hosted a radio show. The family moved to Boulder, Colorado, and then to Los Angeles before settling permanently in Denver. When Collins began piano lessons at the age of five, she was soon considered a prodigy. Her teachers predicted a concert career, a plan that was interrupted when she contracted polio shortly after her family moved to Denver. After her recovery, she continued her piano studies, making her public debut at the age of thirteen with the Denver Businessman's Symphony (conducted by her piano teacher, Antonia Brico) in a performance of Wolfgang Amadeus Mozart's Concerto for Two Pianos. As a teenager, Collins continued to study classical piano, but soon her interest turned to folk music. Collins attended college for one year, but she dropped out in 1958 to marry Peter Taylor. Her only child, Clark, was born the following year. She made her professional debut as a folksinger in a Boulder club in 1959, after which she performed in Denver, Chicago, and Boston. The couple divorced in 1962, and Collins lost a bitter custody battle for her son.

Collins migrated to New York's Greenwich Village, the center of an important folk scene. Like many musicians of the day, she became involved in the Civil Rights and anti-Vietnam War movements and, later, the feminist movement. Personal problems plagued her during the late 1970's and 1980's, including battles with alcoholism and bulimia. After her son committed suicide in 1992, Collins began campaigning on behalf of suicide prevention, and she wrote several books about the healing process after such a tragedy. She has also written an autobiography and a mystery novel, *Shameless* (1995), which includes an album of songs. In 1996 she married Louis Nelson, an industrial designer.

The Music

Early Works. In the early 1960's, New York's Greenwich Village was the center of a folk music revival. Many artists, such as Bob Dylan, John Sebastian, Richie Havens, and Paul Stookey, were attracted to clubs such as Gerde's Folk City and Art D'Lugoff's Village Gate. After she moved there in 1961, Collins signed her first recording contract with Elektra Records, with which she would remain until 1984. Her debut album, *A Maid of Constant Sorrow*, was praised by critics and folk-music audiences alike. Her second album, *The Golden Apples of the Sun*, was released in 1962, followed by *Judy Collins #3* in 1963. Her first live album, *The Judy Collins Concert*, taken from her debut at New York's Town Hall, was released in 1964. During the mid-1960's many of her concerts across the United States and Canada drew standing-room-only crowds.

In My Life. Later in the decade, Collins began to diversify her repertoire and to move away from protest songs and folk material. Her watershed album *In My Life* featured lush orchestral arrangements by Joshua Rifkin, and it included a cabaret song by Jacques Brel, a theater song by Kurt Weill, and contemporary ballads by Canadian poet Leonard Cohen, as well as songs by Bob Dylan, the Beatles, and Randy Newman. In December, 1970, this became her first album (of an eventual six) to be certified gold.

Wildflowers. Collins soon began composing her own songs. Her first songs to be recorded—"Since You've Asked," "Sky Fell," and "Albatross,"— were included on *Wildflowers*, which also featured Rifkin's arrangements. The album's version of Joni Mitchell's "Both Sides Now" became a Top 10 hit for which Collins won a Grammy Award in 1968 for Best Folk Performance.

Judith. Personal problems during the later 1970's limited the number of new albums that Collins released, but rarely did they affect the quality of her work. *Judith*, issued in March, 1975, and certified gold before the end of the year, contains what is often considered the classic version of Stephen Sondheim's "Send in the Clowns."

Judy Collins. (Hulton Archive/Getty Images)

Later Work. During the 1980's, Collins chronicled a personal and spiritual renewal in such albums as *Home Again* and *Sanity and Grace*. In the 1990's, she focused on songs about family life and relationships. She performed children's songs and lullabies on *Baby's Bedtime* and *Baby's Morningtime*, two collections of poems by such writers as Robert Browning and Emily Dickinson, set to music by Ernest Troost. She recorded duets with Tom Chapin for an album of children's songs, *Family Tree* (1992). In 2000 Collins again collaborated with Chapin, this time on an album with an environmental theme, *This Pretty Planet* (2000). Later albums include *Judy Collins Sings Leonard Cohen, Portrait of an American Girl*, and *Judy Collins Sings Lennon and McCartney*.

Musical Legacy

Although Collins was a major figure in the 1960's Greenwich Village folk scene, working in a genre called urban folk that featured songs of social protest, she is also known for a wide variety of other musical styles. Her repertoire is broad, ranging from the Anglo American folk songs that began her career to cabaret songs, theater music, pop and contemporary ballads, children's songs, and soft rock. Many of her compositions attest to her ability as a songwriter. Her vibratoless soprano voice has been described as "liquid silver," and it is characterized by clarity, purity, coolness, and sweetness, if sometimes lacking in emotional depth. Her vocal range is wide, her intonation nearly perfect, and her articulation of lyrics flawless.

Mary A. Wischusen

Further Reading

Cohen, Ronald D. *Rainbow Quest: The Folk Music Revival and American Society, 1940-1970.* Amherst: University of Massachusetts Press, 2002. A comprehensive and scholarly history of the folk music movement in the mid-twentieth century, with references to Collins.

Collins, Judy. *The Judy Collins Songbook.* New York: Grosset and Dunlap, 1969. Along with music to Collins's songs, this includes seven chapters of reminiscences.

_____. *Morning, Noon, and Night: Living the Creative Life.* New York: Tarcher/Penguin, 2005. Collins discusses her approach to singing and songwriting.

_____. *Sanity and Grace: A Journey of Suicide, Survival, and Strength.* New York: Tarcher/Penguin, 2003. A deeply moving memoir about the events leading up to the death of Collins's only child. She illuminates the healing process that took her from pain to survival.

_____. *Trust Your Heart: An Autobiography.* Boston: Houghton Mifflin, 1987. A touching memoir that chronicles the events in Collins's life and her progress from folk musician to multidimensional artist.

Vassal, Jacques. *Electric Children: Roots and Branches of Modern Folkrock.* New York: Taplinger, 1976. An overview of the folk-rock scene in the 1960's and early 1970's in which Collins played.

See also: Baez, Joan; Brel, Jacques; Cohen, Leonard; Crosby, David; Denny, Sandy; Lennon, John; McCartney, Sir Paul; Mitchell, Joni; Newman, Randy; Paxton, Tom; Powell, Bud; Sondheim, Stephen; Stills, Stephen.

Phil Collins

English singer, songwriter, and drummer

Collins gained fame as the drummer and front man for Genesis. This evolved into a successful solo career and writing hits for motion-picture sound tracks.

Born: January 30, 1951; London, England
Also known as: Philip David Charles Collins (full name)
Member of: Brand X; Genesis

Principal recordings

ALBUMS (solo): *Face Value,* 1981; *Hello, I Must Be Going!,* 1982; *No Jacket Required,* 1985; *But Seriously,* 1989; *Both Sides,* 1993; *Dance into the Light,* 1996; *A Hot Night in Paris,* 1999; *Testify,* 2002.

ALBUMS (with Brand X): *Unorthodox Behaviour,* 1976; *Moroccan Roll,* 1977; *Masques,* 1978; *Product,* 1979; *Do They Hurt?,* 1980; *Is There Anything About?,* 1982; *Xcommunication,* 1992; *Manifest Destiny,* 1997; *Missing Period,* 1998.

ALBUMS (with Genesis): *Nursery Cryme,* 1971; *Foxtrot,* 1972; *Selling England by the Pound,* 1973; *The Lamb Lies Down on Broadway,* 1974; *A Trick of the Tail,* 1976; *Wind and Wuthering,* 1976; *Seconds Out,* 1977; *And Then There Were Three,* 1978; *Duke,* 1980; *Abacab,* 1981; *Three Sides Live,* 1982; *Genesis,* 1983; *Invisible Touch,* 1986; *We Can't Dance,* 1991.

The Life

Born into a prosperous family, Philip David Charles Collins had aspirations of being on stage. After receiving a toy drum set for Christmas at the age of five, he practiced so feverishly that his parents purchased a proper kit. To nurture his creativity, he enrolled in the Barbara Speake Stage School at fourteen, and his professional career started as an actor, notably in a childhood role as the Artful Dodger for a London presentation of *Oliver!* (1960). Other early appearances included a cameo in the Beatles' classic film *A Hard Day's Night* (1964).

In his teen years, Collins attended Chiswick Community School, and his passion for music, particularly drumming, blossomed. He formed and joined a variety of bands. By eighteen, he had released an album with the British rock band Flaming Youth. In 1970, he joined Genesis as the band's drummer. Collins became the group's lead singer in 1975, though he also explored jazz fusion as drummer for Brand X. He debuted on a record with Brand X in 1976, and he ceased involvement by the end of the 1970's. Collins branched out for a solo career in 1981, embarking on a whirlwind of band and individual tours throughout the 1980's and 1990's, along with additional acting appearances.

Collins was married to Andrea Bertorelli from 1975 to 1980, and they had a son, Simon. Collins adopted Bertorelli's daughter, Joely. Collins was married to Jill Tavelman from 1984 to 1996, and they had a daughter, Lily. In 1999 Collins married Orianne Cevey, and they moved to Switzerland. The pair had two children, Nicholas and Matthew, but they separated in 2006.

The Music

Collins's tenure in Flaming Youth ended when he answered an advertisement placed by Genesis, which was seeking a percussion player. Though the group played gentle acoustic pop songs throughout the late 1960's, during the 1970's it turned to twelve-string guitars and progressive rock arrangements. Collins fit into the new niche, and after passing an audition, he was hired to play on the album *Nursery Cryme*. At that time, Peter Gabriel served as primary lead vocalist, though Collins provided background (and occasionally lead) vocals while keeping beat.

Genesis. In 1974 Genesis released the grand concept album *The Lamb Lies Down on Broadway*, and the group embarked on an exhaustive tour. Following the extensive time on the road, Gabriel announced his departure, leaving Collins, keyboardist Tony Banks, bassist-guitarist Mike Rutherford, and guitarist Steve Hackett to audition new vocalists. Finding no one suited to the front-man position, Collins reluctantly stepped up to the microphone on *A Trick of the Tail*. The result was the band's best selling album to that point. It was also critically acclaimed, prompting the group to return to the studio to produce *Wind and Wuthering*. (While

singing for Genesis, Collins branched out as drummer for jazz act Brand X, which debuted in 1976.)

Seconds Out *and* And Then There Were Three. Genesis' touring continued, spawning the live project *Seconds Out* (with Chester Thompson at the drums in concert), and Collins steered the group toward a mainstream rock sound. As a result of the constant touring and Genesis' move away from its progressive musical beginnings, Hackett exited the group, paving the way for *And Then There Were Three* (though bassist-guitarist Daryl Stuermer was added to bolster the live sound). The ballad "Follow You, Follow Me" put the group on the charts.

Duke, Abacab, *and* Face Value. *Duke* opened the new decade for Genesis, producing a series of hit singles such as "Turn It on Again" and "Misunderstanding." The creative *Abacab* featured Earth, Wind, and Fire's horn section on "No Reply At All." To launch his solo career, Collins created *Face Value*, an album connected instantly with Genesis listen-

Phil Collins. (AP/Wide World Photos)

ers and introduced him to a new audience that appreciated the percussive "In the Air Tonight" and other songs with soul influences.

Three Sides Live. In 1982 Collins was featured on Genesis' *Three Sides Live* and on his solo follow-up, *Hello, I Must Be Going!*, which was anchored by a cover of the Supremes' "You Can't Hurry Love." By this time, Collins was trying to attract mainstream audiences, and in the process he was alienating some older listeners. With the album *Genesis*, Collins attempted to please both factions of his fan base. Although the project had several radio singles (notably "That's All"), it also concentrated on artistic material (such as "Second Home by the Sea").

No Jacket Required. Collins returned a favor to Earth, Wind, and Fire by dueting with the band's singer, Philip Bailey, on "Easy Lover." Collins sang the power ballad "Against All Odds" for the film of the same name, and he contributed to "Do They Know It's Christmas?," a single to aid African famine victims. Both became major hits for Collins as a solo artist, and they paved the way for a productive 1985 that included two Live Aid concert performances on the same day (London and Philadelphia) and the solo album *No Jacket Required*. Aside from exploring more radio-friendly sounds (the danceable "Sussudio" and the sing-a-long "Take Me Home"), the project was named Album of the Year at 1986's Grammy Awards.

Invisible Touch. Even with his enormous solo acclaim, Collins honored his Genesis commitments to release with the group *Invisible Touch* in 1986. The project was a radio success, with five U.S. Top 10 hits and with several memorable music videos (including MTV staples "Land of Confusion" and "Tonight, Tonight, Tonight"). In 1988 Collins appeared in the movie *Buster* (1988), and with "Two Hearts" and "A Groovy Kind of Love" he had number-one sound-track singles.

But Seriously. *But Seriously* took a serious and sophisticated pop tone, and the socially conscious "Another Day in Paradise" (about aiding the victims of poverty) won a 1990 Grammy Award for Record of the Year. Collins returned to Genesis in 1991 for *We Can't Dance*, which balanced his solo career's commercial aspects with ten-minute tracks of art rock.

Both Sides. Collins exhibited his experimental tendencies in his solo offering *Both Sides*, which

turned to social and political themes, without the mainstream sounds of his earlier solo projects. As a result, the album did not fare well in sales or in radio play. To turn that around, Collins produced 1996's *Dance into the Light* (at which time Collins announced that he was officially leaving Genesis to pursue solo recording full time). Weary of the direction taken in *Both Sides*, fans did not support *Dance into the Light*. In response to slow sales, Collins changed course by forming the Phil Collins Big Band and by returning to drums for a short tour in 1998, which produced the concert album *A Hot Night in Paris*.

Hits *and* Sound Tracks. *Hits* was produced for mainstream fans in 1999, and Collins contributed to the sound track for *Tarzan* (1999), with, among other songs, the ballad "You'll Be in My Heart," which won an Academy Award for Best Original Song. In 2002 Collins's full-length solo project *Testify* was performing poorly.

Collins returned to the concert stage with Genesis in 2006. With Banks, Rutherford, Stuermer, and Thompson, the group embarked on its first tour in fifteen years, resulting in album box sets and the retrospective release *Turn It on Again—The Hits: The Tour Edition*.

Musical Legacy

Collins's early work as a drummer with Genesis helped lay the groundwork for the progressive-art rock movement (along with Yes and Rush). His diverse talents and his influences were exhibited in Brand X, his jazz fusion side project that showcased his playing and his writing abilities. Collins's role as a singer-songwriter in Genesis and as a solo performer made a major mark on pop and commercial rock from the late 1970's through 1990's, with Genesis selling approximately 150 million albums and his solo efforts selling more than one hundred million albums. In addition to this commercial success in music, Collins acted in motion pictures, and he occasionally backed up his screen work with contributions to film sound tracks.

Several acts from different genres have covered his material, from hard rock band Nonpoint reworking the staple "In the Air Tonight" to hip-hop act Bone Thugs-N-Harmony sampling "Take Me Home" within its own hit "Home."

Andy Argyrakis

Further Reading

Banks, Tony, Phil Collins, Peter Gabriel, Mike Rutherford, and Steve Hackett. *Genesis: Chapter and Verse*. New York: St. Martin's Griffin, 2007. The first official book on Genesis, with contributions from its prominent group members. This includes several anecdotes by or about Collins.

Brackett, Nathan, and Christian Hoard, eds. *The New Rolling Stone Album Guide*. 4th ed. New York: Simon & Schuster, 2004. The fourth edition of this exhaustive album guide provides detailed critical assessments of Collins's solo work and extensive time in Genesis.

Coleman, Ray. *Phil Collins: The Definitive Biography*. London: Simon & Schuster, 1997. This text traces Collins's early years through his late 1990's efforts as a solo artist. The book covers his personal life as well as his musical pursuits.

Russell, Paul. *Genesis—A Live Guide, 1969-1975: Play Me My Song*. London: SAF, 2004. The thoroughly researched text covers several Genesis concerts with Gabriel as lead vocalist. Collins's contributions as drummer and songwriter are covered.

Thompson, Dave. *Turn It on Again: Peter Gabriel, Phil Collins, and Genesis*. San Francisco: Backbeat Books, 2005. The text traces the two primary singers for the group, and it outlines Genesis's progressive rock beginnings, its artful stage presentations, and its demonstration of a mainstream sound in the studio and a commercial tone in concert.

Waller, Johnny. *The Phil Collins Story*. London: Zomba Books, 1985. Coverage of Collins's childhood, his early bands, his entry into Genesis, his role as the band's lead singer, his solo career, and his personal life.

See also: Dozier, Lamont; Eno, Brian; Gabriel, Peter; Jones, Quincy; Lennon, John; McCartney, Sir Paul; Plant, Robert; Sting; Turner, Tina.

Willie Colón

American Latin trombonist, singer, and songwriter

A pioneer of salsa music in the United States, Colón and his robust trombone style contributed to the development of the "New York sound" that spurred a renewed interest in Latin popular music in the 1970's.

Born: April 28, 1950; South Bronx, New York

Also known as: William Anthony Colón (full name); El Malo

Member of: Legal Aliens; the Fania All Stars

Principal recordings

ALBUMS (solo): *El malo*, 1967 (with Héctor Lavoe); *The Hustler*, 1968 (with Lavoe); *Cosa nuestra*, 1969 (with Lavoe); *Guisando*, 1969 (with Lavoe); *Asalto navideño*, 1970 (with Lavoe); *La gran fuga* (the big break), 1970 (with Lavoe); *El jucio*, 1972 (with Lavoe); *Asalto navideño*, vol. 2, 1973 (with Lavoe); *Lo mato*, 1973 (with Lavoe); *The Good, the Bad, the Ugly*, 1975 (with Rubén Blades); *There Goes the Neighborhood*, 1975 (with Mon Rivera); *Metiendo mano*, 1977 (with Blades); *El baquiné de angelitos negros*, 1977; *Déjà Vu*, 1978 (with Lavoe); *Siembra*, 1978 (with Blades); *Solo*, 1979; *Doble energía*, 1980 (with Ismael Miranda); *Canciones del solar de los aburridos*, 1981 (with Blades); *Fantasmas*, 1981 (with Blades); *Corazón guerrero*, 1982; *The Last Fight*, 1982 (with Blades); *Vigilante*, 1983 (with Lavoe); *Criollo*, 1984; *Tiempo pa' matar*, 1984; *Especial no. 5*, 1987; *Singers of the Cibao*, 1994 (with Rivera); *Tras la tormenta*, 1995 (with Blades); *Y vuelve otra vez!*, 1995; *Demasiado corazon*, 1998; *Mí gran amor*, 1999; *Idilio*, 2000.

ALBUMS (with Legal Aliens): *Top Secrets*, 1989; *Color Americano*, 1990; *Illegal Alien*, 1990; *Honra y cultura*, 1991; *Hecho en Puerto Rico*, 1993.

The Life

Born in South Bronx to a Puerto Rican family, William Anthony Colón (koh-LOHN) began playing the trumpet at the age of twelve, but he switched to the trombone two years later. He was quickly signed to the nascent record label Fania Records, which produced his first album, *El malo*. Soon after his debut, he became an important member of the Fania All Stars, the large band comprising musicians that performed and recorded for Fania Records. Here he also developed a reputation as a bandleader and composer.

Between 1967 and 1975 Colón collaborated with singer Héctor Lavoe on several albums, including the two *Asalto navideño* albums. While directing the Latin Jazz All Stars in 1975, he formally studied music theory, composition, and orchestration. From 1976 to 1982, a fruitful period for Colón, he recorded several albums with Rubén Blades. In 1983 he began an active career as a bandleader, a lead vocalist, and a producer, often collaborating with salsa and Latin jazz stars such as Ismael Miranda and Celia Cruz. He has appeared on television as an actor, and he has composed music for several tele-

Willie Colón. (AP/Wide World Photos)

vision productions. Colón has long been a champion of Latino rights.

The Music

Colón helped define the salsa and the Latin jazz genres of the late twentieth century. His innovative sound combines Puerto Rican, Cuban, and other Latin rhythms with elements of jazz and rock. As a young musician, he drew inspiration from the charanga music of Eddie Palmieri and the all-trombone brass sections of Mon Rivera's orchestra. Colón's first album, *El malo*, included several tunes in the bugalú style of the 1960's, a fusion of rhythm and blues, rock and roll, and mambo. By the 1970's, however, Colón was experimenting with various Latin rhythms and world music. Typical themes of his lyrics throughout his career include Pan-Latin solidarity, American imperialism, and barrio violence. Especially popular were the socially conscious albums he made with Blades in the late 1970's, including *Siembra*. In the late 1980's he formed a band called Legal Aliens, with which he recorded two albums as lead singer: *Color Americano* and *Honra y cultura*. Colón collaborated once again with Blades in the mid-1990's, recording *Tras la tormenta* and performing a series of concerts that began at the Hollywood Bowl in 1997. With a recording career spanning more than four decades, Colón had a prolific output, producing more than forty albums and earning eleven Grammy Award nominations.

"El malo." Composed in 1967 when he was just seventeen, "El malo" (the bad one) characterizes much of Colón's early career. In the lyrics he styled himself a modern barrio gangster. Taken from his debut album, which featured his "dirty" trombone sound, "El malo" became his nickname.

"Esta navidad." Recorded for Fania Records, *Asalto navideño* (assault on Christmas) almost instantly became a salsa classic. It incorporated Puerto Rican aguinaldos (traditional Christmas folk songs) in the style of salsa. "Esta navidad" (this Christmas), a track from this album, features the voice of Lavoe and the Puerto Rican cuatro, a distinctive guitar-like instrument with ten strings.

"Calle luna calle sol." After the release of *Asalto navideño*, Colón recorded this song of the barrio, "Calle luna calle sol" (moon street, sun street), which became one of his most famous. Like many of his songs, it addressed life in the violent Latin barrio of New York City.

"Plástico." Since both Colón and Blades wrote music that involved social commentary, their collaboration in the mid-1970's proved fruitful. One of the hits from the album *Siembra* was "Plástico," which begins by attacking materialism and superficiality in a pair of archetypal social climbers. The song begins with strings, horns, and a syncopated electric bass line in the distinctive style of disco, which can be read both as mockery (since disco music was quickly going out of fashion) and as a musical way to underscore the message of the lyrics.

Musical Legacy

As a composer, arranger, singer, trombonist, and producer, Colón contributed to recordings that have sold more than thirty million copies. His compositions set standards for the development of salsa and Latin jazz in rhythm, form, and instrumentation. Likewise, the lyrical content of his works combined nostalgia for the tropical land of his ancestors with the harsh realities of city life, a synthesis that defines much of Latin American popular music. In 1995 he became the first member of a minority to serve on the American Society of Composers, Authors, and Publishers (ASCAP) national board of trustees.

Stephanie N. Stallings

Further Reading

Boggs, Vernon. *Salsiology: Afro-Cuban Music and the Evolution of Salsa in New York City.* Westport, Conn.: Greenwood Press, 1992. An introduction to the musical influences evident in salsa music, including interviews with key figures in the salsa industry.

Janson Perez, Brittmarie. "Political Facets of Salsa." *Popular Music* 6, no. 2 (May, 1987): 149-159. Discusses Colón's "El general," an antimilitary song.

Morales, Ed. "The Story of Nuyorican Salsa." In *The Latin Beat: The Rhythms and Roots of Latin Music, from Bossa Nova to Salsa and Beyond.* New York: Da Capo Press, 2003. A detailed study of how Puerto Rican and New York styles of music converged into salsa.

Roberts, John Storm. *The Latin Tinge: The Impact of Latin American Music on the United States.* New York: Oxford University Press, 1998. Discusses

Puerto Rican contributions to salsa, including several useful insights into Colón's music.

Steward, Sue. *Musica! The Rhythm of Latin America: Salsa, Rumba, Merengue, and More.* San Francisco: Chronicle Books, 1999. Contains a preface by Colón.

See also: Blades, Rubén; Cruz, Celia.

John Coltrane
American jazz saxophonist and composer

Coltrane was a leading exponent of extended improvisation in jazz and expanded both the harmonic and modal vocabulary, utilizing his virtuosic saxophone technique to push the boundaries of expression. He also emphasized the spiritual dimension of jazz and its transcendent, transformative potential.

Born: September 23, 1926; Hamlet, North Carolina
Died: July 17, 1967; Long Island, New York
Also known as: John William Coltrane (full name)

Principal recordings

ALBUMS (solo): *John Coltrane and the Jazz Giants*, 1956; *Mating Call*, 1956; *Tenor Conclave*, 1956; *Blue Train*, 1957; *Coltrane*, 1957; *Dakar*, 1957; *The Last Trane*, 1957; *Lush Life*, 1957; *Traneing In*, 1957; *Bahia*, 1958; *The Believer*, 1958; *Black Pearls*, 1958; *Countdown: The Savoy Sessions*, 1958; *Dial Africa*, 1958; *Gold Coast*, 1958; *Settin' the Pace*, 1958; *Soultrane*, 1958; *Stardust*, 1958; *Giant Steps*, 1959; *The Avant-Garde*, 1960; *Coltrane's Sound*, 1960; *My Favorite Things*, 1960; *Africa/Brass*, 1961; *Coltrane Jazz*, 1961; *Olé*, 1961; *Ballads*, 1962; *Coltrane Plays the Blues*, 1962; *Standard Coltrane*, 1962; *Impressions*, 1963; *John Coltrane and Johnny Hartman*, 1963; *Crescent*, 1964; *A Love Supreme*, 1964; *Ascension*, 1965; *First Meditations*, 1965; *The John Coltrane Quartet Plays*, 1965; *Kulu Sé Mama*, 1965; *Om*, 1965; *Sun Ship*, 1965; *Transition*, 1965; *Expression*, 1967; *Interstellar Space*, 1967.

ALBUMS (with Kenny Burrell): *Kenny Burrell and John Coltrane*, 1958.

ALBUMS (with Miles Davis): *The New Miles Davis Quintet*, 1955; *Cookin' with the Miles Davis Quintet*, 1956; *Miles Davis and the Modern Jazz Giants*, 1956; *Relaxin' with the Miles Davis Quintet*, 1956; *'Round About Midnight*, 1956; *Steamin' with the Miles Davis Quintet*, 1956; *Workin' with the Miles Davis Quintet*, 1956; *Milestones*, 1958; *Kind of Blue*, 1959.

ALBUMS (with Thelonious Monk): *Thelonious Monk with John Coltrane*, 1957.

The Life

As a youth, John William Coltrane (KOHL-trayn) was exposed to music by his parents, who both played instruments. His mother's father, the Reverend William Blair, shared with him the ideas of influential writers of the Harlem Renaissance. While attending school in High Point, North Carolina, Coltrane played band instruments such as clarinet and E-flat alto horn. He switched to alto saxophone and began practicing enthusiastically. After his father and his mother's father passed away, his mother, aunt, and cousin moved to Philadelphia, where John joined them after finishing high school in 1943. In Philadelphia, Coltrane studied at the Ornstein School of Music. During a year of service in the Navy, he played in Hawaii and, upon returning to Philadelphia in 1946, resumed studies at Granoff Studios and started to work professionally.

He played in many bands and combos and eventually with Dizzy Gillespie, one of the creators of the complex bebop style. Unfortunately, as his reputation grew, Coltrane fell victim to the drug and alcohol habits that were occupational hazards for jazz musicians at the time. Somehow, he managed to grow musically and attracted the attention of trumpeter Miles Davis, who in 1955 engaged him in a partnership that was to make some of the most influential recordings in jazz. In Davis's group, Coltrane achieved national recognition, although his substance-abuse problems continued. In 1957, after being fired by Davis, who had overcome his addiction to hard drugs, Coltrane freed himself from drugs and soon approached his music with a renewed sense of purpose and energy. While continuing to play with pianist Thelonious Monk and others, Coltrane led his own recording sessions, which included his compositions.

After a second and even more artistically significant period with Davis, Coltrane formed his own group in 1960 and from this time on performed primarily as a leader. Usually leading a quartet with piano, bass, and drums, Coltrane started playing the soprano saxophone, alternating with tenor. With an intense practice regimen that consumed most of his waking hours, he became regarded as one of the great virtuosos of these instruments.

In the process of recovering from addiction, Coltrane had reconnected with the religious background of his childhood, broadening it to Islam through his first wife, Juanita Naima Grubb, and continued to expand his interests through the study of Eastern and African spiritual traditions. He had deep respect for the music of those cultures as well. These trends converged in his 1964 album *A Love Supreme*, accompanied with text indicating that his music was offered as a spiritual expression. Coltrane avoided specific sectarian identification, and his new music was embraced by people of all faiths and backgrounds, who responded to its challenging, intense nature. In the last few years of his life, he continued to assert the spiritual purpose of his music, which became increasingly experimental. He was joined in some of his final projects by his second wife, pianist Alice Coltrane, as well as other colleagues from the jazz community. Tragically, John Coltrane died of liver cancer at age forty.

The Music

During Coltrane's Philadelphia period, he worked in a variety of idioms, including the rhythm-and-blues style, which stressed vocal-style inflections on the saxophone, as well as the more dissonant style of bebop. He developed a vast repertoire of standard pieces and became known as someone with a good memory for chord progressions. Coltrane's initial influences were alto saxophonists: Johnny Hodges, who had contributed to the distinctive sound of the Duke Ellington orchestra, and Charlie Parker, the brilliant innovator who had helped to create bebop. Although Coltrane did not change to tenor saxophone until around 1947, he had listened to tenor saxophonists, including Lester Young, of the rhythmically driving Kansas City style, and Coleman Hawkins, whose bold arpeggios have been considered a precedent for the "sheets-of-sound" style that Coltrane would later develop.

Coltrane's first chance for national prominence came when Gillespie hired him to play in his big band, and Coltrane recorded with the group in 1949. Gillespie attempted to combine the fast tempi and intricate melodies of bebop with the popular appeal and power of the large ensemble. It was an exciting experiment but not commercially viable. After the group disbanded, Gillespie employed Coltrane in a smaller group until 1951. The next prominent musician to employ him was Hodges, who worked in an older style closer to the big band era in sound. A great admirer of Hodges, Coltrane deeply enjoyed this experience, but his debilitating drug habit prevented a long-term association.

'Round About Midnight. In 1955 Coltrane began his first period as a member of the Miles Davis Quintet when Miles needed a replacement for saxophonist Sonny Rollins. In spite of continued substance-abuse problems, Coltrane made significant artistic breakthroughs in his work with Davis during this period, which ended in 1956. Miles allowed his sidemen a great deal of freedom, and this situation encouraged Coltrane to develop a more verbose style that displayed his considerable technique. Also, Coltrane formed strong musical relationships with the other musicians in the quintet, including bassist Paul Chambers, pianist Red Garland, and drummer Philly Joe Jones, consummate players he would soon employ on his own projects. Their harmonic and rhythmic support gave Coltrane the confidence he needed to explore his ideas. In 1956 the quintet recorded four albums for Prestige Records, as well as *'Round About Midnight* for Columbia. Monk, a master of harmonic dissonance who had coauthored "'Round Midnight," hired Coltrane for his own group and encouraged further stylistic developments in the saxophonist.

Trane Albums. Building on his work with Miles, Coltrane engaged some of his colleagues from that

John Coltrane. (Library of Congress)

group, and others, to record his own albums. The first of these, titled simply with his name, was released by Prestige Records, and the second, *Blue Train*, was recorded for Blue Note, both in 1957. *Blue Train* featured several of his original compositions. He also collaborated on recordings with guitarist Kenny Burrell, Garland, and other musicians during this period. A third album, *Soultrane*, was released in 1958, and a fourth, *Lush Life*, was also recorded during this period. These albums contrasted Coltrane's delicate rendering of ballads with exciting, rhythmically precise excursions in the hard-bop style.

Kind of Blue. Coltrane made a triumphant return to Davis's group in 1958, and his dense melodic structures, which had blossomed during the intervening period, formed a perfect contrast to Davis's more minimalist and plaintive soloing. This reunion allowed Coltrane to participate in an important stylistic development for Davis, with a new emphasis on modes. The blues, with its many branches of oral tradition, had always been a modal music. Davis took advantage of this connection as he crafted new pieces, primarily in the mixolydian and dorian modes, which featured slow harmonic rhythm, permitting the soloists to be free and relaxed in their melodic invention. The group recorded two albums, *Milestones* and *Kind of Blue*, and also made live recordings before Coltrane left to pursue his career as a group leader and composer.

Giant Steps. Coltrane's first album to consist entirely of his own compositions, *Giant Steps* was recorded in 1959. Two of the pieces, "Naima" and "Cousin Mary," were named for family members, and a third, "Mr. P.C.," was named for bassist Paul Chambers, who provided a strong foundation for the project. The title piece uses the traditional theme-and-variations approach for a progression that is only sixteen measures long. Although the immediate structures at any given time are familiar, the phrase targets outline the notes of an augmented triad. This, in conjunction with the rapid tempo, weakens the sense of a tonal center. In both "Giant Steps" and "Countdown," which appeared on the same album, the rapid harmonic rhythms of bebop are paired with key areas progressing by major thirds, demanding an unprecedented level of concentration on the part of the soloist. In this premier recording, Coltrane roared through the changes with the same confidence that he displayed in his later work, when he was able to respond immediately and definitively to relatively unpredictable piano chords offered to him in a more open structural context.

A Love Supreme. After *Giant Steps*, Coltrane continued to record many albums under his own name and explored the modal style, frequently playing the soprano sax, which he used for *My Favorite Things*, one of his most popular albums. By this time, he had been joined by McCoy Tyner on piano and Elvin Jones on drums. When Jimmy Garrison joined the group in 1962 to play bass, what came to be regarded as Coltrane's classic quartet was complete. In 1964 this group made its most famous recording, a four-movement suite entitled *A Love Supreme*. Jones, one of the few drummers who could sustain multiple layers of contrasting patterns over a long period of time, provided an unprecedented level of polyrhythmic tension, which would be occasionally released at the beginnings of new phrases. The effect was similar to the great ensemble percussion traditions of West Africa. Although there was plenty of hard swinging jazz content in the suite, for the final movement Coltrane returned to his religious roots, adopting the inflections and phrasing of gospel preaching and spirituals. All of these elements were harmonized with sophisticated modernist voicings that underscored the music's presentation as serious concert music. Tyner's parallel quartal harmonies formed complex inversions and neighboring structures over Garrison's lines and, like Jones's polyrhythms, would occasionally resolve at key points in the structure.

Interstellar Space. During this period, Coltrane's groups played much more experimentally in concert than in the studio and were influenced by the free jazz movement introduced by Ornette Coleman, as well as such modernist composers as Cecil Taylor, Sun Ra, and the musicians in their groups. For Coltrane, melodic lines and intensity became more important than vertical structures, and this became even more pronounced when the piano was dropped. Although the emphasis on melody and rhythm could have made this music more similar to the modal traditions of Asia and Africa, Coltrane often maintained the full chromatic spectrum in his sequences and superimposed lines, obscuring the sense of a strong tonal center and keeping the modernist dimension shared with atonal or pantonal music. Eventually, Coltrane even dropped the bass for his second-to-last recording, *Interstellar Space*, a duo album with drummer Rashied Ali in 1967.

Musical Legacy

Aside from his unquestioned virtuosity on the saxophone, Coltrane has been a powerful influence on subsequent generations of musicians, who continue to be inspired by his intense creativity, his specific musical techniques, and his contributions to the standard repertoire. Along with Davis, he was one of the chief proponents of the modal style, while at the same time pushing the limits of the harmonic vocabulary into polytonality. He provided the world with a deep and lasting affirmation of the essential spirituality of music in general and of jazz in particular. In 2007 the Pulitzer Prize Board awarded him a posthumous special citation honoring his achievements and contributions.

John Myers

Further Reading

Brown, Leonard. "Sacred Music for Secular Space, in Honor of John Coltrane." In *The Triumph of the Soul: Cultural and Psychological Aspects of African American Music*, edited by Ferdinand Jones and Arthur C. Jones. Westport, Conn.: Praeger, 2001. Comprehensive study on the root genre of African American music. Index.

Cole, Bill. *John Coltrane*. New York: Da Capo Press, 2001. Looks at the religious dimension of Coltrane's life and music and his connections to West African traditions. Photographs, music transcriptions.

Kahn, Ashley. *A Love Supreme: The Story of John Coltrane's Signature Album*. New York: Viking Penguin, 2002. Includes interviews with the musicians and others associated with the recording. Photographs, index, extensive notes, discography.

Porter, Lewis. *John Coltrane: His Life and Music*. Ann Arbor: University of Michigan Press, 1998. Well-researched biography focuses on the music and chronology, with music examples, analysis, illustrations, references, index.

Thomas, J. C. *Chasin' the Trane*. Garden City, N.Y.: Da Capo Press, 1975. Biography, including statements from people who knew Coltrane at various periods. Photographs, discography.

See also: Adderley, Cannonball; Corea, Chick; Davis, Miles; Dolphy, Eric; Ellington, Duke; Gillespie, Dizzy; Gordon, Dexter; Hancock, Herbie; Hawkins, Coleman; Jones, Elvin; Jones, Hank; Kirk, Rahsaan Roland; Legrand, Michel; McGuinn, Roger; McPartland, Marian; Marsalis, Wynton; Masekela, Hugh; Monk, Thelonious; Montgomery, Wes; Palmieri, Eddie; Parker, Charlie; Rollins, Sonny; Sanders, Pharoah; Shankar, Ravi; Shorter, Wayne; Taylor, Cecil; Tyner, McCoy.

Sean Combs

American rap vocalist and songwriter

Combs is a rap artist who expanded his involvement in entertainment by founding a record company, Bad Boy Entertainment, that promotes hip-hop and rhythm-and-blues artists.

Born: November 4, 1969; New York, New York
Also known as: Sean John Combs (full name); P. Diddy; Puff Daddy; Diddy

Principal recordings

ALBUMS: *No Way Out*, 1997; *Forever*, 1999; *Thank You*, 2001; *Press Play*, 2006.

The Life

Sean John Combs (kohmz) spent a large portion of his childhood in Mt. Vernon, New York, before attending Howard University. While enrolled at Howard, Combs secured an internship at Uptown Records, and he eventually dropped out of college to focus on a music career. He was quickly promoted to vice president of artists and repertoire at Uptown Records, and he discovered, developed, produced, and styled such acts as Jodeci, Mary J. Blige, and Christopher Wallace, better known as the Notorious B.I.G. In 1993 Combs was fired from Uptown Records, but he quickly found a distributor for his own record label, Bad Boy Entertainment.

Following Combs to his new label were two artists Combs had signed at Uptown Records: Craig Mack and Notorious B.I.G. Mack released the label's first album, *Project: Funk Da World*, in 1994, while the Notorious B.I.G. released his debut, *Ready to Die*, the following year. Produced by Combs, *Ready to Die* propelled the Notorious B.I.G. to the top of the rap world and solidified his position as Bad Boy Entertainment's premier star. Over the next two years, Combs added several other successful acts to the label, such as rhythm-and-blues singer Faith Evans and rapper Mase, and he continued to serve as a producer for such high-profile artists as Mariah Carey and Boyz II Men. This period also saw the development of a rivalry between Bad Boy Entertainment and the West Coast label Death Row Records, which was initiated through accusations by Death Row artist Tupac Shakur that Combs and Wallace been involved in an incident in 1994 in which Shakur had been shot. The feud, which was expressed both lyrically in songs and through public appearances, eventually ended with the shooting deaths of Shakur in 1996 and Wallace in 1997.

In the wake of Wallace's death, his second solo album, *Life After Death*, was released, as was Combs's solo debut as Puff Daddy, *No Way Out*. Both albums were highly successful, but the sales of Combs's next album, *Forever*, were disappointing. In 1999 Combs and Bad Boy Entertainment experienced other setbacks. Prominent rapper Mase and rap group the LOX left the label, and Combs encountered a number of legal problems. He was accused of beating Interscope Records executive Steve Stoute, a charge that was eventually reduced to second-degree harassment, and in December of 1999 he was in attendance at a New York City nightclub when a shooting occurred. Combs, found with an unregistered gun, was charged with illegal possession of a firearm. The charges were eventually dropped, and in the aftermath Combs changed his stage name from Puff Daddy to P. Diddy. Bad Boy Entertainment began to reverse its fortunes with the release of the compilation albums *The Saga Continues* in 2001 and *We Invented the Remix* in 2002, and it was in full resurgence by 2006, when albums by rapper Yung Joc, singer Cassie, the female vocal group Danity Kane, and Combs were released to great success.

In addition to his activities as an artist and label head, Combs has been involved in other successful ventures. His clothing line, Sean John, figures prominently in hip-hop fashion, and he produces the MTV reality show *Making the Band*. As an actor, Combs has appeared in the films *Made* (2001) and *Monster's Ball* (2001) and in the 2004 Broadway revival of *A Raisin in the Sun* (1959).

The Music

Best known as a label head and producer, Combs has also released a number of solo albums since 1997 under the names Puff Daddy, P. Diddy, and Diddy. For these solo efforts he enlists the help of guest artists, and he frequently utilizes his own songs to promote artists on his Bad Boy Entertainment label. Musically, Combs heavily utilizes samples, which frequently serve as the sole basis for his songs. Combs has been criticized for his overreliance on samples, but nevertheless his songs have demonstrated large commercial appeal.

No Way Out. Released after the Notorious B.I.G.'s death in 1997, *No Way Out* marks Combs's debut as a solo artist. A big success, the album has been certified seven times platinum, contains two *Billboard* Hot 100 number-one singles and two number-two singles, and won the 1998 Grammy Award for Best Rap Album. Like all of Combs's solo albums, *No Way Out* features appearances by guest artists, including several artists signed to Combs's Bad Boy Entertainment label. The first single from the album, "Can't Nobody Hold Me Down," established Combs as a solo artist, and it held the top position on the singles chart for six weeks. The song prominently features Bad Boy rapper Mase and relies on samples drawn from previous hit singles "The Message" by Grandmaster Flash and the Furious Five and "Break My Stride" by Matthew Wilder. The next single released from the album was "I'll Be Missing You," which featured Evans and the rhythm-and-blues quartet 112. This song, which won the 1998 Grammy Award for Best Rap Performance by a Duo or Group, is a tribute to the Notorious B.I.G. and samples the melody of "Every Breath You Take" by the Police. The final two singles, "Been Around the World" and "It's All About the Benjamins," both contain posthumous appearances by the Notorious B.I.G. and prominently utilize samples.

The Saga Continues. Released in 2001 under his new stage name P. Diddy, *The Saga Continues* attempted to regain some of the fans that Combs lost apparently because of his legal troubles at the time. The album prominently features other Bad Boy Entertainment artists, especially rappers G-Dep and Black Rob, and it intersperses several spoken interludes and skits between songs. Throughout the album, Combs attempts to reestablish his credibility by declaring his innocence in his legal affairs and by assuring listeners that his Bad Boy Entertainment empire is still intact. Unlike previous albums, *The Saga Continues* relies less on samples and more on original beats, another attempt by Combs to demonstrate his authenticity as an artist.

Press Play. In the middle of Bad Boy Entertainment's resurgence in 2006, Combs released the solo album *Press Play*. Similar to his other albums, *Press Play* features a significant number of collaborators, and they are notable for their prominence in the music business. Among the guest artists are Christina Aguilera, Twista, Nas, Brandy, Mary J. Blige, and Jamie Foxx, and Combs shares production duties with such high-profile producers as Timbaland, Kayne West, and the Neptunes. The music presents an eclectic mix of rhythm and blues, soul, hip-hop, and techno, and Combs, in addition to rapping, debuts as a singer. The album produced five singles, including two that reached the Top 10 on the *Billboard* Hot 100 singles chart. The first Top 10 single, "Come to Me," features Nicole Scherzinger of the group the Pussycat Dolls, and it utilizes a sparse electronic beat that is well suited for a dance club. "Last Night," the other Top 10 single, features rhythm-and-blues singer Keyshia Cole and samples Prince's "Erotic City," creating a 1980's-style beat. The other three singles—"Tell Me," "Diddy Rock," and "Through the Pain (She Told Me)"—feature a prominent guest artist, with the album showcasing his collaborators as much as Combs.

Musical Legacy

Although he began as a rapper, Combs made his primary musical contributions as a producer and record executive. Through his activities as the head of Bad Boy Entertainment, he has launched the careers of numerous acts, such as the Notorious B.I.G., Evans, Mase, and Danity Kane. As a producer, Combs helped popularize rap with mainstream audiences, creating an accessible sound by relying heavily on samples. In addition to the artists he has produced on the Bad Boy record label, he has produced a number of outside acts as well, including Jay-Z, TLC, Mary J. Blige, and Aretha Franklin. His concurrent activities as a record producer, rapper, entrepreneur, label head, and actor have provided the template for other versatile artists to follow. It is now common for rap artists to run their own label, have their own clothing line, and appear in films, just as Combs has done.

Throughout his career, Combs has a received a number of awards and recognitions. In addition to the Grammy Awards he received for *No Way Out* and "I'll Be Missing You," Combs received the 2004 Grammy Award for Best Rap Performance by a Duo or Group, along with Nelly and Murphy Lee, for "Shake Ya Tailfeather," and in 1996 he was named the American Society of Authors, Composers, and Publishers (ASCAP) Songwriter of the Year. He also received MTV Video Music Awards for "I'll Be Missing You" in 1997 and "It's All About the Benjamins (Rock Remix)" in 1998.

Matthew Mihalka

Further Reading

Cable, Andrew. *A Family Affair: The Unauthorized Sean "Puffy" Combs Story*. New York: Ballantine Books, 1998. This book chronicles the early portion of Combs's life and career, from his birth to his work at the MCA Records subsidiary Uptown to his founding of Bad Boy Entertainment and his ascension as a solo artist in the wake of the Notorious B.I.G.'s death. Includes several photographs of Combs with various hip-hop artists.

Nelson, George. *Hip-Hop America*. New York: Viking, 1998. Portions of this book describe Combs's early years at Uptown and the formation of his Bad Boy record label, as well as his role in the East Coast-West Coast feud.

Oliver, Richard, and Tim Leffel. *Hip-Hop, Inc.: Success Strategies of the Rap Moguls*. New York: Thunder's Mouth Press, 2006. This source includes a chapter on Combs's activities as a hip-hop music executive, focusing on Combs as an entrepreneur, as the head of Bad Boy Entertainment and the Sean John clothing line, and as a television and film producer.

Ro, Ronin. *Bad Boy: The Influence of Sean "Puffy" Combs on the Music Industry*. New York: Pocket Books, 2001. This biography of Combs focuses primarily on his activities from the founding of Bad Boy in 1993 to the Notorious B.I.G.'s death in 1997.

_____. *Have Gun Will Travel: The Spectacular Rise and Violent Fall of Death Row Records*. New York: Doubleday, 1998. This book documents the East Coast-West Coast rivalry between Combs's Bad Boy Entertainment and Suge Knight's Death Row Records.

See also: Blige, Mary J.; Carey, Mariah; Franklin, Aretha; Grandmaster Flash; Hammer, M. C.; LL Cool J; Notorious B.I.G.; Prince.

Harry Connick, Jr.

American popular singer, pianist, and composer

Known for reviving jazz vocals in the style of 1940's crooners epitomized by Frank Sinatra, Connick fell in love with jazz and singing as a child and eventually introduced these classic American styles to a new generation. While some critics were initially quick to dismiss him as simply a "Sinatra wannabe," Connick has earned respect as both a consumate performer and a humanitarian.

Born: September 11, 1967; New Orleans, Louisiana

Also known as: Joseph Harry Fowler Connick, Jr. (full name)

Principal recordings

ALBUMS: *Dixieland Plus*, 1977; *Eleven*, 1978; *Harry Connick, Jr.*, 1987; *Twenty*, 1988; *When Harry Met Sally*, 1989 (all songs by Harry Connick, Jr.); *Lofty's Roach Shuffle*, 1990; *We Are in Love*, 1990; *Blue Light, Red Light*, 1991; *Twenty-five*, 1992; *When My Heart Finds Christmas*, 1993; *Imagination*, 1994; *She*, 1994; *Star Turtle*, 1995; *Whisper Your Name*, 1995; *To See You*, 1997; *Come by Me*, 1999; *Songs I Heard*, 2001; *Thirty*, 2001; *Harry for the Holidays*, 2003; *Other Hours: Connick on Piano, Vol. 1*, 2003; *Only You*, 2004; *Occasion: Connick on Piano, Vol. 2*, 2005; *Harry on Broadway, Act 1*, 2006; *Chanson du vieux carré*, 2007; *Oh, My NOLA*, 2007.

The Life

Joseph Harry Fowler Connick (KAH-nihk), Jr., was born in New Orleans, Louisiana, on September 11, 1967. His mother, Anita, who died when Connick was thirteen years old, was a judge, lawyer, and former Louisiana Supreme Court justice. His father, Harry Connick, Sr., was the district attorney of New Orleans for twenty-six years, successfully running against Jim Garrison, who was best known for his investigation into the assassination of President John F. Kennedy. Connick's sister, Suzanna, became an intelligence officer for the U.S. Army.

Growing up in a family of overachievers was not intimidating to Connick. He quickly made his own mark, perhaps influenced by the fact that his parents also owned a record store. He learned to play the keyboard at age three, gave his first public performance three years later, and recorded with a local jazz band when he was ten years old. Under the tutelage of jazz pianists Ellis Marsalis and James Booker, Connick developed his musical talents at the New Orleans Center for Creative Arts. A few years later, he moved to New York City, where he attended the prestigious Manhattan School of Music. In New York, an executive from Columbia Records persuaded Connick to sign a record deal.

After Connick had released a self-titled album of instrumental standards, his reputation in the jazz community quickly grew, and he worked as a pianist in jazz clubs. He added his now-trademark crooner vocals in the album *Twenty*, which garnered even more respect for him within the New York jazz world. Although it would have been easy to develop a career covering already successful jazz standards, Connick instead branched out, alternating between jazz, big band, and funk genres. He also became an actor, earning fame as a guest on several television programs, including *Will and Grace*. In 1994, Connick was married to Jill Goodacre, a former model; the couple would have three daughters.

No matter how famous he became, Connick remained committed to his roots. After Hurricane Katrina wreaked havoc on his hometown of New Orleans in August, 2005, Connick not only helped organize fund-raising efforts but also spent several days touring the city and lending a helping hand. On September 6 of that year, he was made honorary chair of Habitat for Humanity's Operation Home Delivery, a long-term rebuilding plan for families left homeless by the hurricane in New Orleans and along the neighboring Gulf Coast.

The Music

While most of his peers were studying their multiplication tables, Connick was already recording music. In 1977, he recorded *Dixieland Plus* with local New Orleans musicians for ADCO Productions. Only two years later, eleven-year-old Connick recorded *Eleven* with another ensemble cast of New Orleans musicians. Eight years later came Connick's self-titled debut with Sony Records, an instrumental album of jazz standards that showcased his piano-playing prowess.

When Harry Met Sally. Connick officially became a household name with the release of director Rob Reiner's film *When Harry Met Sally*. When Reiner heard of Connick's talent, he asked him to provide the sound track for the film. The movie was a favorite at the box office in 1989, and the accompanying sound track, with Connick's songs, was equally successful. The album went double platinum, with sales of more than two million, and garnered for Connick his first Grammy, for Best Jazz Male Vocal Performance.

We Are in Love. With his silky-smooth vocals, good looks, charm, and a musicial sensibility that spanned genres and therefore appealed to diverse audiences, Connick was well suited to singing romantic ballads, as evidenced by his 1990 release *We Are in Love*. Featuring the wedding favorite "I've Got a Great Idea," as well as classic Connick love songs such as "Recipe for Love," the whimsical title track, and "I'll Dream of You Again," this album solidified his reputation and popularity.

When My Heart Finds Christmas. In 1993, this release of holiday songs would become a classic for the younger generation. The album mixed popular carols and four new contributions by Connick, in-

cluding the spirited gospel song "I Pray on Christmas." The disc enjoyed multiplatinum sales and remains popular.

She. Eager to prove that his musicianship was not limited to jazz or nostalgic standards, in 1994 Connick released *She*. The album ushered in the era of funk experimentation for Connick. While some fans were taken aback by this huge sonic shift, critics applauded his rootsy New Orleans style on "Here Comes the Big Parade" and "Trouble." Crossing over into mainstream pop, as in "(I Could Only) Whisper Your Name," Connick soon proved that he could write more accessible fare as well.

To See You. Connick returned to his jazz roots with his well-received *To See You*. Recorded with a symphony orchestra, this album was, according to Connick, inspired by a flight attendant's request for a romantic album. Adding ambience to the tour that introduced the album, Connick hit the road with a full symphony orchestra. The tour culminated with a Valentine's Day performance in Paris that was aired by the Public Broadcasting Service.

Songs I Heard. Connick's *Songs I Heard* reverted to his childhood with tracks from movies he remembered watching in his youth. Featuring everything from "Ding Dong! The Witch Is Dead!" (from 1939's *The Wizard of Oz*) to "The Lonely Goatherd" (from 1965's *The Sound of Music*), Connick's exploration of his inner child was aimed at both children and adults.

Oh, My NOLA. As a valentine to his beloved hometown, Connick decided to record an album's worth of songs associated with New Orleans, as well as four new songs of his own composition. For the album *Oh, My NOLA*, Connick served not only as a performer, singing and playing the piano, but also as conductor, arranger, and orchestrater. Continuing his charitable work, he directed that a portion of the album's proceeds be donated to Musicians' Village, one of Connick's pet projects in New Orleans.

Harry Connick, Jr. (AP/Wide World Photos)

Musical Legacy

Despite his association with American standards, Connick has never been satisfied with doing something the way it has been done before. Whether serving up a gumbo of funk and blues on 1994's *She* or covering old jazz standards on 2005's *Only You*, Connick always takes his own approach to his material, consistently delivering the high-quality vocals and instrumentals that have earned him the respect of musical legends, contemporaries, and public alike. Hence, while he will be remembered for preserving and renewing jazz classics and popular standards, he has also made his mark as something of a renaissance talent: vocalist, pianist, actor, and humanitarian.

Christa A. Banister

Further Reading

Feather, Leonard, and Ira Gitler. *The Biographical Encyclopedia of Jazz*. New York: Oxford University Press, 1999. Contains and authoritative entry on Connick.

Felix, Antonia. *Wild About Harry? The Illustrated Biography*. Dallas, Tex.: Taylor, 1995. In a revealing biography, Felix gets to know the man behind the music.

See also: Burke, Johnny; Chevalier, Maurice.

Sam Cooke

American soul singer

Cooke was a singer and writer of gospel, rhythm-and-blues, and popular songs. His melding of these three forms in his pure but intense vocals was a major factor in the birth of soul music.

Born: January 22, 1931; Clarksdale, Mississippi
Died: December 11, 1964; Los Angeles, California
Also known as: Samuel Cook (birth name); Dale Cooke

Principal recordings

ALBUMS: *Encore*, 1958; *Sam Cooke*, 1958; *Hit Kit*, 1959; *Tribute to the Lady*, 1959; *Cooke's Tour*, 1960; *Hits of the Fifties*, 1960; *I Thank God*, 1960; *Swing Low*, 1960; *The Wonderful World of Sam Cooke*, 1960; *My Kind of Blues*, 1961; *Twistin' the Night Away*, 1962; *Mr. Soul*, 1963; *Night Beat*, 1963; *Ain't That Good News*, 1964; *Shake*, 1965.

The Life

Samuel Cook was born in Mississippi in 1931, the fifth of eight children of the Reverend Charles and Annie Mae Cook. When Sam was two, his family moved to Chicago, where his father worked at the Reynolds Metal Plant, while pastoring Christ Temple Church and having his children sing in area churches. After graduating from Wendell Phillips High School in 1948, Cooke began singing in gospel groups, and in 1950 he joined the Soul Stirrers. In 1953 Cooke married Delores "Dee Dee" Mohawk; their son Joey was born shortly afterward. Three other women would bear Sam children that year as well. Sam's success with the Soul Stirrers prompted him to start recording popular songs in 1956. His 1957 recording of his composition "You Send Me" became an overnight hit, selling more than a million records and reaching number one on the *Billboard* charts. During this time Cooke left the Soul Stirrers, moved to Los Angeles, divorced Delores, and added an "e" to his last name.

A stream of hits followed as well as appearances in leading theaters and nightclubs, including a live recording at New York's Copacabana. On October 11, 1959, Cooke married his childhood sweetheart, Barbara Campbell, with whom he already had a daughter, Linda. In addition to signing a contract with RCA's flamboyant young record producers Hugo Peretti and Luigi Creatore, Cooke started his own record label. In 1960 his daughter Tracey was born. The following year the family moved into a mansion in an exclusive neighborhood, and Barbara gave birth to their son Vincent. (Tragically, Vincent died in the backyard swimming pool as a toddler.) Cooke became friendly with activist Malcolm X and boxer Cassius Clay, soon to be known as Muhammad Ali, who invited Cooke into the ring after his celebrated knockout of Sonny Liston.

By all accounts Cooke was polite, charismatic, urbane, and handsome. He was an avid reader and a supporter of the Civil Rights movement. However, he could never settle down to married life, which would prove his undoing.

Sam Cooke. (AP/Wide World Photos)

On December 11, 1964, Cooke and a woman named Elisa Boyer went to the Hacienda Motel near the Los Angeles airport. While Cooke was undressed in the bathroom, Boyer fled the motel with his clothes, which also contained his wallet. An inebriated Cooke demanded that the motel manager, Bertha Lee Franklin, produce Boyer. Franklin and Cooke tussled, and Franklin shot Cooke through the heart with her gun. Cooke died minutes later. (A coroner's jury would acquit Franklin on the grounds of "justifiable homicide.")

The Music

Cooke began his musical career with the Singing Children, a group consisting of his siblings that performed in local churches. At sixteen he joined a gospel quartet, the Highway QC's. In 1950 Cooke joined the well-known Soul Stirrers, soon becoming their lead tenor and one of the top stars in gospel music.

"Jesus, I'll Never Forget." Cooke's recording of "Jesus, I'll Never Forget" not only was one of the most acclaimed Soul Stirrer singles but also foreshadowed the hallmarks of his popular music. In this song Cooke began with a melismatic call ("o-o-o-h-h-h, Jesus"). Although his style was calm and lyrical, he instilled his vocals with a subtle passion, intensified by cries of "oh-oh-oh" and "no-no-no" that evoke the call-and-response of the Pentecostal service.

"You Send Me." With Cooke's ascendant star in gospel music, he was approached by record producers to cross over into popular music. In deference to his gospel fans, he made his first pop recordings in late 1956 under the pseudonym Dale Cooke. In 1957 he recorded George Gershwin's "Summertime" for release as a 78-rpm single. The B side featured Cooke's own composition, which his producer thought "ridiculous" as it consisted mostly of Cooke crooning the song's title, "You Send Me." Nevertheless when the record was released, it was the B side that listeners requested and the radio disc jockeys played. Within a few months it had sold more than a million copies and topped both the rhythm-and-blues and pop *Billboard* charts. Cooke's singing represented a unique synthesis of gospel intensity, popular rhythms, and captivating articulation, glissandi, and phrasing. Most of all, many of his fans were able to imagine that he was singing personally to them.

Cooke followed "You Send Me" with a stream of rhythm-and-blues hits that were heartfelt and smooth with a rough-edged core—in other words, soulful. Cooke's composition "Wonderful World" was charming with its lilting rhythms, lighthearted lyrics, and Cooke's mellifluous singing, reinforced at each refrain by his background singers. Cooke flavored the song's conclusion with enchanting "ta-ta-ta's" and "mm-hmm's." In his composition "Chain Gang," Cooke sweetened a tale of convict labor with an array of enticing grunts and moans. In "Cupid," he sang an innocent valentine to Cupid's arrows over an infectious calypso rhythm. In "Ain't That Good News," he recalled his gospel roots with the title's evangelical refrain transformed into an optimistic love call. In 1963 he issued *Night Beat*, an album of blues-inflected songs.

"A Change Is Gonna Come." Cooke was farsighted not only in his style of singing but also in the progress of his musical career. He wrote many of his own songs and increasingly took the lead in producing them. In 1958 he formed his own record company, SAR Records, to develop and record young black singers Cooke thought were mistreated by the established record companies. His last and what many critics consider his greatest song, "A Change Is Gonna Come," recorded a few months before his death, would become an anthem of the Civil Rights movement. Recalling Cooke's gospel roots, it spoke of personal transformation and spiritual longing, and it echoed the call of civil rights leaders for a new society. Accompanied by a mournful French horn, ominous kettledrums, and weeping strings, Cooke's vocal is both elegiac and hopeful, pure but fervent, serene yet stirring.

Musical Legacy

Often described as the inventor of soul music, Cooke drew upon his gospel roots, his affinity for relaxed balladry, and phrasing influenced by Louis Armstrong and Billie Holiday to produce a distinctively lyrical yet intense sound that is the epitome of urbane soul. As Cooke once said, whenever he sang he was trying "to grab hold of someone's heart." His beautiful tenor voice, perfect melisma (singing several notes during a single vocal syllable), floating high notes, charming yodeling phrases, soothing timbre, and precise delivery directly influenced such soul singers as Otis Redding, Smokey Robinson, Al Green, Marvin Gaye, and the Temptations' David Ruffin and Eddie Kendricks, and can be detected in much of soul, Motown, and popular music.

Howard Bromberg

Further Reading

Greene, Erik. *Our Uncle Sam: The Sam Cooke Story from His Family's Perspective*. Victoria, B.C.: Trafford, 2006. By his great-nephew, this questions the accounts of Cooke's death, cynically suggesting he was murdered for financial gain by business syndicates.

Guralnick, Peter. *Dream Boogie: The Triumph of Sam Cooke*. New York: Little, Brown, 2005. Comprehensive life of Cooke and everyone who came into his circle.

McEwen, Joe. *Sam Cooke: The Man Who Invented Soul*. New York: Sire Books, 1977. First full-length biography.

Wolff, Daniel. *You Send Me: The Life and Times of Sam Cooke*. New York: William Morrow, 1995. Lengthy biography with an insider perspective on the recording industry.

See also: Armstrong, Louis; Blackwell, Otis; Brown, Roy; Burke, Solomon; Dylan, Bob; Gaye, Marvin; Green, Al; Hendrix, Jimi; Holiday, Billie; Jagger, Sir Mick; Nelson, Ricky; Neville, Aaron; Pickett, Wilson; Redding, Otis; Robinson, Smokey; Ross, Diana; Rush, Otis.

Aaron Copland
American classical composer

Departing from European styles, Copland helped define the musical identity of America, drawing on American ethnic and folk music and themes and on his assiduous study of the visual arts.

Born: November 14, 1900; Brooklyn, New York
Died: December 2, 1990; North Tarrytown, New York
Also known as: Aaron Kaplan (birth name)

Principal works

BALLETS (music): *Grohg*, composed 1925, first performed 1992; *Hear Ye! Hear Ye!*, 1934; *Billy the Kid*, 1938; *Rodeo*, 1942; *Appalachian Spring*, 1944; *Dance Panels*, 1963.

CHAMBER WORKS: *Vitebsk*, 1928 (for piano, violin, and cello); *Nonet*, 1961 (for three violins, three violas, and three cellos); *Duo for Flute and Piano*, 1971.

CHORAL WORKS: *Four Motets*, 1924; *In the Beginning*, 1947 (for mixed voices); *Canticle of Freedom*, 1955 (text by John Barbour).

FILM SCORES: *The City*, 1939; *Of Mice and Men*, 1939; *Our Town*, 1940; *The North Star*, 1943; *The Cummington Story*, 1945; *The Red Pony*, 1948; *The Heiress*, 1949; *Something Wild*, 1961.

OPERAS (music): *The Second Hurricane*, Op. 2, 1937 (libretto by Edwin Denby); *The Tender Land*, 1954 (libretto by Horace Everett).

ORCHESTRAL WORKS: *Music for the Theatre*, 1925; Symphony for Organ and Orchestra, 1925; Piano Concerto, 1927; Symphony No. 1, 1928; *Dance Symphony*, 1931; *Symphonic Ode*, 1932;

Short Symphony, 1934 (Symphony No. 2); *Statements: Militant, Cryptic, Dogmatic, Subjective, Jingo, Prophetic*, 1935; *El Salón México*, 1937; *Music for Radio: Saga of the Prairie*, 1937; *An Outdoor Overture*, 1938; *The Five Kings*, 1939 (incidental music for Orson Welles's play); *The Quiet City*, 1939 (incidental music for Irwin Shaw's play); *Lincoln Portrait*, 1942 (for speaker and orchestra); *Fanfare for the Common Man*, 1943; *Music for Movies*, 1943; Sonata for Violin and Piano, 1943; *Letter from Home*, 1944; Symphony No. 3, 1946; Clarinet Concerto, 1950 (for clarinet, strings, harpsichord, and piano); *Variations on a Shaker Melody*, 1956; *Orchestral Variations*, 1958; *Connotations*, 1962; *Down a Country Lane*, 1964; *Emblems*, 1964 (for wind band); *Music for a Great City*, 1964; *Inscape*, 1967; *Three Latin American Sketches*, 1972.

PIANO WORKS: *Scherzo Humoristique: The Cat and the Mouse*, 1921; *Passacaglia*, 1923; *Piano Variations*, 1931; *Dance of the Adolescent*, 1933 (for two pianos); Piano Sonata, 1941; *Danzón cubano*, 1942 (for two pianos); Piano Quartet, 1950; *Piano Fantasy*, 1957; *Night Thoughts*, 1972.

VOCAL WORKS: *Old American Songs*, 1950; *Twelve Poems of Emily Dickinson*, 1950 (for voice and piano); *Old American Songs, Set II*, 1952.

WRITINGS OF INTEREST: *What to Listen for in Music*, 1939; *Our New Music*, 1941; *Music and Imagination*, 1952; *Copland on Music*, 1960; *The New Music, 1900-1960*, 1968; *Copland: 1900 Through 1942*, 1984 (with Vivian Perlis); *Copland: Since 1943*, 1989 (with Perlis).

The Life

Aaron Copland (EH-ruhn KOHP-luhnd) was born in Brooklyn of Russian-Jewish immigrant parents who owned and managed a prosperous Brooklyn department store. He grew up in a musically inclined family, and as a teenager he discovered Maurice Ravel and Claude Debussy. He began his musical education with teachers who included Leopold Wolfsohn and Rubin Goldmark (who had taught George Gershwin). Later, Copland studied under Nadia Boulanger, the French music teacher who had taught Astor Piazzolla and Leonard Bernstein.

As a young man, Copland became involved with cultural and political radicals, absorbing the ideas of those who challenged the status quo in the arts and who sought artistic freedom. Novelist and critic Waldo Frank and composer Paul Rosenfeld introduced him to the philosophy of American modernism, bringing him into a circle of like-minded people that included expressionist pianist Leo Ornstein, visual artist William Zorach, and writer James Oppenheim, founder of *The Seven Arts*, a magazine that promoted the modernization of art. Paradoxically, after this long period in search of modernism, Copland was drawn to America's primitive art, and he attempted to redefine the identity of American music.

Copland spent three years studying in Paris under Boulanger, who introduced him into a circle of modernist Parisian artists. After Copland's arrival in Paris in 1921, he developed a friendship with Surrealist painter Marcel Duchamp, and he was exposed to the futurist work of filmmaker Jean Cocteau and composer Francis Poulenc, among others. Copland was impressed by the modernity of avant-garde music, which was reaching audiences in unprecedented ways, both shocking them and enthralling them. Again, paradoxically, Copland's experiences in Paris brought him to the realization that his development as a composer should be tightly connected to his native background rather than to that of Europe.

In June, 1924, he returned to New York to search for his own voice. When he found that voice, Copland became a prominent composer. During this period, along with finding a musical idiom that was innate to America, Copland was developing socialist inclinations, demonstrated by his subscriptions to the liberal journals *The New Republic* and *The Nation*, his avid reading of Vladimir Lenin's and Karl Marx's doctrines, and his active promotion and advocacy of socialist literature among his friends, who at that time included film director Elia Kazan, playwright Clifford Odets, and others who wrote for *The New Masses*, a Marxist publication. With the rise of the fascist Nazi Party in Germany, Copland became sympathetic with the anti-fascist communist cause, identifying with the masses and the proletariat. During this period, his political involvement was directly related to his musical philosophy—music for the common man, for his country, for freedom. His later years were largely free of political activity, bringing a peaceful period that allowed him to teach, to lecture, to write books and articles on music-related subjects, and to conduct his work and that of others. Copland died of Alzheimer's disease in 1990.

The Music

Stimulated by his exposure to the music of his contemporaries, especially Igor Stravinsky, and to the work of visual artists, Copland became prolific in his creative output of a distinctly American musical idiom and in his intellectualization of music. In his writings, Copland used the term "musical cubism" to describe the work of composer Charles Ives; he commented on "musical perspective," drawing from visual-arts terminology; he referred to his work as "using jazz cubistically"; and he coined the phrase "imposed simplicity," describing a style that would reach the masses.

Native Sounds. Copland's affiliation with the Jazz Composers Collective after his return to New York fostered his growing interest in jazz and in folk music. Adding this to his extensive research on ethnic music led to his composition of *Music for the*

Aaron Copland. (Library of Congress)

Theatre in 1925. His search for the native sounds that would enrich his compositional style took him to Mexico, a trip arranged by Mexican composer Carlos Chávez (whose work reflected Indian chants), where he was influenced by the culture and indigenous folk songs. Copland composed a one-movement symphonic piece, *El Salón México*, that was based on four Mexican folk songs and that depicted a scene in a dance hall.

A two-month stay in Santa Fe, New Mexico, revived in him an interest in his ethnicity. Inspired by the Jewish themes the Polish playwright S. Ansky used in his play *The Dybbuk* (1920), Copland composed the chamber piece *Vitebsk*, which portrayed the Russian village that was Ansky's home. By the time his residence in Santa Fe came to an end, his compositional style had solidified in an eclectic amalgam of American rhythms and Jewish melodies that would become the landmark of his musical style.

At a time when art for art's sake was the cultural norm, Copland took an opposing stand. He believed that music should reflect the social and political struggle of the people. While his musical philosophy had been once considered progressive, it soon began to be suspected of being seditious and subversive. Among other accusations, he was said to have signed a letter to President Franklin Delano Roosevelt defending the Communist Party. As a result, in April of 1953, Copland's name was added to the State Department's blacklist, which resulted in his music being banned from American libraries.

Fanfare for the Common Man. This is probably Copland's most recognized work. Eugene Goossens, conductor of the Cincinnati Symphony Orchestra, commissioned several composers to create fanfares that would make, as he said, "stirring and significant contributions to the war effort." They were to be played before concerts. Of the eighteen works that were contributed, Copland's is most enduring. With a title reflecting the composer's social and political ideals, *Fanfare for the Common Man* was written for four French horns, three trumpets, three trombones, tuba, timpani, bass drum, and tam-tam or gong. The bright brasses lift the soaring melodies to a dramatic, crowd-pleasing, and moving conclusion. Copland said about the work that he "used bichordal harmonies that added 'bite' to the brass and some irregular rhythms." With its long-lasting appeal, the piece has been played by such rock groups as the Rolling Stones, Styx, and Emerson, Lake, and Palmer. It is often heard as a theme song for television shows, in the United States and other countries, including Australia, Scotland, Mexico, and Canada.

Billy the Kid *and* Rodeo. *Billy the Kid* was commissioned by Lincoln Kirstein, director of Ballet Caravan, for a ballet to be choreographed by Eugene Loring based on the legend of the cold-blooded killer William Bonney. Copland, who had been exposed to cowboy songs as a child, incorporated some of them in the work. The quotations from "Whoopee Ti Yi Yo (Git Along Little Dogies)" and "The Dying Cowboy" contributed greatly to the work's critical success. Another ballet written by Copland was *Rodeo*. With its rich orchestration evoking the music of the West, *Rodeo* set the stage for the depiction of a barn dance, complete with fiddlers.

Appalachian Spring. Perhaps Copland's most famous music for ballet, *Appalachian Spring* was composed during World War II for choreographer Martha Graham, who shared with Copland an interest in Puritanism. Copland's score shows his manipulation of the basic folk music of the Shakers, a religious sect well established in the United States by the 1840's. The Shakers were noted for their culture of simplicity and their work ethic, elements perfectly suited to Copland's style and reflected in American values in the period from the Great Depression of the 1930's through World War II. Copland repeats several folk-based themes throughout the work, intermingling and layering them to evoke a pastoral, mid-twentieth century America. Horns and violins paint the broad expanse of the American landscape, flutes and piccolos mimic birdsong, and, perhaps most famously, the Shaker hymn "Simple Gifts ('Tis a Gift to Be Simple)" creates the score's emotional climax.

Lincoln Portrait. This thirteen-minute work for narrator and full orchestra was commissioned by the conductor André Kostelanetz after the bombing of Pearl Harbor by the Japanese in 1941. It was a patriotic piece, a portrait of Abraham Lincoln, as Copland described it, an addition to the many representations of the sixteenth president in various art forms: Daniel Chester French's sculpture *Seated Lincoln*, in the Lincoln Monument in Washington, D.C.; Marsden Hartley's several portraits of Lin-coln, including *Young Worshipper of the Truth* and *Weary of the Truth*; and Walt Whitman's *Elegy to Lincoln* (1865).

Symphonies. Copland composed in large scale for orchestras, and he became a sought-after conductor of his music. Symphony for Organ and Orchestra, which was dedicated to Boulanger, was an early three-movement work, and later it was rewritten, omitting the organ, to become Symphony No. 1. Symphony No. 2, only fifteen minutes long, is also known as the *Short Symphony*, and it is arranged for piano, clarinet, and string quartet. Symphony No. 3, which follows the standard symphonic format in four movements, was said to reflect the progressive politics of the era, with an allusion to the speeches of Henry Wallace, the politician made famous for his oration on the common man. In fact, the third movement incorporates references to *Fanfare for the Common Man*. Copland's *Dance Symphony* was part of his unproduced ballet *Grohg*.

Film Scores. In his search for a larger audience and for financial benefits Copland saw in the film industry a fruitful opportunity. His score for *Of Mice and Men*, which was based on John Steinbeck's novel, received two Academy Award nominations, for Best Score and Best Original Score. He subsequently composed scores for films based on famous American plays and novels, such as Thornton Wilder's *Our Town* (1938) and *The Heiress* (1947), inspired by Henry James's novel *Washington Square* (1880). He also composed the music for two documentaries, *The City* and the Office of War Information's documentary *The Cummington Story*.

Musical Legacy

Throughout his life, Copland was concerned with the role of the artist in society. All his creative efforts focused on his country's artistic needs in times of peace and of war, in what has been called his "aestheticization of politics" and his "politization of aesthetics." He believed art should mean something to the everyday citizen. During the passage from World War I to the Great Depression and World War II, he remained committed to making music aesthetically accessible and socially relevant, and he wrote in the simplest possible terms to appeal to all people. His innovative attempts to merge the traditional with the classic and to establish a connection between the composer and the audience earned him praise as well as scorn.

Copland advanced music by incorporating percussive orchestration, changing meter, polyrhythms, and polychords, and he thereby influenced the compositional style of many musicians, including his protégé Bernstein, who became a superb conductor of Copland's works. Copland was awarded the Pulitzer Prize in composition for *Appalachian Spring*, and he earned an Academy Award for his score for *The Heiress*. Copland House, a foundation that is located in the composer's restored house in the Hudson River Valley of New York, supports composers by inviting six to eight artists to live there for three weeks to two months, to work in privacy and to focus on the creative compositional process.

Sylvia P. Baeza

Further Reading

Copland, Aaron, and Vivian Perlis. *Copland: 1900 Through 1942*. New York: St. Martin's Press, 1984. This autobiography covers the early life and career of Copland, beginning with his childhood in Brooklyn and continuing through his years in Paris and his first compositions.

_____. *Copland: Since 1943*. New York: St. Martin's Press, 1989. In this second volume of his autobiography, Copland chronicles the U.S. political scene as it affected his creativity and helped him shape his patriotic pieces and his career as conductor and author. Includes interviews, letters, and previously unpublished scores.

Crist, Elizabeth B. *Music for the Common Man: Aaron Copland During the Depression and War*. New York: Oxford University Press, 2005. Describes communism and the cultural front from the 1930's to the 1950's, covering the intellectual impact of Copland's music rather than its structure or aesthetics. Includes coverage of his collaborative projects for stage and screen, which gave way to creative alliances and artistic community, thereby relating the personal and political to the aesthetic.

Crist, Elizabeth B., and Wayne Shirley. *The Selected Correspondence of Aaron Copland*. London: Yale University Press, 2006. Perhaps the best text to get a view of the composer's personal side, this presents Copland's conception of modern music and his musical triumphs as seen from the man's point of view rather than from the composer's. Copland's correspondence touches on his musical development and the cultural circumstances that informed his compositions during times of both peace and war.

Levin, Gail, and Judith Tick. *Aaron Copland's America: A Cultural Perspective*. New York: Watson-Guptill, 2000. With twenty-four chapters covering every aspect of Copland's rise to the stature of leading American composer, this beautifully illustrated volume documents Copland's travels, friendships, connections, reactionary philosophy, and legacy.

Pollack, Howard. *Aaron Copland: The Life of an Uncommon Man*. New York: Henry Holt, 1999. A detailed portrait of the composer with emphasis on each of his major works, based on documentation from the Copland Collection at the Library of Congress. Drawing from interviews with Copland's colleagues, friends, and lovers, Pollack endows the portrait of Copland the composer with insight into Copland the man.

See also: Beach, Amy; Bernstein, Leonard; Boulanger, Nadia; Carter, Elliott; Chávez, Carlos; Debussy, Claude; Gershwin, George; Gershwin, Ira; Golijov, Osvaldo; Ives, Charles; Koussevitzky, Serge; Lucier, Alvin; Previn, Sir André; Rampal, Jean-Pierre; Rota, Nino; Sandburg, Carl; Seeger, Charles; Seeger, Ruth Crawford; Serkin, Rudolf; Takemitsu, Tŏru; Thomas, Michael Tilson; Thomson, Virgil.

Chick Corea

American jazz pianist and composer

A keyboardist of prodigious technique, Corea was at the forefront of several musical movements, including modal jazz, Latin jazz, avant-garde, and fusion. His compositional style melds large-scale, formal structures and classical developmental processes with the harmonic and rhythmic vocabulary of jazz.

Born: June 12, 1941; Chelsea, Massachusetts
Also known as: Armando Anthony "Chick" Corea (full name)

Member of: Return to Forever; the Elektric Band; the Akoustic Band; Origin; Circle; the New Trio; Touchstone

Principal recordings

ALBUMS: *Inner Space*, 1966; *Tones for Joan's Bones*, 1966; *Jazz for a Sunday Afternoon*, 1967; *La Fiesta*, 1967; *Now He Sings, Now He Sobs*, 1968; *Is*, 1969; *Sundance*, 1969; *Song of Singing*, 1970; *A. R. C*, 1971; *Piano Improvisations, Vol. 1*, 1971; *Piano Improvisations, Vol. 2*, 1971; *Crystal Silence*, 1972 (with Gary Burton); *Return to Forever*, 1972; *The Leprechaun*, 1975; *My Spanish Heart*, 1976; *Corea/Hancock*, 1978 (with Herbie Hancock); *Delphi I: Solo Piano Improvisations*, 1978; *Friends*, 1978; *The Mad Hatter*, 1978; *Secret Agent*, 1978; *Tap Step*, 1978; *Chick Corea, Herbie Hancock, Keith Jarrett, McCoy Tyner*, 1981; *Three Quartets*, 1981; *Trio Music*, 1981 (with Miroslav Vitous and Roy Haynes); *Again and Again*, 1982; *Lyric Suite for Sextet*, 1982 (with Gary Burton); *Touchstone*, 1982; *Children's Songs*, 1983; *Septet*, 1984; *Voyage*, 1984 (with Steve Kajula); *Expressions*, 1993; *Hot Licks: Seabreeze*, 1993; *Paint the World*, 1993 (with Elektric Band II); *Time Warp*, 1995; *Native Sense: The New Duets*, 1997 (with Burton); *Remembering Bud Powell*, 1997 (with others); *Akoustic Band*, 1999 (with the Akoustic Band); *Come Rain or Shine*, 1999; *Spain for Sextet and Orchestra*, 1999; *Waltz for Bill Evans*, 2000; *Past, Present, and Futures*, 2001 (with the New Trio); *Rendezvous in New York*, 2003; *Fiesta Gillespie and Milhaud Jazz*, 2005; *The Ultimate Adventure*, 2006; *Chillin' in Chelan*, 2007; *The Enchantment*, 2007 (with Bela Fleck); *From Miles*, 2007; *Duet*, 2008 (with Hiromi Uehara).

ALBUMS (with the Elektric Band): *The Elektric Band*, 1986; *Light Years*, 1987; *Eye of the Beholder*, 1988; *Inside Out*, 1990; *Beneath the Mask*, 1991; *To the Stars*, 2004.

ALBUMS (with Return to Forever): *Light as a Feather*, 1972; *Hymn of the Seventh Galaxy*, 1973; *Where Have I Known You Before*, 1974; *No Mystery*, 1975; *Romantic Warrior*, 1976; *Musicmagic*, 1977.

The Life

Armando Anthony "Chick" Corea (koh-REE-ah) was born into a musical family in Chelsea, Mas-

sachusetts, on June 12, 1941. His father Armando, a composer and arranger who played trumpet and bass, performed in the Boston area during the 1930's and 1940's. Corea began playing piano at age four and drums at age eight. While still in high school, he played piano in his father's band.

Living in New York City after graduating from high school, he briefly attended Columbia University and then the Juilliard School, but he left school to play professionally. In the 1960's his reputation as a gifted pianist grew, and he worked as a sideman with a number of established musicians. In the late 1960's, primarily through his first recordings as a leader, he gained a reputation as a creative and innovative composer.

In 1968 he replaced Herbie Hancock in Miles Davis's band, and he worked with Davis for two years, performing on the recordings and concerts that defined the emerging style of jazz-rock fusion. His work with electronic instruments, for which he would later become legendary, began at this time. His tenure in Davis's band gave him the stature and recognition he needed to strike out on his own as a bandleader. Corea's strong personal association with Scientology also began at this time.

After working with an avant-garde trio in the early 1970's, he formed the highly influential jazz fusion ensemble Return to Forever. Throughout the 1970's, he recorded and toured with various groups of musicians under this name. While jazz fusion was controversial among musicians, Return to Forever was extremely popular with fans and critics, winning a Grammy Award in 1976.

After disbanding Return to Forever in 1978, Corea recorded and performed in a wide variety of settings and styles, with a number of diverse musicians, including Hancock, Michael Brecker, Eddie Gomez, Steve Gadd, Joe Henderson, Gary Burton, and Freddie Hubbard. In the mid-1980's he revisited jazz fusion, forming the Elektric Band, in which he played a vast array of electronic keyboards. Later in the decade, in an attempt to maintain a musical balance and to find a vehicle for his acoustic piano playing, he formed the Akoustic Band.

In the 1990's and later, Corea was active as a performer and composer, releasing numerous critically acclaimed recordings. He has received fourteen Grammy Awards, and *The Ultimate Adventure*, inspired by L. Ron Hubbard, the founder of Scientology, won Grammy Awards for Best Jazz Instrumental Album and Best Instrumental Arrangement.

The Music

Corea strongly influenced jazz piano and composition. While he was heavily in demand as a sideman when he first began performing professionally, most of his career has been marked by long-term associations with such players as Burton, Gadd, Haynes, and Brecker and with a series of ensembles that have been important vehicles for his compositions and playing. His bands Return to Forever, the Akoustic Band, the Elektric Band, and Origin have performed and recorded widely over the last four decades. Corea's work has been characterized by the freshness and innovation of his writing and the flair and technical prowess of his keyboard playing.

Sideman. In the early 1960's, Corea worked in the Latin jazz idiom as a sideman with percussionists and bandleaders Mongo Santamaria and Willie Bobo. From 1964 to 1966 he played with trumpeter Blue Mitchell. During this time he worked with flutist Herbie Mann and saxophonist Stan Getz. As Corea's reputation began to grow, he performed and recorded with a growing roster of first-rate musicians, such as Cal Tjader, Donald Byrd, Dizzy Gillespie, and Sarah Vaughn.

Corea's most important gig as a sideman came in 1968 when he replaced Hancock in Davis's band. Corea recorded a number of important albums with Davis, including *Filles de Kilimanjaro*, *In a Silent Way*, *Bitches Brew*, and *Live-Evil*. Corea left the band in late 1970, ending his career as a sideman. After his stint with Davis, he was either the leader or co-leader of all of his performing and recording projects.

Now He Sings, Now He Sobs. Through his work as a sideman, Corea came to the attention of the major jazz record labels. His first opportunity to act as a leader in the studio came in 1966, when he recorded *Tones for Joan's Bones* for Atlantic Records. With this recording he began a long association with saxophonist and flutist Joe Farrell.

In 1968 Corea recorded *Now He Sings, Now He Sobs* with Haynes and Miroslav Vitous. Considered one of the greatest trio recordings in jazz history, this album has been enormously influential on the development of the contemporary jazz piano and the piano trio. Corea's linear and harmonic approach represents a distillation and codification of the groundbreaking modal explorations of McCoy Tyner in his work with John Coltrane. The fluidity and inventiveness of his right-hand lines set the standard for jazz piano improvisation in the second half of the twentieth century. His compositions for the recording are wonderfully effective vehicles for the trio's rhythmic interplay.

Return to Forever. His work with Davis and others and the critical acclaim accorded his first two solo recordings established Corea as an important figure in jazz. After leaving Davis's band, he formed a quartet with bassist Dave Holland, called Circle, recording several albums of experimental, avant-garde music for the ECM label. He also recorded a number of improvisations for solo piano, released by ECM Records in a two-volume set in 1971.

In 1971 Corea formed the first incarnation of Return to Forever, featuring the Brazilian husband-and-wife team of Airto Moreira on percussion and Flora Purim on vocals, Stanley Clark on bass, and Farrell on flute and saxophone. This group recorded a number of Corea's compositions that have since become standards, including "Spain," arguably Corea's most well-known piece.

The second edition of Return to Forever, formed in 1973, displayed a heavier rock influence, when Farrell's woodwinds were replaced by Bill Connors's electric guitar and Moreira's light Latin jazz drumming was replaced by Lenny White's funk-rock drumming. Corea added synthesizers to his Fender Rhodes. The group focused on extended compositions, highly complex and difficult individual parts requiring extreme instrumental virtuosity and a broad stylistic palette. Al Di Meola later replaced Connors. Though the group's recordings—like the entire genre of jazz fusion—were highly controversial, 1975's *No Mystery* received a Grammy Award for Best Jazz Instrumental Performance.

The final incarnation of the band included a horn section, Corea's wife Gayle Moran on keyboards and vocals, and the return of Farrell. In 1977, feeling that the band had run its course, Corea disbanded Return to Forever.

Musical Partnerships. Corea formed a number of partnerships throughout his career, to which he would return at various points. Perhaps the most important is with vibist Burton. Their association began with the ECM recording *Crystal Silence* in 1972. The duo has won three Grammy Awards. Other important collaborators include Gadd, Brecker, and Gomez, with whom Corea recorded *Three Quartets* and *Friends*, another Grammy Award-winning record.

Drawing from his wide circle of musical friends, Corea released a number of unique recordings, including *The Leprechaun, The Mad Hatter, My Spanish Heart*, and others.

The Akoustic Band and the Elektric Band. In the mid-1980's, Corea drew on the next generation of virtuoso players to form two bands, one a return to jazz fusion and the other an acoustic jazz trio. Drummer Dave Weckl and bassist John Patitucci played in both ensembles. For the Elektric Band, Corea added guitarist Frank Gambale and saxophonist Eric Marienthal. This group focused on complex compositions, technical virtuosity, and wide stylistic variety. Both bands recorded and toured until 1993, when Corea moved on to other projects.

Origin and the New Trio. In 1997 Corea formed an acoustic sextet, Origin, which recorded several albums, including a critically acclaimed six-compact-disc release of the group's performances at the Blue Note in New York City. In 2001 he began recording and performing with the New Trio, an acoustic trio with drummer Jeff Ballard and bassist Avishai Cohen. Corea also released a number of diverse recordings, including an extended work for orchestra, several albums of solo piano recordings, another duet recording with Burton, and the Grammy Award-winning *The Ultimate Adventure*. Later Corea formed a band with drummer Tom Brechtlein, percussionist Rubem Dantas, saxophonist-flutist Jorge Pardo, and bassist Carles Benavent, called Touchstone.

Musical Legacy

Corea's work is inspiring for its sheer volume and diversity. During his decades-long career, his creativity and output never flagged. As a player, his crisp, fluid lines have been imitated widely by generations of pianists. His codification of the modal language first explored by Tyner has become an important component of the vocabulary of contemporary jazz. His work with electronic keyboards has defined the textural palette of fusion.

His influence as a composer—combining materials and processes from classical music (in particular, extended formal structures) with the methods and vocabulary of jazz—is significant. In both his writing and his playing, he was an important pioneer in fusing the rhythms, textures, and harmonies of Spanish and Latin American music with jazz.

While his writing and his playing exhibit a spirit of playful spontaneity and innovation, the seriousness of his commitment to music has never been questioned, even by those who doubt the validity of the jazz fusion genre.

Matthew Nicholl

Further Reading

Case, Brian, and Stan Britt. *The Harmony Illustrated Encyclopedia of Jazz*. 3d ed. New York: Harmony Books, 1986. An extensive well-written entry about Corea, with profiles of many of his collaborators. Includes a detailed discography.

Corea, Chick. *A Work in Progress, Volume 1*. La Crescenta, Calif.: Chick Corea Productions, 2002. A short but illuminating series of essays about music, playing the piano, and life in general.

Doerschuk, Robert. *88: The Giants of Jazz Piano*. San Francisco: Backbeat Books, 2001. Outlining the history of jazz piano through profiles of important pianists, this book provides details about Corea's style and puts his work in perspective.

Lyons, Len. *The Great Jazz Pianists: Speaking of Their Lives and Music*. New York: Morrow, 1983. After a brief introduction to the history of jazz piano, Lyons presents interviews with a number of important and influential pianists, including Corea.

Nicholson, Stuart. *Jazz-Rock: A History*. New York: Schirmer Books, 1998. A look back at jazz-rock fusion, this book provides historical background and cultural context. Corea's work with Return to Forever and the Elektric Band are chronicled and critiqued. Includes an extensive discography and separate indexes of musicians, group names, and recordings.

Tirro, Frank. *Jazz: A History*. 2d ed. New York: W. W. Norton, 1993. Although this excellent general history of jazz provides only a small amount of information about Corea, the book places the various styles in which he worked—modal jazz, Latin jazz, avant-garde, and fusion—in historical context.

See also: Burton, Gary; Davis, Miles; Evans, Bill; Getz, Stan; Gillespie, Dizzy; Hancock, Herbie; Jarrett, Keith; McFerrin, Bobby; Monk, Thelonious.

Elvis Costello

English rock singer, guitarist, and songwriter

Leader of the British Third Wave of the late 1970's, Costello infused pop punk with a multitude of influences, from soul to big band to reggae.

Born: August 25, 1954; Liverpool, England
Also known as: Declan Patrick McManus (birth name)
Member of: Elvis Costello and the Attractions; Elvis Costello and the Imposters

Principal recordings

ALBUMS (solo): *My Aim Is True*, 1977; *Spike*, 1989; *Mighty Like a Rose*, 1991; *The Juliet Letters*, 1993 (with the Brodsky Quartet); *Brutal Youth*, 1994; *G. B. H.*, 1994 (with Richard Harvey); *Kojak Variety*, 1995; *Costello and Nieve*, 1996 (with Steve Nieve); *Jake's Progress (Original Music from the Channel Four Series)*, 1996 (with Harvey); *Terror and Magnificence*, 1997 (with John Harle); *Painted from Memory*, 1998 (with Burt Bacharach); *The Sweetest Punch: The Songs of Costello and Bacharach*, 1999 (with Burt Bacharach and Bill Frisell); *For the Stars*, 2001 (with Anne Sofie von Otter); *North*, 2003; *Il Songo*, 2004 (with the London Symphony Orchestra); *Piano Jazz*, 2005 (with Marian McPartland); *The River in Reverse*, 2006 (with Allen Toussaint).

ALBUMS (with the Attractions): *This Year's Model*, 1978; *Armed Forces*, 1979; *Get Happy!!*, 1980; *Almost Blue*, 1981; *Trust*, 1981; *Imperial Bedroom*, 1982; *Punch the Clock*, 1983; *Goodbye Cruel World*, 1984; *Blood and Chocolate*, 1986; *King of America*, 1986; *All This Useless Beauty*, 1996.

ALBUMS (with the Imposters): *Cruel Smile*, 2002; *When I Was Cruel*, 2002; *The Delivery Man*, 2004; *Momofuku*, 2008.

SINGLES (solo): "Radio Radio," 1979; "Veronica," 1989; "Thirteen Steps Lead Down," 1994.

The Life

Elvis Costello (kahs-TEHL-loh) was born Declan Patrick MacManus on August 25, 1954, to musician-bandleader Ronald MacManus and record-store manager Lillian MacManus. The family moved to many different locations in and around West London during the first years of Declan's life. When his parents separated in 1962, Declan and his mother relocated to Liverpool. With the early musical training provided by his father and the relocation to Liverpool, Declan explored many genres of music.

By the early 1970's, Declan was writing and singing. Soon he and musician-producer Nick Lowe started a band called Flip City. While the band was not commercially successful, it provided Declan with valuable performance experience and the ability to formulate his own musical voice based on his many songwriting influences (Rick Danko of the Band, Bob Dylan, Van Morrison, and Randy Newman). After Flip City dissolved, Declan needed work in order to support his wife Mary Burgoyne, whom he had married in 1974, and their child, Matthew. Declan recorded acoustic demos in his bedroom and presented them to record labels. He turned down an offer from Island Records and, on the recommendation of Lowe, accepted one from Stiff Records. It was around this time that Declan adopted the last name of his paternal great-grandmother, Costello, and at first used an abbreviation of his first and middle names, forming D. P. Costello. D. P. soon transformed into Elvis, and with his new name, wide-rimmed glasses, and record contract in hand, Elvis Costello launched his musical career.

After forming the Attractions for his second record, *This Year's Model*, the band quickly received attention for its aggressive, cynical attitudes and controversial live shows that often featured Costello berating the audience or performing for only twenty-five minutes before leaving the stage. Raw and unpredictable, the Attractions had a certain appeal that was complemented by Costello's mature songwriting and the band members' fine musicianship. The aggressive nature of Costello and the band dissipated, however, on March 15, 1979, when an intoxicated Costello joked about singers James Brown and Ray Charles in a bar with fellow musician Stephen Stills. Stills's backup singer relayed the comments to the press, and soon Costello was apologizing on national television and declaring he was not a racist. This unfortunate incident stalled Costello's career and cooled the punk fervor for the Attractions.

In 1984 Burgoyne filed for divorce, after a long struggle to keep afloat a marriage that had gone through rough times, including Costello's affair with model Bebe Buell. In 1986 Costello married Caitlin O'Riordan of the Pogues, and they divorced in 2002. In 2003 Costello married jazz pianist and vocalist Diana Krall.

The Music

My Aim Is True. Costello's debut, *My Aim Is True*, was recorded at Pathway Studios in Islington, England, in late 1976 and early 1977. The core backing band was Clover, which, with the addition of Huey Lewis, would later become Huey Lewis and the News. The Lowe-produced record is filled with a wide array of energetic tunes: the Motown-girl-group-inspired "No Dancing"; the popular ballad "Alison"; the humorously crude, punk-inspired "Mystery Dance"; the pop "(The Angels Wanna Wear My) Red Shoes"; the politically charged "Less than Zero"; and the reggae-infused "Watching the Detectives." The album was universally well received, and it introduced to the world stage a skilled songwriter with a penchant for controversy.

This Year's Model. *This Year's Model* was Costello's first with the Attractions, with Steve Nieve on keyboards, Bruce Thomas on bass and backing vocals, and Pete Thomas on drums. Here the Attractions managed to create a sound all their own, with a blend of punk, rock, and soul. The interesting interplay between Bruce Thomas, a rhythmically minded bass player, and Pete Thomas, a melodically driven, composition-conscious drummer, is complemented by the driving Farfisa organ of Nieve. "No Action," the first track, displays the band's raw energy and cohesiveness. The funky, soul-inspired songs "This Year's Girl," "The Beat,"

"(I Don't Want to Go to) Chelsea," and "Living in Paradise" contrast with the energetic arena rockers "Lipstick Vogue," "Radio Radio," and "Pump It Up."

Armed Forces. *Armed Forces* is more musically sophisticated than its predecessors, incorporating a wider variety of keyboards and other electronics, presaging the band's 1980's new wave direction and leaving behind the furious punk elements. Some of the more experimental new wave-influenced tunes ("Goon Squad," "Green Shirt," "Moods for Moderns") along with the new wave pop classics ("Accidents Will Happen," "Oliver's Army," "Party Girl," "(What's So Funny 'Bout) Peace, Love, and Understanding?") resulted in a successful union of musical sophistication and pop success within the new wave format.

Get Happy!! *Get Happy!!*, *Trust*, *Almost Blue*, and *Imperial Bedroom* developed the interplay between the Attractions and Costello's songwriting style. *Get Happy!!* was heavily soul-inspired, with James Jamerson-inspired bass lines (featured prominently in the album's mix) and layered soul harmonies. Representative songs include "Love for Tender," "High Fidelity," and "I Can't Stand Up for Falling Down," a Sam and Dave B-side written by Homer Banks and Alan Jones.

Trust. *Trust* retains some soul elements from *Get Happy!!*, but it largely returns to the new wave-inspired pop punk songwriting with "Clubland," "New Lace Sleeves," and "From a Whisper to a Dream," a collaboration with Glenn Tillbrook and Martin Belmont of Squeeze.

Almost Blue. *Almost Blue* represents the band's foray into country-influenced music, with "I'm Your Toy" the sole hit from this album, which met with mixed critical reviews.

Imperial Bedroom. *Imperial Bedroom*, a concept album produced by Geoff Emerick (the first Costello album not produced by Lowe), was deemed Costello's masterpiece and most cohesive album by countless critics and fans. Whether or not the music compares favorably to the initial Attractions' releases, most reviews commented on the elaborate literary lyrical content and overall musical progression from start to finish. "Beyond Belief," "Shabby Doll," "Man out of Time," "Almost Blue," and "Kid About It" are representative of the sound and content of the 1982 tour de force.

Internal Conflicts. Internal tensions, mostly between Costello and bassist Bruce Thomas, led to some of the harshly reviewed records of Costello's career with the Attractions. *Punch the Clock* featured the hit "Everyday I Write the Book," but the album failed to reach the level of consistency of previous Attractions' records. *Goodbye Cruel World*, created amid countless studio squabbles, was a weak project, and the Attractions disbanded soon after its release.

King of America. Costello took the hiatus from the Attractions to experiment with different musical styles and musicians. He formed the Confederates, a touring band, which featured many of the musicians who performed on his country-roots rock solo record *King of America* (Jim Keltner on drums, Jerry Scheff on bass, and James Burton on guitar; Scheff and Burton played frequently with Elvis Presley). The T-Bone Burnett-produced record is a complete departure from the Attractions' sound, featuring far more acoustic instrumentation. "Brilliant Mistake," "Indoor Fireworks," and "I'll Wear It Proudly" are among the representative tracks.

All This Useless Beauty. The Attractions reunited for a record in 1986, *Blood and Chocolate*; a second reunion in 1996 produced *All This Useless Beauty*. Both records had fine moments, from "Uncomplicated" and "Battered Old Bird" from *Blood and Chocolate* to "All This Useless Beauty" and "Complicated Shadows" from *All This Useless Beauty*. The quality of and critical praise for *All This Useless Beauty* sparked rumors of a permanent reunion, but it ultimately marked the final album billed as Elvis Costello and the Attractions. Costello reformed the Attractions with Davey Faragher (formerly of Cracker and John Hiatt) on bass, Nieve, and Pete Thomas as Elvis Costello and the Imposters. In 2004 they released the critically acclaimed *The Delivery Man*, Costello's second concept album, with highlights including "Country Darkness," "Either Side of the Same Town," and "Monkey to Man."

Solo Work. Between the demise of the Attractions and the rise of the Imposters, Costello released albums under his own name. *Spike* featured collaborations with Paul McCartney and a career-revitalizing hit with "Veronica." *Mighty Like a Rose* began a two-record collaboration with musician-

producer Mitchell Froom. In 1994 the two collaborated on *Brutal Youth*, regarded by critics as Costello's finest solo work. Although billed as a solo record, it featured Nieve, Pete Thomas, Lowe, and Bruce Thomas. In 1993 Costello collaborated with the Brodsky Quartet for a chamber-music-inspired release, *The Juliet Letters*. *Kojak Variety* was a collection of mostly rhythm-and-blues covers, featuring many of the musicians from the *King of America* sessions and Nieve and Pete Thomas. In 2003 Costello released *North*, a collection of jazz-adult contemporary songs backed by a small big band, allowing him to return to his roots by way of his father's long-standing career as a big band vocalist.

Musical Legacy

Costello fused punk, rock, and soul music with the lyrical and musical sophistication of a music historian. His knowledge of doo-wop, big band, folk-rock, blues, and classical music (apart from the punk, rock and roll, and soul that were apparent in his own music) provided him with the freedom to experiment stylistically on his records. With the gifted musicians in the Attractions, he created memorable songs in dynamic performances and influenced the punk and rock bands that followed. At the end of the 1970's and in the early 1980's, when disco was on the decline, Costello and the Attractions arrived from England with their innovative lyrics, music, and live performances, reinvigorating the American music scene. Along with Sting and the Police, they embodied the third-wave attitude that inspired many bands to follow in their footsteps.

Elvis Costello and the Attractions were inducted into the Rock and Roll Hall of Fame in 2003. Costello has twice received the Igor Novello Award for Outstanding Songwriting, and he won a Grammy Award in 1998 for "I Still Have That Other Girl," a collaboration with songwriter Burt Bacharach.

Eric Novod

Further Reading

Hinton, Brian. *Let Them All Talk: The Music of Elvis Costello*. London: Sanctuary, 1999. A biography and discography with emphasis on Costello's musical legacy and its effect on British culture.

Perone, James E. *Elvis Costello: A Bio-Bibliography.* Westport, Conn.: Greenwood Press, 1998. A brief biography with a comprehensive discography, a bibliography, a filmography, and a guide to musical scores.

Sheppard, David. *Elvis Costello.* New York: Thunder's Mouth Press, 2000. A basic biography, with a discography and a section titled "The Legacy," discussing Costello's contribution to post-1980's popular music.

Smith, Larry David. *Elvis Costello, Joni Mitchell, and the Torch Song Tradition.* Westport, Conn.: Praeger, 2004. An academic study of the meaning and progression of elements of confrontation and rebellion in Costello's music and lyrics.

Thomson, Graeme. *Complicated Shadows: The Life and Music of Elvis Costello.* New York: Canongate, 2004. A comprehensive journalistic biography, with equal emphasis on personal life and musical career.

See also: Axton, Hoyt; Bacharach, Burt; Bennett, Tony; Burke, Solomon; Dylan, Bob; Jamerson, James; McCartney, Sir Paul; Mitchell, Joni; Morrison, Van; Newman, Randy.

James Cotton

American blues singer, harmonica player, and songwriter

Virtuosic blues harmonica player for Muddy Waters, James "Superharp" Cotton contributed to the electrification of Delta blues, paving the way for rhythm and blues and rock and roll.

Born: July 1, 1935; Tunica, Mississippi
Also known as: Superharp
Member of: The James Cotton Blues Band

Principal recordings

ALBUMS (with the James Cotton Blues Band): *Cut You Loose!*, 1967; *The James Cotton Blues Band*, 1967; *Cotton in Your Ears*, 1968; *Pure Cotton*, 1968; *Taking Care of Business*, 1970; *100% Cotton*, 1974; *High Energy*, 1975; *Live and on the Move*, 1976; *High Compression*, 1984; *Two Sides of the Blues*, 1984; *Live from Chicago: Mr. Superharp Himself*, 1986; *Live at Antone's*, 1988; *Take Me Back*, 1987; *Harp Attack!*, 1990; *Mighty Long Time*, 1991; *Living the Blues*, 1994; *Three Harp Boogie*, 1994; *Deep in the Blues*, 1996; *Fire Down Under the Hill*, 2000; *35th Anniversary Jam of the James Cotton Blues Band*, 2002; *Got My Mojo Workin'*, 2003; *One More Mile*, 2002; *Baby, Don't You Tear My Clothes*, 2004.

The Life

Born in the Mississippi Delta in 1935, James Cotton was the youngest of eight children of farmers Mose and Hattie Cotton. Hattie gave her little son a fifteen-cent harmonica, and Cotton listened to Sonny Boy Williamson II (aka Aleck Miller) play blues harmonica (or blues harp) on the historic *King Biscuit Time* radio show. Cotton's parents had died by the time he was nine years old, so his uncle, Wiley Creen, brought him to Williamson, who informally adopted him. Cotton played harmonica on the steps of the juke joints where Williamson was performing. When Williamson moved to Milwaukee in 1950, Cotton played with Howlin' Wolf and Hubert Sumlin, recording his first songs. In 1952 he began playing on the radio and working as an ice-truck driver. In December, 1954, after hearing Cotton's recording of "Cotton Crop Blues," Muddy Waters invited Cotton to join his band, replacing Junior Wells. Cotton played with Waters for twelve years, working closely with Waters's pianist Otis Spann and acquiring a commanding stage presence.

Cotton, his wife Ceola, and their child lived upstairs in Waters's Chicago house. In 1966 Cotton was shot five times by a deranged fan. After recovering, Cotton left Waters to form his own band. The James Cotton Blues Band was prolific in the recording studio and in touring. In 1991, after Ceola died, Cotton married Jacklyn Hairston, who served as his manager, and they moved to Austin, Texas. In 1994 Cotton had surgery followed by radiation treatments for throat cancer. Despite his illness, he performed regularly.

The Music

Cotton grew up surrounded by blues music, singing in the fields while he worked. As a protégé of Williamson, he played harmonica on the street

James Cotton. (AP/Wide World Photos)

and in juke joints. In 1952 he had his own show on Arkansas radio station KWEM.

"Cotton Crop Blues." In 1953 legendary music producer Sam Philips invited Cotton to make his first recordings. Cotton recorded "Straighten Up Baby," "Hold Me in Your Arms," "Oh, Baby," and, in 1954, his classic composition "Cotton Crop Blues." When Waters heard "Cotton Crop Blues," he was moved by Cotton's virtuosic harmonica playing and biting lyrics. Cotton's signature piece, "Cotton Crop Blues" is a classic twelve-bar blues in *aab* form that came to life with his characteristic wailing harmonica style and boisterous voice.

"Got My Mojo Workin'." Cotton suggested to Waters that he record a version of a song composed by Preston Foster and recorded by Ann Cole, "Got My Mojo Workin'." It became one of the Waters band's best known songs. Perhaps the definitive version was captured on film when Waters played for the first time at the Newport Jazz Festi-

val on July 3, 1960. Cotton plays an exuberant, attacking harp while Waters roars the lyrics. At one point, Waters grabs Cotton to dance a two-step—although a surprised Cotton looks eager to return to his harmonica. When Cotton formed the James Cotton Band in 1966, "Got My Mojo Workin'" became a standard in the band's repertoire.

James Cotton Band. The band recorded *Cut You Loose!* in 1967. The title song begins with a haunting bass guitar riff, followed by Cotton's plaintive singing to his troublesome woman. The *Pure Cotton*, *Cotton in Your Ears*, and *The James Cotton Blues Band* albums that followed featured Cotton's propulsive, electric blues style with his hard-blowing, explosive harp playing and throaty, rambunctious singing.

"Rocket 88." Cotton's gritty renditions of the early rock-and-roll tune "Rocket 88" associated him with the song. Cotton, a car lover, made the most of the harmonica's limited register, blowing the sounds of a train, a car, and a piston engine.

Taking Care of Business *and* the 1970's. In the 1970's Cotton, like many blues musicians, began playing with rock performers and for rock audiences. *Taking Care of Business* was infused with a rock sound. The James Cotton Band became an opening act for Janis Joplin. Cotton also opened or sat in with leading rock bands such as the Grateful Dead, Santana, and Led Zeppelin. In 1977 he joined with Waters, Pinetop Perkins, and blues rocker Johnny Winter on tour, live recordings of which were released in 2007 on *Breakin' It Up, Breakin' It Down*. Cotton's Buddah label records—*100% Cotton*, *High Energy*, *Live and on the Move*—reflect rhythm-and-blues, soul, and rock influences.

1980's and Later. For the Alligator label, Cotton recorded the funk-oriented *High Compression* as well as *Live from Chicago: Mr. Superharp Himself*, culled from three days of performances with an eight-piece band in Chicago's Biddy Mulligan's. *Take Me Back* on the Blind Pig label reflected a return to his blues roots; *Harp Attack!* featured Cotton with three other blues harmonica players. He recorded *Live at Antone's* (1988) at Antone's nightclub in Austin, Texas; the Antone label also released his

Mighty Long Time album. Cotton's 1996 trio recording, *Deep in the Blues*, won a Grammy Award. His sixty-three years of performing blues harmonica earned Cotton the nickname Superharp.

Musical Legacy

Cotton was a vital figure in the postwar Chicago blues wave that electrified and urbanized Delta acoustic blues. Cotton's blaring, rhythmic harmonica riffs fit well with the added volume and amplification of the electric guitar. Cotton and other Chicago bluesmen were progenitors of rhythm and blues and rock and roll.

Following in the footsteps of his mentor Williamson, Cotton helped establish the harmonica as a vital instrument in an electric blues band. His driving harmonica solos energized such songs as "Cotton Crop Blues," "Rocket 88," and "Got My Mojo Workin'." Cotton popularized the innovative techniques of Chicago blues harpists: microphone amplification combined with varieties of cupped-hand holds to produce moaning and wailing sounds, bending and distorting notes, propulsive harmonica rhythms, and cross-harp technique (playing in the second position to accent the low reeds). Cotton's ferocious singing added to the effect. Modern blues harpists Paul Butterfield and Peter Wolf learned directly from Cotton; Boz Scaggs, Bonnie Raitt, Steve Miller, and Mike Bloomfield have all acknowledged Cotton as a key influence. Canadian guitarist Sue Foley decided to become a blues musician at the age of fifteen after attending a Cotton concert.

Howard Bromberg

Further Reading

Gordon, Robert. *Can't Be Satisfied: The Life and Times of Muddy Waters*. Boston: Little, Brown, 2002. Cotton supplies much of the account of the Waters band in the 1950's and 1960's.

Shadwick, Keith. *The Encyclopedia of Jazz and Blues*. London: Quantum, 2007. Brief article on Cotton.

Williamson, Nigel. *The Rough Guide to the Blues*. London: Rough Guides, 2007. In-depth features on blues musicians, including Cotton.

See also: Howlin' Wolf; Joplin, Janis; Raitt, Bonnie; Waters, Muddy; Watson, Doc; Williamson, Sonny Boy, II.

Sir Noël Coward

English musical-theater and film-score composer and lyricist

Coward wrote music and lyrics of inimitable wit for hundreds of songs. He also composed operettas, film scores, and ballets and wrote plays and films. An actor and singer, he performed on the stage, in film, and on television.

Born: December 16, 1899; Teddington, Middlesex, England
Died: March 26, 1973; Port Royal, Jamaica
Also known as: Noël Pierce Coward (full name); Hernia Whittlebot

Principal works

BALLETS (music and scenarios): *London Morning*, 1958; *The Grand Tour*, 1971 (orchestrated by Hershey Kay).

FILM SCORES: *In Which We Serve*, 1942; *The Astonished Heart*, 1950; *The Grass Is Greener*, 1960.

MUSICAL THEATER (music, lyrics, and libretto unless otherwise stated): *London Calling!*, 1923 (music with Philip Braham); *André Charlot's Revue*, 1924 (music); *On with the Dance*, 1925 (music with Braham); *This Year of Grace*, 1928; *Bitter Sweet*, 1929 (operetta); *Cochran's 1931 Revue*, 1931; *Words and Music*, 1932; *Conversation Piece*, 1934; *Operette*, 1938; *Set to Music*, 1939 (revision of *Words and Music*); *Pacific 1860*, 1946; *Sigh No More*, 1946; *Ace of Clubs*, 1950; *After the Ball*, 1954 (based on Oscar Wilde's play *Lady Windermere's Fan*); *Sail Away*, 1961; *The Girl Who Came to Supper*, 1963 (libretto by Coward and Harry Kurnitz; based on Terence Rattigan's play *The Sleeping Prince*); *Noël Coward's Sweet Potato*, 1968 (revue); *Oh Coward! A Musical Comedy Revue*, 1970; *Cowardy Custard*, 1972 (revue); *Oh! Coward*, 1972 (revue).

WRITINGS OF INTEREST: *Collected Sketches and Lyrics*, 1931; *Present Indicative*, 1937 (first autobiography); *Future Indefinite*, 1954 (second autobiography); *Past Conditional*, 1986 (third autobiography, unfinished).

The Life

Noël Pierce Coward's parents were Arthur Coward, an unsuccessful piano salesman, and Violet Veitch Coward, who took in lodgers to support the family. She encouraged Coward's single-minded childhood desire to succeed onstage, and he entertained wherever he could find an audience. He took dancing lessons and, though he could not read music well, somehow learned how to play the piano. By 1907 he had appeared in school and community concerts and in 1911 made his first professional appearance. A diagnosis of tuberculosis briefly sidetracked him, but in 1916 he toured as Charley in Brandon Thomas's *Charley's Aunt* (1892) and in 1917 appeared as an extra in D. W. Griffith's silent film *Hearts of the World* (1918). In 1918 he entered the military, receiving a medical discharge nine months later.

His first major successes were sketches and songs for André Charlot's 1923 revue *London Calling!* In 1924 he became famous for his play *The Vortex*, in which he starred as the drug-addicted son of a promiscuous mother. The play caused the first of many usually successful confrontations with English censorship. *The Vortex* was still playing in 1925 when two comedies, *Fallen Angels* and *Hay Fever*, and a revue, *On with the Dance*, opened in London. The strain of work brought on his first nervous breakdown. Recovering, he directed and appeared in the New York production of Charles B. Cochran's revue *This Year of Grace* (1928), contributing book, lyrics, and much music.

His successes continued with *Private Lives* (1930), which introduced the song "Someday I'll Find You," and he starred with longtime friend Gertrude Lawrence. *Cavalcade* (1931) was a historical pageant, including the song "Twentieth Century Blues." The American-made Fox film starring British actors Diana Wynyard and Clive Brook won a best picture Oscar in 1934. *Design for Living* (1933) was scandalous for its time, with two men and a woman in love. That year Coward became president of the Actors' Orphanage, initiating reforms and sending the children to America during World War II. (He resigned in 1956 when he decided to live abroad.) In 1936 he directed and played in *Tonight at Eight-Thirty*, a sequence of ten plays, any three of which might be staged on a given night. One, *Red Peppers*, is "An Interlude with Music." Director David Lean created a

classic film, *Brief Encounter* (1945), from another, *Still Life*.

Coward was frequently the target of newspaper criticism, which increased in the late 1930's. Although he was not indifferent to politics and strongly opposed English attempts to appease Adolf Hitler, his plays were not political. Seeking useful work during World War II, he was not taken seriously, and his efforts were sharply criticized. He countered with an escapist comedy about death, *Blithe Spirit* (1941), which ran for almost two thousand performances, then a record, and the film *In Which We Serve* (1942). This account of the sinking of a navy ship and, in flashbacks, the men's lives, brought new confrontations with censorship and objections, probably based on Coward's homosexuality and lower-middle-class origin, to his determination to play a British naval officer. Coward also produced, codirected, and wrote the musical score. He received Oscar nominations for best picture and screenplay, and he accepted a special award for outstanding production achievement. Coward also entertained hospital patients and troops in England and abroad.

During the next ten years, Coward had few successes and suffered much newspaper criticism. From 1951 on, he attracted renewed attention as an entertainer. He appeared in films, most notably in the movie version of Graham Greene's novel *Our Man in Havana* (1959). In 1964 the National Theatre revived *Hay Fever*; which Coward directed. He was knighted in 1970, and his seventieth birthday was marked by gala celebrations and a Tony award for achievement in the theater. Vindicated by renewed interest in his work, Coward died at his Jamaica home after years of failing health, leaving—in addition to his musical works and plays—short stories, poems, revue sketches and parodies, published diaries, essays, an autobiography, and a novel, *Pomp and Circumstance* (1960), which became an American best seller.

The Music

Early Works. Coward's first major song success was "Parisian Pierrot" for *London Calling!* With that revue, Coward began a twenty-year association with Elsie April, who wrote down his music. Of the many songs that followed, some were simple comedy, for example, "Any Little Fish" and "Something to Do with Spring." His most popular songs, however, tended to be either satiric or love songs. Despite his loyalty to England and its traditions, evidenced in such songs as "London Pride" and "There Have Been Songs in England," he satirized the British middle and upper classes in others: "Mad Dogs and Englishmen," "I Wonder What Happened to Him?," "Even Clergymen Are Naughty Now and Then," "The Stately Homes of England," "Uncle Harry," and "What's Going to Happen to the Children?" (revised for Las Vegas as "What's Going to Happen to the Tots?"). Political extremists were skewered in such songs as "Down with the Whole Damn (Darn) Lot!," "When Women Come into Their Own," and "Britannia Rules the Waves." Two World War II songs, the comic "Could You Please Oblige Us with a Bren Gun" and the biting "Don't Let's Be Beastly to the Germans," brought complaints, and the latter was banned from BBC radio. The love songs are marked by wistfulness and yearning, reflecting the sadness at the heart of Coward's art, the realization that human relations are fragile and individuals are at the mercy of time and history. Among these songs are "I'll See You Again," "If Love Were All," "Zigeuner," "That Is the Time to Go," "I Travel Alone," "Someday I'll Find You," and "The Party's Over Now." He ended his cabaret performances with the last.

Bitter Sweet. In the successful operetta *Bitter Sweet* (1929), Coward created one of the strongest female parts in early twentieth century musical theater. The story begins in the present, with Sari Linden, now an old woman and marchioness of Shayne, talking with a girl who must, like Sari in the past, decide whether to defy her parents and social class to marry for love or as society dictates. The second act reveals that, as a girl, Sari had run off with her music teacher, lived with him in poverty, and watched him die protecting her. She has transcended tragedy and pain to become a renowned singer. She regrets nothing; her courage and lack of self-pity are qualities that define heroism in other Coward works. The play's first London appearance ran for 697 performances. It was filmed twice, once in England (1933) and once in a Jeanette MacDonald and Nelson Eddy Metro-Goldwyn-Mayer version (1940) that appalled Coward with its garish Technicolor, sentimentality, and softened portrayal of Sari.

Later Operettas. *Bitter Sweet* was Coward's greatest success. Later works include *Conversation Piece* (1934) with its hit song "I'll Follow My Secret Heart"; *Operette* (1938) with its songs "Dearest Love," "The Stately Homes of England," and "Where Are the Songs We Sung?"; *Pacific 1860* (1946) with "This Is a Changing World"; and *Sail Away* (1961). Musical adaptations of Terence Rattigan's play *The Sleeping Prince* (1953) as *The Girl Who Came to Supper* (1963) and of Oscar Wilde's *Lady Windermere's Fan* (1893) as *After the Ball* (1954) failed.

Performances. While Coward performed as singer and dancer from childhood, only in his final decades was his ability as a performer fully recognized. Recognition began with a series of cabaret performances that won him a new and enthusiastic audience. The first was a concert at the Theatre Royal in Brighton, England, in 1951. From 1951 to 1954 he gave a series of performances at London's Café de Paris and in 1955 was spectacularly successful at the Desert Inn in Las Vegas. He appeared with Mary Martin in 1955 in the first CBS color tele-

Sir Noël Coward. (AP/Wide World Photos)

vision special, *Together with Music* (she had starred in his unsuccessful *Pacific 1860*). He performed on the *Ed Sullivan Show*, a popular television variety show, in 1956 and 1957. NBC honored him with a two-hour "Salute to Noël Coward" in 1963. There were many other appearances. In 1967 he starred in an NBC musical version of George Bernard Shaw's *Androcles and the Lion* (1912); Shaw had been the first major playwright to encourage the young Coward. Coward's seventieth birthday was the occasion for a number of television and other appearances.

Musical Legacy

Many Coward plays—for example, *Blithe Spirit*, *Hay Fever*, *Private Lives*, and *Design for Living*—have proved timeless. In 1964 Hugh Martin and Timothy Gray debuted the successful musical *High Spirits* from *Blithe Spirit*, while Caedmon Audio used excerpts from several comedies in its five-disc *The Noël Coward Audio Collection* (2005). Numerous Coward stories and plays have been televised. Operettas such as *Bitter Sweet*, however, fell out of favor by the mid-twentieth century, when the stage was dominated by the musicals of Richard Rodgers and Oscar Hammerstein II. Similarly, elaborate variety revues such as those staged by Cochran and Charlot were supplanted by television variety shows.

Coward's individual songs are his greatest legacy. Since the musical plays defy revival, a number of revues have been created by anthologizing popular Coward songs. In 1968 Robert L. Steele produced *Noël Coward's Sweet Potato* (originally *And Now Noël Coward*) in New York. Coward biographer Sheridan Morley devised a gala concert, *A Talent to Amuse*, to honor Coward's seventieth birthday and, in 1982, created a play with music, *Noël and Gertie*, from his biographies of Coward (*A Talent to Amuse*, 1969) and *Gertrude Lawrence* (1981). It was produced in America in 1998 and retitled *If Love Were All* in 1999. Another revue, *Cowardy Custard* (1972), ran for almost two years in London. A similar revue was produced in Toronto, Canada (1970), as *Oh Coward! A Musical Comedy Revue* and retitled *Oh! Coward* for its New York production; it ran for 294 performances. Coward's records, transferred to compact discs, have remained popular. The numerous collections include *Noël Coward in New York* (1957), *Noël Coward at Las Vegas* (1955), and *Noël Coward Centenary Celebration* (1998). Many artists have recorded Coward's romantic songs; the comic songs tend to thrive best when sung in his own voice.

Betty Richardson

Further Reading

Citron, Stephen. *Noël and Cole: The Sophisticates.* New York: Oxford University Press, 1993. Biography, detailed musical analysis of Coward's songs, and glossary of musical terms.

Coward, Noël. *Collected Plays.* 8 vols. London: Methuen, 1999-2000. Contains *Bitter Sweet* and dramas, including *Cavalcade* and *Private Lives*, for which Coward wrote important music. Each volume has detailed chronology and is individually introduced.

Day, Barry. *Coward on Film: The Cinema of Noël Coward.* Lanham, Md.: Scarecrow Press, 2005. Illustrated study of productions based on Coward's plays, productions in which Coward was involved, and films in which he acted, including musical television appearances and productions of his plays and short stories.

_____, ed. *Noël Coward: The Complete Lyrics.* Woodstock, N.Y.: Overlook Press, 1998. Comprehensive resource gives lyrics in context with annotations. Includes early songs, lyrics never used, and a list of songs known to exist but now lost.

Hoare, Philip. *Noël Coward: A Biography.* Chicago: University of Chicago Press, 1995. Details of Coward's numerous attacks by government, media, corporate, and individual censors.

Lesley, Cole. *Remembered Laughter: The Life of Noël Coward.* New York: Alfred A. Knopf, 1977. Affectionate biography by Coward's longtime companion.

Mander, Raymond, and Joe Mitchenson. *Theatrical Companion to Coward: A Pictorial Record of the Theatrical Works of Noël Coward.* 2d ed., updated by Barry Day and Sheridan Morley. London: Oberon, 2000. Originally published 1957. Essential resource provides cast lists, descriptions of works, excerpts from critics, and sections on film, radio, and television appearances.

Morley, Sheridan. *A Talent to Amuse: A Biography of Noël Coward.* Boston: Little Brown, 1985. Provides a readable, balanced view. Includes chronology.

Vlasto, Dominic. "The Potency of Cheap Music." In *Look Back in Pleasure: Noël Coward Reconsidered*, edited by Joel Kaplan and Sheila Stowell. London: Methuen, 2000. Discusses songs and contributions of arrangers, important since Coward did not write down his own music.

See also: Hammerstein, Oscar, II; Rodgers, Richard.

Henry Cowell

American classical composer

An eclectic figure in experimental composition, Cowell was a theorist, a teacher, and an indefatigable champion for new American music. His early works challenged the conventional notions of how a piano was to be played, while his later pieces explored techniques and styles of non-Western music and eighteenth century American hymnody.

Born: March 11, 1897; Menlo Park, California
Died: December 10, 1965; Shady, New York
Also known as: Henry Dixon Cowell (full name)

Principal works

CHAMBER WORKS: *Irish Suite*, 1929; String Quartet No. 4, 1936 (*United Quartet*); String Quartet No. 3, 1939 (*Mosaic Quartet*); Suite for Piano and String Orchestra, 1942; Concerto No. 1, 1964; Concerto No. 2, 1965.

ORCHESTRAL WORKS: *Sinfonietta*, 1928; *Four Assorted Movements*, 1939; *Four Irish Tales*, 1940; Symphony No. 2, 1941; Symphony No. 3, 1942 (*Gaelic*); *Exultation*, 1943; Hymn and Fuguing Tune No. 1, 1944; Hymn and Fuguing Tune No. 2, 1944; Hymn and Fuguing Tune No. 5, 1946; Symphony No. 4, 1947; *A Curse and a Blessing*, 1949; Symphony No. 5, 1949; Hymn and Fuguing Tune No. 3, 1951; *Fantasie*, 1952; Symphony No. 7, 1952; Symphony No. 11, 1954 (*Seven Rituals of Music*); Symphony No. 6, 1955; *Persian Set*, 1957; Symphony No. 13, 1959

(*Madras*); Symphony No. 16, 1963 (*Icelandic*); *Twilight in Texas*, 1968.

PIANO WORKS: *Dynamic Motion*, 1916; *The Building of Bamba*, 1917 (performance written by John O. Varian; revised 1930); *The Tides of Manaunaum*, 1917; *The Banshee*, 1925.

WRITINGS OF INTEREST: *New Musical Resources*, 1930.

The Life

Henry Dixon Cowell (KOW-ehl) was born in Menlo Park, California, thirty miles south of San Francisco. His parents, Harry Cowell and Clarissa Dixon, were both writers who espoused the progressive, intellectual bohemianism of late nineteenth century California, and their son's upbringing and education were nontraditional. After a few unsuccessful attempts to integrate young Cowell into the public school system, his mother decided to educate him herself. Her curriculum emphasized literature, politics, and art over such mundane subjects as spelling and mathematics. Cowell's early exposure to music was erratic: He studied the violin and took piano lessons, but he proved to be too free-spirited to accept formal training. He showed great interest in composing, but he lacked the ability to properly notate his ideas. His first pieces reveal an attempt to imitate the classical European masters, while simultaneously defying the traditional rules of form and tonality.

In 1914 Cowell began studies with Charles Seeger at the University of California, Berkeley. Impressed with Cowell's musical potential, Seeger encouraged him to organize his creative and unusual composition methods into theoretically useful concepts. This eventually led to the creation of Cowell's influential book, *New Musical Resources*. Seeger also urged Cowell to broaden his education and in 1916 arranged for him to study in New York at the Institute of Musical Art (later renamed the Juilliard School). Although Cowell rejected the school's conservative approach and returned to California within a few months, he did learn something from Manhattan's cultural life. He met the fiery, virtuosic composer Leo Ornstein, whose piano compositions were famous for aggressive dissonances created through small clusters of notes. Upon his return to the Bay Area, Cowell had a renewed sense of himself as a composer, and he began writing a series of strikingly original compositions for the piano. At this time Cowell began to give regular recitals, and he soon became a significant figure in the American musical avant-garde.

In the 1920's and early 1930's Cowell performed in Europe and in the Soviet Union. At the same time Cowell was actively promoting his own career, he was diligently working on behalf of others. In 1925 he formed the New Music Society, an organization that sponsored concerts and published scores by new American composers. In addition, Cowell taught innovative courses in composition and world music at the New School for Social Research in New York and at Stanford University and Mills College in California.

In May, 1936, Cowell was arrested on a morals charge for engaging in sexual acts with teenage boys. He was sentenced to fifteen years in San Quentin State Prison. The dedicated support of his family and his colleagues ultimately secured his release in 1940, after only four years. During his incarceration, Cowell stayed active as a composer and teacher, leading a band at San Quentin and teaching music to his fellow inmates.

Upon his release in 1940, Cowell took his career and his compositional style in new directions. He married Sidney Robertson in 1941, and he took a job as a music editor for the U.S. Office of War Information. He also resumed his teaching career on the East Coast, and he became more actively involved in the study of world music.

In the late 1950's and early 1960's, he journeyed around the world, visiting more than a dozen countries as both a musical ambassador for the United States and an interested musician. The longest portion of his travels was spent in Iran, where he worked closely with government officials, advising them on the development of their music schools and their radio programming. His experiences abroad resulted in a number of new and significant compositions that showed not only the immediate impact of his firsthand encounters with non-Western musical practices but also a coalescence of his lifelong interest in world music.

Despite suffering a series of painful and debilitating illnesses in the late 1950's and early 1960's, Cowell continued to teach and prolifically compose. He died on December 10, 1965, at the age of sixty-eight.

The Music

Seemingly unconcerned with developing a personal style, Cowell allowed his many interests to guide each of his compositions. No single piece accurately represents his immense catalog of more than nine hundred works. He composed quickly and rarely revised his compositions. His earliest published works are brash and full of experimental devices, such as tone clusters, dissonant counterpoint, elaborately complex polyrhythms, and unconventional playing techniques. The second half of his career, however, is marked by a more judicious use of experimental devices, a greater adoption of traditional tonality and modality, and a deeper exploration of the hybridization of Western art music practices with the practices of non-Western music.

Early Works. Cowell's best-known and most influential compositions are undoubtedly his early solo piano works. Though he already had composed a large number of pieces, it was after visiting New York in 1916 and encountering the ultramodern music of Ornstein that his musical style would find direction. Cowell began cultivating a new repertoire of compositions based on extended methods of producing new sounds from the piano. His *Dynamic Motion*, which depicts the rumbling subways of Manhattan, combines a jovial little melodic motif with crashing groups of clustered, adjacent notes on the piano (known as tone clusters) produced with the performer's fists, palms, and forearms. The following year, Cowell was asked to provide music for a play based on Irish mythology, and he again found an opportunity to employ tone clusters. The overture to *The Tides of Manaunaun* combines a lilting Irish tune with palm and forearm clusters that sonically imitate the crashing of waves upon the shore. As Cowell gained notoriety for his brazen new works and performances, he continued to cull new sounds from the piano. *The Banshee*, again based upon Irish mythology, portrays the deathly screech of a banshee through direct contact with the piano strings, using both the flesh of the finger and the fingernail. The sheer originality and shocking effect of this piece made it one of Cowell's most famous compositions.

String Quartet No. 4. While Cowell gained international fame in the 1920's as a composer and performer of shocking, modern compositions for the piano, his interests had always been much broader. He had long contemplated concertial ideas found in non-Western music, but, aside from a few small examples, this interest is not directly apparent in his early compositions. In his fourth string quartet, which he dubbed the "United Quartet," Cowell sought to reconcile musical techniques and concepts from other cultures with Western art music practices, searching for the commonalities among various musical styles in order to form a hybrid of compatible elements. The melodic and harmonic content of the quartet is derived from intervals and scales that Cowell believed were universally comprehensible. His studies of non-Western music led him to the conclusion that a three-note scale, for instance, was common among primitive musical cultures. Its inclusion in this quartet, along with other globally common musical devices, such as droning fifths, pentatonic scales, and percussive effects, was Cowell's way of bringing the common musical procedures of the non-Western world into harmony with the Western classical tradition of the string quartet, presumably rendering the composition universally comprehensible.

Hymn and Fuguing Tunes. Following his incarceration, Cowell's musical language evolved in unpredictable ways. While many have viewed the more tonal, conservative language of Cowell's compositions during the second half of his career as a regression and a denial of his ultramodern style from the previous decades, it was in fact a deeper, more mature search for a distinctly American musical sound. He found inspiration in the pre-Civil War tradition of shape-note singing, particularly represented by William Walker's 1835 collection of hymns titled *The Southern Harmony*. Cowell was attracted to the modal quality of the melodies and the nonacademic approach to harmonizing them (featuring parallel fifths and octaves, and almost completely eschewing chromaticism). These tunes were often set homophonically as hymns, or they were turned into "fuging tunes" with imitative counterpoint. Cowell adopted these two approaches and combined them with the prelude and fugue structure made famous by Johann Sebastian Bach in order to form a wholly original hybrid genre Cowell called the Hymn and Fuguing Tune. Between 1944 and 1964 Cowell composed eighteen such works, each for a different ensemble of instruments.

Hymn and Fuguing Tune No. 2, scored for strings, is the best-known of this series, and it perfectly exemplifies the style. The opening hymn movement features a completely diatonic setting of a tune that suggests the Dorian mode commonly encountered in early shape-note singing. The harmonization unabashedly explores the parallel sonorities also distinctive to the hymns in Walker's collection. The intertwining imitation of the subsequent fuguing tune movement advances almost entirely in stepwise motion, relying on the beautiful simplicity of clearly comprehensible counterpoint.

Persian Set. At the end of 1956 and the beginning of 1957, during his nearly three-month stay in Iran, Cowell recorded his experience in a composition that again sought to hybridize disparate musical traditions. In *Persian Set*, Cowell merged the Western classical four-movement structure with analogous formal structures found in traditional Persian musical suites, and he also scored the work for a mix of Western and Persian musical instruments. The piece calls for strings, piano, clarinet, and piccolo, as well as a tar (a Persian lutelike instrument) and a drum, which most performers interpret as a Persian tombak drum. In addition, Cowell imitated the largely improvised and monophonic tradition of melodic development and variation found in Persian music, casting it within traditional Western forms with suggestions of harmonic motion.

The first and third movements are pseudoimprovisational dialogues between the melodic instruments, accompanied by droning tonic and dominant tones. The second movement is more rhythmically charged, featuring a strongly defined pattern in the drum, while the main theme is presented monophonically in the strings. Cowell suggests harmonic motion with a subtly articulated bass line in the piano part. The work's finale is a full realization of Cowell's goals toward hybridization. It is simultaneously a rondo, typical of final movements within a Western classical four-movement structure, and a Persian reng, a fast dance movement in triple meter often heard at the end of instrumental suites. *Persian Set* premiered in Tehran in September of 1957, and it remains Cowell's most successful transcultural composition.

Musical Legacy

Despite his large number of works and various methods of composing, Cowell is noted more for his innovative ideas and fearless approach to expanding the Western classical tradition than for his compositions. His writings inspire modern composers to look beyond the inherited traditions of European classicism and to reexamine the ways in which modern music can be constructed. As a teacher, he introduced countless students (including John Cage and Lou Harrison) to musical traditions outside the Western world. Even the U.S. government recognized his unique understanding and employed him as a musical ambassador and as a general source of cultural knowledge. His enormous and eclectic oeuvre—with its exploration of styles and techniques futuristic and retrospective, within and outside Western tradition—presaged the trend toward postmodernism.

Peter Schimpf

Further Reading

Hicks, Michael. *Henry Cowell: Bohemian*. Chicago: University of Illinois Press, 2002. This substantial biographical treatment of the composer examines his life until his incarceration in 1936 and places in context his upbringing within the bohemian culture of early twentieth century California.

Lichtenwanger, William. *The Music of Henry Cowell: A Descriptive Catalog*. New York: Institute for Studies in American Music, Conservatory of Music, Brooklyn College CUNY, 1986. An annotated catalog of Cowell's compositions, including dates of performance, locations of manuscripts and sketches, and detailed commentary on each piece.

Mead, Rita. *Henry Cowell's Concerti, 1925-1936: The Society, the Music Editions, and the Recordings*. Ann Arbor, Mich.: UMI Research Press, 1981. A detailed study of Cowell's New Music Society that traces the specific activities of this organization, including concerts, publications, recordings, and correspondence.

Nicholls, David. *American Experimental Music, 1890-1940*. New York: Cambridge University Press, 1990. In-depth analyses of the most significant and groundbreaking compositions by Cowell and his contemporaries prior to 1940.

_____, ed. *The Whole World of Music: A Henry Cowell Symposium*. The Netherlands: Harwood, 1997. A collection of articles treating various aspects of Cowell's career and music. Personal recollections from Harrison and Sidney Robertson Cowell are included.

See also: Cage, John; Carter, Elliott; Harrison, Lou; Nancarrow, Conlon; Schoenberg, Arnold; Seeger, Charles; Seeger, Ruth Crawford; Theremin, Léon.

Bing Crosby
American singer

In the 1920's Crosby was the first white American jazz singer, borrowing from the work of Louis Armstrong and other black jazz musicians. From the 1930's to the 1950's, he enjoyed success singing popular songs.

Born: May 3, 1903; Tacoma, Washington
Died: October 14, 1977; Near Madrid, Spain
Also known as: Harry Lillis Crosby (full name)

Principal recordings

ALBUMS: *Going My Way*, 1950; *Holiday Inn*, 1950; *Le Bing: Song Hits of Paris*, 1953; *A Musical Autobiography*, 1954; *Some Fine Old Chestnuts*, 1954; *White Christmas*, 1954; *Bing Sings Whilst Bregman Swings*, 1956; *High Society*, 1956; *Bing with a Beat*, 1957; *The Christmas Story*, 1957; *New Tricks*, 1957; *A Christmas Sing with Bing Around the World*, 1958; *Fancy Meeting You Here*, 1958; *Bing and Satchmo*, 1960; *Join Bing and Sing Along*, 1960; *El Señor Bing*, 1961; *101 Gang Songs*, 1961; *Holiday in Europe*, 1962; *I Wish You a Merry Christmas*, 1962; *On the Happy Side*, 1962; *Swingin' on a Star—Bing Crosby and Frank Sinatra*, 1962; *Return to Paradise Islands*, 1964; *Robin and the Seven Hoods*, 1964 (with Frank Sinatra, Dean Martin, and Sammy Davis, Jr.); *Bing Crosby Sings the Great Country Hits*, 1965; *That Travelin' Two-Beat*, 1965 (with Rosemary Clooney); *Hey Jude/Hey Bing!*, 1969; *Bing and Basie*, 1972; *Bingo Viejo*, 1975; *A Southern*

Memoir, 1975; *That's What Life Is All About*, 1975; *At My Time of Life*, 1976; *Beautiful Memories*, 1976; *A Couple of Song and Dance Men*, 1976; *Feels Good, Feels Right*, 1976; *Seasons*, 1977.

WRITINGS OF INTEREST: *Call Me Lucky*, 1953 (autobiography).

The Life

Harry Lillis Crosby was the fourth son of Harry Lowe Crosby and Catherine Harrington. In 1906 the family moved from western to eastern Washington, from Tacoma to Spokane, where Crosby grew up and was educated. An amateur singer, his father loved music. The singer's nickname dated from his childhood fondness for a newspaper feature called the Bingville Bugle. Even his schoolteachers called him Bing.

After graduating from Gonzaga University High School, Crosby attended Gonzaga University. He left shortly before graduation at the urging of his friend Al Rinker, a piano player who urged Crosby to pursue a musical career. In 1925 they went to Los Angeles, and there they became a popular attraction. In 1927 they caught the attention of Paul Whiteman, the successful bandleader. Later the two were joined by Harry Barris, and they performed as Paul Whiteman's Rhythm Boys.

In 1930 Crosby married Dixie Lee, a motion picture actress, and the couple had four boys. In the 1930's, when singers were featured with bands, Crosby became a solo performer. His intimate and nuanced singing style worked well in the new era of the microphone, the use of which Crosby mastered, and he became a popular radio performer. He cultivated a breezy conversational style, and he displayed a knack for comedy routines with his guests. In addition to his many recordings, he appeared in Hollywood films, developing a comedy style that he put to use in the 1940's in *The Road to Singapore* (1940) and in a series of other "road" films with comedian Bob Hope. In a more serious vein were his performances in *Going My Way* (1944) and *The Bells of St. Mary* (1945), in which he portrayed a Catholic priest. In these films, as in the road films, he sang songs, nearly always written by Johnny Burke and James Van Heusen.

Two of his outstanding performances were as an alcoholic husband in *The Country Girl* (1954) and as

a playboy ex-husband in the musical comedy *High Society* (1956). Although his days of film stardom were over by the late 1950's, he continued to perform for the next twenty years.

Dixie died in 1952, and in 1957 Crosby married actress Kathryn Grant. They had two sons and a daughter. Crosby sponsored a major professional golf tournament every year, and he died of a heart attack in 1977 while playing golf near Madrid, Spain.

The Music

Jazz Influences. In Crosby's early years as a performer, he was influenced by minstrelsy, by Al Jolson, and by music from the South, especially as played by jazz musicians, many of whom were black. A great lift came to his career when Whiteman hired him. Although Whiteman was a well-trained musician, the bandleader sought to add jazz musicians to his popular dance band. Most of these performers, including Rinker and Barris, arrived after Crosby joined the band.

Bing Crosby. (AP/Wide World Photos)

315

In 1927 and 1928 Crosby recorded "Mississippi Mud" three times; today this song is considered offensive to blacks, although Crosby would not have thought so at the time. This period saw the rise to prominence of Louis Armstrong, and the Rhythm Boys began to practice the scat singing that Armstrong popularized: the singing of a string of nonsense syllables instead of words. Crosby got to know the great cornetist Bix Beiderbeck, and he also became friends with two men who joined the Whiteman band in 1929, Eddie Lang and Joe Venuti. Lang on guitar and Venuti on violin were ranked as the best jazzmen of their time, and they performed regularly with Crosby. The musicians in Whiteman's band recognized Crosby's keen sense of pitch and rhythm.

"I Surrender, Dear." The Rhythm Boys drifted apart, but one of them aided Crosby early in his solo career by writing the music for "I Surrender, Dear," which Crosby performed to great applause at the Cocoanut Grove nightclub in Los Angeles in 1930. Crosby's handling of the song's changes in key and in tempo distinguished this first hit recording. Singing it in a Mack Sennett short film brought him to the attention of William S. Paley, the president of CBS Radio, who signed Crosby to a radio contract. He recorded the song in 1931, as well as two other notable new songs: Hoagy Carmichael's "Stardust" and a tune that became his radio broadcasts' theme, "Where the Blue of the Night Meets the Gold of the Day."

Crosby's lone recording date with Duke Ellington came in 1932, when he sang "St. Louis Blues." Although he practiced just about every other form of popular music, Crosby seldom sang the blues.

Jazz-Backed Ballads. In the 1930's, Crosby was able to blend recordings backed by top jazz musicians with ballads that his audiences craved, such as "Please," which Crosby introduced in his first full-length film, *The Big Broadcast of 1932* (1932), and "Shadow Waltz" the following year. His jazz style is well represented by a song that became a jazz band standard, "Someday Sweetheart," in 1934. In 1936 he demonstrated his versatile style in a Carmichael song seldom heard today, "Moonburn," complemented by Joe Sullivan's striking piano accompaniment.

Crosby found one of the best of his numerous singing partners in the 1930's: Connee Boswell of New Orleans, who had been performing as part of a sister combination and as a soloist. One of their most successful duets was their 1937 rendition of "Basin Street Blues." Always fond of working with Southerners, Crosby performed with two Texans, Mary Martin and Jack Teagarden, one notable example being "The Waiter and the Porter and the Upstairs Maid," featured in *The Birth of the Blues* (1941).

By 1936 Armstrong was universally recognized as the greatest name in jazz, but he had never appeared in a film. Crosby insisted that Armstrong be prominently featured in *Pennies from Heaven* (1936). Crosby had already successfully recorded a song of the same title, and he sang it again in the film, with Crosby and Armstrong doing separate choruses. "Pennies from Heaven" was one of the most popular of the cheery songs with which performers tried to lift the public's spirits during the Great Depression.

The Mellow Pipe Organ. In the 1930's, Crosby attracted young female admirers, as Frank Sinatra and Elvis Presley did later, but by the end of that decade, his style had changed, along with his audiences. The husky quality of his voice disappeared, and his voice became what one critic called a "mellow pipe organ." Crosby sometimes recorded with the orchestra fronted by his younger brother, Bob. The bassist of that orchestra, Bob Haggart, devised a melody for which Burke, Crosby's favorite songwriter, supplied the lyrics. Crosby's recording of "What's New" illustrates this change in Crosby's style. Although he never lost his penchant for jazz, his singing became mellow and assured.

Other high points include his enormously popular recording of "White Christmas," which appeared in the film *Holiday Inn* (1942), and the musical *High Society* (1956), in which Crosby sang several Cole Porter songs: "Little One," "I Love You, Samantha," "True Love" with Grace Kelly, and "Well, Did You Evah?" with Sinatra. By this period, Crosby was taping radio programs instead of doing them live. He appeared on television in Christmas specials with family members from his second marriage, and even in his seventies he continued to perform in theater concerts, including one at the London Palladium just four days before his death.

Musical Legacy

In his autobiography, Crosby attributed his popularity to the notion that every man in America thought he could sing just as well, especially in the bathroom. Although he was famous for his relaxed, casual style, he expected perfection from himself and from others—a trait that sometimes made working with him difficult. In this respect he was like the great dancer, Fred Astaire: Both made what was difficult look easy. To listen carefully to Crosby's baritone voice is to become aware of his fine sense of rhythm, his true pitch, his skillful use of mordents (the quick alternation of a principal tone with the tone immediately below it), and his sensitive interpretation of lyrics. His recording of "White Christmas," for example—with its respectful attention to songwriter Irving Berlin's artfully simple one- and two-syllable words—is typical of Crosby's considerable contributions to the lyricist's art.

Crosby made about sixteen hundred studio recordings, a number that rivals the output of any other singer in history, and "White Christmas" is among the most popular records ever. Of all these recordings, 368 reached the best-seller charts, more than achieved by Sinatra or Presley. Thirty-eight of Crosby's recordings were number-one hits, more than Presley or the Beatles managed to achieve. In the 1940's, he ranked as the number-one box-office attraction for five consecutive years. On three occasions he was nominated for best actor, and he won the Academy Award for *Going My Way* in 1944.

Robert P. Ellis

Further Reading

Crosby, Bing, with Pete Martin. *Call Me Lucky*. New York: Simon & Schuster, 1953. This autobiography is Crosby's typically relaxed and low-key account of the first fifty years of his life.

Crosby, Gary, with Ross Firestone. *Going My Own Way*. Garden City, N.Y.: Doubleday, 1983. In the course of relating the drug dependency and alcoholism of his life, Crosby's eldest son, who performed with his father, calls attention to his father's deficiencies as a parent.

Friedwald, Will. "Mr. Satch and Mr. Cros." In *Jazz Singing*. Cambridge, Mass.: Da Capo Press, 1996. This chapter in a history of jazz singing focuses on the relationship between a great jazz trumpeter and singer and a man who studied Armstrong's work from his early days as a performer.

Giddins, Gary. *Bing Crosby: A Pocketful of Dreams—The Early Years, 1902-1940*. Boston: Little, Brown, 2001. A jazz expert offers an excellent account of the jazz influences on Crosby. It includes a discography up to 1940, a complete filmograpy, and thorough documentation.

MacFarlane, Malcolm. *Bing Crosby: Day by Day*. Lanham, Md.: Scarecrow Press, 2001. This expansive book contains many details about Crosby, satisfying to readers who find that biographical trivialities can teach much about the subject.

Prigozy, Ruth, and Walter Raubicheck. *Going My Way: Bing Crosby and American Culture*. 2007. Essays relate the importance of Crosby's life to popular music, motion pictures, and the entertainment industry in general.

Shepherd, Donald, and Robert F. Slatzer. *Bing Crosby: The Hollow Man*. New York: St. Martin's Press, 1981. This book offers severe criticisms of Crosby's personality as it affected his family and others who knew him. This provides a one-sided view of the singer.

See also: Andrews, Dame Julie; Basie, Count; Beiderbecke, Bix; Bennett, Tony; Berlin, Irving; Burke, Johnny; Domino, Fats; Ellington, Duke; Garland, Judy; Heifetz, Jascha; Jordan, Louis; Lee, Peggy; Mercer, Johnny; Merman, Ethel; Merrill, Robert; Nichols, Red; Paul, Les; Porter, Cole; Presley, Elvis; Sinatra, Frank; Smith, Kate; Tormé, Mel; Van Heusen, Jimmy; Whiteman, Paul; Willson, Meredith.

David Crosby

American rock singer, songwriter, and guitarist

Crosby was a major contributor to folk-rock, a genre that blended traditional acoustic folk music with electronically amplified rock.

Born: August 14, 1941; Los Angeles, California
Also known as: David Van Cortlandt Crosby (full name)

Member of: Byrds; Crosby, Stills, and Nash;
  Crosby, Stills, Nash, and Young

Principal recordings
ALBUMS (solo): *If I Could Only Remember My Name*,
  1971; *Oh Yes I Can*, 1989; *Thousand Roads*, 1993.
ALBUMS (with the Byrds): *Mr. Tambourine Man*,
  1965; *Turn! Turn! Turn!*, 1965; *Fifth Dimension*,
  1966; *Younger than Yesterday*, 1967; *The
  Notorious Byrd Brothers*, 1968; *Sweetheart of the
  Rodeo*, 1968; *Ballad of Easy Rider*, 1969; *Dr. Byrds
  and Mr. Hyde*, 1969; *Untitled*, 1970; *Byrdmaniax*,
  1971; *Farther Along*, 1971; *The Byrds*, 1973.
ALBUMS (with Crosby, Stills, and Nash): *Crosby,
  Stills, and Nash*, 1969; *CSN*, 1977; *Daylight
  Again*, 1982; *Live It Up*, 1990; *After the Storm*,
  1994.
ALBUMS (with Crosby, Stills, Nash, and Young):
  Déjà Vu, 1970; *American Dream*, 1988; *Looking
  Forward*, 1999.

The Life
Born in Los Angeles, California, David Van
Cortlandt Crosby is the son of Oscar-winning cine-
matographer Floyd Delafield Crosby and artist
Aliph Van Cortlandt Whitehead Crosby. As a student at Montecito's Crane Country Day School, he
often performed in musicals. Shortly after he graduated from Cate School in Carpinteria, his parents
divorced.

Originally intending to become an actor—he
later appeared in several movies and television
shows—Crosby instead took up music, and he sang
folk songs with his older brother Floyd, Jr. (known
as Ethan, who committed suicide in the late 1990's).
By the early 1960's, he had connected with other
musicians who would soon form the core of the
popular group the Byrds. In the late 1960's, he became part of the folk-rock group Crosby, Stills, and
Nash, which periodically performed with Neil
Young as Crosby, Stills, Nash, and Young.

Crosby, who began using drugs and alcohol as a
teenager, sank further into substance abuse after
girlfriend Christine Hinton died in a 1969 automobile accident. Often in legal difficulties throughout
the 1970's and 1980's because of drug use and
weapons possession, he went through rehabilitation after a stint in the Texas State Penitentiary.
However, he was arrested for drug possession as

David Crosby. (AP/Wide World Photos)

late as 2004. His hard living necessitated a liver
transplant in 1995. In 2000 it was revealed that
Crosby was the sperm donor for two children produced by artificial insemination for singer Melissa
Etheridge and her partner Julie Cypher. Married
since 1987 to record producer Jan Dance, he is the
father of their son Django.

The Music
As a songwriter, singer, instrumentalist, and
performer, Crosby first made an impact in the early
1960's with the band the Byrds. The Byrds created a
fresh, new sound that inspired such artists as Bob
Dylan, the Beatles, and many others. After internal
squabbles led to Crosby leaving the Byrds, he
united in the late 1960's with Graham Nash and Stephen Stills to form Crosby, Stills, and Nash, a group
that developed the concept of folk-rock. Featuring
close harmonies, creative arrangements, and musi-

cal subjects that captured the times, Crosby, Stills, and Nash (and later with Young) helped define a generation in song. Crosby, who has released a number of critically acclaimed solo albums since 1971, continues to perform with Crosby, Stills, and Nash; with Crosby, Stills, Nash, and Young; and with Jeff Pevar, and James Raymond.

Fifth Dimension. The third album by the Byrds, released in 1966, featured a number of songs written or cowritten by Crosby. Notable among these was the psychedelic anthem "Eight Miles High," which made it into the Top 20. The album stayed for more than six months on the *Billboard* charts, and it sold well both in the United States and in England.

Crosby, Stills, and Nash. This 1969 debut album combined elements of blues, rock, folk, and jazz to produce an instant classic that rose to number six on album charts, helping to set a new direction in American music. Showcasing Crosby's talent for tapping into society's concerns, Stills's skills in formulating interesting and complicated musical arrangements, and Nash's ability to develop pop hooks, the album produced the Top 40 hits "Marrakesh Express" and "Suite: Judy Blue Eyes" (written for singer Judy Collins), as well as such popular standards as "Guinnevere," "Wooden Ships," "Helplessly Hoping," and "Long Time Gone."

Déjà Vu. The follow-up to *Crosby, Stills, and Nash* and the first to feature Neil Young, this 1970 release solidified the band's position as a musical force. *Déjà Vu* reached the top position on pop album charts—the first of three consecutive album chart-toppers—and it spawned three Top 40 singles: "Teach Your Children," "Our House," and "Woodstock." Flavored with country, Western, rock, folk, and blues, the album offered something for every musical taste, from the soaring harmonies of Stills's "Carry On" to Crosby's tongue-in-cheek "Almost Cut My Hair," which perfectly captured the dichotomy between straight and freak elements existing then.

If I Could Only Remember My Name. Crosby's first solo album, this 1971 release jocularly refers to the artist's well-documented drug problems, and it has remained popular since its debut. Though Crosby is the featured performer throughout, many guest artists contributed to the effort, including Young, Nash, Joni Mitchell, and members of the Grateful Dead, Jefferson Airplane, and Santana. The album rose as high as number twelve on album charts, with such cuts as "Music Is Love," "Laughing," and "I'd Swear There Was Somebody Here."

Musical Legacy

An important member of two seminal folk-rock bands—the Byrds and Crosby, Stills, and Nash—Crosby has had a significant influence on music, both in content and in style. The subject matter of his songs has a wide range, covering the whole of human experience, from concerns about fitting in ("Almost Cut My Hair") to consideration of a ménage à trois ("Triad"). In addition, politically charged and socially relevant statements have always been a mainstay in his compositions. Crosby's music has cut across an amazing variety of genres—folk, country, Western, psychedelic, jazz, and rock—and combinations of styles. His strong voice, capable of carrying lead vocals, has added depth and substance to group efforts. Crosby was inducted into the Rock and Roll Hall of Fame twice: for his work with the Byrds and with Crosby, Stills, and Nash. Crosby makes periodic and highly acclaimed tours with his longtime bandmates, building upon an impressive body of original work.

Jack Ewing

Further Reading

Crosby, David, and Carl Gottlieb. *Long Time Gone: The Autobiography of David Crosby*. New York: Doubleday, 1988. This is Crosby's own story of his role with the Byrds and with Crosby, Stills, Nash, and Young, and it details his abuse of drugs. Includes photographs.

_____. *Since Then: How I Survived Everything and Lived to Tell About It*. New York: Berkley, 2007. A continuation of Crosby's memoir, this takes up where his autobiography left off. Profusely illustrated.

Hoskyns, Barney. *Hotel California: The True-Life Adventures of Crosby, Stills, Nash, Young, Mitchell, Taylor, Browne, Ronstadt, Geffen, the Eagles, and Their Many Friends*. Hoboken, N.J.: Wiley, 2007. This is an overview of the 1960's-1970's California rock scene, as told by those who were there. Includes photographs.

Walker, Michael. *Laurel Canyon: The Inside Story of Rock and Roll's Legendary Neighborhood*. London:

Faber & Faber, 2006. This is an examination of the Los Angeles suburb where many of California's top musicians lived. Includes photographs.

Zimmer, Dave. *4 Way Street: The Crosby, Stills, Nash, and Young Reader*. Cambridge, Mass.: Da Capo Press, 2004. An in-depth look at the popular band over thirty years, comprising articles and interviews.

See also: Browne, Jackson; Collins, Judy; Elliot, Cass; Etheridge, Melissa; King, Carole; Mitchell, Joni; Parsons, Gram; Santana, Carlos; Stills, Stephen; Taylor, James.

Andraé Crouch

American gospel singer-songwriter and pianist

Crouch was one of the first African American gospel musicians to cross over into mainstream modern Christian music and appeal to multiracial audiences. A key artist in the Jesus Music movement of the 1960's and 1970's, he was a pioneer in combining the lyrical, spiritual essence of traditional gospel music with contemporary popular musical styles.

Born: July 1, 1942; Los Angeles, California
Also known as: Andraé Edward Crouch (full name)
Member of: Andraé Crouch and the Disciples

Principal recordings

ALBUMS (solo): *Just Andraé*, 1972; *Don't Give Up*, 1981; *No Time to Lose*, 1985; *Finally*, 1990; *Contemporary Man*, 1991; *Let's Worship Him*, 1993; *Mercy*, 1994; *Pray*, 1997; *Gift of Christmas*, 1998; *Hall of Fame*, 1999; *Legends of Gospel*, 2002; *Kings of Gospel*, 2003; *He's Everywhere*, 2004; *Mighty Wind*, 2005; *Soulfully*, 2005; *Take the Message Everywhere*, 2005; *Platinum Praise Collection*, 2008.

ALBUMS (with Andraé Crouch and the Disciples): *Autograph*, 1970; *I Don't Know Why Jesus Loved Me*, 1974; *Keep on Singin'*, 1971; *Take Me Back*, 1975; *This Is Another Day*, 1977; *Andraé Crouch and the Disciples*, 1978; *I'll Be Thinking of You*, 1979.

WRITINGS OF INTEREST: *Through It All*, 1974 (with Nina Ball).

The Life

Andraé (AHN-dray) Edward Crouch was born into a devout Christian family. Crouch, his twin sister Sandra, and his older brother Benjamin attended Sunday school regularly. Their parents, Benjamin Jerome and Catherine Dorothea Crouch, owned a dry-cleaning business. His father did street-corner preaching in his free time but eventually became minister of a Church of God in Christ (COGIC), a pentecostal church. Crouch enjoyed listening to various styles of music, including gospel, classical, rhythm and blues, rock and roll, and jazz. At the age of nine, he became a church pianist, and he was only fourteen when he wrote his first hit song, "The Blood Will Never Lose Its Power."

In 1960 Crouch formed the COGIC Singers, which included his sister Sandra, Edna Wright, and Billy Preston. Five years later, he founded a gospel rock group, called Andraé Crouch and the Disciples. Crouch's unique combination of diverse musical styles appealed to multiethnic audiences. He and the Disciples appeared on *The Tonight Show* (hosted by Johnny Carson) and *Saturday Night Live*, also performing before sold-out crowds in more than fifty countries. The Disciples disbanded in 1981, but Crouch continued to compose and record.

Between 1993 and 1995, Crouch experienced several life-changing events, the deaths of his mother, father, and older brother. He replaced his father as pastor at Christ Memorial COGIC in Pacoima, California, and moved on, releasing nearly an album per year.

The Music

Crouch revolutionized gospel music with his unique combination of traditional gospel with popular contemporary musical styles. During the 1970's, Andraé Crouch and the Disciples was the best-selling group in a new genre that would be called contemporary Christian music (CCM). Their recordings, all on the Light label, included *Autograph*, *I Don't Know Why Jesus Loved Me*, *Keep on Singin'*, *Take Me Back*, *This Is Another Day*, the self-titled *Andraé Crouch and the Disciples*, and *I'll Be Thinking of You*.

Meanwhile, Crouch had released his first solo album, *Just Andraé*, in 1972. His lyrics reflected traditional themes about personal testimony, God's love, worship, and praise. However, his performances and recordings used jazz, rhythm-and-blues, soul, and other secular styles. Crouch also used a large variety of instruments, including electric guitars, drums, synthesizers, horns, vibraphone, and electric bass. Thus, his music appealed to secular as well as religious audiences.

"The Blood Will Never Lose Its Power." This song, also known simply as "The Blood," was written in 1956, when Crouch was only fourteen. It was an immediate crossover hit, popular among both black and white church congregations and radio listeners. The famous Caravans were the first group to record it. Consisting of thirty-two measures with sixteen bars for the verses and sixteen for the refrain, or chorus, this song has a traditional gospel style. The simple, powerful lyrics affirm the never-ending power of the blood of Jesus to calm fears and provide strength every day. One of Crouch's most commercially successful songs, "The Blood" became part of the standard hymnal repertoire. Many artists have recorded it over the years, including Cece Winans, Selah, and Clay Aiken.

"Through It All." Written in 1971, this song expressed Crouch's total faith and trust in God to help him through any situation. The lyrics expressed thanks for God's blessings "through it all": tears, sorrows, loneliness, and doubt. The score called for a moderate tempo and thirty-two measures, with three sixteen-measure verses and a chorus, but various recordings have rearranged this format. The hymn was so widely identified with Crouch that Crouch named his 1974 autobiography after it. In 1975, he sang the song at a Billy Graham crusade in New Mexico. "Through It All" has become a gospel standard, included in many Christian hymnals.

"My Tribute (To God Be the Glory)." First appearing in 1971 in the classic *Keep on Singin'* album, this slow ballad has become one of the most recorded gospel songs, with more than six hundred versions. Its simple and direct lyrics express

Andraé Crouch. (AP/Wide World Photos)

Crouch's sincere gratitude to God, and the phrase "To God Be the Glory" is repeated nine times. The song is divided into three parts, and rather than the more typical alternation between verses (with the same melody but different words) and a repeated chorus, this piece has a single chorus but two contrasting verses—all of which are repeated musically. Although the original chords were relatively simple, musicians have extended them and used them as vehicles for improvisation. Also, various interpretations of the song have included further embellishments, such as key changes and the addition of extra melodic lines, as well as special endings, all designed to heighten the hymn's emotional impact.

"My Tribute" established Crouch as a pioneer in worship music. In 1996, CCM artists honored Crouch in the recording, *Tribute: The Songs of Andraé Crouch*. "My Tribute" was the finale piece, in which Crouch conduced a seventy-voice all-star choir. In 1997, the album won the Grammy Award for Best Contemporary Gospel Album.

Musical Legacy

One of the most significant artists in modern Christian music, Crouch was a leader in the Jesus Music movement begun in California in the 1960's. This genre's informal worship practices and pop musical styles laid the foundation for the contemporary Christian music industry and many modern evangelical denominations. Crouch's blending of traditional gospel music with soul, jazz, rhythm-and-blues, and mainstream pop styles appealed to diverse audiences. He performed church music in what were then unconventional venues, such as on television and in stadiums and concert halls.

Crouch wrote more than three hundred gospel pieces, many of which have become classics or standards. Major gospel singers and groups have recorded or performed his works, and Crouch himself sold millions of albums and earned many honors: Grammy Awards, GMA (Gospel Musica Association) Dove Awards, and even a star on the Hollywood Walk of Fame. He has collaborated with some of the world's most famous artists, including Whitney Houston, Michael Jackson, Elvis Presley, and Quincy Jones, as well as contributing music to films including *The Color Purple* (1985), *Free Willy* (1993), and *The Lion King* (1994).

Alice Myers

Further Reading

Crouch, Andraé, and Nina Ball. *Through It All.* Waco, Tex.: Word Books, 1974. Crouch's candid autobiography reveals his deep religious faith during difficult times. Illustrated.

Cusic, Don. *The Sound of Light: The History of Gospel and Christian Music.* Milwaukee, Wis.: Hal Leonard, 2002. Describes Crouch's significance in the development of contemporary Christian music. Bibliography, index, notes, and appendix.

Darden, Bob. *People Get Ready! A New History of Black Gospel Music.* New York: Continuum, 2004. The chapter on gospel's evolution establishes Crouch as the first popular proponent of contemporary gospel. Illustrated; discography, bibliography, and index.

Taff, Toni, and Christa Farris. *CCM Top 100 Greatest Songs in Christian Music.* Nashville, Tenn.: Integrity, 2006. Includes the stories behind three of Crouch's songs: "Jesus Is the Answer," "Soon and Very Soon," and "My Tribute." Illustrated.

Terry, Lindsay. *Stories Behind Fifty Southern Gospel Favorites.* Grand Rapids, Mich.: Kregel, 2005. Contains an interview with Crouch about his classic song "The Blood Will Never Lose Its Power." Index.

See also: Cleveland, James; Dorsey, Thomas A.; Grant, Amy; Jackson, Mahalia; Smith, Michael W.; Staples, Pops; Ward, Clara.

George Crumb

American classical composer

Crumb is best known for his idiosyncratic compositional style, which features timbral effects produced by playing instruments or singing in a nontraditional manner. Despite the incorporation of exotic scales, unmetered rhythms, and other twentieth century practices, his music is familiar and deeply expressive.

Born: October 24, 1929; Charleston, West Virginia
Also known as: George Henry Crumb, Jr. (full name)

Principal works

CHAMBER WORKS: *Four Pieces*, 1945; String Trio, 1952; String Quartet, 1954; *Four Nocturnes (Night Music II)*, 1964; *Eleven Echoes of Autumn (Echoes I)*, 1966; *Black Angels: Thirteen Images from the Dark Land (Images I)*, 1970; *Vox Balaenae*, 1971; *Dream Sequence (Images II)*, 1976; *An Idyll for the Misbegotten (Images III)*, 1986; *Quest*, 1994; *Mundus Canis*, 1997.

INSTRUMENTAL WORKS: Sonata, 1955 (for cello); *Pastoral Drone*, 1982 (for organ); *Easter Dawning*, 1991 (for carillon).

ORCHESTRAL WORKS: *Gethsemane*, 1947; Violin Sonata, 1949; Viola Sonata, 1953; *Diptych*, 1955; *Variazioni*, 1959; *Echoes of Time and the River (Echoes II)*, 1967; *A Haunted Landscape*, 1984.

PIANO WORKS: Piano Sonata, 1945; Prelude and Toccata, 1947; *Five Pieces*, 1962; *Makrokosmos, Vol. I*, 1972; *Makrokosmos, Vol. II*, 1973; *Music for a Summer Evening (Makrokosmos III)*, 1974; *Celestial Mechanics (Makrokosmos IV)*, 1979; *A*

Little Suite for Christmas, A.D. 1979, 1980; *Gnomic Variations*, 1981; *Processional*, 1983; *Zeitgeist*, 1987; *Eine Kleine Mitternachtmusik*, 2002 (*A Little Midnight Music*); *Otherworldly Resonances*, 2003.

VOCAL WORKS: Three Early Songs, 1947; *Night Music I*, 1963; *Madrigals, Book I*, 1965; *Madrigals, Book II*, 1965; *Songs, Drones, and Refrains of Death*, 1968; *Madrigals, Book III*, 1969; *Madrigals, Book IV*, 1969; *Night of the Four Moons*, 1969; *Ancient Voices of Children*, 1970; *Lux aeterna*, 1971; *Star-Child*, 1977; *Apparition*, 1979; *The Sleeper*, 1984; *Federico's Little Songs for Children*, 1986; *Unto the Hills*, 2001; *A Journey Beyond Time*, 2003; *River of Life*, 2003; *Winds of Destiny*, 2004.

The Life

George Henry Crumb, Jr., was born in Charleston, West Virginia, on October 24, 1929, a date better known as Black Thursday, the day of the stock market crash that triggered the Great Depression. His parents, George, Sr., a clarinetist, and Vivian, a cellist, were professional musicians who played in the Charleston Symphony. Crumb began clarinet lessons with his father at age seven and by age nine had taught himself to play the piano by ear. Music was an integral part of daily life in the Crumb household, and Crumb and his younger brother, who played the flute, often performed duets, trios, and other chamber music with their parents. Crumb began composing during his high school years, and two of his early works were performed by the Charleston Symphony. He met his future wife, Elizabeth May Brown, in high school. They went on to attend Mason College of Music together and were married in 1949. After graduating from college in 1950 with a bachelor of music degree, Crumb pursued graduate studies at the University of Illinois at Urbana-Champaign, where he studied with Eugene Weigel. He graduated with a master's degree in 1952. During this time Crumb also studied with Boris Blacher at Tanglewood and continued his studies with Blacher at the Hochschule für Musik in Berlin from 1955 to 1956 under a Fulbright fellowship. He completed his doctorate in composition at the University of Michigan at Ann Arbor in 1958 after studying with Ross Lee Finney. Crumb held teaching positions at Virginia's Hollins College (1958-1959), the University of Colorado at Boulder (1959-1964), and the University of Pennsylvania (1964-1997), where he was appointed professor emeritus after retiring. He and his wife had three children, two of whom built successful musical careers of their own. Ann Crumb became a Tony-nominated Broadway singer and actress, and composer David Crumb became a member of the faculty at the University of Oregon.

The Music

Crumb's music can be divided into two distinct periods. The first dates from his student days and ends somewhat abruptly in 1959 upon the completion of his orchestral work *Variazioni*. Crumb's early music incorporates the modernist musical vocabulary characteristic of such twentieth century composers as Béla Bartók, Alban Berg, Anton von Webern, and Arnold Schoenberg. Strongly Western in character, the music of this period follows classical formal schemes and incorporates metrical and rhythmic regularity.

In the late 1950's and early 1960's, Crumb became increasingly unhappy with the direction his music was taking. In recalling this crisis, Crumb once remarked in an interview, "I can remember quite literally waking up one night in a cold sweat with the realization that I had thus far simply been rewriting the music of other composers." In 1962 David Burge, Crumb's friend and colleague at the University of Colorado at Boulder, commissioned Crumb to write a new work for piano. The result of this effort was a piece entitled *Five Pieces*. This composition diverges sharply from the music of Crumb's early period and marks the advent of what Crumb refers to as his "personal style." An important feature of the music of Crumb's second period is the appearance of the scores. Crumb uses cutaway scores in which staves are left out when the corresponding part is silent. This, along with special notation for nontraditional performance techniques, a plethora of expressive markings, and unusual meters, causes the score to take on the appearance of visual art. In some cases, staves form geometric shapes reflective of their titles. In *Makrokosmos*, *Vol. I*, for example, the staves in the fourth movement, "Crucifixus," take the shape of a cross, while the staff in the eighth movement, "The Magic Circle of Infinity," forms a circle.

Aside from the presence of familiar pitch structures, the music of Crumb's mature style departs sharply from traditional Western music, containing unusual meters or lacking meter altogether. In addition, it is saturated with timbral effects created by nontraditional performance techniques. While these sometimes mimic those produced electronically, Crumb does not use synthesizers or other electronic instruments in his compositions. The one exception is the use of microphones for amplification. One of Crumb's common instrumental effects is produced by strumming or picking the strings inside the piano. While this practice originated with John Cage, Crumb's music has little in common with that of the older avant-garde composer. Cage's music is meant to challenge traditional aesthetic values; in contrast, Crumb uses nontraditional sounds and effects as a means to express such extramusical concepts as cyclical conceptions of time, nature, life, death, the human condition, and supernatural events. Although Crumb incorporates radically new sounds, these are meant to recall those heard before, both in music and in nature.

It is a hallmark of the composer's style that motives, themes, and other pitch constructions maintain the same interval throughout a piece. Among the most common devices is the gradual buildup of pitch collections along with the reordering of the notes in subsequent repetitions. Although triads are rare in Crumb's music, other familiar structures, such as pentatonic and whole-tone collections, are prevalent. Crumb often alludes to the influences of his native West Virginia (the sounds of everyday life he heard growing up there as well as its folk traditions and music) and those composers of the past he most admires (Claude Debussy and Bartók). The importance of these influences is manifested in his music by expressive markings that refer to natural sounds, the incorporation of folk instruments such as the musical saw, and the frequent use of musical quotations.

Five Pieces. This 1962 composition is the first of Crumb's mature style. In it may be found nearly all of the features characteristic of his music dating from the early 1960's, such as nontraditional ways of playing, including plucking the strings inside the piano, the use of a microphone placed near the piano strings, graphic notation, unmetered rhythms, and inversional pitch symmetry. Certain aspects of the work—including its title, which reflects the structure rather than, as in many of Crumb's later works, its expressive content—recall the music of Crumb's first period. The work as a whole constitutes an arch form and for this reason Crumb stipulates in the program notes that *Five Pieces* should always be performed in its entirety since the work was conceived as an organic whole." Much of the pitch material is derived from chromatic tri-chords and tone clusters. In keeping with the arch-form organization, the fifth movement ends with the same tri-chord that occurs at the beginning of the first movement, while the tri-chords in the second movement are inverted in the fourth. The middle movement incorporates the arch-form idea on a smaller scale in that the second half of the movement is a near literal retrograde of the first half.

Madrigals, Books I, II, III, and IV. The poetry of Federico García Lorca plays a central role in the music Crumb wrote between 1965 and 1969, and this is

George Crumb. (Hulton Archive/Getty Images)

nowhere more evident than in the four books of madrigals. Characteristic of these pieces and others is Crumb setting to music only a single line or two from García Lorca's poems. Crumb's atmospheric musical settings amplify the brief textual quotes. Each book consists of three madrigals for soprano and a small instrumental chamber group, and the vocal part is often treated as an instrument. For example, in the first madrigal, "Verte desnuda es recordar la tierra" (to see you naked is to remember the earth), the soprano, in addition to singing in a traditional manner, hums and vocalizes nonsense syllables, adding new timbres to those articulated by the vibraphone and contrabass. Always important in Crumb's music, inversional pitch symmetry is prevalent in the madrigals, featured prominently in the three madrigals of books I and II, the first movement of book III, and the last movement of book IV.

An Idyll for the Misbegotten. Many of the devices Crumb uses in the early compositions of his mature style also appear in his later compositions. In *An Idyll for the Misbegotten*, various pitch motives are extracted from the opening theme and altered rhythmically, intervallically, and by means of pitch additions. Like many of Crumb's compositions, the piece sounds improvised but nevertheless has a ternary structure in which the opening material returns at the end. In this work, Crumb seems to express his own philosophical angst over not only humankind's mistreatment of the natural environment but also the silent suffering of nature itself. The original version for flute contains two literal quotations from Debussy's *Syrinx* for solo flute and two lines from a poem by eighth century Chinese poet Ssu-k'ung Shu, which the flutist recites across the flute mouthpiece, producing a flute-like whisper. The mournful quality produced by descending glissando patterns seems to allude to Syrinx's sorrow over her loss of innocence at the hands of Pan, who, according to the Greek myth, turns Syrinx into a pan flute.

Musical Legacy

Crumb has received a number of prestigious awards and grants, including a Pulitzer Prize in 1968 for *Echoes of Time and the River*, the Edward MacDowell Medal for composition in 1995, and a Grammy award for *Star-Child* in 2001. In 2004 he was named *Musical America*'s Composer of the Year. Crumb's most important legacy may well be the elevation of timbre to a central expressive role in musical structure.

Edward Pearsall

Further Reading

Bruns, Steven, and Ofer Ben-Amots, eds. *George Crumb and the Alchemy of Sound: Essays on His Music*. Colorado Springs: Colorado College Music Press, 2005. Analytical and biographical essays on George Crumb and his music.

Cohen, David. *George Crumb: A Bio-Bibliography*. Westport, Conn.: Greenwood, 2002. Annotated listing of Crumb's work along with biographical information.

Gillespie, Don, ed. *George Crumb: Profile of a Composer*. New York: C. F. Peters, 1986. Interviews with, as well as articles by the composer, and excerpts from his published works. Includes photographs of the composer at work, in master classes, and at postperformance receptions.

See also: Bartók, Béla; Berg, Alban; Cage, John; Debussy, Claude; Golijov, Osvaldo; Schoenberg, Arnold; Tan Dun; Webern, Anton von; Wolfe, Julia.

Celia Cruz
Cuban Latin singer

Known as the Queen of Salsa, Cruz was a consummate entertainer, with one of the finest voices ever to come out of Cuba. She gained broad popularity across the United States, performing with distinguished Latin artists from around the world.

Born: October 21, 1924; Havana, Cuba
Died: July 16, 2003; Fort Lee, New Jersey
Also known as: Úrsula Hilaria Celia Caridad Cruz Alfonso (full name)
Member of: La Sonora Mantancera

Principal recordings

ALBUMS (solo): *Canciones premiadas*, 1965; *Cuba y Puerto Rico son*, 1966 (with Tito Puente); *Son con guaguanco*, 1966; *A ti Mexico*, 1967; *Bravo Celia Cruz*, 1967; *La excitante*, 1968; *Serenata guajira*, 1968; *Quimbo quimbumbia*, 1969 (with Puente); *Etc. Etc. Etc.*, 1970 (with Puente); *Celia and Johnny*, 1974 (with Johnny Pacheco); *Tremendo cache*, 1975 (with Pacheco); *Only They Could Have Made This Album*, 1977 (with Willie Colón); *A todos mis amigos*, 1978; *The Brillante*, 1978; *Eternos*, 1978 (with Pacheco); *La ceiba*, 1979; *Celia/Johnny/Pete*, 1980 (with Pacheco and Pete Rodriguez); *Celia and Willie*, 1981 (with Colón); *Feliz encuentro*, 1982; *Tremendo trio*, 1983 (Ray Barretto and Adalberto Santiago); *De nuevo*, 1986 (with Pacheco); *La candela*, 1986; *The Winners*, 1987 (with Colón); *Ritmo en el corazon*, 1988 (with Barretto); *La guarachera del mundo*, 1990; *Canta Celia Cruz*, 1991; *La reina del ritmo Cubano*, 1991; *La verdadera historia*, 1992; *Tributo a Ismael Rivera*, 1992; *Azúcar negra*, 1993; *Homenaje a Beny More, Vol. 3*, 1993 (with Puente); *Homenaje a los santos*, 1994; *Irrepetible*, 1994; *Las guarachera de la guaracha*, 1994; *Merengue*, 1994; *Cuba's Queen of Rhythm*, 1995; *Double Dynamite*, 1995 (with Puente); *Festejando navidad*, 1995; *Irresistible*, 1995; *Celia Cruz*, 1996; *Cambiando ritmos*, 1997; *Duets*, 1997 (with others); *Fania All Stars with Celia Cruz*, 1997 (with Fania All Stars); *También boleros*, 1997; *Afro-Cubana*, 1998; *Mi vida es cantar*, 1998; *Habanera*, 2000; *Inigualable*, 2000; *Salsa*, 2000; *Siempre vivire*, 2000; *La negra tiene tumbao*, 2001; *Unrepeatable*, 2002; *El carnaval de la vida*, 2003; *Regalo del alma*, 2003.

ALBUMS (with La Sonora Matancera): *La incomparable Celia*, 1958; *Mi diario musical*, 1959; *Sabor y ritmo de pueblos*, 1965; *Mambo del amor*, 1994; *Las Estrellas de la Sonora Matancera*, 2003.

The Life

Born Úrsula Hilaria Celia Caridad Cruz Alfonso on October 21, 1924, in Havana, Cuba, Celia Cruz (SEEL-yah krewz). In 1947 she won the *La Hora del Té* talent competition on Radio García Serrá. Although her father, Simón Cruz, believed that music was a disgraceful profession for a woman, her mother, Catalina Alfonso, supported her daughter's ambitions. Cruz studied at the Havana Conservatory and began singing full time. In Cuba she worked with Las Mulatas del Fuego (the Blazing

Mulatto Women) and the Orchestra Gloria Matancera before joining La Sonora Matancera in August of 1950. Cruz worked with La Sonora Matancera for about fifteen years, touring the Caribbean, South and Central America, and the United States. After Fidel Castro's 1959 revolution, Cruz and her band left Cuba. They spent a year and a half in Mexico, performing music and appearing in films. Eventually they moved to New York, and Cruz married the band's trumpeter, Pedro Knight, in 1962.

From the 1960's to the 1990's Cruz was the undisputed top vocalist of salsa, a genre that experienced a significant surge in popularity in the 1970's. Part of her time was spent performing at the Hollywood Palladium, a California venue that commonly promoted swing bands, but to accommodate the large Mexican population, it instituted Latin Holidays. This extended engagement allowed Cruz and her band to apply for U.S. residency. Besides La Sonora Matancera, Cruz regularly worked with Tito Puente, Johnny Pacheco, Willie Colón and their respective bands, as well as several artists from the Fania record label. Mindful of the New York Latin community, Cruz performed on weekends, indicating that these shows allowed the workaday Latin laborers access to their own music. Not completely abandoning her motion-picture career, Cruz appeared in 1991's *The Mambo Kings*. In 2003 Cruz died of a brain tumor at her home in Fort Lee, New Jersey.

The Music

Salsa is an umbrella term that includes many highly specific Cuban, Puerto Rican, Dominican, and other Latin song and dance genres. It also implies a social movement born from a variety of Latin diasporic communities in New York City. As the people took pride in their heritage, the popularity of salsa soared. With her rich, contralto voice, Cruz mastered this genre. She occasionally sang Santería religious chants in the Yoruba language. Incredibly vibrant even in her seventies, Cruz had a quick wit and energetic theatrical stage presence that were as legendary as her voice. Her shouts of "Azúcar!" (sugar), which originated as a punch line to a joke, were sprinkled throughout many songs. Cruz recorded more than seventy albums with the top names in salsa and with several popular American musicians.

"En el tiempo de la colonia." "En el tiempo de la colonia" is closer to a brisk ballad or bolero than to Cruz's typical danceable salsa music. It is a different style of Cuban music, slower and more stately, with a simpler, instrumental accompaniment, particularly in the percussion section. The trumpet takes a brief melodic role, along with its usual solo or percussive function. In this song, Cruz tells the story of colonial Cuba, her nostalgic memories focusing on how the black people played the drums. The irony is that Afro-Cubans were enslaved in colonial times and treated poorly.

"Quimbara." This tune, released on *Celia y Johnny*, is a guaguancó, a type of rhumba. Cruz displays her quick articulation abilities with the repeated phrase "Quimbara cumbara cumaquín bambá." Interestingly, this phrase refers to the sounds and dialogue of Afro-Cuban drums. The chorus section features Cruz and her band engaging in call and response, and while Cruz varies her lyrics, the band repeats the song's signature line. Cruz's love for music and dancing is another subject of the song. "Quimbara" was composed by Puerto Rican Júnior Cepeda, and it became one of the prominent songs of the salsa movement.

"Cúcala." When Pacheco changed the musical style of "Cúcala" from a Puerto Rican bomba plena to a Cuban guaracha, Cruz was interested. It was first recorded live in 1975, at a concert in Madison Square Garden, and later it was studio edited. This developed into one of Cruz's most popular hits. In musical terms, this song showcases the horns during various instrumental breaks as well as a driving piano montuno (highly syncopated melodic and rhythmic ostinatos). Call and response, likely a carryover from assorted African music traditions, is utilized again, as well as a percussion section for punctuation. Lyrically, Cruz is referring to a girl by the name Cúcala, exalting her for her prowess in life and appearance.

"Usted abuso." Although musically upbeat, Cruz presents the listener with lyrics from a broken heart. The theme "you took advantage of me, you took advantage of my love for you" repeats throughout. From *The Brilliante*, "Usted abuso" puts Cruz's powerful and warm vocal timbre at the forefront, rather than her speed and agility. "Usted Abuso" was composed by Antonio Batista, Carlos Figuiero, and Pierre Delanoë. The album was com-

Celia Cruz. (Hulton Archive/Getty Images)

piled in 1978 to feature her works done on the Vaya Records label, a subsidiary of Fania Records.

"La negra tiene tumbao." This song is the title track to the album, which won a Grammy Award for Best Salsa Album. The synthesized instrumentation and stylistic differences heard in this selection are quite unlike the bulk of Cruz's work, but they are an illustration of how diverse her recording and performing career was. Prominent stylistic differences include influences from American rap to Hispanic reggaetón, which is characterized by the "Dem Bow" rhythm. The subject of Cruz's song, the negrita, is being advised on how to live a good and enjoyable life: move straight, avoid obstacles, and consider one's actions. Toward the end, a male rapper attempts to seduce the negrita, calling her beautiful and sweet.

Musical Legacy

Cruz received numerous honors, including two Grammy Awards, three honorary doctorates, a star on the Hollywood Walk of Fame (1990), the Golden Eagle Award (1991), and the National Medal of Arts (1994). These tributes recognized her exceptional musicianship and character. Her tenacity and talent allowed her to become prominent in a male-dominated performance field. Cruz paved the way for later female musicians, such as Gloria Estefan and Sheila Escovedo, and she inspired salsa artists, such as Rubén Blades and Willie Colón. Issues of racism and women's rights were frequently addressed in her lyrics. Musically, she gave a voice to the salsa movement in the United States, a voice with which both immigrant and American-born Hispanics could identify. Moreover, her sound and energy captivated non-Hispanics, introducing the general population of the United States to salsa.

Janine Tiffe

Further Reading

Aparicio, Frances R. *Listening to Salsa: Gender, Latin Popular Music, and Puerto Rican Cultures.* Hanover, N.H.: University Press of New England, 1998. The text focuses on gender issues in salsa music, and several essays discuss Cruz, her repertory, and its feminist implications.

Boggs, Vernon W. *Salsiology.* Westport, Conn.: Greenwood Press, 1992. This resource addresses the history of salsa, significant individuals (such as Cruz) in the genre, popularization, and transculturation. Includes photographs and a musical score for "Gonna Salsalido."

Cruz, Celia, and Ana Cristina Reymundo. *Celia: My Life.* New York: HarperCollins, 2004. Cruz's autobiography recounts her thoughts and feelings regarding her personal life and her career. Includes photographs, discography, and a list of awards and honors.

Gerard, Charley, and Marty Sheller. *Salsa! The Rhythm of Latin Music.* Crown Point, Ind.: White Cliffs Media, 1989. An educational tool that provides historical context, musical samples, two arrangements, a glossary, and a discography to familiarize the reader with the genre of salsa.

Koskoff, Ellen, ed. *The Garland Encyclopedia of World Music: The United States and Canada.* New York: Garland, 2001. This series volume contains a wealth of information, and it places Cruz and her music in a geographical context.

See also: Barretto, Ray; Blades, Rubén; Colón, Willie; Puente, Tito.

Xavier Cugat

Cuban Latin violinist and songwriter

A charismatic bandleader of Latin American dance music, Cugat introduced Latin rhythms to North American audiences through live performance, radio, recordings, television, and motion pictures. During the Latin music craze of the 1930's and 1940's, he helped to popularize rumba, tango, cha-cha-cha, conga, and mambo.

Born: January 1, 1900; Girona, Spain
Died: October 27, 1990; Barcelona, Spain
Also known as: Francisco de Asís Javier Cugat Mingall de Bru y Deulofeo (birth name)

Principal recordings

ALBUMS: *Tropical Bouquets,* 1949; *Xavier Cugat,* 1949; *Relaxing with Cugat,* 1952; *Cugat's Favorite Rhumbas,* 1954; *Mambo at the Waldorf,* 1955; *The King Plays Some Aces,* 1958; *Chile con Cugie,* 1959; *Cugat in Spain,* 1959; *Cugat in France, Spain, and Italy,* 1960; *Cugat Plays Continental Favorites,* 1961; *Viva Cugat!,* 1961; *Cugi's Cocktails,* 1963; *Cugat Caricatures,* 1964; *Xavier Cugat y su oro merengue,* 1986.

The Life

Because of his father's political activities, Xavier Cugat (ZAY-vyahr KEW-gaht), at four years of age, and his family fled Spain, sailing from Barcelona to Havana. In Cuba he received his first violin, a quarter-sized version, and quickly demonstrated his aptitude for playing the instrument. While still young, Cugat played for a silent motion-picture theater, foreshadowing his future endeavors in Hollywood.

Cugat embarked on a career as a classical violinist, touring Europe and North America. He made his professional debut at Carnegie Hall in 1918 to tepid reviews. After the New York concert, he returned to Spain to perform with greater success. During the 1920's he joined Vincent Lopez's dance orchestra at the Casa Lopez in New York.

Encountering difficulties as a professional musician, Cugat moved to Los Angeles and worked as a caricaturist for the *Los Angeles Times.* While in California, he met actor Rudolph Valentino, leading to the formation of a tango orchestra that appeared in the actor's silent film *Four Horsemen of the Apocalypse* (1921). Cugat and his orchestra, known as Cugat and His Gigolos, also began performing at the Coconut Grove Room at the Ambassador Hotel, playing tangos and teaching audience members the Argentine dance. Cugat formed a new orchestra at the Waldorf Astoria Hotel in New York City in 1930, and that same year, he composed music for the film *Gay Madrid*. In 1934 he appeared on a weekly radio show *Let's Dance*. However, he did not reach a national audience until appearing on the radio program *The Camel Caravan*.

Possibly appearing on film more than any other American bandleader, Cugat was extremely comfortable in front of the camera. For Cugat, motion pictures served as a venue to promote his conception of Latin American dance music. Playing himself in film, Cugat appeared in *Let's Go Latin* (1937), *You Were Never Lovelier* (1942), *Stage Door Canteen* (1943), *Two Girls and a Sailor* (1944), *Bathing Beauty* (1944), *Weekend at the Waldorf* (1945), *No Leave, No Love* (1946), *Holiday in Mexico* (1946), *This Time for Keeps* (1947), *A Date with Judy* (1948), *Luxury Liner* (1948), *Neptune's Daughter* (1949), and more.

Making frequent headlines for his numerous marriages and divorces, Cugat carried out stormy relationships with Rita Montaner, Carmen Castillo, Lorraine Allen, Abbe Lane, and Charo. In 1971 he suffered a stroke, becoming partially paralyzed. Because of his medical difficulties, he retired from music and returned to Spain. In 1990 Cugat died of heart failure in Barcelona.

The Music

During the 1930's and 1940's, Cugat was the bandleader associated with Latin American dance music. He recognized that many North Americans were unfamiliar with Latin music, but they enjoyed its rhythms and musical traits. In the United States and to a lesser degree in Latin America, Cugat and his orchestra appeared on stage, radio, records, and motion pictures, performing numerous Latin American dance genres. Primarily marketing his music to a North American public, he performed rumbas, mambos, tangos, sambas, congas, and cha-chachas; however, his music was a hybrid of Latin American models. In Cuban music, ostinatos built around the son rhythm are crucial for performance. In addition, layered percussion and polyrhythms embraced the Afro-Cuban heritage of Cuba. When Cugat worked as a bandleader in New York at the Waldorf Astoria Hotel during the 1930's and 1940's, two styles of Latin music, uptown and downtown, existed. Uptown music catered to a Latin American diaspora living in the Latin barrio of Harlem. Music that was intended for non-Latinos was performed downtown. Initially, Cugat provided audiences with a Latin dance music that was inauthentic, but

Xavier Cugat. (AP/Wide World Photos)

eventually he began moving the music closer to traditional Latin American practices. As a bandleader, Cugat arranged the compositions of others for his Latin jazz ensemble.

"La paloma." Spanish for the dove, the song is by Spanish composer Sebastián Yradier. In Cugat's arrangement, the bandleader employed the characteristic clave rhythm, an Afro-Cuban rhythmic pattern that provides the structural framework of countless Cuban musical works. He arranged the work for a large Latin jazz ensemble, utilizing such Latin percussion instruments as the congas, bongos, and clave. Muted trumpets, piano, and guitar complete the ensemble. Cugat arranged the work as a conga, a song and dance associated with carnival processions that became popular in the United States in the 1940's. The popularity of the conga dance in North America is largely attributed to Desi Arnaz, a former member of Cugat's orchestra, who appeared on the long-running television series *I Love Lucy* as the husband of Lucille Ball. The choreography of the dance consists of three short steps and a leap that accompanies a repeated rhythmic figure. It can be danced as a couples dance or in a conga line. The term conga became synonymous with Latin American music.

"Perfidia." By Mexican composer Alberto Domínguez, the song takes its title from the Spanish word for perfidy. Cugat arranges the treacherous nature of the music in an ironically gleeful manner. An instrumental version, his arrangement opens with a slow and rhythmically free violin introduction. Strict dance rhythms soon follow, providing a rhythmic ostinato. In place of vocals, instruments trace the melody. He orchestrates the bolero for marimba, muted trumpets, saxophones, and piano, with maracas, bongos, and congas marking time. Intended for dancing, the bolero is in duple meter with a characteristic slow-quick-quick rhythm.

"My Shawl." The song opens with the characteristic rhythm of the rumba foxtrot, a hybrid of the Cuban rumba with the ballroom foxtrot. At a slow tempo, the Latin percussion section, consisting of clave, maracas, bongos, and congas, marks the long-long-short-short rhythm of the dance. Cugat's arrangement employs strings to play the melody and countermelody. Intended for North American audiences, the lyrics are in English, and they alternate against the extended instrumental sections.

The rumba originates from Cuba, and Cugat believed that the dance was too difficult for North Americans, especially those he encountered on the dance floor. As a solution, Cugat assembled a simplified version of the Afro-Cuban dance, emphasizing the bass conga-drum accent on the fourth beat. By removing the complex Afro-Cuban polyrhythms associated with the native Cuban model, he made the duple meter of the dance more obvious. In addition, he brought the melody to the forefront of the song.

"Babalú." The song opens with a tribal-like drum introduction, followed by a rhythmically free vocalization on the word babalú. The introduction sets the exotic mood, and claves and cowbell mark the strict dance rhythms within a slow tempo. Highlighted in the arrangement, the piano and muted trumpets alternate with the vocalist. The lyrics are in Spanish, and on occasion the singer comically delivers the lyrics in rapid succession. The song is a mambo, and a large percentage of Cugat's repertoire consists of mambos. In the 1940's, the big band format of North America combined with Afro-Cuban rhythms to create a new genre called the mambo. Arrangers of big band music preferred to write for contrasting instruments in sections. The saxophone section often played an ostinato borrowing from the son, a rhythmic ostinato, and other sections such as trumpet and trombone made musical interjections. Although there are vocals for mambo, it is first and foremost instrumental dance music. Credited with creating the mambo is Cuban bandleader Pérez Prado, and the dance may be described as a slower-tempo rumba.

Musical Legacy

Often leading the band with his violin bow, the engaging bandleader of Latin American dance music introduced Latin rhythms to North American audiences. Believing that North American audiences were more visually than aurally oriented, Cugat created an amalgamated Latin persona. Known for his showmanship and self-parodying, the Spanish-born musician was often seen with a chihuahua in hand, wearing a sombrero, or wrapped in a serape, a traditional blanket shawl. Furthermore, he frequently surrounded himself with beautiful women, perpetuating the image of the Latin lover.

Cugat impacted the popular culture of the United States, appearing in all forms of media. He first reached American homes through the radio, performing his renditions of Latin American music, and then he elevated his persona in motion pictures, in which he portrayed himself.

Most of his childhood musical development occurred in Havana, and the repertoire for Cugat's orchestra included numerous Cuban genres, such as the rumba, conga, mambo, and cha-cha-cha. In addition to the Cuban genres, his orchestra performed Argentine tangos and Brazilian sambas. The Latin music craze of the 1930's and 1940's facilitated the introduction of Latin American music; however, the bandleader altered Latin music to suit the musical tastes of North Americans. Cugat situated the melody in the forefront, as was popular, and simplified the syncopated Latin rhythms by removing layers of percussion. By popularizing Latin American dance music, Cugat paved the way for many other Latin artists, such as Arnaz, Miguelito Valdés, and Tito Rodríguez.

Mark E. Perry

Further Reading

Cugat, Xavier. *Rumba Is My Life*. New York: Didier, 1948. An early autobiography, written after Cugat's successful career in the United States.

Leymarie, Isabelle. *Cuban Fire: The Story of Salsa and Latin Jazz*. London: Continuum, 2002. The author explores the history of Cuban music as it spread throughout the United States. She focuses on the development of hybrid genres. Includes illustrations, glossary, discography, and bibliography.

Lowinger, Rosa, and Ofelia Fox. *Tropicana Nights: The Life and Times of the Legendary Cuban Nightclub*. Orlando, Fla.: Harvest Books, 2005. The authors provide a history of the Tropicana, a Havana nightclub that was significant in the cultural nightlife of prerevolutionary Cuba. The book includes a list of shows at the Tropicana. Includes bibliography.

Morales, Ed. *The Latin Beat: The Rhythms and Roots of Latin Music from Bossa Nova to Salsa and Beyond*. Cambridge, Mass.: Da Capo Press, 2003. The book is a journalistic approach to the study and history of Latin music in the United States. Includes bibliography.

Orovio, Helio. *Cuban Music from A to Z*. Durham, N.C.: Duke University Press, 2004. A reference work that provides comprehensive coverage of Cuban music and musicians.

Roberts, John Storm. *The Latin Tinge: The Impact of Latin American Music on the United States*. 2d ed. New York: Oxford University Press, 1999. The author explores the influence of Latin American music and musicians on music in the United States. Includes illustrations, glossary, discography, and bibliography.

See also: Blades, Rubén; Prado, Pérez; Puente, Tito.

D

D. M. C.

American rapper and songwriter

A pioneer in hip-hop music, McDaniels is one of the founders of the influential hip-hop group Run-D. M. C., which is credited with creating a commercially viable form of rap and with introducing the genre to mainstream music audiences.

Born: May 31, 1964; New York, New York
Also known as: Darryl Matthews McDaniels (birth name); Darryl Lovelace; DMcD; Grandmaster Get High; Easy D
Member of: Run-D. M. C.

Principal recordings

ALBUMS (solo): *Checks, Thugs, and Rock n Roll*, 2006.
ALBUMS (with Run-D. M. C.): *Run-D. M. C.*, 1984; *King of Rock*, 1985; *Raising Hell*, 1986; *Tougher than Leather*, 1988; *Back from Hell*, 1990; *Down with the King*, 1993; *Crown Royal*, 2001.

The Life

Darryl McDaniels taught himself to deejay after being inspired by the work of Grandmaster Flash. In the early 1980's, McDaniels joined with Joseph "Run" Simmons to form Run-D. M. C. McDaniels served as the group's deejay until Jason "Jam Master Jay" Mizell joined the group, at which point Simmons encouraged McDaniels to focus on rapping. The group released six albums between 1984 and 1993.

In the late 1990's, D. M. C. was diagnosed with spasmodic dysphonia, a condition that causes spasms of the larynx, a condition he believed was caused by his singing in Run-D. M. C.'s aggressive vocal style and his years of heavy drinking. As a result of his vocal problems (and rumors of creative differences with Simmons), D. M. C. appeared on only three tracks from Run-D. M. C.'s *Crown Royal*. The group officially disbanded in November, 2002, after Mizell was murdered.

In 2001 McDaniels released his autobiography, *King of Rock: Respect, Responsibility, and My Life with Run-D. M. C.* During the course of his research for this book, he discovered he had been adopted when he was three months old. A documentary on D. M. C.'s search for his birth mother, *D. M. C.: My Adoption Journey*, aired on VH1 in February, 2006. D. M. C. released his first solo album, *Checks, Thugs, and Rock n Roll*, in March, 2006. Later that year D. M. C. was presented with the Congressional Angels in Adoption Award for his work with the Felix Organization, a charity he founded to help provide children waiting to be adopted with a home experience.

The Music

Prior to the work of Run-D. M. C., rap was seen primarily as street music. A few performers, such as the Sugar Hill Gang and Grandmaster Flash, had begun to transform it into a viable recording genre. However, it was the music of Run-D. M. C. that persuaded listeners and recording executives that rap and hip-hop would sell beyond the inner cities. It was one of the first groups to move away from using exclusively background music, or beats, that came from sampling dance records on turntables by tapping into electronic instruments such as synthesizers and drum machines. It also introduced hard rock guitars into a genre that was dominated by the sounds of disco. Run-D. M. C.'s forceful vocal style laid the groundwork for the hardcore rap styles that followed, forcing listeners to pay attention to the words instead of just getting caught up in the music.

"It's Like That." From the first self-titled album, "It's Like That" is largely regarded as the first song to present rap as a commercially viable style. It was one of the first hip-hop songs to use a synthesized accompaniment rather than samples. The song features the two rappers trading lines and uniting for the refrain, "It's like that, and that's the way it is." It is an early example of what has become known as conscious rap, or rap that focuses on social issues rather than boasting or materialism. At times the lyrics forshadow the religious sentiments expressed on *Back from Hell* and *Down with the King*.

"Walk This Way." *Raising Hell* included a cover of Aerosmith's "Walk This Way," in collaboration with Aerosmith's Steve Tyler and Joe Perry. This became the first hip-hop song to break the Top 10 on the *Billboard* Hot 100 (peaking at number four). As such, it is often considered to be the song that introduced rap to mainstream audiences, primarily because of the video's strong presence on MTV.

The song features a combination of sampling and live music. The underlying drumbeat was played on turntables by Jam Master Jay, and so was the song's signature guitar riff. Tyler's vocals and Perry's guitar solos, which follow each chorus, were performed live in the studio.

"Run's House." This song became an unofficial anthem for Run-D. M. C. after its release on *Tougher than Leather*. The song is a fairly typical rap about the artists' skills. The two rappers alternate verses, proclaiming their hip-hop superiority and their disdain for those who think rap is just a passing fad that requires no skill. Unlike some songs of this type, neither rapper boasts about his sexual prowess, his physical toughness, or the acts of violence he has committed. "Run's House" is designed for audience participation in a live setting by encouraging listeners to respond to the question "Whose house?" with the response "Run's house!"

"Can I Get a Witness." Run-D. M. C.'s albums *Back from Hell* and *Down with the King* reflect the spiritual awakening of the two rappers. In "Can I Get a Witness" from *Down with the King*, the lyrics demonstrate the same themes as "Run's House," particularly the skills of both rappers and warnings to those who are "pretenders to the throne." However, Run's verses feature blatant references to his Christian faith. Like many of the songs on this album, "Can I Get a Witness" features some samples of jazz and blues instrumental figures.

"Just Like Me." The first single from D. M. C.'s solo debut, *Checks, Thugs, and Rock n Roll*, "Just Like Me" features D. M. C.'s rapping and the vocals of Sarah McLaughlin. The background is taken from Harry Chapin's "Cat's in the Cradle," the chorus of which is sung by McLaughlin between D. M. C.'s verses. The song is autobiographical, and it focuses on D. M. C.'s adoption.

Musical Legacy

D. M. C.'s legacy is tied to that of Joseph "Run" Simmons and Jason "Jam Master Jay" Mizell. Run-D. M. C. brought rap and hip-hop music out of the inner city to mainstream listeners, encouraging record companies to promote the music of the streets. The group opened the door for a generation of rappers who followed in their footsteps, including LL Cool J, Ice-T, Will Smith, Eminem, and 50 Cent.

Eric S. Strother

Further Reading

Adler, Bill. *Tougher than Leather: The Rise of Run-D. M. C.* Los Angeles: Consafos, 2002. A look at the tough Queens neighborhood in New York, where the members of Run-D. M. C. lived, and at the birth of rap.

Light, Alan. *The Vibe History of Hip-Hop.* New York: Three Rivers Press. 1999. This thorough history covers the origins of rap and hip-hop, the effect of the regional rivalries on the development of the music, and the money and power generated by the successful artists. Includes numerous references to Run-D. M. C., a discography, and photographs.

McDaniels, Darryl. *King of Rock: Respect, Responsibility, and My Life with Run-D. M. C.* New York: St. Martin's Press, 2001. D. M. C. gives an account of his life, including insights into other artists working in rap and hip-hop. He frankly recounts the struggles the members of Run-D. M. C. had with the abuse of drugs and alcohol. His message, "Maturity is not a matter of age," is reflected in his efforts to move rap beyond its sordid gang, sexual, and misogynistic elements.

See also: 50 Cent; Grandmaster Flash; LL Cool J; Simmons, Joseph "Run."

Roger Daltrey

English rock singer and songwriter

Daltrey is considered the voice of the Who, and his energetic stage presence and powerful interpretations of their music were key elements to the success of the band.

Born: March 1, 1944; Hammersmith, London, England
Also known as: Roger Harry Daltrey (full name)
Member of: The Who

Principal recordings

ALBUMS (solo): *Daltrey*, 1973; *Ride a Rock Horse*, 1975; *One of the Boys*, 1977; *McVicar*, 1980; *Parting Should Be Painless*, 1984; *Under a Raging Moon*, 1985; *Can't Wait to See the Movie*, 1987; *Rocks in the Head*, 1992.

ALBUMS (with the Who): *The Who Sings My Generation*, 1965; *A Quick One*, 1966; *Happy Jack*, 1967; *The Who Sell Out*, 1967; *Magic Bus*, 1968; *Tommy*, 1969; *Who's Next*, 1971; *Quadrophenia*, 1973; *The Who by Numbers*, 1975; *Who Are You*, 1978; *Face Dances*, 1981; *It's Hard*, 1982; *Endless Wire*, 2006.

The Life

Roger Harry Daltrey (DAHL-tree) was born to working-class parents in London, and although he excelled at school, he was a born rebel, and he was expelled. After listening to Elvis Presley, he turned to rock music. Initially he played lead guitar in his band, the Detours, which ultimately included members of the Who: John Entwhistle, Pete Townshend, and Keith Moon. When the band's singer departed, Daltrey took over the vocals and Townshend took over the lead-guitar duties.

Daltrey was notorious for being a controlling taskmaster, reportedly hitting band members with whom he disagreed. As the Who's music developed and Townshend became a prolific songwriter, tensions grew, and the band fired Daltrey in 1965. Later they took back the chastened singer in a subordinate role. As the band's popularity grew, its members becoming international stars, Daltrey's stage antics—his bare chest, his microphone twirl-

ing, and his booming vocals—came to be a centerpiece of shows.

Tensions arose once more, and after the death of drummer Moon, Daltrey was outspoken in his dissatisfaction of Kenny Jones, the replacement drummer. As the band wound down its activities, Daltrey embarked on solo music projects and launched a successful film, stage, and television acting career.

The Music

The Who began as a cover band, specializing in rhythm and blues and attracting a passionate following among fans known as the Mods. The band's early signature song, "My Generation," owes as much to Townshend's lyrics as to Daltrey's unique delivery, a stuttering that perfectly captures adolescent frustration and rage. Over a series of albums, Daltrey developed from a passionate shouter into a more refined singer, interpreting Townshend's material with sensitivity and insight.

Tommy. The apogee of this partnership began with *Tommy*, Townshend's rock opera about a deaf, dumb, and blind boy who unwittingly becomes the leader of a generation. Daltrey so energizes and inhabits the songs that he becomes Tommy, as was clearly evident in director Ken Russell's cinematic interpretation of the opera. The range of Daltrey's expression runs the gamut from the sensitive "See Me, Feel Me," to the ecstatic "I'm Free," to the defiant "We're Not Gonna Take It." The record is a tour de force, as much for Townshend's arrangements and often eloquent lyrics as for Daltrey's impassioned singing.

Who's Next. The partnership grew with *Who's Next*, a mixed collection of songs, some of which were left over from Townshend's aborted *Lifehouse* project, another putative rock opera. By this point the formerly marginalized Daltrey was now a confident lead man, again revealing a breadth of vocal interpretations from the wistful "The Song Is Over" to the anthemic "Won't Get Fooled Again," a song that aggressively appraised the loss of generational ideals and the despondent realization that the status quo is not easily dismantled. Many regard this as a quintessential rock album, and Daltrey is a major part of that success.

Quadrophenia. *Quadrophenia* represented another return to Townshend's operatic aspirations, in this case a personal retrospective about his youth as a Mod and about the frustrations and confusions of adolescent yearnings and confused ambitions. The songs chronicle the life of Jimmy, a melancholic teenager who cannot find a comfortable place in the world, except when he is riding his motor scooter or popping pills. Once again, Daltrey metamorphoses into the protagonist, perfectly capturing adolescent angst and trepidation. He delivers another bravura performance, with energetic rocking in "The Real Me" and "Dr. Jimmy," vulnerable pleading in "Sea and Sand," and elegiac serenity in "Love, Reign o'er Me." So involved was he with the project that in 1996 he reunited with Townshend to perform the opera for a royal Prince's Trust concert in Hyde Park. Later, as the band began its tortured disintegration and moved through some desultory offerings, Daltrey delivered stellar performances with "Squeeze Box," "Who Are You," "You Better You Bet," and "Athena."

McVicar. One of Daltrey's most commercially successful solo albums was *McVicar*, the sound track for a film of the same name starring the singer.

Roger Daltrey. (AP/Wide World Photos)

It included contributions from the other members of the Who, and it produced two hit singles, "Free Me" and "Without Your Love." In 1994, in celebration of his fiftieth birthday, Daltrey performed two shows of Who songs at Carnegie Hall, which led to a tour of the United States.

Later Tours and Albums. In 1996 and 1999 Daltrey rejoined Townshend for Who tours, and in 2001 the band once again re-formed to perform at the Concert for New York, after the September 11 attack on the World Trade Center. The success of that venture led to another tour in 2002, during which Entwhistle died of a drug overdose. In 2006 Daltrey and Townshend, along with other musicians, released the first new Who album in twenty-four years, *Endless Wire*.

Musical Legacy

While the success of the Who was always a group effort, Daltrey provided unique vocals and extraordinary stage presence that were essential to the band's long and popular career. A key element of the band's longevity, in spite of all the turmoil and clashes of will, was the magical, hypnotic connection between Townshend and Daltrey. On a number of occasions Townshend admitted that without Daltrey there would be no Who, since no one else was capable of interpreting Townshend's material the way the singer does.

Daltrey became one of rock music's iconic front men, handsome, swaggering, and confident. His work extended into other musical idioms, such as traditional Irish music with the Chieftains, with whom he won a Grammy Award in 1991 for *An Irish Evening: Live at the Grand Opera House*. Daltrey was also extremely supportive of various charities, for which he was given a Commander of the Order of the British Empire for services to music, the entertainment industry, and charity.

David W. Madden

Further Reading

Barnes, Richard. *The Who: Maximum Rhythm and Blues*. London: Plexus, 2004. Examines the development of the band and analyzes the successes and controversies that have affected individual members.

Ewbank, Tim. *Roger Daltrey: The Biography*. London: Portrait Books, 2006. A full-length biography of

Daltrey, placing him in the context of rock history.

Hearn, Marcus. *The Who (Rex Collections)*. Surrey, England: Reynolds & Hearn, 2005. Traces the band's history from its origins to the summer of 2005. Includes impressive photographs.

Marsh, Dave. *Before I Get Old: The Story of the Who*. London: Plexus, 2003. Excellent assessment of the band and individual members by a prolific music critic.

Neill, Andrew, and Matthew Kent. *Anyway, Anyhow, Anywhere: The Complete Chronicle of the Who, 1958-1978*. London: Sterling, 2005. With a foreword by Daltrey, this is a day-to-day diary that chronicles the formation and development of the band.

See also: Morrison, Jim; Plant, Robert; Presley, Elvis; Strummer, Joe; Townshend, Pete.

Hal David

American film and musical-theater composer/lyricist

Best known for his collaboration with composer Burt Bacharach, with whom he wrote dozens of top hits of the 1960's and 1970's, David also wrote lyrics for songs in the big band and country-music genres.

Born: May 25, 1921; New York, New York

Principal works

MUSICAL THEATER (lyrics): *Promises, Promises*, 1968 (libretto by Neil Simon; music by Burt Bacharach); *The Look of Love*, 2003 (libretto by David Thompson; music by Bacharach).

SONGS (written with Burt Bacharach): "The Story of My Life," 1957 (recorded by Marty Robbins); "Magic Moments," 1958 (recorded by Perry Como); "The Night That Heaven Fell," 1958 (recorded by Tony Bennett); "Loving Is a Way of Living," 1959 (recorded by Steve Lawrence); "I Could Make You Mine," 1960 (recorded by the Wanderers); "Gotta Get a Girl," 1961 (recorded by Frankie Avalon); "Don't Make Me Over," 1963 (recorded by Dionne Warwick); "Anyone Who Had a Heart," 1964 (recorded by Warwick); "Send Me No Flowers," 1964 (Doris Day); "(There's) Always Something There to Remind Me," 1964 (recorded by Lou Johnson); "Walk on By," 1964 (recorded by Warwick); "I Say a Little Prayer," 1965 (recorded by Jackie DeShannon); "Make It Easy on Yourself," 1965 (recorded by Warwick); "What the World Needs Now Is Love," 1965 (recorded by DeShannon); "What's New Pussycat?" 1965 (recorded by Tom Jones); "Alfie," 1966 (recorded by Warwick); "Promise Her Anything," 1966 (recorded by Jones); "The Look of Love," 1967 (recorded by Dusty Springfield); "Do You Know the Way to San Jose," 1968 (recorded by Warwick); "Don't Go Breakin' My Heart," 1968 (recorded by Johnny Mathis); "I'll Never Fall in Love Again," 1968 (recorded by Warwick); "This Guy's in Love with You," 1968 (recorded by Herb Alpert); "Raindrops Keep Fallin' on My Head," 1969 (recorded by B. J. Thomas); "One Less Bell to Answer," 1970 (recorded by the Fifth Dimension); "(They Long to Be) Close to You," 1970 (recorded by the Carpenters).

SONGS: "The Four Winds and the Seven Seas," 1949 (with Don Rodney; recorded by Vic Damone); "The Good Times Are Comin'," 1970 (with John Barry; recorded by Mama Cass Elliot); "Ninety-Nine Miles from L.A.," 1975 (with Albert Hammond; recorded by Art Garfunkel); "Almost Like a Song," 1977 (with Archie Jordan; recorded by Ronnie Milsap); "To All the Girls I've Loved Before," 1984 (with Hammond; recorded by Willie Nelson and Julio Iglesias).

The Life

Hal David was the youngest of three sons born to Gedalier David, owner and operator of a delicatessen on Pennsylvania Avenue in Brooklyn, and his wife Lina Goldberg. Though his parents wanted him to be a musician, and his older brother Mack was already writing songs for Tin Pan Alley by the time David was a teenager, David decided to study journalism at New York University. A summer internship in his sophomore year led to a job offer at the *New York Post*. However, when the United States entered World War II, David was drafted, and he was assigned to an entertainment section of Special Services in Hawaii, where he wrote comedy sketches and song lyrics for shows with fellow soldier Carl Reiner, who became a television comedy writer.

After the war, David went to Broadway, but he did not find success until bandleader Sammy Kaye bought "Isn't This Better than Working in the Rain" in 1947 and hired David for his radio show. That Christmas Eve David married schoolteacher Anne Rauchmann. His first hit came in 1949 with "The Four Winds and the Seven Seas," a folksy ballad cowritten with bandleader Guy Lombardo's vocalist Don Rodney. After a string of minor successes, David met composer Burt Bacharach in 1957, and a classic partnership began.

The Music

While his hit-making is popularly linked with Bacharach, David wrote successful lyrics before and after his Bacharach partnership. His first hit with Bacharach was not on the Top 40 pop charts but rather on the country-western charts. "The Story of My Life" hit big for Marty Robbins in 1957. After his success with Bacharach, David would return to country music, and in 1984 he was inducted into the Nashville Songwriters Hall of Fame. The Bacharach-David team scored again with "Magic Moments" for Perry Como in February of 1958. However, it was their collaboration with singer Dionne Warwick that brought Bacharach and David their biggest success.

"What the World Needs Now Is Love." This 1965 hit is David's favorite example of "slow growth" in the creative process and making the lyric fit the mood. The main idea and phrase, "What the world needs now is love," came immediately to him, and then he built the first stanza around it. Then he wanted to contrast the idea with a list of what the world does not need. At first, David listed airplanes and other technological boons, but none of those fit the mood. He put away the lyric for several years, until Jackie DeShannon was looking for an inspirational song. David pulled out the song, intuitively realizing that the contrary elements should be from the natural world. DeShannon recorded the hit version in 1965, but David's personal favorite was Warwick's 1971 recording. It has been covered by several pop and country stars, including Barry Manilow, Wynona Judd, Ed Ames, and the Supremes. Warwick remarked that this song should be a second national anthem.

"Make It Easy on Yourself." David had an astonishing twenty-one Top 40 hits recorded by Warwick throughout the 1960's. David and Bacharach had written "Make It Easy on Yourself" for Warwick, but the more established vocalist Jerry Butler heard her demo, liked it, and recorded his own version first, which went to number twenty. Angry at what she saw as betrayal by the songwriters, Warwick told them, "Don't make me over, man!" David had never heard the idiom, which means "don't try to cheat me," and he turned it into a song for Warwick, which made peace between them—especially when it became a Top 40 hit, peaking at number twenty-five on the *Billboard* Hot 100 and going all the way to number five on the rhythm-and-blues charts. There were multiple Bacharach-David hits for Warwick in the 1960's, and ironically the string ended in 1970 with "Make It Easy on Yourself"—the song that should have been Warwick's first hit. It did not climb as high as the Butler version on the *Billboard* Hot 100, but it reached number two on the rhythm-and-blues charts.

Country-Western. After the Bacharach-David partnership broke up over the failure, artistically and financially, of a film they had scored (*Lost Horizon* in 1972), David wrote a number of country-western hits with various composers. His 1977 "Almost Like a Song" (with music by Archie Jordan) rose to the top spot on the country charts for Ronnie Milsap, and it became a crossover hit in the adult contemporary category, where it hit number seven. Another crossover hit was recorded by the unconventional duo of operatic tenor Julio Iglesias and country superstar Willie Nelson. Written by David with Albert Hammond, "To All the Girls I've Loved Before" reached the top of the country charts in May, 1984, and peaked at number five on the *Billboard* Hot 100.

Musical Legacy

One measure of David's influence on the recording industry is his leadership in its professional organizations. From 1980 to 1986, he served as president of the American Society of Composers, Authors, and Publishers (ASCAP), and in 2008 he served on its board of directors. In 1998 he became chairman of the board of the National Academy of Popular Music, which oversees the Songwriters Hall of Fame, and he continued in the chair for more than a decade. In 1969 David and Bacharach won an Academy Award for Best Song for "Raindrops Keep Fallin' on My Head," from *Butch Cassidy and the Sundance Kid* (1969). Three David songs— "Don't Make Me Over," "(They Want to Be) Close to You," and "Walk on By"—are in the Grammy Hall of Fame (a designation for songs at least twenty-five years old with "qualitative or historical significance").

John R. Holmes

Further Reading

David, Hal. *What the World Needs Now and Other Love Lyrics.* New York: Trident Press, 1968. David gives the lyrics to sixty-two of his hit songs, and they are liberally annotated with background stories.

Friedlander, Paul. *Rock and Roll: A Social History.* 2d ed. Boulder, Colo.: Westview Press, 2006. While this general history specifically focuses on the rock idiom, which was not the category in which David placed his lyrics, it is a good introduction to the musical milieu in which David created his most enduring work.

Platts, Robin. *Burt Bacharach and Hal David: What the World Needs Now.* New York: Collector's Guide, 2003. Although this is primarily a discography and a guide for collectors of David-Bacharach material, this book also includes a substantial biography of both David and Bacharach.

Pollock, Bruce. *In Their Own Words.* New York: Collier Books, 1975. This series of interviews with rock songwriters of the 1960's is prefaced by an interview with David, billed as a transitional figure from the big band era to the 1960's.

Toop, David. *Exotica.* New York: Serpent's Tale, 1999. While this book canvasses exotic music, avoiding the Top 40 material that made David's career, Toop includes a revealing interview with Bacharach discussing his work with David.

See also: Alpert, Herb; Bacharach, Burt; Carpenter, Karen; Elliot, Cass; Garfunkel, Art; Iglesias, Julio; Mathis, Johnny; Milsap, Ronnie; Nelson, Willie; Warwick, Dionne.

Ray Davies

English singer, guitarist, and songwriter

Davies was the leader, singer, and songwriter of the Kinks, one of the most innovative of the British Invasion bands.

Born: June 21, 1944; London, England
Also known as: Raymond Douglas Davies (full name)
Member of: The Kinks

Principal recordings

ALBUMS (solo): *Return to Waterloo*, 1985; *The Storyteller*, 1998; *Other People's Lives*, 2006.

ALBUMS (with the Kinks): *You Really Got Me*, 1964; *Kinda Kinks*, 1965; *The Kink Kontroversy*, 1965; *Face to Face*, 1966; *Something Else*, 1967; *The Kinks Are the Village Green Preservation Society*, 1968; *Arthur: Or, The Decline and Fall of the British Empire*, 1969; *Lola Versus Powerman and the Moneygoround*, 1970; *Muswell Hillbillies*, 1971; *Everybody's in Show-Biz*, 1972; *Preservation, Act I*, 1973; *Preservation, Act II*, 1974; *Schoolboys in Disgrace*, 1975; *Soap Opera*, 1975; *Sleepwalker*, 1977; *Misfits*, 1978; *Low Budget*, 1979; *One for the Road*, 1980; *Give the People What They Want*, 1981; *State of Confusion*, 1983; *Word of Mouth*, 1984; *Think Visual*, 1986; *U.K. Jive*, 1989; *Phobia*, 1993; *To the Bone*, 1996.

WRITINGS OF INTEREST: *X-Ray*, 1994 (autobiography).

The Life

Raymond Douglas Davies was born in a north London working-class district, one of eight children. Davies briefly attended art college, and he then turned to music, playing in jazz bands until he joined his younger brother, Dave (David Russell Gordon Davies), to play rock and roll. Initially known as the Ravens, they changed their name in 1963 to the Kinks, and they scored a huge hit with "You Really Got Me," which topped the British charts and went to number seven in the United States. A string of other popular songs followed, all written by Davies, that established the band as one of the most popular and prolific of the 1960's.

The Kinks produced twenty-three albums over the next three decades, and when their popularity waned in England, they continued to be a major draw in the United States, where their records continued to sell well. In 1990 Davies and the band were inducted into the Rock and Roll Hall of Fame and into England's Music Hall of Fame in 2005. In 2003 he was named a Commander of the British Empire, and shortly thereafter he was shot in the leg by a mugger while visiting a nephew in New Orleans. After the dissolution of the Kinks in 1996, he released several solo albums.

The Music

The Kinks' first two American albums contained some original material, but they also relied upon cover versions of others' songs. Their third album, *The Kink Kontroversy*, included only one cover song (an inspired version of "Milk Cow Blues"), and

Davies compositions, which were tuneful as well as considerably thoughtful. *Face to Face* came after Davies had suffered a nervous breakdown, which he commented on in the sardonic "Sunny Afternoon," and the album included a number of songs of social commentary that would characterize his songwriting throughout his career.

Something Else *and* Concept Albums. *Something Else* continued in the same vein, with songs that moved completely away from the band's hard-rocking early efforts and into an increasingly meditative strain. "Waterloo Sunset," the album's highlight, is considered one of Davies's most beautiful songs. Their next album, *The Kinks Are the Village Green Preservation Society*, was an early concept album built around nostalgic reflections on village life, and it sold poorly. Some criticized the album for its sentimentality, though in later years it has come to be regarded as one of the band's best. *Ar-*

Ray Davies. (AP/Wide World Photos)

thur: Or, The Decline and Fall of the British Empire, originally written as the sound track for an unreleased television play, stands as another concept album, inspired by Davies's, his sister's, and his brother-in-law's emigration to Australia, and it was a critical success.

Lola Versus Powerman and the Moneygoround. *Lola Versus Powerman and the Moneygoround* was Davies's ironic look at the music industry, which he believed had not treated him and the band well. The songs were the most varied of any album up to that point, and it produced the huge hit, "Lola," a mainstay of the Kinks' live shows. After this success, the band switched labels, produced one excellent album that observed their working-class origins (*Muswell Hillbillies*), and then embarked on a series of ill-fated concept albums that offered little in the way of serious music.

Sleepwalker *and* the 1980's. With the release of *Sleepwalker* on yet another new label, the band regained some of its vigor. Gone were the self-conscious concepts and tired performances, as Davies reflected seriously on his career and musical ambitions. *Misfits*, an upbeat work, featured ironic lyrics and an excellent single, "A Rock 'n' Roll Fantasy." *Low Budget* was a strong effort, which found the band playing with renewed energy and which reestablished it as a determinedly rock band. *Low Budget* earned the band its first gold record since the 1960's. A second gold record followed in 1980 with the live recording *One for the Road*.

In the 1980's the band was writing and playing almost exclusively for an American audience, their sound streamlined and punchy. Albums such as *Give the People What They Want*, *State of Confusion*, *Word of Mouth*, and *Think Visual* produced modest radio successes, and they kept the band on the road and in the public eye. Although none of these matched their earlier efforts, many good songs were collected for *Come Dancing with the Kinks*.

To the Bone *and* Solo Works. *To the Bone*, a twenty-nine-song retrospective that includes two excellent new compositions, was recorded just before the Kinks split. After disbanding the group, Davies started a solo tour when his autobiography was published, reading excerpts, then playing various songs, which were collected on the album *The Storyteller*. The success of that show led VH1 to create a series titled *Storytellers*, on which artists would

play selected songs and reminisce about their careers. Another solo album, *Other People's Lives*, appeared in 2006.

Musical Legacy

Davies crafted a remarkable musical career out of an astounding catalog of songs that deal with frustration, social commentary, cultural decay, and a flinty appreciation for the past and traditions. His song "Twentieth Century Man" is a deeply personal anthem of a man trapped in a modern world he finds depraved. Although Davies often betrays his deep emotions, his songs are rarely maudlin, and they are frequently marked by an astringent sense of irony.

Rock musicians have paid tribute to the Kinks for the visceral appeal of their early songs, some even contending that the concept of power chords originated with the band. Davies's sense of theatricality led to many experiments and concept albums, and in the 1970's the group often toured in costume, not only playing music but also acting out the dramas Davies had created. In his songs, Davies has continually denounced power, corruption, and commercialism, always championing the outsider, the iconoclast, and the forgotten. For these reasons, he has been extolled as a rocker with a conscience.

David W. Madden

Further Reading

Davies, Dave. *Kink: An Autobiography*. New York: Hyperion, 1998. Written in response to his brother's autobiography, Davies reveals alternate views of the band and his older brother, who cast such a broad shadow.

Davies, Ray. *X-Ray*. Woodstock, N.Y.: Overlook Press, 1996. An imaginative, often hilarious, look into Ray Davies's life, his inspirations, and his creative ambitions. Full of revealing insights into the band, its inception, its leader's often ambivalent attitudes toward his mates, and its dealings with the music industry.

Marten, Neville, and Jeff Hudson. *The Kinks*. London: Sanctuary, 2001. An authoritative look at the band, revealing details about each member (with a focus on Ray Davies) and about the band's development.

Mendelssohn, John. *The Kinks Kronikles*. New York: Morrow, 1984. The first biography of the band by a journalist who had followed the band for years. Without the cooperation of the band members, the writer relied on band associates for much of his information. Mendelssohn praises the band's early work, but he is a critic of its later efforts in the 1980's.

Savage, Jon. *Kinks: The Official Biography.* London: Faber & Faber, 1985. A straightforward, though superficial, examination of the band and its principal members. Savage gained the band's cooperation in preparing the book, but he is not always successful in exploring personalities or presenting details.

See also: Costello, Elvis; Hynde, Chrissie; Jagger, Sir Mick; Lennon, John; McCartney, Sir Paul; Strummer, Joe.

Miles Davis

American jazz composer and trumpet player

An important figure in jazz, Davis became famous for his trumpet playing, which managed to convey sensitivity and thoughtfulness. In addition, he was influential as a bandleader, with a striking ability to put together highly creative groups of musicians.

Born: May 26, 1926; Alton, Illinois
Died: September 28, 1991; Santa Monica, California
Also known as: Miles Dewey Davis III (full name)
Member of: The Miles Davis Quintet; the Second Quintet

Principal recordings

ALBUMS (solo): *Birth of the Cool*, 1949; *Blue Period*, 1951; *Conception*, 1951 (with Stan Getz); *Diggin'*, 1951; *The New Sounds of Miles Davis*, 1951; *Blue Haze*, 1953; *Miles Davis Quartet*, 1953 (with Miles Davis Quartet); *Bags' Groove*, 1954 (with Modern Jazz Giants); *Miles Davis and the Modern Jazz Giants*, 1954 (with Modern Jazz Giants); *Walkin'*, 1954 (with others); *Miles Davis and Horns, '51-'53*, 1955; *Miles Davis and Milt Jackson Quintet/Sextet*, 1955 (with Milt Jackson); *Miles Ahead*, 1957 (with Gil Evans); *Milestones*, 1958; *Porgy and Bess*, 1958 (with Evans); *Kind of Blue*, 1959; *Sketches of Spain*, 1959; *Someday My Prince Will Come*, 1961; *Quiet Nights*, 1962 (with Evans); *The Man with the Horn*, 1981; *Star People*, 1982; *Decoy*, 1983; *Aura*, 1985; *You're Under Arrest*, 1985; *Tutu*, 1986; *Music from Siesta*, 1987; *Amandla*, 1989; *Bags' Groove*, 1990; *Dingo*, 1990 (with Michel Legrand); *Miles and Horns*, 1990; *Doo-Bop*, 1991.

ALBUMS (with the Miles Davis Quintet): *Miles Davis Quintet*, 1954; *The Musings of Miles*, 1955; *The New Miles Davis Quintet*, 1955; *Round About Midnight*, 1955; *Cookin'*, 1956; *Relaxin'*, 1956; *Steamin'*, 1956; *Workin'*, 1956; *Seven Steps to Heaven*, 1963; *E. S. P.*, 1965; *Miles Smiles*, 1966; *Nefertiti*, 1967; *Sorcerer*, 1967; *Water Babies*, 1967; *Filles de Kilimanjaro*, 1968; *Miles in the Sky*, 1968; *Big Fun*, 1969; *Bitches Brew*, 1969; *In a Silent Way*, 1969; *Live-Evil*, 1970; *A Tribute to Jack Johnson*, 1970; *Get Up with It*, 1972; *On the Corner*, 1972.

The Life

Miles Dewey Davis III grew up in East St. Louis, Illinois, in a middle-class African American family. His father was a respected dentist, and his mother was a capable violinist and pianist. Davis took up the trumpet at the age of nine or ten, beginning lessons with a teacher from the local school district. By the time Davis was sixteen, he was playing professionally around St. Louis. At the age of eighteen, he moved to New York, ostensibly to study at the Juilliard School, but he soon teamed up with his musical idol, Charlie Parker. Davis shared a room briefly with Parker, and Davis began to play in Parker's quintet as well as in other combos and big bands. In the early 1950's, Davis became addicted to heroin. Although he made several recordings for the Prestige label, his work suffered, he became unreliable, and he resorted to pimping and to theft. He reported that he felt himself "sinking . . . toward death." He went back to his parents' house, got off drugs completely, and in 1954 he returned to New York in good health and fully focused on his music.

Davis's comeback was marked by a notable appearance at the Newport Jazz Festival in 1955. As a

Miles Davis. (AP/Wide World Photos)

entirely from performing, living a reclusive existence, listening to music, taking up painting, and indulging in alcohol, cigarettes, and drugs. In 1980 he began to record again, and in 1981 he returned to touring. During this last period of his life, Davis enjoyed his popularity, almost worshipped by his fans and admired by his fellow musicians.

Davis's personal life was revealed in his autobiography and in several biographies. He was a difficult man, abusive to his wives, and an unreliable father to his children. In terms of his musical accomplishments, he is regarded as one of the most creative and influential jazz musicians. After a stroke, Davis died at the age of sixty-five of respiratory failure.

The Music

Davis lived during an active time in jazz history, when musical styles were changing radically every few years. Remarkably, Davis was responsible for many of the stylistic shifts. He despised repetition, and he was constantly reinventing himself and his music. From bop, to cool, to hard bop, to modal, to post-bop and fusion, Davis was either associated with the change or single-handedly introduced it. His trumpet skills were not virtuosic. He preferred a straight vibratoless tone, and he tended to play mostly in the middle register of the instrument. His improvisations were epigrammatic, relying on an expressive use of pauses and silence. After moving to New York, he began playing in a small bebop combo with Parker, whose jazz improvisations were legendary. Early recordings show Davis to be a nervous and uncertain trumpeter playing next to Parker, a saxophone player nearing the height of his powers. By 1949, however, Davis had gained enough musical maturity to be asked to form a temporary group, which, under the guidance of skilled composer and arranger Gil Evans, ultimately recorded twelve sides. A few years later, these became known collectively as the *Birth of the Cool*. After his comeback in the mid-1950's, Davis began to focus on a new technique, in which he played close to the microphone through a Harmon mute without the central stem, creating a sound that was both expressive and intimate. Some of the recordings from this time demonstrate Davis's new

result, Davis was signed to Columbia Records, a company that had money to spend on production and on advertising. New projects included quintet and sextet recordings and some orchestral records in arrangements by Gil Evans. He became a recognizable figure. In 1959 he released one of his most famous recordings, *Kind of Blue*.

In the early 1960's, Davis's life was troubled by illness, by the death of his parents, by another marital failure, and by uncertainty about his own music. Gradually, Davis managed to form a new group, one made up of younger players, which became known as the Second Quintet. It toured widely and produced several recordings. From 1968 to 1975, Davis was involved in jazz-rock fusion. Because of the popularity and greatly enhanced sales of Davis's recordings in this style, he was called variously a visionary and a sell-out.

From the mid-1970's until 1980, Davis withdrew

path, a funky kind of blues known as hard bop. In the late 1950's, new projects included several quintet recordings with Davis's principal foil, John Coltrane, on tenor saxophone, and some orchestral records, with Davis primary in a large group of players in arrangements by Evans. The best of these are *Miles Ahead*, *Porgy and Bess*, and *Sketches of Spain*. Perhaps the most influential recording was the classic *Kind of Blue*.

With his Second Quintet in the mid-1960's, Davis forged flexible and free music known as post-bop. By the late 1960's, Davis took another direction, melding rock music and jazz in fusion. Among Davis's last recordings was a move in the direction of the latest musical trend, toward jazz versions of pop tunes and incorporations of rap music. The recordings of his last ten years were culled by his longtime producer, Teo Macero, from hours of free-flowing performances, involving many players and with Davis's horn fitted out with a microphone and attached electronically to a wah-wah pedal. Critics are strongly divided about the musical quality of these recordings. Davis often attached his own name to compositions by his sidemen, so which pieces are indisputably his is unclear. Nevertheless, several compositions attributed to him have become jazz standards.

Birth of the Cool. These twelve sides from recording sessions in 1949 evoke a new sound—smoother, more contrapuntal, more arranged, and less frenetic than bop—with a nine-piece band made up of only one instrument on each part and weighted toward the mellow range of the sound spectrum. Notable tracks include "Move," "Deception," and "Boplicity."

"Walkin'," "Oleo," and "Bags' Groove." These quintet tracks, whose new expansiveness was made possible by the introduction in the early 1950's of the long-playing record, are trailblazers of the hard bop style—more bluesy, simpler, and catchier than bebop and cool jazz.

Kind of Blue. For this album, the standard quintet group was joined by Julian "Cannonball" Adderley on alto saxophone and by the lyrical and expressive Bill Evans on piano. The new style was later named modal jazz, with its long stretches of unchanging harmony and its unusual scales. The music is moody and introspective. There is one of the most famous albums in the history of jazz.

Miles Smiles. The Second Quintet, with Wayne Shorter (tenor saxophone), Herbie Hancock (piano), Ron Carter (bass), and Tony Williams (drums), toured widely, and it made several recordings in Davis's new approach to the musical possibilities in jazz: post-bop. This flexible style incorporated elements of modal jazz and free jazz, with more balanced and interactive roles among the participants.

In a Silent Way *and* Bitches Brew. These albums were Davis's new challenge to jazz (or capitulation to rock). The music incorporates the bass-heavy, repetitive riffs and electric instruments (particularly bass and keyboard) of rock music, over which Davis improvises with originality and flair. His groups expanded to include a constantly changing mix of participants, including John McLaughlin, Chick Corea, Keith Jarrett, Joe Zawinul, Dave Holland, and others, many of whom went on to form their own fusion groups.

Doo-Bop. Released posthumously, this album features Davis collaborating with rap producer Easy Mo Bee. The instrumental numbers are strong and inventive, though the rapping on the vocal tracks is weak. The experiment shows that Davis never lost his enthusiasm for new music.

Musical Legacy

Davis was far more than a trumpet player: He once said that the trumpet was "just a tool . . . a magic wand." He possessed an uncanny ability to envision significant stylistic shifts in jazz and to make them happen, partly by utilizing his sheer creativity, insight, and ego and partly by putting together groups of musicians who inspired him and each other to play at the top of their abilities. Davis was single-handedly responsible for moving bebop toward cool and then hard bop. He invented (with Bill Evans) modal jazz and (with the Second Quintet) the post-bop style. Finally, he was responsible for creating new styles that merged jazz and rock, jazz and pop, and jazz and rap. His personal style, his intensity, and his signature sound on his muted trumpet influenced generations of jazz musicians. With his remarkable skill in forging new directions for music, he changed the way musicians and listeners regarded jazz.

Jeremy Yudkin

Further Reading

Carr, Ian. *Miles Davis: The Definitive Biography*. Rev. ed. New York: Thunder's Mouth, 1998. The author, a trumpet player, offers a thorough account of Davis's life, with general discussions of albums, a detailed discography, and insightful comments on Davis's playing.

Chambers, Jack. *Milestones: The Music and Times of Miles Davis*. New York: Da Capo, 1998. This full-length biography of Davis gives detailed and thorough discussions of recordings, organized by studio dates.

Cook, Richard. *It's About That Time: Miles Davis On and Off Record*. New York: Oxford University Press, 2005. This source presents a systematic discussion of Davis's recordings.

Davis, Miles, with Quincy Troupe. *Miles: The Autobiography*. New York: Simon & Schuster, 1989. A detailed and unsparing autobiography contains important insights into Davis's views on his life, his music, and that of other musicians.

Tingen, Paul. *Miles Beyond: The Electric Explorations of Miles Davis, 1967-1991*. New York: Billboard, 2003. A thoughtful and sympathetic review of the electric period of Davis's work, from 1967 until his death. With more than fifty interviews, this resource passionately defends the seriousness of Davis's work in this sometimes controversial genre.

Yudkin, Jeremy. *Miles Davis, Miles Smiles, and the Invention of Post-Bop*. Bloomington: Indiana University Press, 2008. A survey of Davis's career and discussions of his best tracks from the late 1940's to the mid-1960's. Includes an analysis of the post-bop album *Miles Smiles* and pinpoints the musical elements of cool, hard bop, modal, and post-bop styles.

See also: Adderley, Cannonball; Alpert, Herb; Belafonte, Harry; Burton, Gary; Carter, Benny; Coltrane, John; Corea, Chick; Evans, Bill; Getz, Stan; Hancock, Herbie; Hawkins, Coleman; Jarrett, Keith; Jones, Elvin; Jones, Hank; Jones, Quincy; Legrand, Michel; Marsalis, Wynton; Montgomery, Wes; Parker, Charlie; Roach, Max; Rollins, Sonny; Shorter, Wayne; Slick, Grace; Stone, Sly; Young, Lester.

Sammy Davis, Jr.

American jazz and popular music singer

Davis's many performances in Las Vegas and nightclubs around the country, as well as his membership in Frank Sinatra's famous Rat Pack, served to make white audiences more accepting of black entertainers. African American entertainers such as Ben Vereen, Gregory Hines, and Michael Jackson would owe much of their success to Davis's trailblazing career.

Born: December 8, 1925; New York, New York
Died: May 16, 1990; Beverly Hills, California
Also known as: Samuel George Davis, Jr. (full name)
Member of: The Will Mastin Trio

Principal recordings

ALBUMS: *Just for Lovers*, 1955; *Starring Sammy Davis, Jr.*, 1955; *Here's Looking at You*, 1956; *Boy Meets Girl*, 1957 (with Carmen McRae); *Sammy Swings*, 1957; *Mood to be Wooed*, 1958; *Porgy and Bess*, 1959; *Sammy Davis Jr., at Town Hall*, 1959; *I Got a Right to Swing*, 1960; *Sammy Awards*, 1960; *Wham of Sam*, 1961; *All-Star Spectacular*, 1962; *Belts the Best of Broadway*, 1962; *As Long as She Needs Me*, 1963; *Forget-Me-Nots for First Nighters*, 1963; *California Suite*, 1964; *Salutes the Stars of the London Palladium*, 1964; *The Shelter of Your Arms*, 1964; *Sings the Big Ones for Young Lovers*, 1964; *If I Ruled the World*, 1965; *The Nat King Cole Songbook*, 1965; *Our Shining Hour*, 1965 (with Count Basie); *Sammy's Back on Broadway*, 1965; *Try a Little Tenderness*, 1965; *The Sammy Davis, Jr. Show*, 1966; *Sammy Davis, Jr. Sings and Laurindo Almeida Plays*, 1966 (with Laurindo Almeida); *Sammy Davis, Jr. Sings the Complete Dr. Doolittle*, 1967; *I've Gotta Be Me*, 1968; *Lonely Is the Name*, 1968; *The Goin's Great*, 1969; *Something for Everyone*, 1970; *Portrait of Sammy Davis, Jr.*, 1972; *Sammy Davis, Jr. Now*, 1972; *Sammy Davis, Jr.*, 1984.

WRITINGS OF INTEREST: *Yes I Can*, 1965; *Why Me?*, 1989.

The Life

The parents of Samuel George Davis, Jr., were vaudeville dancers who separated when he was three. Davis's father taught him to dance, and the boy also learned to play several instruments. Together with Davis, Sr.'s friend Will Mastin, they formed the Will Mastin Trio, which Sammy included in his billing through much of his career. Davis was drafted into the army during World War II, where he served in an entertainment unit and where, for the first time, he also encountered widespread racism. After the war he again joined his father and Mastin to tour the country playing nightclubs. Davis lost his left eye in an automobile accident in 1954, which led to his conversion to Judaism.

The five-foot three-inch Davis began to gain nationwide prominence in the 1950's. His first single, "Hey There," from the musical *Pajama Game* (1954), was a success. In 1959 he joined Frank Sinatra's group of buddies and performers, which the press had dubbed the Rat Pack. Davis made several films with the group and often performed with them in Las Vegas, where he was the headliner at the Frontier Casino.

Davis played an important role in the Civil Rights movement. His political activity attracted controversy when he was snubbed by John F. Kennedy over his marriage to a white woman, the Swedish actress May Britt, and again when he endorsed Richard Nixon for president in 1972. Throughout his life, he fought not only this sort of overt racism but also a subtler form of racism, in that he was often the victim of tokenism as a highly intelligent, articulate, and multitalented African American who found himself touted as a positive example by well-meaning but insensitive whites.

Davis, who smoked six packs of cigarettes per day and struggled with alcohol and drugs, died of throat cancer in 1990. A nation that had witnessed the Civil Rights movement, the decline of segregation, and the beginnings of a transformation in race relations, deeply mourned his death.

The Music

The arc of Davis's career encompassed four periods: his early career as he made a name for himself in clubs and Las Vegas, the years during which he starred in the Rat Pack films and two Broadway musicals, a period of decline brought on in part by Davis's addiction to drugs and alcohol, and his final years, when new audiences cheered his now classic performances of "Mr. Bojangles" and "The Candy Man." The focus here is on his heyday on Broadway, though he later became equally well known for playing the role of Big Daddy Brubeck singing "Rhythm of Life" in Bob Fosse's *Sweet Charity* (1968), along with performances on many television variety shows. A film of Davis performing when he was sixty—only a few years before his death—shows that his singing, dancing, and impersonation skills were as strong as they had been thirty years earlier.

Mr. Wonderful. Composer Jule Styne (later famous for his 1964 musical *Funny Girl*) conceived this 1956 musical about a young New York entertainer who eventually makes it big at a Palm Beach nightclub. The musical was a vehicle to show off Davis's talents, but composer Jerry Bock, who would go on to write *Fiorello!* (1959) and *Fiddler on the Roof* (1964), wrote the songs in his first full score for Broadway. Davis's supporting cast were given most of the songs designed to move the weak plot along, because Davis had little prior acting experience. In "Without You I'm Nothing," however, he was able to display his formidable impersonation skills. Davis's big number from the show, which he included in many of his subsequent nightclub and television performances, was "Too Close for Comfort." The title song was recorded by Sarah Vaughan and Peggy Lee.

Golden Boy. By the time this 1964 musical (based on Clifford Odets's acclaimed 1937 play) was created for Davis, with songs by Charles Strouse and Lee Adams, Davis had honed his acting skills in the Rat Pack pictures. The last, the musical *Robin and the Seven Hoods* (1964), premiered the same year as this musical.

Golden Boy tells the tragic story of young boxer, Joe Wellington (Davis), as he is groomed for success by a white promoter, but he loses his love and ultimately his life in the process. The songs for Davis's second musical have a harder edge than those for *Mr. Wonderful*, reflecting the bitter tone of the plot. The protagonist in Odets's play had been Italian; the racial elements were added for Davis and to make the material relevant to Civil Rights era America. Davis's falling in love with a white woman was a shocking subject for a musical in 1964, although most audiences knew of his marriage to Britt. None of the songs was a major hit, although Davis's performance of "Night Song" prompted a later recording by Sarah Vaughan.

Porgy and Bess. Davis's first film appearance was at the age of seven, when he sang and danced in the twenty-one-minute film *Rufus Jones for President* (1933), with Ethel Waters. His first major film role was as Sportin' Life in director Otto Preminger's troubled 1959 production of George Gershwin's *Porgy and Bess* (1935), costarring Sidney Poitier and Dorothy Dandridge. Cab Calloway sang Davis's songs on the long-playing recording because of contractual conflicts, but a television performance of Davis singing "There's a Boat Dat's Leavin' Soon for New York" was later recorded on DVD in a compilation of Davis performances.

Musical Legacy

Davis was a consummate performer who lived to go on stage and be cheered by an audience. Few performers in his own era or today have matched his ability to sing, dance, play musical instruments, and do dead-on impersonations. Davis possessed a technically remarkable tenor voice; although he never created a distinctive or innovative vocal style, as did singers such as Sinatra and Vaughan, his ability to tell a story in delivering his many signature tunes, such as "Mr. Bo Jangles," moved audiences deeply.

Davis's contribution lay in breaking through the color barrier for black performers in the 1950's and 1960's, becoming the most popular nightclub performer of his era next to Sinatra. Davis was nominated for a Tony for *Golden Boy* and was an honoree at the Kennedy Center Honors in 1987. Equally important to him were his awards from the National Association for the Advancement of Colored People (NAACP) in 1968 and 1989. When Davis died, Las Vegas turned off the lights on The Strip for ten minutes in his honor.

David E. Anderson

Further Reading

Davis, Sammy, Jr., Jane Boyar, and Burt Boyar. *Sammy: The Autobiography of Sammy Davis, Jr.* New York: Farrar, Straus and Giroux, 2000. Burt Boyar revised Davis's two volumes of autobiography, *Yes I Can* (1965) and *Why Me?* (1989), and added new material for this one-volume survey of the singer-actor-activist's extraordinary life.

Davis, Tracey, and Dolores A. Barclay. *Sammy Davis Jr.: My Father*. Los Angeles: General, 1996. Davis's daughter by his second wife, actress May Britt, fleshes out her father's account of his later career, including the poignant story of their reconciliation a year before his death.

Fishgall, Gary. *Gonna Do Great Things: The Life of Sammy Davis, Jr.* New York: Scribner's, 2003. Fishgall tends to skim the surface of Davis's life and focus on the glitz and the glamour, but he includes information gleaned from interviews with Davis's friends and family as well as details of his most important performances.

Haygood, Wil. *In Black and White: The Life of Sammy Davis Jr.* New York: Knopf, 2003. Haygood uses a psychosexual approach to try to explain Davis's swings from Black Power to Richard Nixon, Judaism to devil worship. An excellent portrayal of a complex man trying to fit into an era of social upheaval.

See also: Coleman, Cy; Crosby, Bing; Horne, Lena; Jones, Quincy; Newley, Anthony.

Claude Debussy

French classical composer

Debussy's harmony, melody, and orchestration were radical departures from both classic and Romantic idioms. They promoted a color-based approach to music and foreshadowed the nontonal language of the twentieth century.

Born: August 22, 1862; Saint-Germain-en-Laye, France
Died: March 25, 1918; Paris, France
Also known as: Achille-Claude Debussy (full name)

Principal works

BALLETS (music): *Jeux*, 1913; *La Boîte à joujoux*, 1919 (*The Box of Toys*); *Khamma*, 1947.
CHAMBER WORKS: *Premier Quatuor*, 1894; *Première*

Rapsodie, 1910; *Morceau à déchiffrer pour le concours de clarinette de 1910*, 1910; *Sonata*, 1915; *Syrinx*, 1927; *Premier Trio*, 1986.

OPERAS (music): *Pelléas et Mélisande*, 1902 (libretto by Maurice Maeterlinck); *La Chute de la maison Usher*, 1977 (libretto by Edgar Allan Poe; revised by Claude Debussy); *Rodrigue et Chimène*, 1993 (libretto by Guillén de Castro; revised by Catulle Mendes).

ORCHESTRAL WORKS: *Prélude à l'après-midi d'un faune*, 1895 (*Prelude to the Afternoon of a Faun*); *Deux Gymnopédies*, 1898; *Deux Danses*, 1904; *La Mer*, 1905 (*The Sea*); *Ibéria*, 1910; *Rondes de printemps*, 1910; *Marche écossaise sur un thème populaire*, 1911; *Première Rapsodie*, 1911; *Gigues*, 1913; *Berceuse héroïque*, 1915; *Rapsodie*, 1919; *Fantaisie*, 1920; *Le Triomphe de Bacchus*, 1928; *Symphony*, 1933; *Intermezzo*, 1944.

PIANO WORKS: *Valse romantique*, 1890; *Ballade slave*, 1891; *Deux Arabesques*, 1891; *Rêverie*, 1891; *Tarentelle styrienne*, 1891; *Nocturne*, 1892; *Pour le piano*, 1901; *Estampes*, 1903; *Mazurka*, 1903; *D'un cahier d'esquisses*, 1904; *L'Îsle joyeuse*, 1904; *Masques*, 1904; *Images, Series 1*, 1905; *Pièce pour piano*, 1905; *Suite bergamasque*, 1905; *Children's Corner*, 1908; *Images, Series 2*, 1908; *Sérénade à la poupée*, 1908; *The Little Nigar*, 1909; *Homage à Haydn*, 1910; *La Plus que lente*, 1910; *Préludes, Book 1*, 1910; *Préludes, Book 2*, 1913; *Berceuse héroïque*, 1915; *En blanc et noir*, 1915 (*In Black and White*); *Élégie*, 1916; *Études*, 1916; *Lindaraja*, 1926; *Danse bohémienne*, 1932; *Pièce pour le vêtement du blessé*, 1933; *Images*, 1978.

The Life

Achille-Claude Debussy (ah-KEEL klohd deh-byew-SEE) was the eldest of five children born to Manuel-Achille Debussy and Victorine Manoury. When the family moved to Paris in 1867, the father took a succession of menial jobs, and the mother, who worked as a seamstress, schooled Debussy at home. His first contact with the sea occurred in 1869 at Cannes, in the South of France. The sensitive child was impressed by the size of this body of water and its constant change of color; as an adult, Debussy vividly recalled the sea "stretching out to the horizon."

In Cannes, Debussy took his first piano lessons with the Italian Jean Cerutti; two years later, he be-

Claude Debussy.

came the student of Mme Mauté de Fleurville, the poet Paul Verlaine's mother-in-law, who claimed to have been a pupil of Frédéric Chopin. In 1872 Debussy was admitted to the Paris Conservatory, where he spent twelve years as a student. In 1880 Debussy met Nadezhda von Meck, Peter Ilich Tchaikovsky's patroness, and this enabled him to travel, as a musician of the household, to Switzerland, Italy, and Russia, in the process becoming acquainted with the music of Tchaikovsky, Nikolay Rimsky-Korsakov, and Aleksandr Borodin.

Having unsuccessfully proposed to the sixteen-year-old Sophie von Meck in 1880, Debussy turned his attention to the singer Marie Vasnier, his first true love and his muse, who performed many of the songs he composed in the 1880's. In 1884 he won the prestigious Prix de Rome, for which he had been preparing since 1881.

Debussy spent 1885 and 1886 at the Villa Medici in Rome, where he complained about isolation and "having to compose music to order." However, while there, he had the opportunity to play for Franz Liszt, to listen to the sacred music of

Giovanni Pierluigi da Palestrina and Orlando di Lasso performed at Santa Maria dell'Anima, to study the organ works of Johann Sebastian Bach, and to read the most recent magazines produced by the French Symbolists, whose philosophy was a reaction to realism, advocating a metaphorical and mysterious approach to the truth.

In 1887 he returned to Paris, which was in the midst of a craze for Richard Wagner, a trend of definite appeal to Debussy, and where Symbolist poetry flourished. Within the next two years, the composer met Verlaine, Stuart Merrill, and Pierre Louÿs and embraced their chief aesthetic: Poetry and music should be one. Debussy became acquainted with James McNeill Whistler, the painter of the famous views of the Thames titled *Nocturnes*. Édouard Manet, Edgar Degas, J. M. W. Turner, and Henri de Toulouse-Lautrec were also counted among his favorite painters. In 1891 he befriended the eccentric composer Eric Satie; their friendship lasted for nearly three decades.

The Exposition Universelle of 1889 brought to Paris music from Northern and Eastern Europe, as well as from Africa, Arabia, and the Far East. Debussy was fascinated with the complex rhythmic polyphony, the timbre, and the pentatonic melodies of the Javanese gamelan orchestra, an ensemble comprising single-string instruments, a flute, and gongs and bells. Debussy's later orchestral idiom—especially as seen in *Prélude à l'après-midi d'un faune*, *La Mer*, and the series *Images*—reflected the influence of such rhythmic sophistication. After 1889, pentatonic scales became part of his vocabulary as well.

In addition to being a composer, a conductor, and a performer, Debussy was a perceptive music critic. His first critical writings were published in the literary-artistic magazine *La Revue blanche* (1901) under the nom de plume "Monsieur Croche"; later, he was published in the daily *Gil Blas* (1903) and in *La Revue S. I. M.* (1912-1914). Several of these articles were later selected by Debussy as representative of his musical philosophy, and they were published posthumously as *Monsieur Croche, antidilettant* (1921).

After a tempestuous and long-standing affair with Gabrielle Dupont, Debussy married Rosalie (Lilly) Texier in 1899; the marriage was informally dissolved when the composer met Emma Bardac and started living with her in 1904. They were married in 1908; their daughter, Claude-Emma, affectionately called Chouchou, was the dedicatee of a piano suite Debussy composed between 1906 and 1908, *Children's Corner*. Noted for its humorous slant, the suite incorporates a musical caricature of Muzio Clementi's *Gradus ad Parnassum* and a French nursery song, "Dodo, l'enfant do," which had been alluded to in *Estampes* and would be put to further use in the orchestral *Images* series.

The first signs of cancer, the illness that would ultimately cause the composer's death, appeared in 1909, while Debussy was visiting England. A colonoscopy was performed in 1915, and throughout his last years the composer was in physical pain, as well as depressed because of the events of World War I. He died in Paris on March 25, 1918.

The Music

Debussy's fully matured style, already apparent in works of the late 1880's, fuses several sources into a single, coherent, highly personal language, whose aesthetic foundation is that music should evoke moods and colors. In terms of harmony, this translates into treatment of discords as concords; intense use of chromaticism; abrupt modulations and rapidly shifting key areas; Russian-like modality; exploration of chord structures derived from pentatonic and whole-tone scales; and, above all, understanding harmony as a color-generating device. His melodies are fluid, elastic, and highly ornamental, in the style of Oriental arabesques, and look like embellished improvisations frozen on the page.

Pelléas et Mélisande. Debussy began work on this five-act lyric drama in 1893, two years after returning from his second trip to Bayreuth, Germany, where he had seen Wagner's operas *Parsifal* (1882), *Die Meistersinger* (1867), and *Tristan und Isolde* (1859). Debussy traveled to Ghent, in Belgium, to obtain Maurice Maeterlinck's permission to adapt his Symbolist play as an opera libretto. A tragic love story involving a mysterious princess (Mélisande) and her husband's half-brother (Pelléas), Debussy's *Pelléas et Mélisande* went through a long period of gestation and continuous revisions: The premiere took place in 1902, but the composer continued to revise the score up to and beyond 1905, the year of its publication. Consistent avoidance of cadences, and the intersection of whole-tone scales and their chord-derivatives with chromatic and modal harmonies, infuse the opera with astonishing colors and suggest an atemporal quality. The fluid, quasi-recitative style of the vocal parts, already present in many of Debussy's songs, stems from limited melodic ranges, pitch repetition, and extraordinary rhythmic variety. Somewhat in the spirit of Wagner's music, heroes and situations are characterized through specific motives; these journeys through multiple hypostases suggest alterations in both characters and events. In a similar vein, the orchestral interludes connecting the various scenes take on narrative function and suggest emotions not overtly expressed by the heroes.

Prelude to the Afternoon of a Faun. This orchestral piece was originally intended as incidental music to a dramatic monologue based on a poem by Stéphane Mallarmé. The proposed scope was never achieved; the music was described by Debussy as "a general impression of the poem." The whole work is generated from a single motive heard in the flute in the first four measures, later reprised, transformed, reharmonized, reorchestrated, and extended. Orchestral colors and dynamic ranges are of astounding variety, from subtle and refined pianissimos to luscious fortes. In this, as in his works for piano solo, Debussy showed himself to be the master of an arabesquelike, quasi-improvisatory style, probably based on similar treatments by Rimsky-Korsakov and Borodin in their works of Oriental inspiration. In most of his Symbolist and mature works, Debussy cultivated instrumental color for its own sake and for evoking a certain atmosphere. In *Prelude to the Afternoon of a Faun* Debussy utilized instruments familiar and expected in late Romantic orchestras, but also small, antique cymbals to convey the idea of spatial and temporal remoteness of the lascivious faun's musings. Additional color was created through division of strings as well as muted brass. *Prelude to the Afternoon of a Faun* perhaps best illustrates the composer's belief that the substance of music resides in sound color and rhythm.

The Sea. Debussy's longtime love affair with the sea, his father's sea stories, Turner's sea paintings (which the composer might have seen during his visits to London in 1902 and 1903), and Katsushika Hokusai's Japanese seascapes have all been cited as extramusical sources for these three symphonic sketches composed between 1903 and 1905. *The Sea* might be understood as a cyclical symphony in three related movements, all based on pentatonic material and employing timbre as a building block. A depiction of light and color changes on the sea as the day progresses from early morning to noon, the first movement ("From Dawn to Noon on the Sea") exploits gamelanlike sonorities; the second ("Wave Play") involves ostinatos, chromaticism, and glissandi in the harp as well as timbre innovations, such as the use of muted trumpets in fortissimo to represent perpetual yet unpredictable aquatic motion; and the third ("Dialogue of Wind and Sea") alternates two themes, pitched against each other as if in a state of natural combat, with the sea theme in the lower strings and the wind theme in the oboes, English horn, and bassoon.

Images, Series 1 *and* **Images, Series 2.** This piano suite series comprises six delicate etchings (three in each book); among these are depictions of ephemeral, shimmering reflections of light in water; muffled bell sounds traversing dense leafage; and water splashing as goldfish play in a bowl in a frenzy of trills and tremolos. The second piece in *Images, Series 1* is an homage to Baroque composer Jean-Philippe Rameau, and it tells of Debussy's fascination with the French clavecinists (or harpsichordists) of the eighteenth century. The second piece in *Images, Series 2* uses the gamelan effect to depict the majestic descent of the moon on an Oriental temple.

Préludes. Debussy, who revered J. S. Bach and Chopin (both of whom had penned keyboard preludes), was an exquisite piano player. The two books of *Préludes* offer a singular view of this genre: All pieces (with the exception of No. 11 in Book 2) have descriptive or evocative titles, and all use a fully developed Debussyan idiom. Some are evocative of dances and rhythms of Italy and Spain ("The Hills of Anacapri" in Book 1; "La Puerta del Vino" in Book 2); others are obvious narrative programmatic music ("La Cathédrale engloutie" in Book 1, a musical adaptation of the legendary cathedral of Ys in Brittany, emerging from water to the sound of bells, organ pedal, and Gregorian chant).

Études. Each study in this cycle, composed in 1915 and dedicated to the memory of Chopin, is an in-depth exploration of one major piano technique. There are finger exercises in Nos. 1 and 6; interval-based exercises in Nos. 2, 4, and 5 (studies in thirds, sixths, and octaves, respectively); and chord- and arpeggio-based exercises in Nos. 11 and 12. Thus Debussy turned from symbolism, mystery, and subtle evocation to "pure music," as he described it in a letter to composer Igor Stravinsky.

Musical Legacy

Debussy viewed his works as musical echoes of Symbolist poetry rather than as musical extensions of Impressionist painting. His constant preoccupation with sound color led to instrumentation experiments of unique refinement, possibly equaled only in some of Maurice Ravel's works. Contemporary reception of his music was mixed: Some critics denounced it as unmoving, emotionless, or Impressionistic, and Debussy's stylistic idiosyncrasies were dubbed Debussyism. Stravinsky, Giacomo Puccini, and Béla Bartók admired Debussy's harmonic language, and Max Reger, Gustav Holst, Cyril Scott, and Aaron Copland were all influenced by him. Debussy was France's true musical modernist.

Luminita Florea

Further Reading

Debussy, Claude. *Debussy on Music: The Critical Writings of the Great French Composer Claude Debussy*. Edited by François Lesure, translated by Richard Langham Smith. New York: Alfred A. Knopf, 1977. English translation of all of Debussy's critical works, including *Monsieur Croche, antidilettante* and several interviews Debussy gave to journals and newspapers.

Lederer, Victor. *Debussy: The Quiet Revolutionary*. New York: Amadeus Press, 2007. Discussions of Debussy's piano, orchestral, and operatic music.

Roberts, Paul. *Images: The Piano Music of Claude Debussy*. Portland, Oreg.: Amadeus Press, 1996. Thorough analyses of Debussy's piano music, complemented by studies of fin de siècle Paris and its cultural climate and special references to Debussy's bonds with Impressionist painting and Symbolist poetry. Includes glossary, illustrations, and musical examples.

Thompson, Oscar. *Debussy: Man and Artist*. New York: Dover, 1967. Includes short discussions of all of Debussy's works, arranged by genre, and some illustrations. (The bibliography is outdated.)

Trezise, Simon, ed. *The Cambridge Companion to Debussy*. New York: Cambridge University Press, 2003. Anthology of studies by fourteen authors examining topics as diverse as Debussy the man and music critic, his exploration of nature and the erotic, and his experiments with sound color, rhythm, and form. Includes illustrations, bibliography, and index.

See also: Bartók, Béla; Cliburn, Van; Copland, Aaron; Crumb, George; Evans, Bill; Grappelli, Stéphane; Hancock, Herbie; Heifetz, Jascha; Hindemith, Paul; Kodály, Zoltán; Martin, Frank; Martinů, Bohuslav; Messiaen, Olivier; Mingus, Charles; Paderewski, Ignace Jan; Piazzolla, Astor; Poulenc, Francis; Ravel, Maurice; Rubinstein, Artur; Satie, Erik; Scott-Heron, Gil; Shaw, Artie; Sibelius, Jean; Sousa, John Philip; Stravinsky, Igor; Strayhorn, Billy; Szigeti, Joseph; Takemitsu, Tōru; Tiomkin, Dimitri; Watts, André; Williams, John.

Sandy Denny

English folksinger and songwriter

Denny's songwriting and haunting, stentorian lead vocals set the standard for male and female folk-rock singers on both sides of the Atlantic Ocean in the late 1960's and early 1970's.

Born: January 6, 1948; London, England
Died: April 21, 1978; London, England
Also known as: Alexandra Elene Maclean Denny (full name)
Member of: The Strawbs; Fairport Convention; Fotheringay; the Bunch

Principal recordings

ALBUMS (solo): *The Original Sandy Denny*, 1967; *Sandy Denny*, 1970; *The North Star Grassman and the Ravens*, 1971; *Sandy*, 1972; *Like an Old-Fashioned Waltz*, 1973; *Rendezvous*, 1977.
ALBUMS (with the Bunch): *Rock On*, 1972.
ALBUMS (with Fairport Convention): *Fairport*

Convention, 1968; *Liege and Lief*, 1969; *Unhalfbricking*, 1969; *What We Did on Our Holidays*, 1969; *Full House*, 1970; *Angel Delight*, 1971; *Babbacombe Lee*, 1971; *Nine*, 1973; *Rosie*, 1973; *Rising for the Moon*, 1975; *Gottle o' Geer*, 1976; *The Bonny Bunch of Roses*, 1977; *Tipplers' Tales*, 1978.

ALBUMS (with Fotheringay): *Fotheringay*, 1970.

ALBUMS (with the Strawbs): *All Our Own Work*, 1968; *Sandy Denny and the Strawbs*, 1968.

The Life

Alexandra Elene Maclean Denny was born in London and studied piano and voice at an early age. She became known in the mid-1960's at London-area folk clubs—the Scots House, Bunjies, Les Cousins—as a nursing student who sang old folk songs. She dropped out of nursing school to pursue a solo career, singing traditional folk songs in the public domain as well as covering songs by Tom Paxton and Bob Dylan. A BBC radio broadcast landed her a record deal, and soon she was asked to join the Strawbs.

Denny recorded only one album with the Strawbs, which included one of her first achievements as a singer-songwriter, "Who Knows Where the Time Goes?" While the album was in production in 1968, Judy Collins chose the song as the title track on one of her albums. At the same time the members of Fairport Convention persuaded Denny to replace Judy Dyble in their folk-rock group. Over the next several years, Fairport Convention produced three signature albums of the folk-rock movement: *What We Did on Our Holidays*, *Unhalfbricking*, and *Liege and Lief*.

Denny's romance with guitarist Trevor Lucas contributed to the breakup of Fairport Convention in 1971, and Lucas and Denny formed Fotheringay, the name of the first song on the first Fairport album, which Denny had written.

Denny and Lucas married on September 20, 1973. They briefly rejoined Fairport Convention in 1974 and 1975, touring and releasing a live album, although the group disbanded again. Denny gave birth to a daughter, Georgia, in July, 1977, but her relationship with Lucas was deteriorating. Lucas was seen with other women, and Denny went on drinking binges with John Bonham and Jimmy Page of Led Zeppelin, sometimes joined by actor Peter O'Toole. In March, 1978, at her parents' house in Cornwall, she fell and suffered a head injury. This may have contributed to a brain hemorrhage in April, which put her in a coma from which she never recovered. She died on April 21, 1978.

The Music

Although Denny entered the London folk scene as a vocalist and guitarist who played songs written by others, during the last decade of her life she developed into a premier songwriter.

Early Works. The Strawbs' *All Our Own Work* displays Denny's distinctive voice as well as her songwriting abilities. The first signature song of her own creation, "Who Knows Where the Time Goes?," was included not only on the Strawbs' album but also as the title track on noted American folksinger Collins's album. As the twenty-one-year-old Denny was becoming recognized as a significant singer and songwriter, she was in the process of leaving the Strawbs to join Fairport Convention.

What We Did on Our Holidays. The first Fairport Convention album with Denny was an instant critical and commercial success. Although most of the songs on the album were written by virtuoso guitarist and songwriter Richard Thompson, with covers of songs by Joni Mitchell ("Eastern Rain") and Bob Dylan ("I'll Keep It with Mine"), the first side of the album opens with Denny's "Fotheringay." The album demonstrated the musical prowess and the commercial viability of the band.

Unhalfbricking. This album included more Dylan covers ("Si tu dois partir," "Percy's Song," and "Million-Dollar Bash"); a remarkable eleven-minute arrangement of a traditional British folk song in the public domain ("A Sailor's Life"); and two songs each by Denny and Thompson, showing that the group recognized its two gifted songwriters. Denny's solo song, also recorded with the Strawbs, "Who Knows Where the Time Goes?," finally made a Fairport album, and "Autopsy" provided a poetic lead-in to "A Sailor's Life," which concluded the first side of the album. Unfortunately, in the week before the album's release, drummer Martin Lamble, driving back from a concert in Birmingham with Thompson's girlfriend Jeannie Franklin, crashed, and both perished. The accident had personal and artistic ramifications among the members of Fairport for many years.

Liege and Lief. With Dave Mattacks replacing Lamble on drums and with Dave Swarbick added on violin and viola, Fairport Convention recorded this album in two short weeks late in 1969. The album is mostly traditional British folk songs, except for the opening musical call-to-arms, "Come All Ye," written by Denny with input from bassist Ashley Hutchings. Such songs as "Matty Groves" and "The Deserter" chronicle England's storied past. Thompson's two songs for the album, "Farewell, Farewell" and "Crazy Man Michael," remained in his repertoire after he left Fairport Convention.

Fotheringay. When Denny left Fairport Convention to start Fotheringay with Lucas, she continued her professional relationship with Sound Techniques Studio and producer Joe Boyd, who had produced the last three Fairport albums. The album was a commercial and critical success, but internecine struggles within the band, combined with alcohol and drug abuse, caused the band to break up after the album and a single tour. Denny's songwriting finally achieved center-stage status in this group, which she codirected with Lucas. "Nothing More" and "The Pond and the Stream" are superior works of poetry and music, and "The Sea" and "Winter Winds" are compelling original pieces. She cowrote "Peace in the End" with Lucas, and on the album are the expected Dylan cover ("Too Much of Nothing") and a Gordon Lightfoot cover ("The Way I Feel").

Musical Legacy

Denny's voice was remarkable for its range and clarity, and her songwriting exhibited a remarkable creativity. Her finesse on the guitar complemented the lyrical qualities of her songs. The albums recorded and released between 1968 and 1970, with Fairport Convention and Fotheringay, are among the enduring achievements in the folk-rock movement on both sides of the Atlantic Ocean.

Richard Sax

Further Reading

Brocken, Michael. *The British Folk Revival, 1944-2002.* Aldershot, England: Ashgate, 2003. Details the British postwar folk-music renaissance, including the convergence of folk and pop music in the 1960's.

Heylin, Clinton. *No More Sad Refrains: The Life and Times of Sandy Denny.* London: Helter Skelter, 2001. Drawing on personal interviews (some with British musicians, including Pete Townshend) and other eyewitness accounts, the author places Denny within the social and musical scenes of the era.

Humphries, Patrick. *Meet on the Ledge: A History of the Fairport Convention.* London: Eel Pie, 1982. Brief but well-written and balanced retrospective of the band.

See also: Collins, Judy; Dylan, Bob; Mitchell, Joni; Page, Jimmy; Paxton, Tom.

John Denver

American singer and songwriter

Denver was a successful crossover star in pop, folk, and country music whose wholesome image and memorable songs, celebrating nature and the simple pleasures of life, made him the top-selling solo artist in the 1970's. One of the first musicians from his generation to have a successful film and television career, Denver used his immense popularity to promote environmental and humanitarian causes worldwide.

Born: December 31, 1943; Roswell, New Mexico
Died: October 12, 1997; Monterey Bay, near Pacific Grove, California
Also known as: Henry John Deutschendorf, Jr. (birth name)
Member of: The Chad Mitchell Trio

Principal recordings

ALBUMS (solo): *Rhymes and Reasons,* 1969; *Take Me to Tomorrow,* 1970; *Whose Garden Was This?,* 1970; *Poems, Prayers, and Promises,* 1971; *Aerie,* 1972; *Rocky Mountain High,* 1972; *Farewell Andromeda,* 1973; *Back Home Again,* 1974; *Rocky Mountain Christmas,* 1975; *Windsong,* 1975; *Spirit,* 1976; *I Want to Live,* 1977; *A Christmas Together,* 1979 (with the Muppets); *John Denver,* 1979; *Autograph,* 1980; *Perhaps Love,* 1981; *Some*